THE ROUTLEDGE INTERNATIONAL HANDBOOK OF CRITICAL AUTISM STUDIES

This handbook provides an authoritative and up-to-date overview of Critical Autism Studies and explores the different kinds of knowledges and their articulations, similarities, and differences across cultural contexts and key tensions within this subdiscipline.

Critical Autism Studies is a developing area occupying an exciting space of development within learning and teaching in higher education. It has a strong trajectory within the autistic academic and advocate community in resistance and in response to the persistence of autism retaining an identity as a genetic disorder of the brain.

Divided into four parts

- Conceptualising autism
- Autistic identity
- Community and culture
- Practice

and comprising 24 newly commissioned chapters written by academics and activists, it explores areas of education, Critical Race Theory, domestic violence and abuse, sexuality, biopolitics, health, and social care practices.

It will be of interest to all scholars and students of disability studies, sociology, anthropology, cultural studies, education, health, social care, and political science.

Damian Milton is a Senior Lecturer in Intellectual and Developmental Disabilities at the Tizard Centre, University of Kent. Damian's interest in autism began when his son was diagnosed in 2005 as autistic aged 2 and he was diagnosed with Asperger's in 2009 aged 36. Damian's primary focus is on increasing the meaningful participation of autistic people and people with learning disabilities in the research process and chairs the Participatory Autism Research Collective (PARC).

Sara Ryan is a Professor of Social Care, Manchester Metropolitan University. Her research focuses on autism, learning disabilities, and marginalised groups.

Routledge International Handbooks of Education

The Routledge International Handbook of Research on Dialogic Education
Edited by Neil Mercer, Rupert Wegerif and Louis Major

The Routledge International Handbook of Young Children's Rights
Edited by Jane Murray, Beth Blue Swadener and Kylie Smith

Routledge International Handbook of Women's Sexual and Reproductive Health
Edited by Jane M. Ussher, Joan C. Chrisler and Janette Perz

The Routledge International Handbook of Student-centred Learning and Teaching in Higher Education
Edited by Sabine Hoidn and Manja Klemenčič

The Routledge Handbook of English Language Education in Bangladesh
Edited by Shaila Sultana, M. Moninoor Roshid, Md. Zulfeqar Haider, Mia Md. Naushaad Kabir, and Mahmud Hasan khan

The Routledge Handbook of Language Learning and Teaching Beyond the Classroom
Edited by Hayo Reinders, Chun Lai and Pia Sundqvist

The Routledge Handbook of Dyslexia in Education
Edited by Gad Elbeheri and Siang Lee

The Routledge Handbook of International Social Work
Edited by Stephen Webb

The Routledge International Handbook of Critical Autism Studies
Edited by Damian Milton and Sara Ryan

For more information about this series, please visit: https://www.routledge.com/Routledge-International-Handbooks-of-Education/book-series/HBKSOFED

THE ROUTLEDGE INTERNATIONAL HANDBOOK OF CRITICAL AUTISM STUDIES

Edited by Damian Milton and Sara Ryan

LONDON AND NEW YORK

Cover image: © Getty Images

First published 2023
by Routledge
4 Park Square, Milton Park, Abingdon, Oxon OX14 4RN

and by Routledge
605 Third Avenue, New York, NY 10158

Routledge is an imprint of the Taylor & Francis Group, an informa business

© 2023 selection and editorial matter, **Damian Milton and Sara Ryan**; individual chapters, the contributors

The rights of **Damian Milton and Sara Ryan** to be identified as the authors of the editorial material, and of the authors for their individual chapters, has been asserted in accordance with sections 77 and 78 of the Copyright, Designs and Patents Act 1988.

All rights reserved. No part of this book may be reprinted or reproduced or utilised in any form or by any electronic, mechanical, or other means, now known or hereafter invented, including photocopying and recording, or in any information storage or retrieval system, without permission in writing from the publishers.

Trademark notice: Product or corporate names may be trademarks or registered trademarks, and are used only for identification and explanation without intent to infringe.

British Library Cataloguing-in-Publication Data
A catalogue record for this book is available from the British Library

Library of Congress Cataloging-in-Publication Data
Names: Milton, Damian, editor. | Ryan, Sara (Siobhan), editor.
Title: The Routledge international handbook of critical autism studies / edited by Damian Milton and Sara Ryan.
Description: Abingdon, Oxon; New York, NY: Routledge, 2023. | Series: Routledge international handbooks | Includes bibliographical references and index.
Identifiers: LCCN 2022027791 (print) | LCCN 2022027792 (ebook) | ISBN 9780367521073 (hardback) | ISBN 9780367521011 (paperback) | ISBN 9781003056577 (ebook)
Subjects: LCSH: Autism. | Autism spectrum disorders. | Autism–Social aspects. | Autism spectrum disorders–Social aspects.
Classification: LCC RC553.A88 R6885 2023 (print) | LCC RC553.A88 (ebook) | DDC 616.85/882–dc23/eng/20220912
LC record available at https://lccn.loc.gov/2022027791
LC ebook record available at https://lccn.loc.gov/2022027792

ISBN: 978-0-367-52107-3 (hbk)
ISBN: 978-0-367-52101-1 (pbk)
ISBN: 978-1-003-05657-7 (ebk)

DOI: 10.4324/9781003056577

Typeset in Bembo
By Deanta Global Publishing Services, Chennai, India

CONTENTS

List of figures   *viii*
List of tables   *ix*
List of contributors   *x*

1 Critical autism studies: An introduction   1
   Sara Ryan and Damian Milton

PART 1
Conceptualising autism   **11**

2 First there is a mountain, then there is no mountain, then there is: whither identity?   13
   Larry Arnold

3 Critically contextualising 'normal' development and the construction of the autistic individual   20
   Charlotte Brownlow, Lindsay O'Dell, and Ding Abawi

4 Dimensions of difference   34
   Dinah Murray

5 Heterogeneity and clustering in autism: An introduction for critical scholars   42
   Patrick Dwyer

6 Rational (Pathological) Demand Avoidance: As a mental disorder and an evolving social construct   56
   Richard Woods

7   Community psychology as reparations for violence in the construction
    of autism knowledge   76
    Monique Botha

PART 2
Autistic identity   95

8   Through the lens of (Black) Critical Race Theory   97
    Melissa Simmonds

9   Postponing humanity: Pathologising autism, childhood and motherhood   106
    Francesca Bernardi

10 'It sort of like gets squared': Health professionals' understanding of the
    intersection of autism and gender diversity in young people   122
    Magdalena Mikulak

11 Autistic young people's sense of self and the social world: A challenge to
    deficit-focused characterisations   130
    Emma Rice-Adams

12 A personal account of neurodiversity, academia and activism   150
    Damian Milton

PART 3
Community and culture   157

13 'Autopia': A vision for autistic acceptance and belonging   159
    Luke Beardon

14 The Moulin Rouge and the Rouge Moulin: Language, Cartesianism,
    republicanism and the construct of autism in France   165
    Peter Crosbie

15 Support on whose terms? Competing meanings of support aimed at
    autistic people   182
    Hanna Bertilsdotter Rosqvist, Damian Milton, and Lindsay O'Dell

16 Critical autism parenting   194
    Mitzi Walz

17 "Even though I'm on the spectrum, I'm still capable of falling in love":
A Bourdieusian analysis of representations of autism and sexuality on
Love on the Spectrum 203
Allison Moore

18 Seeking sunflowers: The biopolitics of autism at the airport 218
Katherine Runswick-Cole and Dan Goodley

PART 4
Practice 227

19 Autistic identity, culture, community, and space for well-being 229
Chloe Farahar

20 Contemplating teacher talk through a critical autism studies lens 242
*Nick Hodge, Patty Douglas, Madeleine Kruth, Stephen Connolly,
Nicola Martin, Kendra Gowler, and Cheryl Smith*

21 Models of helping and coping with autism 255
Steven K. Kapp

22 Critical approaches to autism support practice: Engaging situated
reflection and research 270
Joseph Long

23 From disempowerment to well-being and flow: Enabling autistic
communication in schools 277
Rebecca Wood

24 Autistic voices in Autistic research: Towards active citizenship in Autism
research 288
Krysia Emily Waldock and Nathan Keates

Index *303*

FIGURES

6.1	Abbreviated *DSM-5* Autism Spectrum Disorder criteria and the Aggregated PDA Profile	60
6.2	The Demand Management Cycle for PDA	64
11.1	Thematic map: the sense of self elements shared by the autistic adolescents participating in the research study	136
11.2	'People's judgement'	140
11.3	'Special talents'	142
19.1	"Embrace your weird"	236
19.2	"The Great Autismo"	237
19.3	"Awesome"	237
19.4	"Autistic good"	237
24.1	The eight rungs from Arnstein's Ladder of Citizen Participation (1969)	289

TABLES

5.1	Recommendations regarding use of community diagnostic classifications to stratify heterogeneity within the autistic constellation	50
6.1	Questions and sub-questions from PDA diagnostic and screening tools that contain manipulative behaviours and denote intent	70
11.1	Range of methods completed by participants	135
19.1	The key components of the "culture of autism" versus Autistic culture	233

CONTRIBUTORS

Ding Abawi is a student and intern at the University of Southern Queensland, Australia.

Larry Arnold is a specialist in Autism and Disability Studies, and founder of the academic journal *Autonomy* in 2012 with an exclusively autistic editorship.

Luke Beardon is a multiple award-winning Senior Lecturer in Autism at Sheffield Hallam University with a string of publications, including sole-authored books as well as several co-authored papers. Luke is currently the Course Leader for the Post Graduate Certificate in Autism and is dedicated to playing his small part in trying to improve autistic lives as best he can.

Francesca Bernardi is founding chair of the Antonio Gramsci Society UK, and fellow of the Royal Society of Arts. Francesca is a Visiting Lecturer in Childhood Studies at Leeds Beckett University and Arts Therapies at the University of Roehampton. Francesca is a translator, advocate, artist, and creative coach and member of the Disability Without Abuse Project USA.

Hanna Bertilsdotter Rosqvist is an Associate Professor in Sociology and currently a Senior Lecturer in Social work. Her research is primary oriented towards disability, but also on gender, sexuality, and space.

Monique Botha is an autistic and ADHD research-based community psychologist, based at the University of Stirling. They completed their PhD and MSc at the University of Surrey, with a focus on autistic community connectedness as a buffer to the impact of minority stress on mental health.

Charlotte Brownlow is a Professor at The University of Southern Queensland in Australia. Her research focuses on Autism and neurodiversity, and she is particularly passionate about co-production of knowledges with the Autistic and Autism communities. She is currently Co-chair of the Australasian Autism Research Council (AARC).

Stephen Connolly is a Senior Lecturer in Autism at The Autism Centre, Sheffield Hallam University, UK. As an autistic academic Stephen is looking to challenge traditional research power dynamics by working within what he terms an Emanciparticipatory methodology. This focuses on repositioning the power from the researcher to the community being researched.

Peter Crosbie is a husband and father, late-diagnosed as autistic, with a successful career in music and recording behind him.

Contributors

Patty Douglas is an Associate Professor of Disability Studies in Education in the Faculty of Education at Brandon University, Canada. Her work challenges deficit approaches to disability and reimagines exclusionary systems through critical, arts-based, and community-engaged approaches. Patty is a former special education teacher.

Patrick Dwyer is an autistic PhD candidate, UC Davis, CA, USA. His main research interest is autistic sensory processing and attention, including sensory heterogeneity. Patrick also studies community acceptability of autism intervention, postsecondary education, and neurodiversity theory. Patrick co-founded the Autistic Researchers Committee at the International Society for Autism Research. His blog is autisticscholar.com.

Chloe Farahar is an autistic academic whose research interests revolve around her dedicated interests: reducing prejudice with the neurodiversity narrative; supporting autistic people with her discovery programme; reimagining the spectrum as a three-dimension autistic space; creating neurodivergent-inclusive environments; educating learners about autistic experience in training and on her free educative platform, Aucademy.

Dan Goodley is a Professor of Disability Studies and Education in The School of Education at the University of Sheffield, United Kingdom. Dan co-directs iHuman, which sits at the intersections of Critical Disability Studies and Science and Technology Studies.

Kendra Gowler is a Student Services Consultant with Pembina Trails School Division, Canada, and co-chair of the Manitoba Minister's Advisory Council on Inclusive Education. Kendra is a division leader in collaborative and Disability Studies in Education approaches that build school communities so that all children belong. She is a former resource teacher.

Nick Hodge is a Professor Emeritus of Inclusive Practice in the Sheffield Institute of Education, Sheffield Hallam University, UK. Nick is a former special education teacher, supporting disabled children and their families for over 15 years. Nick's research challenges deficit models of disability that mark out children and young people as disordered and other.

Steven K. Kapp is a Lecturer in Psychology, University of Portsmouth, and an autistic self-advocate who has supported systems change work for inclusive employment and influenced the *DSM-5* autism diagnosis. His studies examine how conceptions of autism, neurodiversity, and support associate with identity, lived experiences, and quality of life.

Nathan Keates is a Lecturer and PhD candidate in Intellectual and Developmental Disabilities at the University of Kent with a focus on autistic adults and their lived experiences and exploring an improv comedy intervention for anxiety. His research comes from the social science and psychology perspective investigating autism/neurodevelopmental conditions, disability, and performance.

Madeleine Kruth worked as project coordinator for the Re•Storying Autism project from 2019 to 2021. She is currently coordinating the Safe Places project at Brandon University, Canada, addressing different forms of violence and violence prevention strategies across the long-term care continuum. She is interested in social determinants of health in rural and remote settings.

Joseph Long is Research and Policy Lead for Scottish Autism. He is an Honorary Research Fellow at the University of Edinburgh and an associate of the Edinburgh Centre for Medical Anthropology. His current role draws on several years' experience as a support worker in social care services as well as his academic background as a social anthropologist.

Contributors

Nicola Martin is a Professor of Social Justice and Inclusive Education at London South Bank University (LSBU), a member of the Critical Autism and Disability Studies (CADS) Research Group within the Social Justice and Global Responsibility Research Centre at LSBU, and London Convenor of The Participatory Autism Research Collective (PARC).

Magdalena Mikulak (she/her) is a Senior Research Associate in the Department of Social Care and Social Work, Manchester Metropolitan University. Previously, she worked as a researcher with the Nuffield Department of Primary Care Health Sciences, University of Oxford. She has a PhD in Gender Studies from the London School of Economics and Political Sciences.

Damian Milton is a Senior Lecturer in Intellectual and Developmental Disabilities at the Tizard Centre, University of Kent. Damian's interest in autism began when his son was diagnosed in 2005 as autistic aged 2 and he was diagnosed with Asperger's in 2009 aged 36. Damian's primary focus is on increasing the meaningful participation of autistic people and people with learning disabilities in the research process and chairs the Participatory Autism Research Collective (PARC).

Allison Moore is a Reader in Social Sciences, Edge Hill University. Since graduating with a degree in Applied Social Sciences in 1999, Allison has worked in a variety of settings, including higher education and the voluntary and community sector.

Dinah Murray was an independent researcher and campaigner, former tutor for Birmingham University's distance learning courses on autism (adults) and former support worker for people with varied learning disabilities, including autism. She presented at numerous conferences (world-wide) on varied themes related to autism, including several years of Autscape, an annual conference cum retreat run by and for autistic people. Her autism-related research interests included: medication and its impact on quality of life; information technology for people who don't use speech; the ethics of autism research; and the nature of the human being, with a particular focus on interests. Dr Dinah Murray was a political activist, autistic autism researcher, support worker, writer and mother. She liked to call herself a 'productive irritant'.

Lindsay O'Dell is a Professor and Director of the Graduate School at the Open University, UK.

Emma Rice-Adams is currently the SENCo in a mainstream secondary school. Her research interests include education, autism, sense of self and self-esteem, special educational needs and inclusive practice, and participatory and emancipatory methodologies. These interests are represented in her 2021 PhD, 'Negotiating Self, Autism, Adolescence and School: A Participatory Inquiry'.

Katherine Runswick-Cole is a Professor of Education and Director of Research in The School of Education at the University of Sheffield, UK.

Sara Ryan is a Professor of Social Care, Manchester Metropolitan University, UK. Her research focuses on autism, learning disabilities, and marginalised groups.

Melissa Simmonds is an Adult Project Coordination Manager at Voluntary Action Sheffield, UK.

Cheryl Smith is a high school administrator in Pembina Trails School Division in Manitoba, Canada. She is committed to building inclusive school environments where all students feel a strong sense of belonging. Previously, she was a divisional student services consultant who directly supported school teams on current research-based inclusive practices.

Krysia Waldock is a PhD candidate in Intellectual and Developmental Disabilities and research assistant at the University of Kent (Tizard Centre and Institute for Cyber Security in Society). Her work explores inclusion and belonging of autistic people in religious and non-religious spaces.

Contributors

Mitzi Waltz is a Lecturer at Vrije Universiteit Amsterdam, who actively researches in partnership with autistic people to address societal barriers in areas such as employment, housing, and healthcare. She formerly headed the campus-based Autism Studies programmes at Sheffield Hallam University and the University of Birmingham. She is the author of *Autism: A Social and Medical History*, amongst other books, articles, and policy documents.

Rebecca Wood is a Senior Lecturer in Special Education at the University of East London and Principal Investigator of the Autistic School Staff Project. She completed her PhD at the University of Birmingham and an ESRC postdoctoral Fellowship at King's College London. Her books are *Inclusive Education for Autistic Children* and *Learning from Autistic Teachers*.

Richard Woods is the leading autistic expert on Pathological Demand Avoidance and a PhD student at London South Bank University and a reviewer for *Advances in Autism* and *Autism in Adulthood*. He is involved with the Participatory Autism Research Collective, has delivered training on PDA to postgraduate level, and spoken internationally on the topic.

1
CRITICAL AUTISM STUDIES
An introduction

Sara Ryan and Damian Milton

The importance of critical autism studies was clearly signalled in 1992 with the creation of the Autism Network International by a small number of autistic activists who sought to create an autistic space for autistic people. This early activism lay the foundations of critical approaches to autism and, importantly, was driven by the experiences of those so defined. Despite this development the term 'critical autism studies' only started to gain currency in academic studies following a workshop focused on this subdiscipline organised by Joyce Davidson and Michael Orsini in Ottawa, Canada, in 2010. Davidson and Orsini's (2013) initial conceptualisation of critical autism studies had three core strands: advancing enabling narratives of autism to challenge deficit-focused constructions; a focus on power relations within the autism field; and a commitment to developing new analytical frameworks and theoretical approaches to study the nature and culture of autism. They call for social science research which "demands sensitivity to the kaleidoscopic complexity of this highly individualised, relational (dis)order" (2013, p. 12). This edited volume seeks to explore the development, importance, application, and insights offered by critical autism studies. It draws on the three core conceptual strands identified by Davidson and Orsini and further develops them with the addition of a fourth strand to the original conceptualisation of critical autism studies which locates the work of autistic academics, activists, and professionals at the centre of the discipline.

What is this thing called autism?

Autism remains a contested term or descriptor which is conceived on multiple levels of description, from a biologically based biomedical disorder to a cultural identity. Verhoeff (2012) posed the question "What is this thing called autism?" and a decade later we still have much to learn, particularly from autistic worlds (Davidson and Orsini 2013). Autism has an unusual or even mysterious (McGuire and Michalko 2011) intensity generated by the potential, imaginings, controversy, resistance, and tensions it variously incorporates, engages with, or resists. It has been discursively constructed in different historical, social, political, economic, and cultural contexts, originating as a clinical term, and expanding beyond the clinical realm to mean different things to different people. It is brilliantly and impossibly diverse in terms of experiences, characteristics, 'symptoms', possible biological markers, and social contexts. Controversial and contradictory, it has been perceived as an economic burden (Lavelle et al. 2014), something to be eradicated

(Krcek 2013), and a strength (Milton 2017). At the same time, it is an important life experience that is highly charged and can have devastating consequences for the autistic individual and their families within contemporary cultural contexts (Hirvikoski et al. 2016). Indeed, as Hodge et al. (this volume) ask, how can we somehow undo or avoid the hurt autistic people have often experienced from childhood into adulthood?

The politics and ontological foundations of biomedical research, with its quest for secure, fixed and 'scientific' research outcomes remain strong, with vast sums of money and potential profit available to big pharma. In 2018, for example, around 40% of the US government research funding for autism was spent on biological studies with only 10% on lifespan issues and services (Dattaro 2021). A fundamental schism exists between considerations of the historical, cultural, and social context of the production of autism knowledge, and a biomedically based focus which examines autism through an ableist lens of deviance and inferiority (see, for example, Verhoeff 2012). For McGuire and Milchalko (2011), the use of a puzzle symbol to typically represent autism signifies the idea that there is a currently missing solution to be found, that autism is somehow knowable (and again potentially curable). At the same time, it remains unknown, which implies mono-dimensional manifestations. We should be embracing the ways in which, conceptually, autism always exceeds and confounds, and how it is always 'yet to know', rather than seeking to cure and potentially eradicate it. Most importantly, at the heart of the autism narrative are the experiences of those so defined. This schism in the way that autism is conceptualised is remarkably enduring, and speaks to the commodification of the label, not least given how the cause continues to elude researchers despite the time and resources invested in seeking to discover it. The dominance of the biomedical model has also led to a significant gap between funded research topics and the questions that autistic people would like researched (Milton and Bracher 2013; Milton 2014; Pellicano et al. 2014; Fletcher-Watson et al. 2019). A recent systematic review of studies that report on key stakeholder priorities for autism research found the importance of prioritising initiatives that will result in real life changes for autistic people (Roche et al. 2021). The authors underline the importance of the continued involvement of autistic people and communities in priority-setting research, arguing this is imperative for achieving change in people's lives and for progressing autism research in an ethical and effective way.

The tensions within critical autism studies

These controversies and contradictions extend to the field of critical autism studies, which has been differently interpreted and appropriated by autistic and non-autistic academics and activists, although the power to define autism has long been held by non-autistic or neurotypical clinical professionals and researchers (Evans 2013; Milton 2014). In the Global North there has been a growing community or communities of autistic activists and academics, family members, and allies challenging negative perceptions of autism, facilitated by emerging social media platforms, an increasing number of autistic activist-academics, and interest around critical autism studies within the wider and established field of disability studies (Woods et al. 2018).

The strength of this development has been in part due to resistance to the unwavering dominance of the deficit-laden model which informs biomedical research. Indeed, neurodiversity has become a preferred conceptual paradigm for many autistic people as it is considered to be both socially situated and more value-neutral than medicalised models of autism (Botha et al. 2020). At the same time, embedded within the space of critical autism studies are deeply personal positions on what autism means to different people, whether they are autistic, family members, or the wider public. This includes questions around who has the epistemic authority to research and write about the experiences of being autistic (Milton 2014; Hens et al. 2019, Botha 2021), as well as concerns about the rewriting of the narrative around the development of critical autism studies and the original critical autism studies autistic leadership (Woods et al. 2018). There is strong criticism about the lack of recognition of the importance of epistemological validity and integrity generated by the centrality of autistic input and expertise (Milton 2014; Woods et al. 2018, Gillespie-Lynch et al. 2017), and the importance of critical autism researchers taking seriously a commitment to research that avoids reproducing hierarchical relations with marginalised groups has been highlighted (O'Dell et al. 2016). Critiques of 'cultural imperialism' levelled at neurotypical researchers by autistic researchers and activists (Milton, 2016, Woods et al. 2018) speak to the territorialisation of critical autism studies and the accompanying 'linear containment of thought' (Mercieca and Mercieca 2010). Recent challenges to conventional academic knowledge production by autistic researchers include an account of the impact of experiencing 'scientifically sound' dehumanising accounts (Botha, 2021) and consideration of neurodiverse epistemological communities (Bertilsdottir Roqvist et al. 2019). Without epistemological validity, questions are raised around how meaningful research can be. Indeed, Pellicano et al. (2014 p. 1) argue that "the lack of a shared approach to community engagement in UK autism research represents a key roadblock to translational endeavours".

An alternative position is taken by some activist scholars who provocatively argue that the core questions we should be asking are whether the diagnosis of autism is scientifically valid or useful to autistic people or their families (Runswick, Mallett and Timimi, 2016). It is important to recognise the fluidity (or outright rejection) of autism identity for some and the reasons why such positions are taken up (O'Dell et al. 2016, Runswick-Cole et al. 2016).

There is some evidence of shifting power within the autism research arena. A new study, Spectrum 10K, was launched in the United Kingdom in August 2021 to considerable national media interest. The project, co-led by Simon Baron Cohen from the University of Cambridge and Daniel Geschwind from the University of California Los Angeles aims to "investigate the genetic and environmental factors that contribute to autism and related physical and mental health conditions to better understand well-being in autistic people and their families". After the launch, questions were immediately asked by members of the autistic community and their allies about the lack of involvement of autistic people in the study design. There were also strong concerns around the proposed collection of DNA samples from autistic people and their family members. Despite explicit claims on the project website that the study will not look for a cure or aim to eradicate autism, an autistic-led group, Boycott Spectrum 10K, was founded, and the campaign work of this group and others led to the suspension of the study within weeks. A consultancy firm has been commissioned to conduct retrospective engagement with autistic people and family members to repair the damage caused by the lack of awareness and foresight of the study team and strengthen the research design. As Natri (n.d.) suggests, it is unprecedented for a large-scale study to be paused because of ethical concerns raised by members of the marginalised group targeted by the research.

So what does critical autism studies do?

For us, critical autism studies is a cross-disciplinary endeavour which highlights the constraints of social environment, structures, and cultures. It is essential to recognise and act on these constraints if we want to change things to generate better health and well-being for autistic citizens and their families. Critical autism studies offers the opportunity to have an impact on people's lives. It takes the focus off the autistic person and their 'personal troubles' and recognises the socially situated nature of public issues facing autistic people and their families (Wright Mills 1959).

It creates a space to relieve some of the tensions that percolate around autism and autism research, enabling respectful, open dialogue and discussion. Critical autism studies engages with the use of language and highlights the dangers associated with functional labels which are not only ableist but can generate barriers to appropriate support (Bottema-Beutal et al. 2021). The activist turn within and beyond the autistic community and academia has added anger, clarity, and a hope for pragmatic and meaningful change. From theory to practice, we want this to be practically meaningful and to unsettle positions of power when they are built on shaky, unevidenced grounds, or grounds that have been shown to have a detrimental effect on people.

The production of understandings that perpetuate how we understand phenomena because of the ways in which our research practices are underpinned by the imperialism of common sense – shaped and influenced by the strength of conformist thinking (Guattari 1988) – is, we argue, magnified in a field in which research is dominated by non-autistic researchers and academics. A linear status quo is maintained, reducing space for imagination and opportunities to critically think and do things differently (Deleuze, 1997). There is some irony that this cultural imperialism can be demonstrated through an autistic researcher-led analysis of the referencing of work within critical autism studies (Milton 2018). Authors citing autistic critical theorists in *Disability and Society* are typically other autistic authors, which suggests a systematic sidelining of, or superficial engagement with (Botha et al. 2020), autistic scholarship – a peculiar 'talking over' in the process of writing about the importance of collaborative research and engagement.

Whilst there is a drive towards co-production and interdisciplinarity, with a few notable exceptions, it is autistic scholars who are most likely to cite each other. For critical autism studies to change this, a more participatory and emancipatory ethos is necessary. The contributions and forms of expertise needed (Milton 2014) for such efforts require both autistic and non-autistic scholars and activists, not the erasure of their voices and efforts within the field. Indeed, a compelling case for inclusion on ethical and epistemological grounds has been made (Milton and Bracher 2013; Milton 2014; Gillespie-Lynch et al. 2017; Chown et al. 2017; Fletcher-Watson et al. 2019). We have seen a welcome counter-focus on participatory autism research in the UK (Fletcher-Watson et al. 2019; Milton and Bracher 2013; Milton 2014; Gillespie-Lynch et al. 2017; Chown et al. 2017).

In producing this Handbook, we have embraced how working across these subcultures is possible, productive, and beneficial to all concerned. Critical autism studies offer potential and possibilities to continue to seek the emancipation of autistic people, focus on intersectionality and injustices, and for academics who are autistic and non-autistic to work together in producing important scholarship that has reach and impact. Meaningful collaborative engagement is key and can be demonstrated by the development of a 'neurodiverse collective' in which autistic and non-autistic people (researchers and participants) work together (Bertilsdottir Rosqvist et al. 2019); working in partnership, increasing the inclusion of autistic voices, and revising or reducing the non-autistic voices. Meaningful engagement is a core part of robust research and yet the power relations in the field of autism studies remain unbalanced. We support the summary of autism research advocated by the autistic community (Bottema-Beutal 2021 p. 19): "Accessible, inclusive of autistic participation and perspectives, reflective of the priorities of the autistic community, of high quality and written in a way that doesn't contribute to the stigmatisation of autistic people". Critical autism studies involves the reclaiming of the narratives of autistic people and the centring of these experiences.

There is a strong bias in this volume towards the Global North. The idea of a wider autism spectrum is a Northern European and American concept which means there are fewer autistic people in other parts of the world (Zeidan et al. 2022). In many countries, there is no term for autism, there is no concept of autism as we would define it, and there is a tendency for the Anglo-American representation of autism to be viewed as universal (see Crosbie, this volume). In terms of funding knowledge production and research into autism, there is a highly Americanised weighting. In 2010, for example, the United States spent 89 times more on autism research than the UK (Pellicano, Dinsmore, and Charman 2014). Although there is growing interest in autism across the globalised world and in the spread of information and ways of conceiving issues, in many societies autism still seems a rare disorder of severe learning disability. Autistic activists are often in a difficult position although they are beginning to organise and form autistic activist and family-led groups. This is very early, however, and a strong stigma remains in some parts of the world, related to a strongly medicalised interpretation. Medical clinicians still have the power to label and frame people with more severe learning disabilities and make decisions about people's lives.

Book aims and structure

A key aim of this book is to coalesce the split subcultures within critical autism studies in one place by including contributions from a wide range of perspectives, including autistic and non-autistic activists, academics, practitioners, and professionals. This speaks to the concept of the 'autism wars' (Orsini 2016) and competing meanings generated by *autistic knowledges* (generated by autistic people) and *knowledges of autism* (the knowledge of professionals, parents, and academics) (see Bertilsdottir and colleagues, this volume). This coalescence will provide people – activists, scholars, professionals, students, and others – with a connection to critical voices on the matter of autism, highlighting points of connection with which to build their own activism with, ideas of what to take on and what to disregard as irrelevant, and potential starting points. There is strength in linking theory and practice and improving activism and thereby generating change in people's lives. The collection of authors in this volume gives activism a legitimised voice, a level of respect that activism is often not granted. Indeed, too often activism is not listened to or considered to be part of the academic evidence base.

In terms of structure, the book is divided into four sections: Conceptualising autism; Autistic identity; Community and culture; Practice.

Part 1: Conceptualising autism

In the opening sections, authors conceptualise autism in diverse ways which capture the fluid meaning of the term. In Chapter 2, **Larry Arnold** traces the movement from disorder to identity as autistic people engage with the concept and generate new meanings. For Arnold, 'self' can be viewed as a set of constructions based on contingency and circumstance. He reflects on whether the identity is useful, real, or a mechanism to establish a sense of self. In Chapter 3, **Charlotte Brownlow, Lindsay O'Dell, and Ding Abawi** consider how autistic people are positioned within the dominant discourses of developmental psychology and other psy-disciplines and explore what normative models of development mean for understandings of autism and autistic individuals. The authors highlight the dominance of Western understandings and the powerful role that they have played in constructing 'normal' and 'non-normal'. They further demonstrate how three key developmental concepts manifest within the autism literature are invoked to identify differences, serving to marginalise those labelled. In Chapter 4, **Dinah Murray** makes a strong call for injustices to be exposed as widely as possible, in order to create the passion that is necessary for truly different attitudes towards people who are unable to speak for themselves.

For Murray, language and the power of words are central to this endeavour. In Chapter 5, **Patrick Dwyer** presents an introduction to clustering analyses and, like Brownlow et al., demonstrates how what may be perceived to be an objective process of subgrouping relatively similar autistic people is subjective and can have deleterious consequences, such as reducing support or fracturing communities. In Chapter 6, **Richard Woods** carefully takes us through the process of how the social construction of Pathological Demand Avoidance (PDA) led to the adoption of PDA as a form of autism. For Woods, PDA provides disability studies scholars with an unusual opportunity to study how phenomena are constructed. He again explores the impact of impact of PDA on those assigned with the label. **Monique Botha** completes this section in Chapter 7 by proposing reparations for the gross institutional violence experienced by autistic and other people. Unpacking the presumed neutrality of psychologists, Botha describes how the history and present of autism knowledge is one marked by violence, such as eugenics, dehumanisation, and objectifying narratives, and has rarely fully involved autistic people. Botha suggests Community Psychology could provide a road map for addressing this violence.

Part 2: Autistic identity

Part 2 includes contributions around autistic identity that cover critical race theory, motherhood, gender, and secondary schooling. Autistic identities cut across other, more established identities and this is demonstrated in recent research with studies focusing on gender (Kourti and McCloud 2019, Mandy and Lai 2017), sexuality (Kourti 2021), and race (Brown et al. 2017). **Melissa Simmonds** makes a strong case for the existence of racism in the autistic community and wider society in Chapter 8, demonstrating that it is important to focus not on what it is like to be autistic but what it is like to be Black and autistic. She asks what we are going to do to write the wrongs in the field of autism. In Chapter 9, **Francesca Bernardi** draws on a Gramscian perspective in her qualitative study of Italian mothers of autistic children to highlight hierarchical positions maintained in medical proceedings and contexts, producing practices of control disguised in language as rigour. Her work resonates with contributions from Part 1, including Brownlow et al. and Botha. Bernardi further identifies how the interview space enabled mothers the opportunity to begin to recognise, articulate, and counter marginalisation, ableism, and social distinctions. Chapter 10 stays with mothers, as **Magdalena Mikulak** focuses on the intersection between gender diversity and autism. Drawing on a qualitative study of the experiences of mothers of young trans and gender-diverse children, she asks what ideas and understandings of both gender diversity and autism are reproduced when the two are held together and analysed in relation to one another. In Chapter 11, **Emma Rice Adams** demonstrates an understanding of how the self can be presented in varying social contexts to influence the perceptions of others. She uses the example of young autistic adolescents and the school environment and demonstrates how her findings act as a counter to deficit-focused characterisations of young autistic people. In the process, she illustrates how the sense of self of the autistic young people involved is both conceptualised and negotiated within the social world. Finally, **Damian Milton** offers a personal account of neurodiversity, academia, and activism in Chapter 12. In this chapter Milton examines the power differentials between researchers and autistic people, introduces the reader to the Participatory Autism Research Collective (PARC), a network promoting participatory work within autism studies, and offers advice for others setting out on the path of autistic scholar-activism.

Part 3: Community and culture

Part 3 shifts the focus to community and culture and takes us from a vision of 'utopia' to the Moulin Rouge (or the Rouge Moulin) in Paris, to the reality-TV programme *Love on the*

Spectrum, ending with sunflowers at Manchester airport. **Luke Beardon** starts this section with the presentation of a vision for autistic acceptance and belonging in a future dimension – 'autopia' – in Chapter 13. He returns to the theme of harm that is done to autistic people by narrowly defined normative expectations, arguing that the problems autistic people experience are the result of lack of knowledge, of understanding, acceptance, willingness to listen, and of change. In Chapter 14, **Peter Crosbie** uses the example of France to question the idea that there is a single, universal representation of autism that is understood across all cultures. He challenges the notion that the only way forward for these societies is to adopt the Anglo-American representation of autism as their own. **Hanna Bertilsdotter Rosqvist** and co-authors discuss competing autistic knowledges in Chapter 15 and conceptualise these claims to knowledge and rights of interpretation in terms of struggles for authority within and between different epistemological communities. This again speaks to the aim of this volume, which is to bring together the different subcultures within critical autism studies. **Mitzi Waltz** returns to parents in Chapter 16 with a hard-hitting exploration of the pressures parents experience. She takes us back to the Child Guidance Movement with its focus on the 'maladjustment' of children, which developed in the early 20th century in the UK and the United States, and the subsequent commercialisation of autism. **Allison Moore** brings us back to the present with an examination of the intersection of representation of autism, sex, and intimacy in a US-based reality-TV programme, *Love on the Spectrum*. Using Pierre Bourdieu, Moore demonstrates how it is necessary to move beyond individualised accounts of love and romance, to the structural inequalities autistic people face in the dating world. Finally, in Chapter 18, **Katherine Runswick-Cole and Dan Goodley** provide a biopolitical reading of a story about the use of a sunflower lanyard and the subsequent conversation the authors had about this experience. This allows a consideration of the biopolitics not simply of autism but of life itself and what it means to be human.

Part 4: Practice

The final section in this volume focuses on practice and offers ideas for improving the wellbeing of autistic people. Chapter 19 by **Chloe Farahar** documents the two 'autisms' – autism as a medical disorder and autism as difference – before going on to highlight the importance of an autistic identify as a 'social cure' and the importance of autistic spaces as places of refuge and healing, generating well-being. **Hodge and colleagues** use critical autism studies as a methodological tool in Chapter 20 to analyse how the apparently mundane and ordinary chatter in classrooms conceals and reproduces dominant disabling discourses that deny autistic children personhood and position them as a problem. The chapter is based on a digital story made by Hodge as part of the Re•Storying Autism in Education project. In Chapter 21, **Steven Kapp** compares four attribution models of moral responsibility for the causes of and solution to problems: moral, medical, enlightened, and neurodiverse. He argues the neurodiversity model offers the strongest approach to improving autistic people's lives as it is empowering and encourages people to seek support on their own terms. In Chapter 22, **Joseph Long** considers the insights critical autism studies has to offer autism support services, drawing on his experience of a service-providing organisation, Scottish Autism. For Long, practices and discourses within support services can reflect social norms that have historically marginalised autistic people, but engagement with critical theory has the potential to transform the way services operate. **Rebecca Wood** returns to education practice as she explores communication in the classroom in Chapter 23. Like Hodge et al., she presents evidence of the denial of the value of autistic communication in the classroom, drawing on her doctoral study, which leads to diminished agency on the part of the children. Wood makes the argument for setting aside the unquestioned association between autism and communication to allow children to reclaim their agency and show, themselves, the conditions for communicating more fully. Wood here highlights the values that underpin this volume: a resistance to normative conformity and obedience and an acknowledgement that autistic individuals can stand to gain more from silent resistance. Finally, in Chapter 24, **Waldock and Keates** complete this volume with a chapter that underlines a consistent theme running through the contributions: the colonisation of this thing called autism by non-autistic people and what this has meant for autism 'knowledge'. Examining Arnstein's Ladder of Citizen Participation, the authors underline the importance of the autistic voice in autism research and provide a checklist for autism researchers to use.

References

Arnold, L. (2013). Editorial. Autonomy. *The Critical Journal of Interdisciplinary Autism Studies, North America*. http://www.larry-arnold.net/Autonomy/index.php/autonomy/article/view/ED2>.

Arnold, L. (2016). Rethinking autism, diagnosis, identity and equality. *Good Autism Practice*, 17(2), pp.100–101.

Arnold, L. (2017). Review of rethinking autism. *Autonomy, the Critical Journal of Interdisciplinary Autism Studies*. http://www.larry-arnold.net/Autonomy/index.php/autonomy/article/view/RE7

Autonomy, the Critical Journal of Interdisciplinary Autism Studies (2012) [online]: http://www.larry-arnold.net/Autonomy/index.php/autonomy/index (Accessed 10th December 2017).

Barnes, C. (2003). Disability studies: What's the point? [online]: http://disability-studies.leeds.ac.uk/files/library/Barnes-Whats-the-point.pdf (Accessed 10th Decemebr 2017).

Baxter, A.J., Brugha, T.S., Erskine, H.E., Scheurer, R.W., Vos, T. and Scott, J.G. (2015). The epidemiology and global burden of autism spectrum disorders. *Psychological Medicine*, 45(3), pp.601–613. https://doi.org/10.1017/S003329171400172X

Bertilsdotter Rosqvist, H., Kourti, M., Jackson-Perry, D., Brownlow, C., Fletcher, K., Bendelman, D. and O'Dell, L. (2019). Doing it differently: Emancipatory autism studies within a neurodiverse academic space. *Disability and Society*, 34(7–8), pp.1082–1101. https://doi.org/10.1080/09687599.2019.1603102

Botha, M., Dibb, B. and Frost, D.M. (2020). "Autism is me": An investigation of how autistic individuals make sense of autism and stigma. *Disability and Society*, pp.1–27. https://doi.org/10.1080/09687599.2020.1822782

Botha, M. (2021). Academic, activist, or advocate? Angry, entangled, and emerging: A critical reflection on autism knowledge production. *Frontiers in Psychology*, 12, p.4196.

Bottema-Beutel, K., Kapp, S.K., Lester, J.N., Sasson, N.J. and Hand, B.N. (2021). Avoiding ableist language: Suggestions for autism researchers. *Autism in Adulthood*. https://doi.org/10.1089/aut.2020.0014

Brown, L.X., Ashkenazy, E. and Onaiwu, M.G., eds. (2017). *All the weight of our dreams: On living racialized autism*. Lincoln, NE: DragonBee Press.

Chown, N., Robinson, J., Beardon, L., Downing, J., Hughes, L., Leatherland, J., Fox, K., Hickman, L. and MacGregor, D. (2017). Improving research about us, with us: A draft framework for inclusive autism research. *Disability and Society*, 32(5), pp.720–734. https://doi.org/10.1080/09687599.2017.1320273

Dattaro, L. (2021). https://www.spectrumnews.org/news/autism-research-funding-rises-but-still-falls-short-of-goals/ (Accessed 15th April 2022).

Davidson, J. and Orsini, M., eds. (2013). *Worlds of autism: Across the spectrum of neurological difference*. Minneapolis, MN: University of Minnesota Press.

Deleuze, G. (1997). *Essays critical and clinical*. Minneapolis, MN: University of Minnesota.

Deleuze, G. and Guattari, F. (1988). *A thousand plateaus: Capitalism and schizophrenia* (B. Massumi trans.). London: Athlone Press.

Evans, B. (2013). How autism became autism: The radical transformation of a central concept of child development in Britain. *History of the Human Sciences*, 26(3), pp.3–31. https://doi.org/10.1177/0952695113484320

Fletcher-Watson, S., Adams, J., Brook, K., Charman, T., Crane, L., Cusack, J., Leekam, S., Milton, D., Parr, J.R. and Pellicano, E. (2019). Making the future together: Shaping autism research through meaningful participation. *Autism*, 23(4), pp.943–953.

Gillespie-Lynch, K., Kapp, S.K., Brooks, P.J., Pickens, J. and Schwartzman, B. (2017). Whose expertise is it? Evidence for autistic adults as critical autism experts. *Frontiers in Psychology*, 8, p.438. https://doi.org/10.3389/fpsyg.2017.00438

Hens, K., Robeyns, I. and Schaubroeck, K. (2019). The ethics of autism. *Philosophy Compass*, 14(1), p.e12559. https://doi.org/10.1111/phc3.12559

Hirvikoski, T., Mittendorfer-Rutz, E., Boman, M., Larsson, H., Lichtenstein, P. and Bölte, S. (2016). Premature mortality in autism spectrum disorder. *The British Journal of Psychiatry*, 208(3), pp.232–238.

Kourti, M. and MacLeod, A. (2019). "I Don't Feel Like a Gender, I Feel Like Myself": Autistic individuals raised as girls exploring gender identity. *Autism in Adulthood*, 1(1), pp.52–59. https://doi.org/10.1089/aut.2018.0001

Krcek, T.E. (2013). Deconstructing disability and neurodiversity: Controversial issues for autism and implications for social work. *Journal of Progressive Human Services*, 24(1), pp.4–22.

Lavelle, T.A., Weinstein, M.C., Newhouse, J.P., Munir, K., Kuhlthau, K.A. and Prosser, L.A. (2014). Economic burden of childhood autism spectrum disorders. *Pediatrics*, 133(3), pp.e520–e529. https://doi.org/10.1542/peds.2013-0763

Mandy, W. and Lai, M.-C. (2017) Towards sex- and gender-informed autism research. *Autism of Research and Practice*, 21(6), pp.643–645. https://doi.org/10.1177/1362361317706904

McGuire, A.E. and Michalko, R. (2011). Minds between us: Autism, mindblindness and the uncertainty of communication. *Educational Philosophy and Theory*, 43(2), pp.162–177. doi.org/10.1111/j.1469-5812.2009.00537.x

Mercieca, D. and Mercieca, D. (2010). Opening research to intensities: Rethinking disability research with Deleuze and Guattari. *Journal of Philosophy of Education*, 44(1), pp.79–92.

Mills, C.W. (1959). *The sociological imagination*. Oxford University Press: Oxford.

Milton, D. (2012). On the ontological status of autism: The 'double empathy problem'. *Disability and Society*, 27(6), pp.883–887. https://doi.org/10.1080/09687599.2012.710008

Milton, D. (2014). Autistic expertise: A critical reflection on the production of knowledge in autism studies. *Autism: the International Journal of Research and Practice* (special edition 'Autism and Society'), 18(7), pp.794–802. https://doi.org/10.1177/1362361314525281

Milton, D. (2016). Re-thinking autism: Diagnosis, identity and equality. *Disability and Society*, 31(10), pp.1413–1415. https://doi.org/10.1080/09687599.2016.1221666

Milton, D.E.M. (2017). *A mismatch of salience: Explorations of the nature of autism from theory to practice*. Hove, UK: Pavilion Publishing and Media Ltd.

Milton, D. (2018). *Lancaster disability studies keynote*. Lancaster Disability Studies Conference, 6–8 September.

Milton, D. and Bracher, M. (2013). Autistics speak but are they heard? *Medical Sociology Online*, 7(2), pp.61–69 [online]: http://www.medicalsociologyonline.org/resources/Vol7Iss2/MSo_7.2_Autistics-speak-but-are-they-heard_Milton-and-Bracher.pdf (Accessed 11th January 2022).

Milton, D. and Sims, T. (2016). How is a sense of well-being and belonging constructed in the accounts of autistic adults? *Disability and Society*, 31(4), pp.520–534. https://doi.org/10.1080/09687599.2016.1186529

Milton, D. and Timimi, S. (2016). *Does autism have an essential nature?* [online]: http://blogs.exeter.ac.uk/exploringdiagnosis/debates/debate-1/ (Accessed 10th December 2017).

Murray, D. (2018). Monotropism—an interest based account of autism. *Encyclopedia of Autism Spectrum Disorders*, 10, pp.971–978. https://doi.org/10.1007/978-1-4614-6435-8_102269-1

Natri, H. (2021). Spectrum 10K and the questionable past, present, and future of genetic autism research. https://doi.org/10.13140/RG.2.2.14973.28642

O'Dell, L., Bertilsdotter-Rosqvist, H., Ortega, F., Brownlow, C. and Orsini, M. (2016). Critical autism studies: Exploring epistemic dialogues and intersections, challenging dominant understandings of autism. *Disability and Society*, 31(2), pp.166–179. https://doi.org/10.1080/09687599.2016.1164026

Orsini, M. (2016). Contesting the autistic subject: Biological citizenship and the autism/autistic movement. In *Critical interventions in the ethics of healthcare* (pp.131–146). Routledge.

Pellicano, E., Dinsmore, A. and Charman, T. (2014). Views on researcher-community engagement in autism research in the United Kingdom: A mixed-methods study. *PLOS ONE*, 9(10), p.e109946. https://doi.org/10.1371/journal.pone.0109946

Pring, J. (2021). Autistic campaigners' anger over Spectrum 10K protest lock-out and 'scare tactics'. https://www.disabilitynewsservice.com/autistic-campaigners-anger-over-spectrum-10k-protest-lock-out-and-scare-tactics/ (Accessed 15th April 2022).

Roche, L., Adams, D. and Clark, M. (2021). 'Research priorities of the autism community: A systematic review of key stakeholder perspectives'. *Autism*, 25(2), pp.336–348. https://doi.org/10.1177/1362361320967790

Runswick-Cole, K. (2014). 'Us' and 'them': The limits and possibilities of a 'politics of neurodiversity' in neoliberal times. *Disability and Society*, 29(7), pp.1117–1129. https://doi.org/10.1080/09687599.2014.910107

Runswick-Cole, K., Mallett, R. and Timimi, S. eds. (2016). *Re-thinking autism: Diagnosis identity and equality.* London: Jessica Kingsley Publishers.

Sinclair, J. (2010). Cultural commentary: Being autistic together. *Disability Studies Quarterly*, 30(1). https://dsq-sds.org/article/view/1075

Smith, R. (2006). Peer review: A flawed process at the heart of science and journals. *Journal of the Royal Society of Medicine*, 99(4), pp.178–182.

Snow, C.P. (1961). *The two cultures and the scientific revolution: The Rede Lecture 1959.* New York: Cambridge University Press.

The Autism Centre (2011). *Critical autism seminar day makes an impact* [online]: https://theautismcentre.wordpress.com/2011/01/19/critical-autism-seminar-day-makes-an-impact/ (Accessed 11th January 2018).

Verhoeff, B. (2012). What is this thing called autism? A critical analysis of the tenacious search for autism's essence. *BioSocieties*, 7(4), pp.410–432.

Waltz, M. (2008). Autism = death: The social and medical impact of a catastrophic medical model of autistic spectrum disorders. *Popular Narrative Media*, 1(1), pp.13–23. https://doi.org/10.3828/pnm.1.1.4

Woods, R., Milton, D., Arnold, L. and Graby, S. (2018). Redefining critical autism studies: A more inclusive interpretation. *Disability and Society*, 33(6), pp.974–979. https://doi.org/10.1080/09687599.2018.1454380

Zeidan, J., Fombonne, E., Scorah, J., Ibrahim, A., Durkin, M.S., Saxena, S., Yusuf, A., Shih, A. and Elsabbagh, M. (2022). Global prevalence of autism: A systematic review update. *Autism Research.* https://doi.org/10.1002/aur.2696

PART 1
Conceptualising autism

2
FIRST THERE IS A MOUNTAIN, THEN THERE IS NO MOUNTAIN, THEN THERE IS: WHITHER IDENTITY?

Larry Arnold

The Buddha's Mountain Koan can be seen as a metaphor for first perceiving a thing, then engaging so thoroughly with it that the aspect disappears before one sees it again in a new light. Where can we possibly start such a daunting task as that of examining autistic and neurodivergent identity with all its intersections and pitfalls? Well, as the ancient sages say, the longest journey starts with the first step; but when and where is that? Is the beginning lost in the turbulence and turbidity of those complex sociological and ideological movements such as postmodernism and symbolic interactionalism which are perpetually building on each other, reacting and interacting (Hacking, 2009). It is truly difficult to discern where the individual is – the autobiographical narrative 'I' – because, although discourse is fluid and dialectical, we have a propensity to reinvent the path we came through with the benefit of hindsight, re-signifying the landscape as if we were reflecting on the photographs we took along the way and imbuing them with current rather than contemporary meaning.

For any narrator, myself included, it is not possible to step outside and be objective. We can only approach our inhabited world from the perspective in which we are situated. Before engaging with my PhD thesis, I had the illusion that the question could be approached by quantitative research; however, I learned, through the process, that everything, from the questions I set to my codifying of the responses, was filtered through my own perceptions (Arnold 2015). I resorted to the Constructivist Grounded Theory of Kathy Charmaz to address this paradox (Breckenridge et al. 2012). The best conclusion one can come to is the admission that absolute objectivity is an impossible target and thus one needs to acknowledge oneself as an actor within the process of knowledge production and analysis.

As a narrator, my 'interest' – as much in the Murray, Lesser and Lawson (2005) sense as any other – is in two parts: the first, acknowledging one's situation as being the object of the discourse, identified externally and through self-perception with the 'diagnosis'; the second, from the perspective of an actor within that situation, the essential politics of social and medical engagement with the 'condition', through charity, medicine, and self-advocacy. This has led to my broader engagement with the meaning of autism through academia and critical theory.

Dealing in meaning

What is a 'natural kind'? It is an old philosophical discussion which attempts to separate those realities which would be there independent of the observer from the subjectively created categories fulfilling a real, but not such a universal, function as 'critical realist' discourse.

Autism has its nosological ontology within the wider narrative of mental disorder. It first came to light as a purported 'natural kind' (Bleuler, 1911) within what Bentall (2003) has called the 'Kraepelinian paradigm': the notion that there were a distinct set of biologically derived entities or diseases which were separate from each other. This approach has numerous critiques, not least from the 'mad pride' and 'anti-psychiatry' movements (Szasz, 1960). I do not, however, assume that autism (or any other currently described category of 'disorder') is a 'natural kind'. On the contrary, I assume that the description and social situation of autism (and, by extension, other 'disorders', is a construction born out of a constellation of neurological traits that have come to the fore and been labelled in this way for historical reasons. That which we call autism is contingent on time and era as a form of shifting discourse. That constellation of neurological traits has always existed in one form or another but each of them has been the subject of different foci as to which are the most prominent in terms of what is being constructed as either impairment or maladjustment within a strictly limited context. This context is often invisible to the actors as they are immersed within it; just as the fish does not see water, or we do not see air.

My premise then, from personal experience, observation, and a critical reading of psychiatry, is that autism as it has been understood through the lens of psychiatry is a medical-model view of the world, and a flawed one at that as it does not even accord with neurological, never mind pharmacological, understandings of the brain. It draws from and agrees with the critiques arising within mad studies and the survivor movement which have attempted to build alternatives to hegemonic and damaging psychiatric perspectives (Beresford & Russo, 2016).

This leads me to a troubling question: why would any group of people choose to identify around a purported disorder and does this 'disorder' have anything in common with the psychiatric disorder it originated from? Perhaps this question can be resolved by disengagement from the Kraepelinian paradigm and its current bible (APA, 2014) altogether to consider that possibly the roots of psychiatry are leading to the wrong branches. In essence, this is a restatement of the Duhem–Quine thesis (Harding, 1975), which questions the ability to independently come to any current conclusions without accepting, uncritically as fact, the work of the past. For example, if you are embarking on a study of nuclear physics, you will have to take on trust the early work of Rutherford and others because of the impossibility of independently verifying it for yourself. If any of the fundamental principles are wrong, then what is built on them is open to question. I posit along with others that psychiatry is hopelessly unscientific because it is built on roots that are plainly invalid in the light of more recent discovery showing that the rigid definitions are not discrete, and that they overlap according to customary interpretations in different communities of practice.

I, and other contributors to the field of mad studies (Beresford et al., 2015), suggest, however, that this is what psychiatry needs to do: deliver the externally created identities (diagnoses) and hand them over to another branch of critical knowledge production to deconstruct, to examine the foundations of the discipline as a production of a particularly industrially focused late-19th-century European perspective in order to see if the house it has built still stands firm or if it is now tottering because of its internal contradictions. The resolution of the tensions between mad and neurodivergent identities may then emerge not in opposition, but in new synthesis.

The publication of *DSM-5* in 2013 was merely the latest change to the societal map of autism (Arnold, 2018). Given the history – first, of the condition's emergence in 1980 as a disorder separate from its original context as a subtype of schizophrenia (Bleuler, 1911), then, its change from an infantile disorder in 1987, the entry of Asperger's Syndrome and various subtypes in 1994, and the latest collapse into Autism Spectrum Disorder – it can easily be conceived that the landscape of autism has anything but a clear roadmap and communal understanding. It is more like a set of roadworks attempting to cross an indistinct landscape: not so much, certain knowledge as constant flux. Diagnoses come and go, not necessarily because of the state of medical knowledge at the time but because of societal changes. The elimination of homosexuality as a mental disorder in 1973 is an example. This removal did not mean that the category disappeared from the world as either a natural kind or a focus for restoring the balance of rights in favour of those disadvantaged by the negative nuances of the former category. Rather, it meant that it was no longer considered suitable for psychiatry to engage with the category but more appropriate for the discourse to take place within the social sciences, humanities, and philosophy. Autism can likewise be categorised as a discourse about a presumed category more than it can be described in any way as a Kantian 'noumenon'. What is autism, then, when it is no longer a catalogued disorder? How should society deal with a divergent constellation of that which is currently psychologically recognised?

Everything in this world is, therefore, contingent on something else and while it appears necessary to acknowledge Nadesan (2005) for this deconstruction of autism, Nadesan, too, is contingent and is often not acknowledged by the community, who consider her to be too much of an intellectual colonist. Those of us who were there, exchanging ideas online (Sinclair, n.d., Dekker, 1999), holding conferences of our own, and writing yet-to-be-recognised academic papers, are extinguished, as if by an invasion of anthropologists who come to study our culture and end up throwing us out of our own living space while they make themselves comfortable (Arnold, 2008).

This is not a postmodernist approach, recognising that there are no authors and only texts (Barthes, 1968), but a post-humanist one, going beyond decentring the agency of the author to the idea that the individual makes little difference to the outcome. That is all fictive hindsight, suggesting that the person is not an actor so much as flotsam in a river of change leading us to the present.

Likewise, the history of 'neurodiversity' as a movement grows from a particular time, using the identity afforded by medicine that intersects with a multidimensional reality and ultimately modifies the terrain it inhabits. Kapp (2019) has seminally outlined those beginnings and I am just one part of the continuing narrative using the historically contingent, but useful, social model discourse (Oliver, 1990) to determine how the autistic identity has emerged from disability discourse and seminal rejection of "'person first' language" (Sinclair, 1999) to reclaim formerly negatively nuanced external descriptions of the self.

As a rallying flag, neurodiversity has been at the centre of this as a disputed description originating from within this discourse. This 'neurodiversity', whether reified as a movement or adopted as useful descriptor, has, since its introduction (Singer, 1998), attracted numerous meanings and interpretations by its various proponents and detractors. It has become a political football to be roughly kicked around and beaten in every way but one that leads to better understanding.

Although a term that originated within the autistic community, 'neurodiversity' has an appeal to other communities of interest. The online dyslexic community was where I first came across it while exploring the categories of support available through the alt.support hierarchy. These were pre-existing categories of support through which people like me wandered in and out of before acquiring what became the settled, all-enveloping diagnosis. These categories of difference, which gave rise to categories of personal identification, did not originate within the communities themselves but were donated by pre-existing psycho-medical descriptions that were too readily accepted as factual without question since they were already a taxonomy of pre-existing nosologies as distinct from each other as any Kraepelinian list. Nonetheless, that did not stop people like me cross-posting and sharing between these groups in a way that could often descend into internecine defensive 'territorialism'. Although people often subscribed to more than one group, it was presumed to be bad 'netiquette' to cause these groups to interact by posting the same question to multiple groups while distinct identities and communities were forming; certain commonalities might be observable in many silos rather than just in one.

Even so, this led to the consideration of a multifaceted approach to the problematic definition of 'who is in' and 'who is out', and the concept that neurodiversity did not apply to autism alone was grasped. This is despite it still leading to narrow definitions in and of itself, losing sight of the original conception that in all people there is diversity of neurology just as there is a diversity of body size and shape. The analogy became reified and then became a battle flag, as it were, rallied around by some and defiled by others who cleaved to the supposed safety of a medical definition. The reasons for this could be explored for as long as the concepts of false consciousness have been proposed (see, for example, Gramsci, 1988, Hirst, 1976). This raises the question of acknowledgement of our own myths and legends, as it were; from whom do we seek legitimate authority in the discourse of critical autism studies (Woods et al., 2018)?

Neurodiversity has another significant problem as an all-pervasive meta-identity for the individual because, paradoxically, to go back to where I started and have intimated already, there is the fundamental problem of self in this post-human landscape. 'Self' can be viewed not as an entire and continuous entity, but as a series of constructions based on contingency and circumstance, within the various communities one inhabits in space and time. The very word 'identity' conjures up for me not individual facets but, in a mathematical sense, the congruence of that self with others who one is not different *from* but is 'identical' *to*.

Identity, mind and self, diagnosis and discovery are concepts thrown around with literary abandon, but are any of these concepts deeply seated in cognition, neurological cortices, and modular processes of attention and muscle control? This could be biological reduction taken to the nth degree or it could be that the phenomenon of consciousness that philosophers and scientists alike try to pin down is in fact an illusion. Nothing perhaps exists but shifting patterns of attention, maintaining complex bio-electrical systems surviving in a random landscape of scarce resources and evolutionary contingency. Existence is only given meaning by the fictive narrative creating subjective, and sometimes intersubjective, links simply because the mental apparatus can do that as an epiphenomenon.

This bleak reductionism provides me with (if, after that, I can even use such a term) a perfect background for post-Cartesian introspection and speculation. Could it be said that there is nothing within the sociological and psychological domains that cannot be pinned down to neurobiological substrates of cognition and perception, the way the actual apparatus inside works, and relates phenomenologically to the outside? Whether that be people, rocks, or Bishop Berkeley's trees (Grey, 1952) is not relevant. We are nothing but a collection of molecules, constructed of particles and following a set of prescribed physical laws. It is a wonder we can think at all, but we do, and I believe it is the fundamental neurodiversity stance to take a cognitive rather than a conative view, saving the conative for the bar afterwards.

Where do identity and post-identity sit in this harsh framework? How is it possible to put a phenomenological view back into the discourse where we come to realise that we are not brains in a bottle but all embodied beings in an economy and ecology of physical and discursive exchange? I use the word impairment to describe the bodily and neurological affordances or lack of them that lead to us being treated as disabled, regardless of whether we conceive of ourselves as being so or not, or how we understand and internalise the term disability. It is not perfect, but the distinction works within the context of the social model, and yet I can use metaphor and simile, because these are the affordances of language itself, the innate properties of what can be said.

For instance, to have been given a toxic label is common to many but one is not encouraged to flaunt it in a provocative way, challenging the very existence of normalcy. I think that rather than taking this or that label out, what we need is a thorough humane revision of the psychiatric profession and its practices, bringing it more in tune with the realities that accept that nothing exists in isolation and, unless we live on a desert island, we all have the interface of society to deal with. Our perceptions do not live in isolation; they bang up against the perceptions of other beings and it is the degree to which our affordances facilitate or make difficult those interactions that makes as much difference as any intervention or therapy out there.

Identity as a means of oppression and separation

While I am not a historian, I seek to rationalise from whence the notion of a personal identity has come, and it seems to me that it was a particularly strong concept during the late-19th-, early-20th-century age of falling empires, where individual nationhood and ethnicity gave rise to independence movements. How old these ethnicities are is not my province though a historian of the human psyche could theoretically posit that it must have figured in the Bronze Age given the narratives of Homer and the Old Testament. What concerns me, however, is the aspect of identity that led to the many ethnic conflicts of the 20th century which are still with us, that is, the very toxic notion that one can only derive identity by also identifying the other, who becomes the unwilling adversary. It goes from the point where 'we are we, and not them', to 'we are better than them', and from thence to 'they are not even human', which is, of course, fascism. One can say that the hegemony of imperialism was bad but the world of interethnic conflict that has come from it is not good either.

Nationhood as a given identity has concealed more complex divisions of language, for example, Francophone and Walloon in contemporary Belgium, or Christian vs. Muslim vs. Jew in Lebanon. One can argue as to how real these identities are, but it is difficult to argue that they are not chosen so much as given, in most cases. One may declare oneself to be an ethnic Romanian in the Kosovan Enclave during an independence struggle, but that identity is also tied up in your mother tongue and the religious tradition you are immersed in. It is both the inflexibility and the sense of difference from the other that can lead to conflict when one uses past grievances as an excuse to settle scores and considers the other to be not just different but the oppressor and the enemy.

It may seem a long way to move from the notion of 'collective' identities such as the nation state, religious affiliation, and mother tongue to the current discourses of race, gender, medical oppression (disability), and neurodiversity. At the same time, these intersect and cut across each other within more established identities, raising tough questions rarely asked within academia. For example, not what it means to be autistic but what it means to be an autistic person of colour where class and economic disadvantage further limit one's access to an equal share of the nation's prosperity. Or, what it means to be further disabled within the idealistic notion of autistic union, by physical or sensory impairments, notwithstanding the stigmatisation of being a mental health survivor or 'service user' when notions of autistic integrity are built upon differentiating oneself from one's fellow travellers in the world of psychiatric diminishment.

So much can also be said for 'intergenerationality' or the lack of it, the propensity of every new generation of activists to reinvent the tools and language of self-advocacy without realising that the discourse is diegetic as well as dialectic and synthetic.

This is not so much intended as a deep analysis of the current situation of how atomised identities mesh into wider societal constructs of nationhood and ethnicity; it is a starting point for further consideration.

I am not claiming any exclusive usage of the term 'post-identity' and have seen it used by others quite possibly in a sense I neither mean nor understand. I am instead asking, as Žižek (Gigante, 1998) does, whether strong individual identity is useful as a political tool or part of Marxian false consciousness and internalised oppression. I contend that identity is not a natural position to adopt and is something that only seems to arise strongly in adversity when one's position in society is being externally questioned. It has often been a counter-argument to those who decry labels, that they act as effective pointers to help, but that usefulness is either lost or forgotten when one is prospering or existing in isolation. The very word 'identity' seems perfidious, as it implies the logical position of being identical, without differentiation, whereas it is in practice only likeness to varying degrees; identity is held to be individual, but perhaps it is uniformity. I personally consider I have passed that stage where identity is still central to my conception of who and what I am. I have come over the top of that mountain and now look back from the other side and consider whether it was worth it; whether we could ever arrive at some point in history where we do not need an identity which has proved so divisive in communities both large and small.

Conclusion

For all the debates around the word and meanings of autism, neurodiversity, and the problems of identity politics within a wider sphere of equality politics, there has to be a utility and purpose in identifying within the group vs. identifying outside of it. Or, indeed, not being concerned at all. Assuming the identity gives someone more than authenticity, it provides, as the popular idiom says, 'skin in the game', hazarding a stake at risk. It is, of course, about the power relationships in every field that attempt to limit one's ability to critically engage with the dominant discourse; an imbalance of power that can sometimes be so strong as to render itself invisible to anyone who comes up against it, as thorough and all-embracing as it is. To return to the original metaphor, regardless of whether one still sees it or not, the mountain is still there. We do not live in an ideal world but in one defined externally by identities that are given to us at various points in our lives whether we want them or not. Some of these confer advantage and signification of the elite; others confer disadvantage and the mark of being other, inferior, to be feared. Sometimes it is possible to confront the latter given to us by the former and use it as a rallying call, a flag of convenience or, as a last resort, a port in a storm. If we do not know who we are, can we know what we are fighting for? My final word on our neurodiversity here is that it is not a state but a transition – we are as diverse from ourselves along our life trajectory as we are from each other but at the end "we are all interdependent whether we are aware of the fact or not and if each of us persists in being the centre of our own existence we are all doomed to suffer at each other's hands" (Tantam, 2009).

References

APA, (2014). *Diagnostic and Statistical Manual of Mental Disorders*, 5th ed. Washington, DC: American Psychiatric Association.

Arnold, L., (2008). Discovering the autistic tribes, new territories for the Internet anthropologist. *Perspectives of Autonomy and Autochthoneity in the 21st Century*. Liverpool: Disability and the Internet: Access, Mediation, Representation - Cultural Disability Studies Network Liverpool John Moores University.

Arnold, L., (2015). *The Application of Video in the Education of Autistic Adults*. Birmingham: University of Birmingham.

Arnold, L., (2018). Context and subtext, a part of the world or apart from it? *Lancaster Disability Studies Conference. Lancaster CEDR*, 11th–13th of September, p. 30.

Barthes, R., «La mort de l'auteur» (1968). *ders.: Essais Critiques IV. Le bruissement de la langue*. Paris: Edition du Seuil, 984, pp. 6–67.

Bentall, R., (2003). *Madness Explained: Psychosis and Human Nature in Medicine*. London: Allen Lane.

Beresford, P., McWade, B. & Milton, D., (2015). Mad studies and neurodiversity: A dialogue. *Disability and Society*, 30(2), pp. 305–309. doi: 10.1080/09687599.2014.1000512.

Beresford, P. & Russo, J., (2016). Supporting the sustainability of mad studies and preventing its co-option. *Disability and Society*, 31(2), pp. 270–274. doi: 10.1080/09687599.2016.1145380.

Bleuler, E., (1911). Dementia praecox or the group of schizophrenias. In *Handbuch der Psychiatrie. Spezieller Teil*. 4. Abteilung, 1. Hälfte. Leipzig & Wien: Franz Deuticke.

Breckenridge, J. P., Jones, D., Elliot, I. & Nicol, M., (2012). Choosing a methodological path: Reflections on the constructivist turn. *Grounded Theory Review*, 11(1), pp. 64–71.

Dekker, M., (1999). *On Our Own Terms: Emerging Autistic Culture* [Online] Available at: http://www.awares.org/.

Gigante, D., (1998). Toward a notion of critical self-creation: Slavoj Žižek and the "vortex of madness". *New Literary History*, 29(1), pp. 153–168. doi: 10.1353/nlh.1998.0006.

Gramsci, A., (1988). *The Gramsci Reader* (D. Forgacs, Ed.). London: Lawrence and Wishart.

Grey, D., (1952). The solipsism of Bishop Berkeley. *The Philosophical Quarterly*, 2(9), pp. 338–349. doi: 10.2307/2216814.

Hacking, I., (2009). Autistic autobiography. *Philosophical Transactions of the Royal Society: Biological Sciences*, 364(1522), pp. 1467–1473. doi: 10.1098/rstb.2008.0329.

Harding, S., ed., (1975). *Can theories be refuted?: Essays on the Duhem-Quine* thesis (Vol. 81). Springer Science & Business Media.

Hirst, P. Q., (1976). Althusser and the theory of ideology. *Economy and Society*, 5(4), pp. 385–412. doi: 10.1080/03085147600000009.

Kapp, S., (2019). *Autistic Community and the Neurodiversity Movement: Stories from the Frontline*. Singapore: Springer.

Murray, D., Lesser, M. & Lawson, W., (2005). Attention, monotropism and the diagnostic criteria for autism. *Autism*, 9(2), pp. 139–156.

Nadesan, M., (2005). *Constructing Autism, Unravelling the "Truth" and Understanding the Social*. Oxford and New York: Routledge.

Oliver, M., (1990). The individual and social models of disability. Paper presented at *Joint Workshop of the Living Options Group and the Research Unit of the Royal College of Physicians*. On People with established locomotor disabilities in hospitals July 1990. [Online] Available at: http://www.leeds.ac.uk/disability-studies/archiveuk/Oliver/in%20soc%20dis.pdf [Accessed 10 May 2010].

Sinclair, J., (1999). Why I dislike people first language. [Online] Available at: http://web.archive.org/web/20070715055110/web.syr.edu/~jisincla/person_first.htm [Accessed 20th May 2010].

Sinclair, J., (n.d.) Autism Network International. [Online] Available at: http://www.autreat.com/ [Accessed 1st March 2014].

Singer, J., (1998). Odd people. In *The Birth of Community Amongst People on the Autistic Spectrum: A Personal Exploration of a New Social Movement Based on Neurological Diversity*. BA degree thesis. Sydney: Faculty of Humanities and Social Science University of Technology.

Szasz, T., (1960). The myth of mental illness. *American Psychologist*, 15(2), pp. 113–118. doi: 10.1037/h0046535.

Tantam, D., (2009). *Can the world afford autistic spectrum disorder?: Nonverbal communication, Asperger syndrome and the interbrain*. London: Jessica Kingsley Publishers.

Woods, R., Milton, D., Arnold, L. & Graby, S., (2018). Redefining critical autism studies: A more inclusive interpretation. *Disability and Society*, 33(6), pp. 974–979. doi: 10.1080/09687599.2018.1454380.

3
CRITICALLY CONTEXTUALISING 'NORMAL' DEVELOPMENT AND THE CONSTRUCTION OF THE AUTISTIC INDIVIDUAL

Charlotte Brownlow, Lindsay O'Dell, and Ding Abawi

The establishment of milestones and benchmarks to which individuals and their development are compared, and against which they are assessed, is ingrained in disciplines such as medicine, psychiatry, and psychology. These milestones and benchmarks enable 'normal', 'appropriate' development to be tracked through time and any deviations from the norm identified (Rose, 1979). This view of development has become so ingrained in some disciplines that it has over the years become taken-for-granted knowledge – understandings that do not require any critical consideration but rather are presented as purely factual. Rose (1979) refers to disciplines that draw on and perpetuate such hegemonic knowledge as the 'psy-complex'. This complex reflects the regulated practices and discourses within the field, and the ways in which people are both observed and regulated by psychology and related fields (Parker, 1997). The proposition of 'normative development' renders deficient and other any individual who diverges from expectations. This chapter will explore the constructions of normality and what normative models of development mean for understandings of autism and autistic individuals. In doing so, it will draw on three primary areas of focus within autism research: theory of mind; social connectedness and friendship; and gender identity.

Historical dominance of normative models of development

In a seminal piece of work, Rose (1989) argued that with the development of the psy-complex, psychology as a discipline was implicated in the move to produce a technological, psychological, and psychometric approach to individualising people. Such a focus on the individual meant that people were separated from being considered as part of a larger social grouping, and therefore open for scrutiny and comparison with others. Rose argues that it was through this process of individualisation that the norms of childhood and milestone expectations began to be established, thus enabling the categorisation and labelling of individuals. All these processes could ultimately be governed by appropriately qualified professionals working within the psy-complex. Further, the specific knowledge required to engage with the narratives of psychometrics, drawing on both statistical and psychological jargon, enabled psychology to position itself as the appropriate authority through which to both identify and govern individual differences. Such a position draws on the assumption that there is a 'typical' child, something contested by writers including Taylor (2011) and Hultqvist and Dahlberg (2001), who assert that: "There is no natural or evolutionary child, only the historically produced discourses and power relations that constitute the child as an object and subject of knowledge, practice, and political intervention" (Hultqvist & Dahlberg, 2001, cited in Taylor, 2011, p. 421).

Similarly, Rose (1989) argues that psychometric scales and tests were not just a means of assessing children's abilities, they provided new ways of thinking about childhood that naturalises views of development articulated through milestones of achievement. Such milestones led to the regulating of children's behaviour through practitioners including parents and health workers. Burman (2008) proposes that this position adopted by psychology became taken-for-granted expectations about children's development and had broader-reaching implications concerning the role of parents and families in fostering the development of the 'normal' child. All these narratives and assumptions excluded the expertise of those classified by these systems, and it could be argued that while advocate voices are increasingly more powerful in public discourse, the impact of these on psychologised and medicalised discourse remains limited.

Debates concerning the concept of 'normality' and its measurement, which are common in contemporary work, are entrenched in a history surrounding the construction of abnormality and consequently normality. This is not to say that contemporary psychology ignores history. Indeed, as Parker et al. (1995) have highlighted, once a new concept or classification is described, experts then 'discover' cases of it in the past; for example, the neurologist Oliver Sacks proposed that Henry Cavendish, who discovered hydrogen, was most likely autistic (Harmon, 2004). Jarrett (2020) further reflects on the changing approaches to 'treatment' and the public policies that these approaches reside within. As a result of these changing understandings and approaches, the past is continuously constructed as in some way 'wrong', which the present was required to actively put 'right'. The retrospective reframing or re-diagnosing of 'disorder' serves as a way of warranting the 'real' nature and truthfulness of the concept being described. In doing so, Parker et al. (1995) argue that experts very often ignore discontinuities in history and that words may have very different meanings in different historical contexts. Indeed, recent global events of the COVID-19 pandemic have seen much discussion and media use of the term "the new normal" when referring to a range of activities such as maintaining social distance and interacting with others purely online, suggesting that understandings of specifics change. Therefore, meanings attached to such 'problems', evaluations made about them, and the consequences of such evaluations cannot be isolated from the specific cultural, social, and historical situation in which they are made. The resulting diagnoses are therefore not neutral labels but a reflection of a particular focus by professionals, occurring within a specific historical and cultural location. The normalising focus serves to highlight specifics while reducing others to the periphery of professional attention. Indeed, Milton (2018) has argued that many 'treatment interventions' are situated within ableist understandings promoting particular kinds of normalcy and pathologising others. This frequently results in individuals being required to act 'less autistic'.

Constructions of autism within historical normative models

Autism and the constructions of the autistic individual are intricately intertwined with such dominant understandings of 'normal development'. From the early conceptualisations of Kanner and Asperger, to more contemporary understandings as reflected in the *Diagnostic and Statistical Manual* (*DSM*) and International Statistical Classification of Diseases and Related Health Problems (ICD), autism is presented as something other than the norm. A key example of this is in the framework of the triad, now dyad, of 'impairments', initially proposed by Wing (1997). The original triad comprised social development, communication, and behavioural repertoires, and this has recently been reconceptualised as a dyad in the *DSM-5* with the collapsing of social and communicative development into a single dimension (APA, 2013). Whether we draw on a triad or a dyad, their importance here is on their influence within the field of autism, both clinically and academically, in the role that they play in shaping understandings of autism and focusing gaze on specific characteristics. The focus on key areas therefore highlights attention to specifics and allows more easily for any transgressions from expectations to be quickly and easily identified. For example, hobbies and collecting behaviours are not seen as problematic outside of a lens of a diagnosis of autism, but through a lens of an autism label they can be reconstructed as obsessive, fixed, and rigid (see, for example, Ryder & Brownlow, 2018).

What is interesting in such reflections is that it is not until relatively recently, in the *DSM–III* (APA, 1980), that autism was recognised as an 'official' and distinct diagnostic category (Volkmar, 1998). Since this time, there have been many iterations of classification and reclassification and debates surrounding the similarities and distinctiveness of what were originally two different diagnostic labels of autism and Asperger's syndrome. More recently, in 2013, the *DSM-5* controversially removed the possibility of Asperger's as a diagnostic option, consequently impacting on the identities of a generation of autistic people who had crafted an identity as Asperger's or 'Aspie'.

It is evident from developmental models that neurotypical traits are taken to be positive and something to strive for by non-neurotypical people. A theory or definition of neurotypical is therefore not required, because the focus of the dominant group is on people who are not neurotypical as this is taken as the default majority. In further exploring the construction of the autistic individual against normative milestones and expectations, this chapter will explore three key developmental concepts and tasks against which to interrogate normative development and 'non-normativity' and challenge the positionings afforded by these. All three of these big ideas have been readily taken up within autism and wider related literature and each serves to position autistic people in particular ways, drawing heavily on a deficit narrative. The first of these is theory of mind, often presented as a core 'deficit' in autism and placed at the centre of difficulties in social situations and frequently interchanged with discussions of empathy. The second is social connectedness and friendship, frequently cited as one of the core elements of the triad/dyad argued to characterise autistic people. Finally, the third is gender, both in terms of gender identity and the gendered nature of language used to construct autism.

Theory(ies) of mind

There is a proliferation of theories that seek to explain autism, including psychologically focused theories and those influenced by biology and neurology. The mainstream theories of autism share a common assumption that there is a deficit in autistic people, which should be researched, classified, and potentially modified if the hypothesis suggests that this may be possible. The common link between the theories is therefore an assumption that there is something 'wrong' with the autistic person. In theorising differences, some theories occupy a more influential position than others within the autism literature, and one example of this is theory of mind, which adopts a powerful position in constructing an image of the autistic individual.

Tager-Flusberg (1999) defines theory of mind as referring to "the ability to attribute mental states, such as desire, knowledge, and belief, to oneself and other people as a means of explaining behaviour" (p. 326). Autistic individuals are therefore thought to be 'impaired' in the ability to appreciate their own and other people's mental states (Baron-Cohen, 1998). It is proposed that theory of mind develops in childhood and holds a central influence on the ability of children, and eventually adults, in being able to engage with others in a socially appropriate way. Much of the evidence for theory of mind cites an early study by Baron-Cohen et al. (1985) known as the Sally-Anne experiment. Despite numerous critiques of methodology and interpretation (see, for example, Beaudoin et al., 2020; Guest, 2020; Tager-Flusberg, 1999), the findings are still drawn on to support a characteristic deficit in autistic children and adults and, despite such criticisms, a connection between a theory of mind hypothesis and social difficulties in autism is widely endorsed and accepted. Theory of mind is therefore positioned as a cornerstone in the understanding of autism due to its perceived ability to underpin the 'dyad/triad of impairments'.

The history of the concept of theory of mind is, however, interesting and began with the work of Premack (1978) in their study of primates, and therefore not specific to humans, yet is a concept that has been widely adopted within the discipline of psychology. The use, therefore, of the concept of theory of mind to explain and account for differences by professionals often results in the theory being objectively presented as fact, and while the theory remains a hypothesis, it is frequently presented by writers as an explanatory 'thing'.

In some of our previous work (see, for example, Brownlow & O'Dell, 2009) we have critiqued the way that theory of mind is presented as factual and negates the possibilities for alternative ways of thinking. In this work we have discussed the early work of Sinclair (1993; 2012) and Klein (2002, as cited in Brownlow & O'Dell, 2009), who, two decades ago, critiqued a theory that reflects the dominant way of thinking in society in that it favours neurotypicality. Klein argues that implicit in discussions of theory of mind is the assumption that the neurotypical way is the only correct way, and, as such, autistic people are at fault because they are different from neurotypicals. Klein provides examples as to the way that neurotypical thinking is privileged within the theory of mind hypothesis, which has impacts on the way that autistic and non-autistic individuals are consequently constructed:

> If one of my kind cannot figure out what a normal person is thinking, it is a theory of mind error … it is the fault of the autistic for not being like the NT. If a normal person cannot figure out what one of my kind is thinking, it is because we are not using the proper means to tell you. Again, it is the fault of the autistic for not being like the NT.
>
> *(Klein, 2002, as cited in Brownlow & O'Dell, 2009, p. 476)*

Klein (2002, as cited in Brownlow & O'Dell, 2009) therefore argues that within the theory of mind hypothesis, individuals cannot be simply different. If individuals do not behave in a similar manner to neurotypicals, they are ultimately classified as being 'impaired' and 'failing' the test, and consequently requiring specific intervention. Smukler (2005) further critiques the concept of theory of mind through discussing discrepant positions between how theory of mind is defined and how it is tested. Smukler argues that theory of mind is defined in a very broad way, as an ability to understand the intentions of others, their emotional states etc. However, Smukler notes that, in contrast, it is evaluated in very specific ways, primarily through the design of various false-belief tasks. The inability to specify the exact nature of theory of mind does not seem to be a core requirement in the design of tests to identify transgressions from the norm, which are then used to label some individuals as in some way deficient.

Smukler (2005) further argues that some professionals take the concept that people with autism are 'mind-blind' as uncontroversial. However, these professionals vigorously debate the details of the hypothesis in every other regard. The concept of the lack of theory of mind in autistic individuals could therefore be argued to be hegemonic. Smukler reflects on literature written by autistic people that began to emerge in the late 1980s as evidence for this. Smukler notes that the publication of first-person accounts of autism by people such as Donna Williams (1996) and Temple Grandin (2006) led to the questioning as to whether these individuals could be 'really' autistic (see, for example, Haslem, 1996, for a review of the controversy). The insight expressed by such authors as to the experiences of living as an autistic person in a non-autistic world was considered incompatible with the unquestioned assumption that autistic people could not offer such insights due to their lack of a theory of mind. Indeed Leuder et al. (2004) argue that the hypothesis has become so widely accepted in developmental and cognitive psychology that it is often confused with the phenomena it was introduced to explain. The confusion as to the specifics of theory of mind and a clear articulation of these has been critiqued for many years, with Perkons (1998) being an early discussant. Perkons argues that neurotypicals do not tend to consider the possibility of people living in separate worlds and hence having very different outlooks on the world, which is ironic given that alternative perspectives are a cornerstone of demonstrating the acquisition of a theory of mind. In contrast, Perkons argues that autistic people have a very good theory of mind, but that this is a different theory from that of non-autistic people. Perkons summarises the findings from assorted studies seeking to test and explain theory of mind by highlighting important differences between people with autism and neurotypicals:

The basic difference seems to be:

NT Theory of Mind = Everyone thinks like me, except when shown to be otherwise.
Autistic Theory of Mind = Everyone thinks differently from me – vastly and mysteriously – expect when shown to be otherwise.

(Perkons, 1998, n.p.)

What is interesting from the discussions above is that within the autistic community, the concept of a theory of mind has been critically considered for many years, but its strong hold on dominant developmental narratives remains clear. Indeed, little consideration is given in the dominant academic literature of alternative theories of mind, although there are some examples of a body of research questioning and critiquing traditional concepts of theory of mind (see, for example, Brownlow & O'Dell, 2009; Costall & Leuder, 2004; Milton, 2012). There has more recently been an increase in critique and debate concerning the concept within academia and professional practice (see, for example, Milton, 2014; Milton et al., 2020). However, despite these debates, theory of mind has been used to explain a range of perceived challenges, including language and communication, social skills, and empathy, each of which is positioned within the literature as core 'deficits', constructing autistic individuals as in some way deficient or lacking in specific skills and abilities. This results in the individual being constructed by others in a deficit framework, being in some way incomplete when compared with their neurotypical peers.

With respect to empathy, autistic writer Yenn Purkis, along with others, has questioned deficits in empathy in autistic people reflecting on what Milton (2012) has referred to as the "double empathy problem".

While we [autistic people] are lumbered with the idea that we lack empathy, a lot of autistic people see allistics [non-autistic people] as lacking empathy towards us. The pathologising of autism dictates that this mismatch its usually only seen and written about in one direction [against autistic people].

(Purkis, 2019, n.p.)

For Milton (2012), such experiences render an individual being 'othered' and perceived in some way as being 'pathological', which leads to stigma and isolation. What is particularly interesting for the psy-disciplines is that if there is confidence and evidence put forward in deficits surrounding empathy and given the disciplines' focus on accurate measurements and tools to effectively capture and highlight such deficits, psychometrically robust and appropriate measures for empathy within an autistic population remain conspicuously absent. In a recent COSMIN systematic literature review by Harrison et al. (2020), it was identified that despite the dominant measures of the Empathy Quotient (EQ; Baron-Cohen & Wheelwright, 2004) and the Interpersonal Reactivity Index (IRI; Davis, 1980, 1983) being widely used to identify such difficulties, the development of these measures to understand the construct of empathy was lacking. Indeed, the IRI was developed based on purely the responses of non-autistic individuals. Given the lack of confidence in the scale development and the robustness of the psychometric properties underpinning this, such scales command a disproportionate amount of power in their use to identify those who stray from the 'norm' and are therefore positioned in particular ways. Such positioning is further problematised by propositions that a lack of empathy is at the centre of understanding human actions. An example of this is the book *Zero Degrees of Empathy: A New Theory of Human Cruelty* by Baron-Cohen (2012).

Despite the confidence, or lack thereof, in the tools that have been developed to measure empathy 'deficits' and broader concepts such as theory of mind, these challenges are consistently posed within the literature as a core issue for the development of social relationships. The concept of social relationships and friendship will now be considered.

Friendships

Developmental psychology typically focusses on three aspects of change through time: physical development, cognitive development, and psychosocial development (O'Dell, Brownlow & Bertilsdotter Rosqvist, 2017). Sociality and social relationships, including friendships, are considered central to indications that individuals are developing appropriately. The assumption is that children move from social behaviour that is focused on themselves, including playing in parallel with other children, into more socially 'sophisticated' behaviours such as reciprocity in social relationships and social play. Bukowski et al. (1996) proposed that friendship was characterised by co-operation, equal benefits for each partner, affection, and having fun. Hence, kinds of social behaviour and emotional expressions are naturalised and normalised.

Developmental psychology, and other psy-disciplines, have assumed that autistic children are unable to express meaningful social behaviour (Grinker, 2010). Theory of mind deficits are assumed to prevent autistic children establishing reciprocity in social relationships and hence unable to form friendships (Baumringer et al., 2010). Early research assumed that autistic children were lacking in social development and did not want or need social interaction (Whitehouse et al., 2009). For example, Orsmond et al. (2004) state: "impairments associated with autism are impediments to the development of peer relationships: the more severe the impairments in social skills, the less likely it is for an individual to form peer relationships" (cited in Brownlow et al., 2013, p. 189). Researchers have called for more research to understand how social 'deficits' may affect the formation and development of close relationships for autistic people (for example, Howard, Cohn, & Orsmond, 2006; Locke, Ishijima, Kasari, & London, 2010; see Bertilsdotter Rosqvist et al., 2015).

However, Whitehouse et al. (2009) and others argue that this is not the case. Autistic activists and academics have long demonstrated that social relationships are an essential aspect of their lives (see, for example, Gunilla Gerland, 2003 and Wenn Lawson, 2006). Drawing on critical autism studies to understand friendship and being social enables an alternative view of the normalising and pathologising views of autistic people's social experiences. The approach enables a critique of mainstream research into autistic friendships that identify social behaviours to determine intervention and social skills training. Disciplines which traditionally sit outside of the psy-complex provide alternative conceptualisations of friendship and social experiences. For example, anthropologists Ochs and Solomon (2010) theorise sociality as a 'range of possibilities' rather than a singular expression of being social. They argue that social behaviour is shaped not only by the skills of the individual in terms of social communication and understanding, but also by the socio-cultural environment that such exchanges are being performed in. Hence, they and others (see, for example, Bertilsdotter Rosqvist et al., 2015) examine the socio-cultural conditions that may enable and foster kinds of sociality.

In some of our earlier research we explored the role of Projekt Empowerment, a movement in Sweden that provided autistic spaces in summer camps, educational resources, and a magazine, to create enabling social spaces for autistic people to be with friends and enjoy themselves. For example, a participant described the community as: "a completely voluntary intercourse or joint activity that all participants have sufficient balance and thus not a sacrifice for someone" (Bertilsdotter Rosqvist et al., 2015, n.p.). We highlighted that the context within which to engage socially was, crucially, an enabling space, a space autistic individuals could inhabit freely rather than being the point of difference within a neurotypical dominated space:

> Now I know that the most important thing is not being like everybody else. What is most important is that I have social interaction with others to the extent and in the setting, I feel comfortable with. It's just a shame it took so many years before I understood that how I live my life is up to me.

It is therefore clear that being social and occupying social spaces is a complex arena, and the common comparison of the autistic individual against neurotypical norms and expectations, supported in theories created by neurotypicals, is something to be critiqued and problematised. Another aspect of the shared narratives surrounding autism and the autistic individual is that of gender, a topic that frequently impacts on a range of discussions, including within the friendship literature. For our discussions here we will focus on gender more broadly than purely within friendships but acknowledge that within the friendship literature clear expectations are commonly articulated concerning appropriate 'girl' and 'boy' behaviours and the associated social expectations.

Gender and autism

The concepts of gender and autism have been intertwined since the inception of autism as a distinct state, reflected first in the early work of Kanner (1943) and Asperger (1944), who both presented early case examples indicating a dominance within boys. The strong association between gender, specifically males, and autism has perpetuated since with both researchers and national statistics commonly reporting a prevalence rate of 4:1 for males. Such figures have led to the use of gendered language when discussing autism and theories purporting to explain autism. One such theory is that of the extreme male brain theory of autism (Baron-Cohen, 2002; 2010). At the core of such a theory are two distinct types of brain – one that is more effective in systematising (the male brain) and one that is more effective in empathising (the female brain). Baron-Cohen proposes that autistic individuals have an extreme form of the typical male brain, with an abundance of systematising and a lack of empathising. Of key importance here are two aspects: first, the premise that both male and female brains are significantly different and that autistic brains differ again; and second, that the autistic brain, while excelling in systematising, fails at empathising. Both premises draw and build upon core stereotypes of autistic people as being calculated and systematic but lacking in relational values with others. They also draw on broader social stereotypes about males and females in the relational values placed on girls and women as opposed to the systematic thought processes of boys and men.

It is interesting that while such theories propose a difference between male and female brains in the neurotypical population, the assumption is that such differences are not apparent in autistic brains – the brains of those with autism are therefore presented as in some way without gender distinctiveness, and both male and female autists are positioned as having a 'male brain'. Furthermore, both female and male typical brains are presented as unproblematic, but once discussions turn to the 'extreme male brain' for autistic populations, descriptions of abilities and challenges become problematised.

While traditionally research on gender and autism has disseminated higher prevalence rates of autism diagnosed in boys, giving rise to the assumption of autism being traditionally considered a male condition (Taylor et al., 2016), more recently the under-representation of females has been highlighted, with some researchers arguing that females may exhibit characteristics in different ways, reflecting social expectations of the performance of gender (Cook & Garnett, 2018; Dworzynski et al., 2012). Indeed, new publications and collections written by autistic women have described in detail the different experiences of being autistic that may be specific to women. For example, autistic activists have argued that the normative social expectations of women's behaviour mean that they often mask who they are to appear more neurotypical (see, for example, Cook & Garnett, 2018). Those autistic women who 'succeed' to present themselves in ways that appear more neurotypical, and in effect 'hide' their autism from others, are often further disadvantaged in that they are not identified as needing supports and thus often miss out on supports. Some autistic women report needing to convince neurotypical gatekeepers of supports that they are autistic and in need of and deserving of the same supports more readily given to their male counterparts (e.g., Bargiela, Steward, & Mandy, 2016).

As recognition has increased that women too are autistic, and possibly at a more similar rate to males (Lai et al., 2015), researchers have begun to discuss a 'female' presentation of autism (Hull, Petrides, & Mandy, 2020). In their review of literature, Hull, Petrides, and Mandy (2020) propose that a "female autism phenotype" may be responsible for more autistic women and girls being undiagnosed relative to their male peers. According to this supposed female autism phenotype, autistic women are different from autistic males in that they are more likely to be interested in animals, fiction, psychology, and other 'relational interests', whereas males are more likely to be interested in mechanics and physics – interests traditionally considered typical for autistics. Additionally, as suggested by Hull et al. (2020) autistic women and girls are considered more likely to be 'internalisers' rather expressing their challenges outwardly as males are expected to be more likely to do. Thus, researchers such as Hull, Petrides, and Mandy (2020) have called for taking such gender differences/tendencies into consideration when making diagnostic decisions. While these ideas may be important in demonstrating the power of gendered discourse and practices, they can be critiqued for appealing to, perpetuating, and essentialising 'gender' and gendered stereotypes, including assumptions about interest-based activities and behaviours. Indeed, recent research has shown that such stereotypes and assumptions based on identified gender are largely unhelpful and can have negative impacts on individuals (Brownlow et al., 2021). While research and, more broadly, the autistic community and activist groups are providing some much needed reflection on the important effect that gender may have for an individual, this largely overlooks the intersectional nature of difference, and more attention needs to be given to the effects on an individual of having multiple marginalised identities and how a person might negotiate these. In recent work, Johnson (2018) explored the dominant understandings of gender evident in psychological theories and how a stable identification of oneself as either a girl or a boy has become evident of a key 'normal' developmental marker for individuals. Johnson critiques normative expectations for gender, particularly in childhood, and calls for a more critical reflection on what gender-diverse childhoods might look like. Further, autistic researchers and activists have noted ways in which neurotypical understandings and experiences of gender and sexuality do not easily account for their experiences (Bertilsdotter Rosqvist & Jackson-Perry, 2020).

Recent research suggests that transgender people are more likely than the cisgender population to be autistic (Warrier et al., 2020). However, due to the intersection of being autistic as well as trans or non-binary, some autistic transgender people have reported experiencing additional barriers in obtaining treatments such as gender-affirming hormone therapy (Autistic Self Advocacy Network [ASAN], 2016; Strang et al., 2018). Assumptions that autistic people have deficits such as deficient theory of mind and deficient social relationships, and thus impaired or interrupted socialisation, may influence how they are perceived and treated by professionals. For example, interests in items and wearing clothing deemed 'feminine' and in imitating female characters in autistic people assigned male at birth have sometimes been interpreted as atypical autistic 'preoccupations', possibly due to sensory differences, rather than as potentially indicating a transgender identity (Williams, Allard, & Sears, 1996). Landén and Rasmussen (1997) proposed that in cases of autistic individuals who identify as cross-gender, their gender identities may be thought of as a "paraphilia" resulting from an impairment in the ability to develop normal social and sexual relationships. This paraphilic behaviour could be 'corrected' by the same sort of behaviour medication techniques used to 'correct' other autistic behaviours.

Landén and Rasmussen's work was conducted in the 1990s, when transgender identities were widely considered to be disordered. However, while in some contexts attitudes have become more accepting of transgender people, autistic transgender people have continued to have their gender identities pathologised by many professionals. For example, Robdale (2018) has written about the lack of recognition of transgender identities by professionals, with a focus primarily on an individual's label of autism, thereby neglecting a core part of a person's identity. Such a focus serves to reinforce the narrative that autism is a problem.

Researchers have even sought to explain the occurrence of transgender identities in autistic individuals as due to a deficit of empathy or theory of mind (Glidden et al., 2016). This demonstrates the pervasiveness of the assumption that autistic people are deficient in these regards and these deficits have wide-ranging explanatory power. Through association with these assumed deficits, other aspects of an autistic person – such as their gender identity – may therefore also be framed as deficient. Articles such as one by Kung (2020) entitled, "Autistic traits, systemising, empathising, and theory of mind in transgender and non-binary adults", indicates how constructions of autistic people (as highly systematic, with deficits in empathy and theory of mind) direct the course of research, and therefore what is 'known' about autistic people.

The identification of a higher incidence of autistic people among the transgender community has been used by some professionals to call for caution when assisting autistic individuals to pursue gender transition. Parkinson (2014) is one such clinician urging caution. Parkinson does not argue that autistic people who identify as cross-gender should always be prevented or discouraged from gender transition, but that their identities should be subject to increased scrutiny. Parkinson provided examples of cases he did and did not support in gender transition. Those he did not support included people identifying as female who Parkinson did not perceive to be sufficiently consistent in their feminine expression. Rather than being transgender,

Parkinson suggested these individuals' desires for gender transition were manifestation of autistic 'obsessions'. Parkinson however described one autistic person who identified as male whom he recommended for hormone therapy due to their masculinity being "so well established" (p. 85). Reflecting on writers such as Parkinson, the performance of a 'well established' normative masculinity as a mechanism for accessing therapeutic intervention demonstrates how transgender people, and autistic transgender people especially, may be required to conform to traditional, dominant, and neurotypical constructions of appropriate (stereotypical) gender presentation. In some cases, this may mean that the label of autistic can be used as a mechanism for denying access to transition support.

However, recent research suggests that many autistic people may have understandings of their own gender identities that sit outside the dominant norms. Recent work by Kourti and MacLeod (2018) explored the experience of gender identity in a group of individuals who were assigned female at birth and identified as autistic but who did not necessarily identify as female or as male. Kourti and MacLeod found that their participants did not identify with what could be considered 'typical female presentations' and resisted many gender-based social expectations and stereotypes. They therefore call for more complex understandings to be engaged in with respect to gender identity and autism and focus on the importance of the intersectional influences on an individual of two or more powerful identity components. While the research raises important issues in the need to think more broadly concerning the relationship between autism and gender and challenge some of the previous ways of thinking about these, it falls short in considering the double marginalisation faced by such individuals, and the need to carefully unpack and understand these.

Recent work has suggested that the apparent high co-occurrence of being both autistic and transgender may reflect some mistaken assumptions in the research. Turban (2018) proposed that this co-occurrence is due to measures of autism not being specific enough to differentiate between 'deficits' reflecting 'true' autism and those that are a product of the difficulties faced by transgender people in socialising with their peers due to their gender difference – 'deficits' which in the latter case may be 'reversible'. This reinforces a particular understanding of autism, by which 'true' autism is defined by not only core deficits but by core deficits which are permanent. If one's social difficulties are eased by gender transition, then one's autism is reframed as a mistaken diagnosis. By contrast, 'true' autism is identifiable by autism measures, administered by professionals. This way of defining the boundaries between autistic and non-autistic, based on symptoms as measured by autism questionnaires, ignores/sidelines individuals' own understandings of their identities. It may invalidate or undermine the identities of those transgender individuals, possibly with previous diagnoses of autism, who experience a decrease in 'symptoms' – social difficulties – with gender transition. It seems plausible, however, that autistic people might experience fewer social difficulties when experiencing fewer persistent stressors, and any means of easing gender dysphoria may therefore improve the social functioning of even 'truly' autistic individuals.

(In)conclusions

In this chapter we have presented a critical reflection on three key developmental concepts, and how they are manifest within the autism literature, which are invoked at times to identify differences, serving to marginalise the individuals labelled. Such assumptions about normative development construct a developmental trajectory which normalises behaviours, identities, and cognitive styles, while clearly identifying those who do not align with this as 'other'. We have sought to interrogate the implicit norms that are 'naturalised' through developmental description. What is clear is the need to reflect more fully on intersectionality and complexity in the crafting of individual identities, where multiple aspects of identity are commonly drawn upon to present something unique. Identities, however, are crafted within dominant discourses, which frequently serve to render autistic identities as problematic and, in some way, lacking. While we have focused on theory of mind, sociality and friendship, and gender in this chapter, a much wider consideration of socio-cultural influences needs to be engaged with and the powerful way that language and practice shape identity constructions and experiences. Kapp (2011) argues that autism reflects the socio-cultural constructions and expectations of contexts. He illustrates his position by reflecting on traditional Navajo communities' concept of Hozho which, he argues, fits better with autistic people and ensuring that their needs are supported through the philosophy underpinning the culture being one of wellness and harmony in contrast to the culture of measurement and classification common to Western philosophy and reminiscent of the psy-complex. Similarly, in New Zealand, a new term was recently coined for autism in te reo Māori – "tōku/tōna anō takiwā" – which translates as "my/his/her own time and space". Previously a word for autism did not exist (Opai, 2017). These two examples highlight the dominance of Western understandings and the powerful role that they have played in constructing 'normal' and 'non-normal', and we call for further critical interrogation of these, with space made for alternative theorisations and understandings.

References

American Psychiatric Association (1980). *Diagnostic and Statistical Manual of Mental Disorders (3rd ed.) (DSM-III)*. Washington, DC: American Psychiatric Association.

American Psychiatric Association, DSM-5. Task Force (2013). *Diagnostic and Statistical Manual of Mental Disorders: DSM-5TM (5th ed.)*. Washington, DC: American Psychiatric Publishing, Inc. https://doi.org/10.1176/appi.books.9780890425596

Asperger, H. (1944). 'Autistic psychopathology' in childhood. In U. Frith (ed.), *Autism and Asperger's Syndrome*. Cambridge: Cambridge University Press. https://doi.org/10.1017/CBO9780511526770

Autistic Self Advocacy Network (ASAN) (2016). ASAN joint statement on the death of Kayden Clarke. https://autisticadvocacy.org/2016/02/asan-joint-statement-death-of-kayden-clarke/

Bargiela, S., Steward, R., & Mandy, W. (2016). The experiences of late-diagnosed women with autism spectrum conditions: An investigation of the female autism phenotype. *Journal of Autism and Developmental Disorders*, 46(10), pp. 3281–3294. https://doi.org/10.1007/s10803-016-2872-8

Baron-Cohen, S. (1998). Does the study of autism justify minimalist innate modularity? *Learning and Individual Differences*, 10(3), pp. 179–192. https://doi.org/10.1016/S1041-6080(99)80129-0

Baron-Cohen, S. (2002). The extreme male brain theory of autism. *Trends in Cognitive Sciences*, 6(6), pp. 1904–1906. https://doi.org/10.1016/s1364-6613(02)01904-6

Baron-Cohen, S. (2010). Empathizing, systematizing, and the extreme male brain theory of autism. *Progress in Brain Research*, 186, pp. 167–175. https://doi.org/10.1016/B978-0-444-53630-3.00011-7

Baron-Cohen, S. (2012). *Zero Degrees of Empathy: A New Theory in Human Cruelty and Kindness*. Milton Keynes, UK: Penguin.

Baron-Cohen, S., Leslie, A. M., & Frith, U. (1985). Does the autistic child have a "theory of mind"? *Cognition*, 21(1), pp. 37–46. https://doi.org/10.1016/0010-0277(85)90022-8

Baron-Cohen, S., & Wheelwright, S. (2004). The empathy quotient: An investigation of adults with Asperger syndrome or high functioning autism, and normal sex differences. *Journal of Autism and Developmental Disorders*, 34(2), pp. 163–175. https://doi.org/10.1023/B:JADD.0000022607.19833.00

Baumringer, N., Solomon, M., & Rogers, S. J. (2010). Predicting friendship quality in autism spectrum disorders and typical development. *Journal of Autism and Developmental Disorders*, 40(6), pp. 751–761. https://doi.org/10.1007/s10803-009-0928-8

Beaudoin, C., Leblanc, E., Gagner, C., & Beauchamp, M. H. (2020). Systematic review and inventory of theory of mind measures for young children. *Frontiers in Psychology*, 10. https://doi.org/10.3389/fpsyg.2019.02905

Bertilsdotter Rosqvist, H., & Jackson-Perry, D. (2020). Not doing it properly? (Re)producing and resisting knowledge Through narratives of autistic sexualities. *Sexuality and Disability*, 39(2), pp. 327–344. https://doi.org/10.1007/s11195-020-09624-5

Bertilsdotter Rosqvist, H., Brownlow, C., & O'Dell, L. (2015). 'What is the point in having friends?' reformulating notions of friends and friendship for adults with autism. *Disability Studies Quarterly*, 3(4). https://doi.org/10.18061/dsq.v35i4

Brownlow, C., Bertilsdotter Rosqvist, H., & O'Dell, L. (2013). Exploring the potential for social networking among people with autism: Challenging dominant ideas of 'friendship'. *Scandinavian Journal of Disability Research*, 17(2), pp. 188–193. https://doi.org/10.1080/15017419.2013.859174

Brownlow, C., Lawson, W., Pillay, Y., Mahony, J., & Abawi, D. (2021). "Just Ask Me": The importance of respectful relationships Within schools. *Frontiers in Psychology*, 12, p. 2281. https://doi.org/10.3389/fpsyg.2021.678264

Brownlow, C., & O'Dell, L. (2009). Challenging understandings of "Theory on Mind": A brief report. *Intellectual and Developmental Disabilities*, 47(6), pp. 473–478. https://doi.org/10.1352/1934-9556-47.6.473

Bukowski, M. T., Newcomb, A. F., & Hoza, B. (1996). Popularity as an affordance for friendship: The link between group and dyadic experience. *Social Development*, 5(2), pp. 189–202. https://doi.org/10.1111/j.1467-9507.1996.tb00080.x

Burman, E. (2008). *Developments: Child, Image, Nation*. Hove: Routledge.

Cook, B., & Garnett, M. (2018). *Spectrum Women. Walking to the Beat of Autism*. London: Jessica Kingsley Publishers.

Costall, A., & Leuder, I. (2004). Where is the 'theory' in theory of mind? *Theory and Psychology*, 14(5), pp. 623–646. https://doi.org/10.1177/0959354304046176

Davis, M. H. (1980). A multidimensional approach to individual differences in empathy. *JSAS Catalog of Selected Documents in Psychology*, 10, pp. 85–104.

Davis, M. H. (1983). Measuring individual differences in empathy: Evidence for a multidimensional approach. *Journal of Personality and Social Psychology*, 44(1), pp. 113–126. https://doi.org/10.1037/0022-3514.44.1.113

Dworzynski, K., Ronald, A., Bolton, P., & Happe, F. (2012). How different are girls and boys above and below the diagnostic threshold for autism spectrum disorders? *Journal of the American Academy of Child and Adolescent Psychiatry*, 51(8), pp. 788–797. https://doi.org/10.1016/j.jaac.2012.05.018

Gerland, G. (2003). *A Real Person: Life on the Outside*. Chicago, IL: Souvenir Press Ltd.

Glidden, D., Bouman, W. P., Jones, B. A., & Arcelus, J. (2016). Gender dysphoria and autism spectrum disorder: A systematic review of the literature. *Sexual Medicine Reviews*, 4(1), pp. 3–14. https://doi.org/10.1016/j.sxmr.2015.10.003

Grandin, T. (2006). *Thinking in Pictures and Other Reports from My Life with Autism*. London: Bloomsbury.

Grinker, R. R. (2010). Commentary: On being autistic, and social. *Ethos (Berkley, Calif)*, 38(1), pp. 172–178. https://doi.org/10.1111/j.1548-1352.2010.01087.x

Guest, E. (2020). Autism from different points of view: Two sides of the same coin. *Disability and Society*, 35(1), pp. 156–162. https://doi.org/10.1080/09687599.2019.1596199

Harmon, A. (2004). How about not 'curing' us, some autistics are pleading. Retrieved 25th April 2006, from http://www.cobrass.com/articles_how_about_not_curing_us.htm

Harrison, J., Brownlow, C., Ireland, M., & Piovesana, A. (2020). Empathy measurement in autistic and non-autistic adults: A COSMIN systematic literature review, *Assessment*. https://doi.org/10.1177/1073191120964564

Haslem, B. (1996). Best-selling author denies she faked autism. (Local). (1996-07-30). *The Australian (National, Australia)*, p. 3.

Howard, B., Cohn, E., & Orsmond, G. I. (2006). Understanding and negotiating friendships: Perspectives from an adolescent with Asperger syndrome. *Autism*, 10(6), pp. 619–627. https://doi.org/10.1177/1362361306068508

Hull, L., Petrides, K. V., & Mandy, W. (2020). The female autism phenotype and camouflaging: A narrative review. *Review Journal of Autism and Developmental Disorders*, 7(4), pp. 306–317. https://doi.org/10.1007/s40489-020-00197-9

Hultqvist, K., & Dahlberg, G. (2001). Governing the child in the new millennium. In K. Hultqvist & G. Dahlberg (eds), *Governing the Child in the New Millennium*. New York: Routledge, pp. 1–14.

Jarrett, S. (2020). *Those They Called Idiots. The Idea of the Disabled Mind from 1700 to the Present Day*. London: Reaktion Books. https://doi.org/10.1080/09687599.2021.1890947

Johnson, K. (2018). Beyond boy and girl: Gender variance in childhood and adolescence. In L. O'Dell, C. Brownlow, & H. Bertilsdotter Rosqvist (eds), *Different Childhoods: Non/Normative Development and Transgressive Trajectories*. London, England: Routledge, pp. 25–40. https://doi.org/10.1177/0959353518786522

Kanner, L. (1943). Autistic disturbance of affective contact. *Nervous Child*, 2, pp. 217–250.

Kapp, S. K. (2011). Navajo and autism: The beauty of harmony. *Disability & Society*, 26(5), pp. 583–595. https://doi.org/10.1037/a0028353

Klein, F. (2002). Autistic advocacy. Retrieved June 30, 2009, from http://web.archive.org/web/20050208085225/home.att.net/ascaris1/

Kourti, M., & MacLeod, A. (2018). "I don't feel like a gender, I feel like myself": Autistic individuals raised as girls exploring gender identity. *Autism in Adulthood*, 1(1). https://doi.org/10.1089/aut.2018.0001

Kung, K. T. F. (2020). Autistic traits, systemising, empathising, and theory of mind in transgender and non-binary adults. *Molecular Autism*, 11, p. 73. https://doi.org/10.1186/s13229-020-00378-7

Lai, M.-C., Lombardo, M. V., Auyeung, B., Chakrabarti, B., & Baron-Cohen, S. (2015). Sex/gender differences and autism: Setting the scene for future research. *Journal of the American Academy of Child and Adolescent Psychiatry*, 54(1), pp. 11–24. https://doi.org/10.1016/j.jaac.2014.10.003

Landén, M., & Rasmussen, P. (1997). Gender identity in a girl with autism – A case report. *European Child & Adolescent Psychiatry*, 6, pp. 170–173.

Lawson, W. (2006). *Friendships: The Aspie Way*. London: Jessica Kingsley Publishers.

Leuder, I., Costall, A., & Francis, D. (2004). Theory of mind: A critical assessment. *Theory and Psychology*, 14(5), pp. 571–578. https://doi.org/10.1177/0959354304046173

Locke, J., Ishijima, E. H., Kasari, K., & London, N. (2010). Loneliness, friendship quality and the social networks of adolescents with high-functioning autism in an inclusive school setting. *Journal of Research in Special Educational Needs*, 10(2), pp. 74–81. https://doi.org/10.1111/J.1471-3802.2010.01148.X

Milton, D. E. (2012). On the ontological status of autism: The 'double empathy problem'. *Disability and Society*, 27(6), pp. 883–887. https://doi.org/10.1080/09687599.2012.710008

Milton, D. E. (2014). Autistic expertise: A critical reflection on the production of knowledge in autism studies. *Autism*, 18(7), pp. 794–802. https://doi.org/10.1177/1362361314525281

Milton, D. (2018). Autistic development, trauma and personhood: Beyond the frame of the neoliberal individual. In K. Runswick-Cole, T. Curran, & K. Liddiard (eds), *The Palgrave Handbook of Disabled Children's Childhood Studies*. London: Palgrave Macmillan, pp. 9–29. https://doi.org/10.1057/978-1-137-54446-9_29

Milton, D. E., Heasman, B., & Sheppard, E. (2020). *Double Empathy, Encyclopedia of Autism Spectrum Disorders*. https://doi.org/10.1007/978-1-4614-6435-8_102273-2

Ochs, E., & Solomon, O. (2010). Autistic sociality. *Ethos*, 38(1), pp. 69–92. https://doi.org/10.1111/j.1548-1352.2009.01082.x

O'Dell, L., Brownlow, C., & Bertilsdotter Rosqvist, H. (2017). *Different Childhoods: Non/Normative Development and Transgressive Trajectories*. London: Routledge.

Opai, K. (2017). A time and space for Takiwātanga. https://www.altogetherautism.org.nz/a-time-and-space-for-takiwatanga/#:~:text=The%20word%20I%20have%20coined,her%20own%20time%20and%20space. Accessed 25th October 2020.

Orsmond, G. I., Wyngaarden Krauss, M., & Mailick Seltzer, M. (2004). Peer relationships and social and recreational activities among adolescents and adults with autism. *Journal of Autism and Developmental Disorders*, 34(3), pp. 245–256. https://doi.org/10.1023/B:JADD.0000029547.96610.df.

Parker, I. (1997). *Deconstructing Psychopathology*. London: Sage.

Parker, I., Georgaca, E., Harper, D., McLaughlin, T., & Stowell-Smith, M. (1995). *Deconstructing Psychopathology*. London: Sage.

Parkinson, J. (2014). Gender dysphoria in Asperger's syndrome: A caution. *Australasian Psychiatry*, 22(1), pp. 84–85. https://doi.org/10.1177/1039856213497814

Perkons. (1998). The theory of social delusion. http://erikengdahl.se/autism/isnt/socialdelusion.html. Last Updated 20th September 1998. Accessed 12th March 2021.

Premack, D. (1978). *Intelligence in Ape and Man*. Hillsdale, NJ: Eribaum.

Purkis, Y. (2019). The empathy myth. https://yennpurkis.home.blog/2019/05/09/the-empathy-myth/. Accessed 22nd September 2020.

Robdale, E. (2018). You're not trans… you're autistic. https://disabilityarts.online/blog/emma-robdale/blog-youre-not-trans-youre-autistic/. Accessed 25th October 2020.

Rose, N. (1979). The psychological complex: Mental measurement and social administration. *Ideology and Consciousness*, 5, pp. 5–68.

Rose, N. (1989). *Governing the Soul. The Shaping of the Private Self*. London: Routledge.

Ryder, G., & Brownlow, C. (2018). Exploring leisure, hobbies and special interests: The constructive role of special interests for children with ASD. In L. O'Dell, C. Brownlow, & H. Bertisldotter Rosqvist (eds), *Different Childhoods: Non/Normative Development and Transgressive Trajectories*. London and New York: Routledge, pp. 9–25. https://doi.org/10.1177/0959353518786522

Sinclair, J. (1993/2012). Don't mourn for us. *Autonomy, the Critical Journal of Interdisciplinary Autism Studies*, 1(1). https://philosophy.ucsc.edu/SinclairDontMournForUs.pdf

Smukler, D. (2005). Unauthorized minds: How "theory of mind" theory misrepresents autism. *Mental Retardation*, 43(1), pp. 11–24. https://doi.org/10.1352/0047-6765(2005)43<11:UMHTOM>2.0.CO;2

Strang, J., Powers, M. D., Knauss, M., Sibarium, E., Leibowitz, S. F., Kenworthy, L., Sadikova, E., Wyss, S., Willing, L., Caplan, R., Pervez, N., Nowak, J., Gohari, D., Gomez-Lobo, V., Call, D., & Anthony, L. G. (2018). "They thought it was an obsession": Trajectories and perspectives of autistic transgender and gender-diverse adolescents. *Journal of Autism and Developmental Disorders*, 48(12), pp. 4039–4055. https://doi.org/10.1007/s10803-018-3723-6

Tager-Flusberg, H. (1999). A psychological approach to understanding the social and language impairments in autism. *International Review of Psychiatry*, 11(4), pp. 325–334. https://doi.org/10.1080/09540269974203

Taylor, A. (2011). Reconceptualizing the 'nature' of childhood. *Childhood*, 18(4), pp. 420–433. https://doi.org/10.1177/0907568211404951

Taylor, L., Brown, P., Eapen, V., Midford, S., Paynter, J., Quarmby, L., Smith, T., Maybery, M., Williams, K., & Whitehouse, A. (2016). *Autism Spectrum Disorder Diagnosis in Australia: Are We Meeting Best Practice Standards?* Brisbane, Australia: Autism Co-operative Research Centre.

Turban, J. L. (2018). Potentially reversible social deficits among transgender youth. *Journal of Autism and Developmental Disorders*, 48(12), pp. 4007–4009. https://doi.org/10.1007/s10803-018-3603-0

Volkmar, F. R. (1998). Categorical approaches to the diagnosis of autism. An overview of DSM-IV and ICD-10. *Autism*, 2(1), pp. 45–59. https://doi.org/10.1177/1362361398021005

Warrier, V., Greenberg, D. M., Weir, E., Buckingham, C., Smith, P., Lai, M.-C., Allison, C., & Baron-Cohen, S. (2020). Elevated rates of autism, other neurodevelopmental and psychiatric diagnoses, and autistic traits in transgender and gender-diverse individuals. *Nature Communications*, 11(1), p. 3959. https://doi.org/10.1038/s41467-020-17794-1

Whitehouse, A. J. O., Durkin, K., Jaquet, E., & Ziatas, K. (2009). Friendship, loneliness and depression in adolescents with Asperger's syndrome. *Journal of Adolescence*, 32(2), 309–322. https://doi.org/10.1016/j.adolescence.2008.03.004

Williams, D. (1996). *Autism: An Inside-Out Approach*. London: Jessica Kingsley Press.

Wing, L. (1997). The autistic spectrum. *The Lancet*, 350(9093), pp. 11761–11767. https://doi.org/10.1016/S0140-6736(97)09218-0

4
DIMENSIONS OF DIFFERENCE

Dinah Murray

Speech is obviously energetic and impactful. People use it to draw attention to themselves or the messages they wish to be heard will not be heard; they thus have an impact on other people's thoughts and deeds. Its capacity to do that collectively depends on being part of a shared speech community, with a substantial overlap of word meanings and sentence structures – i.e. a language. This chapter will analyse the way that works in terms of interests – from fleeting and personal to long term and global. All living beings have interests and form communities of interest with others seeking to survive in a complex and changeable universe. The discussion here focuses on individual, hugely varying human beings and their multiple and shifting communities of interest, embedded within the scope of vastly powerful interests such as those of profit-seeking corporations and control-seeking governments and other forces.

This chapter aims to give an informal, naturalistic account of minds and meanings, based on a slightly expanded commonplace concept of interest. It is an account of humanity that accommodates a wide range, including monotropic – single-attention – focused autistic dispositions (Murray, 1992; Murray et al., 2005; Lawson, 2010). Monotropism is a thoroughly embodied and environmentally attuned account of thought and action. As in natural language, interests are conceived here as being informed, aroused, shared, expressed, and they impact on the world which also has an impact on them; they vary in duration, in strength, and in emotional valence. Some interests are selfish, but that is not a default: it is far from true that all interests are self-serving.

Physically the force of speech is expelled, moist, processed air, travelling out of one person's body and expanding and diluting, plus sound waves that have order and meaning they retain as they travel, which endure after the sounds have stopped and the waves dissipated. The written word harnesses other physical forces as it comes into being, is stable and lasts longer, and is much more detached, from the particular moment it is encountered. These differences are sometimes highly significant, but for now, the key commonality of relying on a shared language will be the focus and I will use *saying* and *speaking* to refer to both spoken and written words unless I 'say' otherwise.

So, how does the order and meaning of speech provide opportunities for mutual engagement between speakers and what is the nature of the engagement that ensues? The story here will not focus on syntax and formal definitions but will consider meanings as pragmatic, with linguistic meanings being the most reliable subset for purposes of sharing meaning – with very low maintenance costs, as all co-speakers actively, at low individual cost, contribute to the process. This means that not only can language be used expressively, but also to rather precisely get into other people's heads and alter their directions and flows of thought.

In this respect, language is a brilliant tool for manipulating interest systems, i.e. aligning them as far as possible with one's own. That is a necessary survival capacity for all of us complementarily different beings. *Personal* interest – personal allocation of processing resource – does not equate with *selfish* interest. Any interest system is a value-system on some scale; shared interests and values are the foundation of social alignment.

One main point of this chapter is that languages and linguistic subsystems such as slang, cant, and jargon emerge from interest groups, some more sustained than others, and language meanings always follow currents of interest. There is a self-reinforcing circularity built in as those currents are partly themselves channelled by the vocabulary that expresses them. So members of a community of interest frame the world in roughly the same way, often with an in-group/out-group boundary-patrol function (Becker, 1963; Tajfel et al., 1979).

The other key point is that monotropic (i.e. autistic) people naturally tend *not* to give processing resource to this ongoing negotiation for position – which gets absurdly called 'mind reading' (or 'social imagination') in the privileged world of researchers and practitioners. This is because social positioning for an autistic person will (a) be assumed by them not to need work, because it is a given (either 100% in or 100% out?), (b) will not include regular hierarchical comparison of self with others, and (c) will tend to run as a counter-flow to other thoughts, be uncomfortable, uphill work with uncertain outcomes, and be avoided or never become an attractor at all. This much-vaunted practice of constantly playing to and positioning oneself in relation to others' comparative values has little or nothing to do with either fellow feeling or 'mind reading'. Not engaging with it may make someone awkward or draw unfavourable attention, but it does not make them 'mind blind' – having thoughts others can't hear or read unless I choose is a vital part of my human autonomy, not a defect in relating.

While all concerns or desires are interests, not all interests are goal-oriented concerns or desires. Concerns, aims, and plans are interests with preferred outcomes – people say things like "my main concern is to save lives" or "I'm concerned to be fair": something is sought, an outcome is *desired*. In my PhD I contrasted 'concerns' with the goal-free activity of gazing at the aurora borealis and experiencing wonder and awe. The word 'autotelic' (the intrinsic reward of performing an activity) – which I didn't know then – I think captures that extra realm of awareness, with its intrinsic rather than extrinsic values; it is defined as an important concept in the work of Csikszentmihalyi (1990), who sees some people as more likely to have this as a general disposition. He suggests that an autotelic person needs fewer material possessions, power, status, or entertainment, because what they already are doing is rewarding in and of itself; that they are less easily manipulated by external rewards and punishments, and more involved in their contextual sensorium (Milton, 2017).

The words ardent young autistic naturalist Dara McAnulty (2020) uses to describe how he relates to nature refer again and again to this happy immersion, and support the analysis of McDonnell and Milton (2014) that this is a natural autistic attitude. Much of what Csikszentmihalyi writes regarding this way of relating to life, positions it as a realistic option which will naturally benefit those who have it. That could be true for people in a world where survival was less harried and hurried, but in the current world a blend of autotelic opportunities with externally motivated practicalities of life seems the best hope for all but the most privileged. Retaining one's autonomy and integrity in such a world is an achievement in itself.

Some general features apply to a whole range of interests, from the fleeting to the entrenched. Interests are about the adaptive flow of attention and movement through the world, using and intelligently distributing an energetic processing resource. The more highly aroused an area of interest is, the more likely it is to be expressed, as the more energy will be marshalled to this end; at the same time, the higher an interest's profile, the more likely we are to see it as involving 'paying attention'.

This process occurs within an n-dimensional (unspecified number of dimensions in a multidimensional space) system created from past possibilities explored, enacted, or ruled in or out, in/forming future possibilities as yet unexplored and offering past ones as occasions arise (the technical concept of a Markov blanket described in Clark 2017 captures these key features). A great deal is typically going on that is below awareness; at any given time, only a small part of it can sharpen into clear awareness. The fewer dimensions are channelled the more clearly any stream can emerge into expression and a process of simplification occurs. Meanings are constantly being refreshed, recreated, and exchanged in this way. Common directions and flows harmonised by same resonances are integral to social alignment. They are channelled by serial inhibitions or exclusions creating distinctions between flows and excluding the extraneous. How they are channelled may often be determined by much larger interests which have very different ends in view.

An occasion is a moment for action; concerns seek such moments

The energetic processing resource, which can be thought of as interest or attention, infuses a subset of dimensions, amplifying their signals, 'highlighting' some and excluding the rest, making them distinct so directions of thought can be perceived and relevant expressions can occur and have their own distinct impact. Words and grammars do this job with supreme efficiency: for any individual, to acquire linguistic competence is to acquire a sustained mechanism of resource distribution at minimal personal cost, continually refreshed and maintained by other people's use. The more abundant a directed flow within the system, the less evenly spread and widely distributed the processing resource will tend to be and the more focused the attention will feel. Becoming more aware can be thought of as shedding enough dimensions to allow the mind to 'formulate', i.e. create a little form. The form in the mind's eye cannot be n-dimensional; stripping the dimensions makes awareness possible; it's about leaving out almost everything, then 'it' can begin to become action, including speech. This is how an interest makes itself felt within its owner's awareness as well as in the outside world if uttered.

The brilliance of language creates a whole new world of potential error and illusion (see Milton, 2012) with the spoken word's implicit claims to truth and precision and stability, and its apparently neat overlap of meanings between same speakers.

Language is a tool for manipulating interest systems

The verb 'manipulate' is used here with neutral valence: it is just what happens because a language's expressions activate and resonate with a set of the same restricted dimensions for all speakers of that language. It can be used for benign or malign ends; it can be used honestly and transparently or to hide and distort the truth. It is important to remember that, for any given individual, the meaningful expressions of a language's lexicon resonate beyond their own boundaries every time they are used. Resonating, i.e. amplifying, signals activates overlapping potential. The energetic flow of processing resource goes where the boundaries and branches and gradients take it. Those can be thought of as the accessibility cascades Kahneman (2011) ascribes to his 'System 1' mental process (quick and unconsciously driven). He sees those as the 'quick and dirty' background to more rational thought in the more conscious and time consuming 'System 2' which enables reflection and considered evaluation – yet also potentiates fantasy and self-delusion. The model here notes that this system cannot escape being an expression of the interests that animate System 1: System 2 introduces time: it is the expressive output of System 1; expressions have dimensions pared right down so they can be grasped and noted and shared through overt expression. Thus, one person's interests and meanings can mingle effectively with those of others, and shared happy flows and flappy hows can happen – along with much else.

There are many pleasant alternative ways of creating a degree of this necessary alignment with others' interests; by shared experiences, e.g. via music-making or listening, dancing, rowing a boat, climbing a mountain. What we find in these contexts tends to be mutuality and co-operation, often with an autotelic character, creating happy shared and complementary resonances and rhythms (McDonnell and Milton, 2014). Language has wider scope and adds refined manipulation to interactions, including vulnerabilities and misdirections.

Autistic people, I believe, tend to prefer autotelic pursuits to self-interest, and of course many others share a concern regarding the selfish greedy interests that have been seen as driving 'progress' during recent decades. That has been thanks to Adam Smith's historical baker (1770) who bakes the bread to make a profit for himself, rather than because the bread needs baking or because people need food or because there's nothing to beat the smell of baking bread. It is all simplified and dismissed through the lens of profit.

It's time for the common good to be restored as a fundamental and worthwhile project, and community of interest to be valued as the basic context for all rightful action.

The idea that every human is a gift to the world has begun to seem quaint and has stopped shedding its warm light quite generally, in the most business-oriented cultures. For autistic infants, the situation is even harsher, as they are actually seen as a risk to their parents from the moment of conception and a catastrophe for sure, so that the way autism is framed narrows its meanings into pathological channels and loses its humanity in the process. For people whose assets are not visible in the marketplace, the scope for leading a valued life depends on luck and chance against some rather steep odds. Yet it is surely true that humans, autistic or not, want and need to feel they are a contributing to part of a larger whole.

The words and sentences I have strung together above have hopefully got into your head, dear reader, and done things there in the process, arousing and altering and connecting a range of different interests as you read them. They did that via resonances, enhancing specific signals and setting off cascades of effect within your personal connectome (that is, your interest system as embodied in that body whose eyes take in these words).

Creating such resonances is a human power that is constantly acting upon other humans (and other species, too), with an appearance of neutrality and objectivity, of clarity and truthfulness, of containment and precision that is always, necessarily, partial.

Knowing the jargon is part of getting and keeping the authority of expertise within any community of interest. For example, it is obvious that medical talk is framed to show expertise and strengthen the boundaries so that communication within those bounds is exclusionary, and the person diagnosed is an object whose ignorance reinforces the contrast between inner and outer. When all of this is set in a framework in which measurable profit is seen as a moral good in itself, the commodified person who suffers – i.e. the patient – seems to have very little power. Patients are positioned as faulty, powerless, and sometimes needing their autonomy to be trampled on. This is cited here as a well-known example that is obviously highly relevant to the pathologising of autistic and other atypical strands of human nature, while also showing a general human trend to demonstrate inclusion and exclusion, and/or hierarchy-based relative positions.

Linguistic power play is pervasive and way broader than the medical realm. It is about subtle power lines that enmesh us all by direct and indirect use of language to construct and reinforce attitudes and expectations. We can too easily internalise and adopt those normative expectations and the judgements they encode, and judge ourselves to be defective – a possibly self-fulfilling understanding that can destroy personal hopes (Becker, 1963).

Dear reader, if you have not yourself been given the autism label, try and imagine how a person feels who supposes everyone else 'can' read minds. Please set aside this misleading idea and consider that mismatched interests or salience – different ideas about what matters – are the underlying cause of most misunderstandings, whosoever those are (Milton, 2012; Lawson, 2010).

A neutral translation would read like this: "Autism is a natural variant that leads to unusual or atypical development of reasoning, social interaction, and communication skills". Young people who have received the label have to cope with heavily loaded and stigmatising accounts of their nature, which they may well internalise (Becker, 1963). That means that the identity that is offered can provide a harmful and personally damaging framework for interacting with the world; that it is a false picture that can damage both other people's perceptions of an actual person and that person's own idea of self. Exclusion from full humanity seems to be authorised and legitimised (Hobson, 2011).

There is something 'different' about us that is signalled by the diagnosis but cannot be understood without understanding the social context that highlights this difference and supplies the mismatch of salience (Milton 2012, 2014). It is important that every autistic individual is given access to a positive way to think about who they are – yet the odds are against that, balancing out the amplified signals of rejection which can pepper our daily lives. How can autistic people bring our gifts and let our light shine on the world when judged so dismissively?

When autism is medically framed and simplified, with individuals posited as defective, individuals are seen as maladaptive and 'failure' and 'success' are judged by neoliberal standards and expectations (Milton, 2018). Interests from the marketplace are informing both the practice and the values of many researchers (Wolgemuth et al., 2016). Even when viewed as being potential genuine assets, not just as commodities, autistic people's worth – the criteria for being a true asset – is judged to be about learning how to be a competitive transferable cog, which is sometimes described as 'being independent'. Being independent is construed as an ability to cope, handle challenges, survive without being a drain on anyone else. The idea of contributing to a common good has been reduced to playing a profitable role with minimal nuisance value. Yet I would argue that this is the antithesis of human beings as mutually sharing and socially attuned, with each bringing to the whole their capacities and care (see discussion in Bervoets and Hens, 2020). Contributing to a common interest on the basis of equality and intrinsic human value is a joyful and affirmative experience for anyone, autistic or not. It creates a shared flow that is self-replenishing and sufficient in itself. That nobody is truly independent of others is a fact the current pandemic has vividly highlighted. Perhaps that distortingly individualistic and selfish notion of human relations can finally be put to rest, along with the absurd idea that 'normal' people read each other's minds. This is about powers of influence, direction, and support that play out in daily encounters. Can we rebalance the powers? Can we harness our strengths and change the culture from where we are? If we can, how? Generally, I believe, the argument rests on the common interests of all humanity and ultimately all living things, of which we are but one special case among thousands.

Some of the unluckiest people are those who have wound up in "Assessment and Treatment Units", which neither assess nor treat, and as Duffy suggests, (2019) rather provide containment and imprisonment. A use of language that is not only false and intended to deceive, but also even thus dressed up as benign is stigmatising and belittling of the needs of the young people who enter the locked doors. The – negative, pejorative – assessment happens *before* entering and, among other things, means having your view of yourself set aside in favour of the view of experts who will decide your needs for you. In my view, that is a major harm in itself, though less so than the incarceration and actual loss of autonomy. Just by being contained in such a place one has received an assessment as a failed human, with no opportunity to demonstrate otherwise. Worst of all is that the humans caught in this trap have become commodities, out which others are making profits – an issue that also applies to everyone receiving paid care in our privatised system (Brown et al., 2017).

For those who are lucky enough to escape that particularly grim fate, what powers can we access to protect our well-being? Given the disparity of actual powers between any individual and the forces at work in society that, as Duffy (2019) describes, promote institutionalisation, and undermine effective community support, how can we get our case heard? The case that we are "fully human, fully here" (Postgate, 2008). Can we reclaim the language as has happened in other liberation movements? Unfortunately, unlike say gay liberation or Black Lives Matter, autism's moral authority is subverted by its disordered definition, which is logically inconsistent with its recognition for being as much an asset for humanity as any other human. Identification as disordered by the psychiatric profession is, alas, authoritative.

We also have the public relations problem that it is very hard work for us to bear reputation management in mind at all times and we are likely to forget to give the strokes others may expect – so, as it were 'from the ground up', autistic people experience rejections and barriers despite any amount of goodwill we may be bringing to the social discourse.

A perverse barrier to a fulfilling life is that to be supported outside of paid employment, the reputation management skills of a successful person must be inverted in favour of those of a dud. If one is not demonstrably a dud, the current welfare system in the UK (and many other countries) will offer little or no support. So, we could actually die because we can't play the game according to rules that harm us as they tell us to hide our light and maximise our hopelessness so the boxes get ticked – we are able to survive only by embracing stigmatisation (for arguments that Basic Income is a rational and viable approach to this issue, see Murray, 2017).

So, in reality, we are all enmeshed in enormous and extensive power structures that in many ways curtail our scope and dominate our opportunities. However, I suggest that our distinctive autistic power is that we are not in an obligate state of dual processing in which issues of status – hierarchical or inclusive/exclusive – are constantly affecting our flow of interest, creating shared subjectivities, and strengthening some positions at the expense of others, regardless of the facts. This power of straight thinking can be truly effective when that integrity is combined with the most general power that everybody who speaks has, namely the power to get into other people's heads and do some (partly precise) things there; language is a tool for manipulating interest systems. If what we express meets interests that align with ours then a resonating signal may be amplified again and again and acquire great power thereby.

Language is to some extent always recklessly deployed in active (unritualised) speech; while being the best we've got for sharing truths, it is also a vehicle for any number of interests to find expression, 'directly' or 'lexically' or in many other ways, playing on shared meanings and flows.

This is a true power that anyone who can make themselves 'heard' possesses. Its resonances can have extraordinary reach and longevity. Of course it's a very limited power – but it can have ramified and long-lasting effects: even, say, from the lips of an overpowered Black man in the USA, dying at the hands of four white police. To the everlasting shame of those police officers, his words – "I can't breathe" – didn't have the power to save George Floyd's life; but they did have the power to reach the whole world – where their meaning and meanings are still causing ripples worldwide.

The power of those words of course depended on them being heard so widely; along with the video image of armed and uniformed brutality, they packed a huge punch. It equally crucially depended on the humans who were reached: if there had been indifference – i.e. no concern – in the witnessing world, neither the words nor the images would have had that power; their power depended on reaching people with value-systems where justice, fairness, and compassion are priorities.

So, the words went straight to core values about the worth of human life and the shocking failure of those damned thugs to let their victim breathe. This is a particularly clearcut case of shared meaning being unlocked and unleashed by words expressed, because of a pre-existing and tenacious moral concern that met the words and their story with passion: a passion for justice which takes common humanity as basic and, I postulate, is felt at least as much by autistic people as by anyone. The version of 'empathy' deployed in othering and demoting autistic people may be more about being able to gauge people's roles as customers than as citizens.

The extraordinary reach of George Floyd's words, "I can't breathe", was significantly boosted by individual acts of sharing. Those in turn were only possible because of social media and the capacity to record and disseminate that technology confers. The words alone would have just hung in the air while the man died; instead millions of channels to pass them on became passionately active. From a completely different pathway, we have seen the words of a schoolgirl similarly winging out to the whole world, again because the means exist and the concern that amplifies the words is a passion for many. Greta Thunberg's sharing her knowledge and passion has woken many people up to urgent issues we must all tackle.

I hope that many or most people care about injustice, profiteering, greed, callousness, despite living in a market-dominated society in which those ills are seen as an inescapable part of life, and even pointers to success. The argument I've been making here calls for injustice to be exposed as widely as possible, in order to create the passion that is needed for truly different attitudes towards people who are not positioned to speak for themselves. As well as the young people in ATUs, tens of thousands of others have no means to fight or even expose the slights and cruelties and injustices that can be perpetrated on vulnerable people behind locked (pass-coded) doors. For attitudes to change, effective communication from behind the locked doors must be enabled. Media people like Ian Birrell, Victoria Derbyshire of the BBC, and John Pring of Disability News are vital assets, as are campaigners such as the Rightful Lives group (and AIMS). In the UK, the National Autistic Taskforce is working with an English NHS Trust to develop an easy-to-use 'signposting' app for distribution to those who are still on the wrong side of the digital divide.

Together we can empower the people who are locked up and hidden to have, as a supported and acknowledged right, access to the social media the rest of the world enjoys and which can be fertile ground for a passion for justice once the awareness is there. Then the speech of the disempowered will be heard and can become a real force in the world.

References

Becker, H. (1963). *Outsiders*. New York: The Free Press.
Bervoets, J. and Hens, K. (2020). Going beyond the catch-22 of autism diagnosis and research. The moral implications of (not) asking "What is autism?" *Frontiers in Psychology*, p.3015. https://doi.org/10.3389/fpsyg.2020.529193.
Brown, M., James, E. and Hatton, C. (2017). A trade in people: The inpatient healthcare economy for people with learning disabilities and/or autism spectrum disorder. Briefing Paper 1. *Lancaster University: Centre for Disability Research*.
Clark, A. (2017). How to knit your own Markov blanket: Resisting the second law with metamorphic minds. In T. Metzinger & W. Wiese (Eds.), *Philosophy and Predictive Processing: 3*. Frankfurt am Main: MIND Group. https://doi.org/10.15502/9783958573031.

Csikszentmihályi, M. (1990). *Flow: The Psychology of Optimal Experience*. New York: Harper & Row.

Duffy, S. (2019). Submission to the Joint Committee on Human Rights by the Centre for Welfare Reform. https://www.centreforwelfarereform.org/uploads/attachment/642/close-down-the-atus.pdf.

Hobson, P. (2011). *The Cradle of Thought: Exploring the Origins of Thinking*. London: Pan Macmillan.

Kahneman, D. (2011). *Thinking Fast and Slow*. London: Penguin Books.

Lawson, W. (2010). *The Passionate Mind: How People with Autism Learn*. London and Philadelphia, PA: Jessica Kinglsey Publishers.

McAnulty, D. (2020). *Diary of a Young Naturalist*. London: Ebury Press.

McDonnell, A. and Milton, D. (2014). Going with the flow: Reconsidering 'repetitive behaviour' through the concept of 'flow states'. In: Jones, Glenys and Hurley, Elizabeth (Eds.), *Good Autism Practice: Autism, Happiness and Wellbeing* (pp. 38–47). Birmingham, UK: BILD.

Milton, D. (2012). On the ontological status of autism: The 'double empathy problem'. *Disability & Society*, 27(6), pp. 883–887. https://doi.org/10.1080/09687599.2012.710008.

Milton, D. (2014). Autistic expertise: A critical reflection on the production of knowledge in autism studies. *Autism*, 18(7), pp. 794–802. https://doi.org/10.1177/1362361314525281.

Milton, D. (2017). *A Mismatch of Salience. Explorations in Autism from Theory to Practice*. Hove: Pavilion.

Milton, D. (2018). Autistic development, trauma and personhood: Beyond the frame of the neoliberal individual. In K. Runswick-Cole, T. Curran and K. Liddiard (Eds.), *The Palgrave Handbook of Disabled Children's Childhood Studies* (pp. 461–476). London: Palgrave Macmillan.

Murray, D. (1992). Attention tunnelling and autism. In *Living with Autism: The Individual, the Family, and the Professional*. Durham Conference Proceedings, Obtainable from Autism Research Unit, School of Health Sciences, University of Sunderland, UK.

Murray, D. (2017). Liberating potential – The future I'd like to. National Autism Project. http://nationalautismproject.org.uk/liberating-potential.

Murray, D., Lesser, M. and Lawson, W. (2005). Attention, monotropism and the diagnostic criteria for autism. *Autism*, 9(2), pp. 139–156.

Postgate, S. (2008). Personal communication.

Smith, A. (1770). *The Wealth of Nations*. . London: Penguin Books.

Tajfel, H., Turner, J. C., Austin, W. G. and Worchel, S. (1979). An integrative theory of intergroup conflict. *Organizational Identity: A Reader*, 56(65), p.9780203505984-16.

Wolgemuth, J. R., Agosto, V., Lam, G. Y. H., Riley, M. W., Jones, R. and Hicks, T. (2016). Storying transition-to-work for/and youth on the autism spectrum in the United States: A critical construct synthesis of academic literature. *Disability & Society*, 31(6), pp.777–797. https://doi.org/10.1080/09687599.2016.1205474.

5
HETEROGENEITY AND CLUSTERING IN AUTISM
An introduction for critical scholars

Patrick Dwyer

Background

For several decades, researchers have increasingly come to understand that the label of "autism" refers to a heterogeneous population (see, e.g., Gillberg, 1992, Wing, 1988). Indeed, evidence suggests that the scope of the category and characteristics of autism, which has been described as at least partially socially constructed (Milton, 2012, Grinker, Yeargin-Allsopp and Boyle, 2011, Nadesan, 2008, Grinker, 2007), has grown broader over time, further increasing autism's heterogeneity. Cross-temporal studies suggest that the level of autism characteristics needed to obtain a diagnosis has declined (Avlund et al, 2020, Arvidsson et al., 2018), such that individuals who would once have fallen outside the boundaries of autism are now within its range. Other studies highlight the role of diagnostic substitution, whereby individuals who would once have been given another label (such as learning disability) are instead, or additionally, diagnosed with autism (King and Bearman, 2009, Coo et al., 2008). The considerable and increased heterogeneity of autism poses a challenge to research that aims to understand autism (Rødgaard et al., 2019), and different attempts have been made to break down and describe this heterogeneity. However, researchers' efforts to characterise this heterogeneity have become part of the process whereby autism is socially constructed; defining subgroups of autism changes how autism itself is understood, which could have widespread political and practical consequences. Thus, the heterogeneity of autism is highly relevant to the ontology and politics of autism.

Dimensionality and multidimensionality

One traditional approach to autism's heterogeneity imagines autism as a linear spectrum from greater to lesser "severity" or "functioning". This continuum is sometimes collapsed into discrete, ordinally ranked subgroups, such as "high-functioning" and "low-functioning" autism, or the three levels of severity or support need that are embedded into the *DSM-5* (American Psychiatric Association, 2013). Many autistic advocates have criticised these unidimensional ordinal subgroupings. Levels of severity were included in the *DSM-5* against the advice of an advocacy organisation (Kapp and Ne'eman, 2020). Functioning labels have received even greater opposition (Brechin, 2018, Flynn, 2018, Bonnello, 2015). Advocates have argued against functioning labels on several grounds, but many stress that the term "low-functioning" may be stigmatising and disrespectful, while the term "high-functioning" may ignore or dismiss individuals' challenges.

Moreover, functioning-level classifications in research are typically based on measured cognitive abilities, which are often higher than autistic people's adaptive functioning scores (Alvares et al., 2020). There are even large gaps between autistic people's scores on different measures of cognitive ability (Nader et al., 2016). Indeed, one of the very earliest papers appearing to offer a description of an autistic individual focuses on how quantitative cognitive ability scores can be misleading in this population (Weiss, 1935). These sorts of discrepancies highlight the dangers involved in considering variability on only a single dimension; there may be other relevant dimensions. For this reason, some researchers have begun to use the multidimensional term "constellation" to describe autism in lieu of the unidimensional "spectrum" (e.g. Fletcher-Watson and Happé, 2019, pp. 34–35, Kapp, 2018, p. 364).[1] In addition to recognising different dimensions of autistic characteristics that might vary from individual to individual – such that, for example, one person might have greater sensory sensitivities, while another person might experience greater fear and distress in response to uncertainty – this metaphor of a constellation also acknowledges that individuals could vary in co-occurring characteristics such as mental health symptoms or ADHD features, or indeed in any aspect of personality and individuality in which people might differ from one another. The constellation metaphor further recognises that individuals' positions along different dimensions might change over time, and that individuals' lived experiences of support, acceptance, and person–environment fit might affect their positions along different dimensions. In this sense, the constellation model might be understood in relation to the neurodiversity approach, which is often considered to emphasise dimensionality and inclusivity over biological essentialism and dichotomisation (Kapp, 2020, Russell, 2020 Chapman, 2019).

The existence of this multidimensional variability poses a significant challenge to research attempting to describe subgroups of autism. Although the categories of autism formerly included in the *DSM-IV* (such as "Asperger Syndrome" and "Pervasive Developmental Disorder – Not Otherwise Specified") might have been described as multidimensional in the sense that multiple different domains of autistic characteristics, as well as verbal and cognitive abilities, were relevant to diagnostic classifications (American Psychiatric Association, 1994), the *DSM-IV* also intentionally ignored important dimensions of heterogeneity. For example, it specifically prohibited autistic people from being given a diagnosis of co-occurring ADHD. Furthermore, the *DSM-IV* autism subtypes were applied inconsistently across different clinics (Lord et al., 2012). Thus, the *DSM-IV* subtypes were abandoned in *DSM-5*, and researchers have had to turn to other ways of describing and classifying heterogeneity in autism.

Contemporary approaches to heterogeneity

In the present author's opinion, two approaches to the heterogeneity of autism stand out in contemporary research: first, aetiological explorations aimed at finding "biomarkers"[2] that might relate to the causes of different autism subtypes, and second, phenotyping explorations using clustering, a form of unsupervised machine learning, to classify individuals within a (multi) dimensional space. These two approaches appear to be what Lombardo, Lai, and Baron-Cohen (2019) have in mind when they distinguish "bottom-up" and "top-down" approaches to heterogeneity in autism. This chapter will focus primarily on the top-down, phenotyping approaches, but it may be useful to briefly discuss the bottom-up approach as well.

Briefly, in the bottom-up aetiological approach, researchers strive to identify subgroups of autistic people whose behaviour can be attributed to a biological and aetiological origin common to all members of the subgroup, such as a particular genetic variant.[3] This approach is not without controversy. Although all major stakeholders in the autism world have expressed some degree of support for genetic research, stakeholders also suggest that research in other domains should have higher priority (Pellicano, Dinsmore and Charman, 2014), perhaps because these other domains may be seen as more immediately practical. In addition, autistic individuals may be less interested in understanding aetiology than non-autistics (Kapp, Gillespie-Lynch, Sherman and Hutman, 2013). Indeed, some autistic people and organisations have expressed serious concerns about ethical questions associated with genetics – in particular, the potential for selective abortion or gene editing to be used to simply eliminate disabilities (Autistic Self Advocacy Network, 2019, Ne'eman, 2010 Robison, 2010). On the other hand, information about genetic aetiologies might provide individuals and their families with a better understanding of their neurology, which could be converted into practical interventions or supports, as well as a basis for community with similar individuals.

Regardless of the complex ethical issues surrounding the aetiological approach, it does not appear sufficient to describe the full heterogeneity of autism. For one thing, there appears to be important phenotypic variability within genotypes. Not everyone with autism-associated genotypes will develop clinically diagnosable autism (Richards et al., 2015), and any genetic variants may also be associated with other atypical phenotypes besides autism (Myers et al., 2020). Even monozygotic twins are not always concordant for autism (Hallmeyer et al., 2011) and if they are, they may still differ in their level of autism characteristics (Castelbaum et al., 2019). Crucially, considerable phenotypic heterogeneity can be found even in individuals whose autism shares a common genetic aetiology. Thus, aetiological approaches to decomposing heterogeneity may not be able to, for example, direct individuals towards supports for the specific challenges they may experience in their lives.

Moreover, it does not appear as though all cases of autism can be reduced to a clear primary aetiological origin such as a single genetic origin. Instead, many autistic people's phenotypes reflect complex combinations of many common genetic variants (Klei et al., 2012), as well as gene–environment interactions. In practice, these phenotypes might therefore be seen to vary along multiple continuous dimensions.

Clustering and subgrouping

To investigate this continuous multidimensional heterogeneity, the contemporary top-down, phenotypic exploration approach to research uses unsupervised machine-learning methods such as k-means clustering, agglomerative hierarchical clustering, and Gaussian mixture models to characterise subgroups of participants in large, "big data" samples. Roughly speaking, in these clustering analyses, participants are divided into subgroups based on their score(s) on the variable(s) entered into the analysis; participants with more similar scores are grouped together.[4] While this sort of clustering might, at first glance, appear to offer an "objective" method of defining subgroups, researchers using clustering are in fact making numerous subjective decisions. These begin with the decision to explore subgroups in the first place, continue with the choice of measures used to inform the clustering analysis, and accumulate further as researchers select the final clustering solution and interpret it.

Whether to subgroup?

It is not necessarily clear that using clustering to collapse continuous, dimensional variability into categorically distinct subgroups is the only or best approach to exploring heterogeneity in autism. For example, one could argue that it would be not only simpler, but also sounder, to merely identify relevant dimensions of variability and measure individuals' scores along these continuous dimensions. Reducing continuous variability to categorical classifications entails a loss of information. For example, individuals with different scores on some measure may end up being collapsed into a particular group.

It may be best to discuss the merits of clustering and subgrouping separately in the domain of research and in the domain of community practice. If we begin with research, one important objection to subgrouping might note that, statistically speaking, it is better to study quantitative associations among continuous variables in a dimensional framework than in a categorical one (see MacCallum, Zhang, Preacher and Rucker, 2002). Researchers should examine the continuous correlation between two continuous variables instead of using a median split dichotomisation procedure. However, if research aims to understand the experiences of individuals who come from an extreme end of a dimension, it may be useful to define a subgroup around these individuals. This is, indeed, the strategy used by autism researchers who prefer to study diagnosed or self-identified autistic people instead of autistic traits in the general population. Moreover, subgroups can be used to illuminate how findings from the level of samples might map onto individuals. For example, the abstract knowledge that there is a certain average longitudinal trajectory of scores on a variable, and a certain range around that average, might not be as readily envisioned or interpreted as a graph showing several different averaged trajectories from different subgroups of participants.

There may also be important ways that defining discrete subgroups could be useful in communities, and again, some of these potential advantages may be like justifications for maintaining the discrete category of autism itself. First, as far as decisions regarding eligibility for supports and accommodations are sometimes made on a categorical basis – either one qualifies, or one does not – discrete classifications may help individuals obtain the services and supports they require. From one point of view, the question of whether the supports associated with a classification will be helpful should be the main factor affecting diagnostic decisions. Lorna Wing comments that "diagnostic labels don't mean a damned thing, just use them to get the person the services they need" (in Feinstein, 2010, p. 295). However, concerns have been raised that certain subtypes and classifications, such as *DSM-5*'s category of Social Communication Disorder (Kapp and Ne'eman, 2020, Tager-Flusberg, 2018, Brukner-Wertman, Laor and Golan, 2016), may deprive individuals of access to supports.

Another important way that defining subtypes and discrete classifications could be useful in communities is in fostering positive identity and community among, and political action by/for, individuals with similar experiences or interests. Chapman (2020a, 2020b) suggests that the concept of a "serial collective" (see Young, 1994) may be applicable to autism: that autistic people may, essentially, be unified and defined as a group by similarities in how the external world interacts with them. But because autism is heterogeneous, it does not seem unreasonable to suggest that other, more specific collectives or categories could be defined and (especially if the categories were understood to be defined not by individual characteristics alone, but by the interaction of those characteristics with the external world) that these collectives could also be a useful basis for community or political action. That said, it also seems entirely possible that defining subgroups could instead fractionate and divide communities. Thus, different subgrouping solutions may be more or less useful in community contexts, and care must be taken to ensure that a given subgroup solution is helpful and not harmful.

Choosing constructs to measure

One important factor that may affect whether subgrouping solutions are helpful is what constructs are measured and used to define subgroups. This subjective decision may be affected by the objectives and agendas of researchers. For example, some researchers seek to identify factors that might make children more or less responsive to early behavioural interventions, which could be used to classify children and allocate them to one intervention or another (Sherer and Schreibman, 2005). This goal has explicitly motivated machine-learning subgrouping based on intervention outcomes (Paynter, Trembath and Lane, 2018). Similarly, machine-learning subgrouping analyses aiming to describe different trajectories of "symptom severity" and adaptive functioning have been justified and framed in terms of intervention personalisation (Szatmari et al., 2015). While intervention personalisation does seem valuable, there may be a danger that these analyses could serve the interests of the industry that delivers such interventions, and a decision to define subgroups on these variables would seem to come at the expense of other variables that could otherwise be used for subgrouping, such as personality (Schwartzman, Wood and Kapp, 2016), sensory processing features (Ben-Sasson et al., 2008), or quality of life (Azad et al., 2020).

Furthermore, while it may appear obvious that using a poor measure of a construct will reduce the quality of the subgroups obtained in a clustering analysis, this point still deserves attention. For illustration, several studies have been published using clustering to explore subgroups of autistic individuals based on their profiles of sensory features (see DeBoth and Reynolds, 2017, for a review). These studies typically rely on parent reports of sensory features. However, the internal sensory experiences of individuals are not accessible to external observers: for example, a sensory shutdown that might externally suggest hyposensitivity might reflect an internal experience of hypersensitivity and overload (Grandin and Panek, 2014, see also descriptions of shutdown in Belek, 2018). In addition, some caregiver-report sensory questionnaires contain items that might not always reflect sensory processing; for example, the parent-report Short Sensory Profile (McIntosh, Miller and Shyu, 1999) contains the item, "Has difficulty paying attention". Empirical research comparing identical self- and parent-report sensory measures suggests the former may more closely map onto physiological measures (Keith, Jamieson and Bennetto, 2019). Thus, self-reports (Elwin et al., 2017), neural measures (Dwyer et al., 2020) and autonomic measures may capture information about sensory phenotypes that is not available through the caregiver-report measures used in most sensory subgrouping studies to date. Moreover, these caregiver-report measures have factor structures that typically do not distinguish between different types of sensory sensitivity such as hyperacusis (sensitivity to loud, intense sounds) and misophonia (emotional or physiological responses to specific sounds, which could be soft). At present, intervention strategies for these two sensory phenotypes in autism are not firmly established in research, but it seems reasonable to suggest that misophonia might reflect conditioned associations that might be easily extinguished, whereas hyperacusis might be more problematic in the sense that providing accommodations or technological barriers (e.g. noise-cancelling headphones) to reduce exposure to overwhelming stimuli might be required. Consequently, it might be important in the real world to distinguish subgroups with hyperacusis from those with misophonia.

The context around the individual may also be relevant to decisions regarding measures to be employed in clustering analyses. With rare exceptions (e.g. Wallisch et al., 2019), clustering research in autism is typically based on measurement of the autistic individual's characteristics, not those of their environment. However, someone's environment might influence such factors as exposure to distressing sensory stimuli, or availability of supports paid for out-of-pocket by parents. More broadly, social interactions necessarily involve at least two individuals, and various findings suggest that the judgements of others might play a role in autistic people's social difficulties (e.g. Morrison et al., 2019, Sasson et al., 2017). Heterogeneity in people's surrounding contexts may therefore be relevant to their support needs.

The present author believes that decisions about relevant constructs for measurement in subgrouping analyses should be guided by community voices as well as academic researchers, particularly considering findings that suggest typically developing individuals may sometimes struggle to understand autistic people's mental states and perspectives (Heasman and Gillespie, 2018, Edey et al., 2016). Community-based participatory approaches (Nicolaidis et al., 2019), community advisory boards, and information from qualitative studies may help to ensure that research explores topics relevant to autistic people's well-being and quality of life. Once these topics are identified, relevant measures could be selected or developed. These measures could include behavioural, interview or questionnaire assessments, the dimensional structures of which could be described using approaches such as factor analysis and principal components analysis. Furthermore, measures in other modalities, such as neurobiology, physiology, and eye-tracking, could be valuable, though perhaps more in research than in clinical practice and communities. Measures designed entirely by non-autistic individuals may display biases and value judgements informed by these non-autistic individuals' power over autistic people (Timini et al., 2019), but equal involvement of autistic individuals in measure development may help to mitigate this problem.

Choosing the number of clusters

In clustering analyses, researchers must select the number of clusters that are to be defined. Although there are various indices and methods that aim to aid researchers in selecting an optimal number of clusters (Charrad, Ghazzali, Boiteau and Niknafs, 2014, Nylund, Asparouhov and Muthén, 2007), Fushing and McAssey (2010) argue that determining the optimal number of clusters is an ill-posed problem, at least where clusters are overlapping – and if the multidimensional autistic constellation contained clear subgroups that do not overlap in scores on the assessments commonly used in research and clinical practice, subgrouping debates would probably have been resolved long ago. Indeed, to the extent that heterogeneity in autism may be continuous, the number of subgroups would seem to be arbitrary and defining fewer or more clusters might be of use depending on the research questions of interest and the relevance of the subgroups in the real world. The decision of which set of clusters – a set of four, a set of six? – is most meaningful would seem to be highly subjective.

Interpreting clusters

Finally, researchers must interpret their clusters. While Gaussian mixture models do provide estimates of cluster (or "class") means and variances that describe the boundaries of the different subpopulations identified in the analysis, other clustering methods may not provide this information. In these cases, researchers can use descriptive and perhaps also inferential statistics to characterise patterns. However, after any cluster analysis, researchers will have opportunities to make subjective decisions about the theoretical or practical meaning and implications of obtained patterns, as well as the vocabulary that will be used to describe them. It seems reasonable to assume that researchers' backgrounds and biases could affect these decisions.

Therefore, there are several aspects of the clustering process that require careful judgement and upon which critical autism scholars might wish to offer comment.

Translating clusters into classifications

Critical autism scholars should likewise have much to say regarding the question of how the results of a completed clustering analysis could be translated into subgroups to be used in community settings. Although the foregoing discussion noted some potential advantages to defining subgroups for use in community settings – first, access to supports, and second, identity and community – it was also suggested that these potential advantages could become disadvantages if subgroups are chosen poorly. Furthermore, data-driven clusters obtained from an unsupervised machine-learning analysis are not sufficient in themselves to define useful clinical diagnostic entities: there are further steps required to transform clusters into diagnostic labels. It is also important to note that clustering analyses would not seem to be strictly necessary for diagnostic labels to be described: they might be helpful, but other forms of quantitative and qualitative evidence might be as or more important.

Mutual exclusivity of subgroups

First, different clustering techniques almost invariably assign individuals to one group from a single set of groups; they do not allow for individuals to be assigned to multiple co-occurring subgroups.[5] When a clustering analysis includes multiple measures that could be relevant to classifying autistic people, each subgroup will be based on a particular pattern across multiple measures. Consequently, even though we might imagine a hypothetical subgroup that is characterised by a pattern of severe hyperacusis, low depression, and high intolerance of uncertainty, an individual with a contrary score (e.g. high depression) might still be sorted into that cluster if there was no other cluster better matching their individual profile. Such subgroups would not seem to be practical for purposes such as determining eligibility for supports: an individual with depression should obviously be eligible for mental health supports.

As an alternative, researchers may wish to use multiple successive clustering analyses to describe patterns of variability along different dimensions. The results of these analyses could be used to inform multiple independent sets of co-occurring labels. For example, the individual mentioned above might be described as an autistic person with hyperacusis, depression, and intolerance of uncertainty. Such co-occurring labels might maximise the practical benefits of diagnostic classification, allowing individuals experiencing barriers and challenges in different domains to obtain support in each of these areas – thus perhaps expanding and personalising available support, rather than restricting it.

A greater emphasis on complete diagnosis of all relevant co-occurring labels might also help to address the problem of diagnostic overshadowing. Contemporary diagnosis is often an exercise in determining whether an individual meets criterion for a particular diagnosis: this is, for example, the purpose of autism-specific assessments such as the ADOS (Lord et al., 2000). Gillberg (2010) argues that splitting individuals into discrete groups should only occur *after* a holistic approach has been taken towards recognising all the areas in which an individual might be disabled.

Furthermore, defining sets of co-occurring labels in lieu of hierarchical subgroups would not appear to deny opportunities for positive identity or community-building, as individuals would retain an autism diagnosis alongside additional labels. If anything, an increased number of labels would give individuals more choices regarding identity and community, and perhaps even encourage mixing across the boundaries that presently exist between neurotypes.

Indeed, the earlier example of the autistic person with hyperacusis, depression, and intolerance of uncertainty was deliberately chosen because *at least* two of these co-occurring classifications – depression and hyperacusis – are not unique to autism. While there may be some populations that are largely confined within the boundaries of the autistic constellation, these are groups that extend into and can be informed by heterogeneity in the non-autistic population. For this reason, researchers may wish to conduct subgrouping analyses with both autistic and non-autistic individuals alongside one another. More generally, we should perhaps not aim to "reinvent the wheel" when we stratify heterogeneity in autism, but instead seek to inform our understanding of heterogeneity in autism using concepts from outside autism – and to inform our understanding of heterogeneity outside autism using concepts from autism.

Developmental change

Even if we seek to transform clustering results into useful non-hierarchical, co-occurring sets of labels, practical difficulties remain. Developmental change can complicate phenotyping in so far as individuals might move into and out of different defined groups over time. For example, many autistic people's scores on cognitive assessments increase over time (Simonoff et al., 2019, Solomon et al., 2018). Consequently, individuals who were assigned to one cognitive ability group when being diagnosed could later switch to qualifying for another classification. However, a longitudinal change in scores on a variable could also be an artefact of differences in measures employed at different ages (Farmer, Golden and Thurm, 2016) or might reflect the development of compensatory strategies and camouflaging, in which case the individual might be better classified in their original subgroup. Therefore, age and developmental change could complicate any system of classification based on clustering. Separate clustering analyses might help to describe heterogeneity in separate age bands, including age ranges that are typically understudied in autism research, such as adulthood. Furthermore, as noted earlier, clustering can be used to describe and illuminate different patterns of longitudinal change (e.g. Solomon et al., 2018; Szatmari et al., 2015). Although longitudinal studies of individuals diagnosed at early ages may exclude late-diagnosed individuals, information about trajectories of change from these longitudinal studies can inform decisions about whether and how diagnostic categories should apply at different age ranges.

Other demographic diversity

Although this chapter recommends age-specific and longitudinal clustering analyses, gender- and sex-specific clustering analyses may not be as useful. Lai and Szatmari (2020) argue against gender- or sex-specific diagnostic criteria or measurement cut-offs for autism, suggesting it should be defined in the same way across genders and sexes, albeit of course in a manner informed by its presentation in all of them. As the present author has met male autistics who appeared to display characteristics of the "female phenotype" and vice versa, this argument appears reasonable. The diversity of gender identities found in autism and typical development may also complicate attempts to reduce gender to discrete groups of individuals who could be included in separate clustering analyses. That said, diverse populations should of course be included in research relevant to diagnosis and subphenotyping wherever possible so that differences between these groups can be understood and used to inform definitions of diagnostic labels. These diverse populations might be best clustered alongside one another in a single analysis, so that results can be more easily compared between populations.

Cluster stability

Unfortunately, clustering algorithms do not always yield a stable set of clusters. For example, in an analysis the author conducted using Ward's agglomerative clustering method (Dwyer et al., 2020), when different subsamples were repeatedly drawn and clustered, a small group of participants would seem to continually switch back and forth from a first cluster to a second. Results might vary even more between samples from separate datasets. If clustering is to be used to define diagnostic classifications for use in community settings, researchers may wish to collect more than one sample to explore how clustering solutions change on replication (Wolfers et al., 2019). In addition, researchers should – as alluded to above – explore solutions with different numbers of clusters.

Defining diagnostic criteria

Interpreting clusters is a subjective process. However, in a clustering analysis, all variables are at least quantitative in nature. In community diagnosis, qualitative evidence – clinicians' subjective observations and the subjective observations of other individuals as relayed to clinicians through interviews – may be equally or more important. Thus, when relevant stakeholders – who might include self-advocates, researchers, parents, and clinicians – gather to make decisions about diagnostic entities, they must, without sacrificing clarity, transform a cluster defined by such-and-such a score on such-and-such a measure into a classification described by statements offering greater flexibility. When stakeholders develop these statements and criteria, they should reflect critically on how different language choices might accentuate or reduce stigma. For example, terms such as "autism spectrum disorder" or "restricted, fixated interests" (as used in the present *DSM-5* criteria) not only appear likely to accentuate stigmas,[6] but they reflect subjective, unscientific, and value-laden judgements. Alternative terms such as "autistic constellation development" or "focused, intense interests" might be more neutral.

Conclusions

This chapter has critically discussed the use of unsupervised machine learning and clustering for the purpose of exploring and classifying variability within the multidimensional autistic constellation. It has suggested that clustering could be used in research to help define homogeneous subgroups that might more closely reflect and describe the experiences of specific individuals. Such use of clustering in research requires selecting measures and constructs on which individuals should be clustered, selecting a solution with a given number of clusters, and interpreting the resultant subgroups.

Furthermore, this chapter has discussed how cluster analyses might be used to inform the development of community diagnostic entities to describe heterogeneity within the autistic

Table 5.1 Recommendations regarding use of community diagnostic classifications to stratify heterogeneity within the autistic constellation

---

1. Instead of defining a hierarchy of categorically discrete subgroups beneath the overarching label of autism, stakeholders should accomplish the aim of subgrouping by assigning a set of co-occurring labels to each person qualifying for them. These co-occurring labels could be specific or non-specific to autism.
2. All relevant stakeholders and experts should contribute to decisions regarding diagnostic classifications. These stakeholders/experts should include groups such as self-advocates and parent-advocates, as well as clinicians and researchers.
3. Classifications should be defined in a way that is sensitive to age-related changes as well as different aspects of demographic diversity (e.g. sex, gender, ethnicity).
4. To the extent that clustering analyses are used to inform community diagnostic classifications, the stability of clustering solutions as well as different solutions with different numbers of clusters should be examined.
5. To the extent that clustering analyses are used to inform community diagnostic classifications, quantitative statements defining clustering subgroups should be transformed into clear but flexible descriptive statements defining diagnostic entities.

constellation. It suggests that autism subtypes might help to give people access to supports or put them in contact with communities of similar individuals, but also that some subtyping solutions could reduce access to supports or fracture communities. For these reasons, hierarchical subgroups may not be an ideal approach to classifying and stratifying heterogeneity. Instead, co-occurring labels, whether specific or non-specific to autism, could be used to describe heterogeneity. Although this chapter notes that clustering would seem to be neither strictly necessary nor sufficient for defining such co-occurring diagnostic entities, the diagnostic entities could still be informed by the results of clustering analyses and other research studies, along with perspectives of all relevant stakeholders. It ends with recommendations in Table 5.1 regarding the use of community diagnostic classifications to stratify heterogeneity within the autistic constellation.

Notes

1 When the idea of an autism "continuum" was first introduced, it was also intended in a multidimensional sense, explicitly not as a unidimensional "straight line from severe to mild" (Wing, 1988, p. 92; see also comments by Gould in James, 2018, pp. 162–165). However, this idea of a multidimensional "continuum" was largely displaced by the unidimensional metaphor of a "spectrum" of autism severity.
2 Researchers have begun to use the word "biomarker" in an increasingly broad manner, making its meaning ambiguous. For example, many have used the term "biomarker" to describe observations that are behavioural, not biological (e.g. Frazier and Goodwin, 2020, Murias et al., 2018). While behaviour might indeed be of considerable interest given the biological heterogeneity of autism, in this chapter, the term "biomarker" is used to refer specifically to *biological* markers that are sensitively and specifically associated with a particular phenotype or process, allowing them to be used as an indicator of said process for diagnostic purposes or to measure effects of interventions aiming to alter that phenotype or process. Crucially, the simplest ways that a biomarker can be both sensitive and specific are if it is either the direct etiological origin of the phenotype or process, or at least a consequence of another biological process that is the etiological origin. For example, having an extra copy of chromosome 21 is a biological marker of Down syndrome because trisomy of chromosome 21 causes Down syndrome. Thus, biomarkers (according to the narrow definition used here) are likely to be etiologically relevant.
3 Within the constellation metaphor, these etiological and genetic factors might be seen as particular dimensions that can influence the other dimensions to bring about autistic behaviour and experiences. Usually, these dimensions would be discontinuous, but there are some exceptions. For example, individuals with mosaicism may lie between extreme ends of genetic dimensions, and the continuum of CGG repeat lengths found in the Fragile X spectrum of involvement might be seen as continuous.
4 This approach fundamentally differs from *supervised* machine learning. Briefly, in supervised machine learning, classifications are supplied *a priori* by researchers; the model then attempts to use the available measures (which are often neurobiological) to learn decision rules that would replicate these classifications (see Wolfers et al., 2019). Contemporary use of supervised machine learning in efforts to diagnose autism based on neurobiology raises serious practical and theoretical problems. For one, there is a danger that models could be over-trained, as well as a danger that data acquisition conditions and processing steps might not be perfectly replicated across sites. For another, with rare exceptions (e.g. Rabany et al., 2019), studies routinely attempt only to classify individuals as either autistic or typically developing, ignoring the need for differential diagnosis. Given these problems, and given the heterogeneity of autism, the diagnostic potential of supervised machine learning using neurobiological measures may be extremely limited. Moreover, even if this approach could provide accurate diagnostic labels, a neurodevelopmental evaluation would still be required to provide information about individual strengths and weaknesses and recommended next steps (Kanne and Bishop, 2020).
5 Some approaches, like Gaussian mixture modelling, yield not only discrete class assignments but also continuous probabilities of individuals' belonging in each of the subgroups defined in a particular analysis (Nylund, 2007). However, even these probabilities imply mutual exclusivity insofar as subgroups exist within the same space: an increased probability of belonging to one group entails a reduced probability of belonging to another. Admittedly, it is sometimes possible to cluster an individual twice using two different measurements (e.g. a set of variables measured at two different time points) as in latent transition analysis (e.g. Ausderau et al., 2014), but this is no different from running two separate clustering analyses.

6   It is noteworthy that students who listened to a clinical lecture on autism diagnostic criteria, etiology, and treatment – that is, a lecture in which this sort of negative language was employed – were found to have less understanding of and more negative attitudes towards autism than students who instead watched a television programme featuring an autistic protagonist (Stern and Barnes, 2019).

References

Alvares, G. A. et al. (2020) 'The misnomer of 'high functioning autism': Intelligence is an imprecise predictor of functional abilities at diagnosis', *Autism*, 24(1), pp. 221–232. https://doi.org/10.1177/1362361319852831.

American Psychiatric Association (1994) 'Disorders usually first diagnosed in infancy, childhood, or adolescence'. In: *Diagnostic and Statistical Manual of Mental Disorders*, 4th ed. Washington: American Psychiatric Association, pp. 37–121.

American Psychiatric Association (2013) 'Neurodevelopmental disorders'. In: *Diagnostic and Statistical Manual of Mental Disorders*, 5th ed. https://doi.org/10.1176/appi.books.9780890425596.dsm01.

Arvidsson, O. et al. (2018) 'Secular changes in the symptom level of clinically diagnosed autism', *Journal of Child Psychology and Psychiatry*, 59(7), pp. 744–751. https://doi.org/10.1111/jcpp.12864.

Ausderau, K. K. et al. (2014) 'Sensory subtypes in children with autism spectrum disorder: Latent profile transition analysis using a national survey of sensory features', *Journal of Child Psychology and Psychiatry and Allied Disciplines*, 55(8), pp. 935–944. https://doi.org/10.1111/jcpp.12219.

Autistic Self Advocacy Network (2019) ASAN comments on the clinical use of human germline genome editing [Online]. Available at: https://autisticadvocacy.org/2019/10/asan-comments-on-the-clinical-use-of-human-germline-genome-editing/ [Accessed 19 Mar. 2020].

Avlund, S. H. et al. (2020) 'Time trends in diagnostics and clinical features of young children referred on suspicion of autism: A population-based clinical cohort study, 2000–2010', *Journal of Autism and Developmental Disorders*. Advance online publication. https://doi.org/10.1007/s10803-020-04555-8.

Azad, G. F. et al. (2020) 'Quality of life in school-aged youth referred to an autism specialty clinic: A latent profile analysis', *Journal of Autism and Developmental Disorders*, 50(4), pp. 1269–1280. https://doi.org/10.1007/s10803-019-04353-x.

Belek, B. (2018) 'Articulating sensory sensitivity: From bodies with autism to autistic bodies', *Medical Anthropology*, 38(1), pp. 30–43. https://doi.org/10.1080/01459740.2018.1460750.

Ben-Sasson, A. et al. (2008) 'Sensory clusters of toddlers with autism spectrum disorders: Differences in affective symptoms', *Journal of Child Psychology and Psychiatry and Allied Disciplines*, 49(8), pp. 817–825. https://doi.org/10.1111/j.1469-7610.2008.01899.x.

Bonnello, C. (2015) The labelling issue, by a 'mildly autistic' 'high-functioning' 'person with Asperger syndrome' [Blog], *Autistic Not Weird*. Available at: https://autisticnotweird.com/labels/ [Accessed 19 Mar. 2020].

Brechin, A. (2018) Opening the dialectical Pandora's box [Online], Global Autism Project. Available at: https://www.globalautismproject.org/the-problem-with-functioning-labels-opening-the-dialectical-pandoras-box/ [Accessed 19 Mar. 2020].

Brukner-Wertman, Y., Laor, N. and Golan, O. (2016) 'Social (Pragmatic) Communication Disorder and its relation to the autism spectrum: Dilemmas arising from the DSM-5 classification', *Journal of Autism and Developmental Disorders*, 46(8), pp. 2821–2829. https://doi.org/10.1007/s10803-016-2814-5.

Castelbaum, L. et al. (2019) 'On the nature of monozygotic twin concordance and discordance for autistic trait severity: A quantitative analysis', *Behavior Genetics* [Advance online publication]. https://doi.org/10.1007/s10519-019-09987-2.

Chapman, R. (2019) Is autism really a 'genetically based brain wiring?' [Blog], *Psychology Today*. Available at: https://www.psychologytoday.com/us/blog/neurodiverse-age/201908/is-autism-really-genetically-based-brain-wiring [Accessed 19 Mar. 2020].

Chapman, R. (2020a) Neurodiversity and psychiatric validity: Reconstructing autism as a 'serial collective' [Blog], *Psychology Today*. Available at: https://www.psychologytoday.com/us/blog/neurodiverse-age/202001/neurodiversity-and-psychiatric-validity [Accessed 9 Feb. 2020].

Chapman, R. (2020b) The reality of autism: On the metaphysics of disorder and diversity. *Philosophical Psychology*, 33(6), pp. 799–819.

Charrad, M. et al. (2014) 'NbClust: An R package for determining the relevant number of clusters in a data set', *Journal of Statistical Software*, 61(6). https://doi.org/10.18637/jss.v061.i06.

Coo, H. et al. (2008) 'Trends in autism prevalence: Diagnostic substitution revisited', *Journal of Autism and Developmental Disorders*, 38(6), pp. 1036–1046. https://doi.org/10.1007/s10803-007-0478-x.

DeBoth, K. K. and Reynolds, S. (2017) 'A systematic review of sensory-based autism subtypes', *Research in Autism Spectrum Disorders*, 36, pp. 44–56. https://doi.org/10.1016/j.rasd.2017.01.005.

Dwyer, P. et al. (2020) 'Defining clusters of young autistic and typically-developing children based on loudness-dependent auditory electrophysiological responses', *Molecular Autism*, 11(1), p. 48. https://doi.org/10.1186/s13229-020-00352-3.

Edey, R. et al. (2016) 'Interaction takes two: Typical adults exhibit mind-blindness towards those with autism spectrum disorder', *Journal of Abnormal Psychology*, 125(7), pp. 879–885. https://doi.org/10.1037/abn0000199.

Elwin, M. et al. (2017) 'Sensory clusters of adults with and without autism spectrum conditions', *Journal of Autism and Developmental Disorders*, 47(3), pp. 579–589. https://doi.org/10.1007/s10803-016-2976-1.

Farmer, C., Golden, C. and Thurm, A. (2016) 'Concurrent validity of the differential ability scales, 2nd edn. with the Mullen scales of early learning in young children with and without neurodevelopmental disorders', *Child Neuropsychology*, 22(5), pp. 556–569. https://doi.org/10.1080/09297049.2015.1020775.

Feinstein, A. (2010). *A History of Autism: Conversations with the Pioneers*. Malden: Wiley-Blackwell.

Fletcher-Watson, S. and Happé, F. (2019) *Autism: A New Introduction to Psychological Theory and Current Debate*. Abingdon: Routledge.

Flynn, J. (2018) Why autism functioning labels are harmful -- And what to say instead [Blog], *The Mighty*. Available at: https://themighty.com/2018/07/autism-functioning-labels-low-functioning-high-functioning/ [Accessed 19 Mar. 2020].

Frazier, T. W. and Goodwin, M. S. (2020) 'Developing more clinically useful biomarkers in autism spectrum disorder', *Developmental Medicine and Child Neurology*. https://doi.org/10.1111/dmcn.14414.

Fushing, H. and McAssey, M. P. (2010) 'Time, temperature, and data cloud geometry', *Physical Review*, 82(6 Pt 1), p. 061110. https://doi.org/10.1103/PhysRevE.82.061110.

Gillberg, C. (1992) 'The Emmanuel Miller Memorial Lecture 1991: Autism and autistic-like conditions: Subclasses among disorders of empathy', *Journal of Child Psychology and Psychiatry, and Allied Disciplines*, 33(5), pp. 813–842. https://doi.org/10.1111/j.1469-7610.1992.tb01959.x.

Gillberg, C. (2010) 'The ESSENCE in child psychiatry: Early symptomatic syndromes eliciting neurodevelopmental clinical examinations', *Research in Developmental Disabilities*, 31(6), pp. 1543–1551. https://doi.org/10.1016/j.ridd.2010.06.002.

Grandin, T. and Panek, R. (2014) *The Autistic Brain: Helping Different Kinds of Minds Succeed*. New York: Mariner Books.

Grinker, R. R. (2007) *Unstrange Minds: Remapping the World of Autism*. Philadelphia: Basic Books.

Grinker, R. R., Yeargin-Allsopp, M. and Boyle, C. (2011) 'Culture and autism spectrum disorders: The impact on prevalence and recognition'. In: Amaral, D., Geschwind, D., and Dawson, G. (eds.) *Autism Spectrum Disorders*. New York: Oxford University Press, pp. 62–74. https://doi.org/10.1093/med/9780195371826.003.0008.

Hallmayer, J. et al. (2011) 'Genetic heritability and shared environmental factors among twin pairs with autism', *Archives of General Psychiatry*, 68(11), pp. 1095–1102. https://doi.org/10.1001/archgenpsychiatry.2011.76.

Heasman, B. and Gillespie, A. (2018) 'Perspective-taking is two-sided: Misunderstandings between people with Asperger's syndrome and their family members', *Autism*, 22(6), pp. 740–750. https://doi.org/10.1177/1362361317708287.

James, L. (2018) *Odd Girl Out: My Extraordinary Autistic Life*. Berkeley: Seal Press.

Kanne, S. M. and Bishop, S. L. (2020) 'Editorial perspective: The autism waitlist crisis and remembering what families need', *Journal of Child Psychology and Psychiatry, and Allied Disciplines*. https://doi.org/10.1111/jcpp.13254.

Kapp, S. K. (2018) 'Social support, well-being, and quality of life among individuals on the autism spectrum', *Pediatrics*, 141(Suppl 4), pp. S362–S368. https://doi.org/10.1542/peds.2016-4300N.

Kapp, S. K. (2020) 'Introduction'. In: Kapp, S. K. (ed.) *Autistic Community and the Neurodiversity Movement: Stories from the Frontline*. Singapore: Palgrave Macmillan, pp. 1–19. https://doi.org/10.1007/978-981-13-8437-0_1.

Kapp, S. K. et al. (2013) 'Deficit, difference, or both? Autism and neurodiversity', *Developmental Psychology*, 49(1), pp. 59–71. https://doi.org/10.1037/a0028353.

Kapp, S. K. and Ne'eman, A. (2020) 'Lobbying autism's diagnostic revision in the *DSM-5*'. In: Kapp, S. K. (ed.) *Autistic Community and the Neurodiversity Movement: Stories from the Frontline*. Singapore: Palgrave Macmillan, pp. 167–194. https://doi.org/10.1007/978-981-13-8437-0_13.

Keith, J. M., Jamieson, J. P. and Bennetto, L. (2019) 'The importance of adolescent self-report in autism spectrum disorder: Integration of questionnaire and autonomic measures', *Journal of Abnormal Child Psychology*, 47(4), pp. 741–754. https://doi.org/10.1007/s10802-018-0455-1.

King, M. and Bearman, P. (2009) 'Diagnostic change and the increased prevalence of autism', *International Journal of Epidemiology*, 38(5), pp. 1224–1234. https://doi.org/10.1093/ije/dyp261.

Klei, L. et al. (2012) 'Common genetic variants, acting additively, are a major source of risk for autism', *Molecular Autism*, 3(1), p. 9. https://doi.org/10.1186/2040-2392-3-9.

Lai, M.-C. and Szatmari, P. (2020) 'Sex and gender impacts on the behavioural presentation and recognition of autism', *Current Opinion in Psychiatry*, 33(2), pp. 117–123. https://doi.org/10.1097/YCO.0000000000000575.

Lombardo, M.V., Lai, M.-C. and Baron-Cohen, S. (2019) 'Big data approaches to decomposing heterogeneity across the autism spectrum', *Molecular Psychiatry*, 24(10), pp. 1435–1450. https://doi.org/10.1038/s41380-018-0321-0.

Lord, C. et al. (2000) 'The autism aiagnostic observation schedule - generic: A standard measure of social and communication deficits associated with the spectrum of autism', *Journal of Autism and Developmental Disorders*, 30(3), pp. 205–223. https://doi.org/10.1023/A:1005592401947.

Lord, C. et al. (2012) 'A multisite study of the clinical diagnosis of different autism spectrum disorders', *Archives of General Psychiatry*, 69(3), pp. 306–313. https://doi.org/10.1001/archgenpsychiatry.2011.148.

MacCallum, R. C. et al. (2002) 'On the practice of dichotomization of quantitative variables', *Psychological Methods*, 7(1), pp. 19–40. https://doi.org/10.1037//1082-989X.7.1.19.

McIntosh, D. N., Miller, L. J. and Shyu, V. (1999) 'Development and validation of the short sensory profile'. In: Dunn, W. (ed.) *Sensory Profile: User's Manual*. San Antonio: Psychological Corporation, pp. 59–73.

Milton, D. E. M. (2012) 'On the ontological status of autism: The 'double empathy' problem', *Disability and Society*, 27(6), pp. 883–887. https://doi.org/10.1080/09687599.2012.710008.

Morrison, K. E. et al. (2019) 'Outcomes of real-world social interaction for autistic adults paired with autistic compared to typically developing partners', *Autism* [Advance online publication]. https://doi.org/10.1177/1362361319892701.

Murias, M. et al. (2018) 'Validation of eye-tracking measures of social attention as a potential biomarker for autism clinical trials', *Autism Research*, 11(1), pp. 166–174. https://doi.org/10.1002/aur.1894.

Myers, S. M. et al. (2020) 'Insufficient evidence for 'autism-specific' genes', *American Journal of Human Genetics*, 106(5), pp. 587–595. https://doi.org/10.1016/j.ajhg.2020.04.004.

Nader, A. M. et al. (2016) 'Does WISC-IV underestimate the intelligence of autistic children?', *Journal of Autism and Developmental Disorders*, 46(5), pp. 1582–1589. https://doi.org/10.1007/s10803-014-2270-z.

Nadesan, M. H. (2008) Constructing autism: A brief genealogy. In: Osteen, M. (ed.), *Autism and Representation*. New York: Taylor & Francis, pp. 79–95.

Ne'eman, A. D. (2010) 'The future (and the past) of autism advocacy, Or why the ASA's magazine, *The Advocate*, wouldn't publish this piece', *Disability Studies Quarterly*, 30(1). https://doi.org/10.18061/dsq.v30i1.1059.

Nicolaidis, C. et al. (2019) 'The AASPIRE practice-based guidelines for the inclusion of autistic adults in research as co-researchers and study participants', *Autism*, 23(8), pp. 2007–2019. https://doi.org/10.1177/1362361319830523.

Nylund, K. L. (2007) *Latent Transition Analysis: Modeling Extensions and an Application to Peer Victimization* [Doctoral dissertation]. Available at: https://search.proquest.com/docview/304878179 [Accessed 19 Mar. 2020].

Nylund, K. L., Asparouhov, T. and Muthén, B. O. (2007) 'Deciding on the number of classes in latent class analysis and growth mixture modeling: A Monte Carlo simulation study', *Structural Equation Modeling*, 14(4), pp. 535–569. https://doi.org/10.1080/10705510701575396.

Paynter, J., Trembath, D. and Lane, A. (2018) 'Differential outcome subgroups in children with autism spectrum disorder attending early intervention', *Journal of Intellectual Disability Research*. https://doi.org/10.1111/jir.12504.

Pellicano, E., Dinsmore, A. and Charman, T. (2014) 'What should autism research focus upon? Community views and priorities from the United Kingdom', *Autism*, 18(7), pp. 756–770. https://doi.org/10.1177/1362361314529627.

Rabany, L. et al. (2019) 'Dynamic functional connectivity in schizophrenia and autism spectrum disorder: Convergence, divergence and classification', *NeuroImage: Clinical*, 24, p. 101966. https://doi.org/10.1016/j.nicl.2019.101966.

Richards, C. et al. (2015) 'Prevalence of autism spectrum disorder phenomenology in genetic disorders: A systematic review and meta-analysis', *The Lancet Psychiatry*, 2(10), pp. 909–916. https://doi.org/10.1016/S2215-0366(15)00376-4.

Robison, J. (2010) Of mice and men – Genetic research and its importance in autism [Blog], *Psychology Today*. Available at: https://www.psychologytoday.com/intl/blog/my-life-aspergers/201005/mice-and-men-genetic-research-and-its-importance-in-autism?amp [Accessed 19 Mar. 2020].

Rødgaard, E.-M. et al. (2019) 'Temporal changes in effect sizes of studies comparing individuals with and without autism: A meta-analysis', *JAMA Psychiatry*, 76(11), pp. 1124–1132. https://doi.org/10.1001/jamapsychiatry.2019.1956.

Russell, G. (2020) 'Critiques of the neurodiversity movement'. In: Kapp, S. K. (ed.) *Autistic Community and the Neurodiversity Movement: Stories from the Frontline*. Singapore: Palgrave Macmillan, pp. 287–303. https://doi.org/10.1007/978-981-13-8437-0_21.

Sasson, N. J. et al. (2017) 'Neurotypical peers are less willing to interact with those with autism based on thin slice judgments', *Scientific Reports*, 7, p. 40700. https://doi.org/10.1038/srep40700.

Schwartzman, B. C., Wood, J. J. and Kapp, S. K. (2016) 'Can the Five Factor Model of personality account for the variability of autism symptom expression? Multivariate approaches to behavioral phenotyping in adult autism spectrum disorder', *Journal of Autism and Developmental Disorders*, 46(1), pp. 253–272. https://doi.org/10.1007/s10803-015-2571-x.

Sherer, M. R. and Schreibman, L. (2005) 'Individual behavioral profiles and predictors of treatment effectiveness for children with autism', *Journal of Consulting and Clinical Psychology*, 73(3), pp. 525–538. https://doi.org/10.1037/0022-006X.73.3.525.

Simonoff, E. et al. (2019) 'Trajectories in symptoms of autism and cognitive ability in autism from childhood to adult life: Findings from a longitudinal epidemiological cohort', *Journal of the American Academy of Child and Adolescent Psychiatry* [Advance online publication]. https://doi.org/10.1016/j.jaac.2019.11.020.

Solomon, M. et al. (2018) 'What will my child's future hold? Phenotypes of intellectual development in 2–8-year-olds with autism spectrum disorder', *Autism Research*, 11(1), pp. 121–132. https://doi.org/10.1002/aur.1884.

Stern, S. C. and Barnes, J. L. (2019) 'Brief report: Does watching The Good Doctor affect knowledge of and attitudes toward autism?', *Journal of Autism and Developmental Disorders*, 49(6), pp. 2581–2588. https://doi.org/10.1007/s10803-019-03911-7.

Szatmari, P. et al. (2015) 'Developmental trajectories of symptom severity and adaptive functioning in an inception cohort of preschool children with autism spectrum disorder', *JAMA Psychiatry*, 72(3), pp. 276–283. https://doi.org/10.1001/jamapsychiatry.2014.2463.

Tager-Flusberg, H. (2018) Why no one needs a diagnosis of 'social communication disorder.' *Spectrum* [Online]. Available at: https://spectrumnews.org/opinion/columnists/no-one-needs-diagnosis-social-communication-disorder/ [Accessed 18 Apr. 2019].

Timimi, B. S. et al. (2019) 'Deconstructing diagnosis: Four commentaries on a diagnostic tool to assess individuals for autism spectrum disorders', *Autonomy, the Critical Journal of Interdisciplinary Autism Studies*, 1(6). Available at: http://www.larry-arnold.net/Autonomy/index.php/autonomy/article/view/AR26 [Accessed 19 Aug. 2019].

Wallisch, A. et al. (2019) 'Early identification in autism: Subtypes based on child, family, and community characteristics', *International Society for Autism Research (INSAR)*, Montreal. Available at: https://insar.confex.com/insar/2019/webprogram/Paper29454.html [Accessed 19 Mar. 2020].

Weiss, A. B. (1935) 'Qualitative intelligence testing as a means of diagnosis in the examination of psychopathic children', *American Journal of Orthopsychiatry*, 5(2), pp. 154–179. https://doi.org/10.1111/j.1939-0025.1935.tb06338.x.

Wing, L. (1988) 'The continuum of autistic characteristics'. In: Schopler, E. and Mesibov, G. B. (eds.) *Diagnosis and Assessment in Autism*. New York: Plenum Press, pp. 91–110.

Wolfers, T. et al. (2019) 'From pattern classification to stratification: Towards conceptualizing the heterogeneity of autism spectrum disorder', *Neuroscience and Biobehavioral Reviews*, 104, pp. 240–254. https://doi.org/10.1016/j.neubiorev.2019.07.010.

Young, I. M. (1994) 'Gender as seriality: Thinking about women as a social collective', *Signs*, 19(3), pp. 713–738. Available at: https://www.jstor.org/stable/3174775 [Accessed 9 Feb. 2020].

6
RATIONAL (PATHOLOGICAL) DEMAND AVOIDANCE

As a mental disorder and an evolving social construct

Richard Woods

Pathological Demand Avoidance and Critical Autism Studies – context

There are different interpretations and definitions to Pathological Demand Avoidance (PDA) and Critical Autism Studies[1] (CAS). I need to be clear which definition of each I will be using throughout this chapter. While I will detail divergent PDA interpretations and how they evolved, the CAS definition I use to do this is:

> the "criticality" comes from investigating power dynamics that operate in Discourses around autism, questioning deficit-based definitions of autism, and being willing to consider the ways in which biology and culture intersect to produce "disability".
>
> *(Waltz, 2014, p. 1337)*

This chapter discusses how PDA is a social construct, thus as a concept, and how it has evolved over time, in the process considering how culture and biology intersect to create PDA. This builds on my original article (Woods, 2017); in the process the essay is representative of my thinking in February 2021.[2] While I will be using a medical model of disability to discuss autism[3] and PDA, both in practice are social constructs that interact upon and with prevailing culture. Before I explain how I define PDA and how it is quickly evolving, I will explain why autism, PDA, and other mental disorders are social constructs, using autism and PDA as examples. I then discuss how PDA is different and thus is not autism but is best described as a form of Obsessive-Compulsive Disorder and Related Disorders. This raises the question of *why* autism is viewed as part of the autism spectrum. I describe historical PDA literature and actions of certain stakeholders to control the evolution of PDA to be viewed as a form of autism. Finally, I analyse various PDA behaviour profiles to explain *how* traits of PDA have been amended for PDA to become autism-like.

Mental Disorders as social constructs

Mental disorders, like autism, PDA, Obsessive-Compulsive Disorder (OCD) are highly contentious. There is a continuum of outlooks on their respective utility, with one extreme driven by a scientific-method approach, the other that mental disorders are required as they assist many persons, through providing a model to describe a person and inform suitable support strategies. The central cause of this polarisation of perspectives is that mental disorders are social constructs; when a mental disorder is diagnosed, it is based on observable behaviours and either caregiver or service-user reports. Mental disorders are not diagnosed based on identifiable biological characteristics (Fletcher-Watson and Happé, 2019), and we should not expect this to change for the foreseeable future. Despite substantial effort and resources spent researching biomarkers for it (Pellicano et al., 2014), autism does not have a biomarker and many now accept that it is unlikely to ever gain such evidence (Woods et al., 2019). Hence, mental disorders officially lack features of fixed qualities that are rooted in nature; instead their definitions are based on human understandings and are thus fluid, evolving over time.[4]

This dynamic intangible aspect of mental disorders affects the nature of knowledge surrounding mental disorders, as they can be controlled by human actions and decisions. Clinicians when assessing for features which might be attributed to a disorder, are not seeking concrete information. Instead, they are seeking information they can reliably measure, i.e. information that they can repeatedly measure consistently. Hence, mental disorders are based on reliability and not validity (Christie, 2019, Fletcher-Watson and Happé, 2019). The information a clinician uses to diagnose a mental disorder does not have to be valid, i.e. the characteristic does not have to represent what is being purported. A crucial example of this is how autism is reported to have deficits in Theory of Mind and Empathy (Bishop, 2018, Christie et al., 2012, Baron-Cohen et al., 1985), despite 20% of autistic persons passing Theory of Mind tests (Baron-Cohen et al., 1985). Social communication issues are solely located in autistic persons in the medical model. However, a growing body of empirical research supports the Double Empathy Problem, which posits that social communication problems in autism are related to breakdowns in interactions between autistic persons and those around them (Milton et al., 2020, Milton, 2017).

These challenges around generating deficits to measure, stem from how they are created as a researcher collects data on features in their sample. Statistically, each feature should produce a bell-shaped curve, a Gaussian Curve, and the line under its peak is the average of this characteristic in this population. Under the medical model of disability, the average is referred to as normal, and the extremes at the lower edge of the bell-curve are pathologised with deficits. Anyone who is attributed a deficit should receive intervention to correct the deficit. A problem is that individuals and entire populations can be cured and pathologised based on the definitions used: for example, during the 1970s, when thousands of people of Borderline Mental Retardation were cured by changing how IQ scores are used (Goodley, 2011). Pertinently, just because some persons might fall within the pathologised extreme, it does not mean that the associated features are actually 'deficits', nor that the 'deficits' can be 'repaired' with interventions, or pills. Frequently, there are more complicated processes occurring between the pathologised persons and their environment, which produce the 'deficits'. Mental disorders need to be treated for what they are: abstract representations of a collection of features.

For a mental disorder to be diagnosed reliably it needs to have validated tools and a standardised behaviour profile, and PDA is partly controversial as there is no consensus over what it is, or how to assess for it (Woods, 2020b, O'Nions et al. 2016a, O'Nions et al., 2014a). Lacking both a standardised behaviour profile and validated tools, some argue PDA is best described as a label given to a person (Moore, 2020). However, despite this, the reliability rates for mental disorders are decreasing with each iteration of the *DSM* (Kinderman, 2019) and many clinicians do not find mental disorders useful for prognosis or treatment planning (First et al., 2019).

A critique of PDA is that much of its behaviour profile is difficult to reliably measure, like Surface Sociability, with deficits in social identity, pride, and shame (Garralda, 2003). Some features associated with this trait, like very inappropriate behaviour, and not knowing the difference between right and wrong, are highly subjective and one could question from whose perspective they are being defined. An issue with assessing features that only need to be reliable in nature, is that one can accidentally allow for fallacious assumptions to adversely impact on how one interprets the feature. For PDA, some of the features proposed to indicate deficits in social identity, pride, and shame, include panic attacks and aggression towards others (Newson et al., 2003). When a person is angry, it indicates the person is highly distressed and is highly aroused (Woods, 2019a). The characteristics proposed by Newson et al. (2003) for PDA's social communication issues highlight the potential problems that can occur when one reifies them into a mental disorder.

There are credible arguments for abandoning mental disorders (see, for example, Kinderman 2019). Nonetheless, some mental disorders do seem to be aligned to natural ways of being human. While autism lacks any biomarker evidence (Woods et al., 2019), some argue for discarding the construct (Runswick-Cole et al., 2016). There is a case to be made that autism is associated with autistic features that are valid. First, autistic perspectives are often stronger and more accurate than those of non-autistic stakeholders (Woods and Waltz, 2019). Second, autistic people are forming our own distinct culture (Woods et al., 2018). Third, autistic people frequently also possess co-occurring difficulties, such as anxiety (Woods, 2019a). How such co-occurring mental disorders present in autistic people, is often different to how they present outside of autism (Green et al., 2018a), because autism and co-occurring conditions simultaneously interact with each other (Green et al., 2018a, Brede et al., 2017, Flackhill et al. 2017). Irrespective of whether PDA and other mental disorders are social constructs, it is vital we validate the lived experience and difficulties expressed by those bestowed with a mental disorder.

Features of mental disorders can be arbitrarily chosen for political reasons. For example, when revising the autism criteria for the *Diagnostic and Statistical Manual of Mental Disorders, Fifth Edition (DSM-5)*, a group of autistic persons lobbied (unsuccessfully) for the reduction of number of social communication traits a person needed for a diagnosis (Kapp and Ne'eman, 2019). It means that aspects of mental disorders can be rebranded based on the outlook that is in vogue at any given moment. We can create a mental disorder from a collection of features observed in a particular population. Elizabeth Newson, for instance, reified PDA when she created its first behaviour profile in 1988 (Newson, 1989), making abstract features from her case files suddenly tangible. Additionally, the classification of mental disorders is arbitrary, and it is possible to invent new diagnostic groupings. Newson created her own Pervasive Developmental Coding Disorders group for autism, PDA, dyslexia, and dysphasia (Newson, 1996, 1989). Indeed, leading PDA proponents highlight how clinicians can assign a mental disorder to a specific population, expressing:

> No iteration of either DSM or ICD has acknowledged the fundamental distinction between researchers and practiners … who uses diagnostic classifications and for what purpose?
>
> *(Christie, 2019)*

The crux of this quote is that, if a mental disorder benefits certain stakeholder groups, the diagnostic entity should be accepted and used. The purpose of a definition of a mental disorder should be to describe a constellation of features that adversely affect the diagnosed individual, and/or those around them. Consequently, each mental disorder should represent a discrete set of difficulties and correspond to a particular set of approaches. One of the main justifications for PDA is that it has different strategies[5] to autism and traditional autism approaches do not work with PDA (O'Nions and Eaton, 2020, Eaton and Weaver, 2020, Christie, 2007, Newson et al., 2003). However, this is strongly countered by the number of traditional autism approaches that do not work with many autistic people (Milton, 2017). PDA approaches can be viewed as good practice (Woods, 2019a), replicating strategies that have been practiced with autistic persons, independently of a PDA diagnosis (Green et al., 2018b), such as the Low Arousal Approach. This matters, as it is typical practice for strategies and approaches to be associated with problems, not to be associated with a particular diagnosis.

A primary cause as to why strategies and approaches are not diagnosis specific is that all humans have spiky skills profiles; no-human conforms to all statistical averages, no human can be described as normal (Goodley, 2011). This results from how human features, including psychological features, exist along a continuum within the human population (Kinderman, 2019). We do not fit neatly into boxes. The professional bodies that produce manuals to diagnose mental disorders accept this intrinsic aspect of humanity, and so they create residual mental disorders for each diagnostic grouping for persons who do not meet the clinical threshold for a particular diagnosis (First et al., 2019). When autism subtypes were used in the *DSM-4*, autism was represented by three mental disorders: Asperger's Syndrome; Autistic Disorder; and Pervasive Developmental – Not Otherwise Specified (PDD-NOS) (Christie et al., 2012; Green et al., 2018a); the last one being the residual category for anyone not meeting clinical threshold for either Autistic Disorder and Asperger's Syndrome. Together, these three mental disorders were within the Pervasive Developmental Disorder diagnostic grouping, alongside Childhood Disintegrative Disorder and Rett's Disorder (American Psychiatric Association, 1994). Presently, the consensus is that autism subtypes are unhelpful as it is clinically and scientifically impossible to successfully divide autism (Woods et al., 2019). Yet, some argue that if individuals prefer the name of particular an autism subtype, they should be retained for those who wish to use them (Wing et al., 2011, Frith 1991).

Using autism and PDA as case studies, this section has discussed how mental disorders are social constructs and demonstrated that they do not need to be scientific in nature, they only need to benefit certain stakeholders of a particular population. In the process, mental disorders are not diagnosed on valid features, but on characteristics that can be reliably measured. This can lead to features interpreted based on observer's bias. For instance, panic attacks were assigned to the Surface Sociability trait when it is a sign of distress; more appropriately it should be assigned to the Lability of Mood trait. Due to being social constructs, politics and subjectivity affect how mental disorders are conceptualised and categorised. PDA is known for avoidance of the demands of everyday life (Green et al., 2018a, Christie, 2007, Newson et al., 2003), but these demands vary with each person's situation, cultural background, and lived experience. Later in the chapter I detail how PDA's evolution has been controlled to become more 'autism-like', adopting characteristics that fit this outlook. Before then, I critically evaluate PDA literature, and detail how I conceptualise PDA as a mental disorder.

PDA as a mental disorder

First, I will define what I consider PDA to be, and this can be tricky as PDA means different things to different people. Consequently, there are several different behaviour profiles for PDA, I have amalgamated these to create an Aggregated Profile, as shown in Figure 6.1. I take a medical model of disability approach to describing PDA throughout this chapter, displaying its nature as a social construct and how it interacts with cultural practices.

There are areas of overlap and difference between PDA and autism. The main similarity is that both have Restricted and Repetitive Behaviours and Interests (RRBIs) (Eaton 2018a, Christie et

A—Deficits in social communication and interaction
A1—Deficits in social-emotional reciprocity
A2—Deficits in nonverbal communication
A3—Deficits in relationships

B—Restricted, repetitive behaviour, interests or activities (RRBIs):
B1—Stereotyped/repetitive behaviours
B2—Insistence on sameness and routines
B3—Restricted, fixated interests
B4—Hyper- or hypo-reactivity to sensory input

C—Early onset:
C1 – Early presence.

Criteria A - Surface Sociability (optional trait):
A1 – Atypical interaction and confused world view. Often with extreme behaviours, like violence when angry or panic attacks.

Criteria B – Anxiety based restricted and repetitive behaviours and interests (RRBIs):
B1 - Comfortable in role play and pretending.
B2 - Continues to resist and avoid ordinary demands of life.
B3 - Lability of mood, impulsive, led by need to control.
B4 - Obsessive behaviour.
B5 - Strategies of avoidance are essentially socially manipulative.

Criteria C – Neurodevelopmental (optional traits):
C1 - Language delay, seems result of passivity.
C2 - Neurological Involvement.
C3 - Passive early history in first year.
C4 - Sensory Differences

Figure 6.1 Abbreviated *DSM-5* Autism Spectrum Disorder criteria and the Aggregated PDA Profile. Note: The wording for the *DSM-5* autism spectrum disorder criteria is taken from Evers et al. (2020)

al., 2012, Christie 2007). PDA's RRBIs are clinically different to autism as they are described as obsessive in nature (Newson et al., 2003), and caused by high anxiety (Eaton and Weaver, 2020, Christie et al., 2012, Christie, 2007). Moreover, PDA has five RRBIs whereas autism has three. An essential point of divergence between PDA and autism is the early age of onset of traits, yet some view PDA as being neurodevelopmental in nature (Eaton and Weaver, 2020, Newson et al., 2003).

For social communication issues, the situation is inverted, with autism having three, whereas PDA has an optional one. Akin to RRBIs, PDA's surface sociability is viewed as having a different cause than autism, which is attributed to deficits in Theory of Mind and Empathy. PDA does not have these deficits, but social communication issues in PDA do overlap in some autistic persons, as 20% of autistic persons lack deficits in Theory of Mind (Baron-Cohen et al., 1985). Research suggests that PDA traits have no association with Theory of Mind deficits (Bishop, 2018, O'Nions, 2013). However, PDA developmental aspects were made optional several years ago (Fidler, 2019, Russell, 2018, Green et al., 2018a, O'Nions et al., 2016a). While these differences are present, PDA's behaviour profile is unstable (Eaton, 2018a); its features may in the future become more aligned with autism.

There are many other factors that prohibit PDA being part of the autism spectrum. Key clinical differences between PDA and autism include PDA's use of humour, spontaneity, and novelty, as a PDA strategy which contradicts traditional autism strategies. The fantasy and roleplay characteristics of PDA are typically delayed or absent in autism. PDA's initial gender was one male to one female, which is more balanced than male-biased autism gender ratios (O'Nions et al., 2015, O'Nions et al. 2014b). PDA's socially manipulative demand avoidance behaviours are too frequent and varied when compared to autism, as they preclude a person receiving an autism diagnosis (Trundle et al., 2017, Gillberg et al. 2015, O'Nions et al., 2015, Christie et al., 2012). PDA's surface sociability problems are associated with deficits in social identity, pride, and shame (Newson et al., 2003), unlike autism. The reduction in persons meeting the clinical threshold for PDA, of 44% to 89% is higher than that found in autism; these and other results indicate that features of PDA are developmentally unstable (Woods, 2020), and thus not pervasive.

Certain PDA characteristics could be criminal in nature, such as harassment (O'Nions et al., 2016a, Gillberg et al., 2015), and could risk individuals becoming involved in the Criminal Justice System (CJS). Early PDA research identified a few features, such as stalking and violence (Newson et al., 2003), that increase risk of engagement with the CJS (Egan et al., 2019). Egan and colleagues (2019) found in their first study that around one fifth of their sample had been arrested and about a tenth had a prior conviction. Slightly over 10% of participants in the second study were involved with the CJS (ibid.). Furthermore, Lorna Wing (2002) noted that persons with PDA gain reward from upsetting other individuals and PDA behaviours are found in all autism subtypes. The rates of involvement of PDA in the criminal justice system are higher than those found for autism, with autistic persons no more likely to engage in CJS than their peers (Yu et al., 2021). There is increasing recognition of the adverse impact stigma has for autistic persons, which the criminal conduct aspects of PDA may contribute towards. This raises the question of whether we wish to associate such features with autism, by viewing PDA as a form of autism.

PDA behaviours may not be caused by autism, i.e. a "double-hit" (Wing et al. 2011), and it may be a "triple-hit" of autism, conduct problems, and anxiety (Langton and Frederickson, 2016). Research indicates that PDA is not predicted by autism, but by ADHD, anxiety, and conduct problems (Egan et al., 2020, Green et al., 2018a). Some experts think PDA is seen outside of autism (Green et al. 2018a; Woods 2020b) and has limited supporting evidence (Woods 2020b, Woods 2019a). These, and the previously mentioned factors, support the consistent views of the clinician who first observed PDA: that it is not part of the autism spectrum (Newson et al., 2003, Newson 1996, 1989, 1983).

PDA is commonly portrayed as part of the autism spectrum (O'Nions and Eaton, 2020, Eaton et al., 2018, Russell, 2018, O'Nions et al., 2016, Christie et al., 2012; Christie, 2007). Yet its central impairment is high-anxiety–driven demand avoidance, and anxiety is recognised as a co-occurring difficulty to autism (Woods 2020a, Egan et al., 2019, Gould and Ashton-Smith, 2011). Newson et al. (2003) conceptualised the demand avoidance as being obsessive in nature, and Christopher Gillberg questions if it is a new type of mental disorder (2014). In OCD, there is a simplified cycle of thoughts and actions (OCD-UK, 2020), which matches what happens in PDA. The OCD cycle starts with an obsession (demand), which then causes anxiety or distress to an individual. The individual then responds to the obsession with a compulsion, which is an act or thought that attempts to resist, ignore, and remove the obsessive thought. Subsequently, the individual experiences temporary relief from their anxiety and distress, even only for a few moments, until the next obsessive thought.

Some would argue that a person with PDA has atypical ways of socially interacting and they struggle to maintain social relationships (Eaton and Weaver, 2020, Christie et al., 2012, Newson et al., 2003). Social communication issues and issues maintaining relationships are common in mental disorders (Wilkinson, 2017), for example Attachment Disorders (Flackhill et al., 2017), and Borderline Personality Disorder (Eaton, 2018a). O'Nions et al. (2016a) removed PDA's developmental traits their PDA behaviour profile, as they were too common among autistic persons to be useful in identifying PDA as an autism subgroup. Due to how common social communication issues are outside of autism, we can likewise make the Surface Sociability trait optional.

A logical extension is that if one is primarily diagnosing PDA in autistic persons, the social communications issues are covered by an autism diagnosis and so the Surface Sociability is redundant, as those difficulties are pathologised in an autism diagnosis (Fletcher-Watson and Happé, 2019, Eaton, 2018a). Placing the Surface Sociability trait as optional is in line with the prediction that the diagnostic traits will be reduced as understandings of PDA are refined (Christie et al., 2012). Exclusively utilising traits that are RRBIs reduces PDA's traits down to those that are essential for a diagnosis and reflect the demand avoidance descriptors in its name.

Many of the features of this trait – for instance, panic attacks and violence when angry – suggest the person is highly aroused. This can be viewed as compulsive responses to anxiety from demands; therefore, they are instead attributed to Lability of Mood trait, a RRBI. O'Nions (2019) argues that the demand avoidance behaviours in PDA are developed through a negative reinforcement cycle, where anxiety is temporarily relieved due to the expression of demand avoidance behaviours, which forces other humans away and thus removes the aversive demand. Ergo, these demand avoidance behaviours are viewed as scripted in nature.

In contrast, PDA's demand avoidance behaviours are viewed as manipulative in nature due to how much time and effort a person with PDA expends upon displaying them; it is viewed as their greatest asset (Christie et al., 2012, Newson, 1983). The impact of the demand avoidance behaviours is to change the dynamics of social interaction, often by terminating it, thus removing aversive demands. If a person is frequently expressing such demand-avoidant behaviours, it may lead to the person frequently experiencing chaotic and unpredictable social interactions. This highlights how PDA's obsessive-compulsive aspects interfere with a person's social and occupational functioning (OCD-UK, 2020). Traits of adopting roles and being comfortable with roleplay is viewed as an RRBI due to the obsessive and compulsive nature of these behaviours; for instance, escaping into roles as a coping strategy (Newson et al., 2003, Newson, 1983). PDA's Surface Sociability trait does not necessitate it being a form of autism.

There is substantial overlap between PDA and OCD. Empirical research investigating PDA from caregiver reports of autistic children indicates PDA has a similar cycle to OCD (O'Nions, 2019). Where an individual experiences a demand, which causes distress or anxiety, they respond with avoidant behaviour, which relieves the anxiety and distress until the next demand (O'Nions, 2019). Modern PDA perspectives adopt a transactional approach between individuals and their environment (Fidler and Christie, 2019, Green et al., 2018a, Milton, 2017). Around two thirds of distress (challenging) behaviour is caused by a demand or request by other persons (Woods, 2019a). The compulsive behaviours in PDA include avoiding persons and situations, through behaviours people use to assert their agency, such as pretending to be ill or incapacitating themselves, attempting to negotiate better terms, and running away or hiding (Moore, 2020, Woods, 2019b).

These can be extreme behaviours and difficult for anyone to manage, including the person expressing them. Avoidance, including of certain places, objects, and persons are recognised compulsive acts in OCD (OCD-UK, 2020). PDA's compulsive, avoidant behaviour is a response to a demand, which is an anxiety or distressing thought, typically triggered from their environment, in particular other persons. PDA compulsion behaviours are so extreme that they may cause other persons to remove the demand they are placing on the individual, providing temporary relief to persons with PDA (O'Nions, 2019). Frequently, these compulsive acts impact a person's social relationships. This is reflected in questions in PDA measures, such as "I am good at getting round others and making them do as I want" (Egan et al., 2019, p. 485), and "Would you describe A as good at getting round others and making them do as s/he wants, or playing people off against each other?"[6] Therefore, PDA social demand-avoidance behaviour is pathologising efforts of a person expressing their self-agency (Milton, 2017; Woods, 2017). PDA is a threat to an individual's self-agency as others can ignore a person's legitimate concerns and efforts for self-advocacy, as the person being manipulative (Woods, 2017).

Researchers have found a group of autistic persons who started displaying PDA from around ages 5 to 7, and this usually triggered by aversive school experiences (Eaton and Weaver, 2020, Eaton, 2019). The researchers call this group "Rational Demand Avoidance" as they report these PDA behaviours present less frequently than "Extreme Demand Avoidance" and are not necessarily pervasive (Eaton and Weaver, 2020). However, many of these autistic children and young people (CYP) would not be able to process the reasons behind their demand avoidance behaviour. Many of these 5–7-year-old CYP may have any combination of issues with Theory of Mind, alexithymia, and interoception. They may have difficulty understanding their own mental state, their own emotions, and what their internal bodily signals mean. Consequently, these CYP would not be able to rationalise their demand avoidance. Hence, there cannot be a "Rational Demand Avoidance" group, if many of its members cannot rationalise their demand avoidance and such a distinction between "Rational" and "Extreme" demand avoidance is arbitrary.

The research team themselves consider demand avoidance in their "Rational Demand Avoidance" group to be rational from a non-autistic perspective. Autistic persons, such as Damian Milton and I, argue that PDA should be called Rational Demand Avoidance, as autistic persons will frequently avoid situations we find aversive (Woods, 2019a, Milton, 2017). In our conceptualisation of PDA, there are no distinctions between PDA and Rational Demand Avoidance. This makes sense: when autistic persons live in a world unsuited to our needs, autistic anxiety results from hostile experiences (Pellicano, 2020). This is reflected in high prevalence rates for anxiety-based difficulties, anxiety (42–56%) (Woods, 2019a), Anxiety Disorders (20%), and OCD (9%) (Lai et al., 2019). Anxiety and OCD are associated with trauma and childhood aversive experiences (Allsopp et al., 2019). PDA behaviours can be explained by trauma (Brede et al., 2017, Milton, 2017, McElroy, 2016). When accounting for the psycho-emotional disabling effects non-autistic–led culture has on autistic persons, avoiding demands resulting from said culture would be intrinsically rational.

For OCD, whether or not obsessions and compulsions are understood by those experiencing them is ignored, as children are not necessarily expected to know or express the aims of their actions or mental acts. Additionally, a person meets a threshold when their obsessions/compulsions take up at least an hour a day or when they adversely affect some important areas of functioning, such as social or occupational ones (OCD-UK, 2020). This approach accepts how psychological features present in a continuum and can manifest differently in persons as it does not differentiate between which is more severe between compulsions or obsessions, instead focusing on the universality of the underlying psychological process.[7] A broad conceptualisation of PDA is inherently inclusive as it acknowledges the universal rights to a PDA diagnosis (Summerhill and Collett, 2018).

Modifying the OCD cycle for PDA allows for demands often triggered from external sources, but the obsessional demand is the individual's own thought. With a transactional approach taken in modern PDA understandings (Fidler and Christie, 2019, Green et al., 2018a, Milton, 2017), a demand management[8] cycle is produced, as seen in Figure 6.2.

The following is an example of the Demand Management Cycle describing demand avoidance in PDA. A young autistic child has the demand to attend school. The child becomes anxious from the prospect of facing sensory overload during class and bullying at break times. The child avoids the demand to attend school through school refusal and in the process gains relief from the anxiety of facing a known distressing situation, until the next time they are faced with that demand. It can be more complicated than this in real life, with the caregivers attempting multiple times for the child to attend school each day, initially for at least two weeks, and in response the

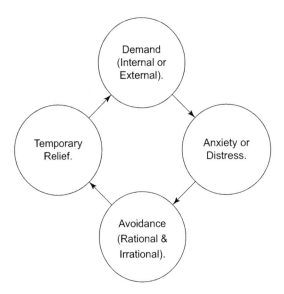

Figure 6.2 The Demand Management Cycle for PDA

child escalates their behaviours to the aversive demand. The child might start with attempting to negotiate with the adult; as this attempt fails, they might try to incapacitate themselves. Finally, the child becomes violent with the caregiver, and at this point the demand to attend school is withdrawn for that day. When this scenario occurs over several months, it conforms to understandings of OCD, as the distressing thoughts are inherently the child's perspective. The compulsive school refusal and violence towards the caregiver would cause clinically significant distress and impairment in social situations and areas of functioning and education (OCD-UK, 2020).[9]

The Demand Management Cycle for PDA is partly derived from the OCD cycle, and it shares similar properties. Firstly, it should be present in most forms of PDA, but it is only a simple model and does not represent all the complex psychological processes that can occur with demand avoidance. PDA is primarily diagnosed in autistic persons (Eaton and Weaver, 2020, O'Nions and Eaton, 2020, Russell, 2018), though this is not universally the case (Woods, 2020b, Green et al., 2018a, O'Nions, 2013, Newson et al., 2003). Anecdotally, many autistic adults report that when demand avoidance forces them to miss an activity they wish to do, they subsequently experience guilt. This extra emotional baggage surrounding demand avoidance behaviours can amplify the reinforcement effects of demand avoidance. Consequently, demand avoidance can become habits and/or negatively impact a person's mental well-being (O'Nions and Eaton, 2020). It is vital that the Demand Management Cycle is not over-reified, to the detriment of the entire psychological processes present in persons with PDA.

The lack of consensus over what PDA is, makes it difficult to directly compare PDA to autism. Yet, there are many factors emerging that indicate PDA is not autism, from it being primarily an anxiety-based condition, to how it appears that PDA is neither necessarily developmental nor pervasive in nature. Furthermore, in my view, PDA is best viewed as a new type of mental disorder that fits within the OCD and Related Disorders diagnostic grouping. Each person with PDA will generally follow the same Demand Management Cycle, in which they receive a demand, which causes the person anxiety or distress. Subsequently, a person with PDA will express avoidance behaviour until the demand is removed and they experience temporary relief. It is appropriate to conceptualise PDA as "Rational Demand Avoidance", supporting the views of Critical Autism Studies scholars (Milton, 2017, Moore, 2020, Woods, 2019a). Such an outlook is intrinsically inclusive, by adopting a low diagnostic threshold and a broad definition, supporting the universal rights of a CYP with PDA (Summerhill and Collett, 2018). However, this outlook does not consider how PDA is mainly diagnosed in autistic persons, and the story of how the present situation occurred is provided in the next section.

PDA and its relationship to the autism spectrum

PDA's traditional diagnostic status is linked to the historic status of autism. Infantile Autism, as proposed by Leo Kanner, was originally viewed as a form of Schizophrenia (Woods, 2019a, Frith, 1991). Autism has since changed diagnostic categories to Pervasive Developmental Disorders with the use of subtypes (American Psychiatric Association, 1994). Presently, autism is viewed as an undividable continuum disorder (Woods, 2020b, Fletcher-Watson and Happé, 2019; Green et al., 2018a). Elizabeth Newson's opinions on PDA's diagnostic identity were consistent over three decades. Newson researched PDA from 1975 to 2003 (Newson et al., 2003), initially creating a new diagnostic grouping into which to place PDA in 1986, two years before the behaviour profile (Newson, 1989). This grouping, used between 1986 to 1996, is the Pervasive Developmental Coding Disorders and was composed of Infantile autism, Asperger's Syndrome, PDA, dyslexia, and dysphasia (Newson, 1996, 1989). Newson later revised this diagnostic grouping into her own version of the Pervasive Developmental Disorders, containing Autistic Disorder, Asperger's Syndrome, PDA, and Specific Language Impairment (SLIs). SLIs contain conditions such as dyslexia and dysphasia. Despite the name change Newson still required all four syndromes to have coding issues (Newson et al., 2003, Newson, 1999).[10]

Newson and colleagues spent 15 years refining the PDA behaviour profile, while fundamentally keeping it the same. Individuals with PDA who displayed autism features were removed from their database. Newson did not base PDA on the Triad of Impairment (Newson et al., 2003) that underpins modern autism diagnostic criteria (Milton, 2017). Vitally, Newson et al. (2003) expressed PDA needs as being distinct and different to Autistic Disorder and Asperger's Syndrome; PDA is not an autism spectrum disorder, and it would be a mistake to envision it as such[11] as early as 1983 (Newson, 1983). The purpose of Newson's PDA research is to demonstrate that PDA is different to Autistic Disorder and Asperger's Syndrome; it is not an ASD and therefore PDA needs to be recognised as a distinct diagnostic entity (Newson et al., 2003). Contrary to Newson's consistent views, PDA is primarily viewed as a form of autism. So how did this occur?

PDA is viewed as a form of autism through two pathways. In 2002, Lorna Wing and Judy Gould argued that Newson's research does not show PDA as a separate syndrome from autism (Milton, 2017, Christie, 2007, Wing, 2002), and that the features of PDA are present throughout the entire autistic population (Milton, 2017, Christie et al., 2012, Christie, 2007). Others have noted that Newson's research does not establish the specificity or validity of PDA (Green et al., 2018a, Garralda, 2003), and that there are not features specific to PDA (Eaton and Weaver, 2020, Woods, 2019a, Garralda, 2003). Later, Gould, with Ashton-Smith (2011), suggested that PDA could be a female form of autism. Wing and Gould's comments have some merit, but seem problematic as their comments came before Newson et al. (2003) article was published. Their critique was premature. Furthermore, I also question whether Wing and Gould have the clinical experience to say exactly what PDA is and how it presents in the general public, considering their history in highly specialised autism settings.

Phil Christie builds on the arguments of Wing and Gould and later discusses how controversy around PDA focuses on whether PDA is a discrete syndrome within broader Pervasive

Developmental Disorders or a syndrome in the narrower Autism Spectrum. While referring to conventional autism and acknowledging that Pervasive Developmental Disorders diagnostic grouping is not the same as the autism spectrum, he attempts to resolve the debate by arguing that PDA should be viewed as an autism subtype, as the public often conflates the Pervasive Developmental Disorders with autism spectrum. He suggests that a prolonged debate on the topic is a distraction from focusing on the true purpose of a diagnosis (Christie, 2007). Essentially, Christie replaced the Triad of Impairment, as the underpinning of autism social construct, with the three descriptors of Pervasive, Developmental, and Disorder.[12]

Christie cites a 1999 diagram by Newson that displays a version of her Pervasive Developmental Disorders diagnostic grouping (Christie, 2007). The 1999 iteration of this diagram is different to the 2003 "The 'family' of pervasive developmental disorders". The earlier version omits Specific Language Impairments (Newson, 1999, Newson et al., 2003). This is a crucial point of divergence when adopting Newson's Pervasive Developmental Disorders as the autism spectrum. Newson's version of Pervasive Developmental Disorders lacks Childhood Disintegrative Disorder and Rett's Disorder of the *DSM-4* (American Psychiatry Association, 1994), adding PDA and SLIs (Newson et al., 2003).

In the *DSM-4*, Pervasive Developmental Disorder- Not Otherwise Specified was the residual category for Autistic Disorder and Asperger's Syndrome; these together with PDD-NOS were autism subtypes (Green et al., 2018a, Christie et al., 2012). Newson had her own definition of PDD-NOS, which is when a person does not meet the threshold for either Autistic Disorder, Asperger's Syndrome, PDA, or SLIs. Newson's definition is clinically broader than the accepted PDD-NOS definition as it includes non-autism constructs of PDA and SLIs. It therefore covers non-autistic persons. Using Christie's logic, one would also be adding SLIs to the Autism Spectrum. The prevalence rate for SLIs is 3% to 7% (Bishop et al., 2017). This would mean using Newson's views on Pervasive Developmental Disorders to add disorders to the spectrum and would add millions of non-autistic persons with SLIs to the autism spectrum. Needless to say, Christie's conceptualisation of PDA as a form of autism contradicts Newson's consistent views on this topic. Controversially, it is through Christie's logic that PDA is commonly viewed as a form of autism (Christie et al., 2012).

Attention on PDA is primarily centred in the UK (Green et al., 2018a), with a major charity adopting the outlook that PDA is part of the autism spectrum (Eaton et al., 2018, Green et al., 2018, Russell, 2018, O'Nions et al., 2016, O'Nions et al., 2014a, O'Nions et al., 2014b) and the inclusion of guidelines for PDA in national autism educational guidelines (O'Nions et al., 2016a, O'Nions et al., 2014a). Furthermore, hundreds and thousands of caregivers partake in surveys (Russell, 2018), petitions that view PDA as an ASD, and annual PDA conferences are oversubscribed (Trundle et al., 2017, O'Nions et al., 2016, O'Nions et al., 2014a, O'Nions et al., 2014b). These awareness-raising activities can lead people to be on the look-out for PDA, potentially biasing PDA diagnoses and research (O'Nions et al., 2016). Outside of clinical settings research heavily relies upon highly motivated caregiver's (O'Nions et al., 2016b), and is noted as being open to bias (Eaton and Weaver, 2020). Caregivers regularly use PDA as a proxy to gain different support strategies (Green et al., 2018b).

There are examples of CYP internalising the outlook that PDA is an ASD (O'Connor and McNicholas, 2020, Finley, 2019), and similarly for autistic adults (Thompson, 2019, Cat, 2018). There are numerous PDA-related activities that support a community of practice around the axiom that PDA is part of autism (Woods, 2019a). As anthropologist Roy Grinker suggests:

> once a diagnosis takes hold and serves as the hub around which so much wealth, so many people, and activities coalesce, it takes on a life of its own as an authentic, natu-

ralized classification (Hacking 2000). This category, in turn, provides an incentive for manufacturing people with the diagnosis of autism whose presence and needs support this financial infrastructure.

(Grinker, 2020, p. 62)

As a result, researchers often primarily portray PDA as being part of the autism spectrum, as an autism subtype, autism subgroup, or an autism profile (Doyle et al., 2020, Bishop, 2018, Russell, 2018, O'Nions et al., 2014a, Eaton and Banting, 2012). In 2011, a research agenda was put forward to get PDA accepted as a form of autism; it included developing new diagnostic screening tools and investigating PDA's cognitive profile in relation to autism theory, such as Theory of Mind. This research was needed to support clinical-based understandings of PDA that it is a form of autism (Christie et al., 2012). Prominent PDA researchers have approached PDA from their understandings of autism (O'Nions et al., 2016b). Subsequently, research into it is dominated by entirely (and suspect) autistic population samples (Doyle et al., 2020, O'Nions and Eaton, 2020; Russell, 2018, O'Nions et al., 2018, Brede et al., 2017, O'Nions et al., 2016a, O'Nions et al., 2014a), or only autistic persons are diagnosed with PDA (Eaton and Weaver, 2020, Gillberg et al., 2015). One could challenge the ethics of such an approach as being unscientific in nature (Woods, 2019a).

For the last few years there has been a concerted research project in PDA between a private clinic and prominent PDA researchers (Eaton, 2019, 2018b). The project involved two research projects operating in tandem, one based on cases from the private clinic (Eaton and Weaver, 2020), the other investigating PDA parenting strategies (O'Nions, 2019). PDA was only diagnosed in autistic persons (Eaton and Weaver, 2020), and PDA parenting strategies were investigated from an entirely autism-caregiver sample (O'Nions, 2019). Researchers involved in this project view PDA as a form of autism (O'Nions, 2019, Eaton et al. 2018, Eaton et al., 2018a). Collectively, they presented findings where they portray PDA as an autism subgroup (O'Nions and Eaton, 2020).

Recently, a PDA charity has publicly said it will campaign for PDA's recognition as part of the autism spectrum. The context to this statement is that the charity collaborates with the lead clinician of the private clinic on their position and campaigning on PDA.[13] They do not discuss that PDA is not based on accepted autism understandings. There appears to be a concerted agenda to have PDA accepted as a form of autism. In the next section PDA's other behaviour profiles are analysed to highlight how PDA has taken on 'autism-like' characteristics.

How has PDA evolved as a mental disorder?

I have discussed the nature of mental disorders, how PDA is viewed as a mental disorder, and the history behind PDA viewed as an autism subtype. Image 1 displays all the PDA diagnostic traits in print across four behaviour profiles, in the Aggregated PDA behaviour profile, and compared to the DSM-5 autism criteria. Newson did not require all features of PDA to be present for a person to meet clinical threshold for a diagnosis (Newson et al., 2003). Some diagnostic traits of Newson are optional, as in they were discarded; these are the developmental traits of neurological involvement, passive early history, and speech delay (Fidler, 2019; Russell, 2018, Green et al., 2018a; O'Nions et al., 2016a).

O'Nions et al. (2016a) removed these diagnostic traits as they viewed PDA as an autism subgroup and developmental traits are too common in the autistic population to be useful to identify PDA as a meaningful subgroup. This outlook on PDA is reflected in main diagnostic and screening tools for PDA, which between them only have one question to assess for Passive Early History (Egan et al., 2019, O'Nions et al., 2016a, O'Nions et al., 2014a), which is Question 26 on the EDA-Q (O'Nions et al., 2014a). Hence, it is easy to conceptualise it as an anxiety-based disorder in practice and research.

There are other signs that PDA has become more autism-like in its behaviour profiles. Image 1 highlights that sensory issues are part of the *DSM-5* autism criteria; the "Sensory Differences trait was included in Eaton et al. (2018), which views PDA as a form of autism. A key point of divergence is with Newson et al.'s (2003) Obsessive Behaviour trait, which was described as such and most of PDA's behaviours are obsessive in nature. This trait evolved into "Obsessive behaviour (often social in nature)" (O'Nions et al., 2016a), and then "Displays obsessive behaviour that is often focused on other people" (Green et al., 2018a). There is a clear progression to the emphasis on this trait having an autism-like special interest, specifically focused on people, instead of special interests on objects, or mundane topics. This is in line with interpretations of a female form of autism (Gould and Ashton-Smith, 2011, Christie, 2007).

The social aspects of PDA seem to have been reinterpreted. The Surface sociability, but lack of sense of identity, pride, or shame (Newson et al., 2003), reflects Newson's assumptions as to the cause of PDA's social interaction issues. They went onto argue that the obsessive demand avoidance seen in their cases is due to CYP knowing no boundaries to their avoidance. O'Nions et al. (2016a) amended the wording to state that PDA had deficits in social identity, pride, or shame. This allows the wording to change to stating there is a lack of understanding – "Appears sociable, but lacks understanding" (Green et al., 2018) – which removes the connotation from deficits not associated with autism.

Predicted PDA populations are largely based on Newson's descriptions (Woods, 2019a, Milton. 2017, McElory, 2016, Gillberg, 2014, Christie, 2007), while these changes derive from autistic population samples (Eaton et al., 2018, O'Nions et al., 2016a), or by organisations that view PDA as a form of autism (Green et al., 2018a, O'Nions et al., 2016a). These revisions to PDA traits matter as they affect how PDA is interpreted. Autism interacts with its co-occurring conditions simultaneously (Green et al., 2018a, Brede et al., 2017, Flackhill et al., 2017), and so these conditions often present differently outside of autism. Thus, these changes to the PDA behaviour cannot be generalised onto other PDA populations.

Beyond the autism-like changes limiting the generalisability of the PDA behaviour profile, they have led to differences to features being assessed by diagnostic and screening tools and their corresponding trait. The trait of "Lability of mood, impulsive, led by need to control" (Newson et al., 2003), has the same wording in O'Nions and colleagues research with the revised PDA Diagnostic Interview for Social and Communication Disorder (DISCO) questions (2016a). Yet, the wording has been changed by the UK-based National Autistic Society to "Experiences excessive mood swings and impulsivity" (Green et al., 2018a). The DISCO question, "Using age peers as mechanical aids, bossy and domineering" (O'Nions et al., 2016, p. 415), has as its sub-question: "Does A use age peers solely as aids in own activities, e.g. to collect materials, to assist in building some construction, to take a specified part in a scenario created by A?"[14] This matters, as such discrepancies between behaviour profiles and screening and diagnostic tools undermines the validity of PDA diagnoses and research.

The most notable change to the PDA behaviour profile is to its social demand-avoidance behaviours trait. Initially, a sub-trait to "Continues to avoid demands of everyday life" was worded as "Strategies of avoidance are socially manipulative" (Newson et al., 2003). Recently, it has adopted autism-like characteristics, first as "Strategies of avoidance that are essentially 'socially manipulative'" (O'Nions et al., 2016a), and "Uses social strategies as part of avoidance, e.g. distracting, giving excuses" (Green et al., 2018a). The first change was made by O'Nions et al. (2016a) who were attempting to make PDA an autism subgroup. Most of its authors had previously written that it is partly problematic fitting PDA into the autism of the manipulative behaviours associated with the profile (Trundle et al., 2017, Gillberg et al., 2015, O'Nions et al., 2015, Christie et al., 2012).

As part of the revising of the wording for strategies of avoidance that are essentially "socially manipulative", quotation marks had been added to suggest that social demand avoidance is not actually manipulative; the associated DISCO question was amended to "Apparently manipulative behaviour" (O'Nions et al., 2016a). The original wording was "Socially manipulative behaviour to avoid demands" (Gillberg et al., 2015). These changes were made based on the opinions of O'Nions et al.'s (2016a) authors. There is some evidence that views PDA social demand avoidance as "socially strategic"; however, this was conducted on an entirely autistic sample and the interview data were coded with the 11 revised PDA DISCO questions (O'Nions et al., 2018). Due to the "apparently" descriptor in the question, coded behaviours in this research could not be manipulative. There is no evidence to suggest that PDA's social demand avoidance is "socially strategic".

There is significant debate around social demand avoidance being manipulative or strategic. It is more empathetic to use "socially strategic", expressing that these behaviours are unsubtle and not like the complex manipulation of those with callous-unemotional traits. It is more compassionate to view social demand avoidance behaviours as strategic rather than manipulative (O'Nions and Eaton, 2020). This stance is from research with entirely autistic population samples (Eaton and Weaver, 2020, O'Nions et al., 2018, 2019). Yet, O'Nions et al. (2015) originally viewed social demand avoidance as manipulative. Most social demand avoidance involves taking advantage of social norms.

Newson et al. (2003) reported that manipulative demand avoidance was universal in PDA. PDA does not have deficits in Theory of Mind and Empathy yet is purported to have deficits in social identity, pride, and shame (Christie et al., 2012, Newson et al., 2003, Newson, 1983, 1989, 1996). Social demand avoidance was described as manipulative due to the empathy required behind the acts (Newson, 1983), and that it is often the greatest skill of CYP with PDA (Christie et al., 2012). Persons with PDA have awareness to "push people's buttons" (O'Nions et al., 2014a), and appear to gain reward from distressing others (Wing, 2002).

Some have argued it is paradoxical to possess sufficient empathy for targeted manipulation while lacking understanding of social hierarchies. Conversely, this research also observed that many social demand avoidance behaviours are astute, relying on social norms and manipulative intent (O'Nions et al., 2015). This replicates the results of Newson et al. (2003). The EDA-Q was designed to assesses for manipulative behaviours (O'Nions et al., 2014a), and this would be reflected in the derived self-report version, EDA-QA (Egan et al., 2019). Accounting for how manipulative behaviours that require intent are found in PDA diagnostic and screening tools, its social demand avoidance is manipulative (see Table 6.1 for examples). Acts such as harassment require intent on the part of the perpetrator, which is something that many autistic persons lack. The fact that PDA contains behaviours that require intent and that persons with PDA pursue what it is they want, strongly suggests PDA social demand avoidance behaviours are manipulative.

Considerable effort has been invested in changing PDA's behaviour profile to become autism-like, demonstrating how mental disorders can evolve over time. This is despite some amendments lacking sufficient evidence to necessarily warrant this approach; for instance the Neurological Involvement trait awaits systematic research into how it relates to PDA (Newson et al., 2003 Newson, 1996, 1989). Such revisions to the behaviour profile have real-life consequences when one is attempting to get PDA accepted by educational, local, medical, and national authorities. The changes outlined above, when added to concerted campaigning efforts on PDA present PDA as a form of autism, regardless of the reasons and evidence to the contrary. This highlights the power clinicians and researchers have over mental disorders as social constructs, and the power disability charities possess to set narratives on mental disorders.

Table 6.1 Questions and sub-questions from PDA diagnostic and screening tools that contain manipulative behaviours and denote intent

Question or sub-question.	Tool and reference.
Good at getting round others and making them do as s/he wants.	EDA-Q (O'Nions et al., 2014a).
I blame or target a particular person/persons.	EDA-QA (Egan et al., 2019).
Does A harass other people? (e.g. writing threatening letters, making verbal threats, stalking, untrue accusations of sexual abuse).	Revised PDA DISCO questions (O'Nions et al., 2016).
Does A frequently tease, bully, refuse to take turns, make trouble.	Revised PDA DISCO questions (O'Nions et al., 2016).
Socially shocking behaviour with deliberate intent	Original PDA DISCO questions (Gillberg et al., 2015).
Lies, cheats, steals, fantasises, causing distress to others.	Original PDA DISCO questions (Gillberg et al., 2015).
Would you describe A as good at getting round others and making them do as s/he wants, or playing people off against each other?	O'Nions and Happé semi-structured interview (O'Nions et al., 2015, 2018).
What strategies does A use to get out of things? Are these strategies targeted at a particular person? • Distracting (e.g. asking questions) • Apologising and making excuses • Withdrawing into role play or toy play • Charm • Passively (e.g. selective mutism) • Other	O'Nions and Happé semi-structured interview (O'Nions et al., 2015, 2018).
Does A ever threaten to hurt him/herself, or do things to hurt him/herself? Is this behaviour impulsive, or does A do it on purpose to show s/he is in control, cause distress or get attention?	O'Nions and Happé semi-structured interview (O'Nions et al., 2015, 2018).

The language of several PDA diagnostic traits has changed in recent years, away from Newson's outlook on PDA being a new type of mental disorder. An important change is in trying to amend how social demand avoidance behaviours are viewed as "strategic" rather than "manipulative", in line with autism understandings. Such changes seem to ignore how PDA diagnostic tools include questions that pathologise a person expressing their wishes. Crucially, the revised interpretations of PDA traits cannot be applied to non-autistic PDA populations, as these predictions are based on Newson's research. These amendments to PDA highlight the power of key stakeholders to control the evolution of mental disorders and how they are treated by broader society. There are important lessons to be learnt from those of PDAs, and future research is required to fully reveal them.

Conclusion

PDA is a new type of mental disorder and is not part of the autism spectrum. As a social construct it represents the pathologising of behaviours that people often express to alleviate anxiety or to simply assert their self-agency. Aspects of PDA diagnostic traits are unstable and are impacted by the politics surrounding the construct. Some features, such as panic attacks, are mistakenly viewed as social communication issues when, in fact, they relate to anxiety-driven

RRBIs. Originally, Newson proposed PDA as a new type of mental disorder that was not part of the autism spectrum. However, a few high-profile autism experts reinterpreted PDA to be as such, and in the last decade various autism stakeholders have been lobbying hard for it to be accepted as part of the autism spectrum. Consequently, the features associated with PDA have taken on more autism-like characteristics, such as changing social demand avoidance behaviours to be "strategic", instead of "manipulative", while discounting how PDA tools assess behaviours that persons typically use to exert their self-agency. As a novel social construct, PDA provides the chance to explore how such phenomena shape both society and those attributed a label of PDA.

Notes

1. For more details, please see Woods et al. (2018).
2. During 2021, the dichotomous debate on PDA has become more entrenched since this chapter was drafted. Three reputable independent parties reviewed the evidence for PDA, concluding there is no good quality evidence to suggest what PDA is and equally respecting divergent opinion. These parties included a systematic review, the British Psychological Society, and National Institute for Health and Care Excellence. While "PDA Profile of ASD" supporters would highlight that PDA has been included in the recent England Autism Strategy. Although, PDA seems not to be mentioned in the England Autism Strategy's document.
3. This chapter discusses different autism conceptualisations over the last 40 years, and in that time-period what has been called autism has expanded significantly. When I refer to Asperger's Syndrome, Autistic Disorder, Infantile Autism, PDD-NOS, these are autism subtypes. Infantile Autism evolved into Autistic Disorder. I use the terms autism and autism spectrum disorder interchangeably.
4. A technical term for describing mental disorders is that they are human-kinds, and they evolve through looping effects. For more information, see Woods (2017).
5. Please see Woods (2019) for a discussion on PDA and comparable approaches.
6. This is Question 2, Sub-question 1, from a semi-structured interview from O'Nions et al. (2018) and can be accessed through this link:
   https://acamh.onlinelibrary.wiley.com/action/downloadSupplement?doi=10.1111%2Fcamh.12242&file=camh12242-sup-0001-Supinfo.pdf
7. *DSM-5* does require specifiers in relation to recognition of the nature of a person's understanding of their obsessions (OCD-UK, 2020).
8. Prof Peter Kinderman suggested that it is preferential to focus on management of demands, rather than on their avoidance.
9. My present view is that demand-avoidance features need to be expressed consistently over, at least 12 months to be pathologised as a Disorder. As many Disorders in DSM-5 require features to be expressed at least several months period. Additionally, when demand-avoidance which is impairing, is expressed for at least a year, it meets the threshold for being disabled under UK's The Equality Act.
10. Coding issues is when a person cannot process or make sense of certain aspects of communication.
11. The latter statement is found in Newson et al.'s (2003) supplementary files and can be accessed through this link:
    https://adc.bmj.com/content/archdischild/88/7/595.full.pdf?with-ds=yes
12. This approach contradicts modern approaches to PDA that do not view it as being developmental or pervasive in nature.
13. For example, see Russell (2018).
14. Wording for the sub-question can be accessed at:
    https://static-content.springer.com/esm/art%3A10.1007%2Fs00787-015-0740-2/MediaObjects/787_2015_740_MOESM1_ESM.pdf

References

Allsopp, K., Read, J., Corcoran, R., & Kinderman, P. (2019). Heterogeneity in psychiatric diagnostic classification. *Psychiatry Research*, 279(209), pp.15–22. https://doi.org/10.1016/j.psychres.2019.07.005.

American Psychiatric Association. (1994). *Diagnostic and Statistical Manual of Mental Disorders*, 4th ed. Washington: American Psychiatric Association.

Baron-Cohen, S., Leslie, A., & Frith, U. (1985). Does the autistic child have a "theory of mind"? *Cognition*, 21(1), pp.37–46. https://doi.org/10.1016/0010-0277(85)90022-8.

Bishop, D., Snowling, M., Thompson, P., Greenhalgh, T., & CATALISE-2 consortium. (2017). Phase 2 of CATALISE: A multinational and multidisciplinary Delphi consensus study of problems with language development: Terminology. *Journal of Child Psychology and Psychiatry*, 58(10), pp.1068–1080. https://doi.org/10.1111/jcpp.12721.

Bishop, E. (2018). *The Relationship between Theory of Mind and Traits Associated with Autism Spectrum Condition and Pathological Demand Avoidance Presentations.* Doctorate of Clinical Psychology, University College London.

Brede, J., Remington, A., Kenny, L., Warren, K., & Pellicano, E. (2017). Excluded from school: Autistic students' experiences of school exclusion and subsequent re-integration into school. *Autism and Developmental Language Impairments*, 2(1), pp.1–20. https://doi.org/10.1177/2396941517737511.

Cat, Sally. (2018). *PDA by PDAers: From Anxiety to Avoidance and Masking to Meltdowns.* London, UK: Jessica Kingsley Publishers.

Christie, P. (2007). The distinctive clinical and educational needs of children with pathological demand avoidance syndrome: Guidelines for good practice. *Good Autism Practice*, 8(1), pp.3–11.

Christie, P. (2019). Towards an understanding of Pathological Demand Avoidance (PDA): Clinical, research and educational perspectives. In: National Autistic Society (Ed.), *Pathological Demand Avoidance Conference.* London: National Autistic Society.

Christie, P., Duncan, M., Fidler, R., & Healey, Z. (2012). *Understanding Pathological Demand Avoidance Syndrome in Children: A Guide for Parents, Teachers and Other Professionals.* London: Jessica Kingsley Publishers.

Doyle, A., Kenny, N., & McNally, S. (2020). *Mapping Experiences of Pathological Demand Avoidance in Ireland: Executive Summary.* (Online Report). Retrieved from: https://www.pdasociety.org.uk/wp-content/uploads/2020/02/Doyle-and-Kenny-2020-Mapping-PDA-in-Ireland-Executive-Summary-1.pdf (Accessed 05 February 2021).

Eaton, J. (2018a). *A Guide to Mental Health Issues in Girls and Young Women on the Autism Spectrum: Diagnosis, Intervention and Family Support.* London: Jessica Kingsley Publishers.

Eaton, J. (2018b). *PDA and Mental Health* (Online Resource). Retrieved from: https://gwladysstreet.org/wp-content/uploads/2020/12/PDA-and-Mental-Health.pdf (Accessed 05 February 2021).

Eaton, J. (2019). *Further Exploring the PDA Profile-Evidence from Clinical Cases* (Online conference paper). Retrieved from: https://www.autism.org.uk/what-we-do/professional-development/past-conferences/pda-2019-presentations (Accessed 12 August 2022).

Eaton, J., & Banting, R. (2012). Adult diagnosis of pathological demand avoidance—Subsequent care planning. *Journal of Intellectual Disabilities and Offending Behaviour*, 3(3), pp.150–157. https://doi.org/10.1108/20420921211305891.

Eaton, J., Duncan, K., & Hesketh, E. (2018). Modification of the coventry grid interview (Flackhill et al., 2017) to include the pathological demand avoidant profile. *Good Autism Practice*, 19(2), pp.12–24.

Eaton, J., & Weaver, K. (2020). An exploration of the pathological (or extreme) demand avoidant profile in children referred for an autism diagnostic assessment using data from ADOS-2 assessments and their developmental histories. *Good Autism Practice*, 21(2), pp.33–51.

Egan, V., Bull, E., & Trundle, G. (2020). Individual differences, ADHD, adult pathological demand avoidance, and delinquency. *Research in Developmental Disabilities*, 105, pp. 103733–103733. https://doi.org/10.1016/j.ridd.2020.103733.

Egan, V., Linenburg, O., & O'Nions, L. (2019). The measurement of adult pathological demand avoidance traits. *Journal of Autism and Developmental Disorders*, 49(2), pp.481–494. https://doi.org/10.1007/s10803-018-3722-7.

Fidler, R. (2019). Girls who "can't help won't": Understanding the distinctive profile of pathological demand avoidance (PDA) and developing approaches to support girls with PDA. In: Carpenter, B., Happé, F., & Egerton, J. (Eds.), *Girls and Autism: Educational, Family and Personal Perspectives* (pp. 93–101). Abbingdon: Routledge.

Fidler, R., & Christie, P. (2019). *Collaborative Approaches to Learning for Pupils with PDA: Strategies for Education Professionals.* London: Jessica Kingsley Publishers.

Finley, C. (2019). Supporting students with autism and PDA: A personal perspective from a 14 year old student. *Good Autism Practice*, 20(1), pp.27–28.

First, M., Erlich, M., Adler, D., Leong, S., Dixon, L., Oslin, D., Siris., S., Koh, S., Levine, B., Berlant, J. L., & Siris, S. G. (2019). How the DSM is used in clinical practice. *The Journal of Nervous and Mental Disease*, 207(3), pp.157–161.

Flackhill, C., James, S., Soppitt, R., & Milton, K. (2017). The coventry grid interview (CGI): Exploring autism and attachment difficulties. *Good Autism Practice*, 18(1), pp.62–80.

Fletcher-Watson, S., & Happé, F. (2019). *Autism: A New Introduction to Psychological Theory and Current Debate.* Abingdon: Routledge.

Frith, U. (1991). *Autism and Asperger Syndrome.* Cambridge: Cambridge University Press.

Garralda, E. (2003). Pathological demand avoidance syndrome or psychiatric disorder? *Archives of Disease in Childhood* (online only article). Retrieved from: https://adc.bmj.com/content/88/7/595.responses (Accessed 05 February 2021).

Gillberg, C. (2014). Commentary: PDA – Public display of affection or pathological demand avoidance? – Reflections on O'Nions et al. (2014). *Journal of Child Psychology and Psychiatry*, 55(7), pp.769–770. https://doi.org/10.1111/jcpp.12275.

Gillberg, C., Gillberg, C., Thompson, Lucy, Biskupsto, R., & Billstedt, E. (2015). Extreme ("pathological") demand avoidance in autism: A general population study in the Faroe Islands. *European Child and Adolescent Psychiatry*, 24(8), pp.979–984. https://doi.org/10.1007/s00787-014-0647-3.

Goodley, D. (2011). *Disability Studies, an Interdisciplinary Introduction.* London: Sage Publications Ltd.

Gould, J., & Ashton-Smith, J. (2011). Missed diagnosis or misdiagnosis? Girls and women on the autism spectrum. *Good Autism Practice*, 12(1), pp.34–41.

Grinker, R. (2020). Autism, "Stigma," Disability A Shifting Historical Terrain. *Current Anthropology*, 61(S21), pp. S55–S67. https://doi.org/10.1086/705748.

Green, J., Absoud, M., Grahame, V., Malik, O., Simonoff, E., Le Couteur, A., & Baird, G. (2018a). Pathological demand avoidance: Symptoms but not a syndrome. *Lancet Child & Adolescent Health*, 2(6), pp.455–464. https://doi.org/10.1016/S2352-4642(18)30044-0.

Green, J., Absoud, M., Grahame, V., Malik, O., Simonoff, E., Le Couteur, A., & Baird, G. (2018b). Demand avoidance is not necessarily defiance: Authors' reply. *Lancet Child & Adolescent Health*, 2(9), p.e21. https://doi.org/10.1016/S2352-4642(18)30221-9.

Kapp, S., & Ne'eman, A. (2019). Lobbying autism's diagnostic revision in the DSM-5. In: Kapp, S. (Ed.), *Autistic Community and the Neurodiversity Movement* (pp. 167–194). New York: Springer Nature.

Kinderman, P. (2019). *A Manifesto for Mental Health: Why We Need a Revolution in Mental Health Care.* London: Palgrave MacMillan.

Lai, C., Kassee, C., Besney, R., Bonato, S., Hull, L., Mandy, W., Szatmari, P., & Ameis, S. (2019). Prevalence of co-occurring mental health diagnoses in the autism population: A systematic review and meta-analysis. *The Lancet Psychiatry*, 6(10), pp.819–829. https://doi.org/10.1016/S2215-0366(19)30289-5.

Langton, E. G., & Frederickson, N. (2016). Mapping the educational experiences of children with pathological demand avoidance. *Journal of Research in Special Educational Needs*, 16(4), pp.254–263. https://doi.org/10.1111/1471-3802.12081.

McElroy, R. (2016). *PDA – Is There Another Explanation?* (Online Magazine). Retrieved from: https://thepsychologist.bps.org.uk/volume-29/january-2016/pda-there-another-explanation (Accessed 05 February 2021).

Milton, D. (2017). *A Mismatch of Salience: Explorations of the Nature of Autism from Theory to Practice.* Hove, UK: Pavilion Publishing and Media Limited.

Milton, D., Heasman, B., & Sheppard, E. (2020). Double empathy. In: Volkmar, F. (Ed.), *Encyclopedia of Autism Spectrum Disorders* (pp. 1509–1517). New York: Springer Nature.

Moore, A. (2020). Pathological demand avoidance: What and who are being pathologized and in whose interests? *Global Studies of Childhood*, 10(1), pp.39–52. https://doi.org/10.1177/2043610619890070.

Newson, E. (1983). Pathological demand-avoidance syndrome. *Communication*, 17, pp.3–8.

Newson, E. (1989). *Pathological Demand Avoidance Syndrome: Diagnostic Criteria and Relationship to Autism and Developmental Coding Disorders* (Online Research). Retrieved from: https://www.autismeastmidlands.org.uk/wp-content/uploads/2016/10/Pathological-Demand-Avoidance-Syndrome.pdf (Accessed 05 February 2021).

Newson, E. (1996). *Pathological Demand Avoidance Syndrome: A Statistical Update* (Online Conference Paper). Retrieved from: https://www.autismeastmidlands.org.uk/wp-content/uploads/2016/10/Pathological-Demand-Avoidance-a-statistical-update.pdf (Accessed 05 February 2021).

Newson, E. (1999). *The "Family" of Pervasive Developmental Disorders: Diagram* (Online Resource). Retrieved from: https://www.autismeastmidlands.org.uk/wp-content/uploads/2016/10/The-family-of-pervasive-development-disorders.pdf (Accessed 05 February 2021).

Newson, E., Le Maréchal, K., & David, C. (2003). Pathological demand avoidance syndrome: A necessary distinction within the pervasive developmental disorders. *Archives of Disease in Childhood*, 88(7), pp.595–600. https://doi.org/10.1136/adc.88.7.595.

OCD-UK. (2020). *Diagnosing OCD* (Online Resource). Retrieved from: https://www.ocduk.org/ocd/diagnosing-ocd/ (Accessed 03rd of February 2021).

O'Connor, C., & McNicholas, F. (2020). Lived experiences of diagnostic shifts in child and adolescent mental health contexts: A qualitative interview study with young people and parents. *Journal of Abnormal Child Psychology*, 48(8), pp.979–993. https://doi.org/10.1007/s10802-020-00657-0.

O'Nions, E. (2019). *Child Behaviour and Parenting Strategies – A Research Update* (Online resource). Retrieved from: https://lizonions.files.wordpress.com/2019/09/1909childbehaviourparentingstrategiessummary.pdf (Accessed 05 February 2021).

O'Nions, E., Christie, P., Gould, J., Viding, E., & Happé, F. (2014a). Development of the 'Extreme Demand Avoidance Questionnaire' (EDA-Q): Preliminary observations on a trait measure for pathological demand avoidance. *Journal of Child Psychology and Psychiatry*, 55(7), pp. 758–768. https://doi.org/10.1111/jcpp.12149.

O'Nions, E., & Eaton, J. (2020). Extreme/'pathological' demand avoidance: An overview. *Paediatrics and Child Health*, 30(12), pp. 411–415. https://doi.org/10.1016/j.paed.2020.09.002.

O'Nions, E., Gould, J., Christie, P., Gillberg, C., Viding, E., & Happé, F. (2016a). Identifying features of 'pathological demand avoidance' using the diagnostic interview for social and communication disorders (DISCO). *European Child and Adolescent Psychiatry*, 25(4), pp.407–419. https://doi.org/10.1007/s00787-015-0740-2.

O'Nions, E., Happé, F., & Viding, E. (2016b). Extreme/'pathological' demand avoidance. *British Psychological Society DECP Debate*, issue 160.

O'Nions, E., Quinlan, E., Caceres, A., Tulip, H., Viding, E., & Happé, F. (2015). *Pathological Demand Avoidance (PDA): An Examination of the Behavioural Features Using a Semi-Structured Interview* (Unpublished Research). Retrieved from: http://www.pdaresource.com/files/An%20examination%20of%20the%20behavioural%20features%20associated%20with%20PDA%20using%20a%20semi-structured%20interview%20-%20Dr%20E%20O'.Nions.pdf (Accessed 05 February 2021).

O'Nions, E., Viding, E., Floyd, C., Quinlan, E., Pidgeon, C., Gould, J., & Happé, F. (2018). Dimensions of difficulty in children reported to have an autism spectrum diagnosis and features of extreme/'pathological' demand avoidance. *Child and Adolescent Mental Health*, 23(3), pp.220–227. https://doi.org/10.1111/camh.12242.

O'Nions, E., Viding, E., Greven, C., Ronald, A., & Happé, F. (2014b). Pathological demand avoidance: Exploring the behavioural profile. *Autism*, 18(5), pp.538–544. https://doi.org/10.1177/1362361313481861.

Pellicano, E. (2020). Commentary: Broadening the research remit of participatory methods in autism science – A commentary on Happé and Frith (2020). *Journal of Child Psychology and Psychiatry*, 61(3), pp.233–235. https://doi.org/10.1111/jcpp.13212.

Pellicano, E., Dinsmore, A., & Charman, T. (2014). What should autism research focus upon? Community views and priorities from the United Kingdom. *Autism*, 18(7), pp.756–770. https://doi.org/10.1177/1362361314529627.

Runswick-Cole, K., Mallett, R., & Timimi, S. (2016). *Re-Thinking Autism: Diagnosis Identity and Equality*. London: Jessica Kingsley Publishers.

Russell, S. (2018). *Being Misunderstood: Experiences of the Pathological Demand Avoidance Profile of ASD* (Online Report). Retrieved from: https://www.pdasociety.org.uk/wp-content/uploads/2019/08/BeingMisunderstood.pdf (Accessed 05 February 2021).

Summerhill, L., & Collett, K. (2018). Developing a multi-agency assessment pathway for children and young people thought to have a pathological demand avoidance profile. *Good Autism Practice*, 19(2), pp.25–32.

Thompson, H. (2019). *The PDA Paradox: The Highs and Lows of My Life on a Little-Known Part of the Autism Spectrum*. London: Jessica Kingsley Publishers.

Trundle, G., Leam., C., & Stringer, I. (2017). Differentiating between pathological demand avoidance and antisocial personality disorder: A case study. *Journal of Intellectual Disabilities and Offending Behaviour*, 8(1), pp.13–27. https://doi.org/10.1108/JIDOB-07-2016-0013.

Waltz, M. (2014). Worlds of autism: Across the spectrum of neurological difference. *Disability and Society*, 29(8), pp.1337–1338. https://doi.org/10.1080/09687599.2014.934064.

Wilkinson, L. (2017). *A Best Practice Guide to Assessment and Intervention for Autism Spectrum Disorders in Schools*. London: Jessica Kingsley Publishers.

Wing, L. (2002). *The Autistic Spectrum: A Guide for Parents and Professionals*. London: Constable & Robinson Limited.

Wing, L., Gould, J., & Gillberg, C. (2011). Autism spectrum disorders in the DSM-V: Better or worse than the DSM-IV? *Research in Developmental Disabilities*, 32(2), pp.768–773. https://doi.org/10.1016/j.ridd.2010.11.003.

Woods, R. (2017). Pathological demand avoidance: My thoughts on looping effects and commodification of autism. *Disability and Society*, 34(5), pp.753–758. https://doi.org/10.1080/09687599.2017.1308705.

Woods, R. (2019a). Demand avoidance phenomena: Circularity, integrity and validity – A commentary on the 2018 National Autistic Society PDA Conference. *Good Autism Practice*, 20(2), pp.28–40.

Woods, R. (2019b). *Is the Concept of Demand Avoidance Phenomena (Pathological Demand Avoidance) Real or Mythical?* (Conference Paper). Retrieved from: https://openresearch.lsbu.ac.uk/item/8v18z (Accessed 07 February 2021).

Woods, R. (2020a). Commentary: Demand avoidance phenomena, a manifold issue? Intolerance of uncertainty and anxiety as explanatory frameworks for extreme demand avoidance in children and adolescents – A commentary on Stuart et al. (2019). *Child and Adolescent Mental Health*, 25(2), pp.68–70. https://doi.org/10.1111/camh.12368.

Woods, R. (2020b). Pathological demand avoidance and the DSM-5: A rebuttal to Judy Eaton's response. *Good Autism Practice*, 21(1), pp.74–76.

Woods, R., Milton, D., Arnold, L., & Graby, S. (2018). Redefining critical autism studies: A more inclusive interpretation. *Disability and Society*, 33(6), pp.974–979. https://doi.org/10.1080/09687599.2018.1454380.

Woods, R., Waldock, K., Keates, N., & Morgan, H. (2019). Empathy and a personalised approach in autism. *Journal of Autism and Developmental Disorders*. https://doi.org/10.1007/s10803-019-04287-4.

Woods, R., & Waltz, M. (2019). The strength of autistic expertise and its implications for autism knowledge production: A response to Damian Milton. *Autonomy, the Critical Journal of Interdisciplinary Autism Studies*, 1(6). Retrieved from: http://www.larry-arnold.net/Autonomy/index.php/autonomy/article/view/CO2/html (Accessed 05 February 2021).

Yu, Y., Bradley, C., Boan, A., Charles, J., & Carpenter, L. (2021). Young adults with autism spectrum disorder and the criminal justice system. *Journal of Autism and Developmental Disorders*, 51(10), pp. 3624–3636. https://doi.org/10.1007/s10803-020-04805-9.

7
COMMUNITY PSYCHOLOGY AS REPARATIONS FOR VIOLENCE IN THE CONSTRUCTION OF AUTISM KNOWLEDGE[1]

Monique Botha

Introduction

The meaning of the term "autism" has evolved rapidly over the last century, from being regarded as a form of psychosis to currently being known mainly as a social and communicational disorder (Evans, 2013). These iterations have been fuelled by multiple factors, including scientific progress, shifts in social and cultural norms, and, increasingly, the involvement of autistic people in autism research (Evans, 2013; Silberman, 2017). Autism has been shaped through technocratic processes in which researchers and professionals have designated meaning to autism, often through a medicalised lens (Evans, 2013).

In this chapter, I highlight how the relationship between psychology and a positivistic standard of science has come to shape how autism has been understood. I highlight how values such as objectivity, epistemological transcendence, and a division between humanistic and scientific goals have excluded autistic people from the science that affects their everyday lives. Further, I point to examples of how autistic people have been objectified and dehumanised in autism research. I demonstrate how issues of epistemological violence permeate research, and how autistic people are othered both theoretically and empirically. Following this, I introduce community psychology as a possible reparation to address this permissive research-based violence. I highlight how the central aims of community psychology are commensurate with the aims of critical autism studies and provide a framework or approach to science that can advance the goals of critical autism studies. Importantly, community psychology provides an approach which is actively anti-objectifying, re-humanises marginalised communities, and does not create a hierarchical knowledge system where knowledge claims by non-autistic people are considered objective (and more accurate) while autistic peoples' experiences and claims are dismissed as "biased".

In the interest of transparency, I am writing from the perspective of an autistic researcher, and autism informs my position on autism just as neurotypicality informs the perspective of neurotypical researchers writing on autism – that is, I am no more biased or unbiased than anyone else – as I will discuss.

Science, psychology, and the infamous "view from nowhere"

During the 20th century, psychology became enmeshed with logical empiricism, which means it adopted the same scientific method you would expect to see in other sciences such as physics (Fondacaro and Weinberg, 2002; Barad, 2007). This shift represented a move away from processes of induction and psychoanalysis. Psychology, underpinned by logical empiricism, aims for deduction through controlled experimentation using operationalised variables, and aims for reproducibility, objectivity, and value-freedom (Tolman, 1992). Psychology moved to operationalise individual variables, control and test them, conduct experiments, and privilege evidence which could be easily distilled and manipulated into controlled environments (Giles and Cairns, 1995). Throughout this process of deduction, scientists are meant to aim for objectivity and epistemological transcendence (Fondacaro and Weinberg, 2002) whereby their evaluation transcends social and cultural predilections and represents an aptly named "view from nowhere" (Nagel, 1989).

Further, by embedding logical empiricism into the fabric of psychology, an artificial divide was created between scientific and humanistic goals, where they are presented as competing and incompatible (Kimble, 1984; Henriques, 2011). This "cultural" divide often sees psychology students enter university with a mix of scientific *and* humanistic ambitions but leave with the idea that one can aim for humanistic *or* scientific ambitions (Kimble, 1984). Quantitative psychology is seen as scientific and claims to be objective, whereas qualitative psychology is seen as humanistic and subjective (Kimble, 1984; Henriques, 2011). This can result in die-hard beliefs around the dichotomy of "realist science" and "post-modern" critiques of power in knowledge generation akin to the "Science Wars" (Ashman and Barringer, 2005) and that often psychologists divide themselves primarily by the methods they use, showing deeply entrenched divisions (Willig, 2020).

The relationship psychology has with the scientific method and logical empiricism has been a complicated and often critiqued one. One critique has been that since the 20th century psychology has aimed to achieve scientific status by applying the scientific method instead of achieving it by acquiring enough knowledge to know how to be one (Koch, 1981; Leary, 2001). Other critiques similarly challenge the fact that psychology is devoted to method over every other part of the processes (aptly named methodolatry – where method leads the question instead of vice versa (Chamberlain, 2000)).

The philosophy of science has moved on from this Newtonian idea of science (including in physics), because we now have a much better understanding about issues of entanglements, whereby we appreciate that what we measure is entangled with how we measure it (Barad, 2007). Further, we can increasingly appreciate that understanding is mediated through language, and value-freedom itself is a value, meaning epistemological transcendence (beyond being an impossibility) is an incoherent request. Despite the philosophy of science having moved on, this movement has been slow to filter down to psychology (Fondacaro and Weinberg, 2002). There is still a need to appeal to concepts such as objectivity in psychology, despite a lack of a road map for how to achieve this (Archer et al., 2013). However, the consequences of these assumptions have in some cases been catastrophic. The presumed neutrality scientists and psychologists hold grants them inordinate amounts of power, giving legitimacy to violence. The main critiques I will focus on in this chapter are with regard to objectivity, the infamous "view from nowhere", and methodolatry. I focus on these critiques because the aim of objectivity and epistemological transcendence, and the prioritisation of method, has resulted in epistemological violence, the marginalisation of minorities from research processes, and in the dehumanisation and objectification of minorities. Given my expertise, I will focus on how these phenomena have shaped autism knowledge and the lives of autistic people.

The guise of scientific objectivity

Scientific objectivity is a termed frequently used to obscure a normative agenda, the social values of the researcher, and to predominate social and temporal values which contextualise research. Objectivity is often defended under the guise of claiming that statistics and numeric-based work is value-free and objective, despite a large body of evidence showing the misuse of statistics (Cumming, 2014; Gigerenzer, 2004). For example, sample sizes are often manipulated in the presentation of data; one study reviewing over 2,500 studies from a leading psychology journal found that in 41% of the studies, reported sample sizes did not reflect the results presented and (potentially unfavourable) data was removed without disclosure (Bakker and Wicherts, 2014). Similarly, another study found that 61% of just under 700 studies had a misrepresented p-value, which in the case of 20% would move the p-value from being non-significant to significant (Veldkamp et al., 2014).

Further, the framing of the research questions we ask, the measures we use in our studies, and our interpretation of the data can be imbued with normative values (Barad, 2007; Teo, 2010). Interpretation of data is an active process (Teo, 2010) in which researchers make, process, and translate research into a hypothesis or study results into meaning. Data do not speak; instead researchers process data and present, frame, and argue for their interpretation (Teo, 2010). This means that who we are as researchers – the values, characteristics, attitudes, and perspectives we hold – are all instrumental to the product of research (Barad, 2007), despite being traditionally packaged as "objective".

Despite claiming science and psychology can be value-free, psychology has had a strong history of racism (Schaffer, 2007), homophobia (Mohr et al., 2009), ableism (Scully & Shakespeare, 2019), cisgenderism and transphobia (Ansara and Hegarty, 2012), and sexism (Ruti, 2015). A racialised psychology has proliferated with arguments around brain size, genetics, and intelligence dominating the works of researchers such as Rushton (Rushton and Templer, 2012) funded by organisations described as holding neo-Nazi, eugenic ideologies (Rosenthal, 1995; see Teo (2011) for an excellent breakdown on empirical race psychology). It was only in 2020 that an article (Rushton and Templer, 2012) that claimed melatonin in skin made Black people less intelligent, more aggressive, and more prone to criminality was retracted. This scientific rationality of objectivity has defended practices such as the pathologisation of minority sexualities and genders; the use of lobotomies and mass institutionalisation; and has installed a focus that removes attention from systematic inequality and blames individuals for having poor mental health instead of addressing social crises (Fondacaro and Weinberg, 2002). Yet, psychologists often ignore these instances and argue that highlighting institutional racism is anti-scientific (Miller, 2020).

The guise of scientific objectivity facilitated, and still facilitates, gross institutional violence such as mass institutionalisation and eugenic programmes (Fondacaro and Weinberg, 2002) which have greatly affected the lives of autistic individuals globally. The result has been that even today, autistic individuals are treated as objects, their subjectivity denied, their boundaries and their rights violated.

Epistemological violence

Epistemological violence is defined as the act of concluding from underdetermined data that a subgroup of people are inferior without considering viable alternatives (Teo, 2010). Epistemological violence stems from a lack of hermeneutical awareness about the constitution of an interpretation in empirical social sciences (Teo, 2010). Scientists in the social sciences (and sciences) present data as if it is a given, without acknowledging the human element of description, re-description, and interpretation. This Newtonian idea of science acts as if a scientist is far removed from the generation or interpretation of empirical data (Barad, 2007) and is commensurate with the kind of scientific method psychology adopted in the 20th century. Scientists in this model are privileged as conveyors of reality. According to Teo (2010), epistemological violence has occurred when researchers have made concrete interpretations of one group's inferiority (in effect "othering" them) without exploring alternative avenues from data. At its essence, it is violence from knowledge creation, where that knowledge is underdetermined.

In a seminal paper, Teo (2010) presents a thought experiment with two groups, where one group has smaller ears than the other. Distinctions around these differences lead to arguments that, for example, small-eared people lack empathy, ought to be segregated in parts of life, and are less capable than larger-eared people. Teo discusses the implications of making othering interpretations and recommendations based on empirical data without an understanding of how this approach is an action. While in the paper it is a thought experiment, autism presents a lively demonstration of this argument – autistic individuals are regularly "othered" in research and argued to lack empathy.

In this example, I point specifically to "theory of mind" literature. Researchers, based on an experiment with a small sample of autistic children (20), argued that autistic individuals lack a fully intact theory of mind – that is, the ability to understand that other people have their own minds, thoughts, emotions, and experiences (Baron-Cohen, Leslie and Frith, 1985). These authors argued it was a universal effect applied to *all* autistic people, and unique to autism. Theory of mind is, and was, deemed to be central to "humanness". The autistic people who passed this test were held to not really be autistic or to be "hackers" (Hollin, 2017). That is, people who passed the test were not deemed to pass by the same means as non-autistic people, instead, by using a different logic, they were deemed to have "hacked" the test and, thus, still not have "normal" theory of mind, thereby preserving the theory. Follow-up studies routinely found that that autistic people used language clearly demonstrating theory of mind (Nuyts and Roeck, 1997), that the effect was either missing (Aldridge et al., 2000; Russell and Hill, 2001; Sebanz et al., 2005), not universal to all autistic people (Ozonoff et al., 1994; Happé, 1995; Peterson, 2002), nor unique to autism (Benson et al., 1993), and heavily dependent on language and age (Yirmiya et al., 1992, 1998). Similarly, autistic people were publishing autobiographies and writing on autism that demonstrates theory of mind, and largely went ignored (Hacking, 2009). For a fuller account of the empirical failings of theory of mind see Gernsbacher and Yergeau (2019). Here I focus on the violence that has followed this literature.

Despite a host of theoretical and empirical issues, researchers continued to argue that theory of mind impairments are unique to autism, universal, and a key trait in autistic people (Baron-Cohen, 2000). By 2002 autistic people were held to be missing a "core" component of humanness (Gernsbacher, 2007). Researchers argued that autistic people lacked empathy, as to have empathy one needs to able to infer the mindedness of other people (Baron-Cohen, 2009a), and shortly thereafter it was also widely circulating that autism was synonymous with an absence of empathy (Smith, 2009). Based on these underdetermined data, it has been argued that autistic people lack full personhood, access to moral community, reciprocal relationships (Barnbaum, 2008; Russell, 2012), and, importantly, it is used to support arguments for the genetic removal of autistic people from society (Barnbaum, 2008).

Epistemological violence occurred because autistic people were othered and routinely singled out, the research was generalised to all autistic people, alternative explanations or interpretations for why autistic children completed the original experiment differently were not sought (Baron-Cohen, Leslie and Frith, 1985), and the argument carried forward into further violent interpretations around the in/abilities of autistic people. Psychology in logical empiricism facilitated this because of the assumption that data speak for themselves, a lack of awareness around the implications of interpretations, and a lack of accountability for the scientist's role in the objects they create.

Dehumanisation

Dehumanisation is defined as the denial of full humanness to other people (Haslam, 2006). In recent literature, two modes of dehumanisation have been outlined – denial of human uniqueness and denial of human nature (Haslam, 2006). With the former, people are denied, or perceived to lack, traits that distinguish them from non-human animals such as civility, refinement, moral sensibility, rationality, or maturity (Haslam, 2006). This can be described as animalistic dehumanisation because humans are reduced to non-human animals. With the latter, individuals are denied or perceived to lack the traits that separate them from objects and are considered to have inertness, coldness, rigidity, passivity and fungibility, and superficiality (Haslam, 2006). This can be described as mechanistic dehumanisation because individuals are reduced to machines.

Accounts of autism in research which perpetrates animalistic dehumanisation or the denial of human uniqueness include comparisons of autistic individuals to Great Apes (Tomasello et al., 2005), to brain-damaged monkeys (Bainbridge, 2008), and chimpanzees (Pinker, 2002). Furthermore, there are arguments that autistic individuals are said to have integrity equivalent only to that of non-human animals (Russell, 2012), and are subhuman and in need of being rebuilt as "proper humans" (Lovaas, Schaeffer and Simmons, 1965). Autistic individuals are held to be lacking domesticated traits at a morphological and physiological level (Benítez-Burraco, Lattanzi and Murphy, 2016), incapable of learning "culture" (Pinker, 2002; Tomasello et al., 2005), incapable of having moral selves or personhood (Barnbaum, 2008), inherently selfish and egocentric (Frith, 2004), or missing a core component of what it means to be human (Falcon and Shoop, 2002). As Barnbuam (2008), interpreting Peter Hobson's work, states:

> The autistic person is outside the moral community, biologically human but not a person in the moral sense.
>
> *(Barnbaum, 2008, p. 92)*

Accounts in autism research which perpetrate mechanistic dehumanisation, or the denial of human nature, can be seen in comparisons of autistic individuals to robots (Pinker, 2006), arguments that they are incapable or deficient in their ability to experience empathy (Baron-Cohen, 2012) or reciprocal relationships and community (Barnbaum, 2008), an economic burden to communities (Ganz, 2006; Tantam, 2009; Lavelle et al., 2014), and in the promotion of the idea that robots might teach autistic children humanness (Kline, 2018). The complete denial of the autistic community (Barnbuam, 2008) similarly could be described within the terms of dehumanisation, whereby there is a denial of the victim's identity and community (Kelman, 1973). These narratives are so prevalent that when people think of autistic individuals, they consider them to be lacking in human uniqueness (Cage et al., 2019).

Dehumanisation allows members of advantaged groups to morally disengage from the harm of the dehumanised minority (Bandura et al., 1996) meaning that this dehumanisation may serve to facilitate discrimination and violence (Moradi, 2013) but also further violence in research (such as the proposal of eugenics (Barnbaum 2008)). Milton (2016), utilising the "five faces of oppression" model by Iris Marion Young (1990), points to the devastating consequences of failing to recognise people as "fully human" – people of certain dispositions (like those who are autistic and or those with significant learning impairments) become socially disposable. One of the earliest examples of the effects of this dehumanisation includes the fact that Hans Apserger, in Nazi-occupied Vienna, routinely and knowingly committed autistic children to a hospital that systematically killed disabled people (Czech, 2018).

The enshrinement of objectivity as the foundation of the science, and the conceptualisation of objectivity as distance from the topic, means that non-autistic scientists are granted a legitimacy that autistic scientists and people can never fully achieve (under this framework). This effectively gives a platform to dehumanising rhetoric because it comes from an "objective" source but blockades marginalised populations from alternative knowledge creation as equals preventing them from using research as an avenue for redress (Harding, 1992). The "machine-like" metaphor of autistic people is exacerbated by the tendency for the scientific community to relegate the expertise of the autistic community itself (Milton, 2014). Autistic autobiographies that challenge the validity of these theories have been dismissed as biased, unscientific, and irrelevant to discussions of psychologists (Hacking, 2009), while psychologists argued that autistic people lacked epistemic authority – that is, the ability to contribute to knowledge production at all (Frith and Happe, 1999).

When autistic people challenge or refute theories, work, or practice relating to autism, or present alternative theories or narratives, they are dismissed as purveyors of partisan complaint. Indeed, the challenge is described in almost "Science War" language and terms, where "objective science" is being challenged by postmodern activists who are lacking "scientific objectivity", or simply misunderstand the complicated science-ness of work. A key example of this is Keenan et al. (2015) rejecting critique of Applied Behavioural Analysis as an attack on science, as being "pseudo-scientific" due to "folk" understandings of psychology, as the result of "propaganda-techniques", and as absurd. Yet, often unmentioned are the widespread conflicts of interest present in such early-intervention research (Bottema-Beutel et al., 2020).

Objectification in the field of autism research

The objectification of autistic people in autism research has had a marked impact on the lives of autistic people. Objectification is defined as the act of treating a person like an object (Nussbaum, 1995) and it has been argued that a person is objectified if one or more of the following properties are applied to them (LaCroix and Pratto, 2015):

1. Instrumentality (the person is treated as a tool for another's purpose)
2. Denial of autonomy (the person is seen as lacking in self-determination)
3. Inertness (seen as lacking in agency and activity)
4. Fungibility (considered interchangeable with other objects)
5. Violability (lacking in boundary integrity, something that is permissible to harm, destroy, smash up, or break)
6. Ownership (as something to be bought, sold, or owned) or
7. Denial of subjectivity (treating the person as though their experience or feelings are unimportant)

Psychologists, ethicists, and researchers have objectified autistic people in research in many ways, including treating autistic people as inert, fungible, violable, and instrumental, and in the denial of autistic autonomy and autistic people's subjectivity. In terms of violability, there is a complex history and contemporary issue of eugenics (the removal of autistic people from the genetic pool) in the field of autism research. Eugenic methods of elimination have been proposed as ethical, both historically (see Czech, 2018) and more recently (Barnbaum, 2008; Russell, 2012; Tantam, 2009). This same violability is seen in the use of invasive, potentially dangerous, procedures in uncontrolled medical studies that involve operating on autistic children (Nguyen Thanh et al., 2020). Further, autistic integrity has been described as "a paradox" (Russell, 2012).

In fact, boundary integrity is predicated on instrumentality for autistic people. Researchers have argued that where the autistic individual is productive as a worker, capable and in employment, and "normal" enough that they do not make other people uncomfortable, that society then might be able to afford them:

> Originality is attractive even in the domestic sphere so long as it does not topple over into uncomfortable eccentricity. However, it is only a few people with ASD who combine originality with high levels of intelligence and industry who are likely to make a sufficiently sustainable salient contribution that their absence might be considered unaffordable.
>
> *(Tantam, 2009, p. 219)*

Essentially, this means only autistic people who conform to a narrow idea of wealth production and normativity (those who mask well enough) are considered viable people. As such, autistic rights are considered in terms of instrumentality to non-autistic people.

In terms of inertness and denial of subjectivity, autistic people have been treated as unreliable narrators to their own experiences, and have had their subjectivity, agency, and activity denied as meaningful. Autistic autobiographies have been side-lined in the production of autism knowledge rather than used as reliable accounts (Hacking, 2009) and research rarely aligns with the goals or interests of autistic people (Milton and Bracher, 2013; Pellicano, Dinsmore and Charman, 2014). Indeed, although autistic individuals tend to fear the use of genetic technologies and research, these protestations have been described as largely unimportant because of the "greater good" (Barnbaum, 2008).

Denial of subjectivity can be seen in discussion around the paradigms of autism promoted in literature, and in debates around the language used to describe autism. Autistic individuals are more likely to endorse neurodiversity instead of pathology as a paradigm (Kapp et al., 2013). Yet, any failure to medicalise or pathologise autism is dismissed as a form of air-brushing the experience of autism – denying struggle or disability experienced by autistic people. Those who endorse neurodiversity tend to have a more balanced perspective of benefits and challenges afforded to autistic people compared to those who medicalise it, who tend to focus strictly on challenges (Kapp et al., 2013) but neurodiversity is dismissed as a rose-tinted view of autism afforded to "high-functioning" autistics (Jaarsma and Welin, 2012).

Similarly, despite evidence that autistic people tend to dislike or find the use of the person-first language ("person with autism") offensive (Kapp et al., 2013; Kenny et al., 2016; Bury et al., 2020), calls to ignore this preference to some degrees have been published (Vivanti, 2020). Worse so, it has been argued that while it is easier for certain autistic people to use identity-first language (autistic person), non-speaking autistic people need person-first language, to remind others of their humanness (Vivanti, 2020). It should be noted that some autistic people (including those who are not always speaking) have described person-first language as actively dehumanising (Botha, Dibb and Frost, 2020), and no group should be so dehumanised that they require special language to remind other people that they are human (Botha, Hanlon and Williams, 2021). The very denial of such established findings around paradigms and language represents a clear and basic denial of subjectivity of a marginalised community – elsewhere described as a "cultural imperialism" (Milton, 2016). This, itself, is objectifying, as it disallows control or consideration for preferences of the very basic terms or approaches used to describe a community.

Similarly, in the debate as to whether society can afford autism, or autistic individuals (or whether genetic options like eugenics should be considered), the argument against it is not predicated on any form of autistic integrity or subjectivity. Instead, the focus is on what would come of non-autistic individuals if they were to erase autistic individuals – that it would mean they relinquish any claim to moral community themselves (Barnbaum, 2008; Tantam, 2009). It means that even in debating whether autistic individuals have the right life, the focus is not on their life, but rather the life of the society objectifying autistic individuals. For example, the argument against the use of eugenics in autism is not because the autistic individual has earned the right to moral community but rather that the non-autistic individual would lose their claim to morality if perpetrating such violence (Barnbaum, 2008).

Community psychology

Community psychology is a transformative value-based praxis that aims to address social injustice, inequality, and real-world issues that face marginalised, relatively less powerful and minority groups (Prilleltensky, 2001; Nelson and Prilleltensky, 2010). It is underpinned by social justice, equity, and ultimately aims for the liberation of humans and communities from oppressive systems (Fondacaro and Weinberg, 2002; Nelson and Prilleltensky, 2010). As such, it focuses on multiple levels of analysis – from the smaller settings in which people find themselves, such as families, schools, or work, to broader communities, countries, cultures, societies, and within historical, structural, and social contexts (Levine, Perkins and Perkins, 2005).

Community psychology embodies critical inquiry, which attempts to address power, inequality, and injustice (Charmaz, 2016). This means that community psychology is equally a tool of social justice, a way of conducting science, and a social critique (Evans, Rosen and Nelson, 2014). The critical history of community psychology extends into a critique of power structures in the creation of science, without descending into an anti-science that rejects all quantitative knowledge (Botha, 2021). It stresses not only a robust theoretical research base but also ways in which this research can be applied to address real-world problems facing minority communities (Orford, 1992; Levine, Perkins and Perkins, 2005). Thus, community psychologists usually have multiple roles such as researcher, activist, or practitioner and engage not only in universities but amongst communities, at a policy level, and with individuals who require assistance (Levine, Perkins and Perkins, 2005). The critical approach of addressing power and normativity, in society and knowledge generation, differentiates it from an "objectivist" social or clinical psychology (Levine, Perkins and Perkins, 2005).

As a field, community psychology developed in the 1960s and 1970s in America and came out of the disenfranchisement researchers and practitioners had with clinical, social, and applied psychology, which was described as individualistic, decontextualising, and responsive to individual crisis, instead of preventative of social crisis (Evans et al., 2014; Orford, 1992; Rappaport, 2005). Within this context, psychologists were frustrated with efforts to address individual issues such as depression, anxiety, and suicide within communities in America, when social issues such as discrimination, poverty, and mass unemployment actively facilitated poor mental health and social crises (Fondacaro and Weinberg, 2002). In essence, psychologists were frustrated with the prevalent victim-blaming approach to mental health that sees people in untenable social circumstances blamed for poor outcomes.

Considerations for implementing community psychology as a praxis include the following: indigenous resources and expertise should be at the forefront of consideration; the power relationship between the researcher and researcher should be closely scrutinised; and finally, interventions and research should be well-informed, empirically based, and grounded in solid theory (Prilleltensky, 2001). An attempt to impact the intricate systems of a community's lives without sound reason would be unethical (Orford, 1992).

Community psychology as reparation for research-based violence

Reparations refer to measures taken to redress gross and systematic violations of human rights. Here, I argue that community psychology should be a basic reparation for the systematic violation of human rights that traditional methods in psychology have facilitated in the construction of autism knowledge. Community psychology provides a framework for science that may act to prevent further objectification, dehumanisation, and violence. I aim to highlight how important it is to engage in reflexive and ethical research practices and avoid contributing work that is "much the same" as what has come before (Carlson and Lewis, 2019). Redress is within the scope of community psychology, through its critical tradition of addressing power in research. Particularly, this opens the door to shaping a way of doing psychology around the need for redress to the autistic community.

Addressing community priorities

Community psychology works with and in communities to promote indigenous resources, solutions, and autonomy (Orford, 1992; Prilleltensky, 2001; Nelson and Prilleltensky, 2010). This approach means being centred in communities to understand what action, knowledge, or resource would be helpful, or can be sought, and to bring about emancipation or social change – something that is sorely lacking in autism research. Instead of biological and genetic research, funding would be redirected into community priorities such as social and health research (Pellicano, Dinsmore, and Charman, 2014) which focuses on issues such as tackling stigma, inequality, quality of life, and mortality disparity in autism (Hirvikoski et al., 2016).

Furthermore, community psychology also provides a structure for further embedding participatory autism research into a basic standard of science for autism research because it is an embodiment of the "Nothing About Us Without Us" tradition (Cornwall and Jewkes, 1995). Participatory research and community psychology require a generation of mutuality, trust, and respect between the parties involved (Fletcher-Watson et al., 2019). The deconstruction of power in knowledge generation can at the same time facilitate a growth of an interactional expertise (Milton, 2014) between autistic people and researchers – making space for different, equally worthy forms and relationships of expertise. Rather than taking the approach where something that is written about being autistic is not meant for the autistic community (see Baron-Cohen, 2009b), research should be not only made available to, but created with, and disseminated through and to the autistic community, by the autistic community, and for the benefit of the autistic community. Community psychology provides a roadmap for this process. It forms a reparation, whereby the attention of research is turned towards the needs of the community, as decided by the community.

Rejecting the false dichotomies

Community psychologists object to the claim that science is or can be "value-free", or objective (Fondacaro and Weinberg, 2002; Prilleltensky, 2001). Psychologists are, after all, humans working to understand and alter the behaviour of other humans, all within the context of a society that has raised them within particular norms and culture (Hacking, 2015). Recognising this, community psychologists instead imbue their work with transparent ideologies, including social justice. Thus, science can be humanistic-orientated, and being transparently value-orientated does not necessarily lead to a lack of scientific rigour or the exclusion of quantitative methods.

Further, by rejecting the objective/subjective and the humanistic/scientific divides, community psychologists can frame the research methods around the actual question at hand and use methods which are shaped individually around the needs of the community. This approach revolts against the methodolatry that sees psychologists divide themselves by method. Qualitative and quantitative methods are no longer divided into scientific versus non-scientific, and instead into generalised versus particular methods (Langhout, 2003). Quantitative methods thus become a tool for general research which can produce enlightenment on important regularities such as mental and physical health disparities that exist between minority and majority communities – including in racial, sexual, and neuro-minorities (see Williams et al., 1997; Matlin, Molock and Tebes, 2011; Hirvikoski et al., 2016; Botha and Frost, 2018; Timmins, Rimes and Rahman, 2019). Yet numbers are limited in their scope to provide platforms for substantial "voice" to relatively powerless groups, and are general in scope, whereas qualitative methods provide narrative, intimate experiential data, and particular detail, which may not be accessed (Bond, García de Serrano and Keys, 2017). Considering this, community psychology has a rich tradition of multi-method and mixed-method research (Bond, García de Serrano and Keys, 2017).

Moving forward with reflexivity

By abandoning objectivity and value-freedom, community psychologists aim instead for reflexive practice and transparency (Suffla, Seedat and Bawa, 2015; Campbell, 2016). This means taking epistemic responsibility for the "cuts" that we make in knowledge and the possibilities each addition to knowledge either opens up or closes down (Barad, 2007). Further, it means engaging reflexively with interpretations we make with data and research and paying attention to *why* we are interpreting the data in the ways we are, *why* we have asked the questions we have, and *what* normative values we have imposed on our work.

Forgoing the guise of objectivity also opens the door for minorities in socially disadvantaged groups to take up their rightful space in the science that affects their everyday lives. While some autistic researchers have discussed their discomfort and described being shunned by science underpinned by logical empiricism (Hooge, 2019), community psychology opens the doors to anyone who will do the reflexive work to acknowledge their values, spreading the onus equally amongst those who are both "close" and "far" from the topic. Community psychology actively aims for indigenous practice that sees members of their own groups involved in the practice of research and action (Orford, 1992). This practice democratises the scientific process instead of overvaluing a small minority because of their perceived distance. Thus, there could be no grounds for dismissing the involvement of autistic people who are partisan when they challenge the dehumanising narratives which proliferate in research. Further, it means autistic people do not need to choose between being a scientist or an activist for their community, and instead can be both.

This reflexive practice should also encompass the process of empirical and statistical inference. The open science approach (Woelfle, Olliaro and Todd, 2011) should be harnessed, alongside a deep reflexive process that questions *all* parts of the research process. This approach can mean deep reflexivity around the kinds of methods and questions we are using, followed by making the data and the process of analysis open. It also means tackling issues such as inappropriate outlier removal (Bakker and Wicherts, 2014) or p-hacking – a process of conscious acknowledgement that individuals have outcomes they are invested in – and further, challenging this culture.

This process of reflexivity forms a reparation because it provides an onus for researchers to engage with their own normative baggage and to take the responsibility or the consequences of the narratives that they impose on autism and, by extension, autistic people. Reflexive practice has been critically missing from the way non-autistic researchers have routinely discussed and referred to autism.

Dismantling ableist academy

In their paper, Hooge (2019) invokes Audre Lorde's famous remark that "the master's tools will never dismantle the master's house". A logical empiricist academia will never achieve change for the autistic community because it is not studying the autistic community, it is attempting to study autism as an ontologically distinct "thing" from the person (Chapman, 2019a; Verhoeff, 2016), despite protestations that autism *only* exists as a person (Sinclair, 1993). But autism is political (Chapman, 2019b). Community psychology acknowledges that science is political, humanistic, complicated, and that no scientist can put down their identity whether marginalised or not, to conduct it – and that the responsibility of the person is to be transparent, open, reflexive, and humanistic in their approach (Orford, 1992; Prilleltensky, 2001; Luke, 2005). For me, community psychology allows me to be an autistic, a researcher, and an autistic researcher creating autism knowledge while acknowledging that psychology and autism are both political and embedded in societal systems that are bigger than me. By extension, it has allowed me the chance to contest the idea that the statement "suffering is inherent to autism" is itself an apolitical statement. It allows for an appreciation of how psychology has been a tool of oppression but also can be something else.

Knowing that as an autistic autism researcher I cannot "sneak in the backdoor of positivism" (Hooge, 2019), instead, I chose the much more transparent front door of community psychology – acknowledging that this work is a product of autism, I am a product of autism, much the way most autism work has been a product of neurotypicality (Yergeau, 2018). As such, I aimed to take meaningful steps to create ethical and re-humanising science. Further, I present community psychology as a path forward that will help to not only achieve the goals of critical autism studies but also be a way of making amends with a community that has suffered horrendous violence and dehumanisation.

Community psychology as commensurate with critical autism studies

Critical autism studies is a new and evolving subdiscipline of autism research which (broadly speaking) aims to explore the power relationships that are involved in constructing autism (both contemporarily and historically), explores enabling narratives that challenge the dogma of dominant medicalised autism, and aims for the creation of theoretical and methodological approaches that are emancipatory in nature (Davidson and Orsini, 2013; Woods et al., 2018). Further, it has been argued that critical autism studies should be embodied and led primarily by autistic people instead of appropriated by non-autistic researchers who do not work in equity with autistic people (Woods et al., 2018). Community psychology may be an overarching framework that is commensurate with the aims of critical autism studies.

First, it challenges the notion of dogmatic dominant narratives as being objective or infallible, especially with concepts that were developed within technocracy. As described earlier, it challenges the notion of detachment and objectivity. The dominant, medicalised model of autism has centralised the experience of autism into individuals and pathologised individuals under a technocratic medicalised gaze – instilling a sense of combat against an amorphous essence instead of recognising people in contexts (McGuire, 2016). Rather than studying individuals in the absence of social and cultural context, community psychology uses ecological-based analysis to consider people within environments (Fondacaro and Weinberg, 2002). This involves appreciating autistic individuals at the centre of social and cultural norms, at the heart of families, peers, communities, and environments that might result in flourishing or floundering, or completely change how we consider the same autistic person. Thus, it helps to achieve the aim of challenging dogmatic ideas of autism and to reframe it within a larger, ecological unit.

Second, community psychology is an inherently emancipatory praxis that aims for emancipation for minorities from the oppressive systems they are embroiled in. A critical realist community psychology also lays an epistemological and ontological framework that can appreciate the multiplicity of experiences of autism experiences without denying the reality or other different autistic experiences, meaning the heterogeneity of the spectrum, and emancipation for the entire autistic spectrum can be aimed for (Botha, in press). Expressly, this means acknowledging that autism, disability, function, and impairment arise from a culmination of mechanisms such as individual capacity, function, support, environment, culture, the conceptualisation of disability and autism, and, further, how these mechanisms interact.

Third, it provides a methodological framework that unites these two aims to produce a guide for emancipatory methods and theory. Community psychology methods (whether qualitative or quantitative) are flexible, creative, and usually made in conjunction with the communities that they are for (Bond, García de Serrano and Keys, 2017). This can mean adaptation from the start of a project and methodological flexibility throughout: for example, in a qualitative project we were approached by autistic individuals who struggled with face-to-face or verbal communication but wanted to take part, so we applied for ethical approval to also include text-based interviewing and email interviews (Botha, Dibb and Frost, 2020). We will ensure these options are available from the onset of a qualitative project.

Conclusions

At the beginning of this chapter, I tell readers that I am autistic. I tell readers this because I am a product of autism discourse, and it is a product of me – I cannot be separated from the rhetoric and narrative that made me an object of scientific inquiry, an example of pathology, and a symptom of disorder or dysfunction. These discourses, however, have unfolded under the impunity of objectivity, and leave me in an odd position – if I (an autistic researcher) and a non-autistic researcher make statements about what it means to be autistic, one is trusted as being more epistemically reliable, and it is not me. Indeed, autistic people have been disenfranchised from research (Hooge, 2019) and described as lacking in authority to describe what it means to be autistic (Frith and Happe, 1999). This follows in the tradition of epistemic oppression that disabled people face in their accounts of disabilities (Wieseler, 2020). The burden of objectivity only ever seems to fall onto the shoulders of minorities who question the dogma of a science which dehumanises them, medicalises, and decontextualises their outcomes from the way in which they are treated by society.

Autism has a long history as an evolving concept (Evans, 2013). The history and the present of autism knowledge are marked by violence such as eugenics (Barnbaum, 2008; Czech, 2018; Tantam, 2009), dehumanisation, and objectifying narratives, and has rarely fully involved autistic people. Psychology underpinned by logical empiricism has provided an impunity for non-autistic researchers writing on autism, as their work is assumed to be an act of scientific rationality, objective, and value-free. Worse, it creates a hierarchy and burdens minorities with a standard of evidence that is impossible to achieve. In actuality, there are values and subjectivities embedded in how we conceptualise questions and interpret data – something psychologists seem intent on learning the hard way through replication crises and data scandals. Yet, the replication crisis and its proposed solutions will not tackle the full issue, until psychologists stand back to reflect on and acknowledge the values inherent to their interpretations and presentations of data – including where they use experimental methods or quantitative analysis.

Community psychology, borne out of disillusionment with this detached form of psychology, may form a road map for addressing this research-based violence while also directing attention to addressing the social inequality that affects the autistic community. Most importantly, it urges and presupposes a detailed introspection and transparency around values and subjectivity that is currently absent in accounts which actively dehumanise autistic people. Further, it invites methods which produce rich data, are flexible around a multiplicity of needs, and are still methodologically robust and rigorous. Finally, it is commensurate with the aims of critical autism studies, both in its aim to question the dominant, detached narrative of a medicalised autism and in its aim for emancipation for minorities. Ultimately, when two researchers (one autistic and one not) make knowledge claims, it should be about evidence and transparency – *both* hold positions and values. Community psychology is not less of a science; it is more of an *equitable* science, and reparation for a history that has been marked by severe violence.

Note

1 The author would like to thank Eilidh Cage for providing feedback on this chapter.

References

Aldridge, M. A., Stone, K. R., Sweeney, M. H. and Bower, T. G. R. (2000) 'Preverbal children with autism understand the intentions of others', *Developmental Science*, 3(3), pp. 294–301. https://doi.org/10.1111/1467-7687.00123.

Ansara, Y. G. and Hegarty, P. (2012) 'Cisgenderism in psychology: Pathologising and misgendering children from 1999 to 2008', *Psychology and Sexuality*, 3(2), pp. 137–160. https://doi.org/10.1080/19419899.2011.576696.

Archer, M., Bhaskar, R., Collier, A., Lawson, T. and Norrie, A. (2013) *Critical Realism: Essential Readings.* 1st edition. Routledge. https://doi.org/10.4324/9781315008592.

Ashman, K. and Barringer, P. (eds). (2005) 'Strange attraction'. In: *After the Science Wars*. Routledge: Abingdon, pp. 147–150.

Bainbridge, D. (2008) *Beyond the Zonules of Zinn: A Fantastic Journey through Your Brain*. Cambridge, MA: Harvard University Press.

Bakker, M. and Wicherts, J. M. (2014) 'Outlier removal and the relation with reporting errors and quality of psychological research', *PLOS ONE*, 9(7), p. e103360. https://doi.org/10.1371/journal.pone.0103360.

Bandura, A., Barbaranelli, C., Caprara, G. V. and Pastorelli, C. (1996) 'Mechanisms of moral disengagement in the exercise of moral agency', *Journal of Personality and Social Psychology*, 71(2), p. 364. https://doi.org/10.1037/0022-3514.71.2.364.

Barad, K. M. (2007) *Meeting the Universe Halfway: Quantum Physics and the Entanglement of Matter and Meaning*. Durham, NC: Duke University Press.

Barnbaum, D. R. (2008) *The Ethics of Autism: Among Them, but Not of Them*. Bloomington, IN: Indiana University Press.

Baron-Cohen, S. (2000) 'Theory of mind and autism: A fifteen year review', *Understanding Other Minds: Perspectives from Developmental Cognitive Neuroscience*, 2(3–20), p. 102. https://doi.org/10.1016/S0074-7750(00)80010-5.

Baron-Cohen, S. (2009a) 'Autism: The empathizing-systemizing (E-S) theory', *Annals of the New York Academy of Sciences*, 1156, pp. 68–80. https://doi.org/10.1111/j.1749-6632.2009.04467.x.

Baron-Cohen, S. (2009b) 'Does autism need a cure?', *The Lancet*, 373(9675), pp. 1595–1596. https://doi.org/10.1016/S0140-6736(09)60891-6.

Baron-Cohen, S. (2012) *Zero Degrees of Empathy: A New Theory of Human Cruelty*. London: Penguin Books.

Baron-Cohen, S., Leslie, A. M. and Frith, U. (1985) 'Does the autistic child have a 'theory of mind' h', *Cognition*, 21(1), pp. 37–46. https://doi.org/10.1016/0010-0277(85)90022-8.

Benítez-Burraco, A., Lattanzi, W. and Murphy, E. (2016) 'Language impairments in asd resulting from a failed domestication of the human brain', *Frontiers in Neuroscience*, 10. https://doi.org/10.3389/fnins.2016.00373.

Benson, G., Abbeduto, L., Short, K., Nuccio, J. B. and Maas, F. (1993) 'Development of a theory of mind in individuals with mental retardation', *American Journal of Mental Retardation*, 98, pp. 427–433.

Bond, M. A., García de Serrano, I. and Keys, C. (eds). (2017) 'Giving voice- and the numbers too'. In: *APA Handbook of Community Psychology*. 1st edition. Washington, DC: American Psychological Association.

Botha, M. (2021) 'Critical realism, community psychology, and the curious case of autism: A philosophy and practice of science with social justice in mind', *Journal of Community Psychology*. https://doi.org/10.1002/jcop.22764.

Botha, M., Dibb, B. and Frost, D. (2020) "Autism is me": An investigation of how autistic individuals make sense of autism and stigma', *Disability and Society*, pp. 1–27. https://doi.org/10.1080/09687599.2020.1822782.

Botha, M. and Frost, D. M. (2018) 'Extending the minority stress model to understand mental health problems experienced by the autistic population', *Society and Mental Health*, 10(1), pp. 20–34. https://doi.org/10.1177/2156869318804297.

Bottema-Beutel, K., Crowley, S., Sandbank, M. and Woynaroski, T. G. (2020) 'Research review: Conflicts of Interest (COIs) in autism early intervention research – A meta-analysis of COI influences on intervention effects', *Journal of Child Psychology and Psychiatry*, 62(1). https://doi.org/10.1111/jcpp.13249

Bury, S. M., Jellett, R., Spoor, J. R. and Hedley, D. (2020) "It Defines Who I am" or "It's Something I have": What language do [autistic] australian adults [on the autism spectrum] prefer?', *Journal of Autism and Developmental Disorders*. https://doi.org/10.1007/s10803-020-04425-3.

Cage, E., Di Monaco, J. and Newell, V. (2019) 'Understanding, attitudes and dehumanisation towards autistic people', *Autism*, 23(6), pp. 1373–1383. https://doi.org/10.1177/1362361318811290.

Campbell, R. (2016) "It's the way that you do it': Developing an ethical framework for community psychology research and action', *American Journal of Community Psychology*, 58(3–4), pp. 294–302. https://doi.org/10.1002/ajcp.12037.

Carlson, M. and Lewis, S. C. (2019) 'Temporal reflexivity in journalism studies: Making sense of change in a more timely fashion', *Journalism*, 20(5), pp. 642–650. https://doi.org/10.1177/1464884918760675.

Chamberlain, K. (2000) 'Methodolatry and qualitative health research', *Journal of Health Psychology*, 5(3), pp. 285–296. https://doi.org/10.1177/135910530000500306.

Chapman, R. (2019a) 'Autism as a form of life: Wittgenstein and the psychological coherence of autism', *Metaphilosophy*, 50(4), pp. 421–440. https://doi.org/10.1111/meta.12366.

Chapman, R. (2019b) 'Autism isn't just a medical diagnosis — It's a political identity'. Available at: https://medium.com/the-establishment/autism-isnt-just-a-medical-diagnosis-it-s-a-political-identity-178137688bd5.

Charmaz, K. (2016) 'The power of constructivist grounded theory for critical inquiry', *Qualitative Inquiry*, 23(1), pp. 34–45. https://doi.org/10.1177/1077800416657105

Cornwall, A. and Jewkes, R. (1995) 'What is participatory research?', *Social Science & Medicine*, 41(12), pp. 1667–1676.

Cumming, G. (2014) 'The new statistics: Why and how', *Psychological Science*, 25(1), pp. 7–29.

Czech, H. (2018) 'Hans Asperger, National Socialism, and "race hygiene" in Nazi-era Vienna', *Molecular Autism*, 9(1), pp. 29–43. https://doi.org/10.1186/s13229-018-0208-6.

Davidson, J. and Orsini, M. (2013) *Worlds of Autism: Across the Spectrum of Neurological Difference*. Minneapolis, MN: University of Minnesota Press.

Evans, B. (2013) 'How autism became autism: The radical transformation of a central concept of child development in Britain', *History of the Human Sciences*, 26(3), pp. 3–31. https://doi.org/10.1177/0952695113484320.

Evans, S., Rosen, A. and Nelson, G. (2014) 'Community psychology and social justice'. In: Johnson, C. et al. (eds) *The Praeger Handbook of Social Justice and Psychology*. Santa Barbara, CA: Praeger.

Falcon, M. and Shoop, S. (2002) 'Stars 'CAN-do' about defeating autism', *USA Today*, 10.

Fletcher-Watson, S., Adams, J., Brook, K., Charman, T., Crane, L., Cusack, J., Leekam, S., Milton, D., Parr, J. R. and Pellicano, E. (2019) 'Making the future together: Shaping autism research through meaningful participation', *Autism*, 23(4), pp. 943–953. https://doi.org/10.1177/1362361318786721.

Fondacaro, M. and Weinberg, D. (2002) 'Concepts of social justice in community psychology: Toward a social ecological epistemology', *American Journal of Community Psychology*, 30(4), pp. 473–492. https://doi.org/10.1023/A:1015803817117.

Frith, U. (2004) 'Emanuel Miller lecture: Confusions and controversies about Asperger syndrome', *Journal of Child Psychology and Psychiatry*, 45(4), pp. 672–686. https://doi.org/10.1111/j.1469-7610.2004.00262.x.

Frith, U. and Happe, F. (1999) 'Theory of mind and self-consciousness: What is it like to be autistic?', *Mind and Language*, 14(1), pp. 82–89. https://doi.org/10.1111/1468-0017.00100.

Ganz, M. (2006) 'The costs of autism'. In: Moldin, S. and Rubenstein, J. (eds) *Understanding Autism*. CRC Press, pp. 475–502. https://doi.org/10.1201/9781420004205.ch20.

Gernsbacher, M. A. (2007) 'On not being human', *APS Observer*, 20(2), pp. 5–32.

Gernsbacher, M. A. and Yergeau, M. (2019) 'Empirical failures of the claim that autistic people lack a theory of mind', *Archives of Scientific Psychology*, 7(1), pp. 102–118. https://doi.org/10.1037/arc0000067.

Gigerenzer, G. (2004) 'Mindless statistics', *The Journal of Socio-Economics*, 33(5), pp. 587–606.

Giles, M. and Cairns, E. (1995) Blood donation and Ajzen's theory of planned behaviour: An examination of perceived behavioural control', *British Journal of Social Psychology*, 34(2), pp. 173–188.

Hacking, I. (2009) 'Autistic autobiography', *Philosophical Transactions of the Royal Society of London Series B Biological Sciences*, 364(1522), pp. 1467–1473. https://doi.org/10.1098/rstb.2008.0329.

Hacking, I. (2015) 'Let's not talk about objectivity'. In: F. Padovani, A. Richardson, and J. Y. Tsou (eds) *Objectivity in Science: New Perspectives from Science and Technology Studies*. Springer International Publishing, pp. 19–33. https://doi.org/10.1007/978-3-319-14349-1_2

Happé, F. G. (1995) 'The role of age and verbal ability in the theory of mind task performance of subjects with autism', *Child Development*, 66(3), pp. 843–855. https://doi.org/10.2307/1131954.

Harding, S. G. (1992) 'After the neutrality ideal: Science, politics, and 'strong objectivity'', *Social Research*, 59(3), pp. 567–587.

Henriques, G. (2011) 'The problem of psychology'. In: Henriques, G. (eds) *A New Unified Theory of Psychology*. New York: Springer New York, pp. 29–42. https://doi.org/10.1007/978-1-4614-0058-5_2.

Haslam, N. (2006) 'Dehumanization: An integrative review', *Personality and Social Psychology Review*, 10(3), pp. 252–264.

Hirvikoski, T., Mittendorfer-Rutz, E., Boman, M., Larsson, H., Lichtenstein, P. and Bölte, S. (2016) 'Premature mortality in autism spectrum disorder', *The British Journal of Psychiatry: the Journal of Mental Science*, 208(3), p. 232. https://doi.org/10.1192/bjp.bp.114.160192.

Hollin, G. (2017) 'Failing, hacking, passing: Autism, entanglement, and the ethics of transformation', *BioSocieties*, 12(4), pp. 611–633. https://doi.org/10.1057/s41292-017-0054-3.

Hooge, A. (2019) 'Binary boys: Autism, aspie supremacy and post/humanist normativity', *Disability Studies Quarterly*, 39(1). https://doi.org/10.18061/dsq.v39i1.6461.

Jaarsma, P. and Welin, S. (2012) 'Autism as a natural human variation: Reflections on the claims of the neurodiversity movement', *Health Care Analysis*, 20(1), pp. 20–30. https://doi.org/10.1007/s10728-011-0169-9.

Kapp, S. K., Gillespie-Lynch, K., Sherman, L. E. and Hutman, T. (2013) 'Deficit, difference, or both? Autism and neurodiversity', *Developmental Psychology*, 49(1), pp. 59–71. https://doi.org/10.1037/a0028353.

Keenan, M., Dillenburger, K., Röttgers, H. R., Dounavi, K., Jónsdóttir, S. L., Moderato, P., Schenk, J. J. A. M., Virués-Ortega, J., Roll-Pettersson, L. and Martin, N. (2015) 'Autism and ABA: The gulf between North America and Europe', *Review Journal of Autism and Developmental Disorders*, 2(2), pp. 167–183. https://doi.org/10.1007/s40489-014-0045-2

Kelman, H. G. (1973) 'Violence without moral restraint: Reflections on the dehumanization of victims and victimizers', *Journal of Social Issues*, 29(4), pp. 25–61. https://doi.org/10.1111/j.1540-4560.1973.tb00102.x.

Kenny, L., Hattersley, C., Molins, B., Buckley, C., Povey, C. and Pellicano, E. (2016) 'Which terms should be used to describe autism? Perspectives from the UK autism community', *Autism*, 20(4), pp. 442–462. https://doi.org/10.1177/1362361315588200.

Kimble, G. A. (1984) 'Psychology's two cultures', *American Psychologist*, 39(8), pp. 833–839. https://doi.org/10.1037/0003-066X.39.8.833.

Kline, R. (2018) 'Robots help autistic kids interact with adults', *Science*. (American Association for the Advancement of Science), 361(6404), pp. 763–764. https://doi.org/10.1126/science.361.6404.763-f.

Koch, S. (1981) 'The nature and limits of psychological knowledge: Lessons of a century qua 'science'', *American Psychologist*, 36(3), pp. 257–269. https://doi.org/10.1037/0003-066X.36.3.257.

LaCroix, J. M. and Pratto, F. (2015) 'Instrumentality and the denial of personhood: The social psychology of objectifying others', *Revue Internationale de Psychologie Sociale*, 28(1), pp. 183–212.

Langhout, R. D. (2003) 'Reconceptualizing quantitative and qualitative methods: A case study dealing with place as an exemplar', *American Journal of Community Psychology*, 32(3–4), pp. 229–244. https://doi.org/10.1023/B:AJCP.0000004744.09295.9b.

Lavelle, T. A., Weinstein, M. C., Newhouse, J. P., Munir, K., Kuhlthau, K. A. and Prosser, L. A. (2014) 'Economic burden of childhood autism spectrum disorders', *Pediatrics*, 133(3), p. e520. https://doi.org/10.1542/peds.2013-0763.

Leary, D. E. (2001) 'One big idea, one ultimate concern. Sigmund Koch's critique of psychology and hope for the future', *The American Psychologist*, 56(5), pp. 425–432. https://doi.org/10.1037/0003-066X.56.5.425.

Levine, M., Perkins, D. and Perkins, D. (2005) *Principles of Community Psychology: Perspectives and Applications*. 3rd edition. Oxford: Oxford University Press.

Lovaas, O. I., Schaeffer, B. and Simmons, J. Q. (1965) 'Building social behavior in autistic children by use of electric shock', *Journal of Experimental Research in Personality*, 1(2), pp. 99–109.

Luke, D. A. (2005) 'Getting the big picture in community science: Methods that capture context', *American Journal of Community Psychology*, 35(3), pp. 185–200. https://doi.org/10.1007/s10464-005-3397-z.

Matlin, S. L., Molock, S. D. and Tebes, J. K. (2011) 'Suicidality and depression among African American adolescents: The role of family and peer support and community connectedness', *American Journal of Orthopsychiatry*, 81(1), pp. 108–117. https://doi.org/10.1111/j.1939-0025.2010.01078.x.

McGuire, A. (2016) *War on Autism: On the Cultural Logic of Normative Violence*. Ann Arbor: University of Michigan Press.

Miller, K. (2020) 'Why I no longer wish to be associated with the BPS'. Available at: https://thepsychologist.bps.org.uk/why-i-no-longer-wish-be-associated-bps

Milton, D. E. (2014) 'Autistic expertise: A critical reflection on the production of knowledge in autism studies', *Autism*, 18(7), pp. 794–802. https://doi.org/10.1177/1362361314525281.

Milton, D. E. (2016) 'Disposable dispositions: reflections upon the work of Iris Marion Young in relation to the social oppression of autistic people', *Disability & Society*, 31(10), pp. 1403–1407.

Milton, D. and Bracher, M. (2013) 'Autistics speak but are they heard?', *BSA Medical Sociology Online*, 7, pp. 61–69.

Moradi, B. (2013) 'Discrimination, objectification, and dehumanization: Toward a pantheoretical framework'. In: Gervais, S. J. (ed.) *Objectification and (De)Humanization*. New York: Springer New York, pp. 153–181. https://doi.org/10.1007/978-1-4614-6959-9_7.

Mohr, J. J., Weiner, J. L., Chopp, R. M. and Wong, S. J. (2009) 'Effects of client bisexuality on clinical judgment: When is bias most likely to occur?', *Journal of Counseling Psychology*, 56(1), pp. 164–175. https://doi.org/10.1037/a0012816

Nagel, T. (1989) *The View from Nowhere*. First Issued as an Oxford University Press Paperback. New York: Oxford University Press.

Nelson, G. B. and Prilleltensky, I. (2010) *Community Psychology: In Pursuit of Liberation and Well-Being*. Basingstoke, UK and New York: Palgrave Macmillan.

Nguyen Thanh, L., Nguyen, H.-P., Ngo, M. D., Bui, V. A., Dam, P. T. M., Bui, H. T. P., Ngo, D. V., Tran, K. T., Dang, T. T. T., Duong, B. D., Nguyen, P. A. T., Forsyth, N. and Heke, M. (2020) 'Outcomes of bone marrow mononuclear cell transplantation combined with interventional education for autism spectrum disorder', *STEM CELLS Translational Medicine*. https://doi.org/10.1002/sctm.20-0102

Nussbaum, M. C. (1995) Objectification. *Philosophy Public Affairs*, 24(4), pp. 249–291. https://doi.org/10.1111/j.1088-4963.1995.tb00032.x

Nuyts, J. and de Roeck, A. (1997) Autism and meta-representation: The case of epistemic modality', *International Journal of Language & Communication Disorders*, 32(2s) Spec No, pp. 113–137.

Orford, J. (1992) *Community Psychology: Theory and Practice*. Chichester [England]. New York: J. Wiley.

Ozonoff, S., Strayer, D. L., McMahon, W. M. and Filloux, F. (1994) 'Executive function abilities in autism and Tourette syndrome: An information processing approach', *Journal of Child Psychology and Psychiatry*, 35(6), pp. 1015–1032. https://doi.org/10.1111/j.1469-7610.1994.tb01807.x.

Pellicano, E., Dinsmore, A. and Charman, T. (2014) 'What should autism research focus upon? Community views and priorities from the United Kingdom', *Autism*, 18(7), pp. 756–770. https://doi.org/10.1177/1362361314529627.

Peterson, C. C. (2002) 'Drawing insight from pictures: The development of concepts of false drawing and false belief in children with deafness, normal hearing, and autism', *Child Development*, 73(5), pp. 1442–1459. https://doi.org/10.1111/1467-8624.00482.

Pinker, S. (2002) *The Blank Slate: The Modern Denial of Human Nature*. New York: Viking.

Pinker, S. (2006) 'The evolutionary psychology of religion', *Humanist-Buffalo-*, 66(5), p. 10.

Prilleltensky, I. (2001) 'Value-based praxis in community psychology: Moving toward social justice and social action', *American Journal of Community Psychology*, 29(5), pp. 747–778. https://doi.org/10.1023/A:1010417201918.

Rappaport, J. (2005) 'Community psychology is (thank god) more than science', *American Journal of Community Psychology*, 35(3–4), pp. 231–238. https://doi.org/10.1007/s10464-005-3402-6.

Rosenthal, S. J. (1995) 'The pioneer fund: Financier of fascist research', *American Behavioral Scientist*, 39(1), pp. 44–61. https://doi.org/10.1177/0002764295039001006.

Rushton, J. P. and Templer, D. I. (2012) 'RETRACTED: Do pigmentation and the melanocortin system modulate aggression and sexuality in humans as they do in other animals?', *Personality and Individual Differences*, 53(1), pp. 4–8. https://doi.org/10.1016/j.paid.2012.02.015.

Russell, B. (2012) 'Reflections on 'autistic integrity'', *Bioethics*, 26(3), pp. 164–170. https://doi.org/10.1111/j.1467-8519.2010.01827.x.

Russell, J. and Hill, E. L. (2001) 'Action-monitoring and intention reporting in children with autism', *Journal of Child Psychology and Psychiatry, and Allied Disciplines*, 42(3), pp. 317–328. https://doi.org/10.1111/1469-7610.00725.

Ruti, M. (2015) *The Age of Scientific Sexism: How Evolutionary Psychology Promotes Gender Profiling and Fans the Battle of the Sexes*. New York: Bloomsbury Publishing USA.

Schaffer, G. (2007) '"Scientific" racism again?": Reginald gates, the mankind quarterly and the question of "race" in science after the Second World War', *Journal of American Studies*, 41(2), pp. 253–278.

Scully, J., & Shakespeare, T. (2019) Report on the impact of ableism in medical and scientific practice. A/HRC/43/41.

Sebanz, N., Knoblich, G., Stumpf, L. and Prinz, W. (2005) 'Far from action-blind: Representation of others' actions in individuals with autism', *Cognitive Neuropsychology*, 22(3–4), pp. 433–454. https://doi.org/10.1080/02643290442000121.

Silberman, S. (2017) *Neurotribes: The Legacy of Autism and How to Think Smarter about People Who Think Differently*. London: Atlantic Books.

Sinclair. (1993) 'Don't mourn for us'. In: *International Conference on Autism*, Toronto. Autism Network International. Available at: https://www.autreat.com/dont_mourn.html.

Smith, A. (2009) 'The empathy imbalance hypothesis of autism: A theoretical approach to cognitive and emotional empathy in autistic development', *The Psychological Record*, 59(2), pp. 273–294. https://doi.org/10.1007/BF03395663.

Suffla, S., Seedat, M. and Bawa, U. (2015) 'Reflexivity as enactment of critical community psychologies: Dilemmas of voice and positionality in a multi-country photovoice study', *Journal of Community Psychology*, 43(1), pp. 9–21. https://doi.org/10.1002/jcop.21691.

Tantam, D. (2009) *Can the World Afford Autistic Spectrum Disorder? Nonverbal Communication, Asperger Syndrome and the Interbrain*. London: Jessica Kingsley Publishers.

Teo, T. (2010) 'Examining the influence of subjective norm and facilitating conditions on the intention to use technology among pre-service teachers: A structural equation modeling of an extended technology acceptance model', *Asia Pacific Education Review*, 11(2), pp. 253–262.

Teo, T. (2011) 'Empirical race psychology and the hermeneutics of epistemological violence', *Human Studies*, 34(3), pp. 237–255. https://doi.org/10.1007/s10746-011-9179-8.

Timmins, L., Rimes, K. A. and Rahman, Q. (2019) 'Minority stressors, rumination, and psychological distress in lesbian, gay, and bisexual individuals', *Archives of Sexual Behavior*. https://doi.org/10.1007/s10508-019-01502-2.

Tolman, C. W. (1992) *Positivism in Psychology Historical and Contemporary Problems*. New York: Springer New York.

Tomasello, M., Carpenter, M., Call, J., Behne, T. and Moll, H. (2005) 'Understanding and sharing intentions: The origins of cultural cognition', *Behavioral and Brain Sciences*, 28(05), pp. 675–691. https://doi.org/10.1017/S0140525X05000129.

Veldkamp, C. L., Nuijten, M. B., Dominguez-Alvarez, L., Van Assen, M. A. and Wicherts, J.M. (2014) 'Statistical reporting errors and collaboration on statistical analyses in psychological science', *PloS One*, 9(12), p. e114876.

Verhoeff, B. (2016) 'Two kinds of autism: A comparison of distinct understandings of psychiatric disease', *Medicine, Health Care, and Philosophy*, 19(1), pp. 111–123. https://doi.org/10.1007/s11019-015-9655-4.

Vivanti, G. (2020) 'Ask the editor: What is the most appropriate way to talk about individuals with a diagnosis of autism?', *Journal of Autism and Developmental Disorders*, 50(2), pp. 691–693. https://doi.org/10.1007/s10803-019-04280-x.

Wieseler, C. (2020) 'Epistemic oppression and ableism in bioethics', *Hypatia*, 1–19. Cambridge Core. https://doi.org/10.1017/hyp.2020.38

Williams, D. R., Yu, Y., Jackson, J. S. and Anderson, N. B. (1997) 'Racial differences in physical and mental health: Socio-economic status, stress and discrimination', *Journal of Health Psychology*, 2(3), pp. 335–351. https://doi.org/10.1177/135910539700200305.

Willig, C. (2020) 'From revision to transformation: Reflections on the impact of the review process across the qualitative/quantitative divide, g 202', *QMiP Bulletin*, 29, p. 4.

Woelfle, M., Olliaro, P. and Todd, M. H. (2011) 'Open science is a research accelerator', *Nature Chemistry*, 3(10), pp. 745–748. https://doi.org/10.1038/nchem.1149.

Woods, R., Milton, D., Arnold, L. and Graby, S. (2018) 'Redefining critical autism studies: A more inclusive interpretation', *Disability and Society*, 33(6), pp. 974–979. https://doi.org/10.1080/09687599.2018.1454380.

Yergeau, M. (2018) *Authoring Autism: On Rhetoric and Neurological Queerness*. Durham, NC: Duke University Press.

Yirmiya, N., Erel, O., Shaked, M. and Solomonica-Levi, D. (1998) 'Meta-analyses comparing theory of mind abilities of individuals with autism, individuals with mental retardation, and normally developing individuals', *Psychological Bulletin*, 124(3), pp. 283–307. https://doi.org/10.1037//0033-2909.124.3.283.

Yirmiya, N., Sigman, M. D., Kasari, C. and Mundy, P. (1992) 'Empathy and cognition in high-functioning children with autism', *Child Development*, 63(1), p. 150. https://doi.org/10.2307/1130909.

Young, I. (1990) *Justice and the politics of difference*. Princeton, New Jersey: Princeton University Press.

PART 2

Autistic identity

8
THROUGH THE LENS OF (BLACK) CRITICAL RACE THEORY

Melissa Simmonds

The individuals contributing to this book are far more qualified to talk about Autism than I am or may ever be. From its conception to current trends, the models of disability, impairments, ad infinitum; there is a wealth of knowledge in this book around the field of Autism. The style of writing I have to adhere to, rules set by the publisher, is unnerving for me, as is why was I approached to contribute and why am I fighting my imposter syndrome on a daily, sometimes hourly, basis to create something barely legible for the audience to consume? It's quite simple: Black people never get an invitation to the metaphorical table, and we collectively need to ask why.

For this chapter, "Black" will refer to people who would be identified as Black/African/Caribbean/Black British, and/or "Mixed/multiple ethnic group" including Black/African/Caribbean/Black British within it (Race Disparity Unit, n.d.). The term "white" or "majority" will be used to describe the Caucasian communities in the United Kingdom and America. It is also probably important for me to add that words that make you uncomfortable should not prevent you from trying to understand the meaning behind them.

For me, growing up, "white supremacy" evokes images of the Ku Klux Klan in white robes burning crosses on Black people's lawns in America. The word supremacy merely means …

I keep rewriting this chapter, I am unhappy with it because I am writing in a way to please the audience, I am imagining who will be reading it. Then I realise the issue. Before I can write about what it is to be a Black Autistic, I need to explain what it is like to be Black. Autism is an invisible disability that I hid well. I did not receive a diagnosis until I was in my late 30s. I can mask my Autism, but I can never hide the colour of my skin. Those who say they do not see colour are liars; my hue is the first thing you see. So, before I can talk about Autism in the Black community, I must help the audience understand what it is to be Black in a Eurocentric, as well as pro-Brexit, country.

A brief history of being Black

There is no need for me to explain how and why the word 'Nigger' is offensive and unacceptable for people who are not Black to say. Even when reading the word aloud, non-Blacks should say "The N-word". And leave it at that, *always*. I cringe when the older generation use 'coloured' to describe me and people who look like me. Far too many people fail to realise it is an offensive and derogatory term. It is most widely used by the older generation and people who feel unsure how to describe people who look like me. They worry 'Black' will offend me.

Black people like to be called Black, and yes there will always be an exception to the rule, but they are in fact the exception.

The term Black has been used as an umbrella term to encompass everybody who is not white. It was used to enhance solidarity, instead hindering the individualism cultures crave. Colonisers will always adopt exercises to homogenise what they steal (Kinouani, 2020) and rename it; so too is the acronym BAME to describe Black, Asian and Minority Ethnic. In the United Kingdom, BAME is defined as all ethnic groups except white ethnic groups.

When organisations, or organisers of national conferences, say they have someone from the BAME or Globalised Majority (Campbell-Stephens, 2021) community to talk about Autism I invite you to look at the List of Ethnic Groups produced by the UK Government Race Disparity Unit and critically think about what this means. Although I can empathise with and probably have a lot in common with a Chinese Autistic person, it would be absurd for me to say I am representing them and giving a voice to their lived experiences. As a cis woman I can argue that my lived experience differs from that of a cis man. So too is my lived experience as an Autistic Black woman different to that of an Autistic Arab woman, yet the majority community has haphazardly placed multiple ethnicities into a single box.

I denounce acronyms such as BME (Black Minority Ethnic) and BAME (Black, Asian and Minority Ethnic). I agree with the communities it encompasses that the shortenings of one's racial identity is misleading and further marginalises disadvantaged people (Bunglawala, 2019). It gives the majority population the opportunity to turn minority populations into a mere tick-box exercise (Majors, Carberry, & Ransaw, 2020). Being colonised and stripped of one's name and identity is a repetitive harmful practice which still occurs (Kinouani, 2020).

White privilege and fragility

It is important to explain, in brief, the terms 'white privilege' and 'white fragility' early on in this chapter, as it is the key component that causes white populations to stop listening and assume the Black person trying to explain it is being racist, is using the race card (which does not exist … imagine being told you are using the "Autism card" each time you try to explain the societal difficulties you are experiencing in a neurotypical-led world!) or is making up an excuse for the difficulties the Black community is facing.

The Black community do not like to be defined as a BAME/BME acronym, yet we are, our descriptors created by white populations. The white communities masterfully assign titles to other populaces at the same time as feeling uncomfortable when they are described by their colour (white) instead of their given names.

In my talk, "Missing *Voices*: The Black Autistic's Journey" (Simmonds, 2020), I explained that because I am a visual thinker and learner, I describe white privilege by showing the audience a picture from a heart-wrenching moment in the movie *Titanic*.

These characters do not have names, and are cast as 'Irish Mommy', 'Irish Little Boy' and 'Little Girl'. The family go back to their third-class cabin to die, as they are locked behind the third-class gates. I explained that this woman has virtually nothing, is invisible to the middle- and upper-class passengers, and because of this she perishes. However, if there had been more lifeboats, almost enough for everyone, and she had been on deck, beside a Black third-class mother and her little Black children, the white mother would have taken precedence and been given seats in the lifeboat. To many, white privilege is an illustration of class and racial prejudice. In fact, all white persons, of whatever class or economic status have hidden benefits by virtue of the colour of their skin, which Black people, *of the same class/status* do not have, because of the colour of their skin (McIntosh, 1988).

White fragility is the unwillingness to have conversations and or be in situations which cause discomfort associated with acknowledging or discussing one's internalised superiority and racial privilege (DiAngelo, 2018).

Critical Race Theory

I stumbled upon the term Critical Race Theory (CRT) in the second year of my master's degree studies and it immediately not only enhanced my understanding of racism and oppression, it also enriched my understanding of the journey of Black Autistics.

Critical Race Theory (CRT) supposes race is not grounded in biology, nor is it natural; it is a socially created concept formulated by the majority (white) population (Curry and Curry, 2018) to maintain their historical advantages and power over minority (Black) people. I find this theory easy to espouse as I favour the social model of disability, which sees disability as a social construct (Durham & Ramcharan, 2018), denouncing the medical (model of disability) supremacy, similar to how CRT condemns white supremacy.

Mistrust in white spaces

The aim of this section in my chapter is not to dishearten the reader. It is here to help you empathise with us and help you appreciate why our mistrust in white spaces, including the National Health Service, is rife.

I rarely attend a meeting where the jarring phrase "hard-to-reach" is not mindlessly bandied around to depict the Black (and brown) (and other marginalised) communities in Western society. We, as a community, are not hard to reach; we merely mistrust the majority communities. In our experience, we find there is always an ulterior motive, an agenda to questions you ask us. We have countless pieces of historical evidence of interacting with and being harmed by the white majority populations we live amongst.

Dr Simons, the "father of modern gynaecology", experimented on female Black slaves without pain relief, the screams so excruciating that his white assistants, often trainee doctors, could no longer aid in holding the women down during their mutilation (Rakatansky, 2017). Instead, fellow female slaves, without power and choice, were made to hold down the patients. His reason for not using any form of medication to sedate or ease the pain of the slaves? The misconception that Black people are subhuman and do not feel pain at the same level of intensity as white people. He was also responsible for experimenting on new-born Black slaves suffering neonatal tetanus (trismus nascentium) (Kenny, 2017) where he would pry their skull bones apart and use shoemaker's awl to realign them as he hypothesised skull-bone movement occurred due to "the sloth and ignorance of their mothers and the Black midwives who attended them" during long labour. The root cause was the unsanitary conditions the slaves were expected to live in and the tools used to deliver the child. Dr Simon's experiments had a 100% fatality rate.

The United States Public Health Service and the Centers for Disease Control and Prevention conducted the Tuskegee Experiment (1932–1972) to observe the natural timeline of untreated syphilis. They purposefully chose the Tuskegee Institute, an HBCU (Historically Black College and University) in Alabama; purposefully lied to the Black men, giving them placebos, telling them they were receiving free health care from the Federal government for their 'bad blood'; and purposefully withheld antibiotics even though penicillin became the certified treatment for syphilis in 1947.

Of the 600 Black men, 399 had latent syphilis but were not made aware of the contagion, which spread to sexual partners and led to children being born with congenital syphilis. A 6-month trial continued for 40 years.

Please do not become complacent whilst reading this section, thinking this is an American issue, and Britain treats/treated Black people more favourably. What is often forgotten is that the Black Africans stolen into slavery were taken primarily to America and the Caribbean, and the UK benefited from the enslavement of Caribbean slaves; hence, whilst atrocities did not take place on British soil, British people profited from the heinous results.

There is insurmountable evidence that racism and bias is inherent across the life cycle of Black people within the UK; from antenatal, neonatal and breastfeeding (Iacobucci, 2020) to geriatric and end-of-life care (Bécares, Kapadia, & Nazroo, 2020). The *British Medical Journal* recently produced a special edition addressing race and health, simply titled "Racism in medicine" (Kmietowicz, 2020). It highlights the irregularities in care for Black and brown patients and staff, as well as the need for a "race equality observatory" in this Eurocentric white country to provide racially unbiased governance, communication and data to address the inequalities faced.

There are greater rates of negative health outcomes, mortality and morbidity rates in Black babies and infants compared to their white contemporaries, as well as white women being five times less likely to die during pregnancy and childbirth than Black women (Seals Allers, 2019).

Inequalities and misdiagnoses also occur around our body's biggest organ – our skin. Melanoma is most common in white skin, yet Black people are more likely to die from it because of late detection (Lyman, Mills, & Shipman, 2017) by practitioners who are trained using images that are primarily of white people displaying skin abnormalities. Even technology has racial bias, as artificial intelligence struggles to detect cancerous moles in darker melanin because images used in training algorithms have almost always been of white skin (Noor, 2020). Though the government plan to invest further in AI (O'Dowd, 2019), little has been said about ensuring that equitable care is the desired outcome or how they will achieve this.

Bécares et al. (2020) rightfully states, "Exclusion from population studies is a form of institutional racism" and this is evident from data retrieved in 2004. The Health Survey for England found maturing (aged 61–70) ethnic minority communities had increased rates of poor mental and physical illness (67% for Black Caribbean, 86% for Bangladeshi people, 69% for Pakistani people and 63% for Indian people) in comparison with 34% of white elderly people of the same age. And whilst Black people were found to be one of the most deprived, excluded and subjugated groups in society, 2004 was the last year the Health Survey for England collected data from this cohort in society, even though it alarmingly showed that the 'fair or bad' health of white English people aged 61 and into their 70s is equivalent to that of Caribbean people in their late 40s or early 50s.

Out of sheer frustration, my Black friends and I devised an imaginary drinking game during COVID-19. Every time a member of the conservative government mentioned Kemi Badenoch during press conferences and interviews, around disparities in Black communities, we could have a shot of alcohol (needless to say, we would have gotten good and drunk had we really been playing the game). Boris Johnson and the cabinet often proudly declare they have the most diverse cabinet ever, with several ethnic minority individuals at the helm of government offices. When the prime minister is asked how many *Black* people they have in the cabinet, an uncomfortable silence always ensues, as the answer is zero!

Cue Kemi Badenoch, the Conservative MP for Saffron Walden since 2017. Much like the fact that applied behaviour analysis (ABA) enthusiasts will always be able to find autistic adults who ferociously believe that such practices are not only justified but necessary for autistic children and young people, so too will you always be able to find influential Black and brown people ready to get up into the pulpit and say that racism isn't too bad in the United Kingdom; some will be willing to sell their soul and say racism no longer exists.

COVID-19 disproportionately impacted the Black, Asian and ethnic minority communities within the UK (Phiri, Delanerolle, Al-Sudani, & Rathod, 2021) when compared to the white population. The key factors were the long-standing inequalities and comorbidities that were exacerbated: increased risk of exposure to and acquisition of COVID-19 due to frontline jobs leading to increased risk of complications and death, racism, discrimination, stigma, fear and distrust. Although COVID-19 does not have the ability to biologically discriminate, the societal discrimination faced by Black, Asian and ethnic minority groups face in the UK meant that fewer people who looked like me had the opportunity to work from home or be placed on furlough and isolate if they or a family member became ill.

Now onto the Black Autistic

I have given you an abundance of evidence about the experience of Black people in white spaces. I, we, are not an anomaly.

My experiential knowledge, as a Black person growing up in a Western society, has countless experience of white fragility (McIntosh, 1988) when one tries to have an honest dialogue about race. Naively, I thought the Autism community would be more sympathetic to the intersections of Black disabled people (Crenshaw, 2016). Unfortunately, I am witnessing the same hierarchical pecking order of white voices intrinsically unable to relinquish power for the bigger cause (Straiton & Sridhar, 2021).

A fellow Sheffield-based Autism educator, David Panther, who specialises in educating people about suicide in the autistic community, recently told me that once an activist, such as myself, takes a position in an organisation, with all the good intentions in the world they will become a part of the unspoken issues occurring in the Autism community.

Having to walk that metaphorical tightrope every day, I cannot deny this issue. Although I am a Black woman with little to no power; I do still have privileges. And when people, like myself, are hired it 'soft-blocks' the individuals who struggle more than I do to be acknowledged or heard.

I am very vocal over being diagnosed with severe prolonged depression at 18, raindrop psoriasis at 19 and chronic fatigue syndrome at 33. All of these were triggered by the fact that I could not cope with the neurotypical world around me. I am also honest about needing 12 tablets a day to function and have required support in my posts to be (somewhat) successful, including in education.

Yet I still have privileges, and because of this, I, as a Black Autistic woman, have to share those things about me in the hope that other Black and brown Autistic families will come out of the shadows and get the help and support they so desperately need. I share embarrassing and taboo things about myself, not because I want to, but because there are so few of us with a platform to highlight that fact that we exist, and we are being neglected by the wider Autistic communities and the infrastructures which support them.

Believe me when I say, if I had my way, I would have written this chapter much like the Autistic women of colour, Brown, Ashkenazy and Giwa Onaiwu, (2017) did in their groundbreaking book *All the Weight of Our Dreams: On Living Racialized Autism*. I, like so many Autistic people I interact with, would like to primarily highlight my area of peak interest: namely, the Marvel Cinematic Universe (MCU), *Star Wars* and *Game of Thrones*. I'd much rather devote my time to dissecting the fact that of the six original Avengers, Clint Barton, although rarely discussed, is the Avenger that the rest are most envious of. Or I would discuss why 'Bucky Barnes' has the greatest MCU arc.

However, I am the only Black Autistic woman being invited to talk about 'Autism and Race', so I have the burdensome task of talking about the daily traumas I experience living in the UK (Hart, 2021). I re-traumatise myself ruminating on the distressing memories so that more people who look like me feel less alone, and seen.

Sara Ahmed (Lorde, 2017) highlights the need of people like myself to "speak through" the following forms of address.

Speaking as, speaking out, speaking from, speaking with and speaking to

'Speaking as' a Black cis woman, and a Black Autistic cis woman, in the microcosmic Autistic world, where, like the wider macrocosmic world, the white cis man has the most privileges, and Autism was perceived as something that only happened to white cis males. 'Speaking out' means I am yet again tasked with the burden of educating those who should already know about racism. Giwa Oniawu (2020) uses the late John Singleton's coming-of-age movie, *Boyz n the Hood*, which globally resonated in Black communities, to poignantly convey the state of the current support the Autism community is experiencing. "They don't know, don't show, or don't care" is a statement uttered by the deuteragonist, who has lived a life of oppression in one of the richest and most influential countries in the world. Giwa Oniawu describes the people and organisations who have influence within the Autistic communities yet do nothing to combat the inequities within it.

I appear nonchalant for two reasons: first, my brain is so incredibly busy, and my body is riddled with chronic fatigue, so I am constantly at civil war with myself (much like Captain America and Iron Man in *Captain America 3*; but I digress). Mainly, I appear nonchalant as a mask (Casimir, 2020) to protect myself in white environments so I am not perceived as the age-old trope of being the 'angry Black woman' (Kent, 2021).

Very recently, I found myself chairing a monthly meeting that increasingly became more difficult as it was repeatedly hijacked by a white cis man who is well respected and a lynchpin in a prominent Autism charity in my region. Every time I chaired the meeting I felt as though I was dishonouring myself and those (Black people) that came before me, as this person felt they had the right to repeatedly question my intentions (Kinouani, 2020).

My mask allowed him to question my identity as I was 'articulate' and 'educated' and therefore they felt I could not speak for Autistics who were struggling with functioning in a neurotypical world. Yes, he was being ableist towards me, however the reader also needs to understand that the Autism community is predominantly led by white cis people, and therefore has racial, colonial and patriarchal regimes that disadvantage me (Cornejo & Jain, 2021).

In meetings with Autistic charities, educators and groups, I am a Black woman burdened with being spoken down to by white people questioning my identity because of the way I conduct myself. The cost of me not speaking out is too high a cost for the Black Autistic community. The cost of me 'speaking out' will have detrimental effects on the way I am viewed within a tightknit gatekeeper community where charities have more weighting than an Autistic person. The cost of speaking out could mean the Black and brown voices will be missed and the white saviour will reign supreme (Jeraj, 2021) as I am the only person championing it. So, do I 'speak out' or shut up?

If we look again at the statement "They don't know, don't show, or don't care", I would not feel burdened to shut up and be spoken down to, to keep my seat at the metaphorical table if those in power within Autism educated themselves on CRT, spoke up to defend people who look like me and ensured we were welcomed and felt safe in the environments we find ourselves in, and actually cared enough to step back and give other people the platform to educate you, the reader, the professionals and the influencers about our lived experiences (Henderson & Majors, 2020).

I capitalise *Black* just as I capitalise *Autism* as they are more than just descriptive words; they are identifiers of communities I am a part of. They describe the very essence of who I am, draping me in pride. In safe spaces, I can not only acknowledge but can discuss the juxtaposition I, and other parents raising Black Autistic children and/or being Black and Autistic themselves, experience. As a parent, I am tasked with ensuring my children are healthy and happy, well-adjusted and balanced individuals; but how are we to achieve this? Teaching them to 'take off the mask' is teaching them to resist the impulse to pretend they are ok and coping. Parents are a masking child's greatest ally, carrying out an assortment of multifaceted activities (Dreyfus & Dowse, 2020) to try to ensure their child's needs are met and reasonable adjustments are adopted in educational, health and social settings, etc. As a Black Autistic however, teaching them to take off their mask is teaching them to expose themselves in white spaces with an audience of conscious and unconscious bias towards them.

Structural racism is entrenched in our education systems and practices throughout one's entire schooling life, from nursery to university, in teacher training, provision and delivery. The lack of Black pastoral and teaching staff in these environments means these spaces must continue to be classified as white spaces and unsafe for Black Autistic children and parents to even contemplate reducing their masks if they wish to improve their long-term health outcomes. There does not need to be revision; instead the whole system needs to be dismantled and excavated and freed from historic prejudice and rebuilt.

We want our kids to be happy and healthy, we want our kids to be their authentic selves. We want them to push boundaries, be inquisitive, cry out at injustices and challenge things they feel need challenging. Having our kids living and breathing and not being incarcerated is the most important thing; so we teach them to suppress themselves. We become their oppressor out of love and necessity, we stifle our kids to keep them free because our colour will always be seen before our disabilities (Brown, Ashkenazy & Giwa Onaiwu, 2017). The lack of equity in the Autism community is not because of my race, it is because of racism, and it puts Black Autistic people at risk of not getting diagnosis, support or a seat at the metaphorical table to empower oneself and/or ones' Black community. The white Autistic community claiming to promote equity whilst being colour-blind will continue to propel white supremacy in the field.

Conclusion

To the reader who came to this chapter for a quick win, you are no doubt disappointed. Much like when Ramsay Bolton told Theon Greyjoy, "If you think this has a happy ending, you haven't been paying attention" (Sakharov, 2013), this chapter does not end in a satisfactory conclusion. The aim of this chapter was never to explain Autism in the Black communities but to help the readers, especially those outside of Black and brown communities, who continue to be primarily in positions to bring about change in the wider Autism community, understand that being Black is not holding people who look like me back from seeking diagnosis.

The structures within Western communities, the accepted designs and structures for living have been and continue to be created to support the majority populations.

What is stopping you, the reader, from questioning the establishment? Asking organisations such as the National Autistic Society and other groups working in collaboration with our government:

1. How many non-white people are a part of their board of directors or top managerial structures?
2. How many non-white people have they actively sought to speak at their conferences? And remunerate, in line with their other speakers?
3. Of the Autistic people contributing to the event, how many of them are from Black and brown communities?
4. What are they actively doing to ensure they are creating structures to educate their organisation on (their inevitable) unconscious bias, CRT, etc.?
5. What are they actively doing to ensure that they are creating structures to educate non-white communities about Autism?

Giwa Onaiwu (2020) believes that "gradual progress is the ancestor of monumental change"; so, I ask you, what are you going to do, to right the wrongs in the field of Autism?

References

Bécares, L., Kapadia, D., & Nazroo, J. (2020). The neglect of older ethnic minority people in UK research and policy: exclusion from population studies is a form of institutional racism. *BMJ, 368*(8233), 1–2. https://doi.org/10.1136/bmj.m212

Brown, L. X., Ashkenazy, E., & Giwa Onaiwu, M. (Eds.). (2017). *All the Weight of Our Dreams: On Living Racialized Autism*. DragonBee Press.

Bunglawala, Z. (2019, July 8). Please, don't call me BAME or BME! Retrieved from https://civilservice.blog.gov.uk/2019/07/08/please-dont-call-me-bame-or-bme/

Campbell-Stephens, R. (2021). *Educational Leadership and the Global Majority: Decolonising Narratives*. Springer Nature.

Casimir, J. N. (2020). The cost of fitting in: An investigative analysis of race-based code-switching and social exclusion. A Senior Honors Thesis, University or North Carolina, Department of Communication Studies, Chapel Hill. Retrieved from https://cdr.lib.unc.edu/downloads/9s161c39g

Cornejo, J., & Jain, S. (2021, March 17). Why racial and gender representation matters in charity boards. Retrieved from *Charity So White*: https://charitysowhite.org/blog/why-racial-and-gender-representation-matters-in-charity-boards

Crenshaw, K. (2016, October). The urgency of intersectionality. *Ted Talk*. Retrieved from https://www.ted.com/talks/kimberle_crenshaw_the_urgency_of_intersectionality

Curry, T. J., & Curry, G. (2018). On the perils of race neutrality and anti-blackness: Philosophy as an irreconcilable obstacle to (Black) thought. *American Journal of Economics and Sociology, 77*(3–4), 657–687.

DiAngelo, R. (2018). *White Fragility: Why It's so Hard for White People to Talk about Racism*. Beacon Press.

Dreyfus, S., & Dowse, L. (2020). Experiences of parents who support a family member with intellectual disability and challenging behaviour: "This is what I deal with every single day". *Journal of Intellectual and Developmental Disability, 45*(1), 12–22. https://doi.org/10.3109/13668250.2018.1510117

Durham, C., & Ramcharan, P. (Eds.). (2018). Understanding the assumptions of major models of disability theory. In: *Insight into Acquired Brain Injury* (pp. 31–51). Springer.

Giwa Onaiwu, G. (2020, December). "They don't know, don't show, or don't care": Autism's white privilege problem. *Autism in Adulthood, 2*(4), 270–272. https://doi.org/10.1089/aut.2020.0077

Hart, A. (2021, November 22). I am not your critical friend. Retrieved from *Charity So White*: https://charitysowhite.org/blog/I-am-not-your-critical-friend

Henderson, M., & Majors, R. (2020). Chapter 11. ASD & cultural competence: An ASD multi-cultural treatment led model. In: Richard Majors, Karen Carberry & Theodore S. Ransaw (Eds.). *The International Handbook of Black Community Mental Health* (pp. 239–256). Emerald Publishing.

Iacobucci, G. (2020). Birthing care without racism: Five minutes with... Kimberly Seals Allers. *BMJ, 368*, m424. https://doi.org/10.1136/bmj.m424

Jeraj, S. (2021). Doing the work to end health inequalities caused by systemic racism. *BMJ, 373*, n821. https://doi.org/10.1136/bmj.n821

Kenny, S. (2017). 'I can do the child no good': Dr Sims and the Enslaved Infants of Montgomery, Alabama. *Social History of Medicine, 20*(2), 223–241. https://doi.org/10.1093/shm/hkm036

Kent, J. (2021, February 19). Scapegoating and the 'angry black woman'. *Group Analysis*, *54*(3), 354–371. https://doi.org/10.1177%2F0533316421992300

Kinouani, G. (2020, March 16). Silencing, power and racial trauma in groups. *Group Analysis*, *53*(2), 145–161. https://doi.org/10.1177%2F0533316420908974

Kinouani, G. (2020, September 26). Whiteness, sovereignty and the body. Retrieved from *Race Reflections*: https://racereflections.co.uk/2020/09/26/whiteness-sovereignty-and-the-body/

Kmietowicz, Z. (Ed.) (2020). Racism in medicine. Retrieved from *The BMJ*: https://www.bmj.com/racism-in-medicine

Lorde, A. (2017). *Your Silence Will Not Protect You*. Silver Press.

Lyman, M., Mills, J., & Shipman, A. (2017). A dermatological questionnaire for general practitioners in England with a focus on melanoma; misdiagnosis in black patients compared to white patients. *Journal of the European Academy of Dermatology and Venereology*, *31*(4), 625–628. https://doi.org/10.1111/jdv.13949

Majors, R., Carberry, K., & Ransaw, T. S. (Eds.). (2020). *The International Handbook of Black Community Mental Health*. Emerald Publishing.

McIntosh, P. (1988, July/August). White privilege: Unpacking the invisible knapsack. *Peace and Freedom Magazine*, 10–12. Women's International League for Peace and Freedom. Retrieved from https://files.eric.ed.gov/fulltext/ED355141.pdf#page=43

Noor, P. (2020, February 12). Can we trust AI not to further embed racial bias and prejudice? *BMJ*, *368*. https://doi.org/10.1136/bmj.m363

O'Dowd, A. (2019). Government pins hopes on £250m AI centre for faster diagnosis and treatment. *BMJ*, *366*, l5106.

Phiri, P., Delanerolle, G., Al-Sudani, A., & Rathod, S. (2021, February 2021). COVID-19 and black, Asian, and minority ethnic communities: A complex relationship without just cause. *JMIR Public Health Surveillance*, *7*(2). https://doi.org/10.2196/22581

Race Disparity Unit. (n.d.). List of ethnic groups. Retrieved from UK.GOV: https://www.ethnicity-facts-figures.service.gov.uk/style-guide/ethnic-groups#2021-census

Rakatansky, H. (2017). The persistence of racially-based health care inequities. *Rhode Island Medical Journal*, *100*(11), 11–12. Retrieved from https://www.proquest.com/scholarly-journals/persistence-racially-based-health-care-inequities/docview/1965028097/se-2?accountid=13827

Sakharov, A. (2013). Season 3. Episode 6: "The climb". *Game of Thrones*. HBO.

Seals Allers, K. (2019). Minding the gap: The lived experience of BAME women in birth & breastfeeding. *The Babyfriendly Initiative Annual Conference*. Unicef. Retrieved from https://www.unicef.org.uk/babyfriendly/wp-content/uploads/sites/2/2020/01/Kimberly-Seals-Allers-slides.pdf

Simmonds, M. (2020). Missing voices: The Black autistics journey. A2ndVoice CIC. Retrieved from https://www.youtube.com/watch?v=UkKwT-3IWfg&feature=youtu.be&t=1

Straiton, D., & Sridhar, A. (2021). Call to action for autism clinicians in response to anti-Black racism. *Autism*. https://doi.org/10.1177%2F13623613211043643

9
POSTPONING HUMANITY
Pathologising autism, childhood and motherhood

Francesca Bernardi

Introduction

This chapter draws on some of the ways in which a medicalised formulation of autism can manifest facets of ableist discourse that reverberate through experiences of childhood and parenthood, as well as having a significant impact on children's identities. In focusing on parental narratives, the chapter draws on some of the findings emerging from a cross-cultural study conducted in Central Italy and North West England, exploring the possibilities of a methodology rooted in respect and creative autonomy in which children participated in making art as experts in rendering visual and material their views and ideas. Children participated in individual creative encounters that fostered liberal self-expression producing their own versions of their identity. Concurrently, I interviewed mothers and fathers on their experiences of parenting and their children's social and educational participation. The study involved 16 children (6–10-year-olds), their mothers, fathers, teaching assistants – or support teachers – and teachers (see Bernardi, 2019). The central thread of the chapter is an invitation to engage with mothers' experiences of the processes leading to and surrounding their children's diagnosis. The chapter is articulated through a critical sociological analysis of interview excerpts and is an attempt to understand the repercussions of conceptualisations of difference based on ableist assumptions maintained through societal hierarchies and reproduced in language use and medical protocols. The narrative provides a metaphorical dialogue between three mothers who took part in the study in the Italian context. While the examples presented in this chapter are situated in a specific geo-cultural setting, it will be argued that, when these accounts are analysed through a process that brings together localised (personal, delicate) views and social structures, it is possible to see practices of control and pathologising ideology at work, which signal a widespread habit towards dehumanising and demonising difference beyond the study sites (Ryan, 2020, Goodley, Runswick-Cole and Liddiard, 2016). While recognising the specificity of place in the analysis, it is possible to capture, in these examples, both situated experiences and the political and economic forces that can destabilise children and mothers' identities beyond the social milieu and time within which participation in the interviews took place.

The themes discussed in this chapter are organised around three symbolic positions within which different relationships and hierarchies are forged: first, the medical position, one of assumed authority, rigour and legitimised control, a "high culture" that reproduces class distinctions through ableist rhetoric and impenetrable language (Bourdieu, 2018/1973, p. 73); second, a transactional position in which the identities of mothers and children are at once scrutinised and reshaped, with consequences visible through unequal participation and isolation; and third, the dialogic position occupied by mothers in the interview space. The latter can be said to provide a context – albeit provisional – for self-reflection, thus the conditions to question the subtle and explicit distinctions expressed by medicalising difference and normalising inequalities. This way the interviews become 'spaces' for assessing cultural habits and engage notions of respect and worth, giving the impetus to question the status quo and highlight the distortions that are produced through the classification of human worth.

A Gramscian lens is used to analyse the hierarchal interactions at play within such symbolic positions and mothers' signalling of a dominant culture that locates some individuals in positions of power while constructing positions of confinement for the 'other', making the process of diagnosis one of subordination and conditional alteration, affecting parents and their children. The pulls determining and maintaining each position denote an insistence on rationalising the desire for a normative identity, one that aspires unequivocally to productivity in social and economic terms (Diez, 2013, Bieler and Morton, 2001, 2004, Gramsci, 1992). These habits on the one hand interfere with familial and parental roles and on the other prompt resistance towards some of the medical practices involved in the process of defining autism. By reflecting on the genesis of diagnosis, through parents' experiences, it is also possible to observe how evolving power relations, orchestrated by the dominant structures (represented by the medical staff, extended family and the preschool), situate mothers and their children in positions of marginalisation and insularity. This chapter seeks to uncover a medical appropriation of motherhood and childhood, from the 'moment' the diagnosis is formalised, and explore how marginalisation and power relations are variously challenged. Consequently, it is possible to appreciate how children and mothers' identities are produced through negotiations and renegotiations, evolve, and are moulded according to the social constructs that attempt to define them. As such, the process of diagnosis becomes a pivotal moment in the life trajectory of a series of – what appear to be – provisional and place-based identities that are subject to scrutiny. Through a collaborative and dialogic research design, the interview space became a place for self-reflection and engagement, eliciting a range of relational strategies that participants used to review and contest the permeation of medical discourse in family life, personal identities and the reductive construction of their roles and their children's prospects (Van Aswegen and Shevlin, 2019, Orton, 2011). Importantly, parents taking part in the study had not previously discussed their views, beyond the familial context. Moreover, parents' interpretations are vital in identifying the persistence of social distinctions, marginalisation and blame that become apparent at the interface of motherhood and ableism.

Methodological considerations

An "explicit and implicit theme" and central thread throughout this work is respect (Alderson, 2008, p. 276). This means respect for participants, their reflections and their human stories; respect for their views, expertise and grit, which guide my discussion.

By upholding this premise, I hope that my contribution to this handbook can go some way to acknowledge the courage of mothers in talking – in their own terms – about the process of diagnosis and to recognise their experiences and feelings, as well as their enthusiasm and openness towards participating in research for the first time. With the informed consent of children, mothers and fathers, extracts from the interviews, conducted in Italy, are analysed to extend the scope of the original study, which focused on children's representations of their identities and the ways these are perceived from different perspectives. Mothers' perspectives and experiences thus offer further entry points for thinking about the experiences of families and the possibilities of alternative narratives countering ableist discourse that permeates their stories.

My affinity with participants, a shared culture and language, my biography, geographical mobility and – in most cases – a mutual working-class identity, although not overtly named in these terms in the Italian language, were pivotal in my own participation in the research encounters, in the ethics of the process of dialogue and in the ways I was received by participants within their familial spaces. On the one hand, sharing an Italian heritage (including local educational trajectories) offered an informal meeting of experiences and important points of contact with participants' realities, enabling participatory trust, understanding and fluidity between non-hierarchical positions. On the other hand, my scholarly activity, situated predominantly in England, became a means for participants to share their curiosity for alternate viewpoints, and for me to begin to draw on emerging commonalities with their English 'counterparts'.

The chapter unfolds through my re-engagement with the interview data and the symbolic positions that emerged progressively as the interviews occurred, demonstrating the benefits of reflexivity and dialogic representation, trust and an organic reimaging of personal agency and consciousness. Parents shared and distinct perspectives give emphasis to the power of self-determination and social action through participation in radical research that is premised on trust and dialogue, highlighting the inferences of medicalised discourse and practices in shaping daily life.

The more deeply I delved into the body of interviews with mothers and fathers in Italy, the more it became necessary to examine the role that societal hierarchies and language play in shaping and interfering with childhood, based on classifications of deviance from normalcy. This type of critical conscious analysis entails interrupting the researcher/researched asymmetry and unpacking experience in spaces that honour participants' stories and engage the radical and political position that researchers (can) occupy, to navigate ableist rhetoric to question and disrupt naturalised and moralised distinctions that precede individuals' self-authoring of their identities and worth in other contexts. The analysis thus opens a space to address the discomfort of language devices that are internalised as inevitable and objective and resist common narratives through a shared agentic alliance. Through this process, it also becomes apparent that contemporary disability discourse, hailed as substantially different from notions of 'subnormalcy' used in the past, continues to be permeated by an ideal and normative conception of personhood, extending the life of historicised ideology in the hegemonic character of current practices and assumptions.

Moreover, the analysis engages with the ways in which, throughout the process of diagnosis, mothers and children's identities become tangled and intimately related, bringing to the surface mechanisms that serve to remove individuality, repositioning motherhood as a social site inducing social isolation and blame, and no longer a relational human experience.

Ethical premise

Finding a coherent correspondence between hearing personal stories in the interviews and developing an ethical discussion in the analysis meant engaging with theory that could do justice to the nature of the encounters with mothers and fathers, through a respectful and reflexive process. I was also mindful that the research encounters should not reproduce existing hierarchical divides. This premise extends to articulating parents' contributions in writing, so it was important to convey a narrative that values the significance of personal stories without contracting these into abstraction. The risk of framing individuals as subjects in 'writing' research, at the expense of social action, not only has important ethical implications, but also reduces the sociological value of participants' agency. Self-expression and personal contributions to research thus become moments of radical intervention.

Gramsci's (1992) notions of collective civic enterprise, the potential of participation and individuals' agency in subverting passivity and inaction, continue to be influential in the development of radical research, despite the persistence of hegemonic forces circulating around it. Tracing the heritage and relevance of Gramsci's sociological and linguistic thinking with his views on intellectuals (researchers) and the privileged opportunity to develop and propel critical consciousness has encouraged me to commit to dialogic research, offering a way to embody an ethical and socially active role – with participants – that counters 'subjectifying' and regulating identities. This type of critical consciousness enables an alliance between insular actors through a research process that engages social action beyond the 'page', making theoretical and practical connections and solidarity explicit. Through a respectful process of dialogue, it is possible to present meaning and personal perspectives in ways that engage their individual and collective value, and political weight. The analysis of localised perspectives thus uncovers common themes, making it possible to denounce systemic habits of disempowerment that can propagate precarity and pathologising redescriptions of humanity, affecting the status of childhood and parenthood.

The work of Antonio Gramsci is often limited, through habit, to reflections and questions of political partisanship and explorations of Marxist thought; this can be reductive. Gramsci's thinking is accidentally unacknowledged or underexplored in dis/ability scholarship and social activism countering ableism and the marginalisation it produces (Bernardi, 2019, Shakespeare, 2014). Gramsci's legacy offers salient indicators that help to map the political inferences that burden individual agency and identity, that are critical factors in the lives of people with disabilities, making the boundaries and hierarchies of political dominance – that exist at a granular level – explicit. Such hierarchies appear to keep those identified as the 'weakest' in society in check and confined, by devaluing difference and resilience and by reconfiguring their social participation and worth. Gramsci primes our thinking and invigorates questioning, rather than soliciting answers. Through a dedicated study of social injustices, resulting from an insistence in maintaining social stratifications, Gramsci – informed by his formal education in linguistics (Ives, 2009) – draws attention to language perpetuating inequality, and is particularly relevant to studying the contours of dis/ability labelling.

Diagnosis as a point of departure

During the fieldwork, I interviewed the parents of each of the children involved in the study individually and as a couple. Although the interviews were conducted with both parents, thus merging and valuing the distinct, shared and equally significant perspectives of mothers and fathers, for the purpose of my contribution to this handbook I have chosen to re-engage with the views and experiences of mothers. A dedicated analysis of mothers' perceptions gives rise to synergies between motherhood and childhood, from the inception of the diagnosis.

In their interviews, parents rarely mentioned the term autism; their rejection or omission gave prevalence to the (word) diagnosis, its effects and the medical 'aura' that circulated around it. Mothers entered, with their children, a territory comparable with chronic illness, oscillating between irremovable 'incurable' disability and correctional ideology, expressed in the sense of urgency to adhere to regulatory norms, therapies (behavioural and medical) and a departure from childhood in its liberal and playful form. New expectations imposed a constant need to be available for appointments, adapting to bureaucratic demands and jargon, interrupting family life as well as parents' employment and children's education (Brewer, 2018). Parents expressed the view that to adhere to these demands was imperative. In their talk, mothers began to explore the tensions between feeling the pressure of following treatments or therapy (with much doubt felt around their efficacy), fear around disrupting children's development if they interrupted any of the prescribed practices, and the unequal and conditional relationship with the individuals acting as gatekeepers for access to specialised assistance. "Life is exhausting" was a recurring comment during the interviews. Mothers expressed and embodied their struggle as a form of conditioning, a sense of dependence on medical protocols and authority, thus attending to a (new) imposed identity while having a natural desire to protect, explore and respect the personhood and personality of their children. To begin to appreciate the significance of such societal and hegemonic pressures, three critical examples are put forward, taken from transcripts of individual unstructured interviews with three mothers, and my field notes. These examples are important in support of some of the themes and facets of experience that emerged across the interviews in dialogue with mothers (and fathers), as well as signalling the value of a non-hierarchical relationship that was formed between participants and me. This type of ethical research relationship was founded on a shared language, my commitment to the delicacy of the stories told and an understanding of mothers' marginal position in everyday life. It became clear that the interviews provided a safe space for reflection and analysis of factors and conditions permeating daily life, childhood and parenthood, and would suggest that my role was perceived to be one of collaboration and allegiance. In drawing attention to the relational and 'listening' character of the interviews, I would argue that this kind of membership in the research process, away from the social gaze invoking judgement and marginalisation, helped to establish and value parents' sociological competence and awareness, expressed in their articulations of complex social dynamics to attempt to resist or challenge the status quo. In contrast, far from promoting participation, the processes that lead to the formulation of the diagnosis serve to create a social imbalance that distinguishes children and disenfranchises parents. To appreciate this imbalance, it is useful to consider the role that language plays in demarcating differences as fault, illness and disadvantage, in ways that can be both pervasive and enduring.

The excerpts presented here are representative of the type of self-reflection that became manifest in mothers' exposition of their experience that led to an understanding of the duality of their role: one of protection and consensus (Runswick-Cole and Ryan, 2019). What mothers chose to share and return to was also indicative of the relationships developed during the period of study (March to May 2017). Mothers planned not only the location and timeframe of the interviews but also the leading thread for exploring their experiences and personal priorities.[1] The testimonies presented here become an explicit attempt to disrupt canonical descriptions of ability, through participation in research as social action, consciousness and dissent.

Mara's story

Mara described herself as a busy mum and secondary maths teacher. Like other mothers, Mara spoke of a simultaneous transformation of her own and her son's identity from the inception of Fabio's diagnosis to his participation in school.

During the first interview, Mara recounted her pregnancy as a time of excitement, reflection, preparation and readiness, and "in spite of an early Caesarean", when Fabio arrived, "all was well". By the time Fabio was 8 months, Mara recalled noticing something "was missing".

Mara: It was only me noticing these differences, shared attention, the gesture of pointing, and so on. I spoke to the paediatrician, and she wasn't too concerned, telling me that all children have their own timings. We arrived at 18 months, 18 months (!), and I returned to the doctor, I was worried it was me.

> We initially took Fabio for an informal observation at the home of friend a neuropsychiatrist (as suggested by our doctor). She watched him play, and she too observed traces of ...[2]
>
> And, within 10, 15 days, admission to hospital was planned and we began the unnerving process.

FB: So you were both, mom and baby, hospitalised. Is this usual in your experience?

Mara: In Italy yes, oh yes, it is.

> And then they practically didn't observe the baby at all. In the sense that they turned him inside out like a sock, blood tests, metabolic tests and chromosomes and ...
>
> and you know, various eye scans. CAN YOU IMAGINE? [at] 20 months, eye scans!
>
> It was a nightmare, he did other tests asleep, a series of checks ... for which all outcomes were in the norm, from a genetic point of view too, but of course we don't know the genetics ... they excluded celiac issues. So, we 'arrived' at the cognitive-behavioural [diagnosis] at 22 months (about 2 years) and in October, so Fabio wasn't even 2 years old, can you imagine?
>
> So small, so when I think back, oh! If I think about it ...

Mara returned to the medical protocol and procedures at different points in this and the subsequent two interviews, noting how a sense of indifference and patriarchy dominated conversations with doctors (almost always male) and how her sense of defeat and impotence determined that she adhered to normative practices, although in retrospect she would have avoided these.

Sofia's story

The following excerpts are taken from two consecutive interviews with Sofia, a quietly spoken and reserved woman, who described herself as a single mum and part-time primary school support teacher. By this stage, Sofia had become familiar with the research activities and gained confidence in sharing her doubts, fears and wishes. And after a notably cathartic rendition of her discontent, Sofia paused to question her right to express her anger at a system that has served to define and redefine her son.

Sofia (second interview)

> He had a thousand diagnoses, all different from each other.
>
> At this point I want a new opinion ... then they discharged him ...
>
> First, they told me the child has problems of attention, then DSA,[3] from DSA he came out, then they told me ADHD. Then ... even Asperger, just because they want to keep control over him, I don't know ... I feel very trapped ...
>
> Can I say those things?
>
> ...
>
> Luigi is such an affectionate son and the views of the clinic are completely different, it makes me and him very angry.
>
> They want to keep control over him.

Sofia's assertive tone and her perplexity and anger at the evolving nature of her son's diagnosis were expressive of her mistrust towards the medical authorities and the individuals progressively involved in trying to impose a medicalised label on her son's identity and personhood. Luigi had been placed in a position of distinction, withdrawing him from an imagined canon of normalcy. Yet, the ever-changing diagnostic outcomes, which could be easily moved and adjusted (on paper), appeared to describe him in different, more or less acceptable terms, interchangeably human and dishuman (Goodley and Runswick-Cole, 2016; Watson, 2018).

Sofia's example shows an attempt to intervene in the expected cycle of dependency on the institution represented by the local clinic, and disabling discourse more generally, by "refusing disability" (Davies, 2018, p. 77, Bernardi, 2019). The stigma of diagnosis and labels therefore not only appears to have an immediate presence within a personal and intimate identity, it also represents a linear trajectory of fear and disempowerment that parents foresee. Sofia was particularly upset by the idea that the diagnosis used to describe her son could be easily removed and changed, with significant implications to be expected in the immediate future and long-term social participation. From a discursive/linguistic perspective it is also important to give weight to the absences that Sofia creates by omitting individual titles and depersonalising roles (the clinic, they) as a way of reinforcing – in her own terms – the structural differentiation between her position and that of the institution pursuing a hegemonic force on her son.

While parents' discourse around medical patriarchy and their perceived "lower position" (Anna, mother) was sometimes only implied, Sofia progressively untangled the social dynamics that had involved – and were continuing to involve – her and her son. By repeating "they want to keep control over him", Sofia assessed the status quo to resist the repositioning of her child. However, when she paused to check the legitimacy of her observations, she demonstrated that the disempowerment and subordination that become inscribed in adults and children's identities are pervasive beyond the place-bound hierarchies from which they originate (Bhabha, 1994, Davies, 2018).

During the third interview, Sofia returned to the issue of imposing labels and linguistic inferences that implied a "problem, something to be monitored and to be seen in a negative light"; the openness and trust that had developed in our conversations appeared to create a sense of alliance that enabled a boundless position of dialogue and denouncement. This way, Sofia introduced her own views and drew attention to how she challenged the redescriptions of qualities and capabilities, while refusing to assume a subordinate identity.

Sofia (third interview)

I call him little engineer, he spends a lot of time building, working with blocks, even wood, he creates model ships, at the [medical] Centre they tell me "that's a restricted interest, if he spends that many hours like that". I say if he has particular attention, attention for these kinds of hobbies, they shut me down with "it's a restricted interest so it's obvious why he spends many hours like that".

Anna's story

The following excerpts are taken from three consecutive interviews with Anna. She works part-time, is married, and has two children, the eldest, Andrea was "diagnosed with autism". Anna began her story by explaining her son had been prescribed medication to "manage behaviour" which teachers and his peers had been "scared of in school". Anna focused on the difference in Andrea's status in spaces regulated by adults in school and at the local clinic.

Anna: At preschool he was like a little robot, he didn't like the rules. At home he was in his territory, while at school he turned into another child. The teacher also had a very high tone of voice so with the very high tone he tended to hit himself on the ears, to hide in any dark hole. They often found him hiding where they hung the coats.

Anna explained she felt the preschool teacher pressurised her to seek medical advice from a neuropsychiatrist, and consequently she began the process of diagnosis; "we are mothers first then become experts in bureaucracy … we [Andrea and his family] were *channelled*" into abnormality (Davies, 2018).

Anna: He had a contrary reaction dependent on how teachers spoke to him, he would put himself and others in danger, but all of this for me was new, the way he was at home didn't reflect what they were describing. I felt disorientated, one of the teachers had no empathy, she didn't greet him when we arrived in the morning, he'd wrap himself around my leg telling me "mummy I don't want to stay"; with the other teacher he was happy for me to leave. She'd take him to draw, she'd wait for him, this helped me relax and able to go to work.

My mother would pick him up every afternoon, and every day would report back that she found him sat alone in punishment.

He was punished every afternoon.

I moved him from the preschool, because at this point he was labelled, whatever happened it was Andrea's fault. You could see the child had a discomfort and it's an enduring thing.

"It was this witnessing of disciplinary power" (Davies, 2018, p. 73) that led Anna to review the context of her son's mood change. The material distinction between Andrea and the other children in the group was perpetuated and justified by the discourses that encircled Andrea's personhood; the diagnosis "was used to separate him instead of getting to know him".

Analysis

Through a symbiotic exchange of parents' narratives on the page, the analysis brings to the fore commonalities of experience and the persistent habit to medicalise difference, pre-empting and dictating outcomes perceived as natural and inevitable, insisting on a common-sense (in the Gramscian connotation) definition of difference, as a problem that produces notions of need, dependency, vulnerability and rehabilitation.

Common themes and experiences become more apparent as mothers begin to weave together different threads, that evidence patterns of subordination and control, merging the genesis of diagnosis with articulations of power and class. Children and mothers enter a process in which their identities merge and co-evolve, thus intimate constructions of childhood and parenthood become open to scrutiny and are depersonalised. The exemplars from the collection of the Italian interviews show that self-reflection strategies and interpretations are adopted, by parents, to respond to social distinctions that serve to anticipate and shape children's prospects, evidencing an external insistence on a reductive construction of their roles and of their children's potential.

Medical authority (authorship) versus motherhood

Mothers' talk and reflections emphasise a feeling of impotence and defeat in their attempts to initiate and enter an equitable dialogue with medical staff as well as with education practitioners, who appear to expand – overtly or inherently – the reach and correctness of medical discourse. The influence of a heavily medicalised culture and the routinisation of testing, the latter seldom accompanied by an explanation of its uses made explicit to parents, evidences a conception of autism as a categorical distinction that delimits participation and humanity.

Medical language dominates exchanges referring to children in and beyond the clinical setting (where therapies are prescribed and visits occur) and, concurrently, medical jargon becomes commonsensical, as it is adopted and used by family members to further scrutinise children's behaviours and mothers' competence (see Anna's example). Pathologising language is also seen to distinguish medical authority and motherhood in ways that resemble class differences (Lareau, 2011), shifting identity authorship to the individuals addressing mothers (usually paediatric neuropsychiatrists), turning children's presence into absence (Watson, 2018) and personhood into abstraction. "Subordination and consensus" (Anna) appeared to be an inevitable characteristic of the shaping of the diagnosis, while concurrently foreclosing mothers' views, interpretations and expertise that pertained to their children, against a tendency to produce a "generic description of symptoms" (Sofia). Furthermore, a culture of insistence on rationalising 'normal' and gathering clout and consensus by labelling and pathologising difference also maintains the asymmetry between medical authority and validating motherhood (Landsman, 2005, Chivers Yochim and Silva, 2013).

Language and disabling distinctions

Language functions in diverse ways to create divisions. This premise engages a reading of Gramsci through his philological education, offering a route to understanding his thought, his philosophy and sociology, preceding and during his incarceration, and thus is crucial in my analysis. Gramsci frequently returns to language in his writings, and particularly to the morphing of language in society and over time. By studying the ways in which institutions (represented here by medical and educational discourse) can appear to promote improvements in equality through 'new' linguistic devices that mimic change, Gramsci acknowledges that such devices – while appealing – are not representative of the assumptions and perceptions that materialise in societal attitudes (Gramsci, 2018/1918, Hodge, 2016). This reading of Gramsci is useful in appreciating the ways in which naming dis/ability has changed while societal structures continue to underscore difference as defect with a propensity to classify human identities. These ideas are critical in the analysis of the language(s) of distinction, participation and resistance and, in a similar vein, Gramsci argues that language can conceal apparent shifts that are evident in dis/ability discourse.

Gramsci's contributions (for example) to critical pedagogy, feminism and dis/ability scholarship that explicitly endorses social justice are not acknowledged directly, making it difficult to engage with his political and civic theories and his own physical condition, the constrictions of his body, his mental and physical health, in ways that account for human sensitivities, struggle and marginalisation that are of vital importance in a dis/ability/human rights context (Goodley, Liddiard and Runswick-Cole, 2018, Ledwith, 2009, Fiori, 2004).

The changing shape of motherhood, disenfranchisement and confinement

Individual testimonies tell equivalent stories, a choral narrative that signals parents and their children are marked by the diagnosis. In the general formulaic social ensemble, being defined as an outsider – an impurity – produces a range of reactions that are variously challenged. In some cases, the sense of injustice is stark. Parents signal the pressures of judgement that transpire in the implicit and explicit views of those situated outside the familial circle, and occasionally from within such an intimate dimension of social life. In philosophical or pragmatic terms, this judgement produces exclusions that imply an inability to contribute to society and daily life and is determined by the medical assumptions that distinguish identities, separating individuals from others who are deemed to be sufficiently fit to have an effective role in the economic mechanisms of local and national productivity. In some cases, parents refuse these assumptions, defending their children's identities from medical views and social glares based on normative and economic imperatives (Davies, 2018, Landsman, 2005).

The diagnosis is initially perceived as a decision, a description, consecrated by the medical authority of the individual producing it; a document upon which a new identity exists, and is forged. In the views of parents, the diagnosis represents the commencement of a "battle against hostile views" towards "not what we had become, but rather what we were not (anymore)" (Mara, mother). The diagnosis is described as a visible block that makes accessing assumed freedoms facilitated by 'normalcy' difficult, determining a deeply segregated family life from its inception. From the mothers' perspectives, this also meant that their paths would seldom intersect with those of other mothers.

> As a mom I have never been integrated, I mean with other mothers, *once* we were 'invited' to a (child's) birthday party, if I could go back, I wouldn't have gone.
> *(Anna)*

For this mother, the defining role of the diagnosis stands in opposition to "freedoms other mothers enjoy" (ibid.), and for whom socialisation in and through motherhood is an intrinsic aspect of their identity (Runswick-Cole, 2014, Farrugia, 2009, Cosslett, 1994). Motherhood after the diagnosis takes a different form, often enmeshed in the tensions of the excessive bureaucratic demands from local clinicians and national protocols (Onnis, 2013, Ryan and Runswick-Cole, 2008). Motherhood also acquires the role of a shield of protection for the intimate life of the family, a space to be defended against "spectators" (Anna). For others, motherhood has the potential of restricting opportunities for self-representation in front of a patriarchal system charged with influencing medical, educational and social decision-making, thus limiting the decisional authority of the parent.

The traditional view of motherhood as the chief carer is encircled within a myriad of further responsibilities, which involve identity negotiations and renegotiations, advocacy and bureaucracy, that group mothers and their children as inevitably different from the mothers and children situated in spaces where privileges and self-made meanings constitute the norm.

> A norm is factual if it has imperative power. On the basis of a factual norm, a person who breaks the rule can be punished or at least criticised.
> *(Huttenen and Heikkinen, 1998, p. 314)*

It looks like it could be a copy-and-paste exercise.

The written diagnosis provoked anxiety in mothers as it resembled a "list of criticisms" of both the mother and the child. One mother reported the use of female pronouns referring to her son, causing anger at the disproportionate scrutiny and testing that had led to the diagnosis while another person's document had been used as a template. Documents pertaining each diagnosis were similar, potentially interchangeable, making tangible some of the underlining dynamics in the relationship with "the clinic". On the one hand, eliciting reflections on a mechanical process detached from any potential shared meaning-making or co-production, albeit between adults constructing a child's identity from – for example – a parental and a clinical perspective; on the other hand, the lack of individual characteristics and character evoked a dehumanising intent, through a stigmatised assessment entailing 'remedial' trajectories (Goodley, 2014, Farrugia, 2009). The diagnosis was an abstract document concerning the initiation of an "uphill struggle" (Sofia) of assigning a specific identity to the child, but also determining significant differences that uphold forms of disablism that reconfigure and redeploy motherhood.

Such a struggle was felt to be debilitating, exacerbated by negotiations with family members embodying the cultural status quo, extending a palpable absence of social solidarity. Gossip, fear of judgement and isolation meant family and work relationships were also impacted by the 'diagnosis' and its power to disrupt expectations that others 'outside' had artificially removed from parents and children's life trajectories (Brewer, 2018). The interviews provided the impetus to examine how abstraction had been produced through language, to revise the fixity implied in the written diagnosis, while offering possibilities to distil identities and extract meaning in ways that could redress the tendency to establish more or less human identities and tangential childhoods.

> In this process, we are also forced to reanalyse what constitutes subversion and resistance, and how the subjective and the political intersect.
>
> *(Steedman et al., 2016, p.2)*

Motherhood and subalternity

The interviews highlight that language becomes a vector of social differentiation. The powers at play in language use produce distinctions that resemble and reinforce class ideology, permeating medical discourse and assigning authority to the individuals and the institutions identifying difference as both meaningful and necessary. The analysis offers a social 'reading' of diagnosis that can help to recognise the political and economic functions of disabling language which, as the Italian exemplars emphasise, not only categorises difference but also serves to initiate a progressive form of control and dependency (Onnis, 2013, Henriques et al., 1998).

Redefining childhood

Medicalised discourse can sift children into 'fields' that maintain the same societal and concrete divisions that situate dis/abled and non-dis/abled lives on parallel routes that rarely merge. In research, this is often the outcome of academic abstraction and fixedness, positioning 'the study' of dis/abled children and childhood into fields/schools with distinct methodological and practical approaches that assume children's ability or inability to participate, *a priori*, at the expense of 'boundless', fair, relevant and autonomous representation (Bernardi, 2020, Alderson, 2017). Children's identities and their agency become the subject of ableist categorisation, denoting who fits and who does not, within a sociology of childhood that also permeates motherhood (Runswick-Cole and Ryan, 2019). This habit prolongs societal divisions and determines that certain freedoms, independence and personal development, enjoyed by some children, are "withheld from children assigned a diagnosis of difference" (Bernardi, 2020, p.67). Avoiding this type of academic fixedness has become the ethical thread of the research and projects I conduct with children and families. Parents' reactions signal that the problem of foreclosing participation produces reductive representations of children, their views, lives, interests and priorities that are not confined to research discourse. In sociological terms, this exposes an attachment to an ideal configuration of childhood that encompasses some children and not others. Disrupting discourses of cognition, language and ability, it is possible to produce a meeting of ideas, intersecting fields and thoughts that engage children's human potential (Goodley and Runswick-Cole 2016, Goodley et al., 2016) and integrate diverse views, feelings and experiences in childhood discourse.

Why the data matters

The interviews with mothers in Italy highlight situated practices characterised by the persistence of descriptions of deviance and pathology that pervade the process of diagnosis, maintaining the assumed authority of medicalised discourses.

While contemporary language and labels are more accommodating of general aspirations for equality, diversity and inclusion (Davies, 2016, Slee, 1997), the discourses and practices discussed in the interviews exposed antiquated, irrelevant and even immoral assumptions, dehumanising children's identities and parents' roles in ways that crystallise positions of subalternity and misappropriate children's and adults' expectancies and rights. Terminology associated with societal advances would appear to be at the core of universally accepted improvements in participation. Such terminology is assumed to have affirmative potential (Gramsci, 1918/2018, Simpson, 2011), yet the intrinsic and, in some instances, substantial insistence on (medicalised) definitions of dis/ability has not been surpassed and determines that current attitudes to difference continue to be the product of historical legacies that pervade the present.

Parents shared their experiences of the Italian medical protocols by unveiling the economic imperative that informs them. The diagnostic frameworks described signal explicit forms of cultural exclusion (Slee, 2019, Oliver, 1996), and their effects on the co-evolving identities of mothers and their children, producing ideological and disabling constructions of motherhood itself. A sociological analysis of these experiences captures the intersections of class, ableism and gender (Kumari Campbell, 2008, Corker and Davis, 2002) that materialise in a medical framing of difference that stifles parental agency, situating children's identities in a position of unsurmountable distinction and marginality.

The three 'stories' presented here can be understood as examples of parents' role in understanding the function of existing social positions to which their agency and social identities are anchored and an attempt to subvert a dominant culture of debilitation and control. These narratives are the contextual outcome of a process of reclaiming a parental identity that is otherwise halted in a deeply segregated experience that produces the kind of motherhood that is tangential, inscribed with loss and blame, and is heavily bureaucratised.

Conclusion

This chapter came into being from conversations on the findings and societal implications of research I conducted in Italy and England with children with a diagnosis of autism and their parents (and school practitioners), resulting in critical reflections on the classification of difference and dis/ability and human worth. These conversations, with scholars who have also contributed to this handbook, specifically drew on the peculiarities of the process of diagnosis in the Italian context and their reverberations on the welfare of children and their parents.

Here I have considered some of the ways in which a medicalised conception of autism can affect the trajectory of childhood and motherhood, providing a critical and detailed account of experiences drawn from the interviews, conducted in Italy, and an analysis of language and culturally situated practices that expose a societal dependency on defining difference. The chapter offers an exploration of the implications of a medicalised diagnosis of autism, which appears to be culturally located, as well as the reverberations of medicalised rhetoric (beyond the Italian context) that can persist despite apparent evolutions in linguistic and societal practices. I have argued that below the surface of new forms of language – used to make disability descriptions appear more malleable – there continues to be an influential hegemonic force that situates those deemed to be economically productive in a role of privilege and distinction, confining the 'other' to spaces of inertia, produced by an ideal of ability and normalcy.

Whether through explicit discriminatory discourse, born in a culture of abstraction and medical patriarchy or, more broadly, in the inclination to amalgamate difference, there appears to be an ongoing appropriation of individual identities, used to group, 'treat' and restrict individual decision-making (during and post-diagnosis) and self-presentation. As well as implications of sociological interest, the analysis has shown the active role that mothers can take in research that is premised on respect, self-presentation and solidarity, highlighting the value of women's agency in a dialogic forum that offers the conditions to review and begin to renegotiate their subject positions.

The themes emerging from the interviews offer a generative analysis that troubles outcomes perceived to be natural and inevitable, exposing social structures that emphasise supremacies and produce a narrative imaginary of dis/ability that enforces methods of disempowerment that can disrupt both parenthood and childhood.

Respecting and engaging with stories of confinement and grit

Importantly, the mothers taking part in the study expressed their appreciation for being able to enter a dialogue in which they were able to outline their priorities, feelings and views while re-establishing their role in my presence. Participation in the interviews enabled the possibility of challenging what appeared to be permanent categorisations of children and their families. It is possible that the opportunity to determine their role, in a context that fostered trust and solidarity, motivated mothers to challenge the structural control tangible in places associated with (medical and educational) authority, at once highlighting and removing the boundaries that marked their positions in other contexts. The interviews invited self-presentation in mothers' own terms, in conversations that did not reflect their prior experiences of talking about their children, where hierarchical tensions played a role in influencing their ability to counter what were explicitly recognised as unjust and ill-informed judgements. The interview space produced a shared sense of purpose and hope in parents' perceptions of research participation, with an interest in the possibilities of symbolic and pragmatic conversations with other families situated beyond their (geographical and discursive) 'border', offering a means to participate in socially active self-presentation, to examine personal difficulties, with potential for social change.

The original study focused on children producing and reclaiming their identities through autonomy and creativity (Bernardi, 2019), to reimage children's participatory choices and rights, disrupting persistent discourses of ableism, as well as assumptions – around disinterest and inability to take part – that can permeate research.

By focusing on the interactions with children's mothers that occurred during the study, this chapter provides salient references to examine both the impact of social hierarchies on the lives and well-being of individuals and the role of language in inducing and prolonging marginalisation and othering, for both mother and child.

It is possible, therefore, to recognise that research participation that values personal priorities, agency and self-made identities, can provide a 'space' to challenge the positions of scrutiny, marginalisation and confinement, that other contexts and relationships can exert over parents and children.

The analysis uncovers the influence of human redescriptions, which are routinely observed by parents, who inevitably enter a trajectory of revision of their role and their children's social identity. Taking Gramsci as a humanist thinker offers a useful route into understanding the ways in which disempowerment, consent and marginalisation can channel and encircle social identities, and particularly those identities that become 'reworked' in the (path to a) diagnosis. Furthermore, if one delves further into Gramsci's biography, it is possible to meet an even more poignant, ethical and sensitive contribution of his thinking to the study of ableist rhetoric and social redescriptions. A critical sociological analysis of the interviews shows a dehumanising phase that begins with the inception of a diagnosis, which situates the persons involved in positions of subalternity and confinement through a medicalised process that is legitimised as necessary and authoritative. Such a process can be unpacked using a Gramscian analysis that draws attention to language, positions of power and societal order that can serve to divide, destabilising the ways in which children and their mothers can authenticate their daily lives. Through a non-hierarchical dialogue, mothers (and fathers) were able to take part in a process of consciousness-building that can be useful in reimaging difference, participation and parenthood, through solidarity and respect.

The analysis therefore takes into consideration an understanding of my role and positioning in the context of this research, an appreciation of societal structures (that can permeate research relationships) and Gramsci's contribution to unpacking the nature of societal interactions and the role of language in regulating these, determining the direction of dominant discourses of privilege and difference. The extracts from the interviews shine a light on the ways parents view their roles and their co-location in a space where the diagnosis becomes an attempt to limit theirs and their children's self-presentation. Moreover, the analysis examines pre-existing social patterns and social factions and a propensity to categorise human potential, in the process of diagnosis.

In this chapter, I have not attempted to produce an assessment of the historical legacy of the habitual segregation of children into disabled and abled identities, nor will my writing function to disperse the relevance and personal value attributed to the diagnosis as experienced – first hand – by the individuals who contributed candidly and generously to the research that led to this discussion. Rather, I have argued that the assumed authority of some social actors over others and the language associated with such authority, continues to demonstrate that contemporary approaches to dis/ability bear the daunting weight of a persistent economic stance towards human value and potential. Such a stance serves to justify sifting individuals and groups according to their assumed economic productivity, upholding ideas of risk posed by the possibility of 'trespassing' on privileged grounds.

Notes

1 Culturally sensitive pseudonyms are used throughout the chapter to maintain anonymity.
　... Indicates moments in which participants paused during the interviews.
2 Like other parents, Mara omits the word autism, which is implied in other interviews.
3 DSA is used here to mean *Disturbi dello Spettro Autistico* (Disorders of the Autistic Spectrum), in other instances it is used as an acronym for *Disturbi Specifici dell'Apprendimento* (Specific Learning Disorders).

References

Alderson, P. (2008) Children as researchers. Participation rights and research methods. In: P. Christensen and A. James (eds), *Research with Children: Perspectives and Practices*, 2nd ed. Abingdon: Routledge, pp. 276–290. https://link.springer.com/chapter/10.1007/978-94-007-1617-9_5.

Alderson, P. (2017) Utopian research with children. In: P. Christensen and A. James (eds), *Research with Children: Perspectives and Practices*, 3rd ed. London: Routledge, pp. 203–222.

Bernardi, F. (2019) *Reclaiming Childhood. Disrupting Discourses of Identity, Autonomy and Dis/Ability, Adopting Arts-Based Methods, Gramsci and Bourdieu. A Cross-Cultural Study in Central Italy and North West England*. Doctoral Thesis. Edge Hill University. Ormskirk. https://research.edgehill.ac.uk/en/studentTheses/reclaiming-childhood-disrupting-discourses-of-identity-autonomy-a.

Bernardi, F. (2020) Autonomy, spontaneity and creativity in research with children. A study of experience and participation, in central Italy and North West England. *International Journal of Social Research Methodology*, 23(1), pp. 55–74. https://doi.org/10.1080/13645579.2019.1672280.

Bhabha, H.K. (1994) *The Location of Culture*. New York: Routledge.

Bieler, A. and Morton, A.D. (2004) A critical theory route to hegemony, world order and historical change: Neo-Gramscian perspectives in international relations. *Capital & Class*, 28(1), pp. 85–113. https://doi.org/10.1177/030981680408200106.

Bieler, A. and Morton, A.D. (eds) (2001) *Social Forces in the Making of the New Europe: The Restructuring of European Social Relations in the Global Political Economy*. Basingstoke: Palgrave Macmillan.

Bourdieu, P. (2018/1973) Cultural reproduction and social reproduction. In: R. Brown (ed.), *Knowledge, Education, and Cultural Change Papers in the Sociology of Education*. Abingdon: Routledge, pp. 71–113.

Brewer, A. (2018) "We were on our own": Mothers' experiences navigating the fragmented system of professional care for autism. *Social Science and Medicine*, 215, pp. 61–68. https://doi.org/10.1016/j.socscimed.2018.08.039.

Chivers Yochim, E. and Silva, V.T. (2013) Everyday expertise, autism, and "good" mothering in the media discourse of Jenny McCarthy. *Communication and Critical/Cultural Studies*, 10(4), pp. 406–426. https://doi.org/10.1080/14791420.2013.841320.

Corker, M. and Davis, J.M. (2002) Portrait of Callum. The disabling of a childhood? In: R. Edwards (ed.), *Children, Home and School: Regulation, Autonomy or Connection?* London: Falmer, pp. 79–91.

Cosslett, T. (1994) *Women Writing Childbirth: Modern Discourses of Motherhood*. Manchester: Manchester University Press.

Davies, K. (2016) How rude? Autism as a study in ability. In: K. Runswick-Cole, R. Mallett and S. Timimi (eds), *Re-Thinking Autism. Diagnosis, Identity and Equality*. London: Jessica Kingsley Publishers, pp. 132–145.

Davies, K. (2018) Going 'off grid': A mother's account of refusing disability. In: K. Runswick-Cole, T. Curran and K. Liddiard (eds), *The Palgrave Handbook of Disabled Children's Childhood Studies*. London: Palgrave Macmillan, pp. 71–80.

Diez, T. (2013) Normative power as hegemony. *Cooperation and Conflict*, 48(2), pp. 194–210. https://doi.org/10.1177/0010836713485387.

Farrugia, D. (2009) Exploring stigma: Medical knowledge and the stigmatisation of parents of children diagnosed with autism spectrum disorder. *Sociology of Health and Illness*, 31(7), pp. 1011–1027. https://doi.org/10.1111/j.1467-9566.2009.01174.x.

Fiori, G. (2004) *Vita di Antonio Gramsci*. Nuoro: Ilisso.

Goodley, D. (2014) *Dis/Ability Studies. Theorising Disablism and Ableism*. Abingdon: Routledge.

Goodley, D., Liddiard, K. and Runswick-Cole, K. (2018) Feeling disability: Theories of affect and critical disability studies. *Disability and Society*, 33(2), pp. 197–217. https://doi.org/10.1080/09687599.2017.1402752.

Goodley, D. and Runswick-Cole, K. (2016) Becoming dishuman: Thinking about the human through disability. *Discourse: Studies in the Cultural Politics of Education*, 37(1), pp. 1–15. https://doi.org/10.1080/01596306.2014.930021.

Goodley, D., Runswick-Cole, K. and Liddiard, K. (2016) The DisHuman child. *Discourse: Studies in the Cultural Politics of Education*, 37(5), pp. 770–784. https://doi.org/10.1080/01596306.2015.1075731.

Gramsci, A. (1992) *Selections from the Prison Notebooks*. Trans. Q. Hoare and G. Nowell Smith. London: Lawrence and Wishart.

Gramsci, A. (2018/1918) *Odio gli indifferenti*. Milano: Chiarelettere Editore Srl.

Henriques, J., Hollway, W., Urwin, C., Venn, C. and Walkerdine, V. (eds) (1998) *Changing the Subject: Psychology, Social Regulation and Subjectivity*. Abingdon: Routledge.

Hodge, N. (2016) Schools without labels. In: K. Runswick-Cole, R. Mallett and S. Timimi (eds), *Re-Thinking Autism. Diagnosis, Identity and Equality*. London: Jessica Kingsley Publishers, pp. 185–203.

Huttenen, R. and Heikkinen, H.L. (1998) Between fact and norms: Action research in the light of Jurgen Habermas's theory of communicative action and discourse theory of justice. *Curriculum Studies. A Journal of Educational Discussion and Debate*, 6(3), pp. 307–322. https://doi.org/10.1080/14681369800200041.

Ives, P. (2009) Global English, hegemony and education: Lessons from Gramsci. *Educational Philosophy and Theory*, 41(6), pp. 661–683. https://doi.org/10.1111/j.1469-5812.2008.00498.x.

Kumari Campbell, F.A. (2008) Exploring internalized ableism using critical race theory. *Disability and Society*, 23(2), pp. 151–162. https://doi.org/10.1080/09687590701841190.

Landsman, G. (2005) Mothers and models of disability. *Journal of Medical Humanities*, 26(2–3), pp. 121–139. https://doi.org/10.1007/s10912-005-2914-2.

Lareau, A. (2011) *Unequal Childhoods: Class, Race, and Family Life*. London: University of California Press Ltd.

Ledwith, M. (2009) Antonio Gramsci and feminism: The elusive nature of power. *Educational Philosophy and Theory*, 41(6), pp. 684–697. https://doi.org/10.1111/j.1469-5812.2008.00499.x.

Oliver, M. (1996) Understanding disability: From theory to practice. *Journal of Sociology and Social Welfare*, 23(3), pp. 191–194. https://scholarworks.wmich.edu/jssw/vol23/iss3/24/.

Onnis, S. (2013) Il dis-positivo. Dal diritto vigente alla nuda vita delle persone con disabilità intellettiva. (The dis-positive. From existing rights to the real life of people with intellectual disabilities). *Italian Journal of Disability Studies*, 1(1), pp. 109–132. http://www.edizionianicia.it/docs/Rivista_Vol1_N1.pdf.

Orton, M. (2011) Flourishing lives: The capabilities approach as a framework for new thinking about employment, work and welfare in the 21st century. *Work, Employment and Society*, 25(2), pp. 352–360. https://doi.org/10.1177/0950017011403848.

Runswick-Cole, K. (2014) 'Us' and 'them': The limits and possibilities of a 'politics of neurodiversity' in neoliberal times. *Disability and Society*, 29(7), pp. 1117–1129. https://doi.org/10.1080/09687599.2014.910107.

Runswick-Cole, K. and Ryan, S. (2019) Liminal still? Unmothering disabled children. *Disability and Society*, 34(7–8), pp. 1125–1139. https://doi.org/10.1080/09687599.2019.1602509.

Ryan, F. (2020) *Crippled. Austerity and the Demonization of Disabled People*. London: Verso.

Ryan, S. and Runswick-Cole, K. (2008) Repositioning mothers: Mothers, disabled children and disability studies. *Disability and Society*, 23(3), pp. 199–210. https://doi.org/10.1080/09687590801953937.

Shakespeare, T. (2014) Antonio Gramsci. In: *Great Lives*. BBC RADIO 4. 2 September. 1630 hrs. https://www.bbc.co.uk/programmes/b04fz6ky.

Simpson, J. (ed.) (2011) *The Routledge Handbook of Applied Linguistics*. Abingdon: Routledge.

Slee, R. (1997) *Ain't Misbehavin': The Politics of Special Educational Needs and Disruption*. London: Goldsmiths.

Slee, R. (2019) Belonging in an age of exclusion. *International Journal of Inclusive Education*, 23(9), pp. 909–922. https://doi.org/10.1080/13603116.2019.1602366.

Steedman, C., Urwin, C. and Walkerdine, V. (eds) (2016) *Language, Gender and Childhood*. Abingdon: Routledge.

Van Aswegen, J. and Shevlin, M. (2019) Disabling discourses and ableist assumptions: Reimagining social justice through education for disabled people through a critical discourse analysis approach. *Policy Futures in Education*, 17(5), pp. 634–656. https://doi.org/10.1177/1478210318817420.

Watson, T. (2018) The construction of life trajectories: Reflections, research and resolutions for young people with behavioural disabilities. In: K. Runswick-Cole, T. Curran and K. Liddiard (eds), *The Palgrave Handbook of Disabled Children's Childhood Studies*. London: Palgrave Macmillan, pp. 263–280.

10

'IT SORT OF LIKE GETS SQUARED'

Health professionals' understanding of the intersection of autism and gender diversity in young people

Magdalena Mikulak

Introduction

This short chapter examines how gender diversity and autism intersect in the narratives of health professionals working with trans and gender-diverse young people in the UK.[1] Health professionals' understandings of the intersection between gender diversity and autism matter in more than one way. Beyond the obvious role of providing healthcare, health professionals are key in producing and upholding ideas and meanings about the populations, with whom they work. The historical burden of pathologisation of both autism (Silverman, 2017) and gender diversity (Pearce, 2018) and the ongoing consequences of this cannot be seen outside of the power that the psycho-medical professions hold over the collective meanings and by extension, individual destinies. In examining health professionals' understandings of the intersection of gender diversity and autism, this chapter also highlights the additional hurdles that exist for young autistic gender-diverse people when seeking gender-affirming care.

Healthcare is a site fraught with difficulties for both gender-diverse and autistic people. Trans and gender-diverse people continue to face discrimination in healthcare settings (Pearce, 2018, Vincent and Lorimer, 2018, Roller et al., 2015, Poteat et al., 2013, Watkinson and Sunderland, 2017). In England and Wales, gender identity care for children and young people is provided within the NHS by the Gender Identity Development Service (GIDS). The service has clinics in London, Leeds, Bristol and Birmingham. To be seen by a specialist team at the GIDS a young person can be referred by any health, social care or education agency, including voluntary groups. The service has a waiting list, which has grown exponentially in recent years, with waiting times for the first appointment exceeding two years at the time of writing (January 2021). The excessive waiting times combined with lengthy treatment pathways have been identified as a source of mental distress for young trans and gender-diverse people and their families (Carlile, 2020).

At the same time, recent anti-trans mobilisations have brought trans rights and healthcare into the public debate (Pearce et al., 2020). In the UK, this debate has also focused on limiting gender-affirming care interventions for young people. In December 2020, in a high-profile case brought against GIDS, the High Court ruled that young people under 16 are unlikely to be able to give informed consent to undergo treatment with puberty blockers; a development that was seen as an assault on not only trans rights, but on the rights of all young people to make decisions about their bodies and health (Stonewall, 2020).

Autistic people experience significant healthcare disparities (Nicolaidis et al., 2012), healthcare facilities and processes are often inaccessible to them (Nicolaidis et al., 2015), and health professionals have been reported to lack confidence in caring for autistic patients (Unigwe et al., 2017). In the UK, these disparities have been recognised and there have been some efforts made to redress them (see for example Westminster Commission on Autism, 2016).

The limited work done on the intersection of gender diversity and autism in young people suggests that people whose lived experience is characterised by both might face a unique set of challenges. Carlile's study (2020) on healthcare experiences of young trans and non-binary people and their parents found that the presence of an autism diagnosis was perceived to 'slow down clinical and therapeutic input' on the young person's gender identity. Strang et al (2018) highlight how autistic gender-diverse young people can be at risk of being misunderstood in terms of their gender and gender-affirming healthcare needs because they are autistic and, further, may face challenges verbalising and self-advocating for their gender 'due to autism-related social communication differences'. The study found participants experienced difficulties navigating the complexities of gender affirmation to stand out as specific to the co-occurrence of gender diversity and autism. In addition, Strang et al. (2018) observed that young autistic gender-diverse people might have little interest in 'outward traditional binary gender presentations', making it more difficult for them to access and negotiate healthcare and to meet expectations of genderidentity specialists who might act as gatekeepers of gender-affirming care (Pearce, 2018).

Arguably, the challenges that young autistic gender-diverse people face in terms of accessing healthcare are only beginning to be analysed and there is an urgent need to centre the voices of the young people themselves. This chapter does not aim to take away from that need; rather, it points to the necessity of also engaging with health professionals' understandings and experiences of working with young autistic gender-diverse people and the arguments presented here are an invitation to consider what is at stake in *how* and *why* we think about gender diversity and autism together.

Gender diversity and autism co-occur

Autism has been noted to occur more frequently in gender-diverse young people than in the general population (Van Der Miesen et al., 2016) although this connection might have been overemphasised. Turban and van Schalkwyk (2018) argue that current research has *not* established an over-representation of autism in gender-diverse young people, or the converse, and one of the plausible explanations they give for the supposed higher prevalence is that autistic young people might be more likely to seek gender-affirming care, as they might be less concerned with social and gender norms. Here I argue that this is important for several reasons. First, studying gender variance and neurodiversity together can offer productive avenues to explore both. However, and second, the focus on *quantifying* the prevalence of autism in gender-diverse people, or gender diversity in autistic people, too often relies on medicalised and at times pathologising understandings of both. Third, we need to ask to what extent such quantifying endeavours are motivated by a quest for aetiology and what does that tell us about conceptualisations behind it. What we do know is that gender diversity and autism *co-occur*.

Note on methods

This chapter is based on data generated as part of a larger research project on Trans Health (funded by the National Institute for Health Research (NIHR); Grant Reference Number 17/51/07). As part of this project, semi-structured qualitative interviews with 20 health professionals working with young trans and gender-diverse people in the UK were conducted. The telephone interviews were conducted between June 2019 and February 2020 by two researchers, including the author. The health professionals interviewed were recruited purposefully through professional networks of the research team, social media routes, Advisory Group members, local and national support groups, and snowballing through research participants. Participants included mental health and primary care practitioners as well as health professionals working for the specialist gender identity services.

The focus of the interviews was participants' experiences working with young trans and gender-diverse people and their families, as well as health professionals' perceived barriers to good-quality care for these groups. Only the data from interviews in which participants discuss autism explicitly – 14 interviews in total – have been used for the purpose of this chapter. The difference in numbers can be explained partly by the overall focus of the interviews as well as by their semi-structured nature. Whilst the topic guide developed for the interviews included a question about factors that might affect the healthcare experiences of young trans and gender-diverse people, autism was not listed explicitly: 'Could you talk me through the young trans patient journey through health care?' Followed by: 'In your experience, are differences of race, class, ability, sexuality, location, or other relevant factors to how that journey looks?' Some participants brought autism up in response to these questions, whilst, in some interviews it was the interviewers who asked about autism explicitly, in relation to something that the participant said.

The interviews were transcribed, and the data generated was coded and analysed thematically using software (NVivo12). The coding was done by the author and checked by another researcher on the larger research project. 'Autism' emerged as a distinct theme in the process. Drawing on feminist methodologies, the combined data relating to 'Autism' as a theme was then analysed discursively. Feminist discourse analysis aims to 'identify, within a text, institutionally supported and culturally influenced interpretive and conceptual schemas ... that produce particular understandings of issues and events', aiming to interrogate these schemas and show how they 'operate to delimit an issue in specific ways' (Bacchi, 2005).

Health professionals' perceived links, barriers and advantages

In the interviews, several participants spontaneously mentioned the link between autism and gender diversity. For example, one person noted 'I do know that there is quite a strong link between ... gender diversity and the autistic spectrum. Though no definite evidence has come about. I think it's about 10% of the young [gender-diverse] people' (HP_1_B; interview). Another participant observed that there tends to be 'a crossover' between autism and gender diversity (HP_10_B; interview). When asked about working with gender-diverse young people who are autistic, another participant shared 'It's a tricky field, the autistic spectrum. We don't know if it's cause or effect' (HP_5_A; interview). However, being autistic was also perceived to be liberating and the same person thought that as autism might lessen social anxiety around gender expectations and expression, autistic gender-diverse people could be more likely to be open about their gender identity, a point I return to later on in this chapter:

> If you are also on the autistic spectrum those social restrictions are less. And, actually, they [the young person] are more able just to say, 'I don't know what you mean. I am

not a boy, I am a girl', because that social fear isn't there. So, that is one reason I think
that and we need more research in this area. That is one reason why I think that people
who are on the autistic spectrum may find it easier to have less restrictions on themselves to come forward and say, my gender doesn't feel right to me.

(HP_5_A; interview)

Whilst most health professionals took the link between autism and gender diversity as a *fact*, one participant's views stood out as they thought the perceived links and, in particular, any attributed causality were indicative of a lack of understanding, or even a 'crisis of understanding', as they put it:

There are clinicians who are very much seeing gender non-conformity as a symptom of autism and then being quite dismissive of it, or sort of very cautious around it … I think we … have a crisis around understanding autism. I think we have a crisis of understanding [of] the way various different divergent traits intersect and that we do have a lot of commonality between the trans population and the autism population and that doesn't mean to say that autism causes transness or transness causes autism, they co-occur.

(HP_4_B; interview)

This is important, if we consider how search for causality and an attachment to a causal relationship between autism and gender diversity, or the reverse, might reinforce pathologising views of gender diversity and autism, or both. In a context where search for causes has historically gone hand in hand with search for cures and treatment, looking for causality is not a value-free endeavour.

Generally, participants acknowledged the additional challenges that young autistic gender-diverse people face when trying to access gender-affirming healthcare and when going through the existing pathway for gender-diverse young people. Whilst some stressed challenges that they perceived as stemming *from* autism, others pointed to the processes involved in accessing gender-affirming care as distinctively disadvantaging autistic people. One participant observed that neurodiversity, including autism, intersects with gender identity in a way that works to multiply the barriers that a person might face in accessing gender-affirming care, in particular if they are young. They noted:

I think is another kind of systemic barrier for a lot of trans people, because, you know, what I am seeing is a ridiculous amount of trans people will have one other issue … whether it's dyslexia or dyspraxia or autism traits or ADHD traits … and actually these things complicate the picture for them and often make them less likely to be taken seriously, particularly when they are young … I think there is a sort of double thing here … It sort of like gets squared.

(HP_4_B; interview)

Moreover, in relation to accessing gender-affirming care, one participant noted, that 'capacity assessment is harder if you have got a learning disability or autism' (HP_5_B). This is particularly pressing given the recent High Court ruling discussed above, that might further limit access to gender-affirming care for young people, based on their perceived ability to consent to treatment.

Another participant pointed out that issues around expectations of *doing* gender might be more difficult for autistic people:

> If you have sensory issues, you might not want to wear make-up. You might find certain clothing difficult to put on. There might be all sorts of sensory issues around the kinds of things that the gender clinic are telling you you need to do in order to … 'present as a woman'. People will then undermine somebody's identity as a woman because they are not performing 'woman' correctly. If you add into that the autistic tendency to go, 'well stuff what anyone else thinks, I am just going to do it my way'. And you often get autistic people who don't necessarily jump through the kinds of hoops that the gender clinic want them to jump through in order to perform their gender. So that can also be a bit of a barrier.
>
> *(HP_4_B; interview)*

This is important, as it signals that whilst autistic people might be more likely to seek gender-affirming healthcare, as they can be less concerned with conforming to societal gender norms and expectations, once they reach the specialist services, they might encounter a new set of norms around being trans and 'correct' gender presentation, with which they might be expected to comply. In consequence, whilst initially liberating, not conforming to gender stereotypes can generate further barriers for young autistic people down the line in the context of gatekeeping of gender-affirming healthcare and interventions.

Further, and echoing Strang et al.'s (2018) insights, communication as an area that might prove challenging for autistic gender-diverse people was also brought up. Communication can be an issue because barriers in communication might mean that autistic people's gender narratives might not be taken seriously, as one participant observed

> Autistic people—I know that there will be some autistic people that might struggle to relate to or understand their gender because of their autism. For the majority of autistic people it's not a barrier to self-understanding … I don't think there is a lack of self-awareness or self-understanding or even empathy in autistic people. What there is, is … sometimes difficulty in communicating and then those barriers of communication can then mean that people won't necessarily take their narratives or stories seriously.
>
> *(HP_4_B; interview)*

Not being taken seriously is a concern that is particularly pressing in the context of accessing gender-affirming care, where trans and gender-diverse people's narratives are often questioned or challenged (Pearce, 2018, Hilário, 2020). It is plausible that being autistic and trans might compound this issue further because of health professionals' perceptions of whose narratives are credible. However, another participant who discussed communication also stressed the need for the 'right support' and noted that autism does not equal *disadvantage* for gender-diverse people:

> We see a large number of patients with autistic spectrum disorders. For them, sometimes there are things around communication … It can be incredibly helpful when thinking what their needs are like and what might support them in the longer term and helping them to express themselves, which can sometimes be challenging. But again, with the right support I wouldn't say it's a disadvantage in any way. Many of those patients flourish and a lot of patients with autistic spectrum disorders tend to flourish all the more, because often they can be less sensitive to what those around them might perceive them and can really feel very confident and happy in their own identity, where some other people might have more social anxiety. They have different challenges.
>
> *(HP_6_B; interview)*

This is key, as it demonstrates that, when adequately supported, autistic gender-diverse young people can thrive. To ensure that they do, they must be met with a system that is aware of their existence and takes them seriously and with health professionals who can help them overcome, rather than reproduce and/or multiply, barriers to healthcare.

One participant who worked for the gender identity development services noted:

> sometimes we have people who come to us who find speaking very very difficult indeed … we spend a lot of time talking and asking questions and that might be quite difficult for some young people. We would use creative ways of engaging with young people and indeed their families to take the pressure off the kind of verbal focus. That might be writing, drawing, creating different formats.
>
> *(HP_3_B; interview)*

Importantly, the processes of seeking referral to the gender identity services or being assessed by the gender identity specialist team can be difficult for any young person and the skills that the health professionals involved in these processes develop to support their patients should be adaptable to also support their autistic patients. The same participant stressed that when working with autistic gender-diverse young people, the services 'adapt the way that we work' and 'have evolved a range of resources … that give much more focus to pictorial representations and figures that don't give such a focus on language and abstract concepts where that is not people's styles or preferred ways of communicating' (HP_3_B; interview). It is plausible that many non-autistic young people could also benefit from having a range of ways to communicate the often-sensitive issues discussed in gender identity services' appointments. This is particularly vital, given that having one's gender narrative understood and taken seriously can be the difference between being able to access gender-affirming care, or having that access denied. This is not only true for how the specialist gender services work with the young person, but also matters for a timely referral to the service.

Looking for solutions instead of 'causes'

This analysis echoes many of the issues discussed in Strang et al. (2018). There is an awareness that a young autistic gender-diverse person might face additional challenges. This can be due to them not being taken seriously because they are autistic, barriers around communication, or because they might be less able/willing to conform to gendered expectations that the current gender identity healthcare model continues to rely on. How we frame these challenges is important. To acknowledge that autistic gender-diverse people might face additional challenges when accessing general and specialist healthcare is not the same as to position autism or gender diversity, or their intersection, as challenging in and of itself. If, indeed, the difficulties and barriers get squared for young autistic gender-diverse people, the question to ask is, who is responsible for that squaring?

Moreover, in some instances, autism is also perceived as an advantage, insomuch as it is associated with lowered sensitivity to social and gender norms. What does this tell us about the norms that might mean some young gender-diverse people are not willing/able to come out and seek gender-affirming care? It signals their weight and oppressive potential, as well as further highlighting the challenges that young people whose gender identity does not align with gender they were assigned at birth have to overcome to be able to access gender-affirming healthcare. I have also argued that any advantage that might come with autistic people's disregard for gender norms might be limited once the young person reaches gender identity services, where they might be expected to comply with a new set of potentially restrictive norms around gender presentation and being trans. Not being able and/or willing to comply with these norms can have grave consequences as it might complicate or impede access to gender-affirming interventions.

Further, that health professionals are aware of existing barriers is an important and positive finding. However, to acknowledge how health systems produce and maintain these very barriers (and one's own complicity in the process) requires individuals working within the system to turn the mirror onto the existing inadequacies, and sometimes on themselves, as opposed to focusing on the difficulties autism and gender diversity might 'present'. This is particularly pressing in relation to the ongoing quest for aetiology when the intersection of autism and gender diversity is discussed. If, as Turban and van Schalkwyk (2018) argue, the link between autism and gender diversity has been overemphasised, it is worth considering the assumption upon which any statements of causality, or other meaningful relationships, rely. Phrases such as 'strong link' and 'cause and effect', signal a belief that gender diversity and autism are linked by more than just statistical co-occurrence. The question that this invites is, can such search for causality be reconciled with the idea that gender diversity and neurodiversity (of which autism is one expression) are expressions of human diversity? Can ideas of autism and gender diversity be held together without the potentially pathologising need to explain one through the other? My argument is that for a truly non-pathologising and affirming approach, they not only can, but also have to.

How the psycho-medical professionals think about an issue and its links to other factors is hugely consequential for what happens to the people whose lived experiences are marked by that issue. Both autism and gender diversity are areas with many dead angles that have proven difficult to address. Yet, the framing of an issue often restricts our ability to engage with it. For example, mental health conditions are said to be more prevalent in autistic people; however, more recently, the minority stress model has been used to explain this disparity, pointing to the centrality of the negative social factors (Botha and Frost, 2020) and away from potentially harmful circular arguments. Similarly, how health professionals understand the relationship between autism and gender diversity affects their ability to respond sensitively, adequately and affirmingly to the needs of young autistic gender-diverse people. Instead of looking for aetiology, their collective energies would be put to better use making sure that the healthcare services upon which young autistic gender-diverse people rely are accessible, inclusive and focused on the individual. Making sure their own understandings of gender diversity and autism, and the intersection of the two, do not contribute to the multiplying of barriers that young autistic gender-diverse people face seems like a good place to begin.

Disclaimer

This chapter summarises independent research funded by the National Institute for Health Research (NIHR) under its Health Services and Delivery Research Programme (Grant Reference Number 17/51/07). The views expressed are those of the author, and not necessarily those of the NHS, the NIHR or the Department of Health.

Note

1 I am aware that 'trans and gender diverse' and 'autism' are not stable categories. I choose these terms over – equally, if not more unstable and contested – medical diagnostic terms such as Autistic Spectrum Disorder or gender dysphoria. This is to emphasise that being autistic or gender diverse is not a medical condition, or a mental health issue, even if some autistic and/or gender diverse people might need support to help them with certain things, in particular in terms of gender affirming care.

References

Bacchi, C. (2005) 'Discourse, discourse everywhere: Subject 'agency' in feminist discourse methodology', *NORA: Nordic Journal of Women's Studies*, 13(3), pp. 198–209. https://doi.org/10.1080/08038740600600407.

Botha, M. and Frost, D.M. (2020) 'Extending the minority stress model to understand mental health problems experienced by the autistic population', *Society and Mental Health*, 10(1), pp. 20–34. https://doi.org/10.1177/2156869318804297.

Carlile, A. (2020) 'The experiences of transgender and non-binary children and young people and their parents in healthcare settings in England, UK: Interviews with members of a family support group', *International Journal of Transgender Health (Print)*, 21(1), pp. 16–32. https://doi.org/10.1080/15532739.2019.1693472.

Hilário, A.P. (2020) 'Rethinking trans identities within the medical and psychological community: A path towards the depathologization and self-definition of gender identification in Portugal?', *Journal of Gender Studies*, 29(3), pp. 245–256. https://doi.org/10.1080/09589236.2018.1544066.

Westminster Commission on Autism (2016) *A Spectrum of Obstacles – An Inquiry into Access to Healthcare for Autistic People*. Huddersfield: The National Children's Group.

Nicolaidis, C., Raymaker, D., McDonald, K., Dern, S., Boisclair, W., Ashkenazy, E. and Baggs, A. (2012) 'Comparison of healthcare experiences in autistic and non-autistic adults: A cross-sectional online survey facilitated by an academic-community partnership', *Journal of General Internal Medicine*, 28(6), pp. 761–769. https://doi.org/10.1007/s11606-012-2262-7.

Nicolaidis, C., Raymaker, D.M., Ashkenazy, E., McDonald, K.E., Dern, S., Baggs, A.E., Kapp, S.K., Wiener, M. and Boisclair, W. (2015) '"Respect the way I need to communicate with you": Healthcare experiences of adults on the autism spectrum', *Autism: The International Journal of Research and Practice*, 19(7), pp. 824–831. https://doi.org/10.1177/1362361315576221.

Pearce, R. (2018) *Understanding Trans Health: Discourse, Power and Possibility*. Bristol: Policy Press.

Pearce, R., Erikainen, S. and Vincent, B. (2020) 'TERF wars: An introduction', *The Sociological Review*, 68(4), pp. 677–698. https://doi.org/10.1177/0038026120934713.

Poteat, T., German, D. and Kerrigan, D. (2013) 'Managing uncertainty: A grounded theory of stigma in transgender health care encounters', *Social Science and Medicine (1982)*, 84, pp. 22–29. https://doi.org/10.1016/j.socscimed.2013.02.019.

Roller, C.G., Sedlak, C. and Draucker, C.B. (2015) 'Navigating the system: How transgender individuals engage in health care services', *Journal of Nursing Scholarship*, 47(5), pp. 417–424. https://doi.org/10.1111/jnu.12160.

Silverman, C. (2017) *Understanding Autism: Parents, Doctors, and the History of a Disorder*. Princeton: Princeton University Press.

Stonewall (2020) *Stonewall Statement on High Court Puberty Blockers Ruling* [Online]. Available: https://www.stonewall.org.uk/about-us/news/stonewall-statement-high-court-puberty-blockers-ruling [Accessed 07/01/2021].

Strang, J.F., Powers, M., Knauss, M., Sibarium, E., Leibowitz, S., Kenworthy, L., Sadikova, E., Wyss, S., Willing, L., Caplan, R., Pervez, N., Nowak, J., Gohari, D., Gomez-Lobo, V., Call, D. and Anthony, L. (2018) '"They thought it was an obsession": Trajectories and perspectives of autistic transgender and gender-diverse adolescents', *Journal of Autism and Developmental Disorders*, 48(12), pp. 4039–4055. https://doi.org/10.1007/s10803-018-3723-6.

Turban, J.L. and Van Schalkwyk, G.I. (2018) '"Gender Dysphoria" and autism spectrum disorder: Is the link real?', *Journal of the American Academy of Child and Adolescent Psychiatry*, 57(1), pp. 8–9.e2., https://doi.org/10.1016/j.jaac.2017.08.017.

Unigwe, S., Buckley, C., Crane, L., Kenny, L., Remington, A. and Pellicano, E. (2017) 'GPs' confidence in caring for their patients on the autism spectrum: An online self-report study', *British Journal of General Practice*, 67(659), pp. e445–e452. https://doi.org/10.3399/bjgp17X690449.

Van Der Miesen, A.I., Hurley, H. and De Vries, A.L. (2016) 'Gender dysphoria and autism spectrum disorder: A narrative review', *International Review of Psychiatry: Gender Dysphoria and Gender Incongruence* (Abingdon, England), 28(1), pp. 70–80. https://doi.org/10.3109/09540261.2015.1111199.

Vincent, B. (2018) *Transgender Health: A Practitioner's Guide to Binary and Non-binary Trans Patient Care*. London: Jessica Kingsley Publishers.

Watkinson, D. and Sunderland, C. (2017) 'How discrimination affects access to health care for transgender people', *Nursing Times* [online], 113(4), pp. 36–39.

11
AUTISTIC YOUNG PEOPLE'S SENSE OF SELF AND THE SOCIAL WORLD

A challenge to deficit-focused characterisations

Emma Rice-Adams

The study reported here considered the sense of self of autistic adolescents through qualitative, participatory research undertaken within a Critical Autism Studies (CAS) approach. It aimed to place autistic adolescents' conceptualisations and presentations of 'self' at the fore, prioritising their insider perspective, and appreciating the complex and varied self that they may wish to present (Orsini and Davidson, 2013; O'Dell et al., 2016). The chapter represents the insider perspectives of eight autistic pupils (two female and six male), aged 12–16 years, who attended a mainstream secondary school. It begins by contextualising the research landscape, identifying how sense of self has been conceptualised in past works, and contemplating the prominence of social influence, within theories of self-development. The chapter then discusses how deficit narratives have positioned autistic young people as lacking social affect, and subsequently challenges such characterisations. It is argued that altering the research methods employed can enable autistic adolescents to share views and experiences which counter such deficit discourses. The views of the autistic young people, who completed a range of alternative visual, verbal and written inclusive methods, are presented in the final part of the chapter. Here, a thematic map offers a visual representation of the varied and complex sense of self the autistic participants shared. Following this, poetic transcriptions further illustrate the relevance of the social world to the sense of self of the autistic adolescents who took part. The research considered in this chapter therefore stands as a counter to deficit-reductive narratives, which diminish the sense of self of autistic young people to one of 'lack', characterised only by what is claimed to be 'missing'.

What is a sense of self in adolescence?

Sense of self has been conceptualised across philosophical, psychological and scientific disciplines, evolving over several centuries of theory and research (Harter, 2012; Hodge, Rice and Reidy, 2019). As my study sits within a Critical Autism Studies approach, it identifies dominant discourses within autism research which are subsequently questioned (Orsini and Davidson, 2013; O'Dell et al., 2016). Therefore, it focuses on psychological concepts, which prevail in autism diagnostic criteria (APA, 2013; Latif, 2016) and in sense-of-self and autism research

(Hodge, Rice and Reidy, 2019; King, Williams and Gleeson, 2017). In following this approach, sense of self is defined as containing both a descriptive self-element, which illustrates who a person *is*, and an evaluative element, which gives a sense of positive or negative self-worth, based on this self-description (Bosacki, 2000; Harter, 2012; Hart and Damon, 1988; Jordan and Powell, 1995). It is asserted that the way a person defines themselves may be based on a range of elements. They may choose to describe themselves in relation to physical descriptors, such as their appearance or material possessions. They may include social aspects, such as their interpersonal relationships and interactions, the groups or individuals they identify with, or consider social traits such as their competence in social situations. Internal elements such as personality, affective traits, private thoughts, feelings, beliefs, dreams or memories may also be included, or capabilities, such as cognitive or sporting ability, may be important to how they define themselves (Damon and Hart, 1982; Epstein, 1973; Hart and Damon, 1988; Harter, 2012; Neisser, 1988). These various domains of description can be evaluated to form a sense of worth, which may include an appraisal of competence or 'success' in these areas (Crocker and Wolfe, 2001; Harter, 2012). Sense-of-self research has also argued that an awareness, or 'sense' of who you are, develops over time (Guardo and Bohan, 1971; Damon and Hart, 1982; Harter, 2012) and is heavily influenced by the social world and the interpersonal relationships within it (Hart and Damon, 1988; Harter, 2012; Hobson, 1990;2002). In these social interactions and comparisons, a person develops a perception of themselves as distinct from others; a separate 'self', which is unique, in comparison with other 'selves' (Guardo 1968; Harter, 2012; Hobson, 1990).

In developmental models, adolescence is considered a time where the *interpersonal* impact of the self becomes central. At this age, a young person focuses on how the 'self' they present interacts with, and is viewed by, others. In this, they prioritise how the perception of their self by others influences how they are treated and their subsequent positioning within the social group (Hart and Damon, 1986;1988; Harter, 2012.) For instance, an adolescent may describe themselves as academically or athletically successful and contemplate how this endears them to their peers *or* places them as someone to be derided. Furthermore, Harter (2012) asserts that whilst early adolescents (aged 11–13) focus on how others appraise them, middle adolescents (aged 14–16), also identify contradictions in their behaviour, with different social groupings. At this age, they begin to consider how their behaviour might change to meet the differing expectations of social groupings such as close friends, peers or family (Harter, 2015; Harter and Monsour, 1992). This leads to a conscious awareness of role-related selves, where a differing self is presented, dependent on which role is being undertaken, in the varying social groups interacted with (Gergen, 1991; 2000; Goffman, 1959/1990; Harter and Monsour, 1992). This can result in conflict for a young person, who struggles to reconcile a "kaleidoscopic self" (Harter, 2012, p. 97), which presents opposing traits depending on the context they are within (Gergen, 2000; Harter and Monsour, 1992).

Further conflict can arise from the opposing expectations of social groups, and which of these expectations should be followed. For example, the academic expectations of parents could be incompatible with the views of peers, who may characterise such success in a negative way (Harter, 2012). Attempting to maintain adherence to varying expectations or 'roles' can be exhausting, with a fear of presenting the 'wrong' self to the 'wrong' group (Goffman, 1959/1990; James, 1892/2001). Moreover, an adolescent may not have full autonomy in the role taken. They may attempt to position themselves in a certain light, but they may also be positioned by others, due to how their behaviour places them within societal beliefs. This can result in increased or diminished status, rights and access (Baines, 2012; Harré and Moghaddam, 2003). Consider the pupil who is positioned by the school as 'naughty', due to their behaviour jarring with the school's rules. Such a student may receive punishments directly attributed to that behaviour, which remove their access to social time such as after school clubs or school trips (Baines, 2012). Whilst they may not wish to be viewed as such, others' perspectives of their behaviour places them within a role, which acts as a barrier to their social experience.

Interaction with various social groups is therefore highly relevant to the sense of self of adolescents and interactions can result in tumultuous feelings, during this significant time for self-definition (Harter, 2012; Molloy and Vasil, 2004).

Deficit narratives, the social self and autism research

Despite the significance of this period for young people, there is a lack of research focus on the multifaceted personhoods of autistic young people *and* the impact of school experience on that sense of self (Bagatell, 2007; Harter, 2012; O'Dell et al., 2016; Williams, Gleeson and Jones, 2017). This may be due to deficit characterisations of autistic adolescents, who are assumed to be detached from the social world, and to have a sense of self lacking in interpersonal influence (Milton, 2014; Williams, Gleeson and Jones, 2017; Winstone et al., 2014).

These deficit narratives are evident in studies which take an 'outsider' quantitative approach to autism and sense-of-self research (Farley, Lopez and Saunders, 2010; Jackson, Skirrow and Hare, 2012; Lee and Hobson, 1998). In such studies, the diverse and complex sense of self of autistic people is diminished in "objective" numerical data (Orsini and Davidson, 2013, p. 1). This can obscure or misrepresent the varied experiences shared, through the reduction of experience to a statistical form and/ or its filtration through an 'outsider' perspective (Orsini and Davidson, 2013; Milton and Bracher, 2013; Pellicano, Dinsmore and Charman, 2014a). In this format, the multilayered self autistic people may wish to be recognised by is not presented as such (Ridout, 2017). Instead, the focus is on what these researchers claim autistic young people are lacking.

In sense-of-self research, non-autistic research teams claim that the autistic person's sense of self lacks interpersonal influence (Farley, Lopez and Saunders, 2010; Jackson, Skirrow and Hare, 2012; Lee and Hobson, 1998). These studies employ the Hart and Damon (1986) self-understanding interview which utilises set questions with answers assigned scores (Hart and Damon, 1988). This developmental model offers levels of self-understanding, which are argued to be 'norms' for the particular age group. In using such a model, autistic adolescents (Farley, Lopez and Saunders, 2010; Lee and Hobson, 1998) and adults (Jackson, Skirrow and Hare, 2012) were compared against the model's 'norms' of development, whilst also being compared with a non-autistic participant group. These studies hypothesised that the autistic participants involved would diverge from a 'normal' socially influenced self and be characterised by a lack of interpersonal focus (Molloy and Vasil, 2004). Comparative methods such as these perpetuate narratives which devalue the sense of self of autistic young people, who are asserted to be lacking a sociality constructed, "essential" part, of a 'normally' developed sense of self (Hobson, 2002, p. 212). This sits within discourses which, present autistic people as "in a world of their own, and, like aliens on the wrong planet ... only spectrally present in ... the world of the 'normal' people" (Davies, 2016, p. 132).

Yet these deficit claims are contradicted in research focusing on the lived experience of autistic people. Such studies demonstrate an awareness of the perceptions of others and their position within social groups. This includes sharing a sense of negative difference in comparison to others, of being not 'normal' (Bagatell, 2007; Humphrey and Lewis, 2008), and attempts to position themselves away from negative discourses surrounding the autism label (Botha, Dibb and Frost, 2020; Johnson and Joshi, 2016). In these attempts, autistic people have reported masking, hiding traits which may mark them out as autistic, and attempting to fit into expectations of 'normality' (Baldwin and Costley, 2016; Davidson and Henderson, 2010; Milton and Sims, 2016). These actions are attributed to wanting to 'succeed' in social environments and to prevent negative treatment from peers (Baines, 2012; Davidson and Henderson, 2010; Pellicano, Dinsmore and Charman, 2014b). Such accounts illustrate an understanding of the social effects of the self which is presented; an appreciation of how the self which is perceived by others can impact on the subsequent treatment by those others. As accounts of masking traits and hiding diagnoses are present in the accounts of autistic adolescents (Baines, 2012; Humphrey and Lewis, 2008; Mogensen and Mason, 2015), this counters the claim that the interpersonal impact of the self is not relevant to these young people, who actively endeavour to be perceived in a certain way. These efforts were further evident in Molloy and Vasil's (2004) narrative research, with autistic adolescents (aged 12–18). Here, participants shared their awareness of being 'outsiders' and a need to have/share the correct hobbies, interests or topics of conversation to 'fit in' with the social group.

Baines' (2012) interviews, with two autistic late-adolescent males (aged 16–18), also demonstrated their consciousness of the interpersonal implications of the self which is presented. For instance, Mark regularly shared concerns about the perceptions of his peers and therefore changed his behaviour, to maintain positive views. Both young men showed their awareness of the expectations, and roles, that could be taken within the school context, and a desire to be positioned in a positive light. They also shared their active efforts to enable such a position, and an understanding of the social consequences of such self-definitions.

These contradictory studies therefore illustrate how characterising autistic adolescents as lacking an interpersonally affected self, and an awareness of the social implications of that self, needs to be challenged (as in Milton, 2014). The research described in this chapter is employed to enact such a challenge, countering deficit-reductive views, and depicting the complex personhood that autistic adolescents want to present (O'Dell et al., 2016; Ridout, 2017).

Challenging conceptions through changing methods

There are a small number of studies which also counter deficit sense-of-self research (King, Williams and Gleeson, 2017; Winstone et al., 2014). These studies particularly critique the self-understanding interview, arguing that this method acts as a barrier to autistic adolescents, perpetuating deficit narratives. They argue that employing alternative, creative methods can enable autistic adolescents to share a sense of self which challenges such discourses.

Support for these method-based critiques can be found in barriers identified in the use of interviews with autistic participants. For example, the face-to-face format can increase anxiety, leading to the withdrawal of autistic children and young people (Beresford et al., 2004; Ellis, 2017). This withdrawal can include not taking part at all, leaving the interview during the questioning process, or giving answers which may not represent their true feelings, to bring the situation to a speedier close (Beresford et al., 2004; Preece and Jordan, 2010; Preece, 2002). In such cases, the data collected would not be an accurate representation of the views or experiences of the autistic participants involved. Furthermore, difficulties with the question format may hinder the depth of response a young person could provide (Cook, Ogden and Winstone, 2016; Preece and Jordan, 2010). King, Williams and Gleeson (2017) argue that the fewer responses provided by autistic participants could illustrate difficulties with the questions themselves, rather than with their social self-understanding.

When addressing such barriers, King, Williams and Gleeson (2017), Ridout (2017) and Winstone et al. (2014) focus on the methods as the area for change. In employing creative methods, such as photo-elicitation, drawing, collage or narrative diary, these studies illustrate how alternative methods can enable rich and detailed responses, which challenge deficit-led discourses. For instance, King Williams and Gleeson (2017) and Winstone et al.'s (2014) research with autistic adolescent boys demonstrates the significance of others to their participants' self-understanding and an increased ease in self-reflection, contradicting the findings of previous self-understanding interviews.

King, Williams and Gleeson's (2017) photo-elicitation interviews particularly highlighted the relevance of the social world. The data gleaned from this method demonstrated a discussion of how self-elements, such as interests, were an important part of interpersonal relationships and an awareness of the interpersonal implications of how their self was perceived. Moreover, all participants in this study spontaneously provided social statements, which made comparisons with peers and family members. As King, Williams and Gleeson (2017) argue, these methods demonstrated a social relatedness, which counters previous deficit claims.

Ridout (2017) and Winstone et al. (2014) further emphasise the impact changing methods can have, by comparing the use of traditional methods with their creative alternatives. In Ridout (2017), collage, with a text- and image-based diary, enabled the sharing of experiences of anxiety and depression in ways that were not accessed through the questionnaire method; whilst for Winstone et al. (2014) activity-orientated interviews, which discussed drawings and collage, provided more detailed and in-depth responses, in contrast with their semi-structured counterpart. One area of noteworthy difference was when autistic adolescents compared themselves with family and peers. In activity-orientated interviews, participants offered a wider range of comparisons and more detail within those comparisons. They discussed differences in personality, preferences, physical, psychological, and social traits, and educational ability. They therefore included more difficult abstract concepts, such as psychological traits, which were directly compared with others. In contrast, in the semi-structured interviews, participants appeared to offer a concrete, physically focused self-description – one which was not differentiated in comparison with others. This highlights how, dependent on method, differing self-understanding can be shown.

Offering a choice of research methods in the research project

Reflections on this research led me to employ alternative approaches to semi-structured interviews. I followed the tenet that it is the researcher's responsibility to ensure participants are enabled to communicate (Ellis, 2017; Scott-Barrett, Cebula and Florian, 2018). Consequently, the focus was on ensuring accessible methods, whilst avoiding any presumptions about how the autistic young people in the study may wish to communicate (Fletcher-Watson et al., 2019; Scott-Barrett, Cebula and Florian, 2018). It was important to appreciate the range of preferences and needs the participants may have (Ellis, 2017; Ridout, 2017). In this, I wanted to ensure that the participants had control, communicating on their own terms, within their own predilections (Ellis, 2017). I did not specify the method participants must complete. Instead, they chose a preferred method from a range of visual, verbal and written options (Ridout, 2017). The choice of methods provided aimed not only to increase accessibility but also to increase enjoyment, which, in turn, can generate deeper and richer responses (Ellis, 2017; Ridout, 2017; Rice, 2018). Participants could select methods which drew on their areas of interest, and which utilised areas of strength, reducing the pressure felt during completion (Beresford et al., 2004).

Within these method choices, further adaptations were available which aimed to increase accessibility. Adaptations were particularly prevalent for verbal or written responses (see Table 11.1). For example, 'conversations' were offered as a form of elicitation interview to avoid the barriers generated by the interview method and to make sure communication needs were prioritised (Clark, 2010). Adaptations included verbal discussion with peers or support

Table 11.1 Range of methods completed by participants

Method type	Method	Adaptations
Visual	Photography	Working with researcher/teaching assistant support.
	Drawing	Discussion with a peer rather than an adult.
	Collage	Dictated notes instead of voice recording.
	Film/Vlog	Typing/written response instead of verbal discussion.
	Videogame design	Typing/asking an adult to write dictated notes.
Verbal	Conversation with prompts	Sentence stems or closed questions as an option to support a written response.
	Conversation without prompts	
	Peer discussion (pairs/ group)	
Written	Diary	
	Typed response	

staff, who they may feel more comfortable with, and nonverbal, written options, which could be completed on a computer, with further literacy supports provided if necessary. The focus throughout was on ensuring the autistic adolescents involved would not be constrained by inaccessible methods, which prevented them from sharing their views (Fletcher-Watson et al., 2019; Ridout, 2017).

Autistic adolescents' sense of self and the social world: findings from the alternative methods employed

The data gathered from the methods described above will now be set out. This data relates to the first research question of the study:

How do autistic pupils negotiate a developing sense of self?

This was supported by the following sub-questions:

What do pupils identify as influencing this sense of self?
What are the pupils' views of the school's enablers or barriers to developing a positive sense of self?

These research questions prioritised the pupils' perspectives of their sense of self and were open to the complexity of self-description that the autistic adolescents involved wished to present (O'Dell et al., 2016; Ridout, 2017). Prioritising autistic voices follows calls for such an approach from autistic scholars (e.g. Bertilsdotter Rosqvist et al., 2019; Milton, 2014; Williams, 1996) and is in line with CAS ideals (Orsini and Davidson, 2013).

This chapter focuses on the social relevance shared by autistic adolescents when discussing their sense of self. However, due to my commitment not to diminish the complex self presented by participants, I have included a thematic map (Figure 11.1), which considers all areas of the self that participants presented. The themes within the map were inductively analysed, and therefore led by participant data (Braun and Clark, 2006; Danker, Strnadová and Cumming, 2016). This meant that data analysis was not framed through a presupposed researcher hypothesis (Crane et al., 2019). Data which did not fit the "dominant story" was retained so that heterogeneity within views would not be obscured (Braun and Clarke, 2006, p. 19; Humphrey and Lewis, 2008). The thematic map therefore represents the entirety of participant data, providing the 'big picture' of what was shared (Attride-Stirling, 2001; Braun and Clark, 2006). The main themes

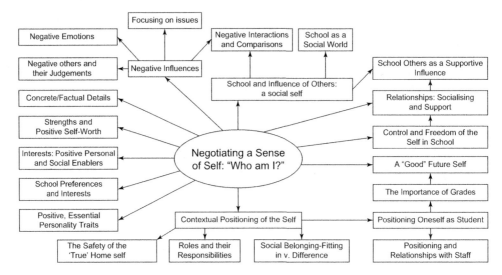

Figure 11.1 Thematic map: the sense of self elements shared by the autistic adolescents participating in the research study

are represented by a thicker arrow and bold font, with linking sub-themes shown through the thinner arrow.

Consequently, the map offers a visual representation of the myriad of influences and elements present in the sense of self for autistic adolescents. Participants shared their interests and preferences, strengths and weaknesses, personality and unique traits, as part of their self-view. They also considered contextual, role-related selves, including 'self' as presented at home, in various roles and responsibilities, and as a 'good' or 'bad' student in school. These discussions demonstrated how the autistic adolescents in the study would aim to 'position' themselves to be viewed in a positive light, with a clear awareness of what 'fitting in' entails. They also illustrated how they felt their grades, behaviour and staff perceptions could impact how they were positioned as a student. Further to this, they explored the 'good' future self they would wish to achieve and how this could be obtained through their school achievements. Additionally, social elements were prominently featured, with relationships with family, friends and the wider peer group explored. Within this, school was considered as a key social space (Harter, 2012; Williams, Gleeson and Jones, 2017). The interpersonal interactions, expectations and comparisons described could be a positive or negative influence on the self-esteem of the young people involved. Negative influences included both the perceived and actual judgements of others, bullying, and comparisons with peers. However, relationships could also offer support, which countered such negative interactions (Milton and Sims, 2016). Moreover, positive relationships and social contact were emphasised as important to the participants involved. Therefore, the relevance of the social world, and the complexity of the sense of self of the autistic adolescents in the study, is evident throughout the thematic map.

Presenting participant data through poetic transcription

During the thematic analysis of the verbal and written data, I began to question how to present that data, to best meet the aims of the study. In seeking to move away from quantifying 'objective' sense of self research, I considered how the emotional depth the autistic adolescents in my study had shared could be fully communicated (Orsini and Davidson, 2013). This brought me to poetic transcription, which employs a literary form, to enable the emotion of participants' experiences to be conveyed (Glesne, 1997; Kookan, Haase and Russell, 2007; Prendergast, 2009). Poetic transcription places the words of participants together into a poetic form (Glesne, 1997). In this form, Kooken, Haase and Russell (2007) argue that poetic transcription "merge[s] the logic of data analysis with human emotional experiences often expressed in qualitative data" (p. 904). Glesne (1997) even claims that this form can "heal wounds of scientific categorization and technological dehumanisation" by introducing "spirit, imagination and hope" (pp. 214–215). As my project was placed in counter to the deficit-based "scientific categorization" of previous sense-of-self studies, I was particularly interested in how poetic transcription could return 'humanity' and 'emotional' soul to the presentation of qualitative data.

The emotional impact of poetic transcription is argued to spring from its compressed form, which can interweave thoughts, feelings and ideas from a range of participants, presenting these in 'one go' (Burdick, 2011; Gasson et al., 2015; Richardson, 2001). By combining participants' contributions, the "essence" of those ideas, experiences or feelings can be immediately accessed (Glesne, 1997; VanWyk et al., 2012, p. 121). Glesne (1997) suggests that this maintains the "wholeness and interconnections of thoughts" (p. 206). When employing this form, I too found that the reader could have immediate access to *all* the participants' views on a theme, enabling them to view the 'big picture' or overriding narrative (Gasson et al., 2015). It also highlighted repeated views or emotional experiences (Henderson, 2018). This emphasised participant feeling in relation to the theme. For Glesne (1997), the reader can then connect with these emotional aspects, empathising with their own similar experiences or comparing different views. This is something which could be lost in the separation of participant quotation in traditional qualitative analysis (Cohen, Manion and Morrison, 2011).

Furthermore, a poetic form can increase accessibility for those outside of academia, by utilising a well-known style (Carroll et al., 2011; Huddleston, 2012; Richardson, 2001). Here, the "essence" or key ideas can be accessed in one condensed form, preventing the need to read dense reports or transcripts (Freeman, 2006; VanWyk et al., 2012, p. 121). Meeting the CAS aim of enabling "empowering narratives" of autism requires stereotypes and deficit misconceptions to be challenged across social groups, including those outside of the research community (Orsini and Davidson, 2013, p. 12; John, Knott and Harvey, 2018; Lakey, Rodgers and Scoble, 2014). Formats which can be accessed by a range of groups therefore support such aims. As well as offering accessibility, the emotional elements of poetic transcription can enhance engagement, with Poindexter (2002) asserting that readers can be "moved by their simplicity and power" (p. 713). In enabling engagement, empathy and understanding, poetic transcription can be a valuable tool in advocacy (MacNeil, 2000; Poindexter, 2002). As my research is committed to advocating for autistic adolescents and their needs, I was particularly interested in how poetic transcription could support those aims.

Here, poetic transcriptions take the form of found poems, where another's text (the participants' words) are arranged into a poetic form (Burdick, 2011; Reilly, 2013). The poetic transcriptions followed the common practice of maintaining participant words as closely to their original form as possible (e.g. Glesne, 1997; Henderson, 2018; Ho, 2012; Kooken, Haase and Russell, 2007). To create fluency in the poems, I changed word endings, e.g. congratulating to congratulated, and added connecting words, such as and or a. I also omitted filler words such as erm or like (Glesne, 1997; Ho, 2012). This process followed the same rules as Ho (2012), limiting additions or omissions to a maximum of ten of each, always aiming for fewer if possible. In doing this, I hoped to maintain the essence of the participants' ideas, and their way of speaking, as closely as possible (Glesne, 1997).

Each poem centres around a main idea or a theme from the thematic analysis and individual verses cluster around elements within that main idea, such as what bullies 'pick on' (Gasson et al., 2015; Henderson, 2018). The titles are also the participants' words. These poems are structured as free verse, meaning there is not a set number of lines to adhere to (VanWyk et al., 2012; Wolosky, 2001). This allowed each poem to combine the entire range and detail of the data, including every participant who contributed a view on that theme, so no participant's opinion was discounted (Madill and Hopper, 2007; VanWyk et al., 2012). This included opposing views, retaining data which stepped away from the dominant narrative, to avoid the presentation of one 'right' answer, which did not represent the views of all the participants involved (Braun and Clark, 2006). I also placed strongly emotional points as individual verses, often at the end of the poem. This further enhanced their emotive impact for the reader (Redmond, 2006).

The poetic transcriptions which will follow represent a small selection from the study. They have been chosen to represent the relevance of the social world to the sense of self of autistic adolescents. Alongside this, where relevant, participant drawings illustrate the poems. In including this data, I will demonstrate how the alternative methods of the study enabled findings which challenged deficit constructions of the autistic adolescents' sense of self as one which lacks social affect.

Poetic transcription: the social self-view of autistic adolescents

The poetic transcriptions below present participant self-description alongside the elements which they feel have a positive or negative influence on their self-view. In this data, the autistic adolescents demonstrate their social awareness and its subsequent influence on their sense of self. This includes comparisons that they make with their peers and the effect of the judgement/comments that those peers make about them. In addition, they discuss presenting a different self at school to who they can be at home; a change in self-presentation based on a desire to 'fit in' and avoid peers' negative judgements. Participants also illustrated awareness of the implications of how their teachers perceived them. In considering these different social groups, participants shared how the perceptions of themselves in a variety of social contexts impacted on, and were therefore relevant to, their self-view.

Comparisons and judgements: the negative influence of peers

Most participants shared how comparing themselves with others had a negative impact on how they felt about themselves. When making comparisons between their grades and school achievements, focus was placed on those which emphasised how they were in a 'worse' position than others. This is demonstrated in the poetic transcription "I sometimes compare grades". The poem illustrates a need to be the "most" or the "best" academically, athletically, or in receiving school credits. If participants felt they were not as 'good' as others, this could have a negative impact on their self-view. However, one participant also felt this could also have a motivating effect, making them "work harder" to achieve.

Listed underneath the poem are the pseudonyms of the participants whose views make up the poem. This illustrates how six of the eight adolescents involved in the study contributed views on comparing themselves with their peers.

I sometimes compare grades

> People try to be like the most something,
> like the smartest or best at football or
> the strongest or other things like most reward credits.

If we're doing a test and I don't do as well
as one of my friends, I like think that,
I am not as good at that.
I wish I was that good at like English as them.

If you have worse subjects than other people,
people might think they're not good enough;
it might make you feel bad about yourself.

It is a weakness because some people like,
get things straight away and then I'm like
"ah what are you supposed to do?"
I feel everyone's ahead of me,
If they finish early it is like,
I am not as good as them.

I sometimes compare grades.
Sometimes it makes me work harder
to become like them.

I aim to be the best I can.

(Connor, Fresh, Harrison, Lightning, Richelle and Skyler)

Two participants also discussed being judged on their appearance, and the impact this had on how they viewed themselves. Again, these were framed as negative judgements, which had a detrimental impact on feeling "not good enough".

Doesn't everyone hate being judged

Doesn't everyone hate being judged on the way they look?
I think we all do.
It could make them feel sad.
Like –
they're the only person who doesn't look very good.
They're not good enough.
When they say bad things.
It makes you feel bad
because you feel worse than everyone else.

It's hurtful.
If someone bragged about their looks
it could hurt someone.
I'd feel like I don't look too good.

(Connor and Harrison)

Harrison also represented judgement as something which "hurts you" in his school video game, shown through a drawing of spikes (Figure 11.2).

Most of the adolescent participants also discussed bullying, mirroring the prevalence of this in the accounts of autistic people across research (Cook, Ogden and Winstone, 2016; Goodall, 2018; Milton and Sims, 2016). Participants experienced this not only with regard to their appearance and academic achievements but also in relation to autism. This is represented in the poetic transcription "It puts people down".

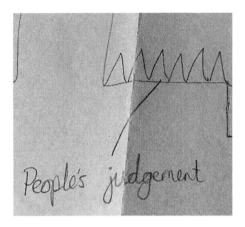

Figure 11.2 'People's judgement'

It puts people down

Bad – bullying.

Bullies can hurt you.
Being hurt, hurtful words,
Insults from people.

Making fun of them,
What they like, what they look like,
bullying about people's appearances,
how they do things, how you act, what grades you get …
Saying like just rude or mean stuff.
Making fun of autistic pupils;
easy target because of my autism.

Get off my friend!
Seeing others being bullied,
makes me feel sympathetic.

They can make you feel bad.
Upset and angry.
It puts people down and makes people's self-esteem low.
You're worth less than other people,
empty inside.
It impacts on that person massively.

Nobody's gonna get like a good outcome-
out of bullying.

(Connor, Fresh, Harrison, Lightning, Richelle, Skyler and Wolf)

Participants therefore characterised comparisons with their peers, and the judgements of those peers, in a negative light (Williams, Gleeson and Jones, 2017). They shared a range of these negative influences and how this impacted on their self-view. This included a sense of reduced value, being worth 'less' in comparison to others (Bolic Baric et al., 2016) and mirror the findings of King, Williams and Gleeson (2017) and Winstone et al. (2014). The alternate methods employed enabled participants to illustrate the relevance of social comparisons with others, and peer feedback, to their self-description. It was also evident how these social influences can impact on the positive or negative evaluation of that self-view (Harter, 2012; 2015; Harter, Waters and Whitesell, 1998). This counters claims that autistic young people are in an anti-social "world of their own" (Davies, 2016, p. 132; Milton, 2012) and that the social world is not relevant to their sense of self (Hobson, 1990; Lee and Hobson, 1998).

Changing to 'fit in': the self in different contexts

Participants also discussed how they might present themselves, depending on the social context they were within. They identified a 'true' self, that existed at home, compared with the "front" employed to 'fit in' at school.

Skyler summarised this, stating:

> you have to put on a front so people accept you but that front like becomes like that personality that you're showing can be completely different to your normal personality, who you really are.

This contrasts with who they can be in the home environment, as illustrated by the following poem. Home is a place of freedom, comfort and a lack of judgement. Participants felt that there was no need to change to 'fit in' in this space.

"At home I can truly be myself"

At home, it's a very relaxed and chilled environment,
where I can feel safe and relaxed.
Relaxing in my room,
I don't have to feel stressed and uncomfortable.

I feel safe and secure,
in where I live and who I live with.
I can truly be myself
and not be judged.
Whatever I do, whatever I say.

I don't have to feel like I have to 'fit in.'

When you're with your friends and family,
You can just be yourself.
Having family around you,
you belong somewhere.

There's no place like home.

(Fresh, Harrison, Lightning and Skyler)

In contrast, school is a place of change; a change required to avoid negative judgements, such as those discussed in the previous section: "When I am at school and in class I may need to act slightly differently, and I need to analyse what I say and do to not stand out in a strange way. People may mock me" (Skyler).

Choices made can therefore be influenced by the perception of what peers or wider society may think. For example, interests which are viewed as unusual may become a source of concern. Skyler, for instance, suggests people can become "paranoid" as to "What would this person think

Special talents

Figure 11.3 'Special talents'

of me doing this, ah, they wouldn't like it so I'm not going to do it". Whilst there was a desire to avoid standing out in this "strange" way, which may be mocked, participants also identified there were some 'right' ways to be different, which would have a positive influence on how you viewed yourself. These included special talents, which may be admired, as represented in Harrison's drawing (Figure 11.3).

They could be unique experiences, such as those experienced by Wolf, who visited places "not open to the public", had been involved in "breaking records" or "had more experiences than most … that very few people have". Certain roles and responsibilities were seen as an acceptable difference, with Harrison feeling "I am proud of my roles because they are what makes you stand out from the crowd". Roles in after school clubs, viewed positively by both Harrison and Wolf, involved responsibility, and helping others, often younger than themselves. Several participants discussed roles they had inside and outside of school, which they felt represented the trust people had in them, and which would garner respect. Participants identified such roles as having a positive impact on their self-view. Standing out and being different was therefore not always a negative; it was dependent on whether something was seen as "strange" by peers and wider society. What was hidden to 'fit in' depended on its interpersonal implications. Talents, experiences, achievements or roles which could be viewed positively, did not need to be treated as such.

Here, autistic adolescents have considered their role-related selves, how they change their behaviour dependent on context (Goffman, 1959/1990; Harter and Monsour, 1992). A different self may be presented at school so that they do not appear "strange". At home, this concern of 'fitting in' or being 'judged' was not present, so they could "truly be myself". In this, the young people in the study demonstrated their social awareness, discussing a need to change in the school setting to avoid the judgements of others (Baines, 2012; Humphrey and Lewis, 2008; Mogensen and Mason, 2015). This also mirrors the adolescents in Molloy and Vasil's (2004) study, identifying the 'right' differences, hobbies and interests which can enable you to 'fit in' with the group. These can therefore be shared, whilst those which appear "strange" may be hidden. Within this, the focus is on maintaining the positive perceptions of peers and avoiding the bullying or victimisation associated with not being 'normal' (Baines, 2012; Botha, Dibb and Frost, 2020; Goodall, 2018). This highlights how the interpersonal effects of the self presented to various social groups form part of the self-awareness of these autistic adolescents (Hart and Damon, 1986;1988).

Teachers' perceptions and the academic self-view

It is not only peers' views which concern adolescents; the interpersonal impact of how teachers perceive them, in the role of pupil, is also of concern. Participants conceptualised themselves in relation to the role of a 'good' or 'bad' pupil, considering their grades, rewards and achievements, behaviour and punishments, and work ethic and resilience. In this, they identified how being perceived as a 'good' or 'bad' pupil positioned them with both their peers and with teaching staff.

This is demonstrated in the poetic transcription "Not a naughty student". Participants did not want to be viewed as troublesome or 'naughty' by teachers. Richelle, Skyler and Wolf all discussed how such perceptions lead to a lack of trust from staff, and disbelief about their claims of innocence in the future. As Skyler felt, "if I'm like good behaved they are more likely to believe somebody who's not really in trouble". Trust was important because, as Harrison shared, "It can make you feel good about yourself if you're like – the teacher thought – like trusts you to put you with your friends or something". Furthermore, four participants identified staff trust as having a positive impact on their sense of self whilst three participants felt conflict with staff would have a negative impact on how they perceived themselves. The autistic young people involved therefore demonstrated their concern over how they were perceived by staff and considered how this influenced of this on their self-view. However, participants also did not want to be viewed as 'too good', an "annoying teacher's pet" or a "try hard". These terms echo the taunting words of peers and imply that participants are wary of how their position as a 'good' pupil might influence how they are viewed by their classmates.

Not a naughty student

I never back down from a difficult task.
A fairly good student,
Do quite well in numerous subjects,
have fairly high targets,
I do my homework.

Teachers say good things about me,
In parents' evenings and things.

I am not a naughty student.
I normally stay out of trouble.

I don't always finish all my work,
can't keep on top of my homework.
I get on with my work –
after 10 mins.

I am an idiot but in a good way.
I can be disrespectful,
catch people out.

You don't want to keep asking the teacher,
In case they should at you for not listening.
You just don't wanna come across as pesky do you?

I am not one of those annoying teacher's pets,
teacher's pet or a try-hard,
where I will be their slave to get good grades.
    (Connor, Fresh, Harrison, Lightning, Richelle, Skyler and Wolf)

In discussing their role of pupil, participants also emphasised the importance of social recognition for their school achievements. This is illustrated in the poetic transcription, "You might get rewarded". Rewards and praise were a marker of doing something "good" and enabled a positive self-view. Participants shared the importance of hard work being "noticed", without which it could be considered "lost". There was a desire for their achievements to be recognised. Praise and reward were characterised as something which enabled success to be "visualise[d]" by the individual *and* were an important marker that others had recognised and appreciated your successes.

You might get rewarded

If you produce a good piece of classwork, homework,
high marks on a test
or answer a question with great detail.
Try your hardest,
have complete respect, for both students and teachers alike,
and contribute to particular activities.
You will be rewarded.

You get rewarded,
praise for achievements,
and it makes you feel good about yourself.
You've done something that's good.

My teachers say good things about me;
my TA or even one of my peers,
recognise my hard work.
My teachers must have been like thinking,
That I was doing well.
People are happy at what you've achieved.
That's gonna erm make me feel like positive about myself.

I have been chosen for like trips,
I have been selected to do things.
Winning a prize in end of term assemblies.
Congratulated me when she knew I did well on exams.

It's like you've been noticed.
I am being noticed as like,
my hard work and reputation.
They can visualise their hard work.

When it's not really recognised by anyone,
you feel like it's lost.

(Fresh, Harrison, Lightning, Richelle and Skyler)

These poetic transcriptions illustrate the young people's awareness of how they are positioned in the role of student, and their aim to be perceived in a particular light. Their discussion considered how the role-related, academic self of 'pupil' was perceived in the school setting (Harter, 2012). In this role, participants wanted to be viewed as a student who has "done something good" and as "not a naughty student" to maintain positive interpersonal relationships with staff (Goodall, 2018; King, Williams and Gleeson, 2017). They also identified how being positioned as 'naughty' resulted in a diminished status, such as a lack of belief or trust from staff, something which they actively tried to avoid (Harré and Moghaddam, 2003). In contrast, trusting, constructive relationships with school staff were identified as having a positive influence on the autistic young people's self-view. In this, recognition and appreciation of their success was desired, as a marker of how staff positively viewed them and their achievements (Fefer, DeMagistris and Shuttleton, 2016). However, participants shared a need to balance teachers' perception of 'good' students, with the negative views of peers, who may view those who are too 'good' as a "try-hard". There were therefore contradictory positions to be negotiated, ensuring that whilst staff viewed them positively, this did not result in negative judgements from peers (Harter, 2012).

A complex self, interacting with a social world

Deficit-focused research has reduced the sense of self of autistic people to one defining characteristic – a lack of interpersonal affect (Farley, Lopez and Saunders, 2010; Jackson, Skirrow and Hare, 2012; Lee and Hobson, 1998). This narrative depicts an autistic adolescents' sense of self as one which does not adhere to the expected 'norms' of development. It is a self which lacks a relationship with the social world, with the implications of how that self leads others to perceive them ignored (Hart and Damon, 1986; Lee and Hobson, 1998; Molloy and Vasil, 2004). However, by addressing the limitations of the methods employed in such studies, these deficit narratives can be challenged (King, Williams and Gleeson, 2017; Winstone et al., 2014). This was evident in the research described in this chapter, which employed alternative methods to address these methodological barriers with the aim of being inclusive to the needs and preferences of all participants. The data illustrates a complex and varied sense of self, one influenced by an awareness of the social world it existed within. This included comparisons with peers and a recognition of the judgements of peers and teaching staff – judgements and comparisons which could have a negative impact on self-worth. This led to strategies to position the self in a positive light, with behaviours, interests and achievements, and actions in the role of 'pupil' changed, hidden, or revealed dependent on how they would influence the perceptions of others. This emphasised the understanding of the autistic adolescents involved with regard to the self in contextual roles, where meeting the expectations of certain social groups is required to be viewed in a positive manner (Gergen, 2000; Goffman, 1959/1990; Harter and Monsour, 1992). In such discussion, the relevance of school as a social world, and a subsequent influence on the sense of self of autistic adolescents, was also emphasised (Harter, 2012; Hodge, Rice and Reidy, 2019; Williams, Gleeson and Jones, 2017). This study has therefore countered deficit-focused characterisations, illustrating how autistic young people's sense of self is a complex and varied form, which is influenced by interactions with their social world.

References

American Psychiatric Association (APA). (2013) *Diagnostic and Statistical Manual of Disorders*, 5th ed. Arlington, VA: APA.

Attride-Stirling, J. (2001) 'Thematic networks: An analytic tool for qualitative research', *Qualitative Research*, 1(3), pp. 385–405. https://doi.org/10.1177/146879410100100307

Bagatell, N. (2007) 'Orchestrating voices: Autism, identity and the power of discourse', *Disability and Society*, 22(4), pp. 413–426. https://doi.org/10.1080/09687590701337967

Baines, A. D. (2012) 'Positioning, strategizing, and charming: How students with autism construct identities in relation to disability', *Disability and Society*, 27(4), pp. 547–561. https://doi.org/10.1080/09687599.2012.662825

Baldwin, S., and Costley, D. (2016) 'The experiences and needs of female adults with high-functioning autism spectrum disorder', *Autism*, 20(4), pp. 483–495. https://doi.org/10.1177/1362361315590805

Beresford, B., Tozer, R., Rabiee, P., and Sloper, P. (2004) 'Developing an approach to involving children with autistic spectrum disorders in a social care research project', *British Journal of Learning Disabilities*, 32(4), pp. 180–185. https://doi.org/10.1111/j.1468-3156.2004.00318.x

Bertilsdotter Rosqvist, H., Kourti, M., Jackson-Perry, D., Brownlow, C., Fletcher, K., Bendelman, D., and O'Dell, L. (2019) 'Doing it differently: Emancipatory autism studies within a neurodiverse academic space', *Disability and Society*, 34(7–8), pp. 1082–1101. https://doi.org/10.1080/09687599.2019.1603102

Bolic Baric, V., Hellberg, K., Kjellberg, A., and Hemmingsson, H. (2016) 'Support for learning goes beyond academic support: Voices of students with Asperger's disorder and attention deficit hyperactivity disorder', *Autism*, 20(2), pp. 183–195. https://doi.org/10.1177/1362361315574582

Bosacki, S. L. (2000). Theory of mind and self-concept in preadolescents: Links with gender and language. *Journal of Educational Psychology*, 92(4), pp. 709–717. https://doi.org/10.1037//0022-0663.92.4.709

Botha, M., Dibb, B., and Frost, D. M. (2020) '"Autism is me": An investigation of how autistic individuals make sense of autism and stigma', *Disability and Society*, pp. 1–27. https://doi.org/10.1080/09687599.2020.1822782

Braun, V., and Clarke, V. (2006) 'Using thematic analysis in psychology', *Qualitative Research in Psychology*, 3(2), pp. 77–101. https://doi.org/10.1191/1478088706qp063oa

Burdick, M. (2011) 'Researcher and teacher-participant found poetry: Collaboration in poetic transcription', *International Journal of Education and the Arts*, 12, pp. 1–12.

Carroll, P., Dew, K., and Howden-Chapman, P. (2011) 'The heart of the matter: Using poetry as a method of ethnographic inquiry to represent and present experiences of the informally housed in Aotearoa/New Zealand', *Qualitative Inquiry*, 17(7), pp. 623–630. https://doi.org/10.1177/1077800411414003

Clark, A. (2010). Young children as protagonists and the role of participatory, visual methods in engaging multiple perspectives. *American Journal of Community Psychology*, 46(1), pp. 115–123. https://doi.org/10.1007/s10464-010-9332-y

Cohen, L., Mannion, L., and Morrison, K. (2011) *Research Methods in Education*. New York: Routledge.

Cook, A., Ogden, J., and Winstone, N. (2016) 'The experiences of learning, friendship and bullying of boys with autism in mainstream and special settings: A qualitative study', *British Journal of Special Education*, 43(3), pp. 250–271. https://doi.org/10.1111/1467-8578.12143

Crane, L., Adams, F., Harper, G., Welch, J., and Pellicano, E. (2019) "Something needs to change': Mental health experiences of young autistic adults in England', *Autism*, 23(2), pp. 477–493. https://doi.org/10.1177/1362361318757048

Crocker, J., and Wolfe, C. T. (2001) 'Contingencies of self-worth', *Psychological Review*, 108(3), pp. 593–623. https://doi.org/10.1037/0033-295X.108.3.593

Damon, W., and Hart, D. (1982) 'The development of self-understanding from infancy through adolescence', *Child Development*, 53(4), pp. 841–864. https://doi.org/10.2307/1129122

Danker, J., Strnadová, I., and Cumming, T. M. (2016) 'Engaging students with autism spectrum disorder in research through participant-driven photo-elicitation research technique', *Australasian Journal of Special Education*, 41(1), pp. 1–16. https://doi.org/10.1017/jse.2016.7

Davidson, J., and Henderson, V. L. (2010) "Coming out' on the spectrum: Autism, identity and disclosure', *Social and Cultural Geography*, 11(2), pp. 155–170. https://doi.org/10.1080/14649360903525240

Davies, K. (2016) 'How rude? Autism as a study in ability', in K. Runswick-Cole, R. Mallett and S. Timimi (eds.), *Re-Thinking Autism: Diagnosis, Identity and Equality*. London: Jessica Kingsley, pp. 132–145.

Ellis, J. (2017) 'Researching the social worlds of autistic children: An exploration of how an understanding of autistic children's social worlds is best achieved', *Children and Society*, 31(1), pp. 23–36. https://doi.org/10.1111/chso.12160

Epstein, S. (1973) 'The self-concept revisited: Or a theory of a theory', *American Psychologist*, 28(5), pp. 404–416. https://doi.org/10.1037/h0034679

Farley, A., Lopez, B., and Saunders, G. (2010) 'Self-conceptualisation in autism: Knowing oneself versus knowing self-through-other', *Autism*, 14(5), pp. 519–530. https://doi.org/10.1177/1362361310368536

Fefer, S., DeMagistris, J., and Shuttleton, C. (2016) 'Assessing adolescent praise and reward preferences for academic behavior', *Translational Issues in Psychological Science*, 2(2), pp. 153–162. https://doi.org/10.1037/tps0000072

Fletcher-Watson, S., Adams, J., Brook, K., Charman, T., Crane, L., Cusack, J., Leekam, S., Milton, D., Parr, J., and Pellicano, E. (2019) 'Making the future together: Shaping autism research through meaningful participation', *Autism*, 23(4), pp. 943–953. doi:10.1177/1362361318786721

Freeman, M. (2006) 'Nurturing dialogic hermeneutics and the deliberative capacities of communities in focus groups', *Qualitative Inquiry*, 12(1), pp. 81–95. https://doi.org/10.1177/1077800405282797

Gasson, N. R., Sanderson, L. J., Burnett, G., and van Der Meer, J. (2015) '"It's all he's going to say": Using poetic transcription to explore students' mainstream and residential school experiences', *Disability and Society*, 30(5), pp. 731–742. https://doi.org/10.1080/09687599.2015.1021762

Gergen, K. J. (1991) *The Saturated Self: Dilemmas of Identity in Contemporary Life*. New York: Basic Books.

Gergen, K. J. (2000) 'The self in the age of information', *The Washington Quarterly*, 23(1), pp. 201–214. https://doi.org/10.1162/016366000560656

Glesne, C. (1997) 'That rare feeling: Re-presenting research through poetic transcription', *Qualitative Inquiry*, 3(2), pp. 202–221. https://doi.org/10.1177/107780049700300204

Goffman, E. (1990) *The Presentation of Self in Everyday Life*. London: Penguin. (Original work published 1959)

Goodall, C. (2018) '"I felt closed in and like I couldn't breathe": A qualitative study exploring the mainstream educational experiences of autistic young people', *Autism and Developmental Language Impairments*, 3, pp. 1–16. doi:10.1177/2396941518804407

Guardo, C. J. (1968) 'Self revisited: The sense of self-identity', *Journal of Humanistic Psychology*, 8(2), pp. 137–142. https://doi.org/10.1177/002216786800800206

Guardo, C. J., and Bohan, J. B. (1971) 'Development of a sense of self-identity in children', *Child Development*, 42(6), pp. 1909–1921. https://doi.org/10.2307/1127594

Harré, R., and Moghaddam, F. (2003) *The Self and Others: Positioning Individuals and Groups in Personal, Political, and Cultural Contexts*. Westport: Greenwood Publishing Group.

Hart, D., and Damon, W. (1986) 'Developmental trends in self-understanding', *Social Cognition*, 4(4), pp. 388–407. https://doi.org/10.1521/soco.1986.4.4.388

Hart, D., and Damon, W. (1988) 'Self-understanding and social cognitive development', *Early Child Development and Care*, 40(1), pp. 5–23. https://doi.org/10.1080/0300443880400102

Harter, S. (2012) *The Construction of the Self: Developmental and Sociocultural Foundations*, 2nd ed. London: The Guildford Press.

Harter, S. (2015) 'Self-development in childhood and adolescence', in J. Wright (ed.), *International Encyclopaedia of the Social and Behavioral Sciences*, 2nd ed. Amsterdam: Elsevier, pp. 492–497. https://doi.org/10.1016/B978-0-08-097086-8.23019-5

Harter, S., and Monsour, A. (1992) 'Developmental analysis of conflict caused by opposing attributes in the adolescent self-portrait', *Developmental Psychology*, 28(2), pp. 251–260. https://doi.org/10.1037/0012-1649.28.2.251

Harter, S., Waters, P., and Whitesell, N. R. (1998) 'Relational self-worth: Differences in perceived worth as a person across interpersonal contexts among adolescents', *Child Development*, 69(3), pp. 756–766. https://doi.org/10.1111/j.1467-8624.1998.00756.x

Henderson, H. (2018) 'Difficult questions of difficult questions: The role of the researcher and transcription styles', *International Journal of Qualitative Studies in Education*, 31(2), pp. 143–157. https://doi.org/10.1080/09518398.2017.1379615

Ho, S. (2012) 'Poetic transcription as a way of data (re)presentation', in *The Association for Qualitative Research Conference 2012*, Charles Darwin University, Northern Territory, Australia.

Hobson, R. P. (1990) 'On the origins of self and the case of autism', *Development and Psychopathology*, 2(2), pp. 163–181. https://doi.org/10.1017/S0954579400000687

Hobson, R. P. (2002) *The Cradle of Thought: Exploring the Origins of Thinking*. London: Macmillan.

Hodge, N., Rice, E. J., and Reidy, L. (2019) '"They're told all the time they're different": How educators understand development of sense of self for autistic pupils', *Disability and Society*, 34(9–10), pp. 1353–1378. https://doi.org/10.1080/09687599.2019.1594700

Huddleston, A. P. (2012) 'Understanding responses to high school exit exams in literacy: A Bourdieusian analysis of poetic transcriptions', *Journal of Adolescent and Adult Literacy*, 55(8), pp. 734–744. https://doi.org/10.1002/JAAL.00088

Humphrey, N., and Lewis, S. (2008) '"Make me normal": The views and experiences of pupils on the autistic spectrum in mainstream secondary schools', *Autism*, 12(1), pp. 23–46. https://doi.org/10.1177/1362361307085267

Jackson, P., Skirrow, P., and Hare, D. (2012) 'Asperger through the looking glass: An exploratory study of self-understanding in people with Asperger's syndrome', *Journal of Autism and Developmental Disorders*, 42(5), pp. 697–706. https://doi.org/10.1007/s10803-011-1296-8

James, W. (2001) *Psychology: The Briefer Course*. New York: Dover Publications Inc. (Original work published 1892)

John, R. P. S., Knott, F. J., and Harvey, K. N. (2018) 'Myths about autism: An exploratory study using focus groups', *Autism*, 22(7), pp. 845–854. https://doi.org/10.1177/1362361317714990

Johnson, T. D., and Joshi, A. (2016) 'Dark clouds or silver linings? A stigma threat perspective on the implications of an autism diagnosis for workplace well-being', *Journal of Applied Psychology*, 101(3), pp. 430–449. https://doi.org/10.1037/apl0000058

Jordan, R., and Powell, S. (1995) *Understanding and Teaching Children with Autism*. Chichester: Wiley.

Kooken, W. C., Haase, J. E., and Russell, K. M. (2007) '"I've been through something": Poetic explorations of African American women's cancer survivorship', *Western Journal of Nursing Research*, 29(7), pp. 896–919. https://doi.org/10.1177/0193945907302968

King, M. C., Williams, E. I., and Gleeson, K. (2017) 'Using photographs to explore self-understanding in adolescent boys with an autism spectrum condition', *Journal of Intellectual and Developmental Disability*, 44(2), pp. 232–243. https://doi.org/10.3109/13668250.2017.1326586

Lakey, J., Rodgers, G., and Scoble, R. (2014) 'What are the different characteristics of research impact?', in P. Denicolo (ed.), *Achieving Impact in Research*. Los Angeles: SAGE, pp. 33–46.

Latif, S. (2016) 'The ethics and consequences of making autism spectrum disorder diagnoses', in K. Runswick-Cole, R. Mallett and S. Timimi (eds.), *Re-Thinking Autism: Diagnosis, Identity and Equality*. London: Jessica Kingsley, pp. 288–299.

Lee, A., and Hobson, R. P. (1998) 'On developing self-concepts: A controlled study of children and adolescents with autism', *Journal of Child Psychology and Psychiatry*, 39(8), pp. 1131–1144. https://doi.org/10.1017/S0021963098003023

MacNeil, C. (2000) 'The prose and cons of poetic representation in evaluation reporting', *American Journal of Evaluation*, 21(3), pp. 359–367. https://doi.org/10.1016/S1098-2140(01)00100-X

Madill, L., and Hopper, T. F. (2007) 'The best of the best discourse on health: Poetic insights on how professional sport socializes a family of men into hegemonic masculinity and physical inactivity', *American Journal of Men's Health*, 1(1), pp. 44–59. https://doi.org/10.1177/1557988306294604

Milton, D. E. M. (2012). On the ontological status of autism: The 'double empathy problem'. *Disability & Society*, 27(6), pp. 883–887. https://doi.org/10.1080/09687599.2012.710008

Milton, D. (2014) 'Autistic expertise: A critical reflection on the production of knowledge in autism studies', *Autism*, 18(7), pp. 794–802. https://doi.org/10.1177/1362361314525281

Milton, D., and Bracher, M. (2013) 'Autistics speak but are they heard?', *Journal of the BSA MedSoc Group*, 7(2), pp. 61–69.

Milton, D., and Sims, T. (2016) 'How is a sense of well-being and belonging constructed in the accounts of autistic adults?', *Disability and Society*, 31(4), pp. 520–534. https://doi.org/10.1080/09687599.2016.1186529

Mogensen, L., and Mason, J. (2015) 'The meaning of a label for teenagers negotiating identity: Experiences with autism spectrum disorder', *Sociology of Health and Illness*, 37(2), pp. 255–269. https://doi.org/10.1111/1467-9566.12208

Molloy, H., and Vasil, L. (2004) *Asperger Syndrome, Adolescence, and Identity: Looking Beyond the Label*. London: Jessica Kingsley.

Neisser, U. (1988). Five kinds of self-knowledge. *Philosophical Psychology*, 1(1), pp. 35–59. https://doi.org/10.1080/09515088808572924

O'Dell, L., Bertilsdotter Rosqvist, H., Ortega, F., Brownlow, C., and Orsini, M. (2016) 'Critical autism studies: Exploring epistemic dialogues and intersections, challenging dominant understandings of autism', *Disability and Society*, 31(2), pp. 166–179. https://doi.org/10.1080/09687599.2016.1164026

Orsini, M., and Davidson, J. (2013) 'Introduction. Critical autism studies: Notes on an emerging field', in J. Davidson and M. Orsini (eds.), *Worlds of Autism*. London: University of Minnesota Press, pp. 1–28.

Pellicano, E., Dinsmore, A., and Charman, T. (2014a) 'Views on researcher-community engagement in autism research in the United Kingdom: A mixed-methods study', *PLOS ONE*, 9(10), pp. 1–11. https://doi.org/10.1371/journal.pone.0109946

Pellicano, E., Dinsmore, A., and Charman, T. (2014b) 'What should autism research focus upon? Community views and priorities from the United Kingdom', *Autism*, 18(7), pp. 756–770. https://doi.org/10.1177/1362361314529627

Poindexter, C. C. (2002) 'Research as poetry: A couple experiences HIV', *Qualitative Inquiry*, 8(6), pp. 707–714. https://doi.org/10.1177/1077800402238075

Preece, D. (2002) 'Consultation with children with autistic spectrum disorders about their experience of short-term residential care', *British Journal of Learning Disabilities*, 30(3), pp. 97–104. https://doi.org/10.1046/j.1468-3156.2002.00179.x

Preece, D., and Jordan, R. (2010) 'Obtaining the views of children and young people with autism spectrum disorders about their experience of daily life and social care support', *British Journal of Learning Disabilities*, 38(1), pp. 10–20. https://doi.org/10.1111/j.1468-3156.2009.00548.x

Prendergast, M. (2009). "Poem is what?" Poetic inquiry in qualitative social science research. *International Review of Qualitative Research*, 1(4), pp. 541–568. https://doi.org/10.1525/irqr.2009.1.4.541

Redmond, J. (2006) *How to Write a Poem*. Malden, MA: Blackwell.

Reilly, R. C. (2013) 'Found poems, member checking and crises of representation', *Qualitative Report*, 18(15), pp. 1–18.

Rice, E. (2018) 'Learning from autistic pupils in mainstream secondary schools: The value of inclusive research methods', *Share: Practice, Knowledge and Innovation*. 50th Anniversary Special Edition, pp. 8–9.

Richardson, L. (2001) 'Poetic representation of interviews', in J. F. Gubrium and J. A. Holstein (eds.), *Handbook of Interview Research Context and Method*. Thousand Oaks, CA: Sage Publications, pp. 876–891.

Ridout, S. (2017) 'The autistic voice and creative methodologies', *Qualitative Research Journal*, 17(1), pp. 52–64. https://doi.org/10.1108/QRJ-07-2016-0046

Scott-Barrett, J., Cebula, K., and Florian, L. (2018) 'Listening to young people with autism: Learning from researcher experiences', *International Journal of Research and Method in Education*, 42(2), pp. 163–184. https://doi.org/10.1080/1743727X.2018.1462791

Vanwyk, C., Rochon, R., Devin, L., Burnell, L., Davidson, J. E., and Virgen, M. (2012) 'Poetic transcription to explore the concept of caring', *International Journal of Caring Sciences*, 5(2), pp. 120–128.

Williams, D. (1996) *Autism: An Inside-Out Approach: An Innovative Look at the "Mechanics" of "Autism" and Its Developmental "Cousins."* London: Jessica Kingsley.

Williams, E. I., Gleeson, K., and Jones, B. E. (2017) 'How pupils on the autism spectrum make sense of themselves in the context of their experiences in a mainstream school setting: A qualitative metasynthesis', *Autism*, 23(1), pp. 8–28. https://doi.org/10.1177/1362361317723836

Winstone, N., Huntington, C., Goldsack, L., Kyrou, E., and Millward, L. (2014) 'Eliciting rich dialogue through the use of activity-oriented interviews: Exploring self-identity in autistic young people', *Childhood*, 21(2), pp. 190–206. https://doi.org/10.1177/0907568213491771

Wolosky, S. (2001) *The Art of Poetry: How to Read a Poem*. Oxford: Oxford University Press.

12
A PERSONAL ACCOUNT OF NEURODIVERSITY, ACADEMIA AND ACTIVISM

Damian Milton

Introduction

Traditionally the field of autism studies has been dominated by biological and psychological research (Pellicano et al., 2013; Milton and Bracher, 2013). Only recently, very large international autism-related projects have been announced such as AIMS-2 (EU-AIMS, 2018) and Spectrum10K framed within a medical model discourse of what autism pertains to be and thus what kinds of intervention would be of potential benefit – i.e. psychopharmacology. In contrast to this are the concerns of community 'stakeholders' who have highlighted the need for social (and social model) research (Pellicano et al., 2013; Milton and Bracher, 2013; James Lind Alliance, 2018).

The neurodiversity movement (in the UK context) can be said to have developed as a form of activism directly opposed to the way academics and clinicians defined particular groups of people purely in terms of pathological deviations from an idealised notion of normalcy. This positionality and resultant ethos have been particularly prevalent within the autistic community which has borrowed heavily from social model (or variations thereof) activist and academic perspectives. Having said this, there are a wide variety of views within the neurodiversity movement and not all would take such a traditional social model approach, including Judy Singer (2017) who coined the term 'neurodiversity'. In different countries the prevalence of social model theorising may be less dominant, and activism will have differing roots and influences.

In this chapter, I reflect upon my position as a scholar-activist working within and between the neurodiversity movement and the academy (within a UK context) and the power differentials that have developed within autism studies, including within critical sociological work, which are reflected in the formation of niche subcultures. Finally, the precarious position of being an 'endorsed insider' (and simultaneously a target of disapproval) scholar-activist will be examined, the potential pitfalls, the expectations and tensions that can come about from others one interacts with, and what can be done to navigate such terrain.

Scholar-activism and the neurodiversity movement in the UK

Autistic people studying autism can be seen across disciplines and theoretical outlooks in ever-increasing numbers. In recent years, the crossover between academia and activism within the neurodiversity movement can be said to have become yet more prevalent, particularly in the UK with the development of the Participatory Autism Research Collective (Milton et al., 2019). This network was formed in 2015 and was heavily influenced by previous autistic-led initiatives such as the 'Theorising Autism Project' (Greenstein, 2014) and the setting up of the autistic-led academic journal *Autonomy, the Critical Journal of Interdisciplinary Autism Studies* in 2012. These projects have all sought to increase the participation of autistic people in research at all levels of the research process.

Alongside these developments, however, is much scepticism and many stories of broken trust within the autistic community regarding the pursuits of researchers in the field of autism studies (Milton, 2014). Many within the autistic community are highly sceptical and distrustful of autism research and are against being 'fishbowled' and 'quote-mined' (Moon, cited in Milton and Moon, 2012). There is concern that lived experience is used to advance the agendas and careers of non-autistic researchers without benefits in return.

Being a scholar-activist means occupying a space between roles that are likely to cause tensions and competing expectations regarding action and discourse (Suzuki and Mayorga, 2014). As an autistic scholar, whilst having been trained in numerous academic disciplines, I have only been partially socialised into academic cultures, often surviving on the periphery of the academy. It was only recently that I took up a position of a part-time lecturer (after 17 years of more precarious academic positions). Although not diagnosed as autistic until my mid-30s, I was already heavily involved in scholarship as well as activist pursuits. My upbringing was steeped in both traditions (and the intermingling of the two) with many family members going on to teach or work in universities and/or becoming involved in political movements. Perhaps the earliest scholar-activist in my family was the rather infamous figure of John Maclean (1879–1923), the Bolshevik consul to Britain once dubbed 'Britain's most dangerous man'. Such an influence inevitably impacted on my own cultural disposition when coming into contact with inequality and discrimination.

> I wish no harm to any human being, but I, as one man, am going to exercise my freedom of speech. No human being on the face of the earth, no government is going to take from me my right to speak, my right to protest against wrong, my right to do everything that is for the benefit of mankind. I am not here, then, as the accused; I am here as the accuser of capitalism dripping with blood from head to foot.
>
> *(Maclean, 1919)*

Growing up in my family, Maclean's ethos impacted on me in terms of how scholarship and activism could be mutually beneficial activities. Maclean was said to be very proud of his studies in Political Science and started his career as a teacher. He took this political understanding to teaching and presenting at rallies of workers on the Clyde in Glasgow. Anything but an academic elitist, he wanted to empower through education as well as challenge social injustices through activism. It is the same ethos that inspires much of my own work as an autistic scholar-activist.

I first came into contact with disability activism and scholarship through a combination of my own academic pursuits in the field of sociology, alongside that of my mother who was studying art at postgraduate level and relating her work to an experience of physical disability following a road-traffic accident. My own experience of being a dispositional 'outsider' and contact with psychiatric professionals led me towards the work of Goffman and Foucault alongside that of radical psychiatrists. Following my son's diagnosis of autism and my own self-identification and subsequent diagnosis of Asperger's, I focused my own scholar-activist efforts into the field of autism studies and the neurodiversity movement.

Establishing oneself as an autistic presenter at autism and academic conferences more widely can be a fraught path. Despite the wide-ranging experiences of autistic people, representations have been at a tokenistic level; a common approach is being asked to talk of one's 'personal story' rather than wider issues. As with other categorisations of disability and mental health there would seem to be a 'sweet spot' of those chosen to represent autistic voices: deemed autistic enough to be seen as exotic, but capable and charismatic enough to be of interest and yet also not too controversial. Being allowed to contribute to the politics of autism and remain subversive is difficult, with negative impressions formed from a normative value base by others creating a barrier. Being academically qualified can help strengthen one's status and potential platform, yet navigating the academic arena as an autistic person is far from straightforward and can be made more difficult when considering intersectional issues people may face. This is not easy for an autistic person to navigate, particularly with the potential for exploitation to suit another's agenda (Botha, 2021).

Power differentials in the field of autism studies

Within the field of autism studies one can see a distinct differential of power between dominant biological and cognitive/behavioural psychological academia and that of social research, particularly that of a participatory nature (Pellicano et al., 2013; Milton and Bracher, 2013; Fletcher-Watson et al., 2018). This imbalance in the field is perhaps exemplified by recent disquiet and critique regarding projects that are biomedical in orientation (Mery et al., 2018). Previously, utilising the theories of Collins and Evans (2007), I have suggested that there is often a lack of interactional expertise – a form of collective tacit knowledge that can only be acquired through immersion in the language and practices of a social group – that researchers in this field have for autistic communities and culture (Milton, 2014). Whilst collaborative efforts can be made to reduce this 'double empathy problem' (Milton, 2012; 2014; Milton et al., 2018) – a breakdown in reciprocity and mutual comprehension between social actors – this is not helped by current power dynamics and funding structures.

The disparity between the research topics that are well funded and the priorities of community interests within the UK context (Pellicano et al., 2013; Fletcher-Watson et al., 2018), between priorities of a more medicalised or social nature, strongly suggest a neoliberal culture of the contemporary academy running counter to community interests. If one has impact within a community, academic impact is often positively improved as a consequence, as more people become aware of one's work and start applying it to practical contexts – which can be seen by the popularity and broader readership of articles concerning topics such as participatory research and the double empathy problem within mainstream academic journals. There are exceptions to this, though, if one does not publish enough in peer-reviewed journals or draw in funding for the university. The labour required to work with communities *and* to publish through other media is not generally paid for, yet if one sets high standards for a participatory ethos in their research practice, such effort is required. In my view, such work often has genuine impact, although of the kind that may not draw attention from the Research Excellence Framework (REF), which is how academic outputs are monitored with the UK context. Organisational agendas regarding higher education, and what is considered 'impact', may jar with what is considered impactful research from within marginalised communities (Derickson and Routledge, 2015), which is often about making a difference to their lives in practical ways. At a recent conference held by PARC in June 2019 at London South Bank University (LSBU), one speaker talked of how they had once naively thought that autism research was for the benefit of autistic people. This was greeted with much amusement by many of the autistic people in attendance. It ought not to be a comical suggestion to have autism research that serves autistic community needs.

In 2015, Professor Nicola Martin and I initiated the Participatory Autism Research Collective (PARC, 2018). PARC was set up with the purpose of bringing together autistic people, including scholars and activists (but not exclusively), together with early-career researchers and practitioners who work with autistic people. The aim was to build a community where those who wished to see more significant involvement of autistic people in research could share knowledge and expertise. Originating with events at LSBU, the network has grown across the UK and invited international interest. It is currently unfunded (although particular events associated with PARC have been) and works somewhat outside of traditional academic structures, subverting traditional ways in which one can have 'impact' with one's work. By not being an official entity, there are few rules as such. This structure has enjoyed popularity, however, amongst many autistic and non-autistic people working across many disciplines. As a way of working, the PARC network is more akin to a 'rhizomatic' structure than a hierarchical one (Milton, 2016). Rhizomatic structures as outlined by Deleuze and Guattari (1980) resist systems modelled on having an 'original source' and conclusion to activities but rather idealise 'nomadic' systems that look to endlessly establish connections, presenting a boundary-less culture as far as possible. Whilst PARC has a simplistic structure of a 'chair' and 'convenors', these are simply to help drive forward and communicate the activities of PARC. As an open network, it has not been confined by strict rules and structures. Whilst there are disadvantages to such systems, particularly for autistic people who prefer clearly laid out rules and structures to work with, this can be alleviated somewhat by partnering more established organisations and working alongside other autistic-led efforts regarding participation in academia.

Critical and participatory work in autism studies is further held back, however, by subcultural divisions within what has come to be termed 'Critical Autism Studies' (CAS) (Davidson and Orsini, 2013; Runswick-Cole et al., 2016; Woods et al., 2018). Recently, colleagues and I undertook a citation survey of this growing area to find a split between differing groups of authors, with many not referencing autistic authors' work who are nevertheless having significant impact upon other autistic authors, or academics working in other disciplines within wider autism studies (Milton, 2018). Whilst there may be a cultural inevitability of competing interests within the field of autism studies it is often the voices of autistic people which have the hardest struggles to become recognised. Such differences must also be seen in the light of intersectional disparities within which these subcultures have emerged.

A precarious position – tensions and reflections

To take a position as a scholar-activist within the contemporary personal and social dynamics of social media is not an easy task. Such forums can often seem to be spaces for the venting of neoliberal populism feeding into a nightmare of Rand-esque legitimation of cultural discrimination, coupled with a sense of entitlement in crisis. Social media provides a platform for endless streams of people seeking self-validation in order to combat feelings of helplessness and alienation. As examples, I have been called the following: "Bigot", "The Katie Hopkins of the autism community", "A master manipulator", "Evil", and charged with "Milton-splaining". If one is to advocate strongly for a position, there are many who may be in agreement, but there will also be those advocating for the opposite position, often with just as much passion and gusto as one's own advocacy. Yet, ad hominem attacks are probably not that effective in terms of reputation management to anybody but the converted to one's ideological 'faith'. A particularly problematic example occurred for me personally in 2018 when a defamatory and inaccurate petition regarding my views on the concept of 'pathological demand avoidance' (PDA) was circulated, which acquired nearly 700 signatories within two days before being removed following threat of legal action. This gave me a valuable lesson, however, regarding online petitions and how easy it can be to see what is written as truthful and jump on bandwagons without knowing the evidence of the situation. Here is a good example of why 'doing one's research' can be helpful in one's activism. For me, informed theoretical reflection through academia informs my activism, and my personal experience and activism informs what I should be reflecting about; scholarship and activism thus creating a virtuous circle for driving social change through one's own agency.

Hughes (2009) makes a distinction between the disabled people's movement in the UK that has challenged the hegemony of the biomedical model and many disability groups that have utilised the specialised medical knowledge associated with their 'condition'. Such 'biological citizens' use their impairment status, diagnosis or classification in their claims to identity. Such a view can create too much of a binary dichotomy, however, particularly when applied to the neurodiversity movement (Woods et al., 2018). Whilst on the surface the claim to an autistic identity reifies the medical model classification of autism, this is often not the case in the narrative regarding autism that many autistic people deploy, which would be more in common with a social model of disability (McWade et al., 2015; Woods et al., 2018).

In order to make sustained change and to be a part of that, one needs to build solidarity with others. In his analysis of rhizomatic structures in activism, Neill (2013) suggests:

> Any movement for diversity and inclusion, must by definition be diverse and inclusive. Sometimes this may lead to unfamiliar, uncomfortable and difficult compromises, but the most creative work happens when people with very different ways of doing things get together, and use the conflicts that happen between them as sources of productive energy rather than allowing them to become destructive rivalries.
>
> *(Neill, 2013:1)*

As a scholar-activist, contemplating what to focus on, and why, can be full of tensions. The often-stated goal of 'consensus' seems a somewhat laughable one, unless one is seeking agreement on a short and widely interpreted set of core principles, perhaps. What does solidarity look like when it encompasses such diversity? Whilst not wishing to appropriate terms from other civil rights movements, a lot can be learnt from the experiences of such social currents more generally. Disability activism also cannot help but become entangled with the activism created from other forms of oppression, or responses to them (Goodley, 2013), and should not be reliant on a few key figures for success (Oliver and Barnes, 2010). This is why it has been essential for autistic people as a collective to begin to claim their own voice when it comes to the production of knowledge about autistic people, in all their diversity.

Conclusion

When trying to convince someone of a rhetorical argument, the philosopher Aristotle suggested one needed to be logical, trustworthy, and appeal to emotion. Following this, one will need to find the allies in one's cause that one can trust to help build a collaborative community of practice or network. One will need evidence and rationale in order to choose targets for efforts wisely. One will need to consider when emotional responses are required and when perhaps they are not. Such social understanding and performance are perhaps not what autistic people are famed for, yet nor are non-autistic people when interacting with autistic people (Milton, 2012; 2014; Milton et al., 2018). One may only be offered token gestures of engagement, but such engagement can create a dynamic where subversion and greater influence are possible. Compromise is always situated within power relations, and therefore there are times when it is best not to do so. A revolution in theory and practice in relation to autistic people is not an outcome that can be accomplished and 'ticked off'; rather, there is a need for a continual sustained effort. As my colleague Dinah Murray once stated, one needs to:

> Proceed like water.
>
> *(Murray, personal correspondence, 2018)*

References

Botha, M. (2021). Academic, activist, or advocate? angry, entangled, and emerging: A critical reflection on autism knowledge production. *Frontiers in Psychology*, 4196. https://doi.org/10.3389/fpsyg.2021.727542.

Davidson, J., & Orsini, M. (Eds.). (2013). *Worlds of Autism: Across the Spectrum of Neurological Difference*. Minneapolis: University of Minnesota Press.

Deleuze, G., & Guattari, F. (1980). *A Thousand Plateaus: Capitalism and Schizophrenia Vol. 2*, trans. Brian Massumi. London: Athlone.

Derickson, K. D., & Routledge, P. (2015). Resourcing scholar-activism: Collaboration, transformation, and the production of knowledge. *The Professional Geographer*, 67(1), 1–7. https://doi.org/10.1080/00330124.2014.883958.

EU-AIMS. (2018). AIMS-2-TRIALS: World's largest autism grant will transform research landscape. Online: https://www.eu-aims.eu/en/news-eu-aims/news-detail/aims-2-trials-worlds-largest-autism-grant-will-transform-research-landscape/3f11df96a37ca7478e7bc8a3d026a3c/, 17/08/18.

Fletcher-Watson, S., Adams, J., Brook, K., Charman, T., Crane, L., Cusack, J., Leekham, S., Milton, D., Parr, J., & Pellicano, E. (2018). Making the future together: Shaping autism research through meaningful participation. *Autism Online*, First, published: August 10, 2018. https://doi.org/10.1177/1362361318786721.

Greenstein, A. (2014). Theorising autism project - Engaging autistic people in the research process. Review of a seminar day at the Institute of Education. *Autonomy, the Critical Journal of Interdisciplinary Autism Studies*, 1(3). Online: http://www.larryarnold.net/Autonomy/index.php/autonomy/article/view/RE4, 17/07/20.

Goodley, D. (2013). Dis/entangling critical disability studies. *Disability & Society*, 28(5), 631–644. https://doi.org/10.1080/09687599.2012.717884.

Hughes, B. (2009). Disability activisms: Social model stalwarts and biological citizens. *Disability & Society*, 24(6), 677–688. https://doi.org/10.1080/09687590903160118.

James Lind Alliance. (2018). Autism top 10. Online: http://www.jla.nihr.ac.uk/priority-setting-partnerships/autism/top-10-priorities/, 17/08/18.

Maclean, J. (1919). Speech from the dock. Online: https://www.marxists.org/archive/maclean/works/1918-dock.htm, 17/08/18.

McWade, B., Milton, D., & Beresford, P. (2015). Mad studies and neurodiversity: A dialogue. *Disability & Society*, 30(2), 305–309. https://doi.org/10.1080/09687599.2014.1000512.

Mery, D., Murray, D., & Brook, K. (2018). Attempting to lift the veil of secrecy over AIMS-2. Online: https://participatoryautismresearch.wordpress.com/2018/08/11/attempting-to-lift-the-veil-of-secrecy-over-aims-2/, 17/08/18.

Milton, D. (2012). On the ontological status of autism: The 'double empathy problem'. *Disability & Society*, 27(6), 883–887. https://doi.org/10.1080/09687599.2012.710008.

Milton, D. (2014). Autistic expertise: A critical reflection on the production of knowledge in autism studies. *Autism*, 18(7), 794–802. https://doi.org/10.1177/1362361314525281.

Milton, D. (2016). Tracing the influence of Fernand Deligny on autism studies. *Disability & Society*, 31(2), 285–289. https://doi.org/10.1080/09687599.2016.1161975.

Milton, D. (2018). "Said the autistic endorsed autistic informed academic": Neurodiversity, Academia and Activism. In: *9th Lancaster Disability Studies Conference*, 11–13 September 2018, Lancaster, UK.

Milton, D., & Bracher, M. (2013). Autistics speak but are they heard. *Journal of the BSA Med.Soc. Group*, 7, 61–69.

Milton, D., Heasman, B., & Sheppard, E. (2018). Double empathy. In *Encyclopedia of Autism Spectrum Disorders* (pp. 1–8). New York, NY

Milton, D., & Moon, L. (2012). The normalisation agenda and the psycho-emotional disablement of autistic people. *Autonomy, the Critical Journal of Interdisciplinary Autism Studies, 1*(1), 1–8.

Milton, D., Ridout, S., Kourti, M., Loomes, G., & Martin, N. (2019). A critical reflection on the development of the Participatory Autism Research Collective (PARC). *Tizard Learning Disability Review, 24*(2), 82–89.

Neill, M. (2013). *Rhizomatic Leadership and Meadian Networking*. Online: http://peoplethinkingaction.blogspot.com/2013/11/rhizomatic-leadership-and-meadian.html, 15/08/18.

Oliver, M., & Barnes, C. (2010). Disability studies, disabled people and the struggle for inclusion. *British Journal of Sociology of Education, 31*(5), 547–560.

Participatory Autism Research Collective (PARC). (2018). Online: www.PARCautism.co.uk, 15/08/18.

Pellicano, L., Dinsmore, A., & Charman, T. (2013). *A Future Made Together: Shaping Autism Research in the UK*. London: Centre for Research in Autism Education.

Runswick-Cole, K., Mallet, R., & Timimi, S. (2016). *Re-thinking Autism: Diagnosis, Identity and Equality*. Jessica Kingsley Publishers. London.

Singer, J. (2017). *NeuroDiversity: The Birth of an Idea*. Self-published.

Suzuki, D., & Mayorga, E. (2014). Scholar-activism: A twice told tale. *Multicultural Perspectives, 16*(1), 16–20. https://doi.org/10.1080/15210960.2013.867405.

Woods, R., Milton, D., Arnold, L., & Graby, S. (2018). Redefining critical autism studies: A more inclusive interpretation. *Disability & Society, 33*, 1–6. https://doi.org/10.1080/09687599.2018.1454380.

PART 3
Community and culture

13
'AUTOPIA'
A vision for autistic acceptance and belonging

Luke Beardon

Based on Luke's presentation of 'Autopia' (a vision for autistic acceptance and belonging in a future dimension) this chapter introduces the author's statement: 'My hypothesis is that there is a pervasive and invidious pattern of thought, behaviour, and belief that is at the heart of a societal "norm" that is, in effect, destroying autistic lives'; identifies various components of autistic existence that appear to be common (current) experiences; and elaborates on some areas of practice that could change in order to reduce harm to autistic children and adults, and redress the (im) balance that appears to be the status quo.

From the mini poem – 'conform to the norm ... or be deemed in the wrong ...' – onwards, the chapter firmly roots itself in direct contrast to the medical model of disability and identifies that the myriad problems faced by autistic people are not as an outcome of being autistic per se, but often (usually) through lack of knowledge, understanding, acceptance, willingness to listen, and change.

Concepts such as 'inclusion' are critiqued in favour of Luke's preferred goal – the autistic quality of life. Education, autistic sociality, and employment are just some of the areas that the chapter will discuss, along with Luke's 'three golden rules' that he promotes as a way of working towards autistic well-being for the future.

Note on terms: by 'we' I refer to society in general; I refer to me, Luke Beardon (and views are my own, based on decades of experience and engaging with the autistic population); 'Autopia' refers to an 'autistic utopia' – a vision for the future that we should, in my view, be striving towards, and is achievable; PNT stands for Predominant Neurotype, my preferred term for the non-autistic population.

Ok – so to be absolutely clear, when I refer to autistic populations for the purposes of this chapter, I am simply doing that; in other words, I am *not* referring to autistic individuals who have additional intellectual disabilities. I am also very well aware of the negative impact that being autistic within current society can bring; please note – language is important. I am not suggesting that being autistic is negative per se, nor that being autistic means that there is invariably a negative impact. I am absolutely of the belief that it is the combination of being autistic within a society that has a misplaced, problematic, and inherently negative view of autism that causes myriad problems for the individual (and wider family). *It is not being autistic that is the problem.* The first of my golden rules that I have written about elsewhere (Beardon, 2017:11) is worth reiterating:

Autism + environment = outcome

This is a simple yet effective way of explaining why the environment has such a huge part to play in the concept of Autopia. Autism in and of itself does not automatically 'lead' to any particular outcome; it is the *combination of the person and their environment* that will dictate outcomes throughout life. If we can't change a person being autistic (which we can't) and if we want to change outcomes for the autistic population, we then by definition must change the environment. Environment literally covers everything that influences the autistic person – so if we understand that the problems faced by autistic people currently are as a result of environmental factors (which, in the main, means 'people') then it is clear that we have an awful long way to go to reach a fair society that doesn't disadvantage the autistic population.

This may sound a little harsh – but I do believe that society in general has an unconscious bias against autistic people; not invariably, but commonly, autistic children and adults are seen as very much second-class citizens. I genuinely think that this is analogous to institutionalised racism – and is widespread across all of Western society. The fact that it is an unconscious bias is perhaps the most troubling – as it denotes just how deep-rooted the problem is: why would anyone be addressing a problem that isn't even in conscious thought? As Milton (2016) notably points out, social oppression of autistic people can be to the extent of such ableism as to deem individuals lesser than human. And yet the issues are hiding in plain sight; they don't need much searching for. Scratching beneath the veneer uncovers horrors that (I hope) most of society would be horrified to be a part of. The tragedy model of autism (Chown and Beardon, 2017) whereby the very existence of a human can be seen as problematic, along with the lower life expectancy of autistics (Bishop-Fitzpatrick and Kind, 2017) and higher incidents of suicide (Cassidy and Rogers, 2017), speaks volumes. I believe that at some point in the future we will look back at these times and wonder what on earth we were thinking; much like the utter, indefatigable, and just contempt we now have for our past whereby homosexuality was deemed a psychiatric condition and individuals were persecuted for their sexuality, so we will wonder why, in order to 'be autistic', one must be clinically assessed as 'lesser'. Current autism criteria and most definitions are rife with deficit-based language – one is referred to as impaired, disordered, and so on; in other words, an imperfect model of what is seen as the 'norm'. This is hateful, unjust, and inaccurate. Being different is not the equivalent of being less; hence the mini poem cited in the introduction that, while terribly written to the point of literary criminality, does sum up how autism seems to be viewed in current society. Any 'difference' identified in the autistic child's development, cognition, sensory world, communication style, and sociality is immediately branded as an impairment, or deficit – as opposed to a different way of being.

I can only briefly identify some of what I understand to be the key areas for change before Autopia becomes more than just a premise. What is clear from the outset, though, is that there needs to be a paradigm shift in thinking as to what autism actually means to those who are autistic. It is astonishing that so little is afforded to 'the autistic voice' when there are so many autistic people who have so much rich experience to share. The very foundations upon which autism is currently understood seem to me to be flawed. The fact that autism is defined within medical manuals – one within a manual for psychiatric conditions, the other within a manual for diseases – speaks volumes. Surely it is safe to say that autism is not a psychiatric condition or a disease, and yet here we are. Until this outdated medical model of autism ceases to be taught as if it were current thinking, we are doing the autistic population a huge disservice. The terms we are encouraged to use to tell autistic people that they are 'disordered' are not helpful; rarely do professionals take a step back and reflect on just what impact referring to humans in this way will actually have. So much of the autism narrative is about dehumanising autistic people; no wonder so many end up on the wrong side of mental well-being.

The Autopia vision aims to reframe autism within the disability framework. Autism is (currently) firmly placed as a disability; this is useful as it helps protect individuals from discrimination and gives some level of guidance within the environment as to how autistic individuals might be better supported. However, it also means that one is required to get a 'medical diagnosis' before being 'allowed' to be autistic. I acknowledge that there are some areas in which self-identification is deemed to be just as valid as a medical diagnosis – for example, some autistic-led research will accept co-researchers who self-identify; these examples could be seen as windows into a future Autopia.

- Autopia recognises that what might be considered disability in one context might be considered an ability in another

Autopia recognises that autistic individuals are likely to have a so-called 'spiky profile'; in other words, they are more likely to have areas of skill and areas of weakness that are more profound than their predominant neurotype (PNT) peers. This is a clue as to how society can adapt to meet the needs of autistic individuals; giving credence to the spiky profile and thus changing education and employment could dramatically alter the life outcomes for the autistic person. 'Allowing' a secondary school pupil to utilise her academic autodidactic strengths so she reaches her potential, or providing autism-friendly job descriptions based on specialism rather than generic skills, could make all the difference to the autistic human. Matching (adapting) the environment to the person (not the other way around) may go a long way to decreasing the uneven playing field that so often autistic people find themselves on.

- Autopia recognises that disability is a fluid concept that requires challenging

Disability is a term that has either no neat definition or, at least, a variety of neat definitions that not everyone can agree upon. As a result, it is unclear to many whether autism should be considered as a disability. Autopia recognises that, irrespective of definition, autism can be disabling (in the extreme) or poorly understood; Autopia promotes the concept that if autism is misunderstood, then the risk of bad practice (which, in some cases, can lead to irreparable harm to the autistic person) will increase.

- Autopia understands autism (currently) as a *disadvantage* rather than an inherent 'problem'

Rather than framing autism automatically as a disability (with all its medical-model deficit-based connotations) I think we are far better off understanding autism as a high-risk disadvantage. And this is no hyperbole. Autistic children and adults can be at a huge disadvantage simply by existing in the PNT world if there are no adaptations to the environment. This can, and must, change. Not only is it unethical to ignore the need for environmental change for autistic people; in many cases it is unlawful. It is clear that autistic people are often at a substantial disadvantage in environments that, with change, could level the playing field and remove that disadvantage. The question remains as to why so many institutions seem reluctant to make those changes.

Autopia understands the harm that can be done from the outset, when autistic people disclose to others that they are autistic. Even this seemingly simple declaration can cause damage; some extraordinary responses to the phrase 'I'm autistic', which are real-life examples that I have been aware of in recent months, include (with additional comment in parentheses):

- But you don't look autistic (what does 'looking autistic' even mean? It's a nonsensical idea that one can 'see' autism)
- But you're nothing like my friend's son (so what? Why would I, an adult woman, be anything like your friend's five-year-old boy?)
- But you're a woman (… thanks for noticing … but what has gender got to do with it? Just because society needs to catch up on the notion that autistic women exist, doesn't mean that they haven't been around for decades)
- But you're an adult (yes, autistic children invariably become autistic adults)
- But you seem so caring (such a damaging thing to say – autistic people can be just as caring, if not more, than the PNT)
- But you can read and write (it is astonishing that anyone might assume that being autistic means that one lacks specific capabilities)
- But you can talk to me (since when has being able to talk led to people thinking one is not autistic?)
- But you're lovely (this one really demonstrates how negatively some people view autism; the fact that there is ever an assumption that being autistic precludes one from being a lovely person shows just how far we need to go before a good understanding is reached)
- But you've got loads of friends (being autistic does not mean that one doesn't like people – contrary to popular belief)
- But you've got a good job (yes, autistic people can work! And many will make for excellent employees so long as the right environment is created)
- But you're married (autistic people can make for fabulous spouses)
- But you're rubbish at maths/music/IT/etc. (this indicates just how 'one-dimensional' much of society is when it comes to understanding autism)
- But you've got kids (er – not to get too gritty but yes, being autistic does not preclude one from engaging in activity that subsequently leads to human creation)

The three Autopian 'golden nuggets' are:

Golden rule: autism + environment = outcome
Golden concept: PNT-based concepts need to be translated
before they are applied to the autistic
Golden notion: the amount of energy put into effecting change
needs to warrant the intended outcome

I have already covered the 'golden rule'. The 'golden concept' in our Autopian future will be embedded as a standard mantra that all those involved with the interaction between self and autistic understand and follow. What it means is that any engagement with an autistic person needs some level of attention and possible translation to make it suitable; that the PNT approach – while useful and suitable for the PNT – may increase risk of detriment if applied without due consideration to the autistic person. So, everything from education (including how we assess knowledge) through to employment (including how we recruit) through to communication, socialising, relationships – everything in life, in fact – should be understood within an autism context. Otherwise, we are at risk of discrimination and disadvantage.

The 'golden notion' identifies that while many autistic people can learn to adapt to conform to PNT expectations, the amount of energy it takes is simply not worth it. And yet, this is still the apparent 'go-to' option in many areas (if not all) for the current-day autistic. It seems almost invariable that the immediate response to an autistic child behaving in a normally autistic manner is to try and change the behaviour to make it more in line with the PNT. It seems almost invariable that the immediate response to an autistic adult behaving in a normally autistic manner is to try and change the behaviour to make it more in line with the PNT. Why can't autistic children and adults be allowed to be themselves if it isn't causing a genuine problem? Why isn't the autistic way of being accepted (even embraced) on a par with the PNT way of being? Of course, critiques will come up with examples of instances which would appear to make this argument a dangerous one, such as self-injury (to give just one example) and claim that I am suggesting that we should all simply 'let' people suffer. This is a nonsense; not all autistic people will self-injure, and self-injury is not an exclusively autistic way of being – any person within humankind who has elevated levels of anxiety that lead to self-injury clearly needs support of one kind or another. What I am referring to is the plethora of variations of being an autistic person that are so often seen as 'lesser', and demands are made to conform – often at great expense to the autistic person – for seemingly extraordinarily little reward. Along with Milton's 'idealisation of normalcy' (2017) concept and the damage it can lead to, Autopia embraces autistic normality and does not impose the need for conformity.

An Autopian educational system understands that how autistic pupils learn might significantly differ from their PNT peers. Therefore, Autopia embraces difference and includes the following in light of autism acceptance and well-being: fully supported learning opportunities outside of traditional school, including home schooling, flexi-schooling, and schooling in alternative venues (e.g. yurts); better support for autistic adults to train as teachers to allow for more access of autistic students to autistic teachers; block learning opportunities readily available – i.e. subjects taught in blocks (e.g. for a day, a week, or a term at a time) for learners who find learning multiple subjects simultaneously disadvantageous; opportunities to complete 'homework' in environments that are not at home; eradication of assessments that disadvantage autistic students and an increase in the range of ways that knowledge is assessed; educational hours made flexible to suit a wide range of needs; the offer of laptops for those who struggle with writing; autodidactic learning opportunities made available; breaktimes created to allow for relaxation, not necessarily socialising; recognition that some subjects simply will not engage an autistic learner and could be substituted for others that are far more appropriate for longer-term interests; assessments should be governed by readiness rather than age; the notion of age-related peers is questioned for validity.

Autopia also questions whether the concept of inclusion requires a revamp. Rather than a focus on inclusion (whatever that might mean), Autopia firmly situates autistic well-being, need, acceptance, and understanding at the forefront of all educational values and beyond; these values are embedded over the breadth and depth of the autistic life. Inclusivity is likely to mean something quite different from one person to the next; indeed, it may well mean something vastly different to one person depending on which environment s/he is in. Therefore, inclusion is based entirely on individual circumstance and wishes, rather than something that is more likely to be imposed on the population as a whole.

Autistic sociality is absolutely recognised as likely to differ qualitatively and quantitatively in comparison to PNT peers. The notion that the more friends one has is an indication of happiness or well-being is rejected; there is absolute acceptance that solitary activity might be beneficial (or necessary) for a person's well-being; that while social skills might differ to the PNT, this does not mean that the autistic person is impaired – it means that there is a valid set of autistic social skills that should be respected; and it means that the PNT conclude that, in the main, they are, in fact, severely impaired in autistic social skills! Autopia also notes that social chit-chat is rarely the (autistic) norm, and it is perfectly acceptable to withdraw from engaging in such activity that might be harmful to the autistic person.

Employment presents its own challenges to many autistic people and Autopia strives to redress this balance. From application to retirement party and everything in between Autopia encourages a different way of engaging with autistic employees in several ways. The way in which people are recruited in Autopia looks vastly different to current processes. Job descriptions ask for specific skill sets rather than an entire range of largely unnecessary skills. Applications forms are just one method of how one might apply for a job; there are other options available, such as presenting one's CV via a video clip. Employers recognise that only having one way of recruitment is likely to disadvantage autistic employees, so endeavour to be more creative and flexible in their approach. Interviews become a thing of the past for those who are at a distinct disadvantage in those kinds of situations. Employers are no longer made to train in skills areas that they do not need to possess – jobs are allocated on a skills level, rather than having to force an employee into working in areas that do not come naturally to them. Open-plan offices are an option, not a rule. Meetings focus on the agenda, not the social life of the PNT, start on time, keep to time, and finish on time. Autistic specialist advocates are the norm and are available via central funding to support autistic employees with their employer to identify areas of potential from the outset and consult on how to avoid them.

So – how might this vision be realised? The development of a genuine relationship between the PNT and autistic populations, whereby the former is willing to be led by the latter in matters relating to autism, would be a start. From research through to well-being concepts we need to establish a far better understanding – not of 'autism' per se (though I would certainly support that!) – but, more importantly, the autistic lived experience. And the best way to do that? Listen to autistics.

References

Beardon, L. (2017). *Autism in Adults*. Sheldon Press, London

Bishop-Fitzpatrick, L., Kind, A.J.H. (2017). A scoping review of health disparities in autism spectrum disorder. *Journal of Autism and Developmental Disorders*, 47(11), 3380–3391. https://doi.org/10.1007/s10803-017-3251-9

Cassidy, S., Rodgers, J. (2017). Understanding and prevention of suicide in autism. *The Lancet Psychiatry*, 4(6), e11. https://doi.org/10.1016/S2215-0366(17)30162-1

Chown, N., Beardon, L. (2017). Theoretical models and autism. In Volkmar, F., ed., *Encyclopedia of Autism Spectrum Disorders*. Springer, New York. https://doi.org/10.1007/978-1-4614-6435-8_102171-1

Milton, D. (2016). Disposable dispositions: Reflections upon the work of Iris Marion Young in relation to the social oppression of autistic people. *Disability and Society*, 31(10), 1403–1407.

Milton, D. (2017). Challenging the ideology of idealised normalcy. In Milton, D., Martin, N., eds., *Autism and Intellectual Disabilities in Adults*. Pavilion Press, Hove, UK, pp. 7–10.

14
THE MOULIN ROUGE AND THE ROUGE MOULIN

Language, Cartesianism, republicanism and the construct of autism in France

Peter Crosbie

Introduction

There is a growing awareness that the knowledge produced around autism in the predominately white, Anglo-American cultures of the Global North is not shared either in their subcultures or in the Global South. However, there has been little examination of how autism is understood across majority cultures in the West, where the underlying assumption is that from Sheffield to Stockholm to Strasbourg, when we use the term "autism", we mean much the same thing.

In this chapter I want to examine the processes by which knowledge about autism is produced in a Western culture outside the Anglosphere, and how even in a European society which most Anglo-Americans would recognise as similar to their own, profound differences arise.

I'll be looking at France. In doing so, I'll examine how Cartesianism, republicanism and the French language combine to frame the construct of autism in a way that is markedly different to its Anglo-Saxon equivalent. I also want to explore how these factors shape a wider discourse around autism in France, including how autism is situated in models of disability.

I intend this not so much as an examination of the situation in France per se, but as an opportunity to hold up a mirror to how social, cultural and linguistic forces combine to shape the identity known as autism in our own cultures. I also see it as an opportunity to question the idea that there is a single, universal representation of autism that's understood similarly across all cultures, and to challenge the notion that the only way forward for non-Anglo societies is to adopt the Anglo-American representation of autism as their own.

Before we plunge in, a couple of definitions. I'm juxtaposing France with similar English-speaking countries. So, North America, UK and Ireland, Australia and New Zealand, and that's about it. In this context, I've used English-speaking, Anglo-Saxon, Anglophone and Anglosphere interchangeably, but I'm not referring to Anglophone cultures in, say, Africa or South Asia. Equally, I'm using French to refer to the country between Spain and Belgium, not to other Francophone societies. I've also used the term "autist" to refer to autistic people – my one-person crusade to give us our own noun.

Finally, and in all transparency, some content here is derived from a blog I wrote on autism in France (Crosbie, 2017).

Language

Where to begin? As the one thing that all French people share is their language, let's start there. After all, we use words to speak our world into existence. In the beginning was the word, and in this case, that word is "autisme".

If we're looking at differences between French and English in the context of factors that could contribute to a uniquely French construct of autism, there's not much to see here, just that additional "e". However, one difference is that in French, nouns need an article and, in this case, the indefinite article. So, "l'autisme". We're not talking about something that's out there – gestures vaguely – but *this* autism *right here*. *The* autism. While in the bigger picture, this is a minor detail, it's another factor in nudging the framing of autism towards a medical model of disability. A pathology is more concrete, more "the …" than a social construct could ever be.

Another difference, and one that French does very well, is that it gives us our own noun. (Gold star to l'Académie Française.) If you're autistic, you're "un/une autiste", depending on gender. This then gives us the French equivalent of "he/she *is* an autist" rather than "he/she *has* autism". Which, in terms of reinforcing the idea of autism as an identity, is a positive – or should be.

There's also the adjectival "autistique", or when you're referring to a person, "autiste". However, French places adjectives after the noun, which is why if you're in Paris looking for a big night out you might head to the Moulin Rouge and not the Rouge Moulin. Thus, you're a "personne autiste", never an "autistique personne". This gives French a get-out-of-jail-free card when it comes to the Person/Identity-first language wars because you're always a person first. Alternatively, as we've seen, you can also be "une autiste". In usage, however, there's a tension between these two formulations, including in the autistic population itself where people can insist on their personhood being acknowledged, i.e. "une personne autiste". This all-too-familiar argument is summed up in the Autisme France language guide: "We don't say 'un autiste' because we don't reduce a person to his or her particularity" (Langage Approprié, 2020).[1]

The other common formulations for someone who's autistic are that they "souffre de l'autisme" (suffer from autism) or are "atteinte de l'autisme" (affected/afflicted by autism). Both carry the same pathologising, pejorative sense that they do in English.

A similar discourse arises around the term "Autism Spectrum Disorder". French has the word "désordre", which means much the same as in English and is a word familiar to both French and English parents in reference to their teenagers' bedrooms. But in French, that's not what you're diagnosed with; you have a "Trouble du spectre de l'autisme" (TSA). "Trouble" has a range of meanings, most of them similar to their English equivalents and all of them negative in this context.

Still, in the larger scheme of things, these differences between French and English in core terminology are comparatively minor, if problematic. It's when we move out into the wider language around disability that linguistic differences start to become more apparent – and consequential.

Let's start with disability itself. Or rather, let's not, because there is no word for disability in French. Or there is, but then there's no word for handicap. Or impairment. Because in practice there's one word that covers all three meanings, and even that word is a comparatively recent borrowing from English: "le handicap". *Le Petit Robert* dictionary dates the use of "handicap" in this sense to 1940.

So where does that get us? Imagine that you're exploring your autism in the context of the social model of disability i.e. that the difficulties you face in a non-autistic world are the result of you and your atypicality bumping up against attitudinal and environmental barriers.

One of the keys to the social model is the differentiation between impairment, disability and handicap. But if you're trying to express this three-way relationship in French, you're off to a bad start because as we've just seen, you only really have one word: "handicap". Which leads us into choppy waters. For example, the whole point of the social model is that a disability is not necessarily a handicap. But in French, disability is by definition always a handicap; these aren't two separate notions.

Further issues arise in that "handicap" is generally only used in this context, so we lose the wider, benign sense, such as handicap in a competition. This use of a specific vocabulary distinct from everyday speech separates people with disabilities from the rest of society in a form of linguistic othering. We also lose the verbal sense, that handicap is not just a thing but is something that you do or is done. The verb "to handicap" exists in French, but I've never come across it in this context.

The same discourse applies to "disabled". Because we effectively lose the word completely, we lose both its vernacular ("Disable the force field Dr Spock") and its verbal sense. In French, disabled ("handicap" is something that you are; society and the environment have nothing to do with it. Further, this "disabled that you are" is anchored in a medical model. The Académie Française, the essential reference for the French language, defines "le handicap" (i.e. disability) as "infirmité, déficience" (Anon, 2005). "Le handicap" pathologises all it touches.

So, handicap, disability; that just leaves "impairment", also commonly translated as "handicap". The confounding of terms throws up the same issues here, for example, that under social model framing, an impairment is not necessarily a disability. Still, unlike the other terms, "impairment" at least has an alternative. Unfortunately, it's "déficience", which needs no translation. There's a gulf between deficiency with its normative notions of "you're missing something" and the idea of impairment as an atypicality.

To push back against these limitations, French disability advocates have taken a leaf out of social model discourse elsewhere and started using the self-explanatory phrase "en situation de handicap", which is gaining currency, even in official circles. However, it's still not a phrase in widespread use. For example, the French version of the UN Convention on the Rights of Persons with Disabilities uses "handicapé" throughout, even though "en situation de handicap" is much closer to the intent of the original.

There are other terms that don't really have a French equivalent and that play a role in shaping the autism and disability discourse, words like "agency" and "empowerment", or even in the sense that English speakers use it, "advocacy". But of all the factors that contribute to the framing of autism in France, it's this inability to clearly articulate the social model and to do so in non-pathologising terms, that is perhaps the most far-reaching. Disability in France is unavoidably situated in the medical model because, as Wittgenstein (1922) pointed out, "The limits of my language mean the limits of my world".

Apart from these specific issues, the other main problem with everyone speaking French is that they're not speaking English. Not a problem per se; of course, you can still buy your baguette and write your novel in French, but a problem in terms of having access to a wider, international autism and disability discourse that's carried out predominantly in English. While there are French translations of books from the likes of Temple Grandin or Donna Williams, the field is notable for the huge number of English-language books that are not available in French. In this basket, and conspicuously absent until 2020, has been Steve Silberman's *Neurotribes*. But this is just the tip of the iceberg. For example, none of the recent books from Luke Beardon, Nicholas Chown, Damian Milton or Melanie Yergeau are available in French, and I'd be very surprised if the one that you're currently holding in your hands ever gets a translation either.

The other problem is, of course, that the majority of academic publications are only available in English – though this hegemony of English in academic fields is not limited either to autism or to French. There are translated versions of both Kanner's and Asperger's original papers, as well as key (?) autism texts such as Baron-Cohen's on theory of mind. But most studies available in French are biomedical or genetic and situate autism in a deficiency/pathology paradigm. There's pretty much zero availability of what I think of as the Nouvelle Vague of autism research, much of it involving autistic researchers. For example, I would be surprised if there were more than a handful of English-speaking cognoscenti who were aware of Damian Milton's paper on the double-empathy problem.

It's not the absence of these specific texts per se which is problematic; it's the near-total absence of a wider discourse around the subjects that they explore. In this vacuum, ideas such as "autists lack empathy" or "autists are deficient in central coherence" circulate unchallenged. Accordingly, they're taken as gospel truth and like much gospel truth become engraved in stone.

We'll return to gospel truths and stone-engraving in more depth in the course of the next section on Cartesianism.

Cartesianism

Newcomers to France can choose from a plethora of books and articles on "how to understand the French", and sooner or later most of them get around to Cartesianism. One such article sums up Cartesianism colloquially as

> a kind of problem-solving founded on the principal of suspicion. You start with a hunch that things may not be as simple as they seem … Then you break it into parts, prioritise the steps of your solution, and march forward in the simplest way possible.
>
> *(Carpenter, 2016)*

At the heart of Cartesian reasoning is Cartesian method, laid out by René Descartes (1637) in his *Discourse on the Method of Rightly Conducting One's Reason and of Seeking Truth in the Sciences*. The first of his precepts was "never to accept anything for true, which I did not clearly know to be such". Which is how he got to "I think therefore I am". Once he'd thrown out everything that he couldn't be certain of, "I am" was about all he had left. We can doubt everything except our own doubting.

According to Descartes' method, when you're confronted with a problem or an unknown, you first seek to bring it back to what you can be sure of. You then take this as your starting point and proceed systematically: if we know this, then we can deduce that: once we know that, we can deduce this other thing, and so on. If you've followed the method correctly, the conclusion must be true because the initial premise is true. Cartesianism basically reduces the world to one big maths problem: if a then b.

Cartesianism plays no major role in Anglo-Saxon culture. If it did, we'd never have had Obama's "Yes we can" or Nike's "Just do it". From a Cartesian perspective, both are reckless and unreliable as they emphasise outcome rather than method. "Les cowboys Anglo-Saxons". I imagine that most people have heard the joke about the French CEO who on seeing a demonstration of an innovative new product declares, "Well, I can see that it works in practice – but does it work in theory?"

But what's all that got to do with autism? A lot as it turns out.

The first factor at play here is that a Cartesian society is one that has a low tolerance for uncertainty. As Nourissier (1968, p. 122) writes "Uncertainty has been, for a long time, officially displaced by cartesian logic". The "if ... then" which is the deductive backbone of the Cartesian method supposes a binary: either it is or it isn't. In other words, everything can be categorised. The French "enjoy distinctions, subtleties; they build boxes within boxes, they seek to codify, to lay down, to plan, to delineate, to structure, to deconstruct all knowledge, all behaviour into neat compartments" (Lannes, 1977).

Autism? In the grand Cartesian scheme of things, it has to *be* something, to fit into one of those neat compartments. But the "is it a bird, is it a plane?" nature of autism with its "if you've met one person with autism" heterogeneity and lack of a "unified physical essence" (Chapman, 2018) doesn't play by these rules.

In order to get round this, to make autism some*thing* and find a box it can be put into, the French pyscho-medico-socio-legal fields turn to what they have at hand, even if the fit leaves something to be desired. After all, any explanation is better than no explanation. And in this case, the oven-ready solution is to see autism as a pathology, a medical problem – with predictable consequences. As Sue Fletcher-Watson (2020) observes: "how the clinical definition of autism is conceived of by psychologists, psychiatrists and other disciplines involved in diagnosis has a big impact on how autistic people are understood in clinical services".

As an example, because autism is medicalised, a French autism diagnosis can only be provided by a medical practitioner. This is nearly always a psychiatrist, but there's nothing to stop a GP giving a diagnosis if they're prepared to do so. Diagnosis by a psychologist, even by a clinical psychologist who specialises in autism, is not officially recognised – thank you, Messrs Attwood and Baron-Cohen, your services will not be required. It goes without saying that self-diagnosis is not recognised either, even within the autistic community itself. Self-diagnosis falls into the "Just do it" school: precipitous and unsound.

Another consequence of France's reliance on Cartesianism stems from the method's requirement that sources are reliable; if not, the whole edifice collapses. Roush (2017) sums up this aspect of Descartes' approach: "Instead of casting doubt on his empirical beliefs one by one, he would doubt the reliability of their source and that would blanket all of them with suspicion".

Accordingly, there is a tendency in France to refer back to canonic texts and authority figures. And this is where we let the genie out of the bottle, because once we medicalise autism, when it comes to human behaviour and psychology there are few more authoritative authority figures than Sigmund Freud. And in particular, someone who followed in Freud's footsteps: local boy Jacques Lacan.

Lacan didn't just pop up one day in the Latin Quarter of Paris wondering "what about if …?" or lean across the table during a lull in the conversation at the Café de Flore with "it occurred to me that …" Being the good Cartesian, his point of departure had to be someone else's point of arrival. So, when he first emerged, it was with "Well, Freud says …" Which in a Cartesian framework is hard to counter, or was at the time. If Freud was right, Lacan had to be right.

Accordingly, we followed Jacques where he led us. Which took us, amongst other places, to toxic mothers and autistic children being removed from their families by social services. Or to autistic kids being wrapped in cold wet towels like mummies to help them achieve "a greater perception and integration of the body, and a growing sense of containment" (Goeb et al., 2008). Yes, "le packing", of which Franck Ramus (2018) noted, "the practice of packing for autism is totally and unambiguously anchored in a psychoanalytical school of thought" where "the main references are the psychoanalysts Freud, Lacan, …"

Of course, not all these practices can be directly attributed to Lacan. But once he gave psychoanalysis legitimacy and his rock-star status gave it a profile, his followers did the rest. It's true that the influence of psychoanalysis has waned, though it's a slow and comparatively recent waning. Mothers of autistic children still report taking their child in for a diagnosis only to find that they're also under examination.

(Though again, this is not limited to autism. In the documentary *Petite Fille* (2020) which follows Sasha, a young trans girl, the family GP asks her mother "Did you, perhaps unconsciously, want to have a little girl?" In a similar vein, when the mother presses the local education authorities for Sasha to be recognised as a girl, they threaten to report her to social services.)

But psychoanalysis doesn't just continue to hang on in France like a limpet on a rock because Lacan had good method and we can't refute his arguments. One of the consequences of all that Cartesian ordering and classifying is that, by definition, you end up with hierarchies, including in society itself. Accordingly, French society is hierarchical, with these pivotal guardians of the truth at the top.

As a result, you do not challenge people in positions of authority – and this applies across the board – as these are our referent figures. Guides to doing business in France are often at pains to point out how hierarchical French businesses are, with ultimate decision-making and the power that goes with it centred on one or two senior figures.

In the field of autism, these authority figures are the heads of departments of psychiatry or psychology in academic and medical establishments, and the upper echelon of administration in the public health sector, all of whom completed their training 20 or more years ago, during which time they will have ingested large doses of psychoanalysis. (Though you don't need to go back 20 years. In France, most courses in psychiatry and psychology still include a healthy dose of psychoanalysis. In fact, many don't just include it, they feature it. For more on this, see Ramus (2020) and Bishop and Swendsen (2020).)

These are the people who determine outcomes for the autistic population, deciding everything from policy to support. They're people whose word is gospel, and because of their training, that word is largely informed by Lacan, Freud or a variant thereof. As Bishop and Swendsen sum up, "the defence of psychoanalysis as a treatment for autism ... is only legitimised because it is promoted by authority figures and maintained by circles of power and influence".

Take, as an example, Dr Pierre Delion, who was until his retirement head of the children's psychiatric department of the Regional University Hospital in Lille. He has been the main advocate and practitioner of packing in France and wrote the book on it (Delion, 2007). There is no evidence base whatsoever to support packing and it has been banned in French socio-medical institutions such as day centres (though not in hospitals), but it continues because it is legitimised by a recognised authority, Dr Delion.

(As an aside here, I don't want to give the impression that such practices aren't challenged in France; they are. But those challenges tend to come from outside the medical and psychiatric establishment and are largely ignored within it.)

Another example is Dr Luc Montagnier, who earned himself a Nobel Prize for his part in the discovery of HIV; which then gave him a free pass in France to do what he wanted, even when that led to a 2012 clinical trial where he gave 50 children long-term treatment with antibiotics because "something something bacteria autism". You don't question an eminent scientist with a Nobel, a Légion d'Honneur and who's a member of the Académie Nationale de Médecine. Unfortunately, this didn't stop there. In the ensuing years, Montagnier built up a network of around 50 doctors (acolytes) prescribing antibiotics, antifungals and antiparasitics for some 5,000 autistic children until a parent whistle-blower tipped off the relevant authorities (Autism: families denounce abuses, 2020).

As well as potentially opening the door to abusive practices, the hierarchical nature of French medico-social structures leaves a younger generation of clinicians with limited scope to implement new approaches. As Vivienne Orchard (2013) commented: "their careers are promoted by posts in hospitals that in turn dictate the kinds of treatment and care that they advocate". While some of these institutions are more enlightened than others, there's still a litany of stories of people being turned down for a diagnosis – "if you can call to make an appointment you can't be autistic" – or of not receiving a diagnosis when they clearly meet the criteria.

Which is, in itself, is a product of Cartesian doubt. Why do you want a diagnosis? Who told you you were autistic (i.e. was it an authority figure)? But that's only the beginning. In a French autism diagnosis, we don't assume that you could be autistic and test whether or not you meet the criteria; we do the reverse. The Method of Cartesian Doubt means that we only accept that you're autistic if we can eliminate every other possibility first. And if along the way we find something that we can get to stick, then that's your diagnosis. Jette Schramm-Nielsen's (2001) summary of decision-making processes in French businesses is relevant here: "The French analyse problems in a systematic way, looking for as many alternatives as possible and trying to evaluate them before coming to a conclusion and then go back to see whether there might be more possibilities to be considered". (Which comes straight from Descartes' fourth rule: "To make enumerations so complete, and reviews so general that I might be assured that nothing was omitted".)

As a result, it's not uncommon for people to receive a range of diagnosis before finally getting the autism diagnosis that was obvious in the first place. After the diagnosis of her son, a woman I know took over ten years to find a clinician who would confirm her own suspicions. In that period, she basically worked her way through the DSM, collecting mental health diagnosis along the way.

But even when you get your precious autism diagnosis, the battle isn't over because you then have to keep it. Woe betide anyone who, for whatever reason, finds themselves back in The System and encounters a different psychiatrist. You might go into a psychiatric hospital as an autist and risk coming out with a diagnosis of "trouble de la personnalité histrionique et syndrome de Peter Pan". (No, I'm not making this up.)

I mentioned the DSM above, and no, it's not universally recognised in France either. This comes down to the same issues we've already seen: the need for categorisation and questions of trust and suspicion, especially of anything that's not French. Since 2005, the official classification in France has been the ICD. But there's also a French system, because as good Cartesians we need to be sure. This is the CFTMEA: *Classification française des troubles mentaux de l'enfant et de l'adolescent*. It loosely aligns with the ICD, but as the relevant French Wikipedia entry sums up, it "complements the less specific international (ICD-10) and American (DSM) systems" (Classification Française des Troubles Mentaux, 2020). Note there the "less specific". To quote myself from above, "a Cartesian society is one that has a low tolerance for uncertainty".

One of the CFTMEA diagnosis that you won't find in the DSM is "Dysharmonies Evolutives" (Developmental Disharmonies). Dr Jacques Boulanger (2011) observes that it's an example of "the old debate between a French approach to the search for clinical finesse and a more pragmatic Anglo-Saxon approach". Finesse? Those Anglo-Saxon cowboys can't even be bothered fitting everything into neat categories. One of the criteria for Dysharmonies Evolutives is "social disinterest, detachment, avoidance, or withdrawal into oneself, in spite of obvious capabilities". Which I'll just leave here without, cough, comment, cough.

As we're starting to see, Cartesianism shapes the social and clinical narratives of autism, which then have a real-world impact on autistic people in France. But it's not done with us yet.

Vivienne Orchard speaks of the need to address "The dire position of both children and adults with autism in France". Amongst other proposals she calls for "the revalidation of 'experiential knowledge'". (She's referring here to the experience of parents of autistic children, but nonetheless ...) Which is a reasonable proposition given how important the input of autists themselves has been in shifting our perceptions.

But let's look at that through the Cartesian lens. One of the key tenets of Descartes' writings is the distrust of experience as a source of knowledge. After all, that's how he got to cogito ergo sum in the first place. If I can't trust my senses, what can I trust?

Accordingly, autists are not seen as reliable witnesses to their own autism. Individual autistic voices such as Donna Williams or Jim Sinclair laying the groundwork for a deeper understanding of autism based on their lived experience are almost impossible to imagine in a French context. Brigitte Chamak (2010), one of the few French researchers to have explored social, as opposed to medical, perspectives on autism noted that "Accounts from autistic people are very rare in France. Only one book, (Bouissac, 2002), has been published".

It's no accident that two of the more high-profile autistic advocates in France, Josef Schovanec and Julie Dachez, both have Doctorates. Their qualifications confirm that they're well-schooled in La Méthode, and are unlikely to fall victim to the siren's call of empiricism.

In France, being autistic does not qualify you to be an autistic voice. Not by yourself anyway. If you try, you'll find that your arguments aren't so much refuted but invalidated on the basis that empirical evidence doesn't count, and because you're not an academic or part of any recognised organisation, your propositions lack referent authority. Consequently, one of the defining features of the French autistic community, such as it is, is the propensity to form associations. We'll look further at some of the reasons why in the next section, but one of them is because an officially recognised association, complete with office bearers and a bank account, is seen as more credible than a lone autist sitting at their kitchen table, no matter their expertise or experience.

To sum up then: Cartesian rationality informs knowledge and reasoning in France and so shapes how the construct of autism is understood. Its need for certainty pushes autism into a medical model; it encourages gatekeeping and inhibits innovation and change, while its rejection of empiricism denies the legitimacy of the personal autistic experience.

But when it comes to narratives around autism, France has another string to its bow. Republicanism.

Republicanism

What does a socio-political ideology have to do with autism? As with Cartesianism, quite a lot. The societies we live in and the way they organise themselves have a direct impact on their members. Including autists. In France, how we see our autistic community, ourselves, what "self" even means, are all shaped by republicanism.

This all starts with *Liberté, Egalité, Fraternité*, and, in particular, the second of those, égalité (equality). Within French republican framing, égalité is understood not just as the presence of equality but as the absence of inequality. In practice, this translates as the erasure of difference. No difference, no inequality and no one getting uppity and bossing you around.

This harks back to the French Revolution, where Article I of the 1789 *Déclaration des Droits de l'Homme et du Citoyen* laid out that "men are born and remain free and equal in rights" and that "social distinctions can be founded only on the common good". The same basic idea turns up in the 1958 French Constitution which states that France is an "indivisible, secular, democratic and social Republic. It shall ensure the equality of all citizens before the law, without distinction of origin, race or religion". Indivisible. Without distinction. As opposed to being particularist or differentialist, which acknowledge the right to a difference or specificity, republicanism is universalist, and doesn't.

Under the French republican model, "the people" are understood to be a single unit and the state eschews making distinctions between them. For example, the French census has no questions on race, ethnicity or religion, and you would never see statistics such as "black women are x times more likely to die in childbirth than white women" because in France it's illegal to collect such data. Everybody is just "French".

French republicanism is the antithesis of the Anglosphere's multiculturalism, which from a republican point of view "sanctions unequal rights and countenances communities closed in upon themselves" (Jennings, 2000). Like many ideas that come in from the Anglosphere, multiculturalism is seen as foolhardy and dangerous. Separatism, tribalisation, plus a couple of self-explanatory French terms – "balkanisation" and "ghettoïsation" – are all ills that are laid at its door.

Accordingly, the French Republic doesn't recognise minority cultures or communities, either in practice or in law. For example, France has not ratified the European Charter for Regional or Minority Languages, nor the European Framework Convention for the Protection of National Minorities, and while it signed the International Covenant on Civil and Political Rights, it contested, and is thus not legally bound by, Article 27, which addresses the cultural rights of minorities.

Abigail Taylor (2018) gives an example of how this plays out on a societal level. She observes that the legalisation of gay marriage in France didn't come about in response to activists' demands, as that would have been seen as acknowledging and giving voice to a minority group. Rather, it came about as a push for "marriage for all" (marriage pour tous). "The language of republicanism was used to point out that a universal – the right to marriage – was not truly universal if it excluded certain groups".

Similarly, accessibility for the disabled is presented as "Universal Accessibility". The relevant government website (Accessibilité Universelle, 2020) sums it up with the catchphrase "à tout pour tous", which clumsily translates as "everything for everyone" or "everywhere for everyone". But as Ravaud and Stiker (2001) point out, "equal rights do not mean equal situations – as the continued social inequalities between groups shows with acuity". This also opens up a Pandora's Box of counterclaims under the guise of this "égalité": if we're all equal, how come Jean-Claude can wear headphones at his desk when I can't? The same counterarguments can be presented in regard to flexible working hours, eating in the staff canteen and so on.

In his governmental report on career paths for French autists, Josef Schovanec (2017) shows how all-pervasive this can be in pointing out that the concept of universal equality doesn't just apply to benefits, but also to disadvantages. You cannot ask to be excused from working in an open-plan office or having your desk near the elevator as these situations are unpleasant for everyone, and the principal of universal equality requires you to experience the same level of unpleasantness as everyone else. Republicanism takes no prisoners.

Consider education in this context, and not just with students who might need additional support. There is effectively no accelerated programme in French schools. Students who are exceptionally capable can skip a year, but it's not encouraged. As one expat parent observed in regard to gifted children: "The schools in France are devoted to the French ideal of 'égalité' so segregating the smart kids for special treatment really goes against the grain" (Bevdeforges, 2012).

It's not hard to imagine the consequences for autistic students. Teachers are reluctant to modify their teaching, schools are reluctant to make adjustments to the sensory environment, and non-autistic students are given no guidance in how to adapt their own behaviours to accommodate an autistic classmate. The solution rests in the autistic child themselves (medical model); the system makes no allowances for those who experience the world differently. And again, it's not just autistic children: sign language was banned in the French education system until 1991, which is somewhat ironic given that the world's first public school for the deaf opened in Paris in 1760.

Right across French society, these notions of égalité are used not just to refuse to make exceptions, but to suppress the idea of difference itself: "The French republican model has traditionally been regarded as the ideal of inclusivity. However, in practice, this amounts to confronting minorities with highly assimilationist demands in terms of language and cultural mores and refuses public recognition of cultural diversity" (Asari, Halikiopoulou and Mock, 2008).

There's a word that acts as a way of policing this: "communautarisme" (not to be confused with the English term, communitarianism, which is a different concept). "Communautarisme" is the fractioning of the population into cultural or identity-based communities. To be seen as a "communautariste" is to be seen as someone who doesn't want to play by the collective rules, someone who's acting against society and worse, against your fellow citizens. It's a term that's employed, usually with some venom, against anyone seeking to further the cause of a minority group.

For example, when Sam Bourcier, Doctorate and Fulbright in hand, attempted to introduce a Masters in Queer Studies at the University of Lille, "I was treated as a communautariste rebel" (Bardou, 2016). Josef Schovanec pointed out that you couldn't even propose an initiative such as Autism Hours in supermarkets without getting into a debate about communautarisme.

Activism/Advocacy

Avoidance of communitarianism acts as a brake on advocacy and activism while shaping the form it takes when it does occur. Chamak (2010) writes in regard to autistic social movements that "the historical and cultural context and in particular the opposition to communitarianism are unfavourable to the development of radical demands". Though I'd question there the use of the term "radical".

Accordingly, what passes for autistic/autism advocacy in France would be largely unrecognisable as such in the Anglosphere. Chamak again: "If in Anglo-Saxon countries groups organise themselves into social movements that challenge normative principles, in France we focus on defending the interests of people with autism and their families". Consequently, much of the French activist discourse revolves around rights and discrimination.

Alongside that, the centralisation of power that republicanism (and Cartesianism) inevitably leads to means that even this rights-based activism incorporates a certain amount of politicking and lobbying. Chamak: "The associations need to diversify their methods of negotiation and forms of pressure at different national, local, political and administrative levels in order to consolidate the links with the State that guarantee their sustainability". For example, AFFA, the association of Francophone autistic women, has as their main objective "to raise the awareness of public authorities regarding the rights and specific needs of autistic girls and women" (Association Francophone de Femmes Autiste, 2020).

Not surprising then that within autistic-led advocacy, "challenging normative principles" takes a back seat. Even when it does occur, it tends to focus on the practical, such as masking, rather than the theoretical. For example, discussion of monotropism or the dual-empathy problem are as good as non-existent in France, either in activist circles or elsewhere.

Community

For me, one of the great casualties of French republicanism is its core denial of the possibility for autists to be recognised as a minority group. Accordingly, there's an absence of what Joseph

Strauss (2013) refers to as a "thriving community of like-minded people committed to celebrating their shared difference". (While there is a newer generation of autists who are starting to forge a nascent sense of community by piggybacking on LGBTQ and feminist approaches to culture and identity, they don't yet have enough critical mass to be mounting autistic-led conferences or establishing a French Autreat.)

This denial extends to the virtual space, which has played such a crucial role in fostering autistic community in the English-speaking world. For example, there are comparatively few French autists on Twitter and there's effectively no French equivalent of the #ActuallyAutistic or #AskingAutistics hashtags, so even making connections with other Francophone autists can be difficult. It's hard to imagine someone going onto Francophone Twitter to announce their autism diagnosis and being met by emojis of gushing champagne bottles.

The impact of this lack of autistic community cannot be underestimated. A community doesn't just support its members, it furthers their shared interests, giving them a common language, a voice, and a role in shaping the discourse, from education and employment to healthcare. No community, no community advocacy or representation. Hannah Thompson (2017) gives an example of one consequence, albeit in a wider disability context: "the relative paucity of user-led disability activism in France means that disabled people are not necessarily at the centre of research conducted about them".

In France, everything about us is without us, as much as anything because there's no acknowledgement of an "us".

Neurodiversity

There's perhaps nowhere where this lack of an autistic-led discourse is more obvious than in attitudes to neurodiversity. It's no exaggeration to say it has been met with suspicion and hostility. Neurodiversity in all its guises is widely criticised, both within the psycho-medical domain and amongst the all-powerful parent groups.

Even putting aside French distrust of anything that comes in from "les Anglo-Saxons", there are a number of reasons. For starters, republicanism's resistance to a fractioning of the population rejects the notion of any kind of subgroup, neurodivergent or not. Then there's the idea of diversity itself. This is not the slam-dunk that it is in the Anglosphere, where from the classroom to the boardroom the advantages of increased diversity are well-documented. In France, cultural diversity is treated with suspicion as a possible Trojan horse for the dreaded multiculturalism. As for the "neuro" part, the philosopher Denis Forest dismisses its use as a prefix here with a wave of the Cartesian hand because "there is no neural explanation for autism" (Forest, 2016). Neuro-something? Get back to us when we can diagnosis autism with an MRI.

It's true that the term has started to gain some currency. But there's still substantial resistance, which leaves France's autistic population without a viable alternative to a medical model.

Disability Studies

To finish off this section on republicanism and its impact, I want to look at Disability Studies.

Let's start with the easy bit. There are no Disability Studies in France. None. But it's in good company. Given that republicanism effectively denies the existence of identity groups, there are no Gender Studies, no Queer or LGBT Studies, no Mad Studies, and there are no fields based on ethnicity such as African American Studies or BAME Studies, even though lord knows France has the communities and history to justify them. So no, no Postcolonial Studies, either.

There's not even a French term for Disability Studies. It's known as "les disability studies". At this point, I was going to offer as evidence the absence even of an entry for Disability Studies in French Wikipedia. But an entry giving a few brief lines of explanation and pointing out that there's not a French equivalent appeared recently (Disability Studies, 2020). I'll return to this later, as there's more to this than meets the eye.

There are a number of commentaries examining the situation of Disability Studies in France, including attempts to both justify its absence and claim its presence in another guise. But when you don't even have a word for it and there's not a single book on the subject available in French, it's hard to claim that it's making inroads.

One of the reasons for the absence of these identity-based fields is that in France, multidisciplinary research domains don't really exist. This stems from Cartesianism and its need for neatly defined categories. A field that might cover history, sociology, politics, ethics and literature is difficult to imagine in a French academic context.

There's an argument put forward that the individual elements exist, but they're not all grouped in one place. Which I'd also contest. The fact that there might be isolated studies on the representation of disability in French films does not foreshadow the emergence of French Disability Studies. (Though even there, you wonder whether such studies would exist in the first place if it wasn't for the success of two recent films featuring disabled protagonists: *The Diving Bell and The Butterfly* (Le Scaphandre et le Papillon) and *Les Intouchables*, with its less successful English-language remake, *The Upside*.)

In any case, much of this work is being undertaken outside of France by non-French academics, where The Absence Of Disability Studies In France is almost becoming its own specialised field. (I look forward to the first international conference on the subject. In English.) Of course, this goes against the raison d'être of these fields in the first place: that they are anchored in and led by their own communities. Which, in itself, gives rise to another problem. In the case of Disability Studies, its symbiotic relationship with the Disability Rights movement with its assertion of "a culture of disability", leads to "a certain proximity to the idea of what has been called multiculturalism" (Albrecht, Ravaud and Stiker, 2001). There be dragons. This is the republican wall Sam Bourcier came up against in his own field: the recognition that if you establish a course in Queer Studies, you're acknowledging that there's a queer community.

The absence of these identity-based fields has a direct impact on the populations concerned. For example, in regard to autism, "only very few French parents have integrated the social model of disability" because "alternative narratives that recognise diversity are still unusual in France" as "disability studies and the disability movement have not developed" (Chamak and Bonniau, 2013).

Given all the above, coupled with what we've already seen with language and Cartesianism, progress to a more enlightened understanding of autism is glacially slow. The biggest recent factor in shifting perceptions has come not from within France but from a single autistic outsider: Greta Thunberg. For many, it's the first time that they will have come across an autistic person in the wider media who's not there by dint of being autistic. The idea that autistic people can participate and contribute as full members of our societies has come as something of a shock to the system. Further, for the first time, many French autists have a model that they can relate to: "Yes, I'm autistic. Like Greta Thunberg". And, also, for the first time, a glimpse of that "thriving community of like-minded people", so critical in the development of an autistic identity, both collective and individual. As Lev Vygotsky (1997) states, "Through others, we become ourselves". But if there's no one like me, who am I? Without "nous sommes", how can I get to "je suis"?

Before wrapping this section up, allow me a postscript regarding republicanism and autism. One criticism that is often levelled at "communautarisme" is the "repli sur soi" aspect, literally of "turning in on yourself", of withdrawal from participation in society either as an individual or as a member of a minority community. But autism itself is widely understood in France as "repli sur soi". In fact, that's how it's defined. For example, the Académie Française gives: "repli morbide sur soi" (Anon, 1992). So the individual autist becomes a personification of and a proxy for "communautarisme" and, as such, an object of suspicion and distrust.

I sometimes feel that autism has been visited upon the French specifically to confront them in their Frenchness: their language, their Cartesianism, their republicanism. Infuriatingly, autism refuses to play by the rules, to be pinned down, to integrate. As such it's a betrayal, with the autist as a traitor not just to Frenchness but to humanness itself, for which autists pay a heavy price. In France, autism is officially "un trouble", and people are troubled by it. An anonymous article on the AFFA site speaks of French society as "not open to difference and where the label of autism is frightening" (Tom, 2019).

One of the consequences of this fear is a reluctance to give an autism diagnosis in the first place. As we saw, the CFTMEA provides a number of possible alternatives, including "Dysharmonies Evolutives" which, as Boulanger points out, in saying the quiet bit out loud, "is often used in France to describe disorders of the autistic series". Another alt-diagnosis that frequently pops up is "Haut Potentiel Intellectuel" (HPI), which we would know elsewhere simply as giftedness. It comes about because the "I spy with my little eye" approach of a French autism diagnosis often includes an IQ test. To a man with a hammer, everything looks like a nail. A further possibility is to diagnose Asperger's Syndrome, even when it's not applicable. Josef Schovanec was initially diagnosed with schizophrenia in 2001, then Asperger's in 2005, even though he doesn't fulfil the criteria for Asperger's as he was nonverbal until the age of six. (He doesn't fulfil the criteria for schizophrenia, either, but see above regarding collecting diagnoses.) In France, Asperger's is code for "autism but not the bad kind" and is routinely used as a substitute. For example, if you were a university who wanted to prioritise inclusion for autistic students, you'd call your scheme "Aspie-Friendly" with the tag line, "An individualised pathway for aspies" (Aspie-Friendly, 2020).

In France we deny autists the right to be autistic or to use the term "autism". It's the word that dare not speak its name.

Conclusions

The aim here has not been to draw attention to France's treatment of its autistic population. Rather, it has been to show how social, cultural, linguistic, even political factors in France work together to write French understandings of autism.

I've treated these independently, but of course in the real world they're interdependent, playing out across a web of interlocking causes and consequences like one of those internet memes where a single falling domino sets off streams of dominoes in all directions. For example, the propensity for French autists to form themselves into associations can be understood through both the Cartesian and republican lens. There's sometimes even the question of which is the cart and which is the horse: would the French be less likely to turn to the medical model in a search for Cartesian certainty if their language allowed for a more precise formulation of the social model?

Beyond an examination of the construct of autism in France, I also hope that this chapter can contribute to a reflection on how such factors play out in shaping these constructs in our own cultures, and in particular, Anglo-Saxon culture. We in the Anglosphere tend to assume that autism looks the same everywhere and that it's our version that everyone sees; which is an idea that sails very close to the winds of cultural imperialism. Alexandre Baril (2016) refers to this English-speaking hegemony as Anglonormativity. He points out that "As with all majority identities, the Anglophone identity remains invisible and under-theorised, particularly by Anglophones". Yes, for the most part France is getting autism terribly wrong. But it's not getting it wrong though failing to do Anglo-Saxon autism correctly.

On the surface, the solutions to "the autism situation in France" would seem fairly obvious, as this is a path that we've been travelling down ourselves for some time. Build on autists' own experiences, give autists a seat at the table and agency to determine their own priorities, address support and accommodations on the basis of the social model of disability, reconceptualise autism within the framework of the neurodiversity paradigm, etc. etc.

But all of these are Anglo-Saxon approaches, developed in places like Dallas and Edinburgh and Brisbane. In France, it's near impossible to articulate the social model, yet alone implement it. Neurodiversity is a dirty word, autistic experience has no validity, the autistic community doesn't exist, autists can't get into the building let alone have a seat at the table, and there's not even a word for agency, still less a way of activating it.

If the French autistic/autism community is to find a way forward, it has to do so in its own way, in its own language, working within its own societal structures and cultural norms. But what form could that take?

I've already referred to a new wave of social-media–savvy autistic activists who don't bother with the political machinations of the existing associations, parents' groups and administrative structures and instead "Just do it"; largely it has to be said, by becoming active participants in the broader minority rights movements in France, starting with the LGBT and women's movements. One of the paradoxes of French republicanism is that while the state is supposedly blind to difference, those who are different see each other. By aligning themselves with other minority groups, autists in France are able to address one of their greatest challenges: visibility. For example, the emerging group CLE, "Collectif pour la Liberté d'Expression des Autistes" have participated, banners aloft, in events from Gay Pride marches to conferences on Feminism.

An interesting development in this respect is the alignment of this movement with the Mad community. This contrasts with the autistic Anglosphere where in an attempt to move on from the framing of autism as a mental illness, there has been a more or less overt distancing. In France, shared grievances around issues such as institutionalisation and abusive treatments with psychotropic drugs are leading to joint advocacy and activism. For example, a recent conference on discrimination and sanism (Psychophobie, 2020), hosted by CLE and Comme Les Fous (Like Fools), whose tag line is "changing the way we look at madness".

Alongside these more visible examples, there's also a small, singular example of how French autistic advocacy is starting to find its own path.

Wikipedia sometimes gets bad press as a reliable source of information as it's relatively easy to hijack entries and skew content. But that goes both ways, and in a quiet corner of French Wikipedia, a lone autistic woman, Amélie Tsaag Valren, has been beavering away to educate, inform and change the autism discourse. In the Anglosphere, we're able to do that through presentations and conferences and through leveraging the vast reach of English-language publications and social media. But as we've seen, most of that is either ineffective or inaccessible to the individual French activist.

But on French Wikipedia – and only on French Wikipedia – you'll find that a three-paragraph English entry under "Discrimination against autistic people" has become a 10K-word entry covering everything from infanticide (or "auticide", as it's referred to here), to discrimination in employment, education and housing, complete with citations and references (Exclusion des personnes autistes, 2020). This article cross-references a 3K-word entry on Prenatal Screening for Autism (Dépistage prénatal de l'autisme, 2020), also by Amélie and also with no equivalent in any other language. In the same French-only category are lengthy entries on Violence and Autism, and Autistic Life Expectancy and Mortality, while a 1500-word entry on Vaccines and Autism in English has become a 10K-word encyclopaedic resource in French. Amélie also acts a moderating influence on Wiki entries on Autism and disability in general, editing, translating and commenting. It was Amélie who added the recent Disability Studies entry.

To my knowledge, there is no equivalent use of Wikipedia in English – but then there doesn't need to be. The unique situation in France has created an equally unique solution. Change will come in France. It's just that when it does, it won't look like what it does in the Anglosphere.

I'll close with another quotation from Alexandre Baril. He's referring here to non-English speakers living in English-speaking cultures, but it seems to me that the basic idea still applies:

> Just as society does not recognise the burden ableist norms and structures impose on disabled people, most Anglophones are unaware of the burden systemic barriers place on non-Anglophones.

Vive la différence.

Note

1 For texts in French where there are no existing English translations, as is the case here, citations are my own translations.

References

Accessibilité Universelle. [online] Available at: <https://handicap.gouv.fr/vivre-avec-un-handicap/acceder-se-deplacer/article/accessibilite-universelle> (Accessed 11 October 2020).

Albrecht, G., Ravaud, J. and Stiker, H. (2001). L'émergence des disability studies: état des lieux et perspectives. *Sciences sociales et santé*, [online] 19(4), pp.43–73. https://doi.org/10.3406/sosan.2001.1535.

Anon. (1992). *Dictionnaire de l'Académie française*, 9e édition [online] Available at: <https://www.dictionnaire-academie.fr/article/A9A3212> (Accessed 11 October 2020).

Anon. (2005). *Dictionnaire de l'Académie française*, 9e édition [online] Available at: <https://www.dictionnaire-academie.fr/article/A9H0140> (Accessed 11 October 2020).

Asari, E., Halikiopoulou, D. and Mock, S. (2008). British national identity and the dilemmas of multiculturalism. *Nationalism and Ethnic Politics*, [online] 14(1), pp.1–28. https://doi.org/10.1080/13537110701872444.

Aspie-Friendly: Construire une université inclusive. (2020). [online] Available at: <https://aspie-friendly.fr/parcours-individualise-pour-les-aspies/> (Accessed 11 October 2020).

Association Francophone de Femmes Autistes. [online] Available at: <https://femmesautistesfrancophones.com/contact/> (Accessed 11 October 2020).

Autism: Families Denounce the Abuses of "Merchants of Hope" - France 24. (2020). [online] Teller Report. Available at: <https://www.tellerreport.com/news/2020-09-19-autism--families-denounce-the-abuses-of-%22merchants-of-hope%22---france-24.HJTTANSXHv.html> (Accessed 11 October 2020).

Bardou, F. (2016). En France, Les «Queer Studies» Au Ban De La Fac. [online] *Libération.fr*. Available at: <https://www.liberation.fr/debats/2016/10/12/en-france-les-queer-studies-au-ban-de-la-fac_1521522> (Accessed 11 October 2020).

Baril, A. (2016). Doctor, am I an Anglophone trapped in a Francophone body? *Journal of Literary & Cultural Disability Studies*, [online] 10(2), pp.155–172. https://doi.org/10.3828/jlcds.2016.14.

Bevdeforges. (2012). *"Gifted" Kids*. [online] Available at: <https://www.expatforum.com/expats/france-expat-forum-expats-living-france/122930-gifted-kids.html> (Accessed 11 October 2020).

Bishop, D. and Swendsen, J. (2020). Psychoanalysis in the treatment of autism: Why is France a cultural outlier? *BJPsych Bulletin*, [online] 45, pp.89–93. https://doi.org/10.1192/bjb.2020.138.

Bouissac, J. (2002). *Qui j'aurai été*. Autisme Alsace, Colmar.

Boulanger, J. (2011). *Dysharmonies évolutives et Troubles envahissants du développement*. [online] Available at: <http://www.jacquesboulanger.com/Jacques_BOULANGER/Publications_files/dysharmonie%20evolutive_TED.pdf> (Accessed 11 October 2020).

Bruno Bettelheim. (2020). *En.wikipedia.org*. [online] Available at: <https://en.wikipedia.org/wiki/Bruno_Bettelheim> (Accessed 11 October 2020).

Carpenter, S. (2016). *Understanding Paris: The Cartesian Method*. Available at: <https://secretsofparis.com/french-culture/understanding-paris-the-cartesian-method/> (Accessed 11 October 2020).

Chamak, B. (2010). Autisme, handicap et mouvements sociaux. *ALTER-European Journal of Disability Research*, 4(2), pp.103–115. https://doi.org/10.1016/j.alter.2010.02.001.

Chamak, B. and Bonniau, B. (2013). Changes in the diagnosis of autism: How parents and professionals act and react in France. *Culture, Medicine, and Psychiatry*, 37(3), pp.405–426. [online] halshs.archives-ouvertes.fr. Available at: <https://halshs.archives-ouvertes.fr/file/index/docid/854648/filename/Autism_in_France6_version_HAL.pdf> (Accessed 11 October 2020).

Chapman, R. (2018). *Did Gender Norms "Cause" The Autism Epidemic?* [online]. Available at: <https://intersectionalneurodiversity.wordpress.com/2016/11/29/did-gender-norms-cause-the-autism-epidemic/> (Accessed 11 October 2020).

Classification Française Des Troubles Mentaux De L'enfant Et De L'adolescent. (2020). *Fr.wikipedia.org*. [online] Available at: <https://fr.wikipedia.org/wiki/Classification_française_des_troubles_mentaux_de_l%27enfant_et_de_l%27adolescent> (Accessed 11 October 2020).

Constitution of 4 October 1958. [online] English ver. Available at: <https://www.conseil-constitutionnel.fr/en/constitution-of-4-october-1958> (Accessed 11 October 2020).

Crosbie, P. (2017). *Autism in France: Why We're 40 Years Behind*. [online] Available at: <https://autism-advantage.com/autism-in-france.html> (Accessed 7 September 2020).

Déclaration des Droits de l'Homme et du Citoyen. [online] English ver. Available at: <https://www.conseil-constitutionnel.fr/sites/default/files/as/root/bank_mm/anglais/cst2.pdf> (Accessed 11 October 2020).

Delion, P. (Ed.). (2007). *La pratique du packing: avec les enfants autistes et psychotiques en pédopsychiatrie*. Toulouse, France: ERES.

Dépistage prénatal de l'autisme. (2020). *Fr.wikipedia.org*. [online] Available at: <https://fr.wikipedia.org/wiki/Dépistage_prénatal_de_l'autisme> (Accessed 11 October 2020).

Disability studies. (2020). *Fr.wikipedia.org*. [online] Available at: <https://fr.wikipedia.org/wiki/Disability_studies> (Accessed 11 October 2020).

Discrimination against autistic people. (2020). *Fr.wikipedia.org*. [online] Available at: <https://en.wikipedia.org/wiki/Discrimination_against_autistic_people> (Accessed 11 October 2020).

Exclusion des personnes autistes. (2020). *Fr.wikipedia.org*. [online] Available at: <https://fr.wikipedia.org/wiki/Exclusion_des_personnes_autistes> (Accessed 11 October 2020).

Fletcher-Watson, S. (2020). *Is Autism a Category or a Dimension?* DART. Available at: <http://dart.ed.ac.uk/autism-category-or-dimension/> (Accessed 11 October 2020).

Forest, D. (2016). Les ambiguïtés de la neurodiversité. *médecine/sciences*, [online] 32(4), pp.412–416. https://doi.org/10.1051/medsci/20163204021.

Goeb, J. L., Bonelli, F., Jardri, R., Kechid, G., Lenfant, A. Y. and Delion, P. (2008). P0362 - Packing therapy in children and adolescents with autism and serious behavioural problems. *European Psychiatry*, 23(S2), pp.S405–S406. https://doi.org/10.1016/j.eurpsy.2008.01.1405.

Jennings, J. (2000). Citizenship, republicanism and multiculturalism in contemporary France. *British Journal of Political Science*, [online] 30(4), pp.575–597. https://doi.org/10.1017/S0007123400000259.

Langage Approprié. (2020). *Autisme France*. [online] Available at: <http://www.autisme-france.fr/offres/doc_inline_src/577/Langage-approprie.pdf?fbclid=IwAR1Vyt3D2pJ1CuNfrhRD6wuTBo1aGeY7q23L9LsT6BsjXbbBwt4i2S8Ti_k> (Accessed 11 October 2020).

Lannes, S. (1977). Les Francais épinglés: L'Expres va plus loin avec Laurence Wylie. *L'Expres* 1–7 August 1977: 52–58.

Nourisier, F. (1968). *The French* (Foulke, A. Trans.). New York: Alfred A. Knopf (cited in Tarro, B. J. 1991. How to cope with the French: Keys to understanding French culture, Paper presented at the Annual Eastern Michigan University Conference on Languages and Communication for World Business and the Professions. Ypsilanti, MI. (10th, Ypsilanti, MI, April 3–5, 1991)).

Orchard, V. (2013). The "rendez-vous manqués" of francophone and anglophone disability studies: The case of autism in cross-cultural context. *Synergies Royaume-Uni et Irlande* n°6 – 2013, pp.53–73.

Petite Fille. (2020). Directed by Sébastien Lifshitz (Film). Paris: Agat Films et Cie.

Psychophobie. (2020). *Facebook.* [online] Available at: <https://www.facebook.com/events/350709136382651> (Accessed 11 October 2020).

Ramus, F. (2020). *Fin De Partie Pour Le Packing Dans L'Autisme.* [online] Ramus Méninges. Available at: <http://www.scilogs.fr/ramus-meninges/fin-de-partie-pour-le-packing-dans-lautisme/> (Accessed 11 October 2020).

Ravaud, J.-F. and Stiker, H.-J. (2001). Inclusion/Exclusion: An analysis of historical and cultural meanings. In G. Albrecht, K. Seelman, and M. Bury (Eds.), *Handbook of Disability Studies.* (pp. 490–512). Thousand Oaks and London: Sage Publications. https://doi.org/10.4135/9781412976251.n21

Roush, S. (2017). Epistemic self-doubt. In Edward N. Zalta (Ed.), *The Stanford Encyclopedia of Philosophy* (Winter 2017 Edition). Available at: <https://plato.stanford.edu/archives/win2017/entries/epistemic-self-doubt/> (Accessed 11 October 2020).

Schovanec, J. (2017). *Rapport présenté à la Secrétaire d'Etat chargée des Personnes handicapées et de la Lutte contre l'exclusion sur le devenir professionnel des personnes autistes.* [online] Available at: <https://solidarites-sante.gouv.fr/IMG/pdf/rapport_josef_schovanec.pdf> (Accessed 11 October 2020).

Schramm-Nielsen, J. (2001). Cultural dimensions of decision making: Denmark and France compared. *Journal of Managerial Psychology*, 16(6), pp.404–423. https://doi.org/10.1108/02683940110402389

Strauss, J. N. (2013). Autism as culture. In Davis, L. J. (Ed.), *The Disability Studies Reader* (pp. 460–484), 4th ed. London: Taylor and Francis. [online] Available at: <https://www.google.com/url?sa=t&rct=j&q=&esrc=s&source=web&cd=&ved=2ahUKEwihq8fpp4ruAhWFzoUKHYMfA6cQFjACegQIAxAC&url=https%3A%2F%2Ffiles.transtutors.com%2Fcdn%2Fuploadassignments%2F1566847_3_straus-autismasculture.pdf&usg=AOvVaw23yxE7lwH8Ynaf8qcJU1yp> (Accessed 11 October 2020).

Taylor, A. (2018). Crimes of solidarity: Liberté, Égalité and France'S crisis of Fraternité. [online] *The Conversation.* Available at: <https://theconversation.com/crimes-of-solidarity-liberte-egalite-and-frances-crisis-of-fraternite-90010> (Accessed 11 October 2020).

Thompson, H. (2017). French and francophone disability studies. *French Studies*, 71(2), pp.243–251. https://doi.org/10.1093/fs/knx019.

Tom, P. (2019). *Handicap Et Protection De L'Enfance: Des Placements Abusifs.* [online] AFFA Association Francophone de femmes autistes. Available at: <https://femmesautistesfrancophones.com/2019/03/05/handicap-placements-abusifs/> (Accessed 11 October 2020).

Vygotsky, L. S. (1997). The genesis of higher mental functions. In R. Reiber (Ed.), *The Collected Works of L. S. Vygotsky: The History of the Development of Higher Mental Functions* (Vol. 4, pp. 97–120). New York: Plennum. https://doi.org/10.1007/978-1-4615-5939-9_5.

Wittgenstein, L. (1922). *Tractatus logico-philosophicus* (Ogden, C. K., Trans.). London: Routledge & Kegan Paul.

15
SUPPORT ON WHOSE TERMS?
Competing meanings of support aimed at autistic people

Hanna Bertilsdotter Rosqvist, Damian Milton, and Lindsay O´Dell

Introduction

Commentators on the "autism wars" (Orsini, 2009; Chamak, 2008) illustrate the competing meanings of autism and what is required in terms of support for autistic people. Meanings have been produced as different *autistic knowledges* (where knowledge is produced by autistic people, such as formulated within groups of autistic self-advocates, adults and academics) and as *knowledges of autism* (as knowledge produced by non-autistic people, such as formulated within groups of non-autistic parents of autistic children, academics and professionals). These knowledges have competed over rights of interpretation including formulating best practice in support aimed at autistic people. In this chapter we conceptualise these claims to knowledge and rights of interpretation in terms of struggles within and between different epistemological communities for authority with a particular focus on support.

We use the conceptual tools of epistemological community and epistemic authority to think about different languages at play within epistemic communities that serve to define and produce meanings of support for autistic people. The conceptualisation of epistemic communities and epistemic authority helps us think through how meanings of support aimed at autistic people are spoken of in different support contexts and to think through positions in relation to autism, specifically in the move for autistic young people to adulthood. This analytic is useful to examine how some knowledges become shared and powerful across communities while others remain within a particular community.

In the following sections we identify the languages at play in the conversations about support aimed at autistic people that we have had with people representing different epistemic communities, situated in different but, in certain ways, also similar, contexts. We are using 'languages' as a way of referencing context, both linguistic (conversations across English and Swedish) but also across autistic/non-autistic worlds and academic/practice. To illustrate our arguments, we will draw on a series of conversations we have had with each other and with others in Sweden and the UK. The discussions took place in a time when, in the UK and Sweden, counter-narratives to the epistemic authority of medicalised and deficit understandings of autism were beginning to be evident in mainstream (non-autistic) discourse. Some were recorded and transcribed, others were informal. Our conversations took place in and from the perspective of different contexts: autism advocacy/activism, researcher, university based, practitioner/NGO, and across the national contexts of

Sweden and the UK. We examine how these conversations draw on different languages of autism and how these position autistic people in need of support. We are using 'autistic people' as a way of referring to people who identify with autism and 'non-autistic' people for those who do not.

Epistemic communities and autism

Feminist theorist Lynn Hankinson Nelson (1993) has conceptualised "epistemological communities" as "agents of epistemology", where "agents or subjects of epistemology" are "embodied and situated in specific social and historical contexts" (p. 121). As such, Nelson suggests that members of these communities contribute to constructing knowledge about their own lives. These communities share knowledge from other sources of information, evaluate the value given to these knowledge sources, and community members both "construct and acquire knowledge" (p. 124). They are therefore both recipients of knowledge about their lives and co-constructors of this same knowledge. However, the process of the evaluation of knowledge requires decision-making by members of these epistemological communities as to what knowledge is credible, and this process can be understood as depending on 'epistemic authority'. Epistemic authority is defined by Oikkonen (2013, p. 284) as "the belief that the proposed account is the most accurate one".

In a condition as highly medicalised as autism, the parameters of which are laid out in medical practitioners' diagnostic manuals, it follows that the most credible testimony which may be assumed to be the most accurate, and which is most published (Murray, 2018), issues from medical science. Therefore, the sources on which a community bases its co-construction, the starting point for discussion, is likely to lean heavily on a medical 'story', which in turn takes an assumption of deficit as its starting point.

While counter-narratives to the medical 'story' have flourished within some autistic-led community spaces, it is perhaps only recently that those rejecting a purely deficit model of representing autism have received much mainstream attention, either in academia or within broader culture. Hence, there was not a formalised language to oppose deficit-oriented talk. It has been argued those from differing communities of practice may lack understandings of effective "cross-neurotype communication" (Hillary, 2020) or "interactional expertise" in understanding the cultural practices of 'outsider' communities (Milton, 2014). This can be particularly problematic in misunderstandings and misrepresentations of autistic community and culture, and concepts such as neurodiversity (Walker, 2014).

Contexts of the discussions

Our conversations took place in, and from, different positions on the non-autistic–autistic spectrum and in different languages (Swedish and English). The people we have had conversations with are all practitioners working with supporting young autistic adults to employment at the regular (non-autistic-led) employment market. They work within a similar frame of thinking about autistic abilities, drawing on a strength-based model on autism informed by neurodiversity ideology (Walker, 2014).

The first conversations were with non-autistic people working at a non-autistic-led service which includes support for autistic people and people with learning disabilities in the UK. The conversations took place between Hanna (a Swedish researcher with English as a second language) and Lindsay (a British researcher) and two non-autistic women working at a charity assisting young people with learning difficulties and/or with autism. The conversations took place in an office space at the charity. One woman took part via telephone.

The second conversations were with autistic people working at an autistic-led support service in Sweden aimed at young autistic adults. Hanna had been a follow-researcher in the Swedish group for two years. The Swedish group was therefore familiar with Hanna and the experience of being participating in a research project as a group (Bertilsdotter Rosqvist, 2019ab). The conversation which took place in Sweden with Hanna and Lindsay and the members of the group can therefore be seen as yet another such follow-researcher meeting, with the difference that the conversation now included a person new to the group (Lindsay) who also did not speak Swedish. The Swedish group consisted of six autistic people: three women and three men. It took place at a conference room near the workspace of the group in a middle-sized Swedish town. The conversation took place partly in Swedish and partly in English. Although all participants understood English, most felt most comfortable expressing their thoughts in their native language, Swedish. The Swedish participants, including Hanna, translated some parts of the discussion in Swedish to Lindsay during the conversation.

A third conversation we had was together as a group of researchers and took place in a British university space. Our positions vary across identifications in and between autistic and non-autistic positions. Among us, Damian (a British researcher) was involved in a neuro-mixed support service where leadership is shared by non-autistic and autistic people.

All conversations were recorded and transcribed by professional transcribers. The recording in the Swedish context was transcribed by a Swedish transcriber who also translated all transcripts into an English-only text.

National policy as language and claim to epistemic authority

A key language that produces epistemic authority is legislative discourse. It conditions ways of working with autistic people, how support oriented towards autistic people is funded and organised.

The UK provision should be seen in relation to the huge cuts to 'welfare' payments that have been a consistent feature of the coalition, and now Conservative, governments. The erosion of the welfare state has meant many services seen as essential to the well-being of disabled people have been cut. Support is provided by a mix of state and third-sector organisations, mainly charities. Hence the language of policy and legislation in the UK is framed around disability rights generally (including the *Disability Discrimination Act*, 1995; the *Equalities Act*, 2010) and specifically in relation to autism, the *Autism Act* (2009) and "Fulfilling and Rewarding Lives: The strategy for adults with autism in England" (2010). The Act and strategy have required local authorities to appoint leads for mapping the needs of autistic people and their families/carers and projects for engaging autistic people in planning and designing services. The policy also refers to the *Children and Families Act* 2014 which sets the expectations for support for autistic children, including the transition to adult services. The update to the strategy in 2014, *Think Autism*, describes autistic people in terms of rights – "people with autism have an equal right to a fulfilling life, just like anyone else"; and seeing the responsibility for fulfilling these rights as something that is shared across services and government – "It is time for us all to think autism". The discourse also views 'people with autism' (in contrast to 'autistic people', which is a term more commonly preferred within the autistic community) as individuals (as seen particularly in the notion of personalisation), with possibilities, with the right kind of support, to "make the most of their talents" (Think Autism, 2014).

In Sweden, support is mainly funded and organised by the welfare state. The Swedish disability reform from 1994 includes the *Swedish Act concerning Support and Service for Persons with Certain Functional Impairments* (LSS). LSS focusses on cooperation between the various authorities to help people with disabilities to participate in society. In LSS, ten forms of assistance are included. Among them are rights to support to daily activities. Daily activities can be carried out within a sheltered employment, such as a day centre, or at the regular employment market with certain support to disabled employees and employers (subsidised wages, certain financial support to workplace adjustments for the disabled employee). The Act divides different disabled people into three "person circle" groups where each group is entitled a degree of support. Autistic people have been included within the first group, which also includes people with learning disabilities, while people with ADHD were added later to the third group, which also includes people with psychiatric disabilities. Most programmes for people with learning disabilities focus on placing people in specific programmes with activities to support their training. For people with psychiatric disabilities, the primary aim is to support the coordination of formal services in order to rehabilitate the person in the community, with the goal of them eventually participating in the regular employment market. A solution regarding autistic people with no learning disabilities or people with ADHD with more support needs is a mix between support directed at people with learning or psychiatric disabilities (Winberg et al., 2019).

Language of policy and 'reasonable adjustments' or tailored support

In British policy the notion of 'reasonableness' is important in determining the extent to which 'mainstream' cultural spaces (Milner and Kelly, 2009) need to be accessible to disabled people. The assumption is that spaces, in particular, workplaces, dominated by non-autistic people, need to be reasonable and proportionate in their adaptation for the (non-autistic) environment and working practices. We reflected on this when we spoke together:

Damian: Just being one of the things that we talked about … is around work. I think a lot of the stuff that's happened around work has been very tokenistic. It's kind of the concept of reasonable adjustment that I've written about and talked about before, because it's kind of reasonable to whom adjusting from what. So reasonable to the person in power adjusting normality to make a special exception for you and your special needs it becomes, and it's very rarely done in practice or acted upon. And one of those words that you hear is compromise, like you just need to compromise more Damian. It's always the autistic people in my mind who are bending over backwards to compromise and change against our better nature sometimes, while you see absolutely none sometimes coming the other way. It's that assumption of normalcy, this is just the way things are done, so get used to it and that's kind of assumed ableism in a way which is so ingrained it's kind of hard to understand at times.

The concept of reasonable adjustment can be contrasted with that of Universal Design (Milton et al., 2016) which rather than making bespoke adjustments that separate out those deserving or not, would seek to ensure environments and products are useable by the widest range of people possible.

Within non-autistic-led support service, the language of individuality – the autistic person as a person "with autism" – is brought into the conversation in which support is framed through a language of personalisation and individualisation. The assumption is that individually adapted or tailored support is an important consideration in service provision. The importance of individually formed solutions is argued through discussions of different ways of offering support depending on an individual's needs.

Central to this are the meanings of strengths and abilities, and the possibility for non-autistic coaches to access abilities or support people to develop and maintain their abilities. This idea of 'ability' is formulated in the talk of the UK practitioners as an individualised capability ("very much around kind of the people themselves", British charity worker, R1). R1 further says:

> And it's quite a kind of detailed in literal assessment and vocational profile around people, kind of really getting to know the level of experiences they've been before, what's worked for them, what hasn't worked for them, what do they want to do, looking at the kind of gaps, and then working with them to match them to jobs really. And working with employers the other way as well, but really looking at what they want from an employee and what is the job. You know, we've even done kind of things where we've done shifts with people just to kind of find out a bit more information about the job.
>
> *Lindsay:* OK, so you've gone along and kind of shadowed someone doing a particular job.
> *R1:* Yes. So, we've got a really good idea of the kind of duties of the job, the dynamics of the job. I think particular with people with autism, the issues we found before was that it might not be the tasks of the job; it's the whole culture of a workplace that can have an impact of it being successful for somebody.

As part of this individualised approach to support for autistic people are references to a concern that the autistic people the non-autistic support service worked with did "not want … to be different" (R1) and hence services were built around bringing them into mainstream (non-autistic–dominated) systems. The idea of "not wanting to be different" sits uncomfortably in relation to meanings of rights of "reasonable adjustment" which is based on accepting one's difference (i.e. support needs). For example, Hanna asked the two British practitioners about their understanding of how 'reasonable adjustments' enable their work and position autistic people:

> *Hanna:* Do the participants in your …, so the people you are kind of coaching, are they getting this idea of reasonable adjustment, as to what they understand about their rights and what is possible for them to kind of get?
> *R1:* I think people's understanding depends on the person themselves. I think people are very scared because I think they think it will make them different. And I think it's about looking at doing it in a kind of not such legal terms, it's what will make you do your job well, rather than … [unclear] in that we need the employer to make a reasonable adjustment, that kind of thing. And I think people themselves, it has to be much more practical for them. So it's really going in-depth with these are the tasks of the job, what do you think, you know, what would you find of support in this, what can we do within these are the structures to help do it better? I think people really struggle with the concept that they're asking the employer for reasonable adjustments and they don't want to be different.

One way of conceptualising the work undertaken as part of the non-autistic practitioner's role is that of a cultural or language broker. This concept was originally developed to understand the work of children (and adults) translating for family members who do not speak the majority language of the place of residence. The activity is not purely a linguistic act of translation but a cultural brokering or mediating between different cultures (Abreu & O'Dell, 2017). A similar concept of mediator or broker was discussed by Brownlow (2007) in her work examining 'autistic cousins', who are not autistic but have awareness and knowledge of autism and work to mediate between autistic and non-autistic worlds and translator of mainstream cultural spaces of work. It also echoes the work of Goffman (1963, cited in Ryan & Runswick-Cole, 2009) who draws on the concept of 'the wise' who, in this context, have an awareness of disability because of knowledge of a disabled family member. A central aspect of this is the task of the non-autistic professionals to talk with their clients about a future in which they can see themselves as "citizen-workers of the future" (Lister, 2003). The support is to translate expectations for the autistic person and enable them to better fit in, 'integrate' with the work culture.

> *R1:* So we had a number of incidents where for example somebody said you can take a break anytime you want, and that person ended up taking a break all the time. And we have to lay down some kind of rules that certain rules that people don't always read, like is it a 'dress-down Friday' place. And we kind of need to get to know some of those things so people integrate much more. You bring a cake on your birthday, those kind of things, because I think sometimes the workplace culture can have quite an impact, and it's also where you see how you communicate. For example, we've got somebody's who's an apprentice with autism at the moment, and one of the issues that we've had is he has got quite distracted, because of where he's been sitting, and he's been talking to lots of other people rather than getting on with his work. So we've had to kind of do some work about how the office runs. And kind of change his desk so he's got kind of separate space and can concentrate.

R1 stresses an important part of her job as coach is to understand workplace culture and how the person learns to work. She also stresses the coach as a messenger and mediator between the autistic person and the employer. This positions the non-autistic support person as someone with epistemic authority to lead cross-neurotype communication (Hillary, 2020), to *cross-neurotype translate* non-autistic work cultures. In this case cross-neurotype translation includes defining what is reasonable adjustment and the task of the autistic employee (to adapt to workspaces dominated by non-autistic people). She says:

> also it's people themselves. You know, people are the best advocates of what works for them. And we've got people that will write down what they want us to tell an employer before they go in. One guy said that he won't interact at a team meeting because he doesn't like talking at team meetings, but he will email after the team meeting his suggestions. And that's what he wanted us to tell the employer: he will go but he won't interact in those team meetings.
>
> *Lindsay:* And the employer's OK with that, I'm assuming, to …
> *R1:* Yes, it's a reasonable adjustment. And because we've done quite a lot of work around disability awareness and working with the kind of staff team around that particular individual, they're fine with it. Because it's not something that we're saying that they can't do the job, it's just an adjustment.
> *Hanna:* What is a reasonable adjustment?
> *R1:* Basically, it's having a reasonable adjustment in terms of, normally at the team meetings people are expected to all contribute. At this team meeting he's not but he will contribute in a different way.

The position of the support worker as cultural broker sits ambivalently in relation to the demands of epistemic authority of the (assumed to be) non-autistic employer. In the narratives of the practitioners we spoke with, employers are positioned as possibly inflexible when it comes to recruitment methods. The practitioners stressed that the job of the non-autistic coaches is to make the employers "a bit flexible" and suggest alternative recruitment methods. Their view was that employers find the approach difficult:

R1: And particularly the public bodies find that very hard to kind of shift things about and why are we doing it differently for one. I think the other thing is that, you know, physical space in offices to have a job coach in can be very difficult. And we have to make some compromises there. I would also say that it's about setting as well, because you might get a couple of good people but it's making sure the whole of the team is aware of somebody's needs. And what we have found is that it's very useful to identify a kind of workplace buddy for somebody. That they've got one person that they answer to and that they can go to if they've got any issues at work. Because if you've got lots of people telling you what to do it can be very difficult, you know, it's very difficult for anybody, that.

The coaches draw on their epistemic authority as knowledgeable about autism and autistic people to show how the employers can learn from the coaches to see the ability of the disabled employees; "I think the other thing is that once people can get over the barrier, if you can see how skilled people are, I think people are worried that people aren't skilled because of their disability".

In these conversations, employers are represented as people in need of a bit of coaxing into becoming supportive to autistic employees. The charity's employment service worked with employers to get people into employment. In conversation it was clear that the practitioners we spoke to assumed that employers were concerned about the additional workload of bureaucratic process, and a sense of not knowing "if we can put the time, will we manage it, etc. etc.". The role of the coaches was described as a broker between autistic clients and non-autistic employers, as someone who works with employers and workplaces, which later become more confident and knowledgeable and can include more disabled employees. For example:

R1: So again, I mean we [R2] and her team have been working with, it's a school catering business and our apprenticeships here are mainly in catering, so we're trying to always find placements and people to move in. So we've worked with the firm about two years now? [name of employer]? Yeah. And they've given four jobs, out of, probably about eight or nine placements that they've had, of people so pretty good. And again he came to speak at this event we had last week and he was saying, you know, it's definitely had its challenges. We've learned what to do and we've learned what does work what doesn't work. But this year now he feels confident enough to offer I think it's about 19 placements. So it's about a trebling of placements that he's willing to offer across all his different businesses and hopefully out of that maybe again, you know, 50% or more will get work out of it, because some people doing the placements won't want to do that sort of job themselves. It's a chance to see it and other people maybe will need a bit more before they will be successful in getting jobs. But it's a very good step. And that sort of partnership, because he feels confident in … team as well, that people are there to support, if anything does prove challenging for them as an employer, that seems very important to that company. It's not a big company but they've got quite a lot of jobs. But it's not a national company or anything like that. And I think they feel confident now to take that forward.

Language of autistic support to autistic people

Central in the formulation of an epistemic community is the real or imagined community space where shared language and concepts, collective "public conceptual schemes" (Nelson, 1993) which structure and make intelligible narratives of experience and legitimate particular sets of theories, concepts and standards, can be taken for granted. Our discussions with the Swedish group exemplified the notion of shared autistic spaces (Sinclair, 2010), seen by the Swedish group as psychosocial space, opposing the "lone autistic self" (Bertilsdotter Rosqvist et al., 2020) as present in the individual approach of the non-autistic coaches. This includes a sense of belonging to that space. For example, the group refers to experiences among autistic participants in those spaces, even those coming there for the first time, to "feel like they are 'home' and they can be themselves" (F1). This is also reflected in the UK context, where autistic-led spaces are seen as often less judgemental and understanding of autistic needs and beneficial to wellbeing (Milton and Sims, 2016). Central in the narratives of this space in the Swedish conversations were particular ways of socialising and communicating. For example, the group refers to a great need among autistic people to discuss with other autistic people things of genuine interest, around a particular topic (cf. Bertilsdotter Rosqvist, 2019a) perhaps reflective of an "interest model" of autistic sociality (Murray, 2018; Bertilsdotter Rosqvist, 2019a). For example, F1 says:

F1: And that we have fact, that we have knowledge, and that we talk within ourselves, from within ourselves. That is very, very essential. And we were thinking of that, that … what might be different is that we have very genuine interest when we communicate … when autistic people communicate, often we communicate with our whole body. And other autistic people understand that the best, because you are very … yeah. We think that is very, very, very important. … it's like … It's a great focus on … the topic. … We are very much 'here'.

In relation to this way of socialising and communicating, the group discussed cultural communication dominant in non-autistic groups, which is defined as "doing all sorts of communication in the same time and that makes it a bit messy" (F2). In the narratives about the autistic space, the common interest and intense focus on what is being discussed is stressed. Understandings of autism within the autistic space are contrasted to understandings of autism within the public realm or to non-autistic understandings of autism. In particular, understandings of autism as something puzzling or associated with learning disabilities, pointing at lack of effective cross-neurotype communication (Hillary, 2020) is stressed by the group.

F1: I think it's very hard for them to … eh. I think the vast majority do not know at all what autism is or how to understand it at all. But what you see is that you see that there are some people who are a little stiff, speak a bit rigidly, so this is the sort of thing that is, too. That there are people who in some way distinguish themselves from, a bit. And that it's a group you do not really understand. I think so … I unfortunately think so. In relation to what [non-autistic] people have seen, they judge an autistic person the first time they met.
F4: Yeah, if you tell someone "I have autism": "No, no, you can't have that. I didn't think … I don't think so".
F1: "You look so normal".
F4: Yeah. "You look so normal".
  …

F4: They think autistic people don't like to be hugged, don't want you to touch their ears, or ... Like to have strange clothes, and ... stuff like that. Like trains. [laughs]

The Swedish group viewed the expectation to 'fit in' in workplaces (evident in discussions with the British practitioners we spoke with) as associated with non-autistic cultural norms of sociality. For example, F4 says:

F4: [unclear] ... you should not stand out. You must not be different, you should well ... dress like the others, you should be just like ... like the others, and laugh at the same things. One laughed at the different ones, as well, and then it was often that you were laughed at. Rather than being included and laugh. And then you thought, uhm, at school, you were mean to each other, and you do not want to be mean, like. And then you were anyway ...You spoke up because others were bad, then became the victim oneself.

The importance of fitting in socially is associated in the group with definitions of social competence in social circles dominated by non-autistic people, which can be thought of as non-autistic epistemic authority when it comes to meanings of communication and sociality.

Questioning non-autistic epistemic authority in support to autistic people

A way in which non-autistic epistemic authority has been challenged by autistic people is through the construction of autistic epistemic communities which break the isolation of autistic people, forming a counter-hegemonic voice in relation to more dominating non-autistic voices. It also suggests the development of autistic communities rather than isolated autistic individuals; for example, in experiences of young autistic people going through university having never knowingly met another autistic person. Damian recalls:

> I went to an alumni group that disability support workers at a university set up, and then there was about 20 autistic young adults in the room who had all gone through their degrees, and one of them early on said why didn't anyone think it was a good idea to do this when we were at the university rather than finished. And a couple of people who've got through university never knowingly met another autistic person and they were in this room sharing stories, empathising with each other within ten minutes or so .... They just took over. And I think what is important sometimes is that awareness of others and strength in numbers. Kind of, if the amount of meetings and forums and working groups I've been on where I'm the only autistic person in the room or one of two or three, we're always in the minority. And when you're in the majority it's like the straight guy at the gay club, it's kind of suddenly the power shifts and that's quite a powerful thing to not be a minority all the time.

The impact of not being a minority, being a majority, illustrated both in the recalling of the Swedish group and in Damian's extract above, illustrate a current move within both support and research, where non-autistic-led research/support is being challenged by autistic-led support or research. During our conversations together we explored histories of autistic-led support and non-autistic-led support albeit in close cooperation with autistic people, both stressing the active involvement or participation of autistic people in the design and implementation of support oriented to autistic people.

In the discussions between the three of us as authors, we picked up on the idea of the different meanings/language of (autistic) collectivity versus (autistic) separateness (the individual approach or the lone autistic self) (cf. Bertilsdotter Rosqvist et al., 2020) associated with different knowledges about support aimed at autistic people among the people we have talked with. The becoming aware of each other as an autistic collective to challenge the separateness and isolation of autistic people from each other is repeatedly stressed by autistic people, while the individuality of an autistic person is stressed by non-autistic people.

A dilemma was brought to the surface when discussing the degrees of involvement or epistemic authority of autistic people. In our discussions, Damien made a distinction between autistic-led research, which refers to something which "tends to be more critical, more sociological, more practical" and "non-autistic research". Our discussion addressed imbalances within critical research on autism. Damien invoked the term "ontological ownership" of autism. Using the "Glass Subheading" (Milton and Bracher, 2013; Milton, 2014) as illustration, non-autistic ontological ownership is mapped out and the risk of tokenism/being bracketed in the corner by non-autistic people within critical research on autism which is not autistic-led but rather is non-autistic-led with the participation of autistic people:

> In articles and in research the autistic person is often misframed, and it is rarely the autistic person writing the conclusion or doing the final interpretation of what this all means. So, the ontological ownership of autism is rarely in the hands of the autistic person, whether it's TV or research or anything else. And the autistic led stuff tends to be very much unfunded people's voluntary goodwill and kind of that grassroots activism type stuff.

Concluding remarks: meanings of collectivity versus separateness in support aimed at autistic people

In this chapter we have used a series of discussions to illustrate the different meaning-making languages of autism and how they position autistic people and support services. Non-autistic support people stressed the importance of providing individually tailored support services where autistic individuals (rather than autistic collectives) are coached in skills to manage a non-autistic work culture. In the autistic discussions the focus was on the sense of being part of a community (a collective) where people meet because they want to do things together rather than to be taught stuff by non-autistic people (in order to be able to integrate more smoothly within worlds dominated by non-autistic people). In terms of epistemic communities, the autistic narratives stress the importance of forming autistic epistemic communities where autistic knowledge is shared and produced within that community, through "shared language and concepts", rather than what can be looked upon as non-autistic epistemic authority in settings dominated by non-autistic people. This can be in settings led by non-autistic people, or a non-autistic talking across non-shared languages (non-autistic versus autistic) and non-autistic–autistic mixed settings where non-autistic ways of being (in this instance in the workplace) are assumed and naturalised. We have conceptualised this in terms of different languages, how languages can be spoken across cultures and frame understandings of support. The language of deficit, personalisation and individualisation can be seen to maintain non-autistic epistemic authority through the isolation/separateness of autistic people from each other (as discussed by Damian in the case of support systems).

The inclusion of autistic researchers and the lived experience of autistic people are becoming more evident in mainstream non-autistic knowledge production and service provision. For example, in a seminar series "Shaping Autism Research UK", participation, alongside autism practice and policy, were key themes from the outset; this became even stronger through the course of the project (Fletcher-Watson et al., 2018). Alongside these efforts was the establishment of the Participatory Autism Research Collective (PARC), an autistic-led network championing participatory research in the field (Milton et al., 2019). Despite these efforts, autism research is still dominated by medicalised deficit-model approaches. These competing knowledges also have their impact on practice, although possibly creating a contradictory and confusing space for practitioners working with autistic people to navigate.

While conflicts over epistemic authority continue, these tensions are worsened by a lack of understanding between perspectives (Milton, 2012; 2014, Hillary, 2020) and what has been described as 'silo mentalities' (Cilliers and Greyvenstein 2012; Arnold 2016) within academia (in relation to barriers to interdisciplinary work). Such a 'double empathy problem' is situated within wider power dynamics (Milton, 2016). While safe autistic-led spaces that can be trusted are growing, they may have limited impact on the epistemic authority of non-autistic people to define the lives of autistic people across the many contexts in which they live. A strength and a weakness perhaps of autistic community efforts are their often fragmented and disparate character.

Through this chapter we have aimed to contribute to a current debate of epistemological authority in meanings of support aimed at autistic people. With this, we also pose some theoretical questions for further consideration: how is epistemic authority (or ontological ownership) of autism invoked and defended in different contexts? What 'autisms' and 'non-autisms' are produced through different contextual epistemic authority or power bases of autistic knowledge production/production of knowledge about autism? How is autistic knowledge/knowledge about autism produced in different autistic or non-autistic spaces? What do non-autist-defined/led and autistic-defined/led services for autistic people constitute – and how could they work together?

References

Abreu, G., & O'Dell, L. (2017). Theorising child language brokering: The example of brokering in health care settings. In R. S. Weisskirch (Ed.), *Language Brokering in Immigrant Families: Theories and Contexts* (pp. 180–204). New York: Routledge/Psychology Press/Taylor and Francis Publishers.

Arnold, L. (2016). *The Application of Video in the Education of Autistic Adults*. Doctoral dissertation, University of Birmingham.

Autism Act. (2009). https://www.legislation.gov.uk/ukpga/2009/15/introduction

Bertilsdotter Rosqvist, H. (2019a). Doing things together: Exploring meanings of different forms of sociality among autistic people in an autistic work space. *Alter*, 13(3), 168–178. https://doi.org/10.1016/j.alter.2019.03.003

Bertilsdotter Rosqvist, H. (2019b). Knowing what to do: Exploring meanings of development and peer support aimed at people with autism. *International Journal of Inclusive Education*, 23(2), 174–187. https://doi.org/10.1080/13603116.2018.1427807

Bertilsdotter Rosqvist, H., Örulv, L., Hasselblad, S., Hansson, D., Nilsson, K., & Seng, H. (2020b). Designing an autistic space for research: Exploring the impact of context, space, and sociality in autistic writing process. In Hanna Bertilsdotter Rosqvist, Nick Chown & Anna Stenning (Eds.), *Neurodiversity Studies. A New Critical Paradigm* (pp. 156–171). London: Routledge.

Brownlow, C. (2007). *The Construction of the Autistic Individual*. PhD thesis, University of Brighton.

Chamak, B. (2008). Autism and social movements: French parents' associations and international autistic individuals' organisations. *Sociology of Health and Illness*, 30(1), 76–96. https://doi.org/10.1111/j.1467-9566.2007.01053.x

Cilliers, F., & Greyvenstein, H. (2012). The impact of silo mentality on team identity: An organisational case study. *Journal of Industrial Psychology*, 38(2), 1–9.

Fletcher-Watson, S., Adams, J., Brook, K., Charman, T., Crane, L., Cusack, J., Leekam, S., Milton, D., Parr, J. R., & Elizabeth Pellicano, E. (2018). Making the future together: Shaping autism research through meaningful participation. *Autism: International Journal of Research and Practice*, 23(4), 943–953. https://doi.org/10.1177/1362361318786721

Goffman, E. (1963). *Stigma: Notes on the Management of Spoiled Identity*. Englewood Cliffs, NJ: Prentice-Hall.

Hillary, A. (2020). Neurodiversity and crosscultural communication. In Hanna Bertilsdotter Rosqvist, Nick Chown & Anna Stenning (Eds.), *Neurodiversity Studies. A New Critical Paradigm* (pp. 91–107). London: Routledge.

Lister, R. (2003). Investing in the citizen workers of the future: Transformations in citizenship and the state under new labour. *Social Policy and Administration*, 37(5), 427–443. https://doi.org/10.1111/1467-9515.00350

Milner, P., & Kelly, B. (2009). Community participation and inclusion: People with disabilities defining their place. *Disability and Society*, 24(1), 47–62. https://doi.org/10.1080/09687590802535410

Milton, D., Martin, N., & Melham, P. (2016). Beyond reasonable adjustment: Autistic-friendly spaces and universal design. In D. Milton & N. Martin (Eds.), *Autism and Intellectual Disabilities in Adults Vol. 1* (pp. 81–85). Hove: Pavilion Publishing and Media.

Milton, D., & Sims, T. (2016). How is a sense of well-being and belonging constructed in the accounts of autistic adults? *Disability and Society*, 31(4), 520–534. https://doi.org/10.1080/09687599.2016.1186529

Milton, D. E. (2012). On the ontological status of autism: The 'double empathy problem'. *Disability and Society*, 27(6), 883–887. https://doi.org/10.1080/09687599.2012.710008

Milton, D. E. (2014). Autistic expertise: A critical reflection on the production of knowledge in autism studies. *Autism*, 18(7), 794–802. https://doi.org/10.1177/1362361314525281

Milton, D. E., & Bracher, M. (2013). Autistics speak but are they heard? *Medical Sociology Online*, 7(2), 61–69.

Milton, D. E. M., Ridout, S., Kourti, M., Loomes, G., & Martin, N. (2019). A critical reflection on the development of the Participatory Autism Research Collective (PARC). *Tizard Learning Disability Review*, 24(2), 82–89.

Murray, D. (2018). Monotropism–an interest based account of autism. *Encyclopedia of Autism Spectrum Disorders*, 10, 971–978. https://doi.org/10.1007/978-1-4614-6435-8_102269-1

Nelson, L. H. (1993). Epistemological communities. In L. Alcoff & E. Potter (Eds.), *Feminist Epistemologies* (pp. 121–159). New York: Routledge.

Oikkonen, V. (2013). Competing truths: Epistemic authority in popular science books on human sexuality. *European Journal of English Studies*, 17(3), 283–294. https://doi.org/10.1080/13825577.2013.867181

Orsini, M. (2009). Contesting the autistic subject: Biological citizenship and the autism/autistic movement. In S. J. Murray & D. Holmes (Eds.), *Critical Interventions in the Ethics of Healthcare: Challenging the Principle of Autonomy in Bioethics* (pp. 115–130). Farnham: Ashgate.

Ryan, S., & Runswick Cole, K. (2009). From advocate to activist? Mapping the experiences of mothers of children on the autism spectrum. *Journal of Applied Research in Intellectual Disabilities*, 22(1), 43–53. https://doi.org/10.1111/j.1468-3148.2008.00438.x

Sinclair, J. (2010). Cultural commentary: Being autistic together. *Disability Studies Quarterly*, 30(1).

THINK AUTISM. (2014). Fulfilling and rewarding lives, the strategy for adults with autism in England: An update. https://www.gov.uk/government/publications/think-autism-an-update-to-the-government-adult-autism-strategy

Walker, N. (2014). Neurodiversity: Some basic terms and definitions [online]. *Neurocosmopolitanism: Nick Walker's Notes on Neurodiversity, Autism, and Cognitive*. Liberty. https://neurocosmopolitanism.com/neurodiversity-some-basic-terms-definitions/

Winberg, K., Bertilsdotter Rosqvist, H., & Rosenberg, D. (2019). Inclusive spaces in post-secondary education – Exploring the experience of educational supports for people with a neuropsychiatric disability. *International Journal of Inclusive Education*, 23(12), 1263–1276. https://doi.org/10.1080/13603116.2018.1445303

16
CRITICAL AUTISM PARENTING

Mitzi Walz

When reading Leo Kanner's initial case studies of children with the condition that he defined as autism (Kanner, 1943), the parents are at times far more present than his erstwhile subjects. They are informants, and figures of suspicion – perhaps guilty of passing on defective genes (a process that was then barely understood), perhaps guilty of cold or indifferent parenting, but firmly positioned as the active agents in his story. Their children, on the other hand, are painted as enigmatic and without agency.

And here it began, the focus on parents as a key factor in autism, although Kanner was simply expanding a narrative of parenting already in vogue for a generation, thanks to the Child Guidance movement (James, 2002). As the saying goes, what isn't counted does not count, and before the advent of Child Guidance clinics in the UK and the United States, it was rare indeed for children to be seen by any kind of mental health professional, much less one with any knowledge of child development. Psychology and psychiatry were new and focused almost entirely on adults. But then, catapulted into action by societal concerns arising out of social and labour unrest on the one hand, and the experience of World War I on the other, the Child Guidance movement emerged to focus on the nebulous topic of 'maladjustment' in childhood (Stewart, 2012).

The word 'maladjustment' could be stretched to fit anything from bed-wetting to shyness to juvenile delinquency, and the practice of Child Guidance put a far greater number of parents than ever before under the clinical gaze. That is because it was parents, not children, who were the real target of Child Guidance professionals. It was parents who required instruction, advice, and intervention so that they could readjust their child.

Of course, we now recognise that child abuse is far more common across every social stratum than was believed even a few decades ago, much less at the start of the 20th century, and that it does indeed cause devastation. There is much to celebrate about the fact that beating your children is no longer viewed as appropriate chastisement, and that robust child protective services exist that can step in when children are at serious risk. However, the Child Guidance movement also created a persistent power dynamic, where rather than encouraging parents to understand and respond to the needs of their actual child, parents find themselves judged for not producing the 'ideal' offspring that our social and economic system has increasingly demanded. Seen through this lens, defining autism as a deviation from expectations, and pathologising parents in relation to autism, can be viewed as part of that ongoing project.

Unfortunately for both autistic people and their parents, being judged and found wanting does not usually bring out the best in people. Evidence ranging from research into the mental health of mothers of autistic children (Bromley, Hare, Davison and Emerson, 2004) to the number of autistic children murdered by parents (Palermo, 2003) suggests that somewhere between real concerns and good intentions, the road to hell has been well and truly paved. In response to finding themselves wrongly in the dock, it is parents themselves – ourselves, because the author is also the mother of an autistic person – who have paved much of that road. We have done so as a form of self-defence, in response to specific neoliberal constructions of childhood and parental duty.

The dangers of self-defence

I have written elsewhere (Waltz, 2013) about parent organisations as key players in the history of autism, including the representation of autistic people as 'puzzles' to be solved and parents as puzzle-solvers. This isn't to apportion blame, because under the circumstances, what else could parents have done? Kanner was followed by a line of clinicians – Bowlby, Tustin, Klein, Bettelheim, and more – who contributed to a narrative claiming that 'incorrect' parenting could cause catastrophic developmental damage to children, with autism firmly positioned at the extreme end of that spectrum of harm (ibid.). We now know that this is not how autism happens. We know that it is largely genetic, encompasses a broad spectrum of expression, and that people so diagnosed can flourish when met with a supportive, individualised response.

This was not the case in 1962, when the National Autistic Society (NAS) emerged after parents of autistic children were rejected by a British organisation of parents of children with intellectual disabilities (ibid.). They were rejected because these parents, also demonised in the popular imagination, feared being associated with child abusers. As late as the 1990s, many professionals pursued the line. For example, psychiatrist Peter Breggin called the 1965-founded Autism Society of America (ASA) a defence group for child-abusers (Breggin, 1994) (actually, he is still at it: see Breggin, 2010).

Their experience of rejection went beyond organisations for parents of disabled children. It included childminders and day-care centres, both mainstream and special schools, other services where parents hoped to find support and guidance, and other parents and often their own families. Having received rejection at every turn, these parents looked for acceptance elsewhere. This was found primarily amongst other parents of autistic children. Together, they tried to find ways to cope, founded their own schools and services, and even became autism researchers in an era when little real research was being done.

But self-defence in the face of parent-blaming has a hidden reverse, in that it is driven by the need for parent-valorisation. Because autism was either ignored by mainstream researchers or addressed by questionable research that reviled parents of children with autism, space was left for entrepreneurs, including not a few cranks, who would succeed by building parents up instead of tearing them down. Parents turned out to be powerful potential allies, especially when they gained a sense of power and prestige from the affiliation.

The late Bernard Rimland, a research psychologist who was also the parent of an autistic son, was one of the first to realise this potential. I got to know Rimland in the early 1990s and spent enough time with him to know that his heart was in the right place. He was not motivated by trying to make himself wealthy. He was also spectacularly wrong on a regular basis. His antipathy to the psychiatric powers-that-were was so great, and his willingness to believe anyone who suggested an alternative approach was so large, that he opened the door to a stream of shysters who have only gained in numbers and grown more sophisticated in their approach. Long after

Rimland had landed the first well-placed shots across Bruno Bettelheim's ship of autism fraud (Rimland, 1964), he launched another one, in the shape of Defeat Autism Now!

I attended a DAN! conference in 2000. Worn down from years of battling my local school system to educate rather than alternately neglecting and abusing my son, I walked into a conference centre whose cheery displays were a showroom for the Autism Industry as we know it today. There was Sidney Baker, with a talk about autism and autoimmune disorders. There was Boyd Haley, bending my ear about supplements. There was Andrew Wakefield showing sciencey-looking pictures that 'proved' a link between autism and vaccinations. There was discussion of updates to the sciencey-sounding 'DAN! protocol', which eventually included everything from elimination diets to mercury chelation; a protocol that was responsible for a few deaths, probably far more sickened or damaged children, thousands of deeply indebted parents, and high earnings for several profiteers. A few of the latter have gotten their just deserts (Barrett, 2019), but most of them got away with the con, and continue to do so.

I took quite a few things away from the conference. Some samples of Rimland's recommended SuperNuThera vitamin formula, pages of notes on diet and supplements and therapies, and a warm memory of having experienced several people who claimed to be qualified professionals giving me the time of day. In fact, many of these professionals listened intently, validated my observations, and applauded the efforts of other parents who stood up to talk about homespun remedies that they thought might be helping their kids.

I now know that what many of these professionals were doing by chatting sympathetically with parents at DAN! was market research. Over the ensuing 20 years, parent-friendly conferences like DAN! have become a primary sales arena for many companies. And although mainstream organisations such as the ASA and NAS are slightly more sceptical than the anything-goes likes of DAN!, their conferences have also become heavily dependent for funding on companies willing to rent booths for product sales or advertise in delegate packs.

Those with something to sell quickly realised that not only were parents a lucrative market, but they were also an excellent sales force. Indeed, even before use of the Web was mainstream, parent-focused autism email lists – one of the few ways for families to learn from each other back in the days when we were actively discouraged from meeting by most clinicians – also functioned as wide-open marketplaces where parent product recommendations were shared (and sometimes fabricated). Therapies were also marketed in this way.

At another parent conference, for the ASA, I encountered the Applied Behaviour Analysis (ABA) marketing juggernaut for the first time. Having failed at using operant conditioning to turn 'feminine boys' into 'normal boys', University of California–based psychologist O. Ivar Lovaas turned his behaviourist tools to work on a new target: autistic children (Gibson and Douglas, 2018). ABA was marketed directly to parents and given the alternative – likely to be lifelong incarceration in a state hospital system where sexual and physical abuse was rife – they lined up to sing his praises. When Lovaas thought he had found a parent with star marketing potential in writer Josh Greenfield, who promised to write a book about the process, he pulled out all the stops. But when his methods did not turn Greenfield's son Noah into a 'normal' child, Lovaas dropped the child and his family like a hot potato. Noah ended up in state care, where he was raped and abused (Greenfeld, 2009). His story was only unusual because it was documented.

Looking back, we now know that Lovaas used deeply questionable research designs (Gresham and MacMillan, 1998), and never published the promised follow-up data on his tiny cohort of successes. And yet ABA was, for many years, touted as the 'gold standard' – the 'Cadillac model' that parents across the US and UK were critiqued for demanding instead of the 'Ford model' that school districts supposedly offered.

There was a problem on both sides of this flawed comparison, of course. ABA was never a Cadillac – autistic adults who were subjected to it tell us that it was abusive and damaging, leading to distress, distrust, and PTSD (McGill and Robinson, 2020). However, the ABA milieu openly welcomed parents, as managers for enthusiastic university students who were the usual therapists for middle-class families who could afford to pay, or as full-time parent-therapists in families of lesser means. School districts kept parents at arm's length at best and were at worst actively hostile. Worse yet, that 'Ford model' could be better characterised as the educational version of an unreliable jalopy cobbled together from spare parts. Lovaas's team had the marketing skills, and they also had a coherent, standardised product. When mainstream psychology journals rejected their papers (behaviourism was considered discredited in the field for anything but blunt-force coercion, suitable only for animals, prisoners, and low-level workers in factories), they set up their own journals and published reams of case studies. These were almost useless scientifically, but they convinced the key audience: parents.

Because parents are positioned in neoliberal education systems as advocates who must compete to obtain 'educational goods' on behalf of their children (Angus, 2013), it was parents who had the most power to demand ABA, or its eventual spin-offs. Because ABA offered an off-the-shelf system delivered (or at least designed) by 'trained professionals', it was easier to demand x number of hours per week of ABA from your school district, local authority, or insurance company than to specify the range of individualised services and supports that could deliver accessible education to your child in an inclusive environment. ABA advocates took other measures to secure their place in the educational marketplace as well, such as setting up a 'credentialling' system for providers and arranging for it to be written into law in various US states and providing 'experts' who could back up parental demands in tribunals and hearings. However, direct marketing to parents was its most effective weapon because it worked within the context of how Individual Education Plans are written and funded.

Unsurprisingly, Lovaas and his acolytes never told parents that at its core, behaviourist theory held that parents were themselves responsible for autism having applied 'incorrect' operant conditioning during infancy. That would have undermined the sales pitch and called the core of their claims into question.

At the University of North Carolina, Eric Schopler and Gary Mesibov were also bringing parents into the fold as parent-therapists. Their methods were kinder, and TEACCH eventually evolved to include support designed for adults, and attention to the sensory and attentional differences that characterise most autistic people (Mesibov, Shea and Schopler, 2005). Their experience of how valuable parents could be as part of the marketing team for TEACCH in the 1970s certainly influenced what came afterwards, however.

ABA and TEACCH are both built on the drive, coming mostly but not entirely from behaviourists, to position parents as therapists. Doing so required redefining the role of parents, encouraging them to see themselves as, to quote the first published review of scientific journal articles on the practice, "the social agents who live with the child" (Berkowitz and Graziano, 1972: p. 278) who carry out "programming" (ibid.: p. 309) within an "interaction system" (ibid., p. 310) These authors also stress that bringing parents into the treatment fold can shift "the focus of treatment several steps closer to a *prevention* model of mental health service ... actively training potential clients to be future problem-solvers rather than future service seekers" (ibid.: p. 279; emphasis in original). This review also notes the potential for saleable products aimed at parent-therapists, such as electronic devices and videotapes, as well as saleable training and supervision hours for behaviour therapists.

In the ensuing years, parents have been pushed into the therapist role not so much by positive choice as through their experience of life in a world of small-government ideologies and privatisation. The pressure to purchase and to achieve the 'right' results is often a role imposed on parents, not a choice, nor is it always experienced as the life-affirming experience it is sold as. For example, in his research on the murder of children with autism by parents, Palermo places the role of parent-therapist as "the essential role parents must play in the rehabilitation of their autistic children" (op. cit.: p. 54), especially in neoliberal contexts where external support is limited, and a key source of stress.

Parents as protective shields

In this environment of planned scarcity, an additional use of parents has emerged that is particularly repugnant: their deployment as human shields when schools and services are under fire. This is a use that gives a lie to the concept of parents acting as informed purchasers of services, because it can only occur in an environment where better services are unavailable, and alternatives are seen as much worse. Only the extreme shortage of any services, much less services that you can afford or that have any positive elements at all, has led parents to defend what should be indefensible.

When parents of one autistic child went to court in the United States, alleging physical abuse at the Higashi School in Boston, others were quickly rounded up to speak to the press.

> "You see these kids achieving things that you never thought … they would achieve," said one. "He's sleeping better, he's eating better. They're opening his world up in a way that in nine years, with a lot of therapy and a lot of intervention and with my love, we weren't getting. We were in quicksand".
>
> *(Barry, 2002: B2)*

This parent was not simply the first name picked from the school director's Rolodex – it was Eileen Naughton, the president of *Time* magazine, and therefore sure to supply a media-friendly quote (ibid.). The quote itself follows the typical pattern of such appeals: our child is benefiting, and there is no viable alternative.

"Mother warriors"

But of course, if you do not play nice, the 'mother warrior' is also a valorised role in the autism community. It is also one that creates huge problems for families, and especially for autistic children and adults, who are rarely asked whether what Mom is fighting for is really what they want or need. Battling school districts, local authorities, and insurance companies for a greater individual share of a tiny pie costs vast amounts of energy. Institutional opponents count on their advantage in these fights with families, doing their utmost to keep any parent they see as mouthy, unsatisfied, or angry at arms' length and on uneven ground.

In the end, what the fight typically devolves to is a preferred selection from a set of products, with experts hired by both sides to advance one commercial interest against another, using 'concerns' about the child or adult in question as positive or negative points on their sales tip sheets. Most such negotiations take place in private – indeed, families and institutional providers are often prevented by non-disclosure agreements from publicising any details of individual cases – but documentation of these sales disputes often ends up online anyway. For example, tribunal documents from a 1999 dispute in which an American parent wanted to move her autistic daughter from the Higashi School to a community-based residential programme using ABA show the mother with her own educational consultant on one side, while on the other the school district has lined up four professionals, including a lawyer, buttressed by five staff members from the Higashi School and a training expert. The parent's argument is that a community-based placement would be safer, offer more opportunities for parent visits, and provide more augmentative and alternative communication support; whereas the district and Higashi argue that the child is meeting learning goals. The school district won, of course, because the child's needs related to parenting were limited in the case to "parental training and involvement" in the school's programme (Commonwealth of Massachusetts, 1999).

No one asked the child about her preferences or needs.

This case also illustrates the reality that few parents will ever be in a position to advocate for one well-resourced residential school versus another. The more typical fight is over whether their child will be allowed a full school day in an unsuitable programme, some hours of speech therapy, or access to teachers with training beyond attendance at an 'Autism Awareness' seminar. For most families, the battle is about the degree of educational neglect or poor care provision that will be provided or permitted. By making access to education and care a private battle, the system incentivises families to make only individual demands, never to question why service provision is so poor for most.

Rhetorics of normativity

The pressures that parents of autistic people experience and respond to are part of a larger picture, in which the family and educational establishments are positioned as having a core duty to create a 'normal' child. I further argue that when it comes to neurological development, the definition of 'normal' has become increasingly constrained, expanding the potential market for products and services aimed at parents but restricting the freedom of people to be themselves. Parents and schools now need to aim not just for 'normal' – which should include a wide degree of diversity, reflecting the general population – but to create the perfect neoliberal subject.

Houghton (2019: p. 623) has defined the "ideal neoliberal subject" as someone who "seeks to make an enterprise of their own life, investing in their human capital to fuel the consumption that will produce their own satisfaction". The personal experience of trying to attain this status puts parents and children alike in a position of constant striving for a goal that will always be slightly out of reach because of the ephemeral nature of the ideal: "no individual will ever fully meet the criteria" (ibid.: p. 622). It is precisely this tension that drives parents of autistic children to 'try everything' within their (consumer) power to prevent their autistic child becoming an autistic adult: they know that not only have the means been privatised, so have the ends. A lack of 'success' on their part will be judged and punished by spending the rest of their lives negotiating with the even worse services and support on offer in the adult system.

An extensive literature has emerged from the confluence of Queer Studies and Childhood Studies that questions these discourses of normativity, and this can be extended to critique how parents and childhood-focused institutions have been deployed around autism as well as around sexuality (for example, Yergeau, 2017; Gibson and Douglas, 2018). Dyer (2017: p. 292) has suggested that "a queer methodological approach to child development and education can more generally disrupt teleologically constructed narratives of growth that require a developmental sequence which culminates in normalcy".

Those of us who have been through the mill can tell other parents what the system will not: responding to this pressure to turn your autistic child into a 'perfect' neoliberal subject through purchase and application of the correct services and products is a losing battle. It will harm you, and it will harm your child. Your child is exactly who they are meant to be, deserving of an appropriate education, good health, and a decent life, none of which should be reliant on whether the child or the family becomes a profit centre. But within the market that has arisen, parents feel inordinate pressure to not only to do their best to help their child, but also to be *seen to be* trying everything possible. That is because autism parenting, once something to be done in secret or handed over to institutional professionals, has become a spectator sport and potential profit centre of its own.

What can't be fixed can still be monetised

Discussion of the family as profit centre brings this article towards one of the latest, and most blatant, uses of parents by the Autism Industry. Even if we are unable to produce a child who will generate profit as a neoliberal subject in their adult life, the autistic child can still be monetised along the way. The service- and product-sellers clearly realised this long ago. But in recent years, parents have been driven to monetise their own children. 'Autism Mom' bloggers, like other online 'influencers', are increasingly in the business of generating clicks for profit and selling products.

When I first joined the online autism world in 1991, the most common sales pitch was from a mom embroiled in a multi-level marketing (MLM) scheme like Amway or Mannitol, usually flogging supplements to generate some household income, or an embarrassed plea to support a frazzled parent's home-based craft business. I stepped away from the screen about ten years later, and a lot has happened in the meantime. A three-minute Google search in December 2020 immediately located a substantial number of 'autism mommy blogs' (and a few 'autism dad blogs') selling products ranging from indigestion relief pills to books to special-needs clothing and toys via a plethora of 'sponsored' posts (not always marked as such), all accompanied by photos and hashtags designed to package up a saleable 'personal brand'.

In 2015, Angela McRobbie dissected the nature of modern competitive femininity by looking at how women now feel pressured to present the perfect image online, even when the reality is something else entirely. The phenomenon is not entirely new – McRobbie mentions Peaches Geldolf's chirpy my-perfect-life women's magazine column coexisting with the heroin addiction that claimed her life; my memory stretches back to Peaches' mother, Paula Yates, writing a series of parenting books retailing her own my-perfect-life stories, starting with *The Fun Starts Here: A Practical Guide to the Bliss of Babies* in 1990 and ending with her own overdose death ten years of 'fun' later. When this form of competitive femininity is limited to B-list celebrities who can employ ghost-writers and assistants to churn out copy, that is one thing, but mothers of autistic children are now encouraged to somehow find the time and energy to cultivate a persona, an audience, and an Instagram-friendly look as cover for shilling products to others. The gulf between reality and carefully curated perception is no less great, but the daily grind here is often about basic survival, reducing parenting to a set of curated performances in response to a world in which money is the great equaliser in the fight to provide your child's basic needs.

This way to the exit

In Houghton's exploration of the ideal neoliberal subject, she concludes with words that suggest the only way out of the role that parents of autistic people find themselves in. The role of the neoliberal subject, she writes, has become so embedded in our culture "because through their acts [individuals] embody it as active subjects" (Houghton, 2019: p. 623).

Within these words lies the solution: stop.

Stop acting as an individual, fighting for your child and yours alone. Collectivise the struggle and demand collective solutions that will be individualised to meet specific needs.

Stop shopping. Reject the brand-name hegemony of ABA, PRT, TEACCH, the branded residential schools and programmes, the product sales pitches.

Stop accepting understandings of autism that are based on comparison to undefined and ever-changing norms. Make common cause with autistic people and take the time to understand how it feels to be the site of person-changing technologies and controls.

Make common cause with good professionals (we all know a few). Make common cause with disabled adults in general and their families and friends, rather than allowing the system to pit autistic people and their families against others in a competition for resources. And if you are still parenting a child under the ae of 18, take steps now to find out about the lived experiences of adults with autism – the poor-quality services, lack of opportunity, discrimination, and written-off lives that are realities for far too many on one hand, and the unaccountably large earnings of companies that profit from this misery on the other.

You are not alone in this fight; you never were. And while you are worth more to the profiteers as an individual neoliberal subject trying to pip others to the post, you are worth more to your autistic family member as part of a broad movement dedicated to realising the rights of autistic people rather than seeking to erase them from the world through homogenisation.

If you work with parents, act as their ally in this fight.

References

Angus, L. (2013) "School choice: Neoliberal education policy and imagined futures," *British Journal of Sociology of Education*, 36(3): pp. 395–413; DOI: 10.1080/01425692.2013.823835.

Barrett, S. (2019) "Government actions against DAN! Doctors," *Autism Watch*, 23 February. Washington, DC: Centre for Inquiry. Online at: https://quackwatch.org/autism/reg/danreg/.

Barry, E. (2002) "Allegations resurface at unique school for autistic children," *Boston Globe*, 1 October. Online at: http://neurodiversity.com/abuse.html.

Berkowitz, B.P. and Graziano, A.M. (1972) "Training parents as behavior therapists: A review," *Behavior Research and Therapy*, 10(4): 297–317; DOI: 10.1016/0005-7967(72)90054-X

Breggin, P.R. (1994) *Toxic Psychiatry: Why Therapy, Empathy, and Love Must Replace the Drugs, Electroshock, and Biochemical Theories of the New Psychiatry*. New York: St. Martin's Press.

Breggin, P.R. (2010) "The new child abuse: The psychiatric diagnosing and drugging of children," *Huffington Post*, 17 December. Online at: https://breggin.com/the-new-child-abuse-the-psychiatric-diagnosing-and-drugging-of-our-children/.

Bromley, J., Hare, D.J., Davison, K. and Emerson, E. (2004) "Mothers supporting children with autistic spectrum disorders: Social support, mental health status and satisfaction with services," *Autism*, 8(4): pp. 409–423; DOI: 10.1177/1362361304047224.

Commonwealth of Massachusetts. (1999) "Lowell public schools—BSEA #98-3521." Online at: https://www.specialedlaw.com/database/lowell-public-schools-bsea-98-3521/.

Dyer, H. (2017) "Queer futurity and childhood innocence: Beyond the injury of development," *Global Studies of Childhood*, 7(3): pp. 290–302; DOI: 10.1177/2043610616671056.

Gibson, M.F. and Douglas, P. (2018) "Disturbing behaviours: Ole Ivar Lovaas and the queer history of autism science," *Catalyst: Feminism, Theory, Technoscience*, 4(2): pp. 1–28; DOI: 10.28968/cftt.v4i2.29579.

Greenfeld, T. (2009) *Boy Alone: A Brother's Memoir*. New York: Harper Perennial.

Gresham, F.M. and MacMillan, D.L. (1998) "Early Intervention Project: Can its claims be substantiated and its effects replicated?," *Journal of Autism and Developmental Disorders*, 28(1): pp. 5–13; DOI: 10.1023/A:1026002717402.

Houghton, E. (2019) "Becoming a neoliberal subject," *Ephemera*, 19(3): pp. 615–626. Online at: http://www.ephemerajournal.org/sites/default/files/pdfs/contribution/19-3houghton_0.pdf.

James, K. (2002) *Taming the Troublesome Child: American Families, Child Guidance, and the Limits of Psychiatric Authority*. Cambridge, MA: Harvard University Press.

Kanner, L. (1943) "Autistic disturbances of affective contact," *Nervous Child*, 2: pp. 217–250.

McGill, O. and Robinson, A. (2020) ""Recalling hidden harms": Autistic experiences of childhood Applied Behaviour Analysis (ABA)," *Advances in Autism*, 7(4): pp. 269–282; DOI: 10.1108/AIA-04-2020-0025.

McRobbie, A. (2015) "Notes on the perfect: Competitive femininity in neoliberal times," *Australian Feminist Studies*, 30(83): pp. 3–20; DOI: 10.1080/08164649.2015.1011485.

Mesibov, G., Shea, V. and Schopler, E. (2005) *The TEACCH Approach to Autism Spectrum Disorders*. New York: Springer Science & Business Media.

Palermo, M.T. (2003) "Preventing filicide in families with autistic children," *International Journal of Offender Therapy and Comparative Criminology*, 47(1): pp. 47–57; DOI: 10.1177/0306624X02239274.

Rimland, B. (1964) *Infantile Autism: The Syndrome and Its Implication for a Neural Theory of Behavior*. New York: Appleton-Centrury-Crofts.

Stewart, J. (2012) ""The dangerous age of childhood": Child Guidance in Britain c. 1918–1955," *Policy Papers*, 1 October. London: History & Policy. Online at: http://www.historyandpolicy.org/policy-papers/papers/the-dangerous-age-of-childhood-child-guidance-in-britain-c.1918-1955.

Waltz, M. (2013) *Autism: A Social and Medical History*. Basingstoke: Palgrave Macmillan.

Yergeau, M. (2017) *Authoring Autism: On Rhetoric and Neurological Queerness*. Durham, NC: Duke University Press.

17
"EVEN THOUGH I'M ON THE SPECTRUM, I'M STILL CAPABLE OF FALLING IN LOVE"

A Bourdieusian analysis of representations of autism and sexuality on *Love on the Spectrum*

Allison Moore

Introduction

Despite increasing representations of autism in popular culture, it is frequently portrayed in narrow, stereotypical ways which serve to reinforce dominant, medical models of autism, underpinned by notions of 'deficit' and 'lack'. Further, there are some aspects of autistic experience that remain taboo and, consequently, invisible or, at best, marginalised. This is particularly the case regarding sex, sexuality and intimacy. Historically, and to a lesser extent today, people with developmental disabilities and cognitive differences, including autistic people, have been portrayed prejudicially as asexual, sexually immature or inappropriate and at times as hypersexual. Sexuality and autism have been constructed as antithetical, with sexuality seen as potentially dangerous and, therefore, something that autistic people should be protected from.

However, in recent years, there have been some popular cultural representations that appear to challenge the assumption that autism and sexuality are mutually exclusive categories. There have been televisual depictions of fictional characters as sexual beings with interests in forming intimate relationships for whom sexual desire and sexual identity are integral to their personhood (*The Good Doctor* (2017–present), *Atypical* (2017–present)). Whilst it can be argued that shows like these can go some way to challenging stereotypes of autism and misconceptions of autistic people as asexual, fictional narratives tend to (re)produce autistic characters who conform to what Murray (2006, 2008) has called the 'sentimental savant' who has a reflective function to shine a light on neurotypical relationships and, in so doing, enrich them. Relationships are almost always normative in so far as they are heterosexual and follow 'conventional' patterns of dating and intimacy. Further, the protagonists are usually male and, therefore, reinforce the myth of autism as a 'male condition'. Although these shows are about autism or "directed *at* autism, ... [they] very rarely engage in conversation *with* autism" (Hartley, cited in West 2018, italics in original).[1]

More promising in presenting positive and representative portrayals of autism, sexuality and intimacy has been the emergence of reality TV format dating shows with a focus on disabled participants, many of whom are autistic (*The Undateables* [(2012–present)]) and, in some shows, exclusively autistic (*Autism in Love* (2016)). These programmes follow disabled and/or neurodivergent individuals, who *The Undateables* refers to as "extraordinary singletons", in their search for love. To 'help' them in their quest is a range of 'experts' and nondisabled/neurotypical friends and family who are on hand to offer advice and guidance and, sometimes, match the individuals up with other similarly 'disabled' singletons. As with fictional depictions of autism and sexuality, there is the potential to undermine and deconstruct stereotypes but given the reality TV format, there are additional opportunities for awareness raising and educating the largely neurotypical audience. However, the promise of moving from fiction to reality is unfulfilled, as like their fictional counterparts, these programmes fall short of their potential. Research indicates that there are higher incidences of homosexuality, bisexuality (Hellemans et al., 2007; Byers et al., 2013; Gilmour et al., 2012) and gender nonconformity (Dewinter et al., 2013; Dewinter et al., 2017) and gender disidentification (Bumiller, 2008) amongst autistic people compared to neurotypical population samples and yet these reality TV formats tend to stick to heteronormative and, very occasionally, homonormative scripts. In formats where dating agencies find prospective partners, autistic participants are never matched with a neurotypical date; they are paired with other autistic people and sometimes with learning disabled individuals. This leads Vertoont (2018) to suggest that these representations of disability and sexuality can have a dis/empowering potential because they perpetuate the notion of a "segregated dating circuit for disabled people" (ibid.: 829), where disabled people can/should only date similarly disabled people.

In 2019, a new cultural text was added to the growing body of reality TV programmes focused on autism and dating. Produced by Northern Pictures for Australian Broadcasting Corporation (ABC) and released on Netflix in July 2020, *Love on the Spectrum* (*LOTS*) follows seven single people as they navigate the highs and lows of dating, some of them for the first time. It also features two couples who share their stories of how they met and fell in love. Northern Pictures describes the show as an

> upifting and insightful series [that] celebrates diversity and difference, with participants who are warm, funny and generously open. It sets out to teach us all lessons of love, romance, intimacy and acceptance.[2]

This chapter will critically consider the intersection of representations of autism, sex and intimacy in *Love on the Spectrum*. Not only is the figure of the sentimental savant ever-present in the show's promotional literature and in its reviews, the show also presents a highly individualised account of love and romance and, by extension, the 'failure' of the participants to achieve their desire for a relationship. In so doing, there is no acknowledgement that sexuality and all its concomitant practices are socially constructed and highly ritualised. It also fails to acknowledge that understandings of and attitudes towards autism are similarly socially contingent and that the ontological status of autism is subject to contestation (Woods et al., 2018). Drawing on the sociology of Pierre Bourdieu and adopting a Critical Autism Studies perspective that is committed to "investigating power dynamics that operate in Discourses around autism, questioning deficit-based definitions of autism, and being willing to consider the ways in which biology and culture intersect to produce 'disability'" (Waltz, 2014: 1337), this chapter will argue that autistic individuals' lived experiences are shaped by the wider sociocultural contexts in which they live and by the power dynamics that exist between neurotypical[3] (NT) and neurodivergent people. From Bourdieu's work, it is particularly his notions of practice, field, capital and habitus that will be important and will be utilised to suggest that, if we are to make sense of why the participants in *LOTS* have not had success in relationships, it is necessary to move beyond individualised accounts of love and romance to look at the structural inequalities that autistic people experience and which make "exploring the unpredictable world of dating even more complicated"[4] for them than it is for neurotypical people.

Love on the Spectrum and genre: resisting categorisation

Love on the Spectrum has been variously described as a documentary, a docuseries and a reality series. That it defies easy categorisation is hardly surprising given the generic hybridity of reality television, which borrows tropes and conventions from other television genres. Now used as an umbrella term to cover a disparate range of formats, what reality TV programmes have in common is "an emphasis on the representation of ordinary people and allegedly unscripted or spontaneous moments that supposedly reveal unmediated reality" (Biressi & Nunn, 2005: 10–11). It also engenders specific types of relationships *"between the camera, the participants, and the viewers"* (Deery, 2015: 16, italics in original), in which the audience has a dual function as a viewer or "voyeur who gains a sense of looking in on other people's lives" (Biressi & Nunn, 2005: 64). However, a viewer does not consume and interpret reality TV objectively; they respond "on conscious and unconscious levels" (ibid.: 84), bringing with them their prior knowledge about the subject. This is illustrative of Mittel's (2001) claim that television genres are best understood as discursive practices, located within specific sociocultural contexts and reflecting dominant cultural conventions and ideologies.

In an explicit reference to the kinds of assumptions that the audience might bring with them, Cian O'Clery, the creator of *Love on the Spectrum*, said his intention in making the series was "to help bust some of the myths about autism—one of the biggest being that people on the spectrum aren't interested in love and uninterested in relationships and intimacy".[5] Whilst O'Clery acknowledges the prevalence of desexualising discourses surrounding autism, he also indicates who the intended audience of the show is: neurotypical people. It is highly unlikely that autistic people will need educating about the fact that *they* may be interested in love, relationships and intimacy. They are unlikely to subscribe to such myths because of their own lived experiences. A further insight into the target audience is evident in O'Clery's aim to "kind of help educate audiences a bit more about autism".[6] As experts by experience, autistic people do not require education about autism, but a NT audience might. Indeed, Milton (2012: 886) has rightfully asserted that autistic people have a deeper level of knowledge of NT experiences than NT people have about autistic experiences because,

> "many autistic people have [...] gained a greater level of insight into non-AS society, and more than vice versa, perhaps due to the need to survive and potentially thrive in a non-AS culture".

A series *about* autism but targeted *at* a neurotypical audience raises issues about the mediation of looking, the power dynamics involved in looking and interpreting, as well as the significance of the neurotypical gaze.

In her now famous 1975 essay, "Visual Pleasure and Narrative Genre", Laura Mulvey draws on psychoanalysis to argue that in a world predicated on sexual inequality, males have been positioned as the active viewer of the passive and objectified female: "The determining male gaze projects its phantasy on to the female figure which is styled accordingly" (Mulvey, [1975] 1999: 837). The male gaze is the product of institutionalised and naturalised sexual differences and the power dynamics that arise from them. I would argue that all representations where there is a power differential between the viewed and the viewer should be subjected to critical scrutiny to examine the "power systems that are at play and [...] which interpretations are privileged so they are made visible, while others are rendered invisible" (Woodward, 2015: 41).

From its identification as a diagnostic category in 1943, autism has been under observation. A (usually neurotypical) clinician or researcher observes autistic behaviour and characterises it as different to and less than the NT norm. Adopting an exterior, rather than interior, standpoint, the neurotypical gaze holds a position of power from which to interpret autistic behaviour. Even today, autism continues to be the *object* of much academic research and autistic scholars are in a significant minority. Contemporary representations of autism must be analysed against a history of autism being scrutinised and being objectified. Increased visibility of autistic people, irrespective of the good intentions of the programme makers to challenge stereotypes or increase understanding, does not inevitably "enable control or the exercise of power over how they [autistic people] are seen" (Woodward, 2015: 42). All texts are polysemic and, regardless of the motivations of the creators of programmes directed at autism, they can be read in multiple ways. As a result, it is important to consider what functions the text is performing for the largely NT audience.

In his critique of *The Undateables*, Richardson (2017) posits that the dating show is analogous to the Victorian freak show, where bodies that transgressed societal expectations were spectacularised for entertainment or presented as a vessel into which the anxieties of the day could be placed. He argues that in the 21st century, emphasis on coupledom and fears about being single permeate society and, as such, the show can be seen as an attempt to alleviate viewers' anxieties; "*we* may find contemporary dating culture difficult, but at least it's not as difficult for '*us*' as it is for the bodies represented in the series" (Richardson, 2017: 334, italics added). The promotional material for *Love on the Spectrum* suggests that the series is conforming to this appeasement function. On Netflix's official site, the brief description of the show is "Finding love can be hard for anyone. For young adults on the autism spectrum, exploring the unpredictable world of dating is even more complicated".[7] In other words, to paraphrase Richardson, 'finding love on the contemporary dating scene can be difficult for *us* neurotypicals but at least it is not as hard as it is for *those* autistics'.

Not only does the show alleviate the anxieties of the neurotypical audience concerning love and intimacy, it also presents autism in a way that enriches the NT viewer. Murray (2008: 13) argues that, in fictional representations, an autistic character frequently "takes on the form of what we might call the 'sentimental savant', especially in realms of creativity and an understanding of core human concerns", amongst which we might include love and relationships. Although he was referring to fictional characters, his argument can also be extended to non-fictional representations. Northern Pictures, who produced *Love on the Spectrum*, state that the series sets out to teach us all lessons of love, romance, intimacy and acceptance" (ibid.). Referring to the couples who featured on the show, it claims "[T]heir love stories are an inspiration to others" (ibid.). These sentiments are also expressed in many of the reviews of the show. It has been described as "heartwarming"[8] and a "show that paints telling portraits of human connection".[9] Although *Love on the Spectrum* was not universally positively received, what these examples illustrate is that "rather than allowing for the presentation of autism within the terms of the autistic individual" (Murray, 2008: 13), representations of autism typically serve a refractive function to shine a light on the neurotypical viewer.

To move beyond stereotypical representations of autism and the perpetuation of the 'sentimental savant' in reality dating series like *Love on the Spectrum*, it is necessary to challenge the highly individualised accounts of why the participants in the shows have failed to find a relationship and to disrupt the dominant, deficit model of autism upon which they are based. It is here that Bourdieu's sociology can be insightful because it is an attempt to understand how "'objective' supra-individual social reality … and the internalised 'subjective' material worlds of individuals and cultural beings and social actors are inextricably bound together" (Jenkins, 2002: 19–20). Autistic people's experiences of love, romance and relationships are shaped not only by individual factors, such as skills, knowledge and opportunity, but by structural factors, such as constructions of autism and attitudes towards autism. In other words, if we are to understand why the participants in reality dating shows are still looking for love, we need a greater understanding of the experiences of being autistic in a neurotypical world.

Insights from Bourdieusian sociology

Bourdieu's sociological project can be understood, fundamentally, as an attempt to transcend the dichotomy between structure and agency and to move beyond the distinction between objectivism and subjectivism, which, he argued, had dominated the sociological tradition. There are four concepts or thinking tools at the core of Bourdieu's sociological project: practice, habitus, field and capital.

Practice can be understood as the social interaction of everyday life. It is concerned with agency and the ways in which people contribute to the reproduction of the social structures which channel and limit their opportunities and life chances. What defines practice for Bourdieu is its historic and sociocultural specificity and its unconscious, or at least, not entirely conscious, nature. He has referred to the taken-for-granted nature of practical logic as *doxa* or *doxic experience*; described by Webb, Schirato and Danaher (2002: xi) as a "set of core values and discourses which a field articulates as its fundamental principles, and which tend to be viewed as inherently true and necessary". Doxa masks the fact that the core values of a society have been imposed through the struggles between dominant and dominated groups. The 'naturalness' or 'taken for grantedness' of doxa renders these struggles invisible, eliminates, or at least limits, the possibilities for the future and, therefore, serves to maintain and reproduce the status quo.

Habitus can be understood as values, behaviours and dispositions which are both structured and structuring; "a subjective but not individual system of internalised structures, schemes of perception, conception, and action common to all members of the same group or class" (Bourdieu, 1977: 86). These values, behaviours and dispositions become embodied, "converted into motor schemes and bodily automatisms" (Bourdieu, 1980: 68). Habitus is relational and has a material reality as far as it exists through our interactions with others. It can also be thought of as embodied because it refers to the way practical taxonomies or binary oppositions, such as male/female, heterosexual/homosexual, neurotypical/neurodivergent are experienced through the senses or through the body. Bourdieu argued that habitus is manifested not only in shared values and dispositions but also in the way social actors physically present themselves in their demeanour, style of dress, cultural tastes and language (Jenkins, 2002).

Bourdieu referred to this as *hexis* or body technique and its function is twofold. First, to succeed in bourgeois society and to secure access to rare resources, including economic, cultural and symbolic capital, it is necessary to have the "right hexis" (Crossley, 2005: 120). Consequently, social actors strategise and adapt their hexis so it more closely resembles that of the 'right', socially recognised hexis. Second, as hexis is learned as part of habitus, it serves to naturalise oppression and inequality and "members of different groups seem *naturally* to belong to those (different) groups" (Crossley, 2005: 120, italics added). Therefore, the existing social order is maintained.

For Bourdieu, the power of the habitus relies on its habitual nature and the unconscious, or, at least, not entirely conscious way in which individuals carry out practices. Another important feature of the habitus is the distinction Bourdieu makes between subjective habitus, as embodied in individuals, and the shared habitus, grounded in "a shared body of dispositions, classificatory categories and generative schemes" (Jenkins, 2002: 80). Everyone's habitus will be unique to them because individuals do not share identical life histories and follow different life trajectories. However, for Bourdieu (1977), these differences represent little more than a 'structural variant' of the wider collective habitus, which has been acquired early in life. Milton (2014) refers to these structural variants as 'dispositional diversity', whereby "human embodied sociality creates a diversity of dispositions and developmental trajectories".[10] However, normative categorisations of the social habitus allow limited space for dispositional diversity and those individuals whose structural variation from the idealised collective habitus are at risk of being 'othered' and assigned an outsider status. Indeed, the greater the structural variant, "the wider the disjuncture in dispositional perceptions of the lifeworld" (Milton, 2012: 884).

Such differences in terms of experience may be accounted for by Bourdieu's concept of social field, a term he used to explain how society is divided into different sectors or "worlds" (Crossley, 2005: 80). He defined a field as "a network, or a configuration, of objective relations between positions" (Bourdieu in Bourdieu & Wacquant, 1992: 97). A field can be understood as a sphere in which a particular type of activity takes place. Social agents occupy different positions within the field, dependent on their access to and accumulation of resources or capital within it.

Bourdieu's concept of field has been developed by some scholars and applied to the sexual field, a sphere within which individuals seek sexual and intimate partners and seek to accrue sexual (or erotic) capital. It emerges

> when a subset of actors with potential romantic or sexual interest orient themselves toward one another according to a logic of desirability imminent to their collective relations and this logic produces, to greater and lesser degrees, a system of stratification.
> *(Green 2014: 27)*

As with all fields, the sexual field is hierarchical, based on *structures of desire* (ibid.: 28), which "eroticize and assign value to certain bodies, affects, and practices while rending others neuter or undesirable" (ibid.).

The term Bourdieu used to describe the goods and resources available in a social field was capital and he identified four main types of capital in his work: economic, cultural, symbolic and social capital. Economic capital refers to monetary capital, including income, wealth and property ownership. It has a tangible quality, and it is, therefore, easy to identify an individual's economic worth. Cultural capital refers to knowledge and can be manifested in one of three ways. It can be represented in an objectified form, an institutionalised form and as embodied "in the sense that one might have culturally valued competences … or one might exude a valued cultural bearing in one's 'bodily hexis' or body techniques" (Crossley, 2005: 29–30). Symbolic capital refers to the social status that is bestowed on an individual, whilst social capital is concerned with the significance of social networks. Whilst Bourdieu used the term to refer to the idea of having "'friends in high places' and 'old boys' networks" (Crossley, 2005: 32), it has a much broader application. Quite simply, an individual with a large social network can be said to have more social capital than an individual who does not.

Bourdieu's focus on embodiment with regards to both cultural capital and habitus has paved the way for the development of 'bodily capital'. Although some scholars have presented bodily capital and its accumulation as an individual pursuit under the conditions of neoliberalism (see, for example, Hakim, 2010), of greater relevance in an analysis of *Love on the Spectrum* is the contribution from disability studies and the critique of compulsory able-bodiedness (and I would argue compulsory neurotypicality), which "requires individuals to find a way to fit within able-bodied [and neurotypical] expectations, spaces, and narratives of tragedy and empowerment" (Connell & Mears, 2018: 569).

The chapter will now draw on these key Bourdieusian concepts to analyse the depictions of autism, love and relationships on *Love on the Spectrum* and argue that, whilst the show presents a highly individualised account of why participants have not formed intimate relationships, it is possible to identify the interplay between agency *and* structure in their accounts.

"Is autism that bad?" (Chloe, Episode 1)

Much of the promotional material for *Love on the Spectrum* indicates that it is autistic people's 'difficulties' that underpin their failure to find love. For example, Northern Pictures' official webpage for the programme states that "difficulties in social interaction and communication are a key feature of autism, which makes finding a partner an often daunting and difficult experience".[11] Similarly, in the opening scenes of the first episode, the narrator reiterates this notion by saying that "People on the spectrum often have difficulty socialising and meeting prospective partners can be difficult" (*LOTS*, 2019: ep. 1). In the press kit for the show, director Cian O'Clery claims that, whilst there are support programmes for autistic people focused on developing work skills to help find employment, some organisations offer social skills training "to help people develop and maintain friendships (arguably not enough) but dating? Close to nothing".[12]

These statements perpetuate a deficit model of autism, locating any 'difficulties' in social interaction within the individual because of *their* autism, rather than recognising the relational and dynamic nature of social communication. However, when autistic people experience 'difficulties' in their interaction with others, it is not a *result* of their autism. Communication is a two-way process (Hacking, 2009; Milton, 2012) and a breakdown in communication is not the fault of one party failing to understand the other. It occurs because *both* parties fail to understand *each other*. Damian Milton calls this the double empathy problem, which occurs when there is "a disjuncture between two differently disposed social actors which becomes more marked the wider the disjuncture in dispositional perceptions of the lifeworld" (Milton, 2012: 884; see also Luke Beardon's notion of cross-neurological theory of mind, 2017). The different life experiences of autistic and neurotypical people, as well as their diverse ways of experiencing the world, are not always conducive to successful communication because of the potential for "a breakdown in reciprocity and mutual understanding"[13] (Milton, 2018).

The asymmetrical dynamics that shape relations between autistic and neurotypical people and which (re)produce deficit discourses of autism is an example of Bourdieu's notion of practice: the unconscious and taken-for-granted social interactions of everyday life predicated on practical logic or doxa. For Bourdieu, "Doxa is a particular point of view, the point of view of the dominant, which presents and imposes itself as a universal point of view" (Bourdieu, 1998: 57). It is through practice and doxa that systemic and structural ableism operate, and which perpetuate taken-for-granted assumptions about normative existence. Two participants reflected the way in which the 'superiority' of neurotypical forms of communication and 'deficits' of autistic communication become engrained and naturalised. When 27-year-old Andrew is asked what he thought the biggest challenge would be for him in a relationship, he replies "Good conversation and, especially, eye contact as well". When the director seeks clarification by asking "So, communication?", Andrew says "Er, yes" (*LOTS*, 2019: ep. 5). In a similar scenario, when Olivia is asked why she thinks so many autistic people fail to find love, her response is "Because of our difficulties, I guess" (*LOTS*, 2019: ep. 4). The narrative of autistic people having 'difficulties' in social interaction and communication is so pervasive that it can become internalised. It is only when neurotypicality is positioned as the norm and neurodiversity judged in relation to, and as lesser than, it that a breakdown in communication between two people can be attributed to autistic people's so-called deficits or difficulties. The assumptions that autistic people have communication deficits become naturalised through practice and doxa and, in so doing, the systematic oppression of autistic people is obscured.

The responses from Andrew and Olivia can also be understood in relation to what Bourdieu called symbolic violence, "a gentle violence, imperceptible and invisible even to its victims exerted for the most part through the purely symbolic channels of communication and cognition (more precisely, misrecognition), recognition, or even feeling" (Bourdieu, 2001: 1–2). Symbolic violence should not be read as a minimisation or trivialisation of actual violence (Bourdieu, 2001). Instead, it is a term used by Bourdieu to describe the process whereby structures of domination have been built throughout history by "singular agents … and institutions – families, the church, the educational system, the state" (Bourdieu, 2001: 34) and which serve to naturalise and reinforce relations of dominance and subordination. It is possible to see analogies between symbolic violence and Iris Marion Young's (1990) famous essay on the five faces of oppression – exploitation, powerlessness, marginalisation, cultural imperialism and violence – in which she argued that structural oppression is reproduced and perpetuated, often unconsciously, and is institutionalised within the very fabric of society. Drawing on the five faces of oppression, Milton (2016) has highlighted that autistic people continue to experience social marginalisation, powerless and cultural imperialism, whereby "[T]hose who have power in society can determine how those in a position of powerlessness are interpreted and talked about" (ibid.: 1404). From the outset, autism has been defined and understood from the outside, with predominantly neurotypical professionals determining what autism looks like and how it manifests.

Social interactions do not take place in a vacuum; they are located in fields, which are hierarchical in nature. In fields, agency and structure interact as an individual's agency is shaped by their social position in the field. In a society predicated on compulsory neurotypicality, autistic people's agency is shaped by dominant discourses that characterise autism as an inability to do some things that neurotypical people purportedly do 'naturally', like finding it easy to engage in social interaction. An individual's position in the field not only shapes their agentic ability; it also determines their access to power and scarce resources within it. This is evident in the social field, but it is also in the sexual field where structural determinants shape an individual's agency because some bodies are constructed as desirable whilst others are deemed undesirable (Green, 2014). The participants in *Love on the Spectrum* demonstrated an awareness of how autism as a condition and, by extension, autistic people are rendered undesirable or, at best, less desirable than neurotypical people.

In Episode 1, 19-year-old Chloe reported, "I was dating a guy and when I told him I was autistic, he left me because he didn't want to be associated with someone who was autistic". Similarly, in Episode 2, 21-year-old Kelvin, who has never been on a date says, "Some girls don't feel like dating with someone with a disability" and, in Episode 4, 25-year-old Olivia is asked what it would mean to her to find love. She replies "Amazing, I guess. I don't know. I never thought about it because I didn't think it was ever going to happen". She then goes on to say that a considerable number of autistic people do not find a partner. In these excerpts, the participants are aware that their autism impacts negatively on their ability to form intimate relationships. From a Bourdieusian perspective, the experiences of the participants are an example of agency and structure interacting. Once structural factors, such as discriminatory discourses of autism, are acknowledged as contributing to an autistic person's potential to form sexual and/or intimate relationships, it is no longer appropriate to suggest that an individual's failure to find love is a result of their 'difficulties' in social interaction. However, because sexual fields, like all fields, are hierarchical and based on, what Green (2014: 27) calls "structures of desire", individuals attempt to accrue more resources to make themselves more desirable. It is here that the programme makers and experts involved in *LOTS* devote much of their attention.

"I'm autistic enough to understand Ruth and she can understand me back" (Thomas, Episode 1)

Bourdieu's notion of habitus "demonstrate[s] the ways in which not only is the body in the social world, but also the ways in which the social world is in the body" (Reay, 2004: 432). Fundamentally, the habitus is a relational concept, concerned with the relationships an individual has with those around them, as well as their environment, which become internalised and embodied. Nick Chown (2012: 58) has suggested that it seems "intuitively correct" that the habitus of an autistic person would be different to that of a neurotypical person. The different habituses or "dispositions of autistic people are misunderstood [...] and ostracised for their otherness. The autistic experience of the lifeworld is often fragmented, but there also exists a double empathy problem between interacting agents of widely differing disposition and perception" (Milton, 2012).[14] I would also argue that it seems "intuitively correct" that the habituses of autistic people would have a great deal in common given the likelihood that they will have had similar life experiences which will have shaped their values, behaviours and dispositions.

Of course, every autistic person's habitus is unique to them, and it is experienced individually but, from a Bourdieusian perspective, it is incorrect to also view those experiences as individually authored because "we share a social position with others, finding ourselves in similar configurations of social relationships and thus enjoying/enduring similar sorts of experiences" (Crossley, 2005: 107).

For some of the participants on *LOTS*, there was a realisation that their autism meant they had something in common with other autistic people because they had similar experiences. In Episode 1, Chloe says "Dating someone on the autistic spectrum might be better because I might be able to talk to them about it and feel like I don't have to be fake and be someone completely different" (*LOTS*, 2019: ep. 1); 23-year-old Maddi also said she would like to date someone on the spectrum (*LOTS*, 2019: ep. 2). During some of the dates, the conversation turned to autism and what the participants' autism meant to them. On Chloe's date (*LOTS*, 2019: ep. 1) with Lotus they talked about the difficulties of getting a diagnosis as a girl and the fact that, frequently, their behaviour was misunderstood or misinterpreted (Gould & Ashton-Smith, 2011). On her date with Thomas, Olivia asked him if he has an accent and he replies, "I like to think I have the autism accent", to which she responded with an understanding "Ahhh" (*LOTS*, 2019: ep. 4). They also discuss how their sensitivities to sounds impacts on them. For both long-term couples who feature on the show, their autism is not only central to their relationship; it is something that strengthens it. When Ruth and Thomas are asked about when they first met, Ruth says "We immediately understood each other" (*LOTS*, 2019: ep. 1) Jimmy did not receive his diagnosis until he was 18. He says that prior to that "I just knew I was different and Sharnae [his girlfriend] just, she just, felt similar to me ... Even before I was diagnosed, she called me autistic" (*LOTS*, 2019: ep. 5).

The differences between the habitus of autistic and neurotypical people are highlighted in the programme by drawing attention to the participants' hobbies and interests and, in so doing, reinforcing the autism diagnostic criteria of "restricted, repetitive patterns of behaviour, interests or activities".[15] In response to Ruth's collection of "probably thousands" of business cards, the director says, "I don't think I've met anyone before who collects business cards" (*LOTS*, 2019: ep.

1). In another episode, after 27-year-old Andrew has shown the camera crew around his hobby room, which contains his jigsaw puzzles and the K'nex models he has built, he is asked "Do you think being on the autism spectrum kind of has something to do with you having these strong interests in things?" (*LOTS*, 2019: ep. 4). In each episode, the narrator introduces the participants' dates by saying what their likes and dislikes are, which typically relate to sensory issues, particularly sound, smell and touch. Although it appears that these examples are an attempt to provide an insight into the lives of the participants so that the viewer can better understand them, their actions and their motivations, I would argue that they also emphasise differences in the behaviours and dispositions of autistic and NT people.

As already highlighted, so-called difficulties that autistic people experience in social interaction and communication are, in fact, attributable to a breakdown in communication *between* parties because of a disjuncture in their dispositions (Milton, 2012). This disjuncture can be a product of individuals' different experiences, but they are just as, if not more, likely to occur between members of different social groups. If autistic people are understood as belonging to distinct social groups, a sociocultural framing of autism and autistic communication is engendered. From a sociocultural perspective, interaction requires "the understanding of other members' expected intentions, beliefs, knowledge, or feelings that are conventionally linked to socioculturally organised practices, roles, institutions, and membership in a social group" (Solomon, 2008: 150). In their ethnographic research on child-directed communication (CDC), Ochs et al. (2005) suggest that the dominant dispositions in CDC in Euro-American cultures of "face-to-face body orientation, [and] speech as the primary semiotic medium" hinders an autistic child's communication abilities. This kind of community speech habitus that privileges face-to-face and verbal communication is synonymous with neurotypicality, at least in the Anglophone West. 'Good' communication skills are, therefore, predicated on the behaviours and dispositions of neurotypical people.

Throughout *LOTS*, there are examples of participants being taught how to improve *their* communication by developing dominant, neurotypically oriented styles of interaction. It is here that Bourdieu's notion of capital is insightful.

"Now you guys have all the tools you need" (Dr Laugeson, Episode 3)

The significance of Bourdieu's concept of cultural capital with regards to sexuality lies in its manifestation as embodied and, particularly, in the notion of bodily hexis, the way in which habitus is expressed through an individual's deportment, posture and accent and which can be used to acquire access to goods and resources. As with all of Bourdieu's concepts, capital is relational and exists within the hierarchical dynamics of social fields. So, to procure goods and resources, one must display the 'right' bodily hexis. Throughout *LOTS*, participants are taught how to perform on their dates. They are told how to behave, how to present their bodies and how to engage in social interaction. In other words, they are told that the embodied habitus and cultural competencies of autistic people are not acceptable to exchange for rewards, which in this case, is the reward of intimate relationships.

The first example of the participants performing the 'right' bodily hexis can be seen in the show's opening image. The seven single participants and one of the couples (Jimmy and Sharnae) are captured in highly staged poses. They are all wearing formal evening wear. The men wear suits, with two of them wearing bow ties, whilst the women all wear long dresses and are immaculately made up. Apart from Olivia, the single participants are looking directly into the camera and Sharnae and Jimmy look into each other's eyes. The shot would not look out of place on the front cover of a glossy fashion magazine, but it is far removed from how the participants dressed during their dates and is indicative of how bodily hexis or body technique is moulded throughout the show.

It is in the encounters with the 'relationship experts' that it is possible to see the modification of bodily hexis most explicitly. During the show, three participants (Michael, Kelvin and Andrew) have one-to-one meetings with Jodie Rogers, a relationship specialist. When she meets Kelvin for the first time (*LOTS*, 2019: ep. 2), they engage in a role play of a first date. At one point, they are talking about anime and manga, two of Kelvin's hobbies. When he discusses a particular anime film, Kelvin turns his body away from Jodie, his upper body learns forward slightly, and he looks at the table in front of him. Jodie stops him quickly and says "So, we start talking about anime and what did you do with your body? … You're looking away". As she asks the question, she uses her own body to mimics what Kelvin had done. Kelvin immediately replies with "And that's a no". He also shakes his finger to indicate 'no' and crosses his arms in front of his body. In this encounter, Kelvin is made to realise that his bodily hexis is not 'right' for a date and he must maintain face-to-face interaction throughout, reinforcing that neurotypical bodily hexis is the 'right' one.

During Jodie's first meeting with Michael (*LOTS*, 2019: ep. 1), she asks him if he has difficulty understanding people's body language. He replies, "I have very little trouble. Facial expressions always give something away … I've been studying human behaviour for many years, specifically in women". He explains that he has always had an interest in it, "in a strange way". Jodie tells him that it is not strange because "If you're on the spectrum and you find understanding body language difficulty, actually studying body language is a really good thing to do". Presumably it is neurotypical body language that should be studied, so that the autistic person can learn how to read and potentially mimic that body language and, in so doing, accrue more capital.

In one of the episodes (*LOTS*, 2019: ep. 3), some of the participants are shown attending a dating workshop run by Associate Clinical Professor, Dr Elizabeth Laugeson at the Department of Psychiatry and Biobehavioral Sciences at the UCLA Semel Institute for Neuroscience and Human Behaviour. She is the director of PEERS, a social skills programmes developed through the University of California for autistic people. Dr Laugeson says that the workshop teaches autistic people skills that many people "take for granted and use naturally in dating situations". Not only are dating situations anything but natural, being highly ritualised and socially and culturally contingent, they also reflect the habitus of a speech community that prioritises neurotypicality. During the dating workshop, we can see a slide behind Dr Laugeson entitled "Time to Practice … Making Conversation on a Date". On the slide is a list of 'dos' and 'don'ts' for successful dating, which include "Use good eye contact", "Smile when Appropriate" and "Give a courtesy laugh". Many autistic people report that making eye contact, or engaging in face-to-face orientation, is extremely challenging and can even feel painful or distressing, so it seems counterintuitive to teach these skills to autistic people in order to be 'successful' in dating.

The work of the relationship experts is clearly well-intentioned and both state they feel it is important that young adults are taught social skills to enable to go on dates and find a relationship. However, the very premise of Dr Laugeson's dating 'boot camp' and Jodie's social skills training is that autistic people have deficits in social interaction. Further, if the skills that are being taught align with neurotypical dating skills and autistic people are required to adopt or adapt to a neurotypical bodily hexis to be seen as desirable, it raises questions about the impact this has on autistic identity and authenticity. There is considerable literature on the negative consequences of camouflaging or masking for autistic people and how having to perform according to neurotypically defined social standards can lead to poor mental health outcomes, such as anxiety, depression and exhaustion (Davidson & Henderson, 2010; Livingstone & Happé, 2017). If autistic young adults are to be supported in their quest for intimate relationships, instead of "*adapting to* a prevailing system or fulfilling certain *standards*" (Späth & Jongsma, 2020: 77) they would be far better served if they are encouraged to decide what kinds of intimate relationships they seek based on their "own idea of what is good for them and how they can integrate themselves best in society" (ibid.).

Conclusion: "I just don't want to be alone for the rest of my life" (Chloe, Episode 1)

Love on the Spectrum does address the under-researched and marginalised issues of sexuality and intimacy in relation to autism. It follows seven single autistic people in their search for love and demonstrates that autistic people can and do have successful intimate relationships through their portrayal of two long-term couples. As such, it does go some way to meeting director Cian O'Clery's aim "to help bust some of the myths about autism" and particularly the myth that autistic people are not interested in relationships or intimacy. The show's relationship expert, Jodie Rogers states that "it doesn't matter whether you're on the spectrum or not on the spectrum, everybody has a basic human right and a basic human need for connection and love" (*LOTS*, 2019: ep. 2). This concurs with the World Association for Sexual Health's (WAS) Declaration of Sexual Rights statement that "sexual rights are grounded in universal human rights"[16] and, as such, are predicated on the "freedom, dignity, and equality of all human beings" (ibid.). However, rights are not natural phenomena, and they are not naturally given. They are the rooted on hierarchical social relations and are usually the outcome of activist struggles (Weeks, 1995). Recognising that autistic people have sexual rights and the basic human right "for connection and love" is not sufficient to actualise those rights.

This chapter has argued that the continuation of deficit models of autism, which position autistic people as having inherent difficulties in social communication and interaction, acts as a significant barrier to the realisation of many autistic people's desire to form intimate relationships. It is not *their* individual 'difficulties' that make it hard for autistic people to find partners but the structural inequalities of the social and sexual fields, predicated on neurotypicality, and their position within those fields which limit their potential. When participants are taught social skills that are more appropriate to the neurotypical dating scene, however well-intentioned, the implication is that autistic ways of being and communicating, or in Bourdieusian terms the habitus of autistic people, are inferior and that to make oneself desirable it is necessary to accrue neurotypically defined capital. There was so much potential in *LOTS* to "bust some of the myths about autism", not least of which included highlighting the sexual and gender diversity of autistic people and their relationships compared to neurotypical population samples. Whilst one participant identified as bisexual and went on dates with a man and a woman in the show, the depiction of sexuality and intimacy was largely heteronormative. As such, the opportunity to queer bodily capital (Connell & Mears, 2018) or what it means to be seen as sexually desirable, was sadly missed and autistic people continue to be 'othered'.

Notes

1. https://www.voicemag.uk/feature/4493/beyond-curious-incident-new-narratives-of-autism-by-david-hartley (viewed 6 September 2020).
2. https://northernpictures.com.au/love-on-the-spectrum (accessed 6 September 2020).
3. The term 'neurotypical' or 'neurologically typical' refers to individuals who are not diagnosed as autistic or as having an intellectual/developmental disability. It is used to challenge 'the assumption of a non-autistic "norm" [which] is, in conventional understandings, unquestioned and naturalised' (O'Dell et al. 2016: 168).

4 https://www.netflix.com/gb/title/81265493 (accessed 6 September 2020).
5 https://www.fastcompany.com/90530421/netflixs-love-on-the-spectrum-celebrates-neurodiversity-amid-the-trials-and-triumph-of-dating (viewed 8 September 2020).
6 https://www.salon.com/2020/07/22/love-on-the-spectrum-autism-dating-netflix-cian-o-clery/ (viewed 9 September 2020).
7 https://www.netflix.com/gb/title/81265493 (accessed 12 September 2020).
8 https://www.independent.co.uk/arts-entertainment/tv/news/love-spectrum-netflix-autism-dating-reviews-release-date-s2-a9635601.html (viewed 31 October 2020).
9 https://mashable.com/article/love-on-the-spectrum-netflix-review/?europe=true (viewed 31 October 2020).
10 http://www.larry-arnold.net/Autonomy/index.php/autonomy/article/view/AR10/html (viewed 5 June 2021).
11 https://northernpictures.com.au/love-on-the-spectrum (viewed 20 October 2020).
12 https://static1.squarespace.com/static/56035a3ae4b08b574e92a643/t/5dca0b25e23407334f7fc44c/1573522247690/LOTS+Press+Kit+%28ABC+FINAL%29.pdf (viewed 20 October 2020).
13 https://network.autism.org.uk/knowledge/insight-opinion/double-empathy-problem(viewed 12 July 2019).
14 http://www.larry-arnold.net/Autonomy/index.php/autonomy/article/view/AR10/html (viewed 5 June 2021).
15 https://www.cdc.gov/ncbddd/autism/hcp-dsm.html (viewed 12 September 2020).
16 https://worldsexualhealth.net/wp-content/uploads/2013/08/Declaration-of-Sexual-Rights-2014-plain-text.pdf (viewed 31 October 2020).

References

Beardon, L. (2017). *Autism and Asperger Syndrome in Adults*. London: Sheldon Press.
Biressi, A., and Nunn, H. (2005). *Reality TV Realism and Revelation*. London: Wallflower Press.
Bourdieu, P. (1977). *Outline of a Theory of Practice*. Cambridge: Cambridge University Press.
Bourdieu, P. (1980). *The Logic of Practice*. Stanford: Stanford University Press.
Bourdieu, P. (1998). *Practical Reason*. Stanford: Stanford University Press.
Bourdieu, P. (2001). *Masculine Domination*. Cambridge: Polity Press.
Bourdieu, P., and Wacquant, L.J.D. (1992). *An Invitation to Reflexive Sociology*. Cambridge: Polity Press.
Bumiller, K. (2008). Quirky citizens: Autism, gender, and reimagining disability. *Signs: Journal of Women in Culture and Society*, 33(4), 967–991. https://doi.org/10.1086/528848.
Byers, E.S., Nichols, S., Voyer, S.D., and Reilly, G. (2013). Sexual well-being of a community sample of high-functioning adults on the autism spectrum who have been in a romantic relationship. *Autism*, 17(4), 418–433. https://doi.org/10.1177/1362361311431950.
Chown, N. (2012). *A Treatise on Language Methods and Language-Games in Autism*, Doctoral Thesis, Sheffield Hallam University. http://shura.shu.ac.uk/7164/, Viewed 10.10.20.
Connell, C., and Mears, A. (2018). Bourdieu and the body. In Medvetz, T., and Sallaz, J. (eds), *The Oxford Handbook of Pierre Bourdieu*. New York: Oxford University Press, 569–576.
Crossley, N. (2005). *Key Concepts in Critical Social Theory*. London: SAGE Publications.
Davidson, J., and Henderson, V.L. (2010). 'Coming Out' on the spectrum: Autism, identity and disclosure. *Social and Cultural Geography*, 11(2), 155–170. https://doi.org/10.1080/14649360903525240.
Deery, S. (2015). *Reality TV*. Cambridge: Polity Press.
Dewinter, J., De Graaf, H., and Beeger, S. (2017). Sexual orientation, gender identity, and romantic relationships in adolescents and adults with autism spectrum disorder. *Journal of Autism and Developmental Disorders*, 47(9), 2927–2934.
Dewinter, J., Vermeiren, R., Vanwesenbeeck, I. and van Nieuwenhuizen, C. (2013). Autism and normative sexual development: A narrative review. *Journal of Clinical Nursing*, 22(23–24), 3467–3483. https://doi.org/10.1111/jocn.12397.
Gilmour, L., Schalomon, P.M., and Smith, V. (2012). Sexuality in a community-based sample of adults with autism spectrum disorder. *Research in Autism Spectrum Disorders*, 6(1), 313–318. https://doi.org/10.1016/j.rasd.2011.06.003.
Gould, J., and Ashton-Smith, J. (2011). Missed diagnosis or misdiagnosis? Girls and women on the autism spectrum. *Good Autism Practice*, 12(1), 34–41.

Green, A.I. (ed.). (2014). *Sexual Fields: Towards a Sociology of Collective Sexual Life*. Chicago: University of Chicago Press.

Hacking, I. (2009). Autistic autobiography. *Philosophical Transactions of the Royal Society: Biological Sciences*, 364(1522), 1467–1473. https://doi.org/10.1098/rstb.2008.0329.

Hakim, C. (2010). Erotic capital. *European Sociological Review*, 26(5), 499–518. https://doi.org/10.1093/esr/jcq014.

Hellemans, H., Colson, K., Verbraeken, C., Vermeiren, R. and Deboutte, D. (2007). Sexual behavior in high-functioning male adolescents and young adults with autism spectrum disorder. *Journal of Autism and Developmental Disorders*, 37(2), 260–269. https://doi.org/10.1007/s10803-006-0159-1.

Jenkins, R. (2002). *Pierre Bourdieu (Revised Edition)*. London: Routledge.

Livingston, L.A., and Happé, F. (2017). Conceptualising compensation in neurodevelopmental disorders: Reflections from autism spectrum disorder. *Neuroscience and Biobehavioral Reviews*, 80, 729–742. https://doi.org/10.1016/j.neubiorev.2017.06.005.

Milton, D. (2014). Embodied sociality and the conditioned relativism of dispositional diversity. *Autonomy, the Critical Journal of Interdisciplinary Autism Studies*, 1, 3. http://www.larry-arnold.net/Autonomy/index.php/autonomy/article/view/AR10/html, Viewed 05.06.2021.

Milton, D.E. (2016). Disposable dispositions: Reflections upon the work of Iris Marion Young in relation to the social oppression of autistic people. *Disability & Society*, 31(10), 1403–1407.

Milton, D. (2018). The double empathy problem. https://network.autism.org.uk/knowledge/insight-opinion/double-empathy-problem, Viewed: 12.07.2019.

Milton, D.E.M. (2012). On the ontological status of autism: The 'double empathy problem'. *Disability and Society*, 27(6), 883–887. https://doi.org/10.1080/09687599.2012.710008.

Mittell, J. (2001). A cultural approach to television genre theory. *Cinema Journal*, 40(3), 3–24.

Mulvey, L. (1975). Visual pleasure and narrative cinema. In Braudy, Leo, Cohen, Marshall (eds), *Film Theory and Criticism: Introductory Readings*. New York: Oxford University Press, 833–844.

Murray, S. (2006). Autism and the contemporary sentimental: Fiction and the narrative fascination of the present. *Literature and Medicine*, 25(1), 24–45. https://doi.org/10.1353/lm.2006.0025.

Murray, S. (2008). *Representing Autism: Culture, Narrative, Fascination*. Liverpool: Liverpool University Press.

Ochs, E., Solomon, E., and Sterpona, L. (2005). Limitations and transformations of habitus in child-directed communication. *Discourse Studies*, 7(4–5), 547–583. https://doi.org/10.1177/1461445605054406.

O'Dell, L., Bertilsdotter Rosqvist, H., Ortega, F., Brownlow, C., and Orsini, M. (2016). Critical autism studies: Exploring epistemic dialogues and intersections, challenging dominant understandings of autism. *Disability and Society*, 31(2), 166–179. https://doi.org/10.1080/09687599.2016.1164026.

Reay, D. (2004). 'It's all becoming a habitus': Beyond the habitual use of habitus in educational research. *British Journal of Sociology of Education*, 25(4), 431–444. https://doi.org/10.1080/0142569042000236934.

Richardson, N. (2017). The invisibles: Disability, sexuality and new strategies of enfreakment. In Smith, C., Attwood, F., and McNair, B. (eds), *The Routledge Companion to Media, Sex and Sexuality*. London: Routledge, 328–339.

Solomon, O. (2008). Language, autism and childhood: An ethnographic perspective. *Annual Review of Applied Linguistics*, 28, 150–169. https://doi.org/10.1017/S0267190508080148.

Späth, E.M., and Jongsma, K.R. (2020). Autism, autonomy, and authenticity. *Medicine, Health Care, and Philosophy*, 23(1), 73–80. https://doi.org/10.1007/s11019-019-09909-3.

Vertoont, S. (2018). Would you date 'the undateables'? An analysis of the mediated public debate on the reality television show 'The Undateables'. *Sexualities*, 21(5–6), 825–839. https://doi.org/10.1177/1363460717699782.

Waltz, M. (2014). Worlds of autism: Across the spectrum of neurological difference. *Disability and Society*, 29(8), 1337–1338. https://doi.org/10.1080/09687599.2014.934064.

Webb, J., Schirato, T., and Danaher, G. (2002). *Understanding Bourdieu*. London: SAGE.

Weeks, J. (1995). *Invented Moralities*. Cambridge: Polity Press.

West, N. (2018). Beyond 'Curious Incident', new narratives of autism by David Hartley. https://www.voicemag.uk/feature/4493/beyond-curious-incident-new-narratives-of-autism-by-david-hartley, Viewed 06.09.2020.

Woods, R., Milton, D., Arnold, L., and Graby, S. (2018). Redefining critical autism studies: A more inclusive interpretation. *Disability and Society*, 33(6), 974–979. https://doi.org/10.1080/09687599.2018.1454380.

Woodward, K. (2015). *The Politics of In/Visibility: Being There*. Houndmills: Palgrave Macmillan UK.

Young, I. [1990] (2005). Five faces of oppression. In Cudd, A.E., and Andreasen, R.O. (eds), *Feminist Theory: A Philosophical Anthology*. Oxford and Malden: Blackwell, 91–104.

Television programmes

Atypical (2017–present, USA: Netflix).
Autism in Love (2016, USA: Independent Lens).
Love on the Spectrum (2019, Australia: Northern Pictures).
The Good Doctor (2017–present, USA: ABC).
The Undateables (2012–present, UK: Channel 4).

18
SEEKING SUNFLOWERS
The biopolitics of autism at the airport

Katherine Runswick-Cole and Dan Goodley

Introduction

What happens when autism is claimed in public spaces? What does it give and take away? In this chapter, we explore the "Sunflower Lanyard Scheme" as one example of claiming autism in public spaces. The lanyard system operates in places such as airports to alert fellow passengers and staff that the wearer has the label of disability. The lanyard 'outs' the person in relation to autism. Frequently, the scheme is used by people who attract or claim the label of autism. In the airport, security concerns mean that the crush of normalcy weighs heavily on all passengers. The risks associated with failing to observe the tacit and explicit rules associated with airport behaviour might be mitigated by the use of the lanyard. The Sunflower Lanyard Scheme seeks to protect people with 'invisible disabilities' from these risks. Wearing the lanyard identifies a passenger as someone in need of 'help' but also as someone who may not conform to 'normal' social rules. Lanyard wearers can use fast-track check-in lanes and go to the front of the passport control queue.

In this chapter we consider the biopolitical work of such schemes in terms of what they give but, at the same time, what they might take away from (all) human beings. We provide a story of lanyard-use in an airport and an account of a conversational exchange between the authors that was provoked by the story. We then pull in a biopolitical reading of the narrative. Often, we argue, biopolitics is drawn upon to make sure of the regulatory effects of discourses. While this is certainly the case, we argue that there is more to biopolitics than regulation; and we unpack the affirmative and excessive effects of biopolitics. This inevitably leads us to consider the biopolitics of not simply autism, but life itself. So, as we contemplate autism, we are contemplating what it means to be human.

An (autism) story

Dan: How was your holiday, KRC? Did you all have a good time?
Katherine (or KRC to her mates): Yeah, good thanks, lovely weather, great food and just nice to spend time together as a family. Ooh, and did I tell you, we used the sunflower lanyard system at the airport for the first time?
Dan: The what?

Katherine: Oh, they've got this system where you go to the special assistance desk, tell them that you are travelling with someone with a hidden disability and they give you a lanyard with sunflowers on it. It means you don't need to queue for check-in and staff are all aware that you might need a bit of extra help or time, you know. Anyway, on the way back there was a massive queue at passport control, and I thought 'Oh no, we can't do that queue' so I just said to one of the staff: 'My son has a lanyard, he's au …'

Dan: You said what?

Katherine: You know, he has a lanyard …

Dan: [mischievously] Come on, let me hear you say it!

Katherine: [with a defiant tone] What?

Dan: You know!

Katherine: [reluctantly] I said 'he's autistic …'

We are friends and colleagues who have written in the field of critical disability studies for several years. In between conversations about work, you might expect us to talk about our kids (not really kids, all quite grown up, but still kids to us). As the story above illustrates, there is no clear dividing line between conversations about 'work' and conversations about 'family'. A casual question about a holiday and we quickly stumble into yet another conversation about disability theory. Katherine has written elsewhere about her reluctance to engage with diagnostic labels in her (now grown-up) children's lives (Runswick-Cole, 2017). She has pondered the meaning of the category of autism and the limits of labelling. And now she reveals, albeit reluctantly, that there, at the end of a queue, she invoked the category of autism to smooth the family's passage through the airport. In this chapter, we try to unravel the biopolitics of autism embedded within this story and how these discussions are entangled with questions of the human.

Sitpoints

So, we began this chapter with a story set in a very specific location – an airport in the UK – because it ignited another discussion about autism and how these reflections are always entangled with questions of the human. It is fair to say that we are wrestling with the concept of autism, as our interaction reveals. Perhaps the idea of wrestling is too aggressive. It also conjures up images of us in Lycra. Never good. Perhaps, on reflection, we are learning to sit with autism. This latter phrasing of our predicament resonates with a paper written by the critical disability studies and feminist scholar Garland-Thomson (2002) in what is now a classic in the field.

Her argument for a *sitpoint theory* of disabled feminism is an intervention into the non-disabled feminist literature that has emphasised – and continues to emphasise – the importance of standpoint. Clearly, standpoint automatically excludes those feminists who don't do standing and Garland-Thomson is at pains to make this exclusion crystal clear through the deployment of her new term, 'sitpoint', which has in mind people who use a wheelchair. But there is a lot more going on in her argument than simply a need to change the terms of reference.

Instead, what she does so well in her paper is to remind feminist orthodoxies that disabled women have a lot to offer in not only furthering feminist analysis but also couching these insights in new nuanced ways that are demanded by the disabled body. Sitting with ideas, then, is firmly locating oneself in a critical disability studies paradigm. This approach, as we have argued elsewhere, starts with disability but never ends with it (Goodley, 2013). Disability provides – just as the sitting feminist philosopher embodies – new insights, perspectives and philosophies for thinking about the human condition.

In this chapter, then, we seek to ask some very human questions. We have provided you with an exchange between the two of us and the background narrative. Both the story and the interaction are very human encounters. Behind the voicing of ideas, the demands for an answer and the troubled response lie some very affective moments. We did not partake in the conversation in a dispassionate manner. Underlying our chat are deeply held feelings, anxieties, concerns and confusions. Autism, as a phenomenon, is deeply affective. To borrow from another fab feminist Ahmed (2004): autism has created a whole host of affect economies. How we come to know autism – like any cultural phenomenon – is through the various circulations of knowledge, economic marketplaces and associated communities of various purveyors of this phenomenon.

People love and hate autism. Autism gives joy and, at other times, is felt as pain. Autism becomes taken up in various communities, from autistic activists to autism specialists, autism professionals, autism practitioners, autism consumers, autism producers and autism researchers. And simply dipping one's toe into this swirling hermeneutic whirlpool we are in danger of being plunged into turbulent waters. Sitting with autism allows us a moment to pause; to consider the kinds of emotions that this phenomenon generates and, by extension, the kinds of affective attachments that it provides. There is no doubt that autism generates feelings of joy, relief and a sense of belonging. The autistic activists represented in this text will convey the potency and potential of autism as a political category and as a pathway into forms of accommodation and inclusion. We know that these affiliations are heartfelt.

But we also know that, for some, autism engenders negative affect. This is especially the case when there is a sense that autism reduces a person to whom it is applied, which has inspired a range of critical approaches to autism, not least in relation to the reclaiming and reconstitution of the very meaning of this phenomenon by activists and their families. We are all more than the categories that are laden on to us. And when one category threatens to dominate a self then that can engender feelings of sadness, anger or disillusionment. Clearly, autism as a phenomenon has cut straight to the emotional hearts of many of us. So, we need to be very careful with others and ourselves when we feel and think about autism.

The biopolitics of autism: a negative reading

We hope that a biopolitical reading of our story may help us to feel and think more carefully about autism. We follow Berlant (2006) in understanding biopower as a force which has the power to determine whether something lives or dies; it is a regulatory force which demands that living or dying occur in prescribed ways. Let us introduce Rabinow and Rose's (2006) conception of biopower and relate this to autism:

(1) One or more truth discourses about the 'vital' character of living human beings with an array of authorities considered competent to speak that truth (for example, autism as a neurological fact described through neuropsychology)
(2) Strategies for intervention upon collective existence in the name of life and health (diagnosis and educational intervention in relation to autistic children)
(3) Modes of subjectification, in which individuals work on themselves in the name of individual or collective life or health (autistic people, their families and a panoply of professionals that work around them internalise the category of autism)

This reading of biopower is fairly standard and standardised in social science analyses (especially of a poststructuralist persuasion). The story goes that we come to know life itself through the regulatory workings of biopolitics. Hence, as discourses circle around a phenomenon, they come to constitute that phenomenon. And discourses do not merely emerge as if by magic. They are created and recreated through modes of reproduction tied to powerful institutions, experts, practitioner communities and policy priorities. So, to take one example, autism becomes known through psychological and psychiatric discourses which, in turn, shape the very ways in which autism is known and then understood by people so labelled and those around them. Psychological and psychiatric discourses speak with authority about the vital character of human beings. And various educational, health and social care policies flock to attend to this vitalised phenomenon.

Before long, of course, participants in this biopolitical milieu come to know themselves and others, in part through the vitalist language of autism. And this happens not simply in places that are directly affected by policy – such as hospitals and schools – but also in everyday and mundane encounters; in life itself. We know that 'on the spectrum' has become a part of everyday parlance. And we know that autism is a powerful ubiquitous cultural trope found in many parts of the world. This reading of biopolitics is helpful in terms of making sense of how categories of the human come to be constituted, known, tendered, applied and used.

Reading autism as biopolitical also permits us to challenge some of the more naively essentialist readings of autism that often masquerade as common-sense and are documented in various iterations of the *Diagnostic and Statistical Manual for Mental Health Disorders* (American Psychiatric Association, 2013). But, where this reading is problematic is when it creates a wholly regulatory reading of autism: as nothing more than a creation of discourse, authority and subjectification. This is a clinical reading of biopower. There is little here to gain for those who feel the joy of autism's promise, the contentment in self-identification, the possibilities of access prompted by its appearance in social settings.

One might read Katherine's reluctance to identify her son with a label, other than his name, as her struggling with the regulatory framing of her son; that he is nothing more than an outcome, a product, a consequence of the biopolitical autistic machine. Many of us struggle with regulations and rules. And one of the joys of the human condition is our apparent tendency to break the rules. Indeed, the standard use of the biopolitical narrative seems at odds with more resistant tendencies of human beings. This is not to say that we can exist outside of discourse or biopower. Katherine's well documented attempts (Runswick-Cole, 2017) to sit without autism feel futile; her refusal to name autism does not mean that she can sit without it; even in the refusal to name it there is an engagement with the category. We are both fairly compliant students of Foucault in this regard: we understand the human condition as a condition constituted through the circulating effects of discourse and the subjectifying effects of biopower. But we think there is more room for play, movement and possibility in the biopolitical. And this leads us to a more affirmative reading of the biopolitics of autism.

The biopolitics of autism: an affirmative reading

Autism is a biopolitical category that cannot help but reproduce itself in infinite, ever-changing and ever-morphing ways (Goodley, 2017). If biopolitics constitutes life itself, then autism's constitution is also tied up with the constitution of life itself. For us, any discussion of the category of autism must engage with the simultaneous study of the category of the human. To consider the biopolitics of autism in isolation from a discussion of the biopolitics of the human would be, for us, a mistake, and a dangerous one at that. To distinguish autism from humanity is not only a separatist and disabling act but also ignores the assertion that life itself is always biopolitical (Rose, 2001). That is to say, how we come to be or become human is always constituted through the generative effects of the workings of biopower.

So, just as autism is diagnosed, it releases a tidal wave of biopolitical possibilities. This reading of biopolitics is in keeping with more affirmative readings which emphasise the generative excesses of biopolitics. Key thinkers here include Hardt and Negri (2000) whose ideas around their concept of Empire sought to understand some of the possibilities that emerge from the globalisation of biopolitics. Their work attends to the biopolitical excesses that are produced through globalisation, economic expansion of late capitalism, rapid developments in digital communication and big data and the resultant impact of this globalised biopower (or Empire) on the subjectivities of global citizens.

Autism is in demand (Mallett and Runswick-Cole, 2012; 2017). A host of products, interventions and training and education services branded as 'autism-specific' are available for consumption; there is a multimillion-pound autism industry, which many of us, including contributors to this volume, are critical of, while at the same time being beneficiaries of the commodification of autism simply by writing this chapter (Mallett and Runswick-Cole, 2012).

In the story at the airport, autism is also in demand, not as a commodity, but as a category which makes it possible for requests to be made of the airport staff. As we've seen before, the category of autism has a hyper-functionality in the context of an airport removing the need to queue at passport control, taking away at least one aspect of the more general inaccessibility of airports (Mallett and Runswick-Cole, 2016). Once the category is offered, and, in this story, confirmed by the presence of the lanyard, the airport staff remove the barrier and accompany the family to the front of the queue. By offering the diagnosis, Katherine expects the staff to perform differently. As Ebben (2020) argues, this type of information exchange is not driven by commodification but by performativity.

Our story is but one example of the biopolitical excesses of autism. There is a pre-existing shorthand set of rules and expectations, collections of already known instructions associated with responding to people with autism. And yet, while the airport staff must perform the role of (literal and metaphorical) barrier removers, one family member must wear the lanyard, and while some people may wear the lanyard with pride and experience the relief it delivers, in this story, Katherine feels constrained by biopower as the force which requires her to perform gratitude, with a faint whiff of embarrassment, as they are ushered past the queue of jet-lagged, grumpy travellers. All eyes are upon the family and silently questioning why *that* family is now at the front of the queue. Here, again, the biopolitics of autism gives with one hand (promoting reasonable adjustment) and takes with the other (introducing a particular kind of known difference). Even in the affirmative excesses of the biopolitical constitution of autism (missing the queues) there are also the negative undertones (found in the stares of the strangers).

And when we turn to the information about the origins and purpose of the lanyard to be found on the Hidden Disabilities web page, we find these biopolitical tensions written through the explanatory text:

> The Hidden Disabilities Sunflower Lanyard originated in 2016 when London Gatwick Airport asked "How can we recognise that one of our passengers may have a non-obvious disability?" The answer was to create a lanyard with a simple sunflower design on a green background. It was intended to be a subtle but visible sign enabling airport staff to recognise that the wearer (or someone with them) may require some extra help, time or assistance when moving through the airport.
>
> *(Hidden Disabilities, no date)*

The question 'How can we recognise that one of our passengers may have a non-obvious disability?' reveals the desire of staff at the airport to 'know' who does and, by implication, who does not, have 'a non-obvious disability'. This, of course, begs several questions, not least, what 'an obvious disability' might look like? And why do staff need to know a person's impairment status before help is offered? After all, staff could offer assistance to anyone who seems to require it. And yet biopolitics demands that we establish the 'truth discourse' about a disabled person before help is offered – does the person *really have* autism? In other words, would the person meet the criteria for a diagnosis of autism as understood in the DSM and which aligns to the ways in which autism becomes known in wider culture (and fit with the culturally dominant ways in which autism comes to be known)? Only then can the intervention, or 'the help', be offered and individuals, and in this case the family, must gratefully subject themselves to the help offered to a lanyard wearer and put up with the gaze of the other passengers (for their own good and for the good of those around them). The lanyard removes the discomfort expressed by the airport staff who are not sure whether the passenger has a hidden disability, but the price for this reassurance, as we've seen, comes at a cost to the lanyard wearer who must work on themselves to perform disability in ways that can be 'known' to the staff at the airport. The queues are avoided, but so is any wider thought or engagement as to how these spaces can be made more accessible for all passengers.

The website goes on to explain the origins of the sunflower motif; it was chosen to suggest "happiness, positivity and strength" (Hidden Disabilities, no date) but this affirmative framing is undermined by the description of the lanyard as allowing a person "to be subtly visible when they need to be" (Hidden Disabilities, no date). Having a hidden disability is not, then, a matter of pride; it is something only to be "visible" *when necessary*, in other words, when it is necessary to satisfy the airport staff's need to know who has (and who does not have) a hidden disability and is legitimately in need of help.

Despite her well-rehearsed resistance to labelling, Katherine offered the category of autism in exchange for the benefits of the sunflower lanyard. She knew the risks of engaging with the discourse, but she also knew the risks of not doing so. The airport is a place where the crush of normalcy (Davis, 1995) is keenly felt by all travellers. As we queue up at security, many of us feel cowed by the need to behave 'normally', not to attract attention to ourselves and to stick closely to the social conventions of the airport in an unfamiliar and busy environment. Many of us find the experience of travel – and the space of the airport – to be an overwhelming experience. Dan is typically known to check on his passport at least 17 times even before he has got to the departure gate! A failure to perform normalcy at the airport carries risks – being questioned, subjected to further searches or being stopped from boarding a fight. These risks are heightened for anyone who does not know, or struggles to follow, the rules.

And here is the conflictual position that Katherine grapples with – of being in use of autism's biopolitical framing while also being simultaneously negatively affected by its potential to other her son and her family. Hence, to read biopolitics is not to seek an either/or – a binarisation – of the phenomenon, but to consider the parallel play of positive and negative affective consequences that are constituted as soon as the biopolitics of autism are enacted.

This holding of tensions and a non-binarised contemplation of biopolitics is commensurate with an affirmative ethics, analysis and politics articulated by Braidotti (2018). She argues for a form of awareness that attends to the *actual* "both what we are and what we are ceasing to be", and the *virtual* "that is to say, what we are capable of becoming" (32). The actual, in our story, refers to the use of the lanyard, the walk past the queues and the stares from the bystanders. The virtual is the conversation between Katherine and Dan; Katherine's reluctance to know her son *as autism*, the desire to seek other ways of being and becoming and Dan's questions about the excesses of autism: what does a biopolitics of autism give and take away? No one escapes biopolitics. A life without biopolitics is not a life at all. But in the debate about biopolitics of autism we query the kinds of life we want to value and the troubles of the kinds of life that are valued and devalued through biopolitics. Braidotti (2018: 34) writes "we are ontologically oriented towards the affirmation of our innermost freedom – the freedom to become all we are capable of, all our bodies can take" (34). In asserting this she is not denying the realities of biopolitics. What Braidotti is demanding us to consider are the kinds of freedoms we are desiring to create with one another in the world.

We want to consider, then, the constraints and the possibilities that are offered by a biopolitics of autism (especially those associated with dominant bio-psychological constructions of the phenomenon). But we are also raising questions about life itself. There is more to Katherine's son than a lanyard and, equally, there is more to autism than easy social scripts. One of the gifts of autism is that it raises more general questions about life itself and therefore, by extensions, questions about the human condition. Autism is but one actual and virtual intervention into a wider inquiry about the human condition.

Autism gives and takes away. Autism offers and holds back. And the human condition is always in the midst of this interplay between the actual and the virtual. What we are and what we might become. Our sense of being and possible becomings. Our knowledge of our past and our present. Holidays end. Flights arrive. Lanyards are taken off. Conversations are never-ending. And this sense of the endless becomings – in this case, as we contemplate autism and then human – should be kept in mind. We are always, endlessly, infinitely constituted, shaped, reconstituted, reshaped in the biopolitics of life itself. And this dynamism which we effortlessly apply to the human condition should also be applied to any contemplation of autism.

COVID postscript

We began to think about this chapter in the heady days of late summer before COVID-19. Air travel has changed dramatically since then. And COVID has seen exponential growth in the number of people wearing lanyards in a wide variety of public spaces. Sunflower lanyards are now not only worn on planes but on buses and trains and in supermarkets and schools. During the pandemic, the function of the lanyard has expanded to indicate that the person wearing it is exempt from the requirement to wear a face covering to stop the transmission of COVID in public spaces. Reading this postscript through biopolitics, we see its seemingly inescapable regulatory effects and insatiable desires, which offer both promise and violation for all human beings inside and outside the airport.

References

Ahmed, S. (2004) *The Cultural Politics of Emotion*. New York: Routledge.
American Psychiatric Association. (2013) *Diagnostic and Statistical Manual of Mental Disorders* (5th ed.). https://doi.org/10.1176/appi.books.9780890425596
Berlant, L. (2006) Cruel Optimism. *Journal of Feminist Cultural Studies*, 17(3), 20–36.
Braidotti, R. (2018) Affirmative Ethics, Posthuman Subjectivity, and Intimate Scholarship: A Conversation with Rosi Braidotti. In *Decentering the Researcher in Intimate Scholarship (Advances in Research on Teaching, Vol. 31)*. Bingley: Emerald Publishing Limited, pp. 30–36. https://doi.org/10.1108/S1479-368720180000031014
Davis, L.J. (1995) *Enforcing Normalcy: Disability, Deafness and the Body*. London: Verso.
Ebben, H. (2020) *Representing Autism as a Discourse within Ableist Economies of Doubt*. Unpublished PhD Thesis, Sheffield Hallam University.
Garland-Thomson, R. (2002) Integrating Disability, Transforming Feminist Theory. *NWSA Journal*, 14(3), 1–32.
Goodley, D. (2013) Dis/entangling Critical Disability Studies. *Disability & Society*, 28(5), 631–644. https://doi.org/10.1080/09687599.2012.717884

Goodley, D. (2017) Autism and the Human. In Runswick-Cole, K., Mallett, R. and Timimi, S. (eds), *Re-thinking Autism: Critical Approaches in a Global Context*. London: Jessica Kingsley Publishing.

Hardt, M. and Negri, A. (2000) *Empire*. Cambridge, MA: Harvard University Press.

Hidden Disabilities. (n.d.) *The Hidden Disabilities Sunflower: About Us*. Available online at: https://hiddendisabilitiesstore.com/about-hidden-disabilities-sunflower. Accessed on: 8th March, 2017.

Mallett, R. and Runswick-Cole, K. (2012) Commodifying Autism: The Cultural Contexts of 'Disability' in the Academy. In Goodley, D., Hughes, B. and Davis, L.J. (eds), *Disability and Social Theory*. Basingstoke: Palgrave MacMillan.

Mallett, R. and Runswick-Cole, K. (2016) The 'Urge to Know' Normal: Theorising how impairment labels function. In Mallett, R., Ogden, C. and Slater, J. (eds), *Theorising Normalcy and the Mundane: Precarious Positions*. Chester: The University of Chester Press.

Mallett, R. and Runswick-Cole, K. (2017) The Commodification of Autism: What's at Stake? In Runswick-Cole, K., Mallett, R. and Timimi, S. (eds), *Re-thinking Autism, Disability, Equality, Identity*. London: Jessica Kingsley Publishing.

Rabinow, P. and Rose, N. (2006) Biopower Today. *BioSocieties*, 1, 195–217. https://doi.org/10.1017/S1745855206040014

Rose, N. (2001) The Politics of Life Itself. *Theory, Culture and Society*, 18(6), 1–30. https://doi.org/10.1177/02632760122052020

Runswick-Cole, K. (2017) Understanding this Thing Called Autism. In Runswick-Cole, K., Mallett, R. and Timimi, S. (eds), *Re-thinking Autism: Disability, Equality, Identity*. London: Jessica Kingsley Publishing.

PART 4

Practice

19
AUTISTIC IDENTITY, CULTURE, COMMUNITY, AND SPACE FOR WELL-BEING

Chloe Farahar

A tale of two "autisms"

As with much human phenomena, multiple narratives can be used to attempt to understand the phenomenon termed "autism". At present, there are largely two opposing narratives: the pathological and paradigmatic narrative that constructs "autism" as a medical neurodevelopmental "disorder"; and the neurodiversity paradigm, constructing Autistic experience as a natural variation within the human species, enacted upon by the societal powers and ideological notions of "normal", in need of acceptance and societal accommodation and support (Bertilsdotter Rosqvist, et al., 2020; Farahar and Bishopp-Ford, 2020; Kapp, 2019; Walker, 2014; Jack, 2011). While I begin by comparing these two narratives of autism and Autistic experience, I wish to assert how Autistic identity, culture, community, and space components are part of a non-linear process. For example, some Autistic individuals enter Autistic spaces and then build their identity as an Autistic person, finding, through their identity development, the community and culture; while others have a keen sense of Autistic identity and thus seek out or create Autistic spaces.

It is important to note that I am not the first to discuss the importance of understanding Autistic experience within and from a perspective of identity, culture, community, and/or space, and there are some thorough and well-reasoned discussions on these dimensions (cf. Botha, 2020; Chapman, 2020; Cooper et al., 2020; Belek, 2019; Kapp, 2019; Fletcher-Watson and May, 2018; Gokh et al., 2018; Cooper et al., 2017; Anderson, 2013; Owren, 2013; Straus, 2013; Sinclair, 2010; Davidson, 2008; Dekker, 1999). Ultimately, my purpose in writing this chapter is to highlight the importance of Autistic identity, culture, community, and space for Autistic well-being, beginning with the harm the "culture of autism" causes members of our community.

The "culture of autism"

Autism as an abstract concept is defined as a persistent impairment in reciprocal social communication and interaction; restricted and repetitive patterns of behaviour, interests, or activities; all of which may relate to hyper-reactivity (avoidance) or hypo-reactivity (sense seeking) to sensory input – with or without accompanying intellectual disability and/or language impairment (World Health Organization, 2019; American Psychiatric Association, 2013). This clinical, abstract way of defining autism is used within the "culture of autism" and applied to human beings, where "people with autism" are disordered, faulty, "normal" people with deficits.

One might wonder how an Autistic culture and collective identity can exist if it is not based on shared medical symptoms or what can connect us if not symptomatology. Much like other minority groups with shared social, sensorial, and political experiences of the world (e.g. LGBTQIA+; Black; Indigenous; Persons of Colour; women), the Autistic community is built on shared Autistic experiences – both positive and negative. While the non-autistic derived medical symptomatology comprises a list of attributes that reflect an Autistic in distress (largely autism "symptoms" can be understood as trauma responses), there is fundamentally more to being Autistic than what the diagnostic manuals reduce us to.

Given that the dominant, existing pathology narrative of autism is predicated solely on the interactional struggles of the "person with autism", it is then no surprise that the culture of autism (and its narrative) harms us collectively and individually (as internalised self-stigma and negative self-worth) (Botha and Frost, 2020). To subvert this negative and dehumanising narrative, many Autistic people come to distance themselves from autism and other "people with autism". This distancing is done to protect themselves by rejecting an autism that is based solely or largely on shared deficits and symptoms, as there is little positive self-esteem or self-worth derived from connecting with others based on such inherently negative experiences and narrative (Cooper, Cooper, Russell and Smith, 2020). This distancing leaves many "people with autism" in purgatory: neither belonging to a non-autistic community, identity, or space (even when they [we] try, when they [we] mask), or Autistic spaces; they are isolated from belonging.

However, the medicalised, pathologising narrative of autism is not the only (or even most persuasive) narrative about Autistic experience.

Autistic culture

We have seen a (laborious, slow, and ongoing) move away from autism as a medical pathology to a social construction, whereby Autistic people "comprise a definable minority group" (Straus, 2013, p. 466), and group cohesion is based on shared experiences, not medical "symptoms". Autistic culture works from a shared understanding of the neurodiversity paradigm, where Autistic experience is a natural variation within the human species, enacted upon by social power relations and ideological notions of "normal" (Farahar and Bishopp-Ford, 2020; Walker, 2014); where Autistic experience needs acceptance and societal accommodation and support, not intervention or "cure". This move from the abstract "autism" to diverse and identified Autistic people is shaped by and perpetuates shared culture and community, where Autistic people (not non-autistic researchers or clinicians) define what Autistic experience is and convey what being Autistic means. This shared, depathologised meaning is in turn transmitted to other Autistic people via "the culture we produce [such as our writing, art, and music]" (Straus, 2013, p. 466). From an Autistic perspective therefore, autism can be defined as:

> [A] neurodevelopmental difference, where Autistic brains work differently to non-autistic people. There are as many different brains and ways of experiencing the world as there are different bodies. There is a variety of Autistic people, just as there is a variety of non-autistic people, but all Autistic people share some similarities. These similarities include:
>
> - differences in experience of the sensory world,
> - differences in communication,

- differences in thinking, socialising and moving.

Some Autistic people need support with day-to-day living, and within this perspective there is no one way to be Autistic.

(Autistic Self Advocacy Network, 2020)

Culture itself can be defined as "[t]he ideas, customs, and social behaviour of a particular people or society" (Oxford University Press, 2020). When you learn about Autistic community and connection, it is not difficult to see that many Autistic people embody this definition of culture: sharing ideas about Autistic experience (as understood within the neurodiversity paradigm[1]); sharing customs and social behaviour (e.g. modes of greeting). As a culture we have our own beliefs, values, and practices, our own language (Davidson, 2008) and understanding of communication. This communication is at odds with non-autistic people, and under the pathological paradigm is argued to be evidence of deficit and disorder. However, in Autistic culture it is understood and shared as valid, understandable, and valued.

In groups of two or more Autistic people this shared language and communication can be straightforward and honest; it can be orally verbal, or gestural, and not understood outside of Autistic interaction (see the double empathy problem; Milton, 2012). For example, known in the culture of autism as "self-stimulatory" behaviour, stimming is a language and communication in and of itself (Kapp et al., 2019; Kim and Bottema-Beutel, 2019; Bascom, 2012). I can discern from the slightest fingernail flicking and rubbing that a fellow Autistic is anxious; from the near imperceptible rocking of an Autistic friend that they are on the verge of meltdown; from the neutral "Autie" face, that they are deep in thought. We talk in spoons[2] (units of energy; Miserandino, 2003), specialisation[3] info-dumps, and echolalia.[4]

Attempts to frame and understand Autistic experience from an anthropological perspective have proven useful. Belek (2019) and Gokh, Mineev, and Viktoruk (2018), for instance, help us see that Autistic experience is not the same as autism in the abstract. Gokh, Mineev, and Viktoruk (2018, p. 1954) argue that Autistic people have an Autistic "community consciousness", one derived from a cultural identity as we as a collective share:

1. Cognitive (mental), communicational, linguistic, and symbolic cohesion
2. [A] feeling of universal oneness of [an] autistic population
3. Group conscience (social awareness, social responsibility)
4. [An] awareness of deep commonality of long-term interests; unity of destiny
5. [A] sense of joint purpose, [a] mindset [for] transformation, [and] personal growth

With research and discussion of Autistic experience from anthropological, ethnographic, sociological, and social psychological perspectives, we are seeing growing evidence for a more three-dimensional understanding of autism, where Autistic people are being taken off "the spectrum" and placed more firmly in a three dimensions[5] Autistic space (Farahar and Foster, 2019). Understanding Autistic people outside of our objectification as "people with autism" may help to humanise our suffering and better focus research and clinical interest on our well-being issues, moving away from focusing on autism in the abstract.

Autistic well-being

Tragically, the Autistic community is subjected to a great deal of trauma due to living in a sensory environment not suited to us, and a society not accepting of us (Crane et al., 2018; Kupferstein,

2018). Consequently, our community experiences high rates of trauma responses (Griffiths et al., 2019). For example, we experience greater levels of anxiety and depression (and other mental health issues, compared to non-autistic, neurotypical controls) due to our "navigating a neurotypical world" (Crane et al., 2018, p. 8). Our community also contends with bullying (Fisher and Taylor, 2016; Cappadocia et al., 2012); loneliness (Lounds Taylor et al., 2017; Orsmond et al., 2013); and abusive and violent victimisation (Griffiths, et al., 2019). We die on average 16 years earlier than our non-autistic, predominant neurotype counterparts, with a mortality rate of age 54 in our community. The leading cause of death for those in our community (without an intellectual/learning disability) is suicide, with an average age at death of 58 years (compare this with the general population mortality rate for the UK of 82 years for women, 79 years for men; Barton and Hawkins, 2018; Hirvikoski et al., 2016). Detrimentally, most intervention focuses on attempting to make us appear non-autistic, even in the face of evidence demonstrating that attempts to do so are correlated with post-traumatic stress responses (Kupferstein, 2018). It is only more recently that we are starting to see a focus on our personal well-being, and how this might be improved with connection to other Autistic people.

The importance of Autistic culture (whether non-autistic or Autistic people alike refuse to relinquish the pathological understanding of autism) comes from its protective properties. What I have seen in the work I do supporting Autistic students, is that those who come to us embodying and living the "culture of autism" narrative (they have deficits; they are a "person with autism spectrum disorder") experience loneliness, isolation, and a negative sense of self. This is what the pathological narrative gives Autistic people – hopelessness, isolation, and loneliness. Autistic culture, on the other hand, has afforded these same people a distinct perspective, one where they can connect with others based on similarity, positive self-worth, hope. Whether you believe that to be Autistic is to *be* a pathology or to *have* a disorder, becomes moot in the face of growing evidence that Autistic identity, culture, community, and space improves well-being (Cooper et al., 2020; Cooper et al., 2017; Spandler and Anderson, 2015; Griffin and Pollak, 2009[6]). It should be enough to relinquish the culture of autism when you learn it harms, and that an alternative narrative improves well-being. And so, I argue, it is fundamental for our population's well-being to foster a positive Autistic identity, and to do this we need to find other Autistic people (see Table 19.1 for the key components of the "culture of autism" versus Autistic culture).

Fostering a positive Autistic identity: the social cure

By virtue of diagnosis, I *belong* to the stigmatised category of "people with autism". Belonging to this category of people means I and others are confronted with stigmatising stereotypes (unsocial, quiet, emotionless; Treweek et al., 2019); prejudicial attitudes (benevolence, anxiety, fear); and discriminatory behaviours (avoided, ignored, not considered for jobs or promotions; Bunt et al., 2020). Not only are we targets of stigma, but we also internalise these attitudes. Bombarded with public stigma, it is easy to see how "people with autism" internalise these attitudes as self-stigma, a phenomenon known to negatively impact self-esteem, efficacy, and well-being (Corrigan, Larson, and Ruesch, 2009). With this pathologising narrative, it is also easy to see why many of us struggle to foster a positive identity.

Fostering a positive identity is further impeded by non-autistic people who will state that we ought not identify as Autistic, that we ought to separate ourselves from the fundamental thing that differentiates and alienates us within current society: our Autistic experience. We are accused of creating an identity based on something that is characterised as an alleged pathology, where it cannot be an identity by virtue of its pathologisation. However, quite simply, those who insist on the pathologising narrative and label of "person with autism" have thrust upon us an

Table 19.1 The key components of the "culture of autism" versus Autistic culture

"Culture of autism"	Autistic culture
• Person with the disorder "autism"	• Neurodiversity paradigm – difference, social models
• Disease/disorder/illness	• Focus on strengths, support for challenges
• Mental illness	• Language and customs – Autistic identification
• Problem/issue	• Stimming language and activities
• Challenging	• Community
• Violent	• Spaces and environments
• Deficit/impairment	• Positive symbols
• Low-functioning	• Fluctuating support needs
• High-functioning	• Specialisations
• Severe/mild autism	• Shared commonalities (no spectrum, but existing in three-dimensional space)
• Pathological	
• Symptoms	• Understanding and acceptance
• On the spectrum	• Research with, for, and by Autistic people
• Cure/treatment	
• Intervention/strategies	
• Risk of autism	
• Special interests	
• Awareness	
• Researched on	

"autism" identity. Calling me a "person with autism" *is* an identity, just one I did not have any say in. There are two key ways of avoiding the negative impact of belonging to a stigmatised group. The first is to distance oneself from the stigmatised group – "I am nothing like those people with autism". The second is to *strongly identify* with the social group.

When belonging to a stigmatised group – i.e. "people with autism" – we can employ several strategies to manage the stigma directed at the group overall, which include individualistic and collectivistic strategies (Perry et al., 2020; Jetten et al., 2012). At the individualistic level, we can attempt to remove ourselves from the group – figuratively or literally – to dissociate from the group "people with autism", to protect our self-esteem, self-worth, and well-being. This, I argue, can lead Autistic people to become isolated. Even when we attempt to "pass" as non-autistic, to connect with social identities that are non-autistic, we never get it quite right. Our natural and inherent "autisticy" (ways of being and interacting in the world, Gates, 2019) is still called out by others, and it still separates us from non-autistic, predominant neurotype others. And so, by deciding to dissociate from the Autistic identity and group, we separate ourselves from the protective properties of the collective, but do not necessarily protect ourselves from future discrimination.

Separating oneself from the stigmatised category of "people with autism" – although a valid means of attempting to maintain positive self-identity – sadly means that many Autistic people do not have the connection to those who could understand and accept them, and who could, importantly, offer collective support. Distancing from Autistic people can mean heavy masking of one's authentic self – to appear as indistinguishable from non-autistic peers as possible. This masking method is known to cause Autistic people harm (erroneously referred to as camouflaging in the literature, but more accurately as masking in the community; Pearson and Rose, 2020; Cage and Troxell-Whitman, 2019). It also means that the protective properties of belonging, and both material and social resources, cannot be accessed, that we run the risk of poor well-being through living inauthentic and overwhelming lives, alone. The opposite of distancing from a stigmatised group – strongly identifying with the social identity of *Autistic person* – brings with it many benefits, and helps individuals protect against the effects of stigma. Simplistically, this can be seen as strength in numbers – a collectivistic "social cure" (Jetten, Haslam, and Alexander, 2012).

At the collectivistic level we can derive resources, symbolic (kind words or feelings of connection) and material (offers of practical support), from fellow community members. When we take pride in not only *belonging* to a stigmatised group but strongly *identifying* with the group, we can collectively combat the discrimination directed at us, together. Importantly, as noted by Jetten, Haslam, and Alexander (2012) in their discussion on the social cure capabilities of social identity, we may be more likely to adopt the collectivistic strategy when we can see our collective ability to alter the intergroup relationship between our stigmatised minority group and that of the powerful majority. As Jetten, Haslam, and Alexander (2012) suggest, for those who adopt the individualistic strategy – i.e. to dissociate from the Autistic community – they may not be able to see the possibility that as a group we can alter the power dynamics that are currently not in our favour. However, when embraced, this "social cure" can improve well-being.

Having a positive Autistic identity can reduce indices of anxiety and depression and does so by increasing collective self-esteem (self-esteem for the Autistic group overall), and consequently increases personal self-esteem (Cooper et al., 2020; Cooper et al., 2017). This is one area of well-being evidenced as improved by strong social identification with the collective *Autistic*. Given the "illegitimate, pervasive, [and] difficult to avoid" (Branscombe, Fernández, Gómez, and Cronin, 2012, in Jetten, Haslam, and Alexander, 2012 p. 118) discrimination Autistic people face in every aspect of daily life (education, employment, medical services, and so on), it is almost inevitable that we should come together as a community to fight for social change of our subordinate position. If as individuals we strongly identify with the Autistic social identity then it, too, is inevitable that we would shape, perpetuate, and maintain an Autistic culture, one connected via an Autistic community.

Creating Autistic communities and space: healing, refuge, and alternatives to diagnosis

The way in which many Autistic advocates and community members challenge the dominant medical narrative of "autism" is, much like the Voice Hearing community, which was pathologised as having "psychosis" or "schizophrenia" (Hart, 2020), by finding others who share similar experiences of the world as Autistic people; within spaces built for Autistic experience of the world; maintained and respected through shared culture and community, which rejects our objectification as "people with autism" for a fuller, reclaimed humanised Autistic identity. It is within these Autistic communities and spaces that we as stigmatised and traumatised individuals can take refuge and begin to heal. We are seeing evidence that what is important for Autistic well-being is Autistic friendship and community, with research starting to focus on peer support (Crane et al., 2018) and understanding the Autistic self:

> I never realised everybody felt as happy as I do when I am around Autistic people.
> *(Crompton et al., 2019, p. 1438)*

Autistic communities and space: healing and refuge

There are numerous Autistic spaces throughout the UK – on and offline – that offer healing for harms done to Autistic people by a rigid society currently not embracing difference. These spaces offer refuge from the stereotyping and prejudicial narrative, and the discriminatory behaviour many of us experience daily outside of these spaces. Community spaces such as Annette Foster's and my University of Kent Autistics social group, spaces such as Autism Inclusive Meets (autisticinclusivemeets.org), events such as the Playing A/Part Inside-out Conference (playingapartautisticgirls.org/inside-out-conference-2019), Autscape (Milton and Sims, 2016), Autcraft (an online Minecraft server; Ringland, 2019), and Scottish Women's Autism Network's Under our Wing mentoring (Stewart, n.d.) are examples of such refuges sheltering Autistic people of varying support needs, allowing attendees to exist in a space where different ways of being, thinking, and behaviour are not only accepted but encouraged and embraced. In these spaces you can see the non-pathologising narrative start to break through and break down internalised ableism, stigma, and invalidation trauma (Gates, 2019); where real friendships can be encouraged and fostered (I met Annette in such a space).

In these spaces, positive Autistic identities begin to form by learning about and becoming a part of Autistic culture, where these small pockets of community protect against the pathologising narratives that exist outside the walls. Where "[t]he walls of the community work to keep community members safe" (Ringland, 2019, p. 132). In these spaces, Autistic people can make their Autistic noises and gestures; share in their stims – placing objects on their head and saying "hat",[7] encouraged to do so because it is a behaviour that is understood; inhabit the space, never having to say a word (due to experiencing situational mutism; social anxiety), but still a vital part of the group; hide behind a curtain throughout a social session because of overwhelm, but wanting to be part of the community – energised by this form of participation, still seen as *participating* in the space in this way.[8]

Autistic communities and spaces are healing refuges because they show Autistic people a different way to inhabit space, one based on positive Autistic identity and Autistic cultural norms. These spaces allow members to be authentic (for many for the first time), *and to not only be accepted but embraced as such*. Perhaps one day these community spaces will be less "ghettoised",[9] when we will not have to protect ourselves so readily from non-autistic spaces. But until that time comes, these spaces are vital to our well-being, social identity, and authenticity. These communities and spaces may also come to be understood as more appropriate contexts with which people come to discover they are Autistic.

Autistic communities and space: an alternative to diagnosis

While I was a PhD student (investigating the reduction of mental health stigma via the neurodiversity narrative), I discovered my Autistic identity.[10] I fully immersed myself in Autistic culture and community and created the Autistic spaces our community desperately needs. With this space (a social space for Autistic university students, of varying support needs, from typical social difficulties creating and maintaining friendships with non-autistic people, to those who are situationally mute and/or minimally orally verbal) I went on to develop a structured support programme for more vulnerable Autistic students, co-developed and facilitated with fellow Autistic, colleague, and friend, Annette (of Super Autie Grrl, and later, Super Autie Gang, fame). The purpose of this structured support programme – So, You're Autistic? (SYA?) – was and is to offer eight small-group sessions to vulnerable Autistic students.

The practicalities and purposes of this structured programme (which among its formal purposes) seek to help deconstruct the harmful internalised pathologisation of typical Autistic experience of its attendees; foster a more positive self-identity; support attendees to find coping mechanisms for feelings and behaviours that distress; as well as foster a sense of community. The latter is something that many attendees have never experienced, alienated as they have been from society and one another by the pathology paradigm. This early alienating effect of being a "person with autism" is demonstrated by one SYA? attendee, who replied with the following when asked "How did you feel about the idea of being Autistic prior to attending SYA? How do you currently feel about being Autistic?":

> [before] It stops me from ever being normal or fitting in and stops me from doing things I want to do, it's a weakness and an excuse to not be able to do things.
>
> [currently] It's okay to be different, there are other people who will understand me and it's okay to need help with things or need to do things differently, I have my own strengths that other people don't.
>
> I thought I could be Autistic on my own and no one had to really know and now I want to tell people and find more people who will relate to the things I do.
> *(SYA? attendee, 23-year-old cis female, Sophie, June 2020)*[11]

Several of our programme attendees come to us with low self-esteem and poor well-being, having internalised negative perceptions of themselves – pathologised perceptions. It is Annette's and my role to help them see that they are not alone, and to help start to reframe their understanding of autism in the hopes they can start to heal from the internalised stigma. When attendees start to see one another's challenges *and* strengths, they reframe negatives into positives, for example "I talk too much about my special interest" becomes "I am knowledgeable about my specialisations and can share them with other Autistic people". To help solidify this reframing, attendee's appliqué positive words or phrases on to clothing, pillowcases, or make banners – something to remind them when they are struggling that there are also strengths to being Autistic.

Figures 19.1–19.4 show appliqués made by SYA? attendees. This is an activity we carry out during the 8-week programme with the aim of helping attendees reframe the negative narrative they have of themselves.[12]

Currently, the process of Autistic discovery is via pathologisation of Autistic experience and expression. For instance, it is rarely the case that an Autistic person – child or adult – is flagged for assessment when they are happy. Parents, educators, general practitioners, and paediatricians push for diagnosis of Autistic children because they are struggling, in distress, and often at their lowest point. Late-discovered Autistic people are diagnosed under similar circumstances: they may have experienced many mental well-being issues growing up and into their adulthood and reach a breaking point where they seek diagnosis, or assessment is recommended by employ-

Figure 19.1 "Embrace your weird"

Autistic identity, culture, community, and space for well-being

Figure 19.2 "The Great Autismo"

Figure 19.3 "Awesome"

Figure 19.4 "Autistic good"

ers, family, and friends, or through self-realisation. This is all based on struggling and distress. A case in point would be parents who request assessment for their child because they know they are Autistic, but the school or general practitioner state that their child is not struggling, or not struggling enough. All these situations set children and adults up to link being Autistic – the diagnosis – with distress, in turn painting being Autistic in a negative and stigmatising light. As already discussed, this pathologisation of difference, from pre-diagnosis through diagnosis, and post-diagnosis, is internalised, isolating, and damages well-being. There is another way.

I argue that Autistic discovery (not diagnosis) ought to be discovered holistically, kindly, and safely, in similar ways to discovering other aspects of one's identity and experience of the world, such as one's gender, sexuality, personality, and so on. A depathologised model would mean we discover we are Autistic when we are in a good place, when our well-being is not poor. This discovery of one's Autistic-ness would be based on positive sensory differences and experiences, not negative ones. This would alter perceptions of Autistic experience for the Autistic person, as well as for society at large. I hear frequently from Autistic children and adults who blame their autism for everything negative in their life, not understanding that when they are doing okay, even thriving, it is because their environment – social, emotional, sensorial – is optimal. We are Autistic in these optimal moments too, and autism should be "blamed" for these experiences and periods in our lives as much as when we struggle and suffer (although our suffering is the result of the interaction between our Autistic needs and the environment not being homeostatic).

I propose that the use of Autistic-led programmes, such as my and Annette's So, You're Autistic? programme, are more effective for discovering ones Autistic-ness as a teen or adult compared to current infantilised and gendered medical diagnosis processes. Within our SYA? programme for instance, all Autistic people – those struggling and in distress, and those who are thriving – are equally able to discover their Autistic identity – the culture, community, and spaces that can educate and support them to understand themselves and other Autistic people. This is what Autistic discovery should be: a journey with similar others.

In summary

In this chapter I have discussed and compared the "culture of autism" with the narrative of Autistic culture, illustrating the damage that the former has on Autistic well-being, devoid as it is of positivity, hope, or connectedness. I have highlighted some of the well-being issues we experience, such as the higher rates of trauma and trauma responses the (my) Autistic community faces: the greater rates of depression, anxiety, suicidality, and mortality compared to many non-autistic populations. I have described how fostering an Autistic identity can act as a "social cure", one that affords Autistic people both symbolic and material support from fellow community members. I demonstrated how the material and symbolic supports an Autistic identity confer can come in the form of Autistic spaces that offer refuge and healing from prejudice and discrimination.

Evidence exists to show that public and internalised, self-stigma can negatively affect well-being (e.g. Botha and Frost, 2020; Link et al., 2017). It is not being Autistic – the differences in experience of the sensory, social, and emotional world – that negatively impacts us. According to the central tenet of the social model of disability, it is the way the environment and those in society treat disabled people that causes us our greatest struggles (Chown et al., 2017). To combat this, there needs to be systemic change. Until then, "people with autism" need support to find and foster a positive Autistic identity to combat the negative effects of the pathologisation of Autistic experience. To foster this positive Autistic identity, we need to find and immerse ourselves in Autistic spaces – spaces where we can learn about our culture and build our community.

As outlined, it is also still my hope that my proposition for an alternative to diagnosis is embraced, where I argue that Autistic-led programmes are better placed to help Autistic people discover their Autistic-ness. It is my fervent wish that one day individuals can discover their Autistic identity in the same way that LGBTQIA+ community individuals come to realise who they are – through seeking answers to feeling different via the community, as opposed to pathologising diagnostic assessment.

Ultimately, I have argued that to improve Autistic well-being, Autistic individuals need a positive social identity (connecting with an Autistic identity); to embrace Autistic culture and its positive narrative (avoiding the "culture of autism" which pathologises Autistic experience, which is in turn internalised); to foster and immerse oneself in an Autistic community; and to create and search for Autistic spaces for healing, refuge, and discovery (as an alternative to diagnosis) of one's Autistic identity. In these ways the Autistic collective can combat the stigma and oppression our community faces, *together*.

Notes

1 Not to be confused with the neurodiversity movement (Walker, 2014).
2 Spoon theory refers to the disability metaphor defined by Christine Miserandino (2003) who has Lupus. To explain the limited energy a disabled person has compared to a non-disabled person Christine had to hand cutlery – spoons – to demonstrate to a non-disabled friend how much energy she expends in a day, which is considerably more than a non-disabled person. Autistic people use spoon theory, and it is not unheard of for us to say "Sorry, I don't have the spoons today" when asked to do something we do not have the energy for.
3 Specialisations, not "special interests".
4 Echolalia is the repetition or echoing of sounds or words.
5 Dimensions, not dimensional, as the three dimensions within the Farahar and Foster Autistic space exist along three axes (internal, external, time).
6 Griffin and Pollak (2009) demonstrate in a small qualitative study that the medical narrative of neurodivergent students correlated with poor self-esteem, finding the opposite in neurodivergent students who embraced the neurodiversity narrative. This is something Annette and I have witnessed and seen improve with students who come to both our University of Kent Autistics group, and So, You're Autistic? support programme.
7 A reference, with permission, to a student who attends my University of Kent Autistics group.
8 A reference, with permission, to a second student, Jessica, who attends my University of Kent Autistics group.
9 A reference to a non-autistic researcher's perspective of these spaces.
10 And was formally diagnosed early 2017.
11 Direct quotes used with permission. Taken from anonymous SYA? programme feedback. Credited, with permission, to Sophie.
12 Photographs of example SYA? attendee appliqués used with permission. Credited, with permission, to Madie, Harvey Bolton, Ben, and Leo Burns.

References

American Psychiatric Association., (2013). *Diagnostic and statistical manual of mental disorders (DSM-5®)*. Arlington, VA: American Psychiatric Publishing. DOI: 10.1176/appi.books.9780890425596

Anderson, J. L., (2013). A dash of autism. In J. L. Anderson, and S. Cushing (Eds.), *The philosophy of autism* (1st ed., pp. 109–142). Plymouth, UK: Rowman and Littlefield Publishers.

Autistic Self Advocacy Network., (2020). *About autism*. Retrieved from ASAN: Autistic Self Advocacy Network: https://autisticadvocacy.org/about-asan/about-autism/

Barton, C., and Hawkins, O., (2018). *Briefing paper number CBP8281: Mortality in the UK*. London: House of Commons Library.

Bascom, J., (2012). *Loud hands: Autistic people, speaking*. Washington, DC: Autistic Self Advocacy Network.

Belek, B., (2019). An anthropological perspective on autism. *Philosophy, Psychiatry, and Psychology*, 26(3), pp. 231–241. DOI: 10.1353/ppp.2019.0038

Bertilsdotter Rosqvist, H., Chown, N., and Stenning, A. (Eds.), (2020). *Neurodiversity studies: A new critical paradigm*. Oxon, UK: Routledge.

Botha, M., (2020). *Autistic community connectedness as a buffer against the effects of minority stress*. (Doctoral dissertation: University of Surrey). DOI: 10.15126/thesis.00854098

Botha, M., and Frost, D., (2020). Extending the minority stress model to understand mental health problems experienced by the autistic population. *Society and Mental Health*, 10(1), pp. 20–34. DOI: 10.1177/2156869318804297

Bunt, D., van Kessel, R., Hoekstra, R., Czabanowska, K., Brayne, C., Baron-Cohen, S., and Roman-Urrestarazu, A., (2020). Quotas, and anti-discrimination policies relating to autism in the EU: Scoping review and policy mapping in Germany, France, Netherlands, United Kingdom, Slovakia, Poland, and Romania. *Autism Research*, 13, pp. 1397–1417. DOI: 10.1002/aur.2315

Cage, E., and Troxell-Whitman, Z., (2019). Understanding the reasons, contexts and costs of camouflaging for autistic adults. *Journal of Autism and Developmental Disorders*, 49(5), pp. 1899–1911. DOI: 10.1007/s10803-018-03878-x

Cappadocia, M., Weiss, J., and Pepler, D., (2012). Bullying experiences among children and youth with autism spectrum disorders. *Journal of Autism and Developmental Disorders*, 42(2), pp. 266–277. DOI: 10.1007/s10803-011-1241-x

Chapman, R., (2020). The reality of autism: On the metaphysics of disorder and diversity. *Philosophical Psychology*, 33(6), pp. 799–819. DOI: 10.1080/09515089.2020.1751103

Chown, N., Robinson, J., Beardon, L., Downing, J., Hughes, L., Leatherland, J., Fox, K., Hickman, L., and MacGregor, D., (2017). Improving research about us, with us: A draft framework for inclusive autism research. *Disability & Society*, 32(5), pp. 720–734. DOI: 10.1080/09687599.2017.1320273

Cooper, K., Smith, L. G., and Russell, A., (2017). Social identity, self-esteem, and mental health in autism. *European Journal of Social Psychology*, 47(7), pp. 844–854. DOI: 10.1002/ejsp.2297

Cooper, R., Cooper, K., Russell, A. J., and Smith, L. G., (2021). "I'm proud to be a little bit different": The effects of autistic individuals' perceptions of autism and autism social identity on their collective self-esteem. *Journal of Autism and Developmental Disorders*, 51(2), pp. 1–11. DOI: 10.1007/s10803-020-04575-4

Corrigan, P., Larson, J., and Ruesch, N., (2009). Self-stigma and the "why try" effect: Impact on life goals and evidence-based practices. *World Psychiatry*, 8(2), pp. 75–81. DOI: 10.1002%2Fj.2051-5545.2009.tb00218.x

Crane, L., Adams, F., Harper, G., Welch, J., and Pellicano, E., (2018). "Something needs to change": Mental health experiences of young autistic adults in England. *Autism*, 23(2), pp. 477–493. DOI: 10.1177/1362361318757048

Crompton, C. J., Hallett, S., Ropar, D., Flynn, E., and Fletcher-Watson, S., (2019). 'I never realised everybody felt as happy as I do when I am around autistic people': A thematic analysis of autistic adults' relationships with autistic and neurotypical friends and family. *Autism*, 24(6), pp. 1438–1448. DOI: 10.1177/1362361320908976

Davidson, J., (2008). Autistic culture online: Virtual communication and cultural expression on the spectrum. *Social and Cultural Geography*, 9(7), pp. 791–806. DOI: 10.1080/14649360802382586

Dekker, M., (1999). On our own terms: Emerging Autistic culture. Retrieved from http://www.autscape.org/2015/programme/handouts/Autistic-Culture-07-Oct-1999.pdf

Farahar, C., and Bishopp-Ford, L., (2020). Stigmaphrenia: Reducing mental health stigma with a script about neurodiversity. In D. Milton (Ed.), *The neurodiversity reader: Exploring concepts, lived experience and implications for practice* (pp. 48–66). Shoreham by Sea, UK: Pavilion Publishing and Media.

Farahar, C., and Foster, A., (2019). Autistic observable and unobservable experiences, and the erroneous use of biological sex as a method to differentiate autistics: Introducing the internal and external autistic space. In *Participatory Autism Research Collective Third Critical Autism Studies Conference*, London, UK.

Fisher, M., and Taylor, J., (2016). Let's talk about it: Peer victimization experiences as reported by adolescents with autism spectrum disorder. *Autism*, 20(4), pp. 402–411. DOI: 10.1177/1362361315585948

Fletcher-Watson, B., and May, S., (2018). Enhancing relaxed performance: Evaluating the autism arts festival. *Research in Drama Education: The Journal of Applied Theatre and Performance*, 23(3), pp. 406–420. DOI: 10.1080/13569783.2018.1468243

Gates, G., (2019). *Trauma, stigma, and autism: Developing resilience and loosening the grip of shame*. London, UK: Jessica Kingsley Publishers.

Gokh, A. F., Mineev, V. V., and Viktoruk, E. N., (2018). Defending identity and diversity: The potential of cultural anthropology for reshaping autism. *Journal of Siberian Federal University. Humanities and Social Sciences*, 12(11), pp. 1947–1961. DOI: 10.17516/1997-1370-0368

Griffin, E., and Pollak, D., (2009). Student experiences of neurodiversity in higher education: Insights from the BRAINHE project. *Dyslexia*, 15(1), pp. 23–41. DOI: 10.1002/dys.383

Griffiths, S., Allison, R., Kenny, R., Holt, R., Smith, P., and Baron-Cohen, S., (2019). The vulnerability experiences quotient (VEQ): A study of vulnerability, mental health and life satisfaction in Autistic adults. *Autism Research*, 12(10), pp. 1516–1528. DOI: 10.1002/aur.2162

Hart, A., (2020). A new alliance? The hearing voices movement and neurodiversity. In H. Bertilsdotter Rosqvist, N. Chown, and A. Stenning (Eds.), *Neurodiversity studies: A new critical paradigm* (pp. 221–225). Oxon, UK: Routledge.

Hirvikoski, T., Mittendorfer-Rutz, E., Boman, M., Larsson, H., Lichtenstein, P., and Bölte, S., (2016). Premature mortality in autism spectrum disorder. *The British Journal of Psychiatry*, 208(3), pp. 232–238. DOI: 10.1192/bjp.bp.114.160192

Jack, J., (2011). "The Extreme Male Brain?" Incrementum and the rhetorical gendering of autism. *Disability Studies Quarterly*, 31(3), pp. 1–18. DOI: 10.18061/dsq.v31i3.1672

Jetten, J., Haslam, C., and Alexander, S. H. (Eds.), (2012). *The social cure: Identity, health and well-being* (1st ed.). Hove, Sussex, UK: Psychology Press.

Kapp, S. K. (Ed.), (2019). *Autistic community and the neurodiveristy movement: Stories from the frontline*. Singapore: Palgrave Macmillan. DOI: 10.1007/978-981-13-8437-0

Kapp, S. K., Steward, R., Crane, L., Elliott, D., Elphick, C., Pellicano, E., and Russell, G., (2019). 'People should be allowed to do what they like': Autistic adults' views and experiences of stimming. *Autism*, 23(7), pp. 1782–1792. DOI: 10.1177/1362361319829628

Kim, S., and Bottema-Beutel, K., (2019). Negotiation of individual and collective identities in the online discourse of autistic adults. *Autism in Adulthood*, 1(1), pp. 69–78. DOI: 10.1089/aut.2018.0029

Kupferstein, H., (2018). Evidence of increased PTSD symptoms in autistics exposed to applied behavior analysis. *Advances in Autism*, 4(1), pp. 19–29. DOI: 10.1108/AIA-08-2017-0016

Link, B. G., Phelan, J. C., and Sullivan, G., (2017). Mental and physical health consequences of the stigma associated with mental illnesses. In B. Major, J. F. Dovidio, and B. G. Link (Eds.), *The Oxford handbook of stigma and health*. New York: Oxford University Press. DOI: 10.1093/oxfordhb/9780190243470.013.26

Lounds Taylor, J., Adams, R., and Bishop, S., (2017). Social participation and its relation to internalizing symptoms among youth with autism spectrum disorder as they transition from high school. *Autism Research*, 10(4), pp. 663–672. DOI: 10.1002/aur.1709

Milton, D., and Sims, T., (2016). How is a sense of well-being and belonging constructed in the accounts of autistic adults? *Disability and Society*, 31(4), pp. 520–534. DOI: 10.1080/09687599.2016.1186529

Milton, D. E., (2012). On the ontological status of autism: The 'double empathy problem'. *Disability and Society*, 27(6), pp. 883–887. DOI: 10.1080/09687599.2012.710008

Miserandino, C., (2003). *The Spoon Theory written by Christine Miserandino*. Retrieved December 2019, from But you don't look sick: https://web.archive.org/web/20191117210039/https://butyoudontlooksick.com/articles/written-by-christine/the-spoon-theory/

Orsmond, G. I., Shattuck, P. T., Cooper, B. P., Sterzing, P. R., and Anderson, K. A., (2013). Social participation among young adults with an autism spectrum disorder. *Journal of Autism and Developmental Disorders*, 43(11), pp. 2710–2719. DOI: 10.1007/s10803-013-1833-8

Owren, T., (2013). *Autreat and autscape: Informing and challenging the neurotypical will and ability to include* (Master's thesis). Bergen University College. Retrieved from http://hdl.handle.net/11250/2481831

Oxford University Press., (2020). *Culture*. Retrieved July 2020, from Lexico: https://www.lexico.com/definition/culture

Pearson, A., and Rose, K., (2020). A conceptual analysis of autistic masking: Understanding the narrative of stigma and the illusion of choice. *OSF Preprints*, pp. 1–25. DOI: 10.31219/osf.io/6rwa5

Perry, E., Hull, L., Mandy, W., and Cage, E., (2020). Understanding camouflaging as a response to autism-related stigma: A social identity theory approach. *PsyArXiv*, pp. 1–37. DOI: 10.31234/OSF.IO/7W2PE

Ringland, K. E., (2019). "Autsome": Fostering an autistic identity in an online minecraft community for youth with autism. In N. Taylor, C. Christian-Lamb, M. Martin, and B. Nardi (Eds.), *Information in Contemporary Society: 14th International Conference, iConference 2019* (Vol. 11420, pp. 132–143). Cham, Switzerland: Springer. DOI: 10.1007/978-3-030-15742-5_12

Sinclair, J., (2010). Being autistic together. *Disability Studies Quarterly*, 30(1), pp. 1–31. DOI: 10.18061/dsq.v30i1.1075

Spandler, H., and Anderson, J. (Eds.), (2015). *Madness, distress and the politics of disablement*. Bristol, UK: Policy Press.

Stewart, C., (n.d.). *Creating a route to the building of self-identity, confidence and inclusion for autistic women and girls: The under our wing peer-mentoring project*. Scottish Women's Autism Network. Retrieved from https://swanscotland.org/wp-content/uploads/2019/10/100705-SA-AE-Swan-Poster-A0_2.pdf

Straus, J. N., (2013). Autism as culture. In L. J. Davis (Ed.), *The disability studies reader* (4th ed., pp. 460–484). London, UK: Routledge.

Treweek, C., Wood, C., Martin, J., and Freeth, M., (2019). Autistic people's perspectives on stereotypes: An interpretative phenomenological analysis. *Autism*, 23(3), pp. 759–769. DOI: 10.1177/1362361318778286

Walker, N., (2014). *Neurodiversity: Some basic terms and definitions*. Retrieved October 9, 2016, from Nick Walker's Notes on Neurodiversity, Autism, and Cognitive Liberty: http://neurocosmopolitanism.com/neurodiversity-some-basic-terms-definitions/

World Health Organization., (2019). *6A02 autism spectrum disorder*. Retrieved May 2019, from International Classification of Diseases 11th Revision: https://www.who.int/news-room/fact-sheets/detail/autism-spectrum-disorders/

20
CONTEMPLATING TEACHER TALK THROUGH A CRITICAL AUTISM STUDIES LENS

Nick Hodge, Patty Douglas, Madeleine Kruth, Stephen Connolly, Nicola Martin, Kendra Gowler, and Cheryl Smith

Introduction

The starting point for this chapter is a short film[1] created within a storytelling workshop as part of the Re•Storying Autism in Education project.[2] The film invites the viewer to reflect on and problematise examples of everyday teacher[3] talk used about and around autistic children in class: the sort of talk that autistic people later report experiencing as wounding and disabling. To support us in identifying these words, understanding their effects and theorising why they might occur we[4] employ Critical Autism Studies (CAS) as a methodological tool of analysis. In doing so, we seek to root out and identify how in classroom chatter the apparently mundane and ordinary conceal and reproduce dominant disabling discourses that deny autistic children personhood and position them as Other and problem (Milton 2017; Milton & Sims 2016). In applying CAS to classroom practice in this way we hope to extend its reach beyond the theoretical to propose new ways of talking to and about children in class that validate and empower rather than reduce and deny.

The chapter begins by introducing the Re•Storying Autism in Education project. We then describe the film made about teacher talk and reflect on the motivations and reasoning behind its construction. To help us with understanding the extent, nature and effects of words that wound in school we put out a request on Twitter for examples of these from autistic people. In spite of us expecting these to be challenging to read we were still shocked by how destructive and devastating some of the comments are that autistic pupils hear said about them. In the chapter we capture these microaggressions before considering the disabling discourses and theoretical constructs that might be in play which permit and leave largely unchallenged such attacks on personhood. We use the term 'microaggression' here to indicate the immediacy and intimacy of the relationships in which they occur. The effects of these attacks though, whether they are singular or cumulative in nature, can have very significant and long-lasting effects on those who experience them.

The Re•Storying Autism in Education project

Re•Storying Autism in Education is an international multimedia storytelling project led by Patty Douglas that brings together autistic people, family members, educators, practitioners and artists (these are not mutually exclusive categories) in storytelling workshops to make short first-person films about their/our experiences of school. The aim of the project is to co-create a proliferation of understandings of autism outside the dominant biomedical one; intervene in deficit understandings of autism as disorder in education; and consider implications for inclusive practice by centring the previously excluded perspectives of autistic people and their/our supporters (Douglas et al. 2019). So far on the project, 34 films have been made, by 17 people who have attracted or claimed the label of autism and/or who identify as autistic (hereafter 'autistic persons') and 17 people who work with and care about autistic people including family members, practitioners and educators (www.restoryingautism.com). Three workshops have been held in Toronto, Canada; one has been held online post COVID-19 with participants in Manitoba, Canada; and one more is currently planned online in spring 2021 with collaborators in Sheffield, England. The Re•Storying Autism project is an intellectual and creative collaboration with our affiliate, the Re•Vision: Centre for Art and Social Justice, University of Guelph, Ontario, Canada, a research creation centre founded and directed by Carla Rice that explores the power of the arts to transform stereotypes of embodied difference and advance social inclusion in health care, education and the arts (Douglas et al. 2019; Rice et al. 2015; Rice et al. 2016). The aim of the Re•Storying Autism project is an explicitly social justice one. Films made on the project often push back against dominant biomedical assumptions about the normative human as nondisabled and the 'critical exigence' (Yergeau 2018) to remedy or 'fix' different bodies and minds before they are thought to be educable (Douglas et al. 2019). The significance of the project is its commitment to justice-facing approaches, including Critical Autism Studies and participatory autism research (Davidson & Orsini 2013; Fletcher-Watson et al. 2019; Milton 2014; Milton et al. 2019; Runswick-Cole et al. 2016; Waltz 2014; Woods et al. 2018; Yergeau 2018) with the potential to enable better outcomes in education and research with and for autistic people.

Films created in Re•Storying Autism workshops are short first-person videos that use multimedia to bring into being new understandings of autism, self and other, and push back against exclusionary systems (Douglas et al. 2019; Rice & Mündel 2018). Our approach is distinct from uses of multimedia in autism research with therapeutic aims (see for example Golan & Baron-Cohen 2006). Briefly, Re•Storying workshops bring together autistic and non-autistic people in 3-day in-person or 3-week online workshops to create short films about their/our experiences of school and knowledge of embodied difference. Workshops provide storytellers with access to computers, training in filmmaking software, cameras, photography support, story development and so on, with approximately 1 month of pre-workshop and post-workshop one-to-one contact to develop and complete stories and access technical and other support. Storytellers in Re•Storying workshops retain ownership of their films and are invited to participate in follow-up research and arts activities as co-researchers including, for example, a co-researcher collective, a day-long post-workshop screening event to begin the work of film analysis, co-authorship on journal articles and chapters like this one, professional development initiatives with educators, disability arts film festivals and academic conference presentations using their/our films. Members of the research team wish to transform deficit narratives and change practice through engagement with the films so that autistic people may feel more known, enabled and valued within educational and other services.

In a recent Re•Storying Autism workshop held in Toronto in November 2019, the idea for this chapter emerged after Nick Hodge, a researcher on the project and former teacher in England made a short film about his experience of teacher talk he overheard in schools about autistic students. The film sparked a conversation with members of the storytelling workshop and research team, who resonated with Hodge's experience of overhearing troubling negative comments as part of everyday life in schools. One autistic participant reported the viewing of the film as a healing experience: for him the film represents an acknowledgement that it is not right to speak of children and young people in this way. This participant had lived in silence for many years with the hurt such words had caused him. Through such discussion we realised that we wanted to explore further why and how this kind of mundane, yet extraordinary, talk can occur, along with how it may impact how autistic people come to view them/ourselves. We begin this consideration with a description of Hodge's film.

So that's who I am: a short film

'Careful she's a biter'; 'He's one of our special needs'; 'He's just an attention seeker. Ignore him'.

These are some of the ways in which we have heard autistic and other disabled children conceptualised and referred to by educators over the years. This is the everyday teacher talk that is used by educators in the presence of children without any apparent awareness of how such comments can have lifelong effects on the young people who hear and absorb them. Nor do educators always reflect upon how frequently children might hear such things said about them and the potential cumulative effects of this drip-feed of negativity on how they come to know and view themselves. Heard often enough, these remarks may come to form how autistic people understand and represent themselves. 'She's a biter' becomes 'I'm a biter'; 'I'm a special need'; 'I'm just an attention seeker' and so on. Currently very little is known through research about the outcomes for children when they come to know themselves in these ways. Some autistic people may absorb these representations of themselves uncritically, accepting that authority figures possess specialist knowledge that empowers them to know and assert how children are. Some, however, may reject these characterisations, relying more on their own evaluation of themselves to decide who and how they are. Others may just be made troubled by these remarks and remain so, repeatedly questioning themselves for many years over what exactly might have been meant by the comment, why it was made and what there was/is about themselves that made someone think and say that about them. Autistic people may find ways to resist the effects of the comments but often at the cost of expending lifelong energy to do so. Whichever category we fall into, for all of us the words that wound will affect us in some disabling ways.

Although he does not identify as autistic, Nick finds himself continuing to dwell on things that educators said about him as a child that still disturb and frustrate him as an adult. One seemingly harmless everyday example occurred when Nick was eight years old. His class teacher looked at Nick's emergent writing and declared, 'Your writing looks like a spider walked across your page'. The class teacher may not have intended harm through this comment; she may even have meant it to be amusing. But 50 years later, Nick still remembers it each time that he writes and experiences again the shame that he felt at the time. Nick still apologises for his handwriting to whomever is receiving the script. It feels to Nick like a lifetime of trying to make sense of and reduce the effects of a comment that the teacher might never have intended to be of particular significance.

Perhaps because of his own experiences of words that wound, scab over but sometimes never fully heal when Nick became a teacher of autistic children, he remained alert to the ways in which educators talked about and to children that Nick felt were not supportive to enabling development of a positive sense of self in young people. Children with a medical diagnosis are often subject to scrutiny by a range of services and various practitioners visit classrooms to observe and invariably discuss pupils. Teaching staff in classrooms rarely have opportunity to be released from the room so find themselves compelled to talk about their pupils even whilst they are sharing the same space. Nick often challenged and debated with colleagues over these concerns. Often when teachers heard their words repeated, they were surprised by what they had said and had not reflected, until that point, on how their words might be received by children (Hodge & Runswick-Cole 2018). Colleagues would respond with assertions such as 'She wouldn't even know I was talking about her', 'He's an autistic – he's not paying attention to what I say', 'She's disabled, she won't remember it tomorrow'. Through the act of being assigned to a medical category such as autistic, ADHD, Fragile X or learning disabled, children were then denied the right to be recognised as fully sentient beings who paid attention to and came to know themselves partly through how others perceived them. In some way, the category seemed to liberate educators from needing to self-monitor what they thought about pupils and how they conveyed this to them through the words that they used about, around and to children.

Curiosity and concern about these practices never left Nick and so he decided to explore this within his story for the Re•Storying Autism Project. In this representation, Nick captures some of the expressions that he remembers using himself as a teacher and that other educators used around him. The story begins with a classroom of children. As they appear to be distracted through activity, it is not immediately apparent who remains alert to what is being said around them. In Nick's story the negative words said about children swirl around them, phrase upon phrase absorbed at least to some extent, however much children may try to resist them. As our examples below from autistic adults demonstrate, these words then set to work, potentially laying the foundations for disturbed well-being and the formation of a troubled sense of self for many years to come (Masten & Barnes 2018; Milton 2017). Words that wound have been argued to contribute to anxiety and depression in later life (Isaacs & Kilham 2017). As it is estimated that 50% of autistic adults experience ongoing significant anxiety and/or depression, this is a matter of real concern (White et al. 2018). We wanted, therefore, through the film and this chapter, to expose and critique what often appear to be only mundane, everyday non-reflective uses of language. To help identify what was taking place in these exchanges, how they might be operating to marginalise, exclude and disable and why they might occur we turned to Critical Autism Studies to provide a critical framework.

Critical Autism Studies as a methodological tool

Critical Autism Studies grounds the Re•Storying Autism project and our analysis of teacher talk as disability microaggressions in this chapter. The initial impetus for the Re•Storying project came out of Patty's troubling encounters with disablism and violence towards autistic 'difference' within education systems as the mother of a son who attracted the label of autism, a special education teacher and a person who lives with neurodivergence and invisible disability. Patty wanted to build a project to challenge problem-saturated understandings of autism in education and create space to bring into the world new representations of autism and inclusive practices that centre the perspectives and experiences of autistic people and their/our supporters (Douglas et al. 2019). On the Re•Storying project, this means our methodology is participatory; we take up calls by autistic scholars, activists and critical allies for autistic voices to be at the centre of autism research (Davidson & Orsini 2013; Fletcher-Watson et al. 2019; Milton 2014; Milton et al. 2019; Runswick-Cole et al. 2016; Woods et al. 2018; Woods & Waldock 2020). We do this by prioritising mentorship of and by autistic researchers; democratic and inclusive leadership; employment of autistic and disabled people; and co-authorship. We also organise a co-researcher collective, a group of autistic co-researchers, artists, activists and critical allies directing research priorities on the project as well as autistic-led spaces, arts initiatives and representation from Black, trans, women-identified, Indigenous and other autistic communities excluded from diagnosis, services and conventional autism research.

For this chapter, we employ Critical Autism Studies as a methodological tool to challenge the ableism and exclusions of conventional autism research (Fletcher-Watson et al. 2019; Milton 2014; Milton et al. 2019; Woods et al. 2018; Yergeau 2018). After autistic participants in the storytelling workshop responded to Nick's video by recalling experiences of negative teacher talk of their own, we surveyed a wider group of autistic people to learn if they, too, recalled examples of teacher talk that wounded them in some way. On 21 April 2020 we posted the following tweet[5] on the Re•Storying Autism Twitter account @ReStorying:

> We are asking autistic people to share in this thread examples of things you heard school staff say about you that wounded you in some way. Some of these will be used as examples in a chapter about "teacher talk" in a book being edited by @milton_damian & @sarasiobhan.

To analyse responses to our tweet about talk by school staff that wounds, we draw methodologically on the elements put forward by Davidson and Orsini (2013) about Critical Autism Studies in *Worlds of Autism* as articulated by Waltz (2014) in her review of the book. Waltz summarises Davidson and Orsini, asserting that the 'criticality' in Critical Autism Studies 'comes from investigating power dynamics that operate in discourses around autism, questioning deficit-based definitions of autism, and being willing to consider the ways in which biology and culture intersect to produce "disability"' (Waltz 2014, p. 1337). In this chapter, we share Nick's story and analyse tweets to interrogate neuro-normative and ableist power dynamics – disability microaggressions – that operate in educational discourse to identify and flush out deficit-based understandings of autism. In so doing, we also theorise about how such talk, which interferes with autistic people's sense of self and well-being, can be possible at all.

Critical Autism Studies directs us to understand disability as co-constituted by the intertwining of 'different' bodies and culture. This means we do not 'fix' the meaning of autism in a biology/culture binary, whether as a deficit-based disorder in biomedicine and psychology or as a positive brain-based difference as it appears in some versions of neurodiversity discourse (Runswick-Cole et al. 2016). Rather, we hold open the meaning of autism in our approach and orient to embodiment through new materialist ontology – an anti-essentialist processual and relational approach. This places at the centre of our Critical Autism Studies methodology the inextricable entanglement of 'different' autistic bodies and world, between knowledge/power, discourse, material realities, affect, objects and stubborn bodies that 'push back' against normative expectations (Douglas et al. 2019). This is an ontology that understands body and world as in a constant relation of becoming, rather than as settled matters. This is not to deny the reality of 'different' bodies or disablism and neuro-normativity, but rather to recognise the serious disabling effects of how bodies/minds and world are entangled in everyday talk, as witnessed in this chapter in examples of the long-term effects of teacher talk. More, it is to assert that paying attention to autism as a material-discursive entanglement offers a methodological beginning point from which new possibilities for a more just world might emerge (Douglas et al. 2019). This is because such an approach embraces autism and embodied difference as valid and valuable ways of being that are not in need of professional remedy but, instead, are fully human ways of being. Our approach thus combines a Critical Autism Studies critique of power/knowledge and autism discourse with a disability studies politic of possibility around 'different' bodies (Douglas et al. 2019; Rice et al. 2016). In doing so we seek to identify, interrogate and counter deficit practices, as well as trouble teacher talk and understandings that can produce devastating material and discursive effects for autistic pupils. Reductionist and disabling everyday attacks on personhood are sometimes referred to within Critical Disability Studies literature as 'microaggressions' (Keller & Galgay 2010). It is the nature and operation of microaggression that we now expose and trouble within the making of the film and the writing of this chapter.

Microaggressions in practice

The microaggressions that Nick captured within his film were those remembered from his own experience as a teacher in schools. As shared above, when we viewed the film with other practitioners, autistic people and family members at the storytelling workshop, some people reported either having heard educators talk about autistic children, and/or themselves having been talked about, in these ways. This inspired us to try and capture some of these experiences from across the autistic and autism communities.[6] We sought approval therefore from the Brandon University Research Ethics Committee to put out the call via Twitter for autistic people to share with us examples of educator talk that had wounded them in some way.

Some debate occurred within the pursuant Twitter discussion about how it might not be experienced as enabling for autistic people and practitioners for a book chapter to be developed around a 'negative' focus of talk that wounds. One contributor suggested that it might be more helpful to balance this with some examples of positive practice. We recognise that these comments were motivated by concern for the well-being of the autistic people and/or the practitioners who might read the tweets and/or the chapter. However, we wanted in this instance to maintain the focus on the words that wound in the hope that, as in the earlier example of the workshop member, the naming of these words and the damage that they do might be a healing process for some readers.

Autistic children are socialised like all others into ableist and normative cultural understandings that position them as odd, abnormal, challenging and deviant; as being in need of intervention, treatment or even cure. Autistic people are observed by, attend meetings with, and hear themselves discussed by an extensive array of health, education and social care practitioners. These practitioners, through their qualifications and accepted status, speak about the nature and value of children with a perceived authority (Mallett & Runswick-Cole 2014; Sarrett 2016). Bombarded with these daily representations of themselves as being at fault, autistic children, like other disabled people, often consciously or unconsciously take on responsibility for any disruptions of fit between how they are and the environments in which they find themselves (Thomas 1999; Williams et al. 2018).

Autistic people have told us in our discussions on Twitter that because of this, when they heard what was said, it made them feel upset, but they did not perceive of themselves as having the power or means to challenge it. Some people find ways to rationalise and resist these harms but for others the words seem to sit resentfully with their recipients and trouble them throughout their lives. Some autistic viewers of the film at the storytelling workshop informed us that hearing others now critiquing these statements and revealing them as the illegitimate practices of ableism and normalcy supports them with exercising agency over the words that have wounded them. Bringing the comments into debate helped these autistic people towards accepting their own evaluation of themselves as a more legitimate representation of who they are rather than how they have heard others speak of them.

Some of the authors of this chapter used to be teachers in schools. It is not our intention or desire to disparage the practice of education or to demean and vilify the actions of well-intended educators. Rather we have always seen reflective practice as a critical contributor to our own development as practitioners (Minott 2019; Schon 1991). In this analysis of educator talk we are not critiquing what educators say but rather seeking to expose the systems and structures that permit and promote such ways of understanding and talking about autistic children. We are interested in what is revealed about how society understands and responds to autism and disability when educators use words that wound.

In response to our tweet we had 57 responses: 27 of these were from autistic people and 10 were from parents reporting on incidents that had happened to their children (these categories are not mutually exclusive – some respondents spoke of both their own experiences and those of their children). These were made by a total of 36 individual contributors. We have not treated the tweets as research data in the sense of them being critical contributors to a full and detailed examination of how autistic people experience words that wound in educator talk. Instead, we have utilised them to illustrate the nature of such comments and the effects that they have on the children who hear them. In helping us to reflect upon these we have employed the ten categories of disability microaggressions that were identified by Keller and Galgay (2010): denial of personal identity; denial of disability experience; denial of privacy; helplessness; secondary gain; spread effect; infantilisation; patronisation; second-class citizen and desexualisation. In our reflections we have also taken into account the two additional categories suggested by Olkin et al. (2019): symptoms not being believed by medical professionals[7] and disability being discounted by others based on looking healthy and young. Within this reflective process we have attempted to highlight how ableism and normalcy appear to be operating to position autistic people as Other and lesser.

This examination of educator talk reveals how having a diagnosis of autism or being perceived as significantly 'different' in some way permits others to attack even one's fundamental nature without any expectation or care for how this may make the recipient feel as a person. We did not consider that any of the 12 categories above sufficiently captured the unbridled ferocity and cruelty that some of the collaborators' tweets bore witness to. Therefore, we suggest here that a thirteenth category should be added to those suggested by Keller et al.: denial of personhood. This is perhaps a more overarching category and one which encompasses some of the 12 that have already been identified. We suggest though that it is more than a failure to recognise a person's identity; rather it is the denial of them as a person.

Our autistic respondents and parents reported young children being referred to by educators in ways that dehumanised and reduced them. Children were referred to by educators as 'feral', a 'perfect pest', 'a liability', 'special needs' and objectified as unwelcome additional labour: 'Look what I have to deal with'. Even though we were prepared for some distressing responses, the destructive savagery of a number of these still surprised us. Annie Sands, for example, wrote of how a teacher had shockingly told her son, 'The best thing you can do is get in a boat and sail out to sea, without oars or a sail'. Reading this made us wonder how a child would be able to maintain any positive sense of self when faced with an authoritative summary of their worth that asserts that the world would be better off if they were dead. A denial of disability experience takes place within this as the actions of children that gave rise to this educator talk were at times the result of impairment effects, part of the very embodiment of being autistic. These included challenges with controlling motor skills that led to a spilling of milk and a seven-year-old child unwittingly transgressing a social rule that had not yet been explicitly taught: looking in a bag without permission that was being held by a teacher.

Even where children's skills and abilities were recognised, personhood could still be denied through what Keller and Galgay (2010) referred to as the 'spread effect'. Alex Adams for example was described by a teacher as an 'untapped resource' and derided for not exhibiting his intelligence within class discussion. Even less respectfully, JoJo was described as 'selfish' for 'refusing' to share the answers to questions that were directed to the class. Ableism is revealed, therefore, even within what the educators might have intended as positive or complimentary remarks: whilst recognising the individual ability of Alex and JoJo, the teachers reproduce the trope of the autistic savant whose talents should always be 'on tap' in the same way as one can retrieve information from a computer, regardless of what it might cost an individual to make a public contribution. Midbook Review reminded us too of the pressure that is put upon children when they then feel obliged to live up to this construction of themselves. For Midbook Review, performing being the 'smart' one became too challenging to maintain as they got older: 'I struggled as I got older and felt like I was failing at being me'.

Another of the categories identified by Keller and Galgay (2010) is the assumption of lack of ability; a downgrading or disregard of knowledge and skills simply because that person had been medically categorised in some way. Our respondents provided several illustrations of this. A parent, Josiejo, shared how an art teacher stated about her son, 'I'm not having someone like him in my class. I'm not here to teach colouring in'. This remark continues to trouble her son even though he is now aged 19. Within this one remark, a child was reduced from person to category through being constructed as 'someone like him', i.e. as 'an autistic person'. He was homogenised into the single category of the mythical autistic who is 'like this' and so we must teach them 'like that'. In referring to this child in this way, the teacher's talk reveals an ableist, reductionist understanding of autistic people as necessarily being limited in what they can do and achieve. In not recognising the child as an individual learner this teacher fails to identify and appreciate this person's capabilities and interests. Through such ableist acts autistic people are then denied opportunities to achieve (Hedley et al. 2017).

Another example of this came from Chloe Farahar Âû[8] who now has a PhD. Chloe was advised by a teacher that there was no point in her taking A-levels[9] as she was 'not capable of further education'. A school report for Damian Milton,[10] who also has a PhD and is a university academic, declared, 'I'm afraid that Damian is not very bright, and his lack of effort only compounds the problem'. Similarly, a teacher informed Connective, who now has a Master's in Education, that 'she should go into clothes or fashion' as she was 'not the brainy type'. Even more starkly, Smurf was advised in the 11th grade[11] by a creative writing teacher that she would 'never amount to anything' whilst JoJo aged 13 was similarly informed that she would never get anywhere because of her personality. Even when children demonstrate capability, this is sometimes still denied by educators who frame it as cheating. Windy Malone's creative writing abilities, for example, were dismissed by a teacher as '(t)here's no way you wrote that poem'. Connective's child was also charged unwarrantedly with cheating over his creative writing and Miche_Marples told us that when her daughter self-reported in front of the class her test results of ten out of ten the teacher replied with 'well that can't be right, not for you'. Deficit is automatically assumed if a child does not demonstrate capabilities within expected norms. Alex Adams, for example, was told, 'I used to think you were dumb because you never talked', making explicit the link often made by educators between non-speaking autistic students and presumed lack of ability or intelligence (Yergeau 2018). These attitudes have very real potential to limit opportunities for autistic pupils to progress to university. Even though there are effective support systems in higher education for disabled students, it is quite possible that autistic people miss out through lack of encouragement at school (Martin et al. 2019).

Behaviours and characteristics associated with autism, such as reduced social verbal interaction with peers, emotional responses that are not always obvious to neurotypical others, issues with spatial awareness resulting in what others term as clumsiness and not readily recognising social rules unless these are made explicit, were all constructed within educator talk as individual failings in either ability or attitude. This is perhaps a manifestation of a different kind of spread effect as some contributors would not have had a diagnosis of autism at the time the remarks were made. Ableism and normalcy assume that all bodies are made and behave in the same way; that they all meet developmental norms (Campbell 2009; Davis 1995). In actuality this is a different kind of spread effect: the Ableism-and-Normalcy spread effect. For the undiagnosed autistic child, the ways in which they operate within the world go unnoticed and so remain misunderstood by educators. Absence of an official diagnosis does not protect autistic children from being positioned within a category of deficit. An autistic academic shared how when she was 12 or 13 a teacher, through the use of one short phrase, 'shyness problem', constructed her as being both shy and as having a problem. Similarly, a parent, Abi Myers, revealed how she has been asked by several PE (Physical Education) teachers if English was her daughter's first language, presumably because her daughter did not interpret and respond to language within expected 'norms'. Lucy Stokes' challenges with writing were not named as dyslexia so were defined as being 'slow at my work'.

With reference to how their bodies operated within time and space, four contributors remembered being asked if they were on drugs. Damian Milton was 14 years old and did not know what this meant. Ross Henley still remembers that happening to him, aged six, 48 years later and the lack of power to challenge the same accusation reduced an autistic student nurse to tears. Children are made individually responsible for breakdowns in social communication and understanding. They are expected to change the fundamentals of who they are as though being autistic is some sort of lifestyle choice. Aspie Jedi Lisa, for example, was told, 'If you acted/dressed/talked like the other kids, they wouldn't bully you'. Smokey, on alerting a teacher that she was being bullied by peers was advised, 'If you weren't so weird they wouldn't notice you'. Joanne was held accountable for not demonstrating sufficient affect through expected modes: 'Smile – you won't crack your jaw'. School reports stated that 'Jorn could participate more in class' without recognition that Jorn Bettin did not know how to do this. For as Jorn states, 'We never received instructions on when and how to participate'. Similarly, for It's not Schrödinger's Autism their fine motor-control dyspraxia was reinterpreted by an art teacher as a lack of effort that generated a burdensome bother: 'You're not even trying, stop wasting my time'. Like Nick's handwriting experience, which has stayed with him throughout life, this contributor was also told by a social studies teacher that their handwriting was 'disgusting' and so they too remain conscious of their writing and embarrassed over it in adulthood.

Ableism in positioning disabled people as lesser and outside of 'normal' seems to remove the protection of respect and dignity that would typically be afforded fellow human beings. It is almost as though it provides an amnesty from typical social conventions in which we are expected to watch what we say and allows educators, and others, then to critique and define children within earshot and without filter. This corresponds with what Keller and Galgay (2010) categorised as 'denial of privacy'. Our autistic contributors gave examples of how they had been publicly humiliated by educators who attacked their ways of being in front of the class. Andy Jordyn (A.J.) Carlisle, for example, as a non-speaking nine-year-old child, was hauled before their classmates who were then told, 'You do not want to be friends with Andy, because they are retarded and will be a welfare bum when they grow up'. The hands of Ann Memmott PGC were beaten with a wooden ruler in front of everyone, Iain was slapped three times with a slipper and a teacher kept open a personal folder on Harriet Axbey during a lesson. In response to K's (knife symbol) selective mutism they were 'commanded' by a teacher to speak in front of the class. On apologising for being late to class after attending an assessment for autism, Chrissie Fiddle's teacher publicly announced, 'Ah yes, sit down, you've been at your psychiatrist assessment haven't you'. n.v.b. experienced a traumatic incident in class that resulted in a 'meltdown' in their behaviour. Rather than recognising and responding empathically to n.v.b's distress, the teacher responded to this by joining in with the laughter of classmates.

It can be seen therefore that a single tweet calling for examples of teacher talk that wounds and reduces revealed a whole range of microagressions at play in our schools. Some of these microagressions are overtly aggressive and apparently intended to injure, whilst others were more subtle and disguised in humour or made carelessly without an appreciation of the lifelong harm that they might cause.

Conclusion

Within this chapter we have employed a short film that was made within a Re•Storying Autism in Education workshop as a starting point for exposing and critiquing examples of teacher talk that is experienced by autistic people as wounding and disabling. In doing so we have advanced Critical Autism Studies as a methodology that directs us to reflect on what these examples of microaggressions within teacher talk might reveal about how autistic children and young people are framed, valued and responded to within our society. The tweets we received from autistic people and their allies responding to the themes of the film reveal the nature and extent of the lifelong damage that can be caused through some of the comments that teachers make about children, either directly to them or within their vicinity. The things we hear said about us as children clearly play a part in constructing the adults that we become. The words of teachers carry a particular significance for many children because children are taught to conceive of teachers as bearers of knowledge and authority figures. When we talk to teachers after watching the film about these comments, many tell us that they recognise these words as being part of classroom talk. Some teachers report having used them themselves as have some of the authors of this chapter during their times as teachers. Often this has been done with the intention of the comment being humorous rather than hurtful or just made carelessly without consideration for how a child might receive the words heard. The emotional effects of hearing these comments, as shared by our Twitter contributors, illustrate, however, that humour is personal and is easily lost and/or distorted as it travels the space between communicators. Similarly, what might have been intended as a 'throwaway' comment by a teacher to a child continues to be ruminated over by our Twitter contributors in their adult lives.

We have sought here to expose the mundane and everyday microaggressions that many autistic pupils experience through careless teacher talk within our schools. We appreciate that the recognition of these by teachers and the realisation of the potential effects of these on pupils may make this chapter difficult to read. However, we trust in the desire and capacity of teachers for reflective practice that can enrich and support their work. None of us are perfect in our craft; most of us learn about the nature and effect of microaggressions through committing them ourselves and then later coming to know and understand how children really experience them. In the example we provided from Nick's childhood, when his ability to form letters was critiqued as a child, we illustrated how insidiously ableist culture inhabits and forms even those comments that might be intended as throwaway or humorous. The cultural messages embedded within and received through these remarks are experienced bodily and psychically. The example demonstrates, too, the power and potential of using such experiences to help us recognise and empathise with the wounding effects of careless talk on others.

The examples that autistic adults and their allies have shared with us demonstrate how important teacher talk is and how carefully it needs to be practised. Our analysis of the comments we received in response to our tweet provides a set of indicators of the ways in which, as teachers, we should take care of the words we use. The most important of these is that we should always remain alert as to how our words are received and processed by others. We need to become practised in recognising when our words wound and then seek to counter the effects of these. In monitoring our talk, we should seek to catch out those occasions when ableism and normalcy creep into our thoughts and speech. We must resist their desire to cast disabled children as Other, as permitted objects of speculation whom we can reduce through critique of their ways of being without concern for how our words might affect them.

As well as capturing the wounding effects of careless teacher talk, the examples within this chapter also illustrate how autistic children and young people desire to hear themselves talked to and about: in ways that communicate recognition of, and value for, who they are and how they engage the world. They want the words they hear to reflect the positive aspects of their personalities, abilities and skills as well as appreciating the things that challenge them. We must therefore always respond to the challenge set us by Critical Autism Studies and Critical Disability Studies: to remain vigilant to the ways in which ableism and normalcy replicate themselves through our understandings of disability and the ways in which we communicate these. Here we have focused on talk but as one of our Twitter contributors, Maura Campbell (2017), reminds us, as powerful as words is the stare:

> The teacher, a stern woman of a certain age, folded her arms across her ample bosom and stared intently over the top of her thick-rimmed glasses. The reason for her evident irritation cowered before her – a painfully shy seven-year-old girl.
>
> *(Campbell 2017)*

Looks of dismissal and disappointment can wound as deeply as words.

Acknowledgement

This work was supported by the Social Sciences and Humanities Research Council of Canada Grant (435-2019-0129).

Notes

1. To view this film, go to https://www.restoryingautism.com/teacher-talk and enter the password 'teacher-talk'.
2. https://restoryingautism.com/
3. We use 'teacher' here as a term to represent all those who, in whatever role, support children and young people within education.
4. We are a collective of academics, some of whom identify as autistic and some who do not. Some are also parents of autistic people.
5. https://twitter.com/ReStorying/status/1252582659764748290
6. We adopt McGuire and Michalko's (2011) definition of these terms here. The autism community generally refers to the parents and carers of autistic people and practitioners working in the field. The autistic community refers to autistic people.
7. Olkin et al. (2019) focused in particular on medical practitioners in their study. However, here we have applied the concept to all practitioners who work within education.
8. Chloe Farahar Âû is a contributor to this volume.
9. A-levels in the UK are exams taken by pupils when they are aged around 18 years old.
10. Damian Milton is a contributor to this volume.
11. Eleventh grade in Canada is attended by pupils usually aged around 17 to 18 years old.

References

Campbell, F 2009, *Contours of ableism: The production of disability and abledness*, Palgrave MacMillan, London, UK. https://doi.org/10.1057/9780230245181

Campbell, M 2017, 'The glass of milk-Maura Campbell', *Spectrum Women Magazine*, web post, July 24, viewed April 24 2020, https://www.spectrumwomen.com/my-life/the-glass-of-milk-maura-campbell/

Davidson, J & Orsini, M (eds.) 2013, *Worlds of autism: Across the spectrum of neurological difference*, University of Minnesota Press, Minneapolis, MN.

Davis, L 1995, *Enforcing normalcy: Disability, deafness and the body*, Verso, London, UK.

Douglas, P, Rice, C, Runswick-Cole, K, Easton, A, Gibson, M, Gruson-Wood, J, Klar, E & Shields, R 2019, 'Re-storying autism: A body becoming disability studies in education approach', *International Journal of Inclusive Education*, 1464–5173, pp. 1–12. https://doi.org/10.1080/13603116.2018.1563835

Fletcher-Watson, S, Adams, J, Brook, K, Charman, T, Crane, L, Cusack, J, Leekam, S, Milton, D, Parr, JR & Pellicano, E 2019, 'Making the future together: Shaping autism research through meaningful participation', *Autism*, vol. 23, no. 4, pp. 943–953. https://doi.org/10.1177/1362361318786721

Golan, O & Baron-Cohen, S 2006, 'Systematizing empathy: Teaching adults with Asperger syndrome or high-functioning autism to recognize complex emotions using interactive media', *Developmental Psychopathology*, vol. 18, no. 2, pp. 591–617. https://doi.org/10.1017/S0954579406060305

Hedley, D, Uljarević, M & Hedley, DFE 2017, 'Employment and living with autism: Personal, social and economic impact', in S Halder & L Assaf (eds.) *Inclusion, disability and culture: An ethnographic perspective traversing abilities and challenges*, pp. 295–312, Springer Publishing International, Cham, Switzerland. https://doi.org/10.1007/978-3-319-55221-8

Hodge, N & Runswick-Cole, K 2018, '"You say … I hear …": Epistemic gaps in practitioner-parent/carer talk', in K Runswick-Cole, T Curran & K Liddiard (eds.) *The Palgrave handbook of disabled children's childhood studies*, pp. 537–555, Palgrave MacMillan, London, UK. https://doi.org/10.1057/978-1-137-54446-9_33

Isaacs, D & Kilham, H 2017, 'Words that wound', *Journal of Pediatrics & Child Health*, vol. 53, pp. 433–434. https://doi.org/10.1111/jpc.13545

Keller, RM & Galgay, CE 2010, 'Microaggressive experiences of people with disabilities', in DW Sue (ed.), *Microaggressions and marginality: Manifestation, dynamics, and impact*, pp. 241–267, John Wiley & Sons Inc., Hoboken, NJ.

Mallett, R & Runswick-Cole, K 2014, *Approaching disability: Critical issues and perspectives*, Routledge, London, UK.

Martin, N, Barnham, C & Krupa, C 2019, 'Identifying and addressing barriers to employment of autistic adults.' *Journal of Inclusive Practice in Further and Higher Education*, vol. 10, no. 1, pp. 56–77.

Masten, AS & Barnes, AJ 2018, 'Resilience in children: Developmental perspectives', *Children*, vol. 5, no. 7. https://doi.org/10.3390/children5070098

McGuire, AE & Michalko, R 2011, 'Minds between us: Autism, mindblindness and the uncertainty of communication', *Educational Philosophy and Theory*, vol. 43, no. 2, pp. 162–177. https://doi.org/10.1111/j.1469-5812.2009.00537.x

Milton, D 2014, 'Autistic expertise: A critical reflection on the production of knowledge in autism studies', *Autism*, vol. 18, no. 7, pp. 794–802. https://doi.org/10.1177/1362361314525281

Milton, D 2017, 'Autistic development, trauma and personhood: Beyond the frame of the neoliberal individual', in K Runswick-Cole, T Curran & K Liddiard (eds.) *The Palgrave handbook of disabled children's childhood studies*, pp. 461–476, Palgrave MacMillan, London, UK. https://doi.org/10.1057/978-1-137-54446-9_33

Milton, D & Sims, T 2016, 'How is a sense of well-being and belonging constructed in the accounts of autistic adults?', *Disability & Society*, vol. 31, no. 4, pp. 520–534. https://doi.org/10.1080/09687599.2016.1186529

Milton, DEM, Ridout, S, Kourti, M, Loomes, G & Martin, N 2019, 'A critical reflection on the development of the Participatory Autism Research Collective (PARC)', *Tizard Learning Disability Review*, vol. 24, no. 2, pp. 82–89. https://doi.org/10.1108/TLDR-09-2018-0029

Minott, M 2019, 'Reflective teaching, inclusive teaching and the teacher's tasks in the inclusive classroom: A literary investigation', *British Journal of Special Education*, vol. 46, no. 2, pp. 226–238. https://doi.org/10.1111/1467-8578.12260

Olkin, R, Hayward, H, Abbene, MS & VanHeel, G 2019, 'The experiences of microaggressions against women with visible and invisible disabilities', *Journal of Social Issues*, vol. 75, pp. 757–785. https://doi.org/10.1111/josi.12342

Rice, C, Chandler, E, Harrison, E, Liddiard, K & Ferrari, M 2015, 'Project Re • Vision: Disability at the edges of representation', *Disability & Society*, vol. 30, pp. 513–527. https://doi.org/10.1080/09687599.2015.1037950

Rice, C, Chandler E, Liddiard, K, Rinaldi, J & Harrison, E 2016, 'Pedagogical possibilities for unruly bodies', *Gender and Education*, vol. 30, pp. 663–682. https://doi.org/10.1080/09540253.2016.1247947

Rice, C & Mündel, I 2018, 'Story-making as methodology: Disrupting dominant stories through multimedia storytelling', *Canadian Review of Sociology*, vol. 55, pp. 211–231. https://doi.org/10.1111/cars.12190

Runswick-Cole, K, Timimi, S & Mallett, R (eds.) 2016, *Re-thinking autism: Diagnosis, identity and equality*, Jessica Kingsley, London, UK.

Sarrett, JC 2016, 'Biocertification and neurodiversity: The role and implications of self-diagnosis in autistic communities', *Neuroethics*, vol. 9, pp. 23–36. https://doi.org/10.1007/s12152-016-9247-x

Schon, D 1991, *The reflective practitioner: How professionals think and act*, Avebury, Oxford, UK.

Thomas, C 1999, *Female forms: Experiencing and understanding disability*, Open University Press, Buckingham, UK.

Waltz, M 2014, 'Worlds of autism: Across the spectrum of neurological difference', *Disability & Society*, vol. 29, no. 8, pp. 1337–1338. https://doi.org/10.1080/09687599.2014.934064

White, S, Simmons, G, Gotham, K, Conner, C, Smith, I, Beck, K & Mazefsky, C 2018, 'Psychosocial treatments targeting anxiety and depression in adolescents and adults on the autism spectrum: Review of the latest research and recommended future directions', *Current Psychiatry Reports*, vol. 20, no.10, pp. 1–10. https://doi.org/10.1007/s11920-018-0949-0

Williams, V, Tarleton, B, Heslop, P, Porter, S, Sass, B, Blue, S, Merchant, W & Mason-Angelow, V 2018, 'Understanding disabling barriers: A fruitful partnership between disability studies and social practices?', *Disability & Society*, vol. 33, no. 2, pp. 157–174. https://doi.org/10.1080/09687599.2017.1401527

Woods, R, Milton, D, Arnold, L & Graby, S 2018, 'Redefining critical autism studies: A more inclusive approach', *Disability & Society*, vol. 33, no. 6, pp. 974–979. https://doi.org/10.1080/09687599.2018.1454380

Woods, R & Waldock, KE 2020, 'Critical autism studies', in FR Volkmar (ed.) *Encyclopedia of autism spectrum disorders, 2nd edition*, pp. 1–9. https://doi.org/10.1007/978-1-4614-6435-8_102297-1

Yergeau, M 2018, *Authoring autism: On rhetoric and neurological queerness*, Duke University Press, Durham, NC.

21
MODELS OF HELPING AND COPING WITH AUTISM

Steven K. Kapp

Introduction

Better understanding parents' and autistic people's different approaches to addressing the problems they face may help to shed light on the ethical and practical issues raised by tensions among and between these primary stakeholders in the autism community (Pellicano & Stears, 2011). Empirical evidence suggests key differences and overlap between autism's cure movement (led by parents and supported by academics and practitioners) and the neurodiversity movement (led by self-advocates: Gillespie-Lynch, Kapp, Brooks, Pickens, & Schwartzman, 2017; Kapp, Gillespie-Lynch, Sherman, & Hutman, 2013), although a growing number of non-autistic parents have joined the movement as allies (Langan, 2011). This chapter traces the history of autism from the perspective of parents and autistic people, applying Brickman et al.'s (1982) models of helping and coping to paradigms of autism not limited to but culminating in the medical model and neurodiversity movement. In the process, like Brickman et al. (1982), this analysis provides evaluations of which views and actions promote subjective well-being, recognising the importance of toxic stress to development (Singh, 2012) and happiness to quality of life (Ne'eman, 2010).

Brickman et al. (1982) take care to distinguish between attribution of responsibility for problems and solutions, a distinction with critical implications for helping and coping. They argue that in terms of the origin of problems, it is most beneficial not to blame people, because then people will be more willing to seek help and be perceived as deserving it. With regard to finding solutions, they present strong evidence that it is more effective to hold people, and view oneself as, responsible, because attributing solutions to oneself increases motivation and competence. People have the most power to get help and cope when not blamed for problems but given credit for solutions, because they are more likely to have the respect and opportunity to get help and can more actively control help towards solutions.

Parents and autistic people have made or been subjected to attributions of responsibility for all combinations of onset and offset of problems related to autism. Professionals and society have unjustly blamed parents for causing autism, isolating and judging their family. As scientific progress absolved parents of blame, parents organised a dominant movement to cure autism, viewing it as separate from their innocent children. Instead of leaving families on their own or breaking them up as before, now autistic people often receive too much and inappropriate help, suffering mistreatment and becoming dependent, as others do for them what they could do for themselves. Autistic people also often develop learned helplessness from other experiences, such as trying to fit in but getting rejected, feeling ashamed and lonely. When offered help for their disability, many try to avoid it, not wanting that which could mark them as different. Yet, increasingly, autistic people come to embrace their differences through the neurodiversity movement, which attributes disability mostly to systemic factors that problematise those outside the norm. As self-advocates, autistic people must take control over our lives with the support needed for full participation in society.

Models

Moral model: refrigerator mother theory and parent-blaming

Under the moral model, people are held responsible for problems (which they supposedly create because of personal failings) and for solutions to them (Brickman et al., 1982). Over the course of autism's history, the most prominent example (as applied to the parents' perspective) is the refrigerator mother theory of autism, which harmfully blamed mothers (and fathers to a lesser degree) for causing autism (Sarrett, 2011).

The refrigerator mother theory damaged parents and their autistic children. Amid a clinical climate in which psychoanalysis and mother-blaming dominated, a psychiatrist who recognised autism as a distinct condition, Leo Kanner (1949), blamed what he considered parents' coldness and obsessiveness for their child's withdrawal into autism. While the moral model tries to encourage people to gain motivation for self-improvement, including from peers (Brickman et al., 1982), this professional orientation caused parents to feel guilty and shunned by society. This is consistent with the weaknesses of the moral model stated by Brickman et al. (1982), especially its tendency towards loneliness. Many families suffered further, as psychologist Bruno Bettelheim offered autism's first purported cure, breaking up families by institutionalising children (Offit, 2008).

Since then, the refrigerator mother theory has become discredited. Aside from the fraudulence of Bettelheim's work on treating autism (Offit, 2008), the premises on autism itself were untrue. Regarding causation, a neurological revolution demonstrated the biological basis of autism (Silverman & Brosco, 2007). Regarding autism's features, parents and their autistic children tend to form secure attachments (Gernsbacher et al., 2005). Indeed, the depth of the child's autism appears unrelated to the quality of the parent–child relationship (Beurkens et al., 2013).

Public, professional, and self-blaming of parents abound. Given autistic children's generally typical physical appearance and behaviours that others often experience as disruptive, onlookers may regard them as spoiled, rude brats, reacting angrily and insensitively (Gray, 1993b). Similarly, moral judgements and rejection happen more frequently to autistic people with subtler manifestations of autism and who make more active social attempts (Shtayermann, 2007), probably because they are more likely to be perceived as odd rather than disabled (Weiner, 1993). Many professionals, especially (and unfortunately) some of those who clinically work with families, still hold parents as at least partially responsible for "invisible" neuropsychiatric disabilities, although understandably familiarity with the parent disability community (such as support groups) tends to reduce blaming (Johnson et al., 2000). Even parents often blame themselves, regardless of the perceived cause, such as feeling guilty for passing on their genes if they make a biological attribution (Mercer et al., 2006), or for environmental exposures if they believe toxins (for example, in vaccines) trigger autism (Fitzpatrick, 2008). This may produce insecurities that detract from the child's needs.

A variety of cultures have blamed parents for causing autism, and while often harmful, these beliefs do not always interfere with helpful parenting. Few psychoanalysts practice with autistic people anymore in the West, except in France, where the misguided approach has caused increasing controversy (Chamak, 2008; Houzel, 2018). South Koreans (among other cultures) sometimes blame mothers for causing autism, associating it with reactive attachment disorder; the stigma isolates families and poses obstacles to obtaining needed services (Kim, 2012). Yet the Navajo, while traditionally regarding autism as the result of witchcraft for punishment of past wrongdoing by the family, immediately come to accept autism after a healing ceremony and proactively include autistic people in society (Kapp, 2011).

Meanwhile, Western society at times continues to insinuate that parental influence such as parent–child interaction and the screen time their baby receives may contribute to the development of autism (e.g. Gordon, 2020). For example, the media pounced during the height of the COVID-19 pandemic on a poorly designed recent study (Heffler, Sienko, Subedi, McCann, & Bennett, 2020) that failed to show this using a weak screening instrument (Guthrie et al., 2019). Reflecting not only the flaws of the study but also the backlash against the legacy of the refrigerator mother model, scientists leapt to critique the study (Science Media Centre, 2020), which also received publicity (e.g. Haridy, 2020).

Medical model: pro-cure movement

According to the medical model, the sick or diseased person is neither responsible for the origin nor the solution to his or her problems; instead, the professional knows best. This combination stands opposite the moral model; the medical model seeks to absolve people of blame and encourages the use of help (Brickman et al., 1982; Weiner, 1995). Nevertheless, it fosters dehumanisation and dependency (Brickman et al., 1982; Kapp, 2019), of major concern given the model's dominance in autism. Its aggressive interest in a cure also hinders more helpful coping.

While the transition from the moral to the medical model reduces judgement and empowers parents (Farrugia, 2009), it lowers expectations for autistic people (Chambres et al., 2008), with destructive effects at times. After Bernard Rimland, through his credibility as both a psychologist and father of an autistic son, organised parents into a medical movement, the field began to adopt Rimland's view at the time of autism as an organic disorder (Silverman & Brosco, 2007). Yet with professionals' emerging position on autism as a developmental disability rather than parent-induced psychosis came expectations of little learning or remediation and instead institutionalisation, devastating prospects that parents defied with belief in a cure (Gray, 1993a; Stone & Rosenbaum, 1988). Psychologist Ivar Lovaas claimed to offer recovery through intensive behavioural intervention (Ne'eman, 2010), but thought that autistic children were so deficient in social motivation that he needed to abuse (e.g. electric shock, slap, scream) them so they would learn (Koegel, 2011; Larsson & Wright, 2011). While those aversive practices have mostly ended, behaviourists continue to defend Lovaas (Koegel, 2011; Larsson & Wright, 2011) and questionable treatment continues as desperate parents experiment with unproven and sometimes dangerous types of alternative medicine (Fitzpatrick, 2008).

Damage from such low expectations often extends into interfering with family and community life, as seen from the example of bilingualism. Learning two languages does not harm, and may even help, autistic children's development of language and communication (Hambly & Fombonne, 2012; Ohashi et al., 2012; Peterson et al., 2012; Valicenti-McDermott et al., 2013). For young children generally it helps to promote theory of mind, executive functioning, and pragmatics (Akhtar & Menjivar, 2012). Yet many professionals and some parents think learning multiple languages will stunt the child's growth (Yu, 2013), even though the family may speak and value the native language (Jegatheesan, 2011).

Similarly, the medical model operates from a deficit basis that pathologises neutral differences and even strengths, illustrated through oxytocin as a treatment for autism. Oxytocin, while famous for helping people trust and bond with in-group members, also raises conformity with the in-group, and promotes envy, gloating, conflict, and ethnocentrism towards out-group members (see Stallen et al., 2012, for a review). It is not necessarily different in autistic children (Miller et al., 2013), as acknowledged by a group of researchers (Dadds et al., 2014). Yet they studied it as a treatment for autistic children anyway, and found it did not help, recommending caution against it (Dadds et al., 2014). One might question the ethics of trying to increase oxytocin and whether it might remove autistic people's possible tendency towards reduced prejudice against out-groups (Kirchner et al., 2012), yet the medical model encourages compliance with even coercive treatments so long as they are provided by experts (Brickman et al., 1982).

Among further evidence against the medical model, parents and their child cope better when parents take a more positive approach. In cultures such as where religious or spiritual beliefs hold that a child with a disability is a blessing (Blacher et al., 2013; Carr & Lord, 2013; Dychess et al., 2004), or interdependent social structure means that parents expect to have closer, more personal social networks and more time caregiving as a normal fact of life, as in Cuba (Sotgiu et al., 2011), parents perceive more positive impact from having an autistic or otherwise disabled child. Parents who begin with a medical orientation also tend to cope better over time by moving towards a positive perspective, reframing their attitude towards their child (such as an exciting challenge rather than a threat: Cappe et al., 2011; Roesch & Weiner, 2001) and making appropriate lifestyle adaptations. For example, religiosity and spirituality themselves tend to help, while participation in religious activities (which may be overwhelming for the child) may hinder, parents' well-being (Ekas et al., 2009). Seeing the child's autistic traits as positive characteristics rather than as symptoms not only reduces parents' stress but also instils more confidence in the child's ability to do things for him- or herself and in the child's future (as with ADHD: Lench et al., 2013). This encourages the young person to take risks and make personal discoveries through experience, reducing parents' tendency towards overprotectiveness (for example, discouraging their teenager's interest in dating: Nichols & Blakeley-Smith, 2009).

Unfortunately, while this model of autism has adapted and encountered resistance, the medical model remains the dominant lens through which society views autism. Despite heavy personal and financial investment in early intensive behavioural interventions, no autism therapies for young children show strong evidence, due to weak study designs or risk of bias (Sandbank et al., 2020). Applied behavioural analysis-based studies especially suffer from conflicts of interest for which they rarely account (Bottema-Beutel, Crowley, Sandbank, & Woynaroski, 2020). The approaches with the most evidence have responsive, naturalistic, developmental principles, such as following the child's lead (Kapp, 2018; Sandbank et al., 2020). Nevertheless, autistic people continue to be dehumanised, pathologised, and essentialised because of the pervasiveness of the medical model, not least approaches that reduce autism to a social disorder (Kapp, 2019).

Enlightenment model: learned helplessness

Like the moral model, the enlightenment model holds people responsible for creating their problems, but instead of people solving the problems themselves (which they are seen as unwilling or unable to do), the model has authorities help people work through problems. Under both models, people may have caused their problems through low motivation. The closest match in autism is social motivation theory, according to which reduced interest in people from infancy on causes young children to withdraw from or less actively engage in social interaction, reducing social learning and leading to the cascading impairments of autism in need of treatment (Chevallier et al., 2012). A comprehensive challenge to this theory is beyond the scope of this chapter, but evidence shows that autistic people often show strong social drives (strong emotional empathy, reduced prejudice, and diverse relationships) but often struggle to interact with at least non-autistic people (Kapp, Goldknopf, Brooks, Kofner, & Hossain, 2019a). Before becoming aware of their autism, many autistic people do blame themselves for their differences, until diagnosis (e.g. in adulthood) offers a sense of explanation and relief (Leedham, Thompson, Smith, & Freeth, 2020; Punshon, Skirrow, & Murphy, 2009). Yet the tenets of social motivation theory appear incorrect, and ironically the negative self-image required by the enlightenment model (Brickman et al., 1982) perpetuates learned helplessness rather than motivation to comply with interventions.

Consistent with the enlightenment model's requirement that people must accept a starkly negative self-concept (in order to submit to others' control, a point addressed later in this section), as autistic people become more "enlightened" about their differences, they tend to view themselves as more incompetent, which increases distress. Children and adults with subtler autism (Mazurek & Kanne, 2010; Sterling et al., 2008), more emotional awareness (Capps et al., 1995), closer friendships (Mazurek & Kanne, 2010), and higher cognitive abilities (Mazurek & Kanne, 2010; Sterling et al., 2008; Vickerstaff et al., 2007) tend to regard their autism as more severe and endorse more anxiety and depression, likely reflecting increased internalisation of stigma of difference. Similarly, during adolescence, a time when identity and fitting in become most salient, social anxiety tends to increase for autistic youth even as it decreases for typically developing peers (Kuusikko et al., 2008). Autistic youth with higher cognitive abilities and anxiety – and, thus, probably, self-awareness – are more likely to take risks, motivated by fear of failure, even as that increased anxiety tends to inhibit typically developing peers (South et al., 2011).

Despite growing self-awareness and willingness to take risks, many autistic youth make attempts to fit in that prove unsuccessful. Many make regular initiations towards peers but suffer high rates of loneliness-inducing rejection (Bauminger et al., 2003). Many students face alarming rates of peer victimisation, with heightened sensitivity to ridicule and memory of past mocking experiences; some sadly come to expect it (Sreckovic, Brunsting, & Able, 2014). Loneliness; low support from classmates, friends, and parents; anxiety; and withdrawal all contribute to depression among autistic youth (Kapp et al., 2011).

Autistic youth have options that could improve their relationships or coping but require some acceptance of their differences in contrast with the enlightenment model. They might have better relationships if they pursued them with other social "misfits". Rejected children report the most interest in interacting with autistic peers once aware of their disability (Campbell et al., 2005). In turn, autistic children, adolescents, and adults often prefer the atypical communication style of one another (Granieri, McNair, Gerber, Reiffler, & Lerner, 2020; Morrison et al., 2020), because of their similarities in communication behaviours (Granieri et al., 2020) and assumptions or demands (Heasman & Gillespie, 2019). Many autistic people experience a sense of belonging together or find they relate to one another exceptionally well (Crompton, Hallett, Ropar, Flynn, & Fletcher-Watson, 2020; Schilbach et al., 2013), with autistic people matching non-autistic people in the effectiveness of their communication among their own group (Crompton, Ropar, Evans-Williams, Flynn, & Fletcher-Watson, 2020). Furthermore, some support services may help, but autistic youth may dislike them for fear of stigma and harm to their reputation (Camarena & Sarigiani, 2009; Humphrey & Lewis, 2008) – and supports become less available after secondary school (Gerhardt & Lainer, 2011; Shattuck et al., 2011).

Self-perceptions aligned with the enlightenment model lead autistic and other people to become fixated on their problems and redesign their lives around ultimately gaining the self-control to deal with them, even when the real problem lies in external factors. Most autistic youth perceive themselves as different, which many blame for social failures (Barnhill, 2001) and negative events (Barnhill & Myles, 2001), all of which tends to depress them (Hedley & Young, 2006; Meyer et al., 2006). Many such self-conscious youth and adults exert effort to inhibit unusual behaviours or "pass" for neurotypical. Such attempts to mask autism or camouflage tend to worsen mental health, but many autistic people feel obligated to engage in it (e.g. to reduce bullying: Mandy, 2019). While they may receive more acceptance from typically developing peers with more passive interaction styles given the stigma of atypical social approaches (Jones and Frederickson, 2010), that phenomenon reflects unfair norms. Instead of attributing social rejection to individual differences such as in personality, it may be more accurate to attribute them to attempts of the in-group to maintain status over out-group members, requiring social change (Killen et al., 2013). Indeed, despite the listing of social-emotional reciprocity as a deficit of autism, reciprocity must work both ways, and frequently non-autistic people fail to demonstrate it (Milton, 2012).

A growing body of evidence supports the double empathy problem model that the social challenges autistic people experience lie in the mismatch between autistic and non-autistic people's communication styles (Milton, 2012). While autistic people and non-autistic people share information well among their own group, communication breakdowns happen *between* autistic and non-autistic people (Crompton et al., 2020b). Non-autistic people often fail to read autistic people's behaviour (Sheppard, Illai, Wong, Ropar, & Mitchell, 2016), such as facial expressions (Brewer et al., 2016), and this misunderstanding appears to contribute to unfavourable impressions both via experimental performance (Alkhaldi, Sheppard, & Mitchell, 2019) and self-report (Gillespie-Lynch et al., 2021). Indeed, non-autistic children and adults tend to quickly make negative judgements against autistic peers (Stagg et al., 2014; Sasson et al., 2017) based on factors that have more to do with the non-autistic perceivers than the autistic people (Morrison, DeBrander, Faso, & Sasson, 2019). Autistic and non-autistic people implicitly acknowledge this mismatch by self-reporting more autistic traits when interacting with or perceived by their out-group than their in-group (fellow autistic or non-autistic people: Gernsbacher, Stevenson, & Dern, 2017). Despite these data demonstrating the empirical failures of the enlightenment model but providing support for Milton (2012), fellow autistic scholar Chapman (2021) offers a compelling social ecological model that society benefits from this neurodiversity, such as from a cognitive division of labour.

Compensatory model: neurodiversity movement

According to the compensatory model, people suffer not from internal deficiencies but the failure of the social environment to provide the resources they deserve, requiring people to take the lead in solving their problems or transforming the environment. Brickman and colleagues (1982) imply that the civil rights movement belongs under this model, offering the Reverend Jesse Jackson as an example. Similarly, the neurodiversity movement operates out of the civil rights tradition. As Brickman et al. (1982) note, this model may be superior because it encourages people to seek help (since they are not responsible for the problems), but they must exert control over their lives (since they must determine how to leverage help towards solutions).

The neurodiversity movement believes that autistic people's disability lies mostly in an inaccessible, oppressive society designed for the privileges of the neurotypical majority, but that they must solve the problem through identifying as a community in solidarity with other minority groups (Baker, 2011). It began in response to self-advocates' perceived exclusion by parents' advocacy efforts and seeks the full participation of autistic people in society, especially in matters about them (Chamak, 2008; Sinclair, 2005). Family-led autism advocacy organisations continue to focus predominantly on causation and children, creating alarms about an autism "epidemic" and the urgent need for early intervention while neglecting the reality and needs of adults (Gerhardt & Lainer, 2011; Milner and Cho, 2014; Stevenson et al., 2011). Like other stigmatised groups (Frable et al., 1998; Salmon, 2013), self-advocates in the movement obtain social support from meeting with others with similar experiences, but they also encourage one another to take pride in autism as a natural, essential part of themselves (Chamak, 2008; Kapp, 2020). Although acceptance of autism both personally and from others (Cage, Di Monaco, & Newell, 2018), and outness as an autistic person and autistic community connectedness benefit autistic adults' mental health (Botha, 2020), the movement has attracted most controversy for its opposition to curing autism.

In particular, the chief claim against neurodiversity is that it does not apply to or serve the interests of "low-functioning" autistic people (see, for example, Jaarsma and Welin, 2012), which appears related to Brickman et al.'s (1982) main critique of the compensatory model – that it puts pressure on people (presumably especially the most vulnerable) to solve problems they did not create. Yet leaders of the neurodiversity movement prioritise ensuring that everyone has a reliable means of communication (Ne'eman, 2010; Robertson, 2010), such as through augmentative and alternative communication methods, which work best when matched with the user's preference (Van der Meer et al., 2012). Similarly, parental following of their autistic child's lead tends to increase the child's language, especially for more language-impaired children (Kapp, 2018; Kapp, 2013). Autistic people with self-injurious, aggressive, or destructive behaviours (Ruef and Turnbull, 2002) and who struggle to communicate (Rossetti et al., 2008), likewise stress the need to exercise control over their lives. It is a matter of ethics and quality of life, as increasingly recognised by the developmental disabilities field, that all people should exert as much self-determination over their lives as possible, regardless of intellectual ability or support needs (Petry and Maes, 2009). Furthermore, much of the controversy seems intertwined with misunderstanding the overlap of the neurodiversity framework and the medical model in that advocates of both recognise that autism can inherently challenge quality of life and support (certain) means of ameliorating those aspects, as demonstrated empirically (Kapp et al., 2013; Gillespie-Lynch et al., 2017) and voiced by autistic scholars and activists (Bottema-Beutel, Kapp, Lester, Sasson, & Hand, 2020; Kapp, 2020).

The compensatory model seeks to build deprived people's power, and the critique of the neurodiversity movement often falls into a pattern of underestimating the "hidden" abilities of autistic people with higher support needs (Courchesne, Meilleur, Poulin-Lord, Dawson, & Soulières, 2015; McGonigle-Chalmers et al., 2013). Although excessive emphasis on autistic strengths might play into savant or "shiny aspie" tropes (Broderick & Ne'eman, 2008), even non-speaking autistic children deemed "untestable" often demonstrate visuospatial peaks of ability typical of autistic people (Courchesne et al., 2015), which are more common in individuals with lower verbal skills (Bölte, Dziokek, & Poustka, 2009). Most autistic adults have reported strengths they associate with autism when asked (Russell et al., 2019) and a social identity as autistic enhances the impact of these strengths on autistic people's self-esteem (Cooper, Cooper, Russell, & Smith, 2020; Cooper, Smith, & Russell, 2017) and quality of life (McDonald, 2020; 2017). Adopting an identity as an autistic person (for example, viewing autism as an equally valid way of being) similarly benefits the well-being and reduces stigma for both formally and self-diagnosed autistic people (McDonald, 2020; 2017), which suggests the benefits of the neurodiversity movement for self-diagnosed people's coping. While thinking of one's autistic traits as adaptable rather than static also benefits quality of life (McDonald, 2020, 2017), this again does not necessarily conflict with the neurodiversity movement, given the movement's support for mitigating challenges. Indeed, some autistic traits or diagnostic behaviours help to cope with others. For example, repetitive movements or vocalisations (which have been reclaimed by autistic advocates as *stimming*) help to soothe overwhelming sensations and emotions (Kapp et al., 2019b).

The neurodiversity movement offers a variety of possible solutions to problems. In addition to social solutions such as services, non-discrimination protections, and respectful attitudes (Baker, 2011), the movement appears compatible with some clinical solutions. Direct evidence suggests near-universal recognition of autism's challenges and support for some means of mitigating them, with the goal of adaptive skills to navigate society (Kapp et al., 2013) rather than normalisation for its own sake (Ne'eman, 2010).

Some problematic treatments may be modified in their goals and what they target, such as parents who consider themselves allies applying behavioural therapy in ways they consider compatible with neurodiversity (Savarese, 2010). Intense and focused interests that typify autism provide intrinsic motivation for knowledge and a positive "flow state" of engagement when immersed in them (Grove, Roth, & Hoekstra, 2016; McDonnell & Milton, 2014), and incorporating interest-based activities into daily life often has the therapeutic effect of improving functioning (Dunst, Trivette, & Hamby, 2012; Gunn & Delafield-Butt, 2016; Winter-Messiers, 2007; see also Murray & Lawson, 2005). Self-advocates also benefit from collaborating with non-autistic allies (Schwartz, 2004), which also helps parents (Greenburg & Des Roches Rosa, 2020). Accepting their autistic child helps parents understand them, which in turn improves the parent–child relationship (Oppenheim et al, 2012). Critically, the quality of support, rather than disability characteristics, appear to promote quality of life from autistic people's perspective (Renty & Roeyers, 2006).

As awareness of the neurodiversity movement has grown, so have attitudes aligned with it: viewing autism as a positive identity that needs acceptance rather than a cure, yet still supporting amelioration of challenges (Kapp et al., 2013; Kim, 2020). Similarly, the networks of autistic co-researchers who join participatory autism research teams (Willingham, 2020) and of professional autistic autism researchers (Nuwer, 2020), continue to grow and make an impact (Nuwer, 2020; Willingham, 2020). For example, co-authoring articles that demonstrate the stigmatising effect of autism's puzzle piece symbol (Gernsbacher, Raimond, Stevenson, Boston, & Harp, 2018) and of ableist language practices (Bottema-Beutel et al., 2020). This has led respectively to the journal *Autism* abandoning that representation of autism (Pellicano et al., 2018) and *Autism in Adulthood* adopting the language guidelines. This chapter began in 2009 (as university coursework) and the empirical evidence that has since emerged in support of the mismatch of autistic and non-autistic people's communication styles and the damage of camouflaging exhibit how the neurodiversity movement continues to change the autism research landscape and beyond. Change cannot come soon enough; poor coping for too many autistic people results in *autistic burnout* (chronic exhaustion, skills loss, and reduced tolerance of stimuli: Raymaker et al., 2020). Autistic people are more likely to experience trauma but the relationship with suicidality is weaker than for non-autistic people (Pelton et al., 2020), yet people's resilience has a limit.

Conclusion

The neurodiversity movement has earned its match with Brickman et al.'s (1982) overall preference for attribution of responsibility for the offset but not onset of problems. Through its social rather than personal deficit orientation, the neurodiversity movement has encouraged autistic people to accept and seek help that they might otherwise find too stigmatising. As a rights-based movement, it empowers autistic people to get the help they need, which in turn helps them and their family cope.

As Brickman et al. (1982) note, models work best when the help-givers and help-recipients operate from the same model, suggesting the need for widespread acceptance of neurodiversity. This has already begun to happen as, for example, most countries have signalled their commitment to disability rights as a human right (Harpur, 2012). Societies respect these rights when they balance (inter)dependence with respect for individuality and diversity (Sarrett, 2012). Nevertheless, the examples are non-exhaustive, and everyday practices often fall within multiple models (Brickman et al., 1982), suggesting the need for further study into the nuances of what people believe helps and what actually helps.

References

Akhtar, N. and Menjivar, J.A. (2012) Cognitive and linguistic correlates of early exposure to more than one language. *Advances in Child Development and Behavior* 42: 41–78. https://doi.org/10.1016/B978-0-12-394388-0.00002-2.

Alkhaldi, R.S., Sheppard, E. and Mitchell, P. (2019) Is there a link between autistic people being perceived unfavorably and having a mind that is difficult to read? *Journal of Autism and Developmental Disorders* 49(10): 3973–3982. https://doi.org/10.1007/s10803-019-04101-1.

Baker, D.L. (2011) *The Politics of Neurodiversity: Why Public Policy Matters*. Boulder, CO: Lynne Rienner Publishers.

Barnhill, G.P. (2001) Social attributions and depression in adolescents with Asperger syndrome. *Focus on Autism and Other Developmental Disabilities* 16(1): 46–53. https://doi.org/10.1177/108835760101600112.

Barnhill, G.P. and Myles, B. (2001) Attributional style and depression in adolescents with Asperger syndrome. *Journal of Positive Behavioral Intervention* 3(3): 175–190. https://doi.org/10.1177/109830070100300305.

Bauminger, N., Shulman, C. and Agam, C. (2003) Peer interaction and loneliness in high-functioning children with autism. *Journal of Autism and Developmental Disorders* 33(5): 489–507. https://doi.org/10.1023/A:1025827427901.

Beurkens, N.M., Hobson, J.A. and Hobson, R.P. (2013) Autism severity and qualities of parent–child relations. *Journal of Autism and Developmental Disorders* 43(1): 168–178. https://doi.org/10.1007/s10803-012-1562-4.

Blacher, J., Begum, G.F., Marcoulides, G.A. and Baker, B.L. (2013) Longitudinal perspectives of child positive impact on families: Relationship to disability and culture. *American Journal on Intellectual and Developmental Disabilities* 118(2): 141–155. https://doi.org/10.1352/1944-7558-118.2.141.

Bölte, S., Dziobek, I. and Poustka, F. (2009) Brief report: The level and nature of autistic intelligence revisited. *Journal of Autism and Developmental Disorders* 39(4): 678–682. https://doi.org/10.1007/s10803-008-0667-2.

Botha, M. (2020) *Autistic Community Connectedness as a Buffer against the Effects of Minority Stress* (Doctoral dissertation, University of Surrey).

Bottema-Beutel, K., Crowley, S., Sandbank, M. and Woynaroski, T.G. (2020) Research review: Conflicts of Interest (COIs) in autism early intervention research–A meta-analysis of COI influences on intervention effects. *Journal of Child Psychology and Psychiatry*. https://doi.org/10.111/jcpp.13249.

Bottema-Beutel, K., Kapp, S.K., Lester, J.N., Sasson, N.J. and Hand, B.N. (2020) Avoiding ableist language: Suggestions for autism researchers. *Autism in Adulthood*. https://doi.org/10.1089/aut.2020.0014.

Brewer, R., Biotti, F., Catmur, C., Press, C., Happé, F., Cook, R. and Bird, G. (2016) Can neurotypical individuals read autistic facial expressions? Atypical production of emotional facial expressions in autism spectrum disorders. *Autism Research* 9(2): 262–271. https://doi.org/10.1002/aur.1508.

Brickman, P., Rabinowitz, V.C., Karuza Jr., J., Dan, C., Ellen, C. and Louise, K. (1982) Models of helping and coping. *American Psychologist* 37(4): 368–384.

Broderick, A.A. and Ne'eman, A. (2008) Autism as metaphor: Narrative and counter-narrative. *International Journal of Inclusive Education* 12(5–6): 459–476. https://doi.org/10.1002/aur.1508.

Cage, E., Di Monaco, J. and Newell, V. (2018) Experiences of autism acceptance and mental health in autistic adults. *Journal of Autism and Developmental Disorders* 48(2): 473–484.

Camarena, P.M. and Sarigiani, P.A. (2009) Postsecondary educational aspirations of high-functioning adolescents with autism spectrum disorders and their parents. *Focus on Autism and Other Developmental Disabilities* 24(2): 115–128.

Campbell, J.M., Ferguson, J.E., Herzinger, C.V., Jackson, J.N. and Marino, C. (2005) Peers' attitudes toward autism differ across sociometric groups: An exploratory investigation. *Journal of Developmental and Physical Disabilities* 17(3): 281–298.

Cappe, E., Wolff, M., Bobet, R. and Adrien, J.L. (2011) Quality of life: A key variable to consider in the evaluation of adjustment of parents of children with autism spectrum disorders and in the development of relevant support and assistance programs. *Quality of Life Research* 20(8): 1279–1294.

Capps, L., Sigman, M. and Yirmiya, N. (1995) Self-competence and emotional understanding in high-functioning children with autism. *Development and Psychopathology* 7(1): 137–149.

Carr, T. and Lord, C. (2013) Longitudinal study of perceived negative impact in African American and Caucasian mothers of children with autism spectrum disorder. *Autism* 17(4): 405–417.

Chamak, B. (2008) Autism and social movements: French parents' associations and international autistic individuals' organisations. *Sociology of Health and Illness* 30(1): 76–96.

Chambres, P.C., Auxiette, C., Vansingle, C. and Gil, S. (2008) Adult attitudes toward behaviors of a six-year-old boy with autism. *Journal of Autism and Developmental Disorders* 38(7): 1320–1327.

Chapman, R. (2021) Neurodiversity and the social ecology of mental functioning. *Perspectives on Psychological Science*. Advance online publication. https://doi.org/10.1177/1745691620959833.

Chevallier, C., Kohls, G., Troiani, V., et al. (2012) The social motivation theory of autism. *Trends in Cognitive Sciences* 16(4): 231–239.

Cooper, R., Cooper, K., Russell, A.J. and Smith, L.G. (2020) "I'm proud to be a little bit different": The effects of autistic individuals' perceptions of autism and autism social identity on their collective self-esteem. *Journal of Autism and Developmental Disorders* 51(2): 704–714.

Cooper, K., Smith, L.G. and Russell, A. (2017) Social identity, self-esteem, and mental health in autism. *European Journal of Social Psychology* 47(7): 844–854.

Courchesne, V., Meilleur, A.A.S., Poulin-Lord, M.P., Dawson, M. and Soulières, I. (2015) Autistic children at risk of being underestimated: School-based pilot study of a strength-informed assessment. *Molecular Autism* 6(1): 12.

Crompton, C.J., Hallett, S., Ropar, D., Flynn, E. and Fletcher-Watson, S. (2020) 'I never realised everybody felt as happy as I do when I am around autistic people': A thematic analysis of autistic adults' relationships with autistic and neurotypical friends and family. *Autism* 24(6): 1438–1448. https://doi.org/10.1177/1362361320908976.

Crompton, C.J., Ropar, D., Evans-Williams, C.V., Flynn, E.G. and Fletcher-Watson, S. (2020) Autistic peer-to-peer information transfer is highly effective. *Autism* 24(7): 1704–1712. https://doi.org/10.1177/1362361320919286.

Dadds, M.R., MacDonald, E., Cauchi, A., Williams, K., Levy, F. and Brennan, J. (2014) Nasal oxytocin for social deficits in childhood autism: A randomized controlled trial. *Journal of Autism and Developmental Disorders* 44(3): 521–531.

Dunst, C.J., Trivette, C.M. and Hamby, D.W. (2012) Meta-analysis of studies incorporating the interests of young children with autism spectrum disorders into early intervention practices. *Autism Research and Treatment*. Article ID 462531. https://www.hindawi.com/journals/aurt/2012/462531/

Dyches, T.T., Wilder, L.K., Sudweeks, R.R., Obiakor, F.E. and Algozzine, B. (2004) Multicultural issues in autism. *Journal of Autism and Developmental Disorders* 34(2): 211–222.

Ekas, N.V., Whitman, T.L. and Shivers, C. (2009) Religiosity, spirituality, and socioemotional functioning in mothers of children with autism spectrum disorder. *Journal of Autism and Developmental Disorders* 39(5): 706–719.

Farrugia, D. (2009) Exploring stigma: Medical knowledge and the stigmatisation of parents of children diagnosed with autism spectrum disorder. *Sociology of Health and Illness* 31(7): 1011–1027.

Fitzpatrick, M. (2008) *Defeating Autism: A Damaging Delusion*. London: Routledge.

Frable, D.E., Platt, L. and Hoey, S. (1998) Concealable stigmas and positive self-perceptions: Feeling better around similar others. *Journal of Personality and Social Psychology* 74(4): 909–922.

Gerhardt, P.F. and Lainer, I. (2011) Addressing the needs of adolescents and adults with autism: A crisis on the horizon. *Journal of Contemporary Psychotherapy* 41(1): 37–45.

Gernsbacher, M.A., Raimond, A.R., Stevenson, J.L., Boston, J.S. and Harp, B. (2018) Do puzzle pieces and autism puzzle piece logos evoke negative associations? *Autism* 22(2): 118–125.

Gernsbacher, M.A., Rogers, S., Mundy, P., Mundy, P.C., Rogers, S.J. and Sigman, M. (2005) Autism and deficits in attachment behavior. *Science* 307(5713): 1201–1203.

Gernsbacher, M.A., Stevenson, J.L. and Dern, S. (2017) Specificity, contexts, and reference groups matter when assessing autistic traits. *PLOS ONE* 12(2): e0171931.

Gillespie-Lynch, K., Daou, N., Obeid, R., Reardon, S., Khan, S. and Goldknopf, E.J. (2021) What contributes to stigma towards autistic university students and students with other diagnoses? *Journal of Autism and Developmental Disorders* 51(2): 459–475. https://doi.org/10.1007/s10803-020-04556-7.

Gillespie-Lynch, K., Kapp, S.K., Brooks, P.J., Pickens, J. and Schwartzman, B. (2017) Whose expertise is it? Evidence for autistic adults as critical autism experts. *Frontiers in Psychology* 8: 438.

Gordon, S. (2020, April 20) Screen time for tiniest tots linked to autism-like symptoms. *U.S. News & World Report.* https://www.usnews.com/news/health-news/articles/2020-04-20/screen-time-for-tiniest-tots-linked-to-autism-like-symptoms.

Granieri, J.E., McNair, M.L., Gerber, A.H., Reifler, R.F. and Lerner, M.D. (2020) Atypical social communication is associated with positive initial impressions among peers with autism spectrum disorder. *Autism* 24(7): 1841–1848. https://doi.org/10.1177/1362361320924906.

Gray, D.E. (1993a) Negotiating autism: Relations between parents and treatment staff. *Social Science and Medicine* 36(8): 1037–1046.

Gray, D.E. (1993b) Perceptions of stigma: The parents of autistic children. *Sociology of Health and Illness* 15(1): 102–120.

Greenburg, C. and Des Roches Rosa, S. (2020) Two winding parent paths to neurodiversity advocacy. In S.K. Kapp (Ed.), *Autistic Community and the Neurodiversity Movement: Stories from the Frontline* (pp. 155–166). Singapore: Palgrave Macmillan.

Grove, R., Roth, I. and Hoekstra, R.A. (2016) The motivation for special interests in individuals with autism and controls: Development and validation of the special interest motivation scale. *Autism Research* 9(6): 677–688.

Gunn, K.C. and Delafield-Butt, J.T. (2016) Teaching children with autism spectrum disorder with restricted interests: A review of evidence for best practice. *Review of Educational Research* 86(2): 408–430.

Guthrie, W., Wallis, K., Bennett, A., Brooks, E., Dudley, J., Gerdes, M., … & Miller, J.S. (2019) Accuracy of autism screening in a large pediatric network. *Pediatrics* 144(4): e20183963.

Hambly, C. and Fombonne, E. (2012) The impact of bilingual environments on language development in children with autism spectrum disorders. *Journal of Autism and Developmental Disorders* 42(7): 1342–1352.

Haridy, R. (2020, April 20) Experts slam new study linking baby screen time to autism-like symptoms. *New Atlas.* https://newatlas.com/health-wellbeing/screen-time-baby-child-autism-asd-journal-critics/.

Harpur, P. (2012) Embracing the new disability rights paradigm: The importance of the convention on the rights of persons with disabilities. *Disability and Society* 27(1): 1–14.

Heasman, B. and Gillespie, A. (2019) Neurodivergent intersubjectivity: Distinctive features of how autistic people create shared understanding. *Autism* 23(4): 910–921.

Hedley, D. and Young, R. (2006) Social comparison processes and depressive symptoms in children and adolescents with Asperger syndrome. *Autism* 10(2): 139–153.

Heffler, K.F., Sienko, D.M., Subedi, K., McCann, K.A. and Bennett, D.S. (2020) Association of early-life social and digital media experiences With development of autism spectrum disorder–like symptoms. *JAMA Pediatrics* 174(7): 690–696. https://doi.org/10.1001/jamapediatrics.2020.0230.

Houzel, D. (2018) Autism and psychoanalysis in the French context. *The International Journal of Psycho-Analysis* 99(3): 725–745.

Humphrey, N. and Lewis, S. (2008) 'Make me normal': The views and experiences of pupils on the autistic spectrum in mainstream secondary schools. *Autism* 12(1): 23–46.

Jaarsma, P. and Welin, S. (2012) Autism as a natural human variation: Reflections on the claims of the neurodiversity movement. *Health Care Analysis* 20(1): 20–30.

Jegatheesan, B. (2011) Multilingual development in children with autism: Perspectives of South Asian Muslim immigrant parents on raising a child with a communicative disorder in multilingual contexts. *Bilingual Research Journal* 34(2): 185–200.

Johnson, H.C., Cournoyer, D.E., Fisher, G.A., et al. (2000) Children's emotional and behavioral disorders: Attributions of parental responsibility by professionals. *American Journal of Orthopsychiatry* 70(3): 327–339.

Jones, A.P. and Frederickson, N. (2010) Multi-informant predictors of social inclusion for students with autism spectrum disorders attending mainstream school. *Journal of Autism and Developmental Disorders* 40(9): 1094–1103.

Kanner, L. (1949) Problems of nosology and psychodynamics of early infantile autism. *American Journal of Orthopsychiatry* 19(3): 416–426.

Kapp, S. (2019). How social deficit models exacerbate the medical model: aAutism as case in point. *Autism Policy & Practice*, 2(1),: 3–28.

Kapp, S.K. (2011) Navajo and autism: The beauty of harmony. *Disability and Society* 26(5): 583–595.

Kapp, S.K. (2013) Empathizing with sensory and movement differences: Moving toward sensitive understanding of autism. *Frontiers in Integrative Neuroscience* 7(38): 1–6.

Kapp, S.K. (2018) Social support, well-being, and quality of life among individuals on the autism spectrum. *Pediatrics* 141(Supplement 4): S362–S368.

Kapp, S.K. (2020) Introduction. In S.K. Kapp (Ed.), *Autistic Community and the Neurodiversity Movement: Stories from the Frontline* (pp. 1–19). Singapore: Palgrave Macmillan.

Kapp, S.K., Gantman, A. and Laugeson, E.A. (2011) Transition to adulthood for high-functioning individuals with autism spectrum disorders. In M.R. Mohammadi (Ed.), *A Comprehensive Book on Autism Spectrum Disorders* (pp. 451–478). InTech. http://www.intechopen.com/books/a-comprehensive-book-on-autism-spectrum-disorders.

Kapp, S.K., Gillespie-Lynch, K., Sherman, L.E. and Hutman, T. (2013) Deficit, difference, or both? Autism and neurodiversity. *Developmental Psychology* 49(1): 59–71.

Kapp, S.K., Goldknopf, E., Brooks, P.J., Kofner, B. and Hossain, M. (2019a) Expanding the critique of social motivation theory of autism with participatory and developmental research. *Brain and Behavioral Sciences* 42(e82): 26–27. https://doi.org/10.1017/S0140525X18001826.

Kapp, S.K., Steward, R., Crane, L., Elliott, D., Elphick, C., Pellicano, E. and Russell, G. (2019b) 'People should be allowed to do what they like': Autistic adults' views and experiences of stimming. *Autism* 23(7): 1782–1792.

Killen, M., Mulvey, K.L. and Hitti, A. (2013) Social exclusion in childhood: A developmental intergroup perspective. *Child Development* 84(3): 772–790.

Kim, H.U. (2012) Autism across cultures: Rethinking autism. *Disability and Society* 27(4): 535–545.

Kim, S.Y. (2020) The development and pilot-testing of the autism attitude acceptance scale: An instrument measuring autism acceptance. *Autism in Adulthood* 2(3): 204–215. https://doi.org/10.1089/aut.2019.0066.

Kirchner, J.C., Schmitz, F. and Dziobek, I. (2012) Brief report: Stereotypes in autism revisited. *Journal of Autism and Developmental Disorders* 42(10): 2246–2251.

Koegel, R. (2011) O. Ivar Lovaas (1927–2010). *American Psychologist* 66(3): 227–228.

Kuusikko, S., Pollock-Wurman, R., Jussila, K., et al. (2008) Social anxiety in high-functioning children and adolescents with autism and Asperger syndrome. *Journal of Autism and Developmental Disorders* 38(9): 1697–1709.

Langan, M. (2011) Parental voices and controversies in autism. *Disability and Society* 26(2): 193–205.

Larsson, E.V. and Wright, S. (2011) O. Ivar Lovaas (1927–2010). *The Behavior Analyst* 34(1): 111–114.

Leedham, A., Thompson, A.R., Smith, R. and Freeth, M. (2020) 'I was exhausted trying to figure it out': The experiences of females receiving an autism diagnosis in middle to late adulthood. *Autism* 24(1): 135–146.

Lench, H.C., Levine, L.J. and Whalen, C.K. (2013) Exasperating or exceptional? Parents' interpretations of their child's ADHD behavior. *Journal of Attention Disorders* 17(2): 141–151.

Mandy, W. (2019) Social camouflaging in autism: Is it time to lose the mask? *Autism* 23(8): 1879–1881.

Mazurek, M.O. and Kanne, S.M. (2010) Friendship and internalizing symptoms among children and adolescents with ASD. *Journal of Autism and Developmental Disorders* 40(12): 1512–1520.

McDonald, T.A.M. (2017) Discriminative and criterion validity of the autism spectrum identity scale (ASIS). *Journal of Autism and Developmental Disorders* 47(10): 3018–3028.

McDonald, T.A.M. (2020) Autism identity and the "lost generation": Structural validation of the autism spectrum identity scale and comparison of diagnosed and self-diagnosed adults on the autism spectrum. *Autism in Adulthood* 2(1): 13–23.

McDonnell, A. and Milton, D. (2014) Going with the fow: Reconsidering 'repetitive behavior' through the concept of 'fow states'. In Glenys Jones and Elizabeth Hurley (Eds.), *Good Autism Practice: Autism, Happiness and Wellbeing* (pp. 38–47). Birmingham: BILD.

McGonigle-Chalmers, M., Alderson-Day, B., Fleming, J. and Monsen, K. (2013) Profound expressive language impairment in low functioning children with autism: An investigation of syntactic awareness using a computerised learning task. *Journal of Autism and Developmental Disorders* 43(9): 2062–2081.

Mercer, L., Creighton, S., Holden, J.J.A. and Lewis, M.E. (2006) Parental perspectives on the causes of an autism spectrum disorder in their children. *Journal of Genetic Counseling* 15(1): 41–50.

Meyer, J.A., Mundy, P.C., Van Hecke, A.V. and Durocher, J.S. (2006) Social attribution processes and comorbid psychiatric symptoms in children with Asperger syndrome. *Autism* 10(4): 383–402.

Miller, M., Bales, K.L., Taylor, S.L., Yoon, J., Hostetler, C.M., Carter, C.S. and Solomon, M. (2013) Oxytocin and vasopressin in children and adolescents with autism spectrum disorders: Sex differences and associations with symptoms. *Autism Research* 6(2): 91–102.

Milner, L.C. and Cho, M.K. (2014) Focusing on cause or cure? Priorities and stakeholder presence in childhood psychiatry research. *AJOB Empirical Bioethics* 5(1): 44–55.

Milton, D.E. (2012) On the ontological status of autism: The 'double empathy problem'. *Disability and Society* 27(6): 883–887.

Morrison, K.E., DeBrabander, K.M., Faso, D.J. and Sasson, N.J. (2019) Variability in first impressions of autistic adults made by neurotypical raters is driven more by characteristics of the rater than by characteristics of autistic adults. *Autism* 23(7): 1817–1829.

Morrison, K.E., DeBrabander, K.M., Jones, D.R., Faso, D.J., Ackerman, R.A. and Sasson, N.J. (2020) Outcomes of real-world social interaction for autistic adults paired with autistic compared to typically developing partners. *Autism* 24(5): 1067–1080.

Murray, D., Lesser, M. and Lawson, W. (2005) Attention, monotropism and the diagnostic criteria for autism. *Autism* 9(2), 139–156.

Ne'eman, A. (2010) The future (and the past) of autism advocacy, or why the ASA's magazine, *The Advocate*, wouldn't publish this piece. *Disability Studies Quarterly*, 30. http://dsq-sds.org/article/view/1059/1244.

Nichols, S. and Blakeley-Smith, A. (2009) "I'm not sure we're ready for this…": Working with families toward facilitating healthy sexuality for individuals with autism spectrum disorders. *Social Work in Mental Health* 8(1): 72–91.

Nuwer, R. (2020, June 10) Meet the autistic scientists redefining autism research. *Spectrum*. https://www.spectrumnews.org/features/deep-dive/meet-the-autistic-scientists-redefining-autism-research/.

Offit, P.A. (2008) *Autism's False Prophets*. New York: Columbia University Press.

Ohashi, J.K., Mirenda, P., Marinova-Todd, S., et al. (2012) Comparing early language development in monolingual-and bilingual-exposed young children with autism spectrum disorders. *Research in Autism Spectrum Disorders* 6(2): 890–897.

Oppenheim, D., Koren-Karie, N., Dolev, S. and Yirmiya, N. (2012) Maternal sensitivity mediates the link between maternal insightfulness/resolution and child–mother attachment: The case of children with autism spectrum disorder. *Attachment and Human Development* 14(6): 567–584.

Pellicano, E., Mandy, W., Bölte, S., Stahmer, A., Lounds Taylor, J. and Mandell, D.S. (2018) A new era for autism research, and for our journal. *Autism* 22(2): 82–83.

Pellicano, E. and Stears, M. (2011) Bridging autism, science and society: Moving toward an ethically informed approach to autism research. *Autism Research* 4(4): 271–282.

Pelton, M.K., Crawford, H., Robertson, A.E., Rodgers, J., Baron-Cohen, S. and Cassidy, S. (2020) Understanding suicide risk in autistic adults: Comparing the interpersonal theory of suicide in autistic and non-autistic samples. *Journal of Autism and Developmental Disorders* 50(10): 3620–3637. https://doi.org/10.1007/s10803-020-04393-8.

Petersen, J.M., Marinova-Todd, S.H. and Mirenda, P. (2012) Brief report: An exploratory study of lexical skills in bilingual children with autism spectrum disorder. *Journal of Autism and Developmental Disorders* 42(7): 1499–1503.

Petry, K. and Maes, B. (2009) Quality of life: People with profound intellectual and multiple disabilities. In J. Pawlyn and S. Carnaby (Eds.), *Profound Intellectual and Multiple Disabilities: Nursing Complex Needs* (pp. 15–36). Chichester, UK: Wiley-Blackwell.

Punshon, C., Skirrow, P. and Murphy, G. (2009) The 'not guilty verdict' psychological reactions to a diagnosis of Asperger syndrome in adulthood. *Autism* 13(3): 265–283.

Raymaker, D.M., Teo, A.R., Steckler, N.A., Lentz, B., Scharer, M., Delos Santos, A., … & Nicolaidis, C. (2020) "Having all of your internal resources exhausted beyond measure and being left with no clean-up crew": Defining autistic burnout. *Autism in Adulthood: Challenges and Management* 2(2): 132–143. https://doi.org/10.1089/aut.2019.0079

Renty, J.O. and Roeyers, H. (2006) Quality of life in high-functioning adults with autism spectrum disorder: The predictive value of disability and support characteristics. *Autism* 10(5): 511–524.

Robertson, S.M. (2010) Neurodiversity, quality of life, and autistic adults: Shifting research and professional focuses onto real-life challenges. *Disability Studies Quarterly* 30(1). https://dsq-sds.org/article/view/1069/1234

Roesch, S.C. and Weiner, B. (2001) A meta-analytic review of coping with illness: Do causal attributions matter? *Journal of Psychosomatic Research* 50(4): 205–219.

Rossetti, Z., Ashby, C., Arndt, K., Chadwick, M. and Kasahara, M. (2008) "I like others to not try to fix me": Agency, independence, and autism. *Intellectual and Developmental Disabilities* 46(5): 364–375.

Ruef, M.B. and Turnbull, A.P. (2002) The perspectives of individuals with cognitive disabilities and/or autism on their lives and their problem behavior. *Research and Practice for Persons with Severe Disabilities* 27(2): 125–140.

Russell, G., Kapp, S.K., Elliott, D., Elphick, C., Gwernan-Jones, R. and Owens, C. (2019) Mapping the autistic advantage from the accounts of adults diagnosed with autism: A qualitative study. *Autism in Adulthood* 1(2): 124–133.

Salmon, N. (2013) 'We just stick together': How disabled teens negotiate stigma to create lasting friendship. *Journal of Intellectual Disability Research* 57(4): 347–358.

Sandbank, M., Bottema-Beutel, K., Crowley, S., Cassidy, M., Dunham, K., Feldman, J.I., … & Woynaroski, T.G. (2020) Project AIM: Autism intervention meta-analysis for studies of young children. *Psychological Bulletin* 146(1): 1–29. https://doi.org/10.1037/bul0000215.

Sarrett, J. (2012) Autistic human rights – A proposal. *Disability Studies Quarterly* 32(4). http://dsq-sds.org/article/view/3247/3186.

Sarrett, J.C. (2011) Trapped children: Popular images of children with autism in the 1960s and 2000s. *Journal of Medical Humanities* 32(2): 141–153.

Sasson, N.J., Faso, D.J., Nugent, J., Lovell, S., Kennedy, D.P. and Grossman, R.B. (2017) Neurotypical peers are less willing to interact with those with autism based on thin slice judgments. *Scientific Reports* 7(1): 1–10.

Savarese, R.J. (2010) Neurodiversity and caregiving: A roundtable with parents and siblings of children with autism. *Disability Studies Quarterly* 30(1). http://dsq-sds.org/article/view/1061/1236.

Schilbach, L., Timmermans, B., Reddy, V., Costall, A., Bente, G., Schlicht, T. and Vogeley, K. (2013) Toward a second-person neuroscience 1. *Behavioral and Brain Sciences* 36(4): 393–414.

Schwarz, P. (2004) Building alliances: Community identity and the role of allies in autistic self-advocacy. In S. Shore (Ed.), *Ask and Tell: Self-Advocacy and Disclosure for People on the Autism Spectrum* (pp. 143–176). Shawnee Mission, KS: Autism Asperger Publishing Co.

Science Media Centre (2020, April 20) Expert reaction to study looking at screen time in infants and autism spectrum disorder-like symptoms. https://www.sciencemediacentre.org/expert-reaction-to-study-looking-at-screen-time-in-infants-and-autism-spectrum-disorder-like-symptoms/.

Shattuck, P.T., Wagner, M., Narendorf, S., Sterzing, P. and Hensley, M. (2011) Post–high school service use among young adults with an autism spectrum disorder. *Archives of Pediatrics & Adolescent Medicine* 165(2): 141–146.

Sheppard, E., Pillai, D., Wong, G.T.L., Ropar, D. and Mitchell, P. (2016) How easy is it to read the minds of people with autism spectrum disorder? *Journal of Autism and Developmental Disorders* 46(4): 1247–1254.

Shtayermman, O. (2007) Peer victimization in adolescents and young adults diagnosed with Asperger's syndrome: A link to depressive symptomatology, anxiety symptomatology and suicidal ideation. *Issues in Comprehensive Pediatric Nursing* 30(3): 87–107.

Silverman, C. and Brosco, J.P. (2007) Understanding autism: Parents and pediatricians in historical perspective. *Archives of Pediatrics and Adolescent Medicine* 161(4): 392–398.

Sinclair, J. (2005) *Autism Network International: The Development of a Community and its Culture*. Autism Network International. https://www.autreat.com/History_of_ANI.html.

Singh, I. (2012) Human development, nature and nurture: Working beyond the divide. *BioSocieties* 7(3): 308–321.

Sotgiu, I., Galati, D., Manzano, M., Gandione, M., Gómez, K., Romero, Y. and Rigardetto, R. (2011) Parental attitudes, attachment styles, social networks, and psychological processes in autism spectrum disorders: A cross-cultural perspective. *The Journal of Genetic Psychology* 172(4): 353–375.

South, M., Dana, J., White, S.E. and Crowley, M.J. (2011) Failure is not an option: Risk-taking is moderated by anxiety and also by cognitive ability in children and adolescents diagnosed with an autism spectrum disorder. *Journal of Autism and Developmental Disorders* 41(1): 55–65.

Sreckovic, M.A., Brunsting, N.C. and Able, H. (2014) Victimization of students with autism spectrum disorder: A review of prevalence and risk factors. *Research in Autism Spectrum Disorders* 8(9): 1155–1172.

Stagg, S.D., Slavny, R., Hand, C., Cardoso, A. and Smith, P. (2014) Does facial expressivity count? How typically developing children respond initially to children with autism. *Autism* 18(6): 704–711.

Stallen, M., De Dreu, C.K., Shalvi, S., Smidts, A. and Sanfey, A. G. (2012) The herding hormone: Oxytocin stimulates in-group conformity. *Psychological Science* 23(11): 1288–1292.

Sterling, L., Dawson, G., Estes, A. and Greenson, J. (2008) Characteristics associated with presence of depressive symptoms in adults with autism spectrum disorders. *Journal of Autism and Developmental Disorders* 38(6): 1011–1018.

Stevenson, J.L., Harp, B. and Gernsbacher, M.A. (2011) Infantilizing autism. *Disability Studies Quarterly* 31(1). http://dsq-sds.org/article/view/1675/1596.

Stone, W.L. and Rosenbaum, J.L. (1988) A comparison of teacher and parent views of autism. *Journal of Autism and Developmental Disorders* 18(3): 403–414.

Valicenti-McDermott, M., Tarshis, N., Schouls, M., et al. (2013) Language differences between monolingual English and bilingual English-Spanish young children with autism spectrum disorders. *Journal of Child Neurology* 28(7): 945–948.

Van der Meer, L., Sutherland, D., O'Reilly, M.F., Lancioni, G.E. and Sigafoos, J. (2012) A further comparison of manual signing, picture exchange, and speech-generating devices as communication modes for children with autism spectrum disorders. *Research in Autism Spectrum Disorders* 6(4): 1247–1257.

Vickerstaff, S., Heriot, S., Wong, M., Lopes, A. and Dossetor, D. (2007) Intellectual ability, self-perceived social competence, and depressive symptomatology in children with high-functioning autistic spectrum disorders. *Journal of Autism and Developmental Disorders* 37(9): 1647–1664.

Weiner, B. (1993) On sin versus sickness: A theory of perceived responsibility and social motivation. *American Psychologist* 48(9): 957–965.

Weiner, B. (1995) *Judgments of Responsibility: A Foundation for a Theory of Social Conduct*. New York: The Guilford Press.

Willingham, E. (2020, April 29) 'Autistic voices should be heard.' Autistic adults join research teams to shift focus of studies. *Science*. https://www.sciencemag.org/news/2020/04/autistic-voices-should-be-heard-autistic-adults-join-research-teams-shift-focus-studies?fbclid=IwAR18W4aHTuB6sReOkZAFg9uyhMx-yHB0-FSqP-3DL6v_dNE7a7nU6qLpTKo.

Winter-Messiers, M.A. (2007) From tarantulas to toilet brushes: Understanding the special interest areas of children and youth with Asperger syndrome. *Remedial and Special Education* 28(3): 140–153.

Yu, B. (2013) Issues in bilingualism and heritage language maintenance: Perspectives of minority-language mothers of children with autism spectrum disorders. *American Journal of Speech-Language Pathology* 22(1): 10–24.

22
CRITICAL APPROACHES TO AUTISM SUPPORT PRACTICE
Engaging situated reflection and research

Joseph Long

Introduction

The field of Critical Autism Studies has important insights to offer professionals and practitioners working in autism support services. The field has problematised dominant conceptions of autism that underpin both autism research and service provision (O'Dell et al., 2016; Woods et al., 2018). In particular, critiques of deficit-based understandings of autism that inform support models (e.g. Kapp et al., 2013; Sinclair, 2012) have significant implications for social care provision. Practices and discourses found within support services can reflect social norms that have historically marginalised autistic people, but engagement with critical theory has the potential to transform the way services operate.

In this chapter, I discuss the ways in which Critical Autism Studies is increasingly influencing providers of supported living services usually defined in the UK as social care. In addition, I argue that situated research within services can provide a useful opportunity for critical reflection upon practice. Such research can both draw from, and contribute to, the field of Critical Autism Studies as well as to autism research more widely. These reflections are drawn from one service-providing organisation, Scottish Autism, where I facilitate a programme of research, and provide insights relevant to the broader service context in the UK and beyond.

Service provision and changing models of support

For many years, autism support services were heavily influenced by clinical paradigms for defining both autism itself and the support that autistic people would receive. The deficit-based view of autism that has prevailed in psychological literature, and classifies autism as a disorder (APA, 2013) was replicated in community-based services. According to this model, autism as an 'impairment' in communication demanded a focus on communication supports and skills, while impairment in social interaction required working on 'social skills' for autistic people to live successfully in their local community. While these approaches identified core difficulties for many autistic people, the implicit role of services was seen as remediating these impairments so that autistic people would fit a normative definition of life in the community, rather than to recognise and validate neurodiversity. Indeed, Wolfensberger's principle of 'normalisation' was employed for many years in the learning disability services in which so many autistic people were supported (Brown and Smith, 2012). While the term itself was jettisoned some decades ago, an implicit orientation towards normative understandings of what constitutes a valued life lingers on in many support models.

A significant achievement of critical autism scholars – and the social activism with which many are allied – has been the departure of some service providers from a pathologised model of autism as a disorder to be remediated, 'treated', or even 'fixed', to one of accepting diversity and difference in thinking styles and supporting autistic people to live a meaningful life on their own terms. The shift is far from universal, however, and the relationship between critical thinking around how autism is defined and perceived on the one hand, and support provision focused on autistic well-being on the other, is crucial in advocating for the development of enabling services.

One of the biggest points of difference between competing models of support provision is the extent to which service providers label and treat autistic 'behaviour' as a focus of their practice. Such a focus remains common in many services, particularly those that utilise Applied Behaviour Analysis (Baer et al., 1968; Lovaas, 1987), and its progeny in the UK, Positive Behaviour Support (Gore et al., 2013). These practice models ultimately focus on remediating behaviour that is deemed 'challenging' and rewarding behaviour that is deemed desirable.

Autistic theorists and activists have been instrumental in provoking a rethink of such approaches. A key proponent of behaviourist approaches, Ole Ivar Lovaas, memorably lauded the results of behavioural intervention in making autistic children 'indistinguishable from their normal friends'(Lovaas, 1987). This quote is frequently cited by critics as an offensive denial of autistic people's unique means of self-expression and, in the case of 'repetitive behaviours', practices that help self-regulation. Indeed, many autistic people feel that they have been harmed by their experiences of this approach (Dawson, 2004; Kupferstein, 2018; McGill and Robinson, 2021). Critical scholars have questioned what behaviours should be seen as 'desirable' and 'undesirable' and by whom (Milton, 2014b). The apparent lack of insight into the lived experience of autistic people undergoing these therapies exemplifies what Damian Milton has termed the 'double empathy problem' (Milton, 2012). The formulation describes the ironic situation in which autistic people are labelled with deficits such as 'lacking empathy' by professionals who themselves show little empathy for autistic experience in devising therapies and interventions. Moreover, the sociological orientation of critical theorists takes account of the wider social milieu in which such approaches become possible, not least the lucrative marketplace for therapies and cures in contemporary capitalist societies (Broderick and Roscigno, 2021; Grinker, 2020).

In the UK, a small but growing number of services have taken heed of these critical accounts, focusing on the experience, feelings, and well-being of supported autistic people, rather than remediating cognitive 'impairments' or autistic behaviour. Often, new approaches have been developed in conversation with critical theory. For example, McDonnell and colleagues at the organisation Studio III have sought to reframe incidents and interactions once classed as 'challenging behaviour' as expressions of stress and distress. The organisation's approach, centred on low-arousal environments and interactions, emphasises the role of practitioners in reducing transactional stress in interactions between themselves and supported people (McDonnell, 2019; McDonnell et al., 2015). In a similar vein, the Synergy programme, developed by Mills and McCreadie seeks to decentre the behaviour of the supported person and encourages practitioners to take responsibility for elements of their own behaviour in promoting calm and empowering interactions (Mills and McCreadie, 2017). The National Autistic Taskforce, led by autistic professionals, researchers, and advocates in the UK, has produced its own set of guidelines for social care practice, accentuating the human rights of supported autistic people as a basis for service provision (National Autistic Taskforce, 2019).

At Scottish Autism, practitioners have brought these approaches into dialogue with processes of organisational learning and participatory research to develop a model of value-based and relational support. Working communities of practice (Wenger, 1998) have come together from across a diverse range of services to review practice models, and to undertake systematic inquiry into questions arising from support practice. The initiatives have engaged with key themes from critical theory and autistic self-advocacy: acceptance of difference rather than deficit or disorder; a focus on well-being; and an ethical commitment to upholding human rights. The initiatives and research projects have also sought the meaningful involvement of supported autistic people (Long and Clarkson, 2017). These processes have provided an opportunity for collective, critical reflection grounded in the day-to-day dynamics of autism services (Long, 2020).

The Ethical Practice Framework developed by Scottish Autism is a result of these processes of critical reflection. The approach proceeds from seven standards that frame autism-specific well-being needs as practice imperatives. To give three examples: rather than simply state that autistic people have difficulties or differences in communication, the practice framework stipulates that 'understanding communication allows us to listen to a person's voice and choice'; rather than repeat the diagnostic label of 'impaired social interaction', the framework stipulates that 'positive interactions nurture meaningful relationships and supportive communities'; recognising that autistic people have sensory processing difficulties, the framework reminds practitioners that 'providing low stress environments creates safe spaces for personal growth'. This shift recognises the specific needs of autistic people and outlines the practice imperatives to promoting well-being: choice and control, positive relationships, low-stress environments.

These kinds of paradigm shifts are possible when spaces are made for critical reflection, and where the voices and experiences of autistic people are part of critical dialogue. This entails nurturing the role of the critical practitioner (Glaister, 2008) and encouraging reflective practice (Long, 2020; Schön, 1983) as well as creating opportunities for supported voices to be heard through involvement in support forums and participatory research (Long and Clarkson, 2017). At Scottish Autism, critical communities of practice have been vital in creating cross-organisation dialogue, harnessing multiple perspectives, and making opportunities to 'stand back' from the day-to-day demands of services to undertake that critical reflection. The resulting changes to support provision have been informed by the body of work recognised as Critical Autism Studies, but they have also entailed broadening the loci for critical thought beyond academic and research institutions.

Situated research and the production of autism knowledge

A crucial role of Critical Autism Studies has been to question how and where autism knowledge is produced. The move to broaden autism research from neuroscience, psychology, and clinical studies to include social sciences and humanities has opened up a space for critical interdisciplinary debate. But this broadening of the field must comprise more than the inclusion of social scientists working within academia if it is to open up possibilities for alternative processes of knowledge production. An inclusive field, in which critical inquiry can be made from multiple perspectives, must include evidence and insights generated from diverse contexts – from lived experience, practice settings, and participatory research.

The establishment of a practice research programme at Scottish Autism provides one example of this diversification. As a resident researcher within the organisation, I have collaborated with supported autistic people and support practitioners to address issues arising from day-to-day support practice through systematic inquiry. We have done so by capturing the experiences of different social actors; examining the dynamics of support contexts; providing forums for reflection and discussion; and tracking and evaluating the changes to practice that result.

While this follows an established model for action research (Altrichter et al., 1993) or 'practitioner research' (Keeping, 2007; Shaw et al., 2014), the approach – in foregrounding lived experience and critical reflection – has more in common with Critical Autism Studies than it does with models of research 'translation', or practice as 'intervention' that dominate autism research and practice. The latter paradigms work on the assumption that knowledge and expertise are generated in one context (research institutions) and applied in another (practice settings).

In contrast, insights from the social sciences that knowledge is often tacitly held (Collins, 1974, 2010) and gained through 'situated learning' in practice settings (Lave and Wenger, 1991) is as true for understanding autism support practice as it is for other kinds of situated knowledge (Long, 2020; Milton, 2014a). Research that makes visible the knowledge and experience of autistic people and support practitioners and takes as its point of departure everyday life and practice might usefully be thought of as situated practice research. I use the term to refer to research in which both questions for inquiry, and the evidence to answer them, are drawn from the day-to-day concerns and experiences of supported autistic people and those around them.

Working with a team of practitioners who are skilled at supporting autistic people with a range of communication and thinking styles has allowed our organisation to take a participatory approach to research, involving supported people in guiding and contributing to research in ways that are meaningful to the individuals in question (Long and Clarkson, 2017). Practice research topics have included voice and involvement in autism services (Long et al., 2017), friendship and social opportunities for supported autistic people (Long et al., 2018), and auditing of sensory needs. In trying to gain a holistic picture of social care services, Scottish Autism's research team has looked to the anthropological heuristic of participant observation as a key to understanding how services facilitate or hinder the well-being of supported people (Long 2020). In undertaking case studies for the projects above, practitioner researchers have sought to understand how practitioner knowledge, organisational systems and processes, and everyday practical considerations impact the experiences of supported people by grounding enquiry in the dynamics and exigencies of life in services. By engaging practitioners who have longstanding relationships with supported people with intellectual disabilities, many of whom do not communicate verbally, or have unique means of expression, such research projects have also been better able to meaningfully include the voices and opinions of those supported people.

Situated practice research of this kind draws more on the methods and theoretical concerns of anthropology and social sciences than on scientific paradigms. The approach has a kinship with other kinds of situated autism research. Participant observation and first-person reflection both generate crucial insights for critical debate. In documenting lived autistic experience, the systematic reflection of autistic people might take the form of auto-ethnography (what Milton (2015) terms 'Aut-Ethnography'), or it may employ creative methods for capturing embodied experience that is otherwise hard to verbalise (e.g. Cain, 2020). Concomitantly, situated practice research can be deployed to better understand the relationships, discourses, and social dynamics found in autism support services from a range of perspectives.

Of course, auto-ethnography and practice research are not entirely of the same order. Where first-person accounts can provide a direct expression of autistic experience, practitioner-facilitated projects may entail some degree of mediation or selection by practitioners or professional researchers in representing the voices of supported autistic people. This runs the risk that practitioner perspectives may occlude the perspectives of supported people and reproduce inequalities (Keeping, 2007; Woods and Waltz, 2019). However, if ethical considerations are taken seriously and such risks mitigated as far as possible, the involvement of practitioner researchers can provide a means to facilitating the involvement of autistic people with learning disabilities or unique communication styles who are often excluded from autism research (Russell et al., 2019). Thus, while these different types of situated research differ in the degree to which they directly communicate autistic experience, they share a commitment to a 'ground up' approach to capturing lived experience and illuminating the everyday social contexts of lives and services.

Scottish Autism's focus on the relational elements of autism support has stemmed directly from the organisation's practice research programme. A participatory research project investigating friendship and social opportunities initially focused on relationships between supported autistic people but revealed the importance of relationships between supported people and practitioners in social care services (Long et al., 2018). This led to further research seeking to better understand those relationships and interactions, which are vital to the well-being of autistic people in supported living services. The team have drawn on the language of social science to better understand the diverse sociality found in autism services, and to foreground social relationships within services over a clinical analysis of 'social skills' or 'social functioning' located in a deficit-based model of autism. Much of this shift is possible because of the in-house research programme and nurturing links with the autism research world, including critical theorists and others committed to participatory research. Consequently, autism services have become a location for critical enquiry rather than simply a place where research insights are translated or applied.

The value of context

A defining characteristic of Critical Autism Studies is the commitment to understanding the contexts in which autism and autistic people operate. At the broadest macro-sociological level, this implies studying institutions of science and medicine; the emergence of diagnostic labels; policymaking; advocacy and activist movements; and markets for autism treatments and supports. Such critical study provides one perspective from which to understand the definitions, discourses a,nd power relations navigated by autistic people. At the micro-level, more ethnographically informed work looks at the way these discourses are replicated or challenged in day-to-day interactions and practices.

In the latter case, studies of the social dynamics of social care services, and the interactions between supported people and practitioners, have much to tell us. Applied autism research is dominated by the logic of clinical 'intervention', in which the practitioner's role is simply to reproduce an intervention method devised in a trial. This model may be helpful in focusing on acute clinical issues, or in difficulties that can be reduced to a single variable, but it tells us little about social care services, which aim at holistic and individualised support for a person's well-being. For a person in supported living services, relationships with the practitioners that support them, day in and day out, are likely to have an enormous impact on well-being – for good or ill (Ryan, 2020). Autism research all too often occludes these relationships, relegating practitioners to exist invisibly somewhere between the (pathologised) cognition of the autistic person and the replicable 'intervention' designed to remediate that thinking. Situated research should always have the concerns and experiences of autistic people at its centre, but it should also place those experiences in context. Overlooking interactions with those people with whom supported individuals have some of their most intense and long-lasting relationships does little to enlighten us as to how meaningful change in services might come about.

Concluding remarks

The emancipatory potential of Critical Autism Studies lies not just in the field's mission to illuminate and critique the contexts of autism knowledge production, but also in broadening sites and spaces for critical engagement and democratising the production of autism knowledge. Contributions to Critical Autism Studies have provided service providers with grounds to carefully rethink the paradigms that inform support practice. Moving from models of remediating autistic 'deficits' to models based on acceptance of diversity and the promotion of well-being on autistic people's own terms can best be achieved when critical theory and practice development work in dialogue with one another. This can be better achieved when we move from unidirectional paradigms of research translation and application to enable multiple sites and contexts for knowledge generation. This pluralistic vision of autism research includes various kinds of situated research, including practice research that is based upon a reflexive engagement with service contexts. Critical inquiry that is based upon situated research and reflection offers a better understanding of service contexts and, through that understanding, the possibility of transforming services into spaces in which autistic people can flourish.

Acknowledgements

This chapter documents the insights, critical discussions, and hard work of many supported autistic people, practitioners, and service leaders. As such, it represents a collective endeavour and I wish to acknowledge the contributions of so many people in the Scottish Autism community to this work.

References

Altrichter H, Posch P and Somekh B (1993) *Teachers Investigate Their Work: An Introduction to the Methods of Action Research*. Routledge.
Association AP (2013) *Diagnostic and Statistical Manual of Mental Disorders (DSM-5®)*. American Psychiatric Publishing.
Baer DM, Wolf MM and Risley TR (1968) Some current dimensions of applied behavior analysis. *Journal of Applied Behavior Analysis* 1(1): 91–97. https://doi.org/10.1901/jaba.1968.1-91.
Broderick AA and Roscigno R (2021) Autism, Inc.: The autism industrial complex. *Journal of Disability Studies in Education* 1: 1–25. https://doi.org/10.1163/25888803-bja10008.
Brown H and Smith H (2012) *Normalisation: A Reader*. Routledge.
Cain P (2020) 'How do I know how I think, until I see what I say?': The shape of embodied thinking, neurodiversity, first-person methodology. *Idea Journal* 17(02): 32–57. https://doi.org/10.37113/ij.v17i02.400.
Collins H (2010) *Tacit and Explicit Knowledge*. University of Chicago Press.
Collins HM (1974) The TEA set: Tacit knowledge and scientific networks. *Science Studies* 4 (2): 165–185.
Dawson M (2004) *The Misbehaviour of Behaviourists: Ethical Challenges to the Autism-ABA Industry*. Available at: http://www.sentex.net/~nexus23/naa_aba.html (accessed 8 June 2016).
Glaister A (2008) Introducing critical practice. In *The Critical Practitioner in Social Work and Health Care*, eds. Sandy Fraser and Sarah Matthews. Sage Publications, 8–26.
Gore NJ, McGill P, Toogood S, et al. (2013) Definition and scope for positive behavioural support. *International Journal of Positive Behavioural Support* 3(2): 14–23.
Grinker RR (2020) Autism, "stigma," disability: A shifting historical terrain. *Current Anthropology* 61(S21): S55–S67.
Kapp SK, Gillespie-Lynch K, Sherman LE, et al. (2013) Deficit, difference, or both? Autism and neurodiversity. *Developmental Psychology* 49(1): 59. https://doi.org/10.1037/a0028353.
Keeping C (2007) Practitioner research. In *The Critical Practitioner in Social Work and Health Care*, eds. Sandy Fraser and Sarah Matthews. SAGE, 132.

Kupferstein H (2018) Evidence of increased PTSD symptoms in autistics exposed to applied behavior analysis. *Advances in Autism* 4(1): 19–29. https://doi.org/10.1108/AIA-08-2017-0016.

Lave J and Wenger E (1991) *Situated Learning: Legitimate Peripheral Participation*. Cambridge University Press.

Long J, Brown J, Daly S, et al. (2018) Friendship and sociality in autism services. *Good Autism Practice (GAP)* 19(1): 22–31.

Long J and Clarkson A (2017) Towards meaningful participation in research and support practice: Effecting change in autism services. In *Autism and Intellectual Disability in Adults*, eds. Damian Milton and Nicola Martin. Pavillion, 41–45.

Long J, Panese J, Ferguson J, Hamill MA and Miller J (2017) Enabling voice and participation in autism services: Using practitioner research to develop inclusive practice. *Good Autism Practice (GAP)* 18(2): 6–14.

Long JJ (2020) Reflective practitioners and participant observers in autism services: Managing knowledge in UK social care. *Anthropology in Action* 27(1): 35–45. https://doi.org/10.3167/aia.2020.270104.

Lovaas OI (1987) Behavioral treatment and normal educational and intellectual functioning in young autistic children. *Journal of Consulting and Clinical Psychology* 55(1): 3.

McDonnell A (2019) *The Reflective Journey*. Studio III.

McDonnell A, McCreadie M, Mills R, et al. (2015) The role of physiological arousal in the management of challenging behaviours in individuals with autistic spectrum disorders. *Research in Developmental Disabilities* 36: 311–322. https://doi.org/10.1016/j.ridd.2014.09.012.

McGill O and Robinson A (2021) "Recalling hidden harms": Autistic experiences of childhood applied behavioural analysis (ABA). *Advances in Autism* 7(4): 269–282. https://doi.org/10.1108/AIA-04-2020-0025.

Mills R and McCreadie M (2017) Knowing me - Knowing me: Changing the story around stigma and 'behaviours of concern'; promoting self awareness, self control, and a positive narrative. In *Autism and Intellectual Disability in Adults*, Volume 2, eds. Damian Milton and Nicola Martin. Pavillion, 47–50.

Milton D (2015) *Aut-ethnography: Working from the Inside Out*. Blog post available at: https://theautismanthropologist.wordpress.com/2015/01/19/aut-ethnography-working-from-the-inside-out/ (accessed 19 February 2021)

Milton DE (2012) On the ontological status of autism: The 'double empathy problem'. *Disability & Society* 27(6): 883–887. https://doi.org/10.1080/09687599.2012.710008.

Milton DE (2014a) Autistic expertise: A critical reflection on the production of knowledge in autism studies. *Autism* 18(7): 794–802. https://doi.org/10.1177/1362361314525281

Milton DE (2014b) So what exactly are autism interventions intervening with? *Good Autism Practice (GAP)* 15(2): 6–14.

National Autistic Taskforce (2019) *An Independent Guide to Quality Care for Autistic People*. National Autistic Taskforce. Available at: https://nationalautistictaskforce.org.uk/an-independent-guide-to-quality-care-for-autistic-people/ (accessed 19 February 2021).

O'Dell L, Bertilsdotter Rosqvist H, Ortega F, et al. (2016) Critical autism studies: Exploring epistemic dialogues and intersections, challenging dominant understandings of autism. *Disability & Society* 31(2): 166–179. https://doi.org/10.1080/09687599.2016.1164026.

Russell G, Mandy W, Elliott D, et al. (2019) Selection bias on intellectual ability in autism research: A cross-sectional review and meta-analysis. *Molecular Autism* 10(1): 9. https://doi.org/10.1186/s13229-019-0260-x.

Ryan S (2020) *Love, Learning Disabilities and Pockets of Brilliance: How Practitioners Can Make a Difference to the Lives of Children, Families and Adults*. Jessica Kingsley Publishers.

Schön DA (1983) *The Reflective Practitioner: How Professionals Think in Action*. Basic Books.

Shaw IF, Lunt N and Mitchell F (2014) *Practitioner Research in Social Care: A Review and Recommendations*. NIHR School for Social Care Research.

Sinclair J (2012 [1993]) Don't mourn for us. *Autonomy, the Critical Journal of Interdisciplinary Autism Studies* 1(1). Available at: http://larry-arnold.net/Autonomy/index.php/autonomy/article/view/AR1 (accessed 20 August 2019)

Wenger E (1998) *Communities of Practice: Learning, Meaning, and Identity*. Cambridge University Press.

Woods R, Milton D, Arnold L, et al. (2018) Redefining critical autism studies: A more inclusive interpretation. *Disability & Society* 33(6): 974–979. https://doi.org/10.1080/09687599.2018.1454380.

Woods R and Waltz M (2019) The strength of autistic expertise and its implications for autism knowledge production: A response to Damian Milton. *Autonomy, the Critical Journal of Interdisciplinary Autism Studies* 1(6). Available at: http://www.larry-arnold.net/Autonomy/index.php/autonomy/article/view/CO2 (accessed 20 August 2019).

23
FROM DISEMPOWERMENT TO WELL-BEING AND FLOW
Enabling autistic communication in schools

Rebecca Wood

Introduction

It is very difficult to escape the notion that autism and communication difficulties are inextricably interconnected. When mighty diagnostic manuals such as the *DSM-5* (American Psychological Association [APA] 2013) pronounce on the multiple "deficits" in the communication of autistic people, such as an "abnormal social approach and failure of normal back-and-forth conversation", or "a total lack of facial expressions and nonverbal communication",[1] it is hardly surprising that such ideas are deeply entrenched in medical, professional, media and family circles. Even the ICD-11 (2016), in which it is asserted that autistic people "exhibit a full range of intellectual functioning and language abilities", their communicative aptitudes are reduced to the notion of "functional language" used for "instrumental purposes".[2]

In my view, "functionality", not only in relation to autistic communication but also more broadly in the autism context, is a deeply problematic concept, suggesting that it is even possible to define what is functional for anyone other than ourselves. We know already that despite research to the contrary (Sterponi and Shankey 2014; Gernsbacher, Morson and Grace 2016), echolalia (a tendency to repeat words and phrases), for example, is generally considered to be of little functional value and so can be targeted through "treatments" via speech and language interventions (Neely et al. 2016). And while it is difficult to define "functionality", I think we can agree that this concept is not usually considered to incorporate a tendency to say the same words again and again for the sheer, mellifluous pleasure of it, as some autistic people explain, or having the vocabulary to describe all aspects of a particular interest, but not be able to ask for a cup of tea. Moreover, within this framing, there is little cognisance of the fact that the ways autistic people might "function" can vary hugely according to environmental factors, such as noise levels, accommodations and general understanding.

So even if we do accept, as I think we must, that a number of autistic people may well experience difficulties in language and communication, within such formulations we are already nudging towards the profoundly troubling issues which too often underpin autism and communication: stigmatisation, power relationships and a concomitant lack of agency. The ways in which these modalities can operate in school settings, drawn from my own research evidence, will be explored in this chapter.

DOI: 10.4324/9781003056577-27

Autism and communication

The *DSM-5* (APA 2013) and the ICD-11 (2016) outline posited impairments in the social aspects of communication, sometimes referred to as "social (pragmatic) communication disorder" (Norbury 2014), but this has not prevented other manifestations of language and interaction being subject to scrutiny. Autistic people have been described as manifesting an "odd" tone of voice (Tager-Flusberg, Paul and Lord 2005), "bizarre" responses to questions (Loveland et al. 1990), an impaired use of pronouns (Lee, Hobson and Chiat 1994), and flawed narrative delivery and style (Tager-Flusberg, Paul and Lord 2005). Similarly, having too many pauses in conversation, exhibiting poor turn-taking (Ochi et al. 2019) and manifesting "peculiarities" of "gaze" (Noris et al. 2012), are all phenomena which can be considered problematic in relation to autistic communication, as is "incoherent discourse, unresponsiveness to questions, aberrant prosody, and lack of drive to communicate" (Rapin and Dunn 2003, 166). Here, the conceptual hinterland to autistic communication is that it is always, somehow *wrong*.

Allied with these negative portrayals of autistic expression is the fact that descriptions of autism often rely on reductive binaries and classifications situated within an unhelpful mathematical narrative, with references to "scales" and "spectrums", for example. Terms such as "high" and "low functioning", "mildly" and "severely" autistic, and of course, "verbal" and "nonverbal", are deeply embedded within professional and research discourses. No one is ever placed in the middle, considered "averagely functioning", "fairly autistic" or deemed to communicate "a reasonable amount". In these ways, autistic communication is graded and commodified, with autistic people positioned as the passive receptors of interventions from unimpaired, fluent others, whose own communicative expertise is insufficiently scrutinised.

Autistic people can also be described as "minimally verbal", generally considered to apply to those who have fewer than 30 "functional" (that word again!) words or other forms of expression (Brignell et al. 2018). There tends to be an unthinking assumption that a lack of spoken language equates to learning disabilities, even though there are many examples to contradict this view. One only has to think of the comedian Lost Voice Guy (Lee Ridley), who communicates via voice output software or, within the autism context, DJ Savarese, a nonspeaking autistic man who, as well as graduating with a double major in Anthropology and Creative Writing, is also a poet, teacher and an activist. Regardless, the longer-term outcomes of autistic people with limited speech are especially poor (Howlin, Mawhood and Rutter 2000), although the question remains as to whether this is de facto because of having few spoken words, or due to a lack of support, understanding and opportunities, or indeed both.

Communication interventions

There is a considerable amount of research into communication interventions for autistic children and they are often the "go-to" approach in schools (Parsons et al. 2011) for children with SEND (special educational needs and disabilities) in general. For example, Roulstone et al. (2012) identified 158 separate interventions for children with speech and language communication difficulties. This report was one of a range of studies funded by the Department for Children, Schools and Families following the Bercow Review (2008) and included, for example, a focus on the profiles of need of autistic children and those with language impairments in mainstream schools by Dockrell et al. (2012). When this was followed up ten years later (I CAN and RCSLT 2018), it was asserted that significant numbers of children do not receive the support they need for their language and communication development, and that many do not even have their difficulties diagnosed. So, the pressure is on schools to ensure that children with speech and language problems do not slip through the net.

For autistic children, support can be in the form of specific techniques such as PECS (Picture Exchange Communication System) or, less frequently, Makaton (a simplified form of British Sign Language), as well as broader intervention approaches including social stories, "now and next" boards and the ubiquitous visual timetable. There is a strong emphasis on pictures and the visible manifestations of support – teaching assistants who are not comfortable with the laminator and applying copious quantities of Velcro, need not apply – based on the assumption that all autistic children are "visual learners" and additionally giving the outward impression that *something* is being done. However, evaluating the impact of communication interventions, especially in school settings, is notoriously difficult, given the vast range of variables that can operate, not least the natural process of maturing that children typically undergo, regardless of adult input. Indeed, Brignell et al. (2018, 25), in conducting a systematic review of interventions for minimally verbal children, concluded that "clinicians, families and consumers should be aware of the lack of evidence for the effectiveness of communication interventions for minimally verbal children with ASD".

Speech difficulties

While it was beyond the scope of my study (as well as my own expertise) to conduct a specialist assessment of the speech and language competencies of the ten autistic child participants in my own study, based in five primary schools in England, it was evident that they all, to a greater or lesser extent, experienced problems with speech. According to their parents, some had been slow to develop spoken language compared with their peers, while the youngest two, both aged four, were described as "nonverbal" (although, as we will see, this was not in fact the case). A boy I have called Alex in previous publications (Wood 2019; 2020), aged five, was a lively and engaging talker, who enjoyed conversation, but he nevertheless struggled with pronunciation, language recall and narrative order. He stated, for example, that "an ambulance got in and he went to hospital" when recounting an anecdote about a man who had an accident near where he lived. Similarly, Rashan, aged nine, found it difficult to relate anecdotes and pronounce words, and Lucy, aged seven, sometimes struggled to answer my questions during our interviews.[3]

However, the situation was a little more complex than this. For example, although it is true that neither of the two youngest children used spoken language very often, I certainly heard them speak on several occasions. Piotr tended to produce words when he objected very strongly to what he was being asked to do, pronouncing "no, no, no!" or asserting "want to go out!" when he was truly fed up. Bobby was a little different, as he would say words when he was absorbed in an activity, such as the names and the sounds of animals, a subject of great interest to him. This led his well-intentioned teaching assistant to laminate each page of his favourite pop-up book, *Dear Zoo* by Rod Campbell, in the hope that this could be used as a teaching aid. It was a testament to Bobby's good nature that when he was asked to name the animal hidden underneath each flap, he did not manifest any evident frustration as he scratched fruitlessly at the hermetically sealed surface of the page in an attempt to reveal the creature beneath.

"Choosing"

The example with Bobby indicates the complexities of the issues surrounding communication support in schools and what can go wrong when good intentions are not allied with engagement, understanding and, from the point of view of school staff, appropriate guidance. In my study, sometimes the true purpose of communication support seemed to get lost in the focus on the Velcroed and laminated paraphernalia of speech interventions, as well as a tendency to impose these from on high (quite literally, given some of my participants were small).

Piotr had a "choosing board" that had been set up by a speech and language therapist, and the idea was that by selecting cards for different activities, he could express what he wanted to do, conform better with the school routine, and integrate more into the class. Unfortunately, Piotr was not always allowed to choose what he wanted to do and was sometimes made to put down the card he had picked (usually the "outside" picture, because that was a way of avoiding the activity the TA (Teaching Assistant) had in mind) and replace it instead with the card that represented the adult-led task. This led to some illogical and concerning scenarios whereby the adult would be effectively forcing Piotr to "choose" something he really didn't want to do. We have to question what possible benefit this could have brought to Piotr, at the very least from the point of view of his communication. Indeed, if anything, Piotr was being taught that communicating in the way he was asked was somehow to his detriment, and that he stood to gain more from not expressing his wishes than actually doing so.

Even gentler examples showed Piotr's actual communication being ignored if it did not fit with adults' intentions. He had been handed a book by the teacher as she knew this was one of his favourites, and this led to a nice activity with his TA when they looked through the book together. However, after about 15 minutes, Piotr did not want to look at the book any longer, upon which I observed the following:

> Piotr draws the TA's hand to book, says to her "finished", which she doesn't recognise. At the end, he closes the book and puts her hand on it – he is trying to communicate that he has had enough. She seems to recognise this, but carries on anyway.

What is noticeable here is that even though Piotr is communicating his wishes and intentions very clearly and appropriately, both verbally and nonverbally, he is neither being heard nor his requests are respected.

These scenarios indicate how the labels that can be applied to categorise autistic people, including "nonverbal", can be detrimental, because it means that their unanticipated speech simply disappears into the mire of preset expectations. This example also reveals that the response to some children's communication can be highly selective, and dictated by the adult's motivations and intentions, rather than the child's aspirations and needs.

It was also evident that school staff felt under some pressure in relation to supporting the communication of autistic children, meaning that the bigger picture of the true purpose of this support can be lost. There was an occasion when Bobby was crouched on the floor, deeply absorbed in a large book about animals, turning contently to the different pages that interested him. No doubt with the best of intentions, his TA took the opportunity to try to get Bobby to point to different animals and name them. However, the result was simply that Bobby became frustrated that his interest in the book was now being directed by an adult and there was certainly no communicative benefit that I could observe.

Moreover, these scenarios did not just occur with the children who were deemed to be "nonverbal". Rashan was asked to copy a section from his exercise book onto a leaflet he was designing. His TA had copied the sentences from his book onto a whiteboard (somewhat pointlessly, but that is a whole other discussion), and asked him to write those onto his leaflet. However, in doing so, she had omitted a sentence from Rashan's book for no other reason, it seemed to me, than it would not fit onto the white board. Rashan was frustrated by this and stated multiple times that he wanted this sentence to feature in his leaflet. Indeed, this whole copying exercise was dominated by a sense of irritation and boredom on his part:

> But I'm hungry. It will take too long. It's killing me. It's annoying. It's annoying me.

This was not least because once Rashan had, after much delay and distraction, copied the sentences from the white board onto the leaflet, the TA then asked him to copy the same sentences *back into* his exercise book. In fact, Rashan even turned to me, as I was filming this activity, and pulled an "argh" face, to which his TA responded with irritation. Consequently, on multiple levels, Rashan's communication was ignored and devalued in this situation, and by extension, his agency and independence were denied.

Indeed, there were several occasions when the children in my study expressed their thoughts and intentions very clearly, only to be either ignored or made to assert something different to correspond with the adult agenda. In these instances, the communication interventions were not so much for the benefit of the child, but to support the adults' intentions. Moreover, when I was interviewing Rashan later during break time, in the presence of his TA, he started telling me that he was being bullied, but his TA interrupted him and tried to change the subject, thus potentially preventing him from sharing an important piece of information relating to his well-being.[4] Within school settings, where the emphasis is usually on conformity and uniformity – a circumstance the autistic child is often considered to disrupt – support for communication sometimes lapsed – no doubt unintentionally – into control of communication.

Agency

What matters here is not so much the ineffective and, at times, detrimental nature of the communication support for the autistic children in my study, but to understand the factors that enabled them to take place. Interestingly, interviews with TAs and teachers would sometimes take on a confessional tone when they would express sadness and frustration that the abilities of the autistic children were not being recognised and that their time in school was not as happy as it could have been. There were also some instructive and heart-warming examples of particularly effective communication support – sometimes from the same members of staff – suggesting that the issue was not individual failings, but structural, organisational and attitudinal circumstances which prevented staff from listening to their own better instincts.

Michael, aged eight, had a very good relationship with his TA, who had a wonderful way of engaging with him, and so the TA conducted his interview, using the questions I had prepared. Before we started, the TA helped Michael to go through the assent form, guiding him with great sensitivity, which can be seen in this extract:

TA: Do you know what an interview is?
Michael: Yes. An interview? When someone records videos.
TA: An interview is when you ask someone some questions and you want to find out what they think.
Michael: Yeah.
TA: And Rebecca would like to interview you and me.
Michael: Yeah.
TA: But one of the things you have to do when you do an interview, you have to agree to be recorded. Now I've already agreed, and your mum's agreed, but we'd like you to agree as well. So do you want to read this, because this tells you all you need to know about what you're agreeing to.
Michael: OK.

(The TA then helps Michael to go through the assent form).
TA: Very good. And are you sure you're happy with all of this?
Michael: Yeah.
TA: Good boy.

In this example, we can see how the TA is reassuring and supporting Michael and presenting him with choices and control. I noticed this on numerous occasions, as the TA would negotiate gently with Michael to get him to do some curriculum work, offering him different options of activities interspersed with copious amounts of time on the computer watching CBeebies, Michael's favourite activity. Moreover, when our interview took an unexpected turn – Michael said that he was afraid of being expelled from school – rather than trying to deflect this or change the subject, the TA stopped asking questions to give him a hug and provide some reassurance.[5]

Similarly, in another school, after I had reached the end of an interview with Valentin, aged eight, his TA offered him three ways he could be rewarded for his efforts: a personal, tangible reward (e.g. extra golden time), a personal, token reward (points individual children are awarded in class which are then totted up at the end of the week) or a group personal award (points added towards the whole class total, which are then compared with other classes in school). He went for the third option, as it was important to Valentin to be perceived as someone who brought value to his whole class. As in the example with Michael, Valentin is being given genuine options and his choices are being respected. Importantly though, the adult is still in charge, and following the child's lead results in more, not less compliance and co-operation in these examples.

The communicative power of interests

These demonstrations of positive support for communication point us in the direction of what should surely be the main aim of all communication interventions, to "create opportunities, relationships and environments that make individuals want to communicate" and to support individuals "to understand and express their needs in relation to their health and wellbeing" (Royal College of Speech and Language Therapists 2013, 5). Fortunately, in my own study, the autistic children provided some strong indications of what aided their communication and wellbeing. Indeed, it was when staff worked with their intentions and dispositions, not against them, that effective communication took place.

The most striking example of this was with Lucy. During our interviews, she was quite hesitant and unsure, being unable to answer quite a few of my questions about how she liked to work, her attitude towards tests (in all honesty, the questions were probably a bit dull), etc. Lucy was also subdued in some curriculum activities when she struggled to understand their purpose, not least because they were not always communicated especially clearly to her; for example, blocks for doing fractions were used for a number game, described by her TA as a "puzzle numbers". However, Lucy's great interest was the natural world, and she was completely transformed during a reading activity when she was looking at a book about snakes. Lucy was extremely enthusiastic, exclaiming "wow" a few times, and appeared much more confident than she had on previous occasions. She also exhibited a variety of aptitudes such as reading aloud, finding synonyms and asking questions e.g. "Does the milk snake drink milk?" Lucy paid attention to detail, commented spontaneously and on request on the text ("The sunbeam snake is so shiny!"), related the book to her own experiences watching films about snakes at home and carried out independent, silent reading. In so doing, she was demonstrating a range of high-level reading skills identified by the Department for Education (2015) as being linked to positive longer-term educational, health and employment outcomes.

Another striking example was Marcus, aged nine, who also found my interview questions quite difficult to answer, a circumstance that frustrated him as he struggled to find the words to express himself. However, his great interest in life was computers, and he was able to develop this in Coding Club, his favourite school activity, telling me it was "epic" and describing in some detail the latest game he had designed, Pixel Rush, which was also "epic" and "cool". In fact, unlike during other parts of our interviews, when talking about Coding Club, Marcus was speaking at greater length, was less inclined to trip over his words, volunteered information, and responded to open questions without difficulty.

Crucially, in these scenarios, when the autistic children were being loud and clear about what facilitated their communication, the staff helping them seemed to benefit too, becoming more relaxed, and by extension, more effective in their support. For example, when Lucy was looking at the book about snakes, I made the following observation:

> The TA is interacting with her very well in this activity too – guiding her well with questions, getting her to find out information for herself, congratulating her etc. At one point the TA explains something and Lucy says (confidently) – "I was going to say that!" The TA and I laugh and a flicker of a smile from Lucy.

Similarly, the TAs of Bobby and Piotr both showed skilled and effective support on the occasions when they followed their lead, and encouraged and guided them, rather than imposing their own intentions. In an early handwriting activity that Piotr had chosen, his TA let Piotr guide her hand to make swirling shapes with felt-tipped pens on a white board, to which she responded with warmth, stating "beautiful" and "good boy". Importantly, Piotr was being much more compliant on this occasion, and carried out the TA's instructions when she asked him to select another pen or wipe the board clean. By enabling Piotr to genuinely "choose", he was in fact much more likely to carry out adult requests.

Silent resistance

It is important too that we do not present children with communication difficulties as passive victims of adult control, even if their wishes and intentions could be frustrated and ignored on occasions. For example, Bobby was given a colouring-in sheet that had outlines of lots of animals on it, and his TA asked him to colour in the horse, which was the largest animal, in the centre of the sheet. Bobby sat down with his felt-tipped pens and set to colouring in the sheep, the pigs, the hens etc., while his TA asked repeatedly "colour in the horse Bobby!", a request he silently ignored. In the end, Bobby had coloured in all the animals on the sheet, except the horse, an impressive act of resistance for this little four-year-old boy. In fact, as I spent time observing Bobby, he most enjoyed "free flow" activities, when the children were able to move indoors and outdoors at will and choose their own activities. On these occasions, Bobby seemed relaxed, purposeful, and content, and required little, if any, adult support. And apart from quietly saying the names of animals to himself or imitating their sounds, he was usually silent in these circumstances.

Similarly, Rashan, following the leaflet activity, was fatigued by the time it came to our interview, and so his speech was quite fractured and not always coherent. Moreover, as his great interest was superheroes, he would end up talking about this topic in some detail, no matter what I asked him. I tried negotiating with Rashan, such as by suggesting that if he answered some of my questions, he could then talk about what he wanted. Rashan agreed enthusiastically to this, but he continued to talk about superheroes, regardless. Nevertheless, we got through my questions, whereupon it was Rashan's turn to talk about his own interests. However, instead of talking, Rashan asked me to video him carrying out some action hero moves of his own invention, all of which he had named. Consequently, not only had Rashan chosen to express something important about himself in a nonverbal way, but he was demonstrating his inventiveness and ability to define his own self-image, strengths and resistance to bullying. What was striking about Rashan too was that he spoke two languages (as a different language was spoken in the home) and that he was very skilled in his use of gesture, and so he had developed multimodal forms of communication, despite some speech and language difficulties.

Discussion

As we have seen, the communication and interaction of autistic children in schools is complex and multifaceted, suggesting a need for thought and sensitivity rather than generic interventions predicated on a presumption of autistic communicative dysfunction. I am certainly not arguing that autistic children in our schools do not require support with their speech and interaction skills, but my research suggests that we must question the impact of widespread diagnostic and scientific associations of autism with communication impairments. As such formulations filter down to professional circles and school settings, this perspective can result in a failure to recognise and understand the communication of autistic children and young people, the imposition of ill-thought-out interventions and a denial of agency for those pupils. Indeed, laudable intentions can founder within typical presumptions of expert adult to impaired child dynamics, leading to a lack of reflexivity in the part of the supporting adult. Add to this the typical sorts of pressures school educators are under in terms of time and staffing (National Education Union 2018), and the consequences can be the opposite of what everyone surely intends.

To experience problems in speech is to be unquestioningly considered "disabled, disordered or dysfunctional" (Lawson 2008, 74), and so perceived as intellectually deficient, even minacious, as well as devoid of reason, civility and plausibility. By extension, the emphasis on support for communication can shift unavoidably towards control of what the child communicates and, inevitably, how the child acts. This denial of agency is surely the antithesis of what communication support should provide (National Autistic Taskforce 2019).

I also found that such unchallenged associations can mean that the more evident verbal and nonverbal communication of the autistic children is ignored. Indeed, it is these "abnormality discourses" (Thibault 2014, 80) which can impede more effective forms of engagement, particularly if the child is not on message with what the adult has in mind. Furthermore, misleading, and dysfunctional labels – such as "nonverbal" – can mean that communication is unanticipated, and so neither seen nor heard. This "confirmation bias" (Jonas et al. 2001), whereby conflicting evidence is ignored once a decision has been fixed, underscores how damaging such labels can be (Runswick-Cole and Hodge 2009).

Furthermore, the certainty of these "deficit-oriented discourses" (Liasidou 2012, 99) can be contrasted with the disbelief that results from indications of cogency, particularly when unanticipated (Erevelles 2002). The flames of such formulations are fanned by the insidious presence of behaviourist models which increasingly underpin governmental school policy documents (Department for Education 2016), whereby the non-conforming child is perceived as a dangerous spark who could easily ignite an uncontrolled conflagration. Several school staff told me that the autistic children failed to follow the school routine and instead seemed fixed on their own agenda, without recognising that they were describing a clash of natural dispositions and itineraries rather than behavioural difficulties on the part of the child (Milton 2012).

When school staff have the confidence, support and resources to step away from such unhelpful positionings, a light is shone on the approaches needed to provide help and facilitate child independence and identity. It was noticeable in my study that when staff members created enabling circumstances for the communication of the children, they were not also expected to multitask by supporting additional members of the class, or to provide support in noisy and cluttered environments. Many of the examples of positive support took place in quiet places, with staff more broadly facilitated by pedagogical approaches, such as "free flow" time or (genuine) choosing activities, thus providing adult and child with the space within which to engage authentically. Such circumstances are more likely to permit "interactional participation rather than remediation of individual deficit" (Muskett 2016, 314), whereby communication becomes a shared act, rather than an imposed discipline and a means of control.

The autistic children in my study also provided important clues to their own communicative motivations and showed, in some cases, striking improvements in engagement and speech when focused on their interests (Wood 2019). Counter-intuitively, the children in these circumstances became more, not less compliant, providing possibilities for greater self-efficacy on the part of staff, too. In addition, the children indicated that nonverbal or silent communication can – and should be – a positive choice (Autistic Self-Advocacy Network 2012) and not thought of as "a lack" or "the void in which speech occurs" (Acheson 2008, 552). Moreover, their silent resistance showed an ability to assert and define themselves beyond the limitations of the labels imposed on them, or the restrictions unwittingly placed on their actions and expressions. This also suggests that we need to think more broadly about the concept of "functionality", and to consider specifically what role language plays for the individual, whether it is for everyday needs and wants, the aesthetics of sonority, or to process meaning. It is only by rethinking our approach to communication support in school that autistic children can be provided with the circumstances, tools and agency they need and deserve.

Acknowledgements

With thanks to my research participants, particularly the children who briefly shared their world.

Notes

1. Source: https://www.cdc.gov/ncbddd/autism/hcp-dsm.html (accessed 29 September 2020.
2. Source: https://icd.who.int/browse11/l-m/en#/http://id.who.int/icd/entity/437815624 (accessed 29 September 2020).
3. All children's names in this chapter have been changed.
4. Rashan was in fact being bullied, which I reported to the school SENCo (Special Educational Needs Co-ordinator).
5. I also reported Michael's anxiety to the school SENCo.

References

Acheson, K. (2008) 'Silence as Gesture: Rethinking the Nature of Communicative Silences.' *Communication Theory* 18(4): 535–555. https://doi.org/10.1111/j.1468-2885.2008.00333.x

Autistic Self Advocacy Network (2012) *Loud Hands: Autistic People, Speaking*. Washington: The Autistic Press.

Brignell, A., Chenausky, K.V., Song, H., Zhu, J., Suo, C. and Morgan, A.T. (2018) 'Communication Interventions for Autism Spectrum Disorder in Minimally Verbal Children: Review.' *Cochrane Database of Systematic Reviews 2018*(11): CD012324. https://www.cochrane.org/CD012324/BEHAV_are-communication-interventions-effective-minimally-verbal-children-autism-spectrum-disorder

Department for Children, Schools and Families (2008) *The Bercow Report: A Review of Services for Children and Young People (0 – 19) with Speech, Language and Communication Needs*. DCSF-OO632-2008. Nottingham: DCSF Publications. https://webarchive.nationalarchives.gov.uk/20130321005340/https://www.education.gov.uk/publications/standard/publicationdetail/page1/DCSF-00632-2008

Department for Education (2016) 'Behaviour and Discipline in Schools: Advice for Headteachers and School Staff.' https://www.gov.uk/government/publications/behaviour-and-discipline-in-schools

Dockrell, J., Ricketts, J., Palikara, O., Charman, T. and Lindsay, G. (2012) 'Profiles of Need and Provision for Children with Language Impairments and Autism Spectrum Disorders in Mainstream Schools: A Prospective Study.' *Research Report DFE-RR247-BCRP9*. London: Department for Education. https://assets.publishing.service.gov.uk/government/uploads/system/uploads/attachment_data/file/219635/DFE-RR247-BCRP9.pdf

Erevelles, N. (2002) 'Voices of Silence: Foucault, Disability and the Question of Self-Determination.' *Studies in Philosophy and Education* 21(1): 17–35. https://doi.org/10.1023/A:1014473121819

Gernsbacher, M.A., Morson, E.M. and Grace, E.J. (2016) 'Language and Speech in Autism.' *Annual Review of Linguistics* 2: 413–425. https://doi.org/10.1146/annurev-linguistics-030514-124824

Howlin, P., Mawhood, L. and Rutter, M. (2000) 'Autism and Developmental Receptive Language Disorder - A Follow-Up Comparison in Early Adult Life. II: Social, Behavioural, and Psychiatric Outcomes.' *Journal for Child Psychology and Psychiatry* 41(5): 561–578. https://doi.org/10.1111/1469-7610.00643

I CAN and Royal College of Speech and Language Therapists (2018) *Bercow: Ten Years On. An Independent Review of Provisions for Children and Young People with Speech, Language and Communication Needs in England*. https://www.bercow10yearson.com/

Jonas, E., Schultz-Hardt, S., Dieter, F. and Thelen, N. (2001) 'Confirmation Bias in Sequential Information Search after Preliminary Decisions. An Expansion of Dissonance Theoretical Research on Selective Exposure to Information.' *Journal of Personality and Social Psychology* 80(4): 557–571. https://doi.org/10.1037/0022-3514.80.4.557

Lawson, W. (2008) *Concepts of Normality (The Autistic and Typical Spectrum)*. London: Jessica Kingsley Publishers.

Lee, A., Hobson, R.P. and Chiat, S.J. (1994) 'I, You, Me, and Autism: An Experimental Study.' *Journal of Developmental Disorders* 24(2): 155–176. https://doi.org/10.1007/BF02172094

Liasidou, A. (2012) *Inclusive Education, Politics and Policymaking*. London: Continuum International Publishing Group.

Loveland, K., McEvoy, R., Tunali, B. and Kelley, M. (1990) 'Narrative Story Telling in Autism and Down's Syndrome.' *British Journal of Developmental Psychology* 8(1): 9–23. https://doi.org/10.1111/j.2044-835X.1990.tb00818.x

Milton, D. (2012) 'The Ontological Status of Autism: The "Double Empathy Problem".' *Disability & Society* 27(6): 883–887. https://doi.org/10.1080/09687599.2012.710008

Muskett, T. (2016) 'Examining Language and Communication in Autism Spectrum Disorder – In Context.' In *Re-Thinking Autism: Diagnosis, Identity and Equality*, edited by K. Runswick-Cole, R. Mallett and S. Timimi, 300–316. London: Jessica Kingsley Publishers.

National Autistic Taskforce (2019) *An Independent Guide to Quality Care for Autistic People*. https://nationalautistictaskforce.org.uk/

National Education Union (2018) *Teachers and Workload*. https://neu.org.uk/

Neely, L., Gerow, S., Rispoli, M., Lang, R. and Pullen, N. (2016) 'Treatment of Echolalia in Individuals with Autism Spectrum Disorder: A Systematic Review.' *Review Journal of Autism and Developmental Disorders* 3: 82–91. https://doi.org/10.1007/s40489-015-0067-4

Norbury, C.F. (2014) 'Practitioner Review: Social (Pragmatic) Communication Disorder Conceptualization, Evidence and Clinical Implications.' *Journal of Child Psychology and Psychiatry* 55(3): 204–216. https://doi.org/10.1111/jcpp.12154

Noris, B., Nadel, J., Barker, M., Hadjikhani, N. and Billard, A. (2012) 'Investigating Gaze of Children with ASD in Naturalistic Settings.' *PLOS ONE* 7(9): e44144. https://doi.org/10.1371/journal.pone.0044144

Ochi, K., Ono, N., Owada, K., Kojima, M., Kuroda M., Sagayama, S. and Yamasue, H. (2019) 'Quantification of Speech and Synchrony in the Conversation of Adults with Autism Spectrum Disorder.' *PLOS ONE* 14(12): e0225377. https://doi.org/10.1371/journal.pone.0225377

Parsons, S., Guldberg, K., Macleod, A., Jones, G., Prunty, A. and Balfe, T. (2011) 'International Review of the Evidence on Best Practice in Educational Provision for Children on the Autism Spectrum.' *European Journal of Special Educational Needs* 26(1): 47–63. https://doi.org/10.1080/08856257.2011.543532

Rapin, I. and Dunn, M. (2003) 'Update on the Language Disorders of Individuals on the Autistic Spectrum.' *Brain & Development* 25(3): 166–172. https://doi.org/10.1016/S0387-7604(02)00191-2

Roulstone, S., Wren, Y., Bakopoulou, I., Goodlad, S. and Lindsay, G. (2012) 'Exploring Interventions for Children and Young People with Speech, Language and Communication Needs: A Study of Practice.' *Research Report DFE-RR247-BCRP13*. London: Department for Education. https://www.gov.uk/government/publications/exploring-interventions-for-children-and-young-people-with-speech-language-and-communication-needs-a-study-of-practice

Royal College of Speech and Language Therapists (2013) *Five Good Communication Standards*. London: RCSLT.

Runswick-Cole, K. and Hodge, N. (2009) 'Needs or Rights? A Challenge to the Discourse of Special Education.' *British Journal of Special Education* 36(4): 198–203. https://doi.org/10.1111/j.1467-8578.2009.00438.x

Sterponi, L. and Shankey, J. (2014) 'Rethinking Echolalia: Repetition as Interactional Resource in the Communication of a Child with Autism.' *Journal of Child Language* 41(2): 275–304. https://doi.org/10.1017/S0305000912000682

Tager-Flusberg, H., Paul, R. and Lord, C. (2005) 'Language and Communication in Autism.' In *Handbook of Autism and Pervasive Developmental Disorders*, edited by F. Volkmar, R. Paul, I. Klin and D. Cohen. Volume 1, 3rd ed., 335–364. New Jersey: John Wiley & Sons, Inc. https://doi.org/10.1002/9780470939345.ch12

Thibault, R. (2014) 'Can Autistics Redefine Autism? The Cultural Politics of Autistic Activism.' *Trans-Scripts* 4. https://www.academia.edu/7234120/Can_Autistics_Redefine_Autism_The_Cultural_Politics_of_Autistic_Activism

Wood, R. (2019) 'Autism, Intense Interests and Support in School: From Wasted Efforts to Shared Understandings.' *Educational Review*. https://doi.org/10.1080/00131911.2019.1566213

Wood, R. (2020) 'The Wrong Kind of Noise: Understanding and Valuing the Communication of Autistic Children in Schools.' *Educational Review* 72(1): 111–130. https://doi.org/10.1080/00131911.2018.1483895

24
AUTISTIC VOICES IN AUTISTIC RESEARCH
Towards active citizenship in Autism research

Krysia Emily Waldock and Nathan Keates

A lack of active citizenship in Autism research

Autism research is a dynamic and broad field covering many disciplines. However, the Autistic voice is not always present in Autism research, notably empirical Autism research, despite its necessity for epistemological validity (Woods, Milton, Arnold & Graby, 2018). In this chapter, we will examine Arnstein's (1969) Ladder of Citizen Participation (from hereon in, we will refer to 'the ladder') as a model for good practice for inclusive Autism research due to its prospective beneficial impact; evaluate the scope of current Autism scholarship in regard to 'the ladder' and the potential impact on Autistic people; explain how such an approach is compatible with taking an intersectional approach and why the voices of marginalised Autistics are important; explore benefits and limitations of encouraging active citizenship in Autism research and the practical aspects researchers may need to undertake; and give a short checklist at the end of the chapter for researchers to consider if they wish to undertake this.

We will resist using person-first language (e.g. person with Autism). The first author is an Autistic academic, and both authors wish to respect the voice of the British Autistic community, where amongst Autistic people, identity-first language is generally preferred (Kenny et al., 2016). Reasons for this include the experience of being Autistic as innate to the individual's lived experience (Williams, 1996, p. 14) and therefore influencing how the world is processed and understood. Furthermore, many Autistic people also see being Autistic as inseparable from their identity (Sainsbury, 2000, p. 12) and identity-first language resists this separation of identity and self.

The ladder is a useful framework for understanding citizen power. Envisaged within a post-war context in the literature on city and town planning, it remains highly used and referred to in contemporary academic literature and is the most cited article from the urban development planning literature (Innes & Booher, 2004). However, it is not only applicable to city and town planning, and remains applicable to a variety of fields, notably participatory and inclusive literature in the case of Autism research (as argued by Gowen et al. 2019; Pellicano, Dinsmore & Charman, 2014) and intellectual disability research (Ham et al., 2004; Ward & Trigler, 2001). This is important with the growing dialogue around participatory and inclusive research methods in relation to Autism (e.g. Fletcher-Watson et al., 2019; den Houting, Higgins, Isaacs, Mahony & Pellicano, 2020; Pellicano, 2014; Pellicano et al., 2014).

Autistic voices in Autistic research

An eight-rung ladder represents the framework that illustrates the differing levels of citizen power within participation (Arnstein, 1969) (see Figure 24.1); however, Arnstein has alluded that there may be up to 150 levels. Within this chapter, we will only refer to the main eight rungs that Arnstein refers to in her seminal work. The eight rungs include: manipulation; therapy; informing; consultation; placation, partnership; delegated power; citizen control. In 'the ladder', participation is equal to citizen power, as Arnstein (1969, p. 216) describes: 'It is the redistribution of power that enables the have-not citizens, presently excluded from the political and economic processes, to be deliberately included in the future'. This is critical in reference to contemporary Autism research and science, as part of Critical Autism Studies is a reflexivity on power differentials (Waltz, 2014; Woods & Waldock, 2020) and criticality more widely (Woods et al., 2018), and therefore improving the current evidence base. There needs to be an examination of who holds the power in Autism research currently.

Participation and power are often seen as different things; however, in relation to the impact, it is important to consider participation and power alike. Arnstein's (1969) model describes an 'emancipatory claiming of rights by citizens' (Blue, Rosol & Fast, 2019, p. 364). This demonstrates clear social justice leanings of the framework which is key to critical disability studies. Furthermore, participation is also considered as a neutral entity in many instances; however, as Blue et al. (2019) argue, normative assumptions about how things are done can underpin the ability and desire to participate. This further increases our need for criticality and guidance within the realm of Autism research.

The stigmatised nature of being Autistic means that Autistic people have reduced citizen power, particularly within research. With our current understanding of Autism consistently growing and developing, it is vital to remember that some Autistic people would have

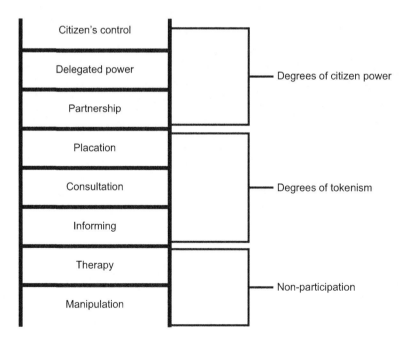

Figure 24.1 The eight rungs from Arnstein's Ladder of Citizen Participation (1969) Source: {Arnstein, S. R. (1969). A ladder of citizen participation. Journal of the American Institute of planners, 35(4), 216-224. } reprinted by permission of The American Planning Association, www.planning.org.>

been counted amongst the mentally ill, the eccentric, and amongst other stigmatised groups of individuals not long ago. Many Autistic people would have been in institutions historically. Beginning with deinstitutionalisation, disabled people, including Autistic people, were brought into the community to live an 'ordinary life' (Nirje, 1969; Wolfensberger, 1972). However, this normalisation has been critiqued by scholars (e.g. Szivos-Bach, 1993; Walmsley, 2001), including Autistic scholars (e.g. Chown et al., 2017; Milton & Moon, 2012); normalisation of this accord places responsibility on the disabled party. Those who cannot, or wish not to, 'normalise' in this manner may face higher levels of 'othering' and psycho-emotional disablement (Milton, 2013; Reeve, 2010). Notably in relation to Autism, there has been continued negative stereotyping and infantilisation of Autistic people (Huws & Jones, 2011). This has reduced the power of Autistic people, i.e., people who 'appear' Autistic or identify as 'Autistic'. Therefore, this relates to the potential citizen power they have, in relation to Autism research.

Neglecting the Autistic voice

Historically, numerous groups of Autistic people have been neglected within research, due to the developing understanding of the phenomenon of 'Autism' being shaped by these changes. This has included Autistic women, people who identify as LBGTQIA+ (including non-binary and Transgender people), ethnic minorities and older Autistic people (e.g. Crompton, Michael & Fletcher-Watson, 2020; Hickey, Crabtree & Stott, 2018; Mason et al., 2019). It is of note that not all the groups would have been conceptualised as groups historically, for example non-binary people. However, as the conceptualisation of identities progresses, so should research.

Historically Autism research participants have been limited to a narrow demographic which creates a bias and difficulty in how that research may be interpreted – notably the under-representation of Autistic people from ethnic minorities, although there exists also a gender bias (male-driven diagnostics and screening tools) in historic conceptualisation of Autism and subsequent diagnostic materials (Haney, 2016; Loomes, Hull & Mandy, 2017; Parish-Morris et al., 2017; Young, Oreve & Speranza, 2018). Considering this in relation to being 'active citizens' in Autism research in accordance with 'the ladder', these people gained no inclusion in the research: they were experimented *upon* and not *with*. Therefore, there is not even an attempt to delegitimise their existence. It is possible that there are other factors that will impact this under-representation, including the absence of the dissemination of culturally sensitive information on Autism, cultural stigma, and the set of beliefs and understandings around disability generally (e.g. Daley, 2004; Singh & Bunyak, 2019). One example is the role religious beliefs play in understanding disability; for example, Waldock and Forrester-Jones (2020) identified in a small exploratory study that some churchgoers may use their belief system (in this case, interpretations of Biblical teachings and scripture) to help make sense of phenomena such as disability (in this case, Autism and Autistic people).

Using Goffman's social stigma theory, Autistic people who 'appear' Autistic and/or openly identify as Autistic are 'stigmatised' as having a 'blemished' identity (Goffman, 1963, p. 1). This demonstrates how stigma operates in society, which buys into an enactment of the pathology lens of Autism, which is often the main narrative surrounding being Autistic, presenting Autism as a deficit which 'blemishes' the Autistic individual, discrediting their voice. In this manner, individuals are taught that they, as people, are 'wrong'. This refers to the manipulation rung on 'the ladder' and conceptualises Autistic people within a medical model framework (Milton & Moon, 2012). Not being stigmatised is further favoured in wider society through the endorsement of those that comply with the norms of sociality and emotionality (O'Dell, Bertilsdotter Rosqvist, Ortega, Brownlow & Orsini, 2016). Stigma may also have a differing effect on the stigmatised individual, particularly in relation to their cultural background. In collectivist cultures, the stigma of having a disabled child is wide-reaching, potentially leading the family in some cultures to hide their child. In others, medical racism may be rife (Jones et al., 2020). This shielding of the child and medical racism lead to not accessing a diagnosis or support and inadvertently misses the support needs of Autistic people.

Ableism and the 'therapy' of Autism research

'The ladder' suggests that the focus on changing the citizens ('therapy' rung), in this case Autistic people, is a method to cure and pathologise their 'wrongness'. The language often used in Autism research reflects the medical model of disability and how Autistic people are in deficit of the necessary components (e.g. Theory of Mind, Baron-Cohen, Leslie & Frith, 1985; Weak Central Coherence, Happé, 1996; in some cases, casting them as subhuman, see first sentence in Baron-Cohen, 2000, p. 3: 'A theory of mind remains one of the quintessential abilities that makes us human'). Autistic people who 'appear' Autistic (e.g. showing signs of distress at stimuli not considered 'normative' by society, communicating in a literal manner, having sensory processing differences, having preferred routines) can be perceived as 'other' (e.g. Botha, Dibb & Frost, 2020; Farrugia, 2009; Grinker, 2020; Kinnear, Link, Ballan & Fishbach, 2016; Milton & Sims, 2016). Definitions of Autism as a phenomenon have historically been defined from an outsider's perspective, that being of a non-autistic person or at least someone who does not identify as Autistic. This is in much the same manner that Simone de Beauvoir argues that what it means to be a woman is defined from a male perspective (1949, p. 16). This is exemplified by normativity as preponderant and valued in society and social structures (one example being the valuing of verbal communication over alternate methods when face to face), further placing Autistic people as the 'othered outsider' (Milton, 2013). Although some more 'partnered' research studies (as per 'the ladder') may take place, ableism may still occur. The 'call for participants' could be normative and 'othering' through its use of ableist language (for example, using functioning labels to describe participants sought), or procedures not considering Autistic lived experience (for example, not considering the sensory environment of an interview and requesting only verbal communication in an interview).

Power, stigma and 'getting heard'

As Autistic people learn the apparent need to be 'normal'; this can produce Autistic camouflaging, which in turn reduces stigma (e.g. Cage, DiMonaco & Newell, 2018; Gray, 1993, p. 114; Pearson & Rose, 2021). 'Masking Autism' covers the so-called 'blemished identity' that Autistic people have, further complicating the landscape. Camouflaging amongst the Autistic population is not a homogenous phenomenon, and camouflaging successfully, as Goffman argues (1963, p. 73) can hide the social stigma, therefore making that individual not 'othered'. This adds complexities to the degree of discreditation of the Autistic voice and who is listened to, with potentially only certain 'types' of Autistic voices listened to, again highlighting the importance of taking considerations of intersectionalities (e.g. race, gender identity, sexual orientation, other disabilities). Autistic people who are 'othered', for example, non-speaking Autistics, Autistics who do not camouflage or Black Autistic people, may therefore be seen as less 'credible' than their non-othered counterparts. These individuals are therefore branded as 'not able to participate' and excluded from having any voice or citizen power in relation to 'the ladder', not even placing them on a rung of the ladder. Autistic people being stigmatised, and the complexities surrounding this, impacts the information base (for example, practitioner knowledge and information imparted in teaching) that is available; this may potentially have an impact on the subsequent research base, echoing what Milton (2014a) argues (translating it for research followed and carried out) regarding the varied and polarised information and resources available in relation to Autism interventions.

The implications of this for Autistic people

Previous stereotypes of Autism continue to inform current ideas (for example, the historic idea that Autistic people were incapable of empathy (Nicolaidis et al., 2018) and the infantilising of Autistic people (Stevenson, Harp & Gernsbacher, 2011)). It has been argued that these enduring stereotypes have been harmful to the relationship between Autistic and non-Autistic people (Stevenson et al., 2011); Autistic voices are needed to inform a more honest and realistic understanding of Autistic people and living as an Autistic person (Milton 2014b).

The impact of being on the 'therapy' rung of the ladder is that Autistic people are seen as people upon whom to experiment rather than people with agency. In this chapter we use Schalock et al.'s (2002) Quality of Life (QoL) framework when discussing the conceptualisation of QoL, as it gives useful domains which are relevant to all populations. It is the domains as broadly defined which are of interest rather than the specific components of which may constitute the domains. Using Schalock et al.'s (2002) QoL framework, Autistic people may be determined as lacking self-determination at the 'therapy' rung (otherwise stated as being voiceless). Potentially, this could lead to diminishing respect, inflicting a decrease in emotional well-being (Schalock et al., 2002). Given that respect is a key element of person-centred care and 'quality' within services supporting Autistic people and people with intellectual disability (Schalock, 2000), viewing stakeholders as having agency is vital in terms of the research process. Feelings of exclusion from the processes of research could potentially lead to social exclusion (Kroll & Morris, 2009), especially if dissemination of information sustains misconceptions of Autistic people to wider society. The views that remain unaccounted for are the voiceless people in research: there is research about Autistic people without Autistic people's inclusion, which identifies bad practice that must be examined and replaced by Autism research *with* Autistic people. Research not using a citizen control or delegated power model could lead to disempowered people who are not valued (Chambers, 1994; Milton, 2014b); fractious dialogue where polarised disagreements may occur (see, for example, Oliver, Kothari & Mays, 2019 in relation to relationships between stakeholders in health research); and distress (both physical and emotional well-being) (Murdoch & Caulfield, 2016). Fundamentally, this would lead to 'lost scholarship', which means further knowledge which could be useful may not be discovered (Milton 2014b).

How can researchers improve their practice
Current research

The current research landscape is slowly opening to examining a greater variety of lived experiences of Autistic people and their families, including Autistic women (e.g. Bargiela et al., 2016; Leedham, Thompson, Smith & Freeth, 2020; Sedgewick, Crane, Hill, & Pellicano, 2019); gender expression amongst Autistic people (e.g. Kourti & Macleod, 2019); traveller families' experiences of Autism (e.g. Gray & Donnelley, 2013); and Black families of Autistic children (Munroe, Hammond & Cole, 2016). The freshness of these research studies demonstrates a recent push towards increasing the diversity of voices present in research, and away from a homogenous interpretation of Autism, and therefore Autistic people. Recent research on camouflaging (Hull et al., 2017) has additionally complicated perceptions of how we may envision Autistic people (e.g. further disrupting preconceptions and stereotypes of our expectations of how Autistic people 'should' behave or appear). This can be seen through the perceptions of Autistic people from different socio-cultural backgrounds, particularly through how stereotypes impact our image of what an Autistic person should be like.

The current research landscape is also beginning to include work by Autistic scholars, amongst the most influential being Dr Damian Milton, Dr Steven Kapp and Dr Melanie Yergeau in our field, and an increasing number of Autistic people seeking to do research. This is demonstrative of pockets of the top rung in Arnstein's ladder (1969): citizen control. Autistic people in the research landscape can challenge our perceptions of Autistic people and how Autistic people are defined, and bring original research ideas which have the potential to positively impact the quality of life of Autistic people (Bölte, 2019; Fletcher-Watson et al., 2019; Pellicano, 2020).

An intersectional approach

A variety of voices are needed due to the differing lived experiences that Autistic people can have. Much like the general population, not all Autistic people will experience life in the same manner. It is essential this is considered, as Autistic people have the potential to be misunderstood due to heterogeneous experiences (Williams, 2020, p. 35). Intertwined with issues pertaining to identity (Ortega & Choudhury, 2011), this may cause misunderstanding of support needs or 'homogenisation'. One example includes the assumption that Autistic people are all under- or over-sensitive to the same stimuli (Crane, Goddard & Pring, 2009). This also links to the stereotypes mentioned above, as we can often embody Autistic people within a particular 'body' or 'space', for example, a white, cis-male child in a Western country. This can be exemplified by the under-diagnosis of Autistic women in comparison to men (Halladay et al., 2015) due to a 'stereotypical male' bias in the screening tools (Young et al., 2018) and the 'whiteness' of the Autism landscape (Jones et al., 2020; Gina Onaiwu, 2020). For example, much information available to parents of ethnic minority Autistic children is not culturally appropriate and information is often assumptive that the recipient is white and Anglophone.

There is also a current lack of Autism research originating from the Global South (O'Dell et al., 2016), with a need to break away from the current bias. We believe intersectionality to be necessary in understanding the differing lived experiences amongst Autistic people alongside 'the ladder' and acquiring citizen power. In one way, this is meta-'partnership', due to the researcher including (or partnering with) all voices. This forms *accountable* research that provides citizen power in a different way. Furthermore, an intersectional approach can add nuance to our understanding of the phenomenon we call Autism, and of the lived experiences of Autistic people. As Shmulsky and Gobbo (2019, p. 648) argue, intersectionality 'more accurately conveys real life complexity', allowing the phenomenon we know as Autism not to be seen in just one dimension, i.e. homogeneously. This is vital if the citizen control rung is to be aimed for on the Ladder of Citizen Participation (since this is an ever-evolving goal; Rosen & Painter, 2019).

Intersectionality fundamentally provides insight into the social inequalities and prospects for social change (Collins, 2019). This is key, given the social justice focus within 'the ladder' and the focus of authentic dialogue, interaction and collaboration (Innes & Booher, 2004). Crenshaw (1989) produced the seminal work on the intersection of Black women in the Criminal Justice System; however, Patricia H. Collins (2015, 2019) remains one of the key academic thinkers on intersectionality. Intersectionality, however, now scopes a much wider range of personal identifiers. Social problems can arise from the intersection of race, gender, class, sexuality, age, ethnicity, ability, capitalism and colonialism (Collins, 2019). Furthermore, some aspects of race, ethnicity and nation can encapsulate religion, which Carbado and Harris (2019) include in their intersectional research, as a belief system can be an integral part of culture. In the past, having two or three identifiers has been termed as double or triple jeopardy (Fujiura, 1998, p. 7). These were viewed as being added onto the struggle, but for King (1988), multiple jeopardy leads to more intensifying experience – multiplying the issues.

Thus, this is a long-term and systemic issue. No one solution will automatically create a more inclusive dialogue on Autism involving Autistic people, especially in avoiding tokenistic inclusion (as is necessary for 'Active Citizens'). We recommend a multifaceted approach including multiple stakeholders to address this issue and to take steps towards using a more intersectional approach in research and increasing citizen power. In relation to looking at marginalised populations which may not otherwise be heard, some research has taken an intersectional approach in elucidating experiences of Autistic people (Singh & Bunyak, 2019; Toft, Franklin & Langley, 2019; 2020), showing the value of this approach in understanding the heterogeneous nature of Autistic people and the multiple identities they can have. This knowledge is likely to be of high importance in terms of understanding those who are currently voiceless and invisible regarding citizen power. As part of this, further qualitative and mixed-methods studies and approaches are keenly recommended in eliciting the views, perspectives and world views of Autistic people. This would effectively ground further work not only in the lived experiences of a broader pool of Autistic people, but it would also allow for greater depth in the nuances of the phenomenon called Autism and Autistic people.

Autistic stakeholders

Partnership in research and other projects between Autistic and non-autistic stakeholders is a phenomenon that is starting to take hold in some projects (as per 'the ladder'); for example, the Playing A/Part project (for further information see: University of Kent, 2021). Both authors are actively seeking to involve Autistic people meaningfully in their research through advisory groups, steering groups and participatory methods. We see this as central to the aims of our research, contrasting the paucity of research acquiring experiential and embodied knowledge from Autistic people (Dossa, 2008; Milton, 2014b; Duncan & Oliver, 2017; Stewart & Liambo, 2012). However, care needs to be taken, when involving marginalised groups, that merely tokenistic involvement is not reached, thus stunting the potential for growth and true ownership of projects by Autistic people. This includes potential creativity and breaking away from norms in roles. For example, advisory group roles and co-researchers' roles need to be designed flexibly and creatively to meet the needs (e.g. physical, sensory) of the populations being sought for the role. Without such creativity, it is possible that roles may be conceptualised which inadvertently exclude the very people sought for the role. It is important not to stunt the citizen power and control of Autistic people in research, notably through not limiting Autistic input to steering groups, advisory group members or informal advisors.

Another aspect to consider is the historical mistrust that some Autistic people have in regard to Autism research and researchers (Milton, 2014b) and the impact this has on the current Autism research landscape. Transparency of research aims and goals (Harrison et al., 2019) is of vital importance in participatory work, which can also be considered with Autism research, aims and processes. One example is clarity regarding the recruitment process and subsequent write-up and/or publication. Autistic academics are a key part of furthering citizen power, with Autistic-led projects and scholarship a crucial part of this. This is one avenue into the development of trust between researchers and participants, especially where the researchers may share ideology with participants (e.g. the social model of disability). However, systemic barriers in academia more broadly can disadvantage disabled and neurodivergent people (including Autistic people), leading them to be 'invisible' (Brown & Leigh, 2018).

Much current research that seeks to be participatory or inclusive remains at the tokenistic inclusion level of citizen control on 'the ladder', with full citizen control (projects being led by Autistic people) yet to be reached. Reasons for this are plural, including time constraints from research budgets and grants to difficulty in the preparation of potential co-researchers, especially if they are not academics or in newly defined roles, and a lack of precedence of such work in certain fields. Participatory research may be regarded with caution by some other researchers, in relation to the time implications it may demand (Chambers, 1998) or the ending of research relationships in participatory work (Northway, 2000). However, as Christopher, Watts, McCormick and Young (2008) argue, including the voice of the community you are working with is vital in incorporating them into the academic literature.

Meaningful inclusion of Autistic people in research

Meaningful inclusion in research involves engagement with knowledge already accrued by Autistic people and rightful attribution. An 'Autistic culture' encapsulates a shared knowledge amongst many Autistic people of varying support needs, backgrounds and ages (Sinclair, 2012). This fits the current understanding of a culture, as argued by Schein (1991, p. 313), where a key part of a 'culture' is shared knowledge. The Autistic and neurodivergent communities have influenced scientific work, both academic and non-academic, within the Autism field increasingly over the last 20 years (e.g. the Participatory Autism Research Collective, Milton et al., 2019). Enabling dialogue between this epistemic community (composed of activists and self-advocates, as described by Kapp, 2020, p. 306) and the research community has the potential to produce further ideas for research which may further benefit Autistic people.

Meaningful involvement is a significant part of ethical Autism research (Milton, 2014b), as the voices of Autistic people then become a key part of the research itself. Gillespie-Lynch et al. (2017) recommend that Autistic people, as experts in Autism, should be research partners. Guidance and checklists have been published citing steps researchers can take to increase the inclusivity of their research both on a practical and theoretical level (Chown et al., 2017; Fletcher-Watson et al., 2019; Gowen et al., 2019). These papers are Autistic-led (Chown et al., 2017) or have significant Autistic input into them, demonstrating positive collaborative practices (Fletcher-Watson et al., 2019, Gowen et al., 2019). Gowen et al. provide guidelines on pre- and post-study considerations, recruitment of participants, and addressing the anxiety provoking nature of travelling to and visiting buildings for research. Furthermore, Chown et al. (2017) have produced guidance on each site in research with advice on how to avoid conflict of interest between funders and the Autistic community. The papers mentioned above, as complementary to our chapter, are a key part of building a more comprehensive, participatory and inclusive research base in the field of Autism.

The research-to-practice gap

The authors of this chapter, alongside other researchers (e.g. Dingfelder & Mandell, 2011; Parsons et al., 2013), have also noted a research-to-practice gap amongst work in this field. A bridging of this gap is not likely to be a quick or easy solution, however bridging knowledge across epistemic communities may increase the knowledge shared, including cultural knowledge amongst Autistic people. This is vital in terms of hearing the variety and multiplicity of Autistic lived experiences, and to resist homogenising Autistic persons by reducing them to their diagnostic label and the stereotypes associated with this label. The 'citizen power' of individuals within such dialogue would also need to be considered by the involved parties and stakeholders, which is a step to be taken. Reflecting on standpoints, beliefs and views is acknowledged by the authors as potentially novel for some involved parties, given the vested interest of some stakeholders of the phenomenon we know as 'Autism'. However, as exemplified by Brookfield (1998) in regard to educational practices and 'the reflective teacher', reflection encourages growth; it is only through the consideration of how others view us that some of our preconceptions can be challenged. Reflexivity is also a key component of high-quality qualitative research (Finlay, 2002). Models and provision of support for Autistic people are likely also to be positively impacted through the acknowledgement of the experiences of Autistic people, including barriers to such support. This may have a subsequent impact on improving the quality of life of Autistic people from diverse backgrounds, cultures and lived experiences, and further research in this area is necessary.

The benefits for the Autistic community and Autism science

As a culmination of thought, it is important to identify the potential benefits of this approach. The 'A Future Made Together Report' (Pellicano, Dinsmore & Charman, 2013) highlights the discrepancy between the research carried out in the field of Autism, the funding distribution, and research that Autistic people feel would improve their QoL. While we understand that research that is not participatory or inclusive in nature might also benefit Autistic people's QoL, the value of the Autistic voice in research, and the subsequent impact on QoL, must be acknowledged as key stakeholders within the research process. Autistic-led papers (for example, Robertson, 2009, Waldock, 2019) have argued for the QoL of Autistic people to be differently conceptualised, supporting other work on the ASQoL[1] (McConachie et al., 2018). This is not to say that only Autistic people should research Autism, rather to celebrate the richness of the scholarship they bring and how it complements research by researchers who are either non-autistic or undisclosed. The presence of the Autistic voice in Autism research improves epistemic validity (Woods et al., 2018) and is vital (Milton, 2014b), and is an example of new undiscovered knowledge, bringing 'richness' to academia. Through the delegation of power to Autistic people, research projects, and subsequent empowerment, less pejorative attitudes towards Autistic people, notably those who are 'stigmatised', may be facilitated. In turn this would lead to further new, yet undiscovered, knowledge.

Barriers faced by the academic community in acting on this are important to consider. For example, the way academia is constructed may be difficult for intersectional Autistic people with intellectual disability (ID) to lead a research project. Nonetheless, citizen control will enable a building of trust and dialogue between Autistic people and researchers (for example, in Autism research, Milton, 2014b; in other fields, Goodman & Sanders Thompson, 2017; Harrison et al., 2019; Trimble & Berkes, 2013).

Through successfully achieving this, the research process and citizen power will improve; the Autistic community will be empowered and feel valued. Through gaining lived experiences, Autism science will develop and enhance the accuracy and fit of the findings to the heterogeneity of the Autistic population. The knowledge developed will account for more Autistic people's experiences. The priorities in Autism science will be better directed to benefit the research, and thus the practices and lives of those within the Autism community. This is echoed by the assertation that many Autistic scholars are aiming for the emancipation of the Autistic population (as originally described in Woods et al., 2018 in regard to Autistic scholars) through their research. Thus, this is a practical development for the stakeholders (Pellicano et al., 2013).

Conclusion

In conclusion, 'the ladder' is a valuable tool in relation to the growth and future of Autism research, as well as taking an intersectional approach to this field of study. Much research is stuck at the 'therapy' rung and there is scope for growth in terms of citizen power. There is a need for research with cultural considerations and sensitivity, and increased knowledge dissemination to support the lives of Autistic people from all cultural backgrounds. With a past focus on Autism in the Global North and on cis-male-gendered Autistic people, meaningful inclusion of all voices is yet to happen. Autistic people need to have citizen control or delegated power as part of meaningful change, including Autistic voices at all intersections and not only those who are convenient to work with. We also recommend that researchers and others who work with or for Autistic people work creatively, in order to enable and facilitate accessible ways and means for Autistic people's involvement and engagement with research. Finally, there are numerous benefits for the Autistic community and for Autism science (e.g. increased epistemic validity, potential for undiscovered knowledge to be found, increased trust in researchers).

A summary of what is needed

- A bridge between research and practice to overcome the current gap
- Further diversity, including further QoL research, to understand the nuances of Autistic lives
- Research must seek under-researched populations and their voices
- Time must be taken to gain trust (which is a longitudinal goal), through being transparent in research aims and processes, and welcoming dialogue
- Reflexivity on the researchers' own position as a researcher and the outcomes sought by themselves as a researcher
- Creative thinking in terms of roles and how to accredit 'citizen power'

Note

1 ASQoL – Autism-Specific QoL, i.e. items added to the WHOQoL-BREF (World Health Organization's measure for QoL).

References

Arnstein, S. R. (1969). A ladder of citizen participation. *Journal of the American Institute of Planners*, 35(4), 216–224. https://doi.org/10.1080/01944366908977225

Bargiela, S., Steward, R., & Mandy, W. (2016). The experiences of late-diagnosed women with autism spectrum conditions: An investigation of the female autism phenotype. *Journal of Autism & Developmental Disorders*, 46(10), 3281–3294. https://doi.org/10.1007/s10803-016-2872-8

Baron-Cohen, S. (2000). Theory of mind and autism: A review. In *International Review of Research in Mental Retardation* (Vol. 23, pp. 169–184). Academic Press. https://doi.org/10.1016/s0074-7750(00)80010-5

Baron-Cohen, S., Leslie, A. M., & Frith, U. (1985). Does the autistic child have a "theory of mind"? *Cognition*, 21(1), 37–46. https://doi.org/10.1016/0010-0277(85)90022-8

Blue, G., Rosol, M., & Fast, V. (2019). Justice as parity of participation: Enhancing Arnstein's ladder Through Fraser's justice framework. *Journal of the American Planning Association*, 85(3), 363–376. https://doi.org/10.1080/01944363.2019.1619476

Bölte, S. (2019). Hey autism researcher, what's on your mind today about inclusion? *Autism*, 23(7), 1611–1613. https://doi.org/10.1177/1362361319870994

Botha, M., Dibb, B., & Frost, D. (2020). "Autism is me": An investigation of how autistic individuals make sense of autism and stigma. *Disability & Society*, 1–27. https://doi.org/10.1080/09687599.2020.1822782

Brookfield, S. (1998). Critically reflective practice. *Journal of Continuing Education in the Health Professions*, *18*(4), 197–205. https://doi.org/10.1002/chp.1340180402

Brown, N., & Leigh, J. (2018). Ableism in academia: Where are the disabled and ill academics? *Disability & Society*, *33*(6), 985–989. https://doi.org/10.1080/09687599.2018.1455627

Cage, E., Di Monaco, J., & Newell, V. (2018). Experiences of autism acceptance and mental health in autistic adults. *Journal of Autism & Developmental Disorders*, *48*(2), 473–484. https://doi.org/10.1007/s10803-017-3342-7

Carbado, D. W., & Harris, C. I. (2019). Intersectionality at 30: Mapping the margins of anti-essentialism, intersectionality, and dominance theory. *Harvard Law Review*, *132*(8), 2193–2239.

Chambers, R. (1994). The origins and practice of participatory rural appraisal. *World Development*, *22*(7), 953–969. https://doi.org/10.1016/0305-750X(94)90141-4

Chambers, R. (1998). Foreword. In J. Holland and J. Blackburn (Eds.), *Whose Voice? Participatory Research and Policy Change* (pp. xv–xviii). Intermediate Technology Publications.

Chown, N., Robinson, J., Beardon, L., Downing, J., Hughes, L., Leatherland, J., ... & MacGregor, D. (2017). Improving research about us, with us: A draft framework for inclusive autism research. *Disability & Society*, *32*(5), 720–734. https://doi.org/10.1080/09687599.2017.1320273

Christopher, S., Watts, V., McCormick, A. K. H. G., & Young, S. (2008). Building and maintaining trust in a community-based participatory research partnership. *American Journal of Public Health*, *98*(8), 1398–1406. https://doi.org/10.2105/ajph.2007.125757

Collins, P. H. (2015). Intersectionality's definitional dilemmas. *Annual Review of Sociology*, *41*(1), 1–20. https://doi.org/10.1146/annurev-soc-073014-112142

Collins, P. H. (2019). *Intersectionality as Critical Social Theory*. Duke University Press. https://doi.org/10.1215/9781478007098

Crane, L., Goddard, L., & Pring, L. (2009). Sensory processing in adults with autism spectrum disorders. *Autism*, *3*(3), 215–228. https://doi.org/10.1177/1362361309103794

Crenshaw, K. (1989). Demarginalizing the intersection of race and sex: A black feminist critique of antidiscrimination doctrine, feminist theory and antiracist politics. *University of Chicago Legal Forum*, *1*. http://chicagounbound.uchicago.edu/uclf/vol1989/iss1/8

Crompton, C. J., Michael, C., Fletcher-Watson, S., Crompton, C., & Tower, K. (2020). Co-creating the Autistic Satisfaction with Care Holistic Interview (ASCHI) to examine the experiences of older autistic adults in residential care. *Autism in Adulthood*, *2*(1), 77–86. https://doi.org/10.1089/aut.2019.0033

Daley, T. C. (2004). From symptom recognition to diagnosis: Children with autism in urban India. *Social Science & Medicine*, *58*(7), 1323–1335. https://doi.org/10.1016/s0277-9536(03)00330-7

De Beauvoir, S. (1949). *The Second Sex*. Random House Group Ltd.

den Houting, J., Higgins, J., Isaacs, K., Mahony, J., & Pellicano, E. (2020). "I'm not just a guinea pig": Academic and community perceptions of participatory autism research. *Autism*, 1–16. https://doi.org/10.1177/1362361320951696

Dingfelder, H. E., & Mandell, D. S. (2011). Bridging the research-to-practice gap in autism intervention: An application of diffusion of innovation theory. *Journal of Autism & Developmental Disorders*, *41*(5), 597–609. https://doi.org/10.1007/s10803-010-1081-0

Dossa, P. (2008). Creating alternative and demedicalized spaces: Testimonial narrative on disability, culture, and racialization. *Journal of International Women's Studies*, *9*(3), 79–98.

Duncan, S., & Oliver, S. (2017). Motivations for engagement. *Research for All*, *1*(2), 229–233. https://doi.org/10.18546/RFA.01.2.01

Farrugia, D. (2009). Exploring stigma: Medical knowledge and the stigmatisation of parents of children diagnosed with autism spectrum disorder. *Sociology of Health & Illness*, *31*(7), 1011–1027. https://doi.org/10.1111/j.1467-9566.2009.01174.x

Finlay, L. (2002). "Outing" the researcher: The provenance, process, and practice of reflexivity. *Qualitative Health Research*, *12*(4), 531–545. https://doi.org/10.1177/104973202129120052

Fletcher-Watson, S., Adams, J., Brook, K., Charman, T., Crane, L., Cusack, J., ... & Pellicano, E. (2019). Making the future together: Shaping autism research through meaningful participation. *Autism*, *23*(4), 943–953. https://doi.org/10.1177/1362361318786721

Fujiura, G. T. (1998). Demography of family households. *American Journal of Mental Retardation*, *103*(3), 225–235. https://doi.org/10.1352/0895-8017(1998)103<0225:dofh>2.0.co;2

Gillespie-Lynch, K., Kapp, S. K., Brooks, P. J., Pickens, J., & Schwartzman, B. (2017). Whose expertise is it? Evidence for autistic adults as critical autism experts. *Frontiers in Psychology*, *8*, 438. https://doi.org/10.3389/fpsyg.2017.00438

Giwa Onaiwu, M. (2020). "They don't know, don't show, or don't care": Autism's white privilege problem. *Autism in Adulthood*. https://doi.org/10.1089/aut.2020.0077

Goffman, E. (1963). *Stigma: Notes on the Management of Spoiled Identity*. Penguin Books.

Goodman, M. S., & Sanders Thompson, V. L. (2017). The science of stakeholder engagement in research: Classification, implementation, and evaluation. *Translational Behavioral Medicine*, 7(3), 486–491. https://doi.org/10.1007/s13142-017-0495-z

Gowen, E., Taylor, R., Bleazard, T., Greenstein, A., Baimbridge, P., & Poole, D. (2019). Guidelines for conducting research studies with the autism community. *Autism Policy & Practice*, 2(1), 29.

Gray, C., & Donnelly, J. (2013). Unheard voices: The views of traveller and non-traveller mothers and children with ASD. *International Journal of Early Years Education*, 21(4), 268–285. https://doi.org/10.1080/09669760.2013.842160

Gray, D. E. (1993). Perceptions of stigma: The parents of autistic children. *Sociology of Health & Illness*, 15(1), 102–120. https://doi.org/10.1111/1467-9566.ep11343802

Grinker, R. R. (2020). Autism, "stigma," disability: A shifting historical terrain. *Current Anthropology*, 61(S21), S55–S67. https://doi.org/10.1086/705748

Halladay, A. K., Bishop, S., Constantino, J. N., Daniels, A. M., Koenig, K., Palmer, K., … & Singer, A. T. (2015). Sex and gender differences in autism spectrum disorder: Summarizing evidence gaps and identifying emerging areas of priority. *Molecular Autism*, 6(1), 36. https://doi.org/10.1186/s13229-015-0019-y

Ham, M., Jones, N., Mansell, I., Northway, R., Price, L., & Walker, G. (2004). 'I'm a researcher!' Working together to gain ethical approval for a participatory research study. *Journal of Learning Disabilities*, 8(4), 397–407. https://doi.org/10.1177/1469004704047507

Haney, J. L. (2016). Autism, females, and the DSM-5: Gender bias in autism diagnosis. *Social Work in Mental Health*, 14(4), 396–407. https://doi.org/10.1080/15332985.2015.1031858

Happé, F. G. (1996). Studying weak central coherence at low levels: Children with autism do not succumb to visual illusions. A research note. *Journal of Child Psychology & Psychiatry*, 37(7), 873–877. https://doi.org/10.1111/j.1469-7610.1996.tb01483.x

Harrison, J. D., Auerbach, A. D., Anderson, W., Fagan, M., Carnie, M., Hanson, C., … & Weiss, R. (2019). Patient stakeholder engagement in research: A narrative review to describe foundational principles and best practice activities. *Health Expectations*, 22(3), 307–316. https://doi.org/10.1111/hex.12873

Hickey, A., Crabtree, J., & Stott, J. (2018). "Suddenly the first fifty years of my life made sense": Experiences of older people with autism. *Autism*, 22(3), 357–367. https://doi.org/10.1177/1362361316680914

Hull, L., Petrides, K. V., Allison, C., Smith, P., Baron-Cohen, S., Lai, M. C., & Mandy, W. (2017). "Putting on my best normal": Social camouflaging in adults with autism spectrum conditions. *Journal of Autism & Developmental Disorders*, 47(8), 2519–2534. https://doi.org/10.1007/s10803-017-3166-5

Huws, J. C., & Jones, R. S. (2011). Missing voices: Representations of autism in British newspapers, 1999–2008. *British Journal of Learning Disabilities*, 39(2), 98–104. https://doi.org/10.1111/j.1468-3156.2010.00624.x

Innes, J. E., & Booher, D. E. (2004). Reframing public participation: Strategies for the 21st century. *Planning Theory & Practice*, 5(4), 419–436. https://doi.org/10.1080/1464935042000293170

Jones, D. R., Nicolaidis, C., Ellwood, L. J., Garcia, A., Johnson, K. R., Lopez, K., & Waisman, T. C. (2020). An expert discussion on structural racism in autism research and practice. *Autism in Adulthood*. http://doi.org/10.1089/aut.2020.29015.drj

Kapp, S. (2020). Conclusion. In S. K. Kapp (Ed.), *Autistic Community and the Neurodiversity Movement: Stories from the Frontline* (pp. 305–318). Springer Nature. https://link.springer.com/book/10.1007%2F978-981-13-8437-0

Kenny, L., Hattersley, C., Molins, B., Buckley, C., Povey, C., & Pellicano, E. (2016). Which terms should be used to describe autism? Perspectives from the UK autism community. *Autism*, 20(4), 442–462. https://doi.org/10.1177/1362361315588200

King, D. K. (1988). Multiple jeopardy, multiple consciousness: The context of a black feminist ideology. *Signs: Journal of Women in Culture & Society*, 14(1), 42–72. https://doi.org/10.1086/494491

Kinnear, S. H., Link, B. G., Ballan, M. S., & Fischbach, R. L. (2016). Understanding the experience of stigma for parents of children with autism spectrum disorder and the role stigma plays in families' lives. *Journal of Autism & Developmental Disorders*, 46(3), 942–953. https://doi.org/10.1007/s10803-015-2637-9

Kourti, M., & MacLeod, A. (2019). "I don't feel like a gender, I feel like myself": Autistic individuals raised as girls exploring gender identity. *Autism in Adulthood*, 1(1), 52–59. https://doi.org/10.1089/aut.2018.0001

Kroll, T., & Morris, J. (2009). Challenges and opportunities in using mixed method designs in rehabilitation research. *Archives of Physical Medicine & Rehabilitation*, *90*(11), S11–S16. https://doi.org/10.1016/j.apmr.2009.04.023

Leedham, A., Thompson, A. R., Smith, R., & Freeth, M. (2020). "I was exhausted trying to figure it out": The experiences of females receiving an autism diagnosis in middle to late adulthood. *Autism*, *24*(1), 135–146. https://doi.org/10.1177/1362361319853442

Loomes, R., Hull, L., & Mandy, W. P. L. (2017). What is the male-to-female ratio in autism spectrum disorder? A systematic review and meta-analysis. *Journal of the American Academy of Child & Adolescent Psychiatry*, *56*(6), 466–474. https://doi.org/10.1016/j.jaac.2017.03.013

Mason, D., Mackintosh, J., McConachie, H., Rodgers, J., Finch, T., & Parr, J. R. (2019). Quality of life for older autistic people: The impact of mental health difficulties. *Research in Autism Spectrum Disorders*, *63*, 13–22. https://doi.org/10.1016/j.rasd.2019.02.007

McConachie, H., Mason, D., Parr, J. R., Garland, D., Wilson, C., & Rodgers, J. (2018). Enhancing the validity of a quality of life measure for autistic people. *Journal of Autism & Developmental Disorders*, *48*(5), 1596–1611. https://doi.org/10.1007/s10803-017-3402-z

Milton, D. (2013). Reversing the vicious circle of psycho-emotional disablism in the education of autistic people. In P. Banajee, R. Barrie, M. Hand and Michael (Eds.), *Championing Research, Educating Professionals: How Compatible Are Elitism, Inclusion and Social Justice?* Annual Conference (11). University of Birmingham, Birmingham, UK, pp. 127–134.

Milton, D. E. (2014a). So what exactly are autism interventions intervening with? *Good Autism Practice (Gap)*, *15*(2), 6–14.

Milton, D. E. (2014b). Autistic expertise: A critical reflection on the production of knowledge in autism studies. *Autism*, *18*(7), 794–802. https://doi.org/10.1177/1362361314525281

Milton, D., & Moon, L. (2012). The normalisation agenda and the psycho-emotional disablement of autistic people. *Autonomy, the Critical Journal of Interdisciplinary Autism Studies*, *1*(1).

Milton, D., & Sims, T. (2016). How is a sense of well-being and belonging constructed in the accounts of autistic adults? *Disability & Society*, *31*(4), 520–534. https://doi.org/10.1080/09687599.2016.1186529

Milton, D., Ridout, S., Kourti, M., Loomes, G., & Martin, N. (2019). A critical reflection on the development of the Participatory Autism Research Collective (PARC). *Tizard Learning Disability Review*, *24*(2), 82–89. https://doi.org/10.1108/tldr-09-2018-0029

Munroe, K., Hammond, L., & Cole, S. (2016). The experiences of African immigrant mothers living in the United Kingdom with a child diagnosed with an autism spectrum disorder: An interpretive phenomenological analysis. *Disability & Society*, *31*(6), 798–819. https://doi.org/10.1080/09687599.2016.1200015

Murdoch, B., & Caulfield, T. (2016). Doing research with vulnerable populations: The case of intravenous drug users. *Bioéthiqueonline*, *5*. https://doi.org/10.7202/1044290ar

Nicolaidis, C., Milton, D., Sasson, N. J., Sheppard, E., & Yergeau, M. (2018). An expert discussion on autism and empathy. *Autism in Adulthood*, *1*(1), 4–11. https://doi.org/10.1089/aut.2018.29000.cjn

Northway, R. (2000). Ending participatory research? *Journal of Learning Disabilities*, *4*(1), 27–36. https://doi.org/10.1177/146900470000400102

Nirje, B. (1969). The normalization principle and its human management implications. In R. Kugel & W. Wolfensberger (Eds.), *Changing Patterns in Residential Services for the Mentally Retarded* (pp. 179–195). President's Committee on Mental Retardation.

O'Dell, L., Bertilsdotter Rosqvist, H., Ortega, F., Brownlow, C., & Orsini, M. (2016). Critical autism studies: Exploring epistemic dialogues and intersections, challenging dominant understandings of autism. *Disability & Society*, *31*(2), 166–179. https://doi.org/10.1080/09687599.2016.1164026

Oliver, K., Kothari, A., & Mays, N. (2019). The dark side of coproduction: Do the costs outweigh the benefits for health research? *Health Research Policy & Systems*, *17*(1), 33. https://doi.org/10.1186/s12961-019-0432-3

Ortega, F., & Choudhury, S. (2011). "Wired up differently": Autism, adolescence and the politics of neurological identities. *Subjectivity*, *4*(3), 323–345. https://doi.org/10.1057/sub.2011.9

Parish-Morris, J., Liberman, M. Y., Cieri, C., Herrington, J. D., Yerys, B. E., Bateman, L., … & Schultz, R. T. (2017). Linguistic camouflage in girls with autism spectrum disorder. *Molecular Autism*, *8*(1), 48. https://doi.org/10.1186/s13229-017-0164-6

Parsons, S., Charman, T., Faulkner, R., Ragan, J., Wallace, S., & Wittemeyer, K. (2013). Commentary–bridging the research and practice gap in autism: The importance of creating research partnerships with schools. *Autism*, *17*(3), 268–280. https://doi.org/10.1177/1362361312472068

Pearson, A., & Rose, K. A. (in print). A conceptual analysis of autistic masking: Understanding the narrative of stigma and the illusion of choice. *Autism in Adulthood*, *3*(1), 52–60. https://doi.org/10.1089/aut.2020.0043

Pellicano, E. (2020). Commentary: Broadening the research remit of participatory methods in autism science—A commentary on Happé and Frith (2020). *Journal of Child Psychology & Psychiatry*, *61*(3), 233–235. https://doi.org/10.1111/jcpp.13212

Pellicano, E., Dinsmore, A., & Charman, T. (2013). *A Future Made Together: Shaping Autism Research in the UK*. Institute of Education.

Pellicano, E., Dinsmore, A., & Charman, T. (2014). Views on researcher-community engagement in autism research in the United Kingdom: A mixed-methods study. *PLOS ONE*, *9*(10), e109946. https://doi.org/10.1371/journal.pone.0109946

Pellicano, L. (2014). A future made together: New directions in the ethics of autism research. *Journal of Research in Special Educational Needs*, *14*(3), 200–204. https://doi.org/10.1111/1471-3802.12070_5

Reeve, D. (2010). Ableism and disability studies: The myth of the reliable and contained body. Paper presented at *Critical Disability Studies Conference: Theorizing Normalcy and the Mundane*, Manchester Metropolitan University, 12–13 May.

Robertson, S. M. (2009). Neurodiversity, quality of life, and autistic adults: Shifting research and professional focuses onto real-life challenges. *Disability Studies Quarterly*, *30*(1). https://doi.org/10.18061/dsq.v30i1.1069

Rosen, J., & Painter, G. (2019). From citizen control to co-production: Moving beyond a linear conception of citizen participation. *Journal of the American Planning Association*, *85*(3), 335–347. https://doi.org/10.1080/01944363.2019.1618727

Sainsbury, C. (2000). *Martian in the Playground: Understanding the Schoolchild with Asperger's Syndrome*. Lucky Duck Publishing.

Schalock, R. L. (2000). Three decades of quality of life. *Focus on Autism & Other Developmental Disabilities*, *15*(2), 116–127. https://doi.org/10.1177/108835760001500207

Schalock, R. L., Brown, I., Brown, R., Cummins, R. A., Felce, D., Matikka, L., … & Parmenter, T. (2002). Conceptualization, measurement, and application of quality of life for persons with intellectual disabilities: Report of an international panel of experts. *Mental Retardation*, *40*(6), 457–470. https://doi.org/10.1352/0047-6765(2002)040<0457:cmaaoq>2.0.co;2

Schein, E. H. (1991). What is culture? In M. Godwyn and J. Hoffer Gittell (Eds.), *Sociology of Organisations: Structures and Relationships* (pp. 312–314). Pine Forge Press.

Sedgewick, F., Crane, L., Hill, V., & Pellicano, E. (2019). Friends and lovers: The relationships of autistic and neurotypical women. *Autism in Adulthood*, *1*(2), 112–123. https://doi.org/10.1089/aut.2018.0028

Shmulsky, S., & Gobbo, K. (2019). Autism support in a community college setting: Ideas from intersectionality. *Community College Journal of Research & Practice*, *43*(9), 648–652. https://doi.org/10.1080/10668926.2018.1522278

Sinclair, J. (2012). Autism network international: The development of a community and its culture. In J. Bascom (Ed.), *Loud Hands: Autistic People, Speaking* (pp. 17–48). The Autistic Press. http://www.autreat.com/History_of_ANI.html

Singh, J. S., & Bunyak, G. (2019). Autism disparities: A systematic review and meta-ethnography of qualitative research. *Qualitative Health Research*, *29*(6), 796–808. https://doi.org/10.1177/1049732318808245

Stevenson, J. L., Harp, B., & Gernsbacher, M. A. (2011). Infantilizing autism. *Disability Studies Quarterly*, *31*(3). https://doi.org/10.18061/dsq.v31i3.1675

Stewart, R., & Liabo, K. (2012). Involvement in research without compromising research quality. *Journal of Health Services Research & Policy*, *17*(4), 248–251. https://doi.org/10.1258/jhsrp.2012.011086

Szivos-Bach, S. E. (1993). Social comparisons, stigma and mainstreaming: The self esteem of young adults with a mild mental handicap. *Mental Handicap Research*, *6*(3), 217–236. https://doi.org/10.1111/j.1468-3148.1993.tb00054.x

Toft, A., Franklin, A., & Langley, E. (2019). Young disabled and LGBT+: Negotiating identity. *Journal of LGBT Youth*, *16*(2), 157–172. https://doi.org/10.1080/19361653.2018.1544532

Toft, A., Franklin, A., & Langley, E. (2020). 'You're not sure that you are gay yet': The perpetuation of the 'phase' in the lives of young disabled LGBT+ people. *Sexualities*, *23*(4), 516–529. https://doi.org/10.1177/1363460719842135

Trimble, M., & Berkes, F. (2013). Participatory research towards co-management: Lessons from artisanal fisheries in coastal Uruguay. *Journal of Environmental Management*, *128*, 768–778. https://doi.org/10.1016/j.jenvman.2013.06.032

University of Kent. (2021). Playing A/part: Project summary, aims and objectives. Accessed January 4th 2021. https://playingapartautisticgirls.org/project/

Waldock, K. E. (2019). Commentary on "Thinking differently? Autism and quality of life". *Tizard Learning Disability Review, 24*(2), 77–81. https://doi.org/10.1108/tldr-02-2019-0006

Waldock, K. E., & Forrester-Jones, R. (2020). An exploratory study of attitudes toward autism Amongst Church-Going Christians in the South East of England, United Kingdom. *Journal of Disability & Religion, 24*(4), 349–370. https://doi.org/10.1080/23312521.2020.1776667

Walmsley, J. (2001). Normalisation, emancipatory research and inclusive research in learning disability. *Disability & Society, 16*(2), 187–205. https://doi.org/10.1080/09687590120035807

Waltz, M. (2014). Worlds of autism: Across the spectrum of neurological difference. *Disability & Society, 29*(8), 1337–1338. https://doi.org/10.1080/09687599.2014.934064

Ward, K., & Trigler, J. S. (2001). Reflections on participatory action research with people who have developmental disabilities. *Mental Retardation, 39*(1), 57–59. https://doi.org/10.1352/0047-6765(2001)039<0057:ROPARW>2.0.CO;2

Williams, D. (1996). *Autism – An Inside-Out Approach: An Innovative Look at the Mechanics of 'Autism' and Its Developmental 'Cousins'*. Jessica Kingsley Publications.

Williams, G. L. (2020). Perceptual deviants: Understanding autistic subjects in a (not so) predictable world. In D. Milton, D. Murray, N. Martin, S. Ridout and R. Mills (Eds.), *The Neurodiversity Reader: Exploring the Concepts, Lived Experience and Implications for Practice* (pp. 35–40). Pavilion Publishing.

Wolfensberger, W. (1972). *The Principle of Normalization in Human Services*. National Institute of Mental Retardation.

Woods, R., Milton, D., Arnold, L., & Graby, S. (2018). Redefining critical autism studies: A more inclusive interpretation. *Disability & Society, 33*(6), 974–979. https://doi.org/10.1080/09687599.2018.1454380

Woods, R., & Waldock, K. E. (2020). Critical autism studies. In *Encyclopedia of Autism Spectrum Disorders*, 1–9. https://doi.org/10.1007/978-1-4614-6435-8_102297-2

Young, H., Oreve, M. J., & Speranza, M. (2018). Clinical characteristics and problems diagnosing autism spectrum disorder in girls. *Archives de Pédiatrie, 25*(6), 399–403. https://doi.org/10.1016/j.arcped.2018.06.008

INDEX

Page numbers in *italics* mark figures or illustrations, while page numbers in **bold** represent tables.

Abawi, D. 5, 20–30
ableism 160, 291; impacts on identity 106; internalized 38, 235, 259; and the medical model of autism 106; and motherhood 107; and normalcy 21, 247, 250; by teachers 248–251; and treatment interventions 21; and whiteness 102
Ableism-and-Normalcy spread effect 249–250
academia, barriers in 296
accessibility cascades 36–37
Adams, A. 248–249
adolescence, and the sense of self 131, 133, *136*
ADOS assessment 47
agency 210, 281–282, 292; lack of 277
Ahmed, S. 102, 219
AIMS-2 project 150
airports 218–219, 222–223
Alexander, S. H. 234
All the Weight of Our Dreams: On Living Racialized Autism (Brown, Ashkenazy and Giwa Onaiwu) 101
anger 58
Anglonormativity 177–178
animals, dehumanizing comparisons to 80
anxiety 61; and autism 63, 232
Applied Behavioural Analysis (ABA) 262, 271; critiques of 81, 197; marketing of 196
Aristotle 154
Arnold, L. 5, 13–18
Arnstein, S. R. 288–289
Arnstein's Ladder of Citizen Participation 8, 288, *289*, 291–293, 297
artificial intelligence, and Black people 100
Ashkenazy, E. 101
Asperger, H. 21, 26, 81, 168

Asperger's Syndrome 15, 43, 59, 66, 71*n*3, 177
"Assessment and Treatment Units" 38–39
attention deficit hyperactivity disorder (ADHD) 43; and PDA 61
authenticity, and identity 18
autism 71*n*3, 161, 219–220, 224; and biopolitics 221–224; books on 167–168; as constellation 43, 51*n*3; defined 1–2, 76, 229–231; DSM recognition of 22; French term for 166, 177; genetics of 44; heterogeneity of 42–44, 47; history of 14–15, 22, 65, 76, 81–82, 87–88, 194, 255; as label 42, 219–221; as linear spectrum 42, 50, 51*n*1; presumptions about 162, 189–190, 209, 236, 278, 290; self-diagnosis of 161; and sexuality 203
autism activism 234, 261; and autism scholarship 150–154; in France 174, 178; and friendships 25; global 5, 150; need for collectivism in 201; and the neurodiversity movement (United Kingdom) 150; and social media 2–3
autism community 230, 234, 259; in France 172, 174–175; and hierarchies of power 101; lack of representation of 152; shared spaces for 189
autism cure movement 255, 261
autism diagnoses 3, **50**; adult 151; and clustering 50; community diagnostic entities **50**, 51; co-occurring conditions with 47; diagnostic substitution 42; and the *DSM-IV* 43; female underdiagnoses 27; in France 169, 171, 177; and gender 26–29, 48, 293; and gender affirming therapies 28; and gendered language 27; and high/low-functioning labels 42–43, 278; and psychiatry 14; self-diagnosed 161, 169, 261; timing of 236–238
autism identity 3, 15, 229, 232–235, 238, 261, 288
Autism in Love 204

Index

Autism Industry 196, 200, 222
Autism Network International 1
autism research 150, 288–289; and agency 292; by autistic people 150–152, 190–191, 273–274, 294–295; and autistic stakeholders 294–295; biological/genetic 43–44, 152; changing methods of 133–134, **135**, 292–297; clustering 44–50, 51*n*4; community-based 47; concerns about 44, 47; and 'cultural imperialism' claims 3; and dehumanization 76, 80–81; and the denial of subjectivity 82; and ethics 108–109; and eugenics 81–82; and exclusion 87; individual experiences 45; lived experiences in 132, 292–293; and machine-learning 44–45, 47; and multimedia 243; and objectification 81–83; and objectivity claims 78; participatory autism research 84, 152, 262, 288, 290, 292; and PDA 67; phenotyping 43; qualitative methods of 85; quantitative methods of 85; questions for 3; research-to-practice gap 295–296; on sense of self 132–133; into sensory processing issues 46; situated research 272–274; statistical misuse in 78; study designing 3; subgrouping 44–49; through the Re•Storying Autism project 245–246; in the United Kingdom 3; in the United States 2, 5; *see also* critical autism studies
Autism Spectrum Disorder 15, 50, 59, *60*, 66; and French 166
autism wars 5, 182
autisme 177; linguistics of 166–168
autistic burnout 262
autistic collectivity 191, 234
Autistic culture 230–232, 259, 295; *vs.* "culture of autism" 232, **233**
Autistic discovery process 236–238
autistic knowledges 5, 7, 182
autistic separateness 191
Autistic space 231, 234–235
autistic writers 79, 82, 153; controversies over 24, 81; in France 172; *see also* autobiographies
autobiographies 82, 273–274; controversies over 24, 81; and identity 13
auto-ethnography 273
Autonomy, the Critical Journal of Interdisciplinary Autism Studies 151
Autopia 159, 161; educational system 162; employment in 163; and the environment 160–161; golden concept 162–163; golden notion 162; golden rule 160–162
autotelic pursuits 35, 37

Badenoch, K. 100
Baines, A. D. 133
Baker, S. 196
Baril, A. 177–179
Barnbuam, D. R. 80
Baron-Cohen, S. 3, 23, 25–27, 168

Beardon, L. 7, 159–164
Bécares, L. 100
behaviourism 197
Belek, B. 231
Bentall, R. 14
Berlant, L. 219
Bernardi, F. 6, 106–119
Bertilsdotter Rosqvist, H. 7, 26, 182–192
Bettelheim, B. 196
bias: against autistic people 160; *see also* racism
bilingualism 257–258
biological reductionism 16
biomarkers 43, 51*n*2
biomedical research 2
biopolitics 218–221; and autism 221–224
biopower 219, 222
Birrell, I. 40
Bishop, D. 170
Black people: and artificial intelligence 100; defined 97; healthcare statistics 100; and medical training 100; mistrust by 99; speaking out 102
blame, and problems 255
Blue, G. 289
Borderline Mental Retardation, and IQ score changes 57
Botha, M. 6, 76–88
Boulanger, J. 171, 177
Bourcier, S. 174, 178
Bourdieu, P. 7, 204, 206–211
Boyz n the Hood (film) 102
Braidotti, R. 223–224
the brain: and autism 14; and gender 26–27; 'male' 26–27
Breggin, P. 195
Brickman, P. 255–256, 260–263
Brignell, A. 279
British Medical Journal 100
Brookfield, S. 296
Brown, L. X. 101
Brownlow, C. 5–6, 20–30, 186–187
bullying 140
Burman, E. 21

Campbell, M. 252
Carbado, D. W. 294
Carlile, A. 123
Cartesianism 168–172, 175, 177
Cavendish, H. 21
Chamak, B. 172, 174
Chapman, R. 45, 260
Charmaz, K. 13
Child Guidance movement 194
childhood, redefined 116
Childhood Disintegrative Disorder 59, 66
children 199–200; and identity 107, 113, 116; and mental health 194; and mother warriors 198–199; and PDA 63; Rose on 20–21

Index

Chown, N. 211, 295
Christie, P. 65–66
Christopher, S. 295
Classification française des troubles mentaux de l'enfant et de l'adolescent (CFTMEA) 171, 177
Collins, P. H. 293
common good: need to restore 37; shifting values of 38
communication 209–210, 212; changing methods for research 133–134, **135**; child-directed 212; defined as "functional" 277; and the DSM-5 277; ignored 280–281; and interests 282–285; and the neurodiversity movement 261; non-autistic 189, 260; and resistance 283–284; Scottish Autism Ethical Practice Framework 272; scrutiny of 278; and speech difficulties 279; therapeutic interventions for 278–285; whole body 189; *see also* language; speech
communitarianism 174, 176–177
communities of interests 37
communities of practice 272
community psychology 6, 83–87; and critical autism studies 86–87
compensatory model (autism) *see* social model (autism)
compromise 155; by autistic people 185
concerns 35
Connolly, S. 242–252
Constructivist Grounded Theory 13
context, importance of 274
co-occurring labels 58; and developmental change 48; and neurodiversity 47
COVID-19 21, 224; and independence 38; in the United Kingdom 100–101
Criminal Justice System and PDA 61
critical autism studies 1, 153, 191, 242, 245–246, 251, 270, 272, 275, 289; and autism 246; and community psychology 86–87; and context 274; defined 3–5, 56; and disability 246; in the Global North 2–5; *see also* autism research
critical disability studies 219
Critical Race Theory (CRT) 99
Crosbie, P. 7, 165–179
Csikszentmihalyi, M. 35
cultural capital 208, 212
'cultural imperialism' claims, and autism research 3
culture 231
"culture of autism" 229–230, 232, 238; *vs.* Autistic culture 232, **233**; harms of 229–230, 232

Dachez, J. 172
Dahlberg, G. 21
Damon, W. 132
'DAN! protocol' 196
Danaher, G. 207
Davidson, J. 1
de Beauvoir, S. 291

death 232
Defeat Autism Now! 196
deficit models of autism 22, 57, 130, 192, 214, 246–247, 258, 275, 284–285, 290–291; and critical autism studies 270; and gender affirming therapies 28; in popular culture 209, 213; rejection of 183; and sense of self 130, 132, 145; and supports 270; *see also* medical model (autism)
dehumanization 117, 161; and autism research 76, 80–81; medical model of autism 257; person first language 82–83; by teachers 248
deinstitutionalisation 290
Deleuze, G. 153
Delion, P. 170
denial of personhood/identity 248
denials of disability experiences 248
Derbyshire, Victoria 40
Descartes, R. 168
development: and milestones 20; normative 20, 25, 29–30, 132, 145, 199, 291
developmental change, and co-occurring labels 48
diagnoses: of mental disorders 57; and societal changes 15
Diagnostic and Statistical Manual (DSM) 21; and France 171; and mental disorders 57; *see also* DSM-5
Diagnostic Interview for Social and Communication Disorder (DISCO) 68–69
disability: and critical autism studies 246; in the French language 166–167; lack of definition of 161; recognition of 222–223; and religion 290; research about 175
disability activism 175
disability studies, and France 175–177
disablism 245
disclosure responses 162
Discourse on the Method of Rightly Conducting One's Reason and of Seeking Truth in the Sciences (Descartes) 168
discourses 219–220
dispositional diversity 208
Dockrell, J. 278
double-empathy problem 24–25, 57, 192, 209, 211, 260, 271
Douglas, Patty 242–252
Down Syndrome 51n2
doxa 207, 209
DSM-5 14–15, 22, 42, 50, 60, 68, 71n9, 277; Social Communication Disorder 45, 278; *see also* Diagnostic and Statistical Manual (DSM)
DSM-III 22
DSM-IV 43, 59, 66
Duffy, S. 38–39
Duhem–Quine thesis 14
Dwyer, P. 6, 42–52
Dyer, H. 199

Index

Eaton, J. 68
Ebben, H. 222
echolalia 231, 239n4, 277
economic capital 208
EDA-Q 67–69
educational systems: Autopian 162; French 173–174, 177–178; and language supports 278–284; and negative comments 243–250; neoliberal 197; and PDA 63; racism in 102; and the sense of self 131–132, 142–145; and supports 259, 283; *see also* teachers assistants, supports from
educators: dehumanisation by 248; talking about children 243–251
empathy: measuring 25; and othering 24–25; presumed deficits of 28, 57, 79, 168
employment, support for 186–188
energetic processing resource 36; *see also* interests
enlightenment model (autism) 258–260
epistemic authority 182–183; non-autistic 190–191; and workplace supports 187–188
epistemological communities 182–183, 189–191
epistemological violence 78–80
equality, and republicanism 173
ethnic minorities, underrepresentation of 290, 293
eugenics: and autism research 81–82; debates over 83; and scientific objectivity 78

Fabio 110–111
Farahar, C. 7, 229–239, 249
female autistic phenotypes 27
female autistics, lack of supports for 27
female brains 26–27
fields 208, 210–211
fitting in 132–133, 138, 141–142, 187, 190, 256, 259
Fletcher-Watson, S. 169
flow states 262
Floyd, G. 39–40
Forest, D. 175
Forrester-Jones, R. 290
Foucault, M. 151, 221
France 165, 257; autism activism in 174–175, 178; and disability studies 175–177; educational systems in 173–174, 177–178; and empirical evidence 172; hierarchies of power 170–171; mothers in 169–170; and neurodiversity 175; and packing 169–170; and republicanism 172–174, 178
Freud, S. 169
friendships 25–26; and gender 26; and theory of mind 25
Fushing, H. 47
'A Future Made Together Report' 296

Galgay, C. E. 248–250
Garland-Thomson, R. 219
Geldolf, P. 200

gender: and autism diagnoses 26–29, 48, 203, 211, 293; and the brain 26–27; and friendship 26; and intersectionalism 27–28; normative expectations for 28, 125–128
gender affirming therapies: and autism diagnoses 28–29, 123, 125–126, 128; in the United Kingdom 122–123, 127–128
gender diversity 6, 128n1; and autism 123, 204; and childhood 28; health professional perceptions of 124–125; and normative gender constructions 29, 125–128; statistics 124; in the United Kingdom 122; *see also* transgender people
gendered language, and autism diagnoses 27
Geschwind, D. 3
Gillberg, C. 47, 61
Gillespie-Lynch, K. 295
Giwa Onaiwu, M. 101–103
Gleeson, K. 133–134, 140
Glesne, C. 137
Gobbo, K. 293
Goffman, E. 151, 187, 290–291
Gokh, A. F. 231
Goodley, D. 7, 218–224
Gould, J. 65
Gowler, K. 242–252
grade comparisons 138–139
Gramsci, Antonio 109, 114, 118–119
Gramscian lens 107
Grandin, T. 24, 167
Green, A. I. 211
Greenfield, J. 196
Griffin, E. 239n6
Grinker, R. 66–67
Guattari, F. 153

Haase, J. E. 137
habitus 207–208, 211, 213–214
Haley, B. 196
"handicapped" 167
handwriting 244
Hardt, M. 222
Harris, C. I. 294
Harrison, J. 25
Hart, D. 132
Harter, S. 131
Haslam, C. 234
healthcare disparities, for autistic people 123, 126–127, 232
Henley, R. 250
hexis 207, 212–214
hierarchies of power 291–292; in France 170–171; and parents 109–112, 114–115
high/low-functioning labels 42–43, 278
Ho, S. 137
Hobson, P. 80
Hodge, N. 2, 7, 242–252
home 112–113, *136*, 138, 141–142, 189

Index

homophobia, and psychology 78
homosexuality, as mental disorder 15, 160
Hooge, A. 86
Houghton, E. 199–200
Hozho 30
Hughes, B. 154
Hull, L. 27
Hultqvist, K. 21
human rights, disability rights as 263
humor 251
hyperacusis 46

'idealisation of normalcy' 162, 199
identity 5, 16, 229; and ableism 106, 116; and authenticity 18; and autobiographies 13; children's 107, 113, 116; diagnoses as 14, 154, 288; and disability 154; distancing from autism 233; and intersectionality 17; and masking 213; and nationhood 17; as oppression 17; and othering 17; post-identity 18; and sense of self 131; as transgender 28–29, 124–125; *see also* autism identity
inclusion 159, 162
Infantile Autism 65
infantilisation 248, 290, 292
institutionalisation 290; promotion of 38–39, 257; and scientific objectivity 78
interests 35–36, 211–212; and communication 282–283; communities of 37; *see also* energetic processing resource; special interests
intergenerationality 17
International Statistical Classification of Diseases and Related Health Problems (ICD) 21, 171, 277–278
Interpersonal Reactivity Index (IRI) 25
intersectionalism 291–294; and gender 27–28
intersectionality, and identity 17
IQ scores, 1970's measurement change of 57

Jarrett, S. 21
Jetten, J. 234
Johnson, K. 28
judgements 139, *140*, 260

Kahneman, D. 36–37
Kanner, L. 21, 26, 65, 168, 194, 256
Kapp, S. K. 7, 15, 30, 255–263, 293
Keates, N. 8, 288–297
Keenan, M. 81
Keller, R. M. 248–250
King, D. K. 294
King, M. C. 133–134, 140
Klein, F. 23
knowledges of autism 5, 7, 165, 182–183
Kooken, W. C. 137
Kourti, M. 29
'Kraepelinian paradigm' 14

Kruth, M. 242–252
Kung, K. T. F. 28

labelling 42, 219–221; negative effects of 280–281; nonverbal 277–280, 284
Lacan, J. 169
ladder *see* Arnstein's Ladder of Citizen Participation
Lai, M. C. 48
Landén, M. 28
language 182; and divisions 114, 116; French 166–168, 174; and interests 34–35; manipulation of 36–37; and meaning 35, 40; person first 15, 82–83, 288; and power 37–40, 110–114; reclamation of 39
Laugeson, E. 213
Lawson, W. 13
learned helplessness 256, 258–260
Lesser, M. 13
Leuder, I. 24
life-outcomes 232; improving 161
lived experiences, in autism research 132, 292–293
logical empiricism 86; and psychology 77
Long, J. 7, 270–275
Lorde, A. 86
Lost Voice Guy 278
Lovaas, O. I. 196, 257, 271
love, and autistic people 206–207
Love on the Spectrum 6–7, 204, 212–214; and the bodily hexis 212–214; description 205–206; neurotypical audience of 206; promotional material for 209

McAnulty, D. 35
McAssey, M. P. 47
McCormick, A. K. H. G. 295
McCreadie, M. 271
McDonnell, A. 35, 271
McGuire, A. E. 2
machine-learning 51*n*4; and autism research 44–45, 47
Maclean, J. 151
MacLeod, A. 29
McRobbie, A. 200
maladjustment 194
male brains 26–27
males: and autism diagnoses 26–29, 203; *see also* gender
Malone, W. 249
Mandy, W. 27
marketplace/business-oriented societies 37–38
Markov blankets 36
Martin, N. 242–252
masking 233, 260, 291–292; and Blackness 97, 102; children 102; and dating 212–213; and sense of self research 132–133; by women/girls 27
meaning, and language 35, 40

medical model (autism) 14, 38, 76, 87, 106, 113–114, 117, 160–161, 183, 229–230, 236, 238, 239n6, 243, 257–258, 261, 271, 291; and communication 277; in France 169, 173–174, 178; and parents 106–107, 109–112, 114
medical model (disability) 56–57, 99, 291
medical racism 291
medical 'story' (autism) 183
mental disorders: clinician/researcher power over 69; defining 58; diagnoses of 57; and politics 58, 67–69, 86; social construction of 56–59; *see also* Pathological Demand Avoidance (PDA)
mental health, victim-blaming approaches to 78, 83
Mesibov, G. 197
microaggressions 242, 247–251
Mikulak, M. 6, 122–128
Milchalko, R. 2
milestones 20; parental regulation of 21
Mills, R. 271
Milton, D. 1–8, 21, 24–25, 35, 63, 80–81, 150–155, 160, 162, 182–192, 205, 208, 210, 271, 292–293
mind reading/social imagination 35, 38
Mineev, V. V. 231
minority groups: Autistic people as 174–175, 178, 230; lack of recognition of 173–174
Miserandino, C. 239n1
misophonia 46
"Missing Voices: The Black Autistic's Journey" (Simmonds) 98–99
Mittel, J. 205
modern competitive femininity 200
Molloy, H. 133, 142
monotropic autistic dispositions 34–35
monotropism 34
Montagnier, L. 170
Moore, A. 7, 203–215
moral model (autism) 194–195, 256–257
motherhood: and ableism 107, 114–115; views of 115
mothers 117–118; blamed for autism 194–195, 256; and expectations 109; in France 169–170; mother warrior role 198–199, 201
Moulin Rouge 6
multiculturalism, *vs.* French republicanism 173, 175
Mulvey, L. 205
Murray, D. 5–6, 13, 34–40, 155, 203, 206
Myers, A. 250

Nadesan, M. 15
nationhood, and identity 17
Natri, H. 3
natural kinds 14
Naughton, E. 198
Negri, A. 222
Neill, M. 154
Nelson, L. H. 183

neoliberalism: and bodily capital 208–209; and educational systems 197; "ideal neoliberal subject" 199–201
neurodiversity 229; and co-occurring labels 47; in France 175; and gender diversity 123; and gender identity 124–125; history of 15–16; *vs.* neurotypicality 210; research dismissal of 82; and the strength-based model of autism 183
neurodiversity movement 255, 260–262
neurotypical gaze 205; autistics as entertainment to 206, 212; and power 206
neurotypicality 22, 214n3; autistic peoples' knowledges of 205; and communication 212; *vs.* neurodiversity 210; and objectivity 76; studying 213; and theory of mind 23; *see also* Predominant Neurotype (PNT)
"new normal" 21
New Zealand, term for autism in 30
Newson, E. 58, 65–71
normalcy: and autism supports 270; pressures for 223, 290
normative development 20, 25, 29–30, 199, 291; and autism supports 217, 270; and sense of self 132, 145
"Nothing About Us Without Us" 84
Nourissier, F. 168–169
N-word 97–98

objectification: and autism research 81–83; of autistic people 76, 206, 231, 248; defined 81; of women 205
objectivity: claims of 78; and dehumanization 81; impossibility of 13, 84–85; and neurotypicality 76; scientific objectivity 78; as "view from nowhere" 77
Obsessive-Compulsive Disorder 56, 61–63; Demand Management Cycle 64; social construction of 56–57
Ochs, E. 26
O'Clery, C. 205, 209, 214
O'Dell, L. 5, 20–30, 182–192
Oikkonen, V. 183
Olkin, R. 248
O'Nions, E. 61, 67–68
online petitions 153–154
oppression 210; and identity 17
Orchard, V. 170–172
Orsini, M. 1
Orsmond, G. I. 25
othering 291–292; and biopolitics 223; and empathy 24–25; as epistemological violence 79; and identity 17
oxytocin 258

packing 169–170
Palermo, M. T. 198
Panther, D. 101

Index

paradigm shifts, needed 160
parent organisations 195
parents 201; and the autism cure movement 255; and autism diagnosis process 236–237; and childhood milestones 21; and hierarchies of power 109–112, 114; in Kanner's research 194; as market for products 196–197, 199–200; and masking 102; and the medical model of autism 106–107, 109–110; and the neurodiversity movement 262; pathologisation of 194–195, 255; positive impacts of 258; scammers taking advantage of 195–196; self-defence by 195; as shields 198; as therapists 197–198
Parker, I. 21
Parkinson, J. 28
participation, in Autistic spaces 235
Participatory Autism Research Collective (PARC) 6, 151–153, 192
Pathological Demand Avoidance (PDA) 6, 56, 64–65, 154; and ADHD 61; *vs.* autism 58–59, *60*, 64–65, 67; defined 59, *60*, 61; Demand Management Cycle 63, *64*; evolution of 67–69, **70**; as "Extreme Demand Avoidance" 63; as "Rational Demand Avoidance" 63; and self-agency 62–63, 71; social construction of 56–57; Surface Sociability 57–58, 61–62; *see also* mental disorders
pathologization of autism 24–25, 37
PEERS program 213
Pellicano, E. 3
performativity, and sunflower lanyards 222–223
person first language 15, 288; dehumanization of 82–83; and French 166
"Pervasive Developmental Disorder–Not Otherwise Specified" 43, 59, 65–66
Petrides, K.V. 27
Playing A/Part project 294
poetic transcription 136–138; on school 143–145; social self-view 138–141
Poindexter, C. C. 137
Pollak, D. 239*n*6
popular culture: autism representations in 203–204, 206, 209; *see also Love on the Spectrum*; reality TV shows
practice 207, 209
Predominant Neurotype (PNT) 159, 161; *see also* neurotypicality
Premack, D. 23
Pring, J. 40
Projekt Empowerment 26
psychiatry 194; authority of 220; and autism 14
psychoanalysis 77, 205; in France 169–170
psychology 20–21, 194; authority of 220; divisions in 77; and history 21; and homophobia 78; and logical empiricism 77, 86; and racism 78; and sexism 78; and transphobia 78; *see also* community psychology

'psy-complex' 20; on friendships 25–26
public conceptual schemes 189
public relations, and reputation management 39
Purkis, Y. 24

Quality of Life (QoL) framework 292, 296
questions: about autism diagnoses 3; for the National Autistic Society 102–103; normative values of 78; sense of self 135

Rabinow, P. 220
racism 6, 291; compared to anti-autistic biases 160; in educational systems 102; and healthcare 100; and psychology 78; in the United Kingdom 100
Ramus, F. 169
Rasmussen, P. 28
Ravaud, J. F. 173
reality TV shows 203–204; *see also* popular culture
reasonable accommodations 185–188
reflexivity 85–86, 296
refrigerator mother theory 256
relationships: between autistic people 211; stereotypes about 203–204
reparations 84
republicanism 172–174, 177–178
reputation management: inversion of 39; and public relations 39
research-to-practice gap 295–296
respect 107–108
Re•Storying Autism in Education project 7, 242–243, 245, 251
Rett's Disorder 59, 66
'rhizomatic' structures 153
Rice, C. 243
Rice-Adams, E. 6, 130–145
Richardson, N. 206
Ridout, S. 133–134
Rimland, B. 195–196, 257
Robdale, E. 28
Rogers, J. 212, 214
Rose, N. 20, 219
Roulstone, S. 278
Roush, S. 169
Runswick-Cole, K. 7, 218–224
Rushton, J. P. 78
Russell, K. M. 137
Ryan, S. 1–8

Sacks, O. 21
Sands, A. 248
Saverese, D. J. 278
Schalock, R. L. 292
Schein, E. H. 295
Schirato, T. 207
schizophrenia 65, 177
Schopler, E. 197
Schovanec, J. 172–174, 177

Schramm-Nielsen, J. 171
science: and epistemological violence 78–79; philosophy of 77
Scottish Autism 7, 272; Ethical Practice Framework 272; research programme at 272–273
self-injury 162
self-stimulatory behaviour 231
sense of self 130–131; during adolescence 131; and deficit models of autism 130; and identity 131; and normative development 132; researching 132–133; social self-view 138–141; teachers' impacts on 142–145; thematic map of *136*; and varying roles 131–132, *136*, 142
sensory processing issues 211–212; questionnaires about 46; *see also specific types of sensory issues*
sexism, and psychology 78
sexuality 214; and autism 203; and cultural capital 212
shared autistic spaces 189
Shmulsky, S. 293
Simmonds, M. 6, 97–104
Simons, Dr. 99
Sinclair, J. 23, 172
Singer, J. 150
sitpoint theory (disabled feminism) 219
sitpoints 219
situated learning 273
slavery, and the United Kingdom 100
Smith, A. 37
Smith, C. 242–252
Smukler, D. 23–24
So, You're Autistic? (SYA?) support program 235–236, *236–237*, 238
social behaviors 26, 259; neurotypical judgements of 46
social communication issues 24–25, 57, 59, 69
social-emotional reciprocity 260
social fields 208
social interactions 210
social justice 114, 289; and community psychology 83, 85; and the Re•Storying Autism project 243
social media: and autism activism 2–3, 153–154; and George Floyd 40i; *see also* Twitter
social model (disability) 99, 167, 176, 178, 238, 260–262
social positioning 35
social situation of autism 14, 42, 59
social skills 162–163
social stigma theory 290
societal norms, impacts on autistic lives 159
solidarity 154
Solomon, O. 26
solutions, motivation for 255
speaking out 102
special interests 68, 101–102, 141–142, 236; *see also* interests
Specific Language Impairments (SLIs) 66

Spectrum 10K study 3
speech 34, 284; *see also* communication; language
spiky profiles 161
spoon theory 231, 239*n*1
spread effects 249–250
staring 252
statistics, misrepresentation of 78
stereotypes 232, 290; impact on diagnoses 293; in popular culture 203
stigmatization: of autistic communication 277; of autistic people 289–291
stigmatized groups 233–234
Stiker, H. J. 173
stimming 231, 262
Stokes, L. 250
Strang, J. F. 123, 126–127
Strauss, J. 174–175
structures of desire 211
suicide 232
Sunflower Lanyard Scheme 218, 222; and performativity 222–223
supports 191; as controls 281; as cultural/language broker 186–187; and the deficit-based model of autism 270; fights over 198–199; and individuality 185–186; lacking 199; Makaton 279; PECS (Picture Exchange Communication System) 279; and stigma 259
Sweden: autism support in 184–185; *Swedish Act concerning Support and Service for Persons with Certain Functional Impairments* (LSS) 184–185
Swendsen, J. 170
symbolic capital 208
symbolic violence 210
Synergy program 271
Szatmari, P. 48

Tager-Flusberg, H. 22
Taylor, A. 21, 173
TEACCH 197
teachers assistants, supports from 280–283
Teo, T. 79
theories of mind 22–25, 67; presumed deficits of 57, 79; and transgender identities 28
'Theorising Autism Project' 151
Thompson, H. 175
Thunberg, G. 40, 176
"toku/tona ano takiwa" ("my/his/her own time and space") 30
tragedy model (autism) 160
transgender people 128*n*1; and autism diagnoses 28, 122–123, 128; discrimination against 122–123; in France 170; and gender affirming therapies 28–29, 123, 127–128; statistics about 124; *see also* gender diversity
transphobia, and psychology 78
trauma 231–232, 235; of negative comments 243–245, 247–251; and PDA 63

Index

treatment interventions: and ableism 21; personalization of 46
Triad of Impairment 66
Turban, J. L. 29, 128
Tuskegee Experiment (1932–1972) 99–100
Twitter 247–248; hashtags 175; *see also* social media

UN Convention on the Rights of Persons with Disabilities (French version) 167
uncertainty, and Cartesianism 168–169
The Undateables 204, 206
United Kingdom: *Autism Act* (2009) 184; autism research in 3, 152; autism support in 184–188, 191; Autistic spaces in 234–235; BAME 98; Bercow Review 278; "Fulfilling and Rewarding Lives: The strategy for adults with autism in England" (2010) 184; gender diversity in 122; Gender Identity Development Service (GIDS) 122–123; mortality rates in 232; National Autistic Society 68, 102–103, 195; National Autistic Taskforce 40, 271; neurodiversity movement 150, 154; Participatory Autism Research Collective (PARC) 6, 151–153, 192; and racism 100; reasonable accommodations 185–188; Research Excellence Framework (REF) 152; Scottish Autism 7, 272; "Shaping Autism Research UK" 192; and slavery 100; social discrimination in 100–101; Spectrum 10K study 3; Synergy program 271; Trans Health research project 124; welfare system of 39
United States: autism research in 2, 5; Autism Society of America (ASA) 195; Higashi School (Boston) 198–199; Tuskegee Experiment (1932–1972) 99–100
Universal Accessibility 173
Universal Design 185
usenet groups, and neurodiversity 15–16

Valren, A. T. 178–179
van Schalkwyk, G. I. 128

Vasil, L. 133, 142
Verhoeff, B. 1
Vertoont, S. 204
viewed/viewer power relationships 205–206
Viktoruk, E. N. 231
violence 6; epistemological violence 78–80; symbolic 210
"Visual Pleasure and Narrative Genre" (Mulvey) 205
Vygotsky, L. 176

Wakefield, A. 196
Waldock, K. E. 8, 288–297
Walz, M. 7, 194–201
Watts, V. 295
Webb, J. 207
white fragility 98–99, 101
white privilege 98–99
white supremacy 97, 102
Whitehouse, A. J. O. 25
whiteness, and ableism 102
Wikipedia 178–179
Williams, D. 24, 167, 172
Williams, E. I. 133–134, 140
Wing, L. 22, 45, 61, 65
Winstone, N. 133–134, 140
Wittgenstein, L. 167
Wolfensberger, W. 217, 270
Wood, R. 7–8, 277–283
Woods, R. 6, 56–71
World Association for Sexual Health's (WAS), Declaration of Sexual Rights 214

Yates, P. 200
Yergeau, M. 293
Young, I. M. 80–81
Young, S. 295

Zero Degrees of Empathy: A New Theory of Human Cruelty (Baron-Cohen) 25

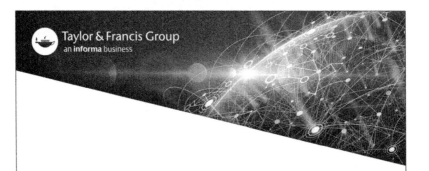

Printed in Great Britain
by Amazon